I WILL
BEAR
WITNESS

I WILL

A DIARY OF

BEAR

THE NAZI YEARS

WITNESS

1933 — 1941

VICTOR KLEMPERER

Translated by Martin Chalmers

 RANDOM HOUSE NEW YORK

First published in Germany under the title *Ich will Zeugnis ablegen bis zum letzten:
Tagebücher 1933–1945 von Victor Klemperer.* Copyright © Aufbau-Verlag GmbH,
Berlin, 1995.

Library of Congress Cataloging-in-Publication Data

Klemperer, Victor.
[Ich will Zeugnis ablegen bis zum letzten. English]
I will bear witness: the diaries of Victor Klemperer.
p.   cm.
Contents: [1]. 1933–1941.
ISBN 0-679-45696-1 ([1] : alk. paper)
1. Klemperer, Victor, 1881–1960—Diaries.
2. French teachers—Germany—Diaries.   3. Philologists—Germany—Diaries.
4. Germany—History—1933–1945—Sources.   I. Title.
PC2064.K5A3   1998
943.086'092—dc21
[B]   98-15429

Random House website address: www.atrandom.com
Printed in the United States of America on acid-free paper
24689753
First U.S. Edition

DESIGN BY MERCEDES EVERETT

Frontispiece photograph of Victor Klemperer by Eva Kemlein, Berlin.
Photograph on p. vi © Aufbau-Verlag GmbH.

I shall go on writing. That is my heroism.
I will bear witness, precise witness!

—May 27, 1942

Eva and Victor Klemperer, c. 1940.

PREFACE

The Lives of Victor Klemperer

Escape

At the beginning of February 1945, there were 198 registered Jews, including Victor Klemperer, left in the city and the district of Dresden. The remainder of the 1,265 who had been in the city in late 1941 had been deported to Riga, to Auschwitz, to Theresienstadt.[1] Many were shot or gassed on arrival. Some had committed suicide on receiving notice of deportation. A handful survived.[2]

All the remaining Jews in Dresden had non-Jewish wives or husbands. This had placed them in a relatively privileged position[3] but dependent on the courage and tenacity of their marriage partners. If the "Aryan" spouse died or divorced them, they would immediately be placed on the deportation list. The majority of such couples and families had been ghettoized, together with the less privileged Jews, in a dwindling number of "Jews' houses."

On the morning of Tuesday, February 13, all Jews considered capable of physical labor were ordered to report for deportation early on Friday, February 16. The "mixed marriages" of Dresden were finally to be split up. Victor Klemperer regarded this as a death sentence for himself and the others. Then, "on the evening of February 13 the catastrophe overtook Dresden: the bombs fell, the houses collapsed, the phosphorus flowed, the burning beams crashed onto the heads of Aryans and non-Aryans alike, and Jew and Christian met death in the same firestorm; whoever of the bearers of the star was spared by this night was delivered, for in the general chaos he could escape the Gestapo."[4]

Victor Klemperer and the other Jews who survived the Allied raid and the subsequent firestorm had experienced a double miracle, had been doubly lucky.

In the confusion following the destruction of the city, Victor Klemperer pulled off the yellow Jew's star, and he and his wife merged with the other inhabitants fleeing the city. It was easy enough for them to claim they had lost their papers. Nevertheless, afraid of being recognized and denounced, they went on the run across Germany for the next three months, until the village they had reached in southern Bavaria was occupied by American forces.

Contradictions

On the night of the Dresden firestorm, when Victor Klemperer escaped both the Allied bombs and the Gestapo, he was already sixty-three. He was born in 1881, the youngest child of Wilhelm Klemperer, rabbi in the little town of Landsberg on the Warthe (today the Polish town of Gorzow Wielkopolski), in the eastern part of the Prussian province of Brandenburg. Three brothers and four sisters survived into adulthood; the famous conductor Otto Klemperer was a cousin, but there was little contact between the two parts of the family. By the time Victor was nine, his father, after an unhappy interlude with the Orthodox congregation at Bromberg (today Bydgoszcz), had been appointed second preacher of the Berlin Reform Congregation. The whole family appears to have felt relieved at the change, and according to his autobiography, Victor immediately relished the freedom and excitement of the big city.

Observance at the Reform Synagogue was extremely liberal. The services themselves were conducted almost entirely in German, and on a Sunday, heads were not covered, and men and women sat together. There was no bar mitzvah; instead, at the age of fifteen or sixteen, boys and girls were confirmed together on Easter Sunday. There were neither Sabbath restrictions nor dietary proscriptions. The sermons seem, to some degree, to have expressed the ethical tradition of the German Enlightenment. In other words, services approximated Protestant practice, and Judaism here became as rational and progressive as it could be while retaining a Jewish identity. This was not the norm of Jewish congregations, but it is nevertheless exemplary of a tradition of merging with the dominant culture. The Reform Synagogue can perhaps be regarded as something of a halfway house to conversion to Protestantism, which had become common in Prussia since the early nineteenth century. (The parents of Karl Marx and Felix Mendelssohn were among only the most prominent examples; conversion, of course, remained for a long time a condition of state service.) Wilhelm Klemperer raised little objection when his own sons were baptized as Protestants. Indeed, Victor Klemperer's three elder brothers seem to have gone out of their way to deny their Jewish origins. The biographical note prefacing the doctoral thesis of Georg Klemperer, the oldest brother, begins with the words, "I was born the son of a country cleric."

Georg Klemperer, sixteen years Victor's senior, was only in his thirties by the time he had become a noted surgeon and one of Germany's most respected medical men. Felix and Berthold Klemperer were also successful, the former as a doctor, the latter as a lawyer. Berthold even married a general's daughter. The sisters were much less free and had Jewish husbands more or less chosen for them.

Wearying of school and perhaps even more of the tyranny of Georg, who dominated the family after the move to Berlin, Victor Klemperer did not continue into the upper grades. He became a commercial apprentice in a company that exported trinkets and souvenirs for sale in English seaside resorts. This move seems to have convinced the eldest brother of Victor's lack of ability and determination. Victor Klemperer was never to shake off the feeling that his brother condescended to him and regarded him as a dilettante.

The apprenticeship, at any rate, did not lead anywhere. Victor Klemperer had entered it with dreams of future independence. Within three years, however, intellectual and literary interests gained the upper hand; he also became a passionate theatergoer. (It was during this period, in his seventeenth year, that he began to keep a diary.) He went back to school, attending the same grammar school in Landsberg as his brothers, and lived in lodgings in the town. This time he completed his schooling and became *primus* in his final year—something like head prefect.

He then enrolled at Munich University to study literature and languages and was increasingly drawn to French literature. He spent terms in Geneva and Paris before returning to Berlin to complete the first part of his university studies. It was in Geneva that he discovered Voltaire as a writer and found his own spirit of tolerant skepticism confirmed. "Ferney [where Voltaire lived in exile from France] was the best thing about Geneva," Klemperer later wrote, and the visit to Voltaire's house was like a pilgrimage.

Victor Klemperer had now found his way intellectually, but a commitment to a figure like Voltaire was unlikely to make for a smooth academic career. Before 1914, the study of Romance literatures and culture in German universities was dominated by hostility to the "superficial" ideas of the French Enlightenment. In fact, Klemperer was unable to find a suitable professor with whom to undertake a doctoral thesis on Voltaire and, to his brothers' consternation, threw up his studies once again. For the next few years, from 1905, he tried to make a living as a writer and literary journalist. At this point it may be worth noting that, for all the scholarliness he was to display in the future, Klemperer never seems to have felt really comfortable with other academics, even liberal ones, or in conventional middle-class settings in general. Although he loved teaching, he did not deal very well with the social aspects of his profession. In his diaries he often appears more at ease with "practical" people or with craftsmen.[5]

Relations with several of his siblings went from bad to worse with Klemperer's romance with Eva Schlemmer, a musician from a Protestant family in Königsberg. They married in 1906. The wedding did not find favor with either family—on Eva's side because some of her relatives objected to her marrying a Jew, on Victor's side because his brothers did not consider her a good enough match. Nevertheless, Victor Klemperer was to share his life with her for the next forty-five years. And in this marriage, "share" is the appropriate word. In a speech on the occasion of Klemperer's seventy-fifth birthday in 1957, the couple's longtime friend Auguste "Gusti" Lazar, who appears in the diaries under her married name Wieghardt, said, "What especially fascinated me about the two Klemperers, was the 'community of intellectual property' in which they lived and worked."[6] In his autobiography, *Curriculum Vitae*, Klemperer wrote that as a young man he had been convinced of the justice of women's emancipation. Whatever difficulties in the relationship are evident and implied from the diaries and given that Victor Klemperer's writing and then academic career took precedence, it is clear that every aspect of intellectual and political life was subjected to intense discussion.

Having abandoned the university and living in Berlin once more, Klemperer demonstrated a tremendous energy in producing poems, stories, anthologies, articles, reviews, and biographies, largely on contemporary German themes. One of his most reliable sources of income came from lectures on literary subjects that he gave to Jewish societies throughout Germany, though it was in fact toward the end of this period that he converted fully to Protestantism. The young couple had a particular enthusiasm for the cinema and, in addition to a number of shorter pieces, Victor Klemperer wrote a study of Berlin film theaters and their audiences. It was also at this time that he became friends with Siegfried "Friedel" Kracauer, later to become famous for his writings on film and as a cultural historian and theorist. They lost touch during the First World War.

It was a struggle to make ends meet in Berlin's literary world. Nevertheless, *Der Kinematograph*, of September 25, 1912, as part of a feature entitled "The Cinema in the Opinion of Prominent Contemporaries," introduced Victor Klemperer in the following terms: "A young combative literary man who writes with rare courage and is not afraid to speak out against established authorities."[7]

Inclination, as well as the need to make a living, pushed Klemperer toward literary journalism, which he clearly practiced with some success. He did not, however, make his mark as an author. He judged his efforts to be failures, later even refusing a publisher's offer to reprint one of his stories. Subsequently, he also had mixed feelings about his freelance years altogether, not least because he never quite managed to shake off the accusation or suspicion that his scholarly work still had something journalistic about it.

Incidentally, although Klemperer was undoubtedly progressive in his views, his "bohemian phase" did nothing to modify a lifelong aversion to bohemian lifestyles, and he retained an enduring suspicion of long hair and extravagant dress.

Return to University

Klemperer concluded that a doctorate would, if nothing else, enhance his position as a journalist. Financially supported by his brothers once again, he returned to Munich, found a sympathetic professor and in 1913 quickly completed a dissertation on Friedrich Spielhagen, a nineteenth-century German novelist. Spielhagen had been a liberal-democratic supporter of the ideals of the 1848 revolutions and was one of the favorite writers of

Klemperer's father. In Munich, Victor Klemperer also made the acquaintance of Karl Vossler, a liberal professor of Romance literature and language. For all the differences—and resentments, not always justified, on
Klemperer's side—that emerged later, Vossler was to remain an abiding
influence. Klemperer wrote a postdoctoral habilitation thesis (in Germany
a habilitation thesis is a condition for professional appointment) on Montesquieu. In it he argued for Montesquieu to be seen as a writer as well as
a theorist or philosopher and that esthetic criteria were of determining importance in the composition of the latter's major works. This dissertation
too was completed very rapidly, and with the distinction summa cum
laude. Then, in 1914, as he was turning the Montesquieu study into a
book, he accepted a post as lecturer in German literature at the University
of Naples, although still continuing as one of Vossler's assistants.

War

Finally at ten o'clock we were sitting in the garden of the Hotel "Zur Sonne" [in
Riva, then in Austria]. *It was June 28. The waiter came running toward us and
cried out: "The heir to the throne and his consort have been murdered in Sara-
jevo!" I said regretfully: "Oh!" and added with an apologetic smile: "But we are
dreadfully hungry."*[8]

What was to become known as the First World War began just as Victor
and Eva Klemperer had returned to Munich for the summer from Naples.
In 1940, when Klemperer was working on his autobiography, he chose to
interrupt the narrative at this point. Not to falsify his own responses, he
simply let his diary entries speak for his mood in the weeks immediately
preceding and following the outbreak of hostilities. From these it appears
that although he was not carried away by bellicose sentiments, he was
convinced, as a good liberal and patriot, that Germany's cause was a just
one. He nevertheless returned to his post in Naples, where he remained
until shortly before Italy entered the war on the Allied side in May 1915.

Back in Munich, Klemperer was declared fit for military service—he
had been rejected in 1903—and was enlisted as a cannoneer in the Bavarian field artillery. He saw duty on the Western Front from November 1915
to March 1916 before succumbing to serious illness and being hospital-
ized. (His front-line service would be a source of "privilege" during the
Third Reich.) Klemperer was out of danger for the rest of the war. Following convalescence, he was transferred to the army's book censorship office
on the eastern front, working first in Kovno (now Kaunas) in Lithuania,
then in Leipzig, where he was allowed to live in private accommodations
with his wife.

An Academic Career

The year and a half after the armistice in November 1918 was a period
in which Klemperer's disappointment at not being given a professorship

merged with his disquiet at what was going on around him in Leipzig, Munich and throughout Germany. As a liberal he had little sympathy for the excesses and foolishness, as he saw it, of the Munich Councils Republic (the name, referring to workers' councils, given to the final phase of Socialist revolutionary activity in the Bavarian capital in the spring of 1919). He did, however, have an insight into the latter episode, because his oldest and closest friend, Hans Meyerhof, who had been his fellow apprentice in Berlin between 1897 and 1900, was involved on the revolutionary side. At the same time Klemperer was filled with unease and dread at the open expressions of anti-Semitism on the part of the government troops and the irregular units that suppressed the Left in Bavaria and elsewhere. Politically, nothing gave him encouragement. At the time of the attempted right-wing coup d'état known as the Kapp Putsch, he wrote in his diary, "I would gladly see the people of the present coup put up against the wall, and I truly cannot feel any enthusiasm for an army which has broken its oath [i.e., to the Republic] . . . but not really for the 'legitimate' Ebert government either, and even less for the radical Left. I detest them all. What is there that embodies the democratic, the German, the humane ideal? I am a neutral observer." A few days later he corrected himself: In politics there were greater and lesser evils. "My sympathies are with no one, but if I have to choose, then rather the Councils Republic than the gentleman officers and anti-Semites."[9]

"What is there that embodies the democratic, the German, the humane ideal," Klemperer asked himself in his diary. For his own life, of course, he already knew the answer: It lay in the tireless curiosity, the questioning, the generous standards of debate of his heroes Voltaire and Montesquieu and of the other thinkers of the Enlightenment.

Thanks to Vossler, Klemperer was called to the chair of Romance languages and literature at Dresden Technical University in 1920. From then until his dismissal in 1935, he pursued his scholarly work and university commitments with extraordinary energy, just as he had done as a literary journalist fifteen years before. He introduced modern French literature in histories and anthologies for students and general readers, presented his own approach in numerous specialized essays, edited a scholarly journal, and wrote a study of the dramatist Corneille before embarking on extended study and comparison of "the century of Voltaire and Rousseau." During this time, he was still partly guided by notions of "essential national characters," which the events of 1933 and after forced him to reject. Despite that, it would be right to see Klemperer's work during these years as a contribution to Franco-German understanding and as an ongoing critique of the German academy's dominant francophobia. There were also distinguished mediators between France and Germany outside the universities, Siegfried Kracauer, for example, and Walter Benjamin and his mentor Franz Hessel, to mention names known outside Germany. Nor was Klemperer's the only voice within the universities to challenge the opposition postulated between supposed German "depth" and French "superficiality."[10] Nevertheless, Klemperer was certainly part of a minority.

These were not, in fact, years of unalloyed happiness for the Klemperers. In professional terms, the humanities section of a technical university did not rank very highly. The Dresden professorship should have been a stepping stone to a more respected university chair, and Klemperer experienced considerable frustration as he saw himself passed over for appointments at "proper" universities. Already somewhat isolated from the mainstream, he made his situation worse by quarreling with Vossler, who felt Klemperer's work drew in too much historical and general cultural material. Of Erich Auerbach, later to become famous as the author of *Mimesis,* who had succeeded Leo Spitzer at Marburg University, he notes in his diary—four years later, which shows how much being passed over on this occasion must have rankled—"A young man, who was still unknown as a scholar when I was already a professor. A Jew, an esthete—and he has managed it, and I am growing old, am the 'previous generation,' have been left behind in a second-rate post, once and for all. Again and again I tell myself that the pain of vanity is pointless, that fame, even great fame, always exists only among a small circle and for a short time; but all such philosophical comfort does not get one anywhere. Only work helps, work without thought for its worth."[11]

During these years also, Eva Klemperer suffered increasingly from ill health, perhaps hypochondria, certainly depression, possibly related to the subordination of her career to that of her husband. At times the couple seem bound together by their illnesses, real and imagined. Nevertheless, nothing appeared to stem Victor Klemperer's prodigious work rate. In addition to his writing and a relatively modest teaching load, he was also involved in educational reform in the state of Saxony, of which Dresden was—and is again—the capital, and was constantly traveling to conferences and to give lectures. It should not be thought, however, that the Klemperers led a quiet life. They were very sociable and had time for lengthy cruises to South America and to the Mediterranean. But what perhaps gave the couple the greatest pleasure was their shared and continuing passion for the cinema, for cinema at its most populist; their "cinema mania" was only temporarily dampened by the advent of sound, which Victor Klemperer, like so many others at the time and after, held to represent a dilution of the power of film images.

1933–45

There is no need to summarize Victor Klemperer's life, experiences, and survival during these twelve years. The diaries for this period, as published in the present volume, begin rather abruptly. Inevitably so, since they represent only a section of the journals that Victor Klemperer kept all his life. But this section chronicles in unparalleled detail the progressive elimination of every private space, the arbitrary cruelty toward those whom the regime defined as Jews, and finally the operation of an opaque (to those who were its victims) apparatus of extermination, that worked slowly, stretching out time to impose an agony of anticipation. Not only does it do so *from the inside*, as it were, from the perspective of those subjected, but uniquely it does so from the first day to the last of the Third Reich.

Victor Klemperer was not dismissed from his post, a state appointment, when the Nazis came to power at the beginning of 1933. Because of his war record, he was allowed to lecture to an ever dwindling band of students. Even when he was dismissed in 1935, officially it was not because he was a Jew, but because he was surplus to requirements as the government cut back student numbers and deemed French literature irrelevant to a technical university. This was lucky for Klemperer, because it meant that he was allowed a pension, which continued to be paid to him, even though, after the November 1938, pogrom, there were increasingly ingenious and draconian deductions.

This pension helped give the couple a certain room to maneuver. At Eva Klemperer's urging they had already built a house in Dölzschen, a village to the west of Dresden. After he lost his job, Victor Klemperer took driving lessons and bought a car. These were two ways of gaining a little more freedom in the face of dictatorship. The Klemperers continued to hope that soon the whole thing would blow over like a bad dream, that the Nazis would devour each other or that someone—the army, foreign powers—would put an end to it. But, above all, the defiance that Victor Klemperer practiced, the space he asserted, was that of his scholarship. The very fact that he continued to write expressed his conviction that the Nazis would not and could not last and prevented him from falling into despair at the blows to his professional self-esteem, to his confidence in the German nation and to himself as a German. When he can no longer work on his book on the eighteenth century, he begins his autobiography, *Curriculum Vitae*. When he can no longer work on his autobiography, he holds fast to his diary and intensifies his observations and reflections on Nazi language, drawing on material that is all around him. He gives his notes the title LTI, for *Lingua tertii imperii*, to be at once his own code and to mock the dictatorship's obsessive use of abbreviations and foreign words.

The point at which some kind of normal life, under the conditions of a racist dictatorship, becomes impossible is the November 1938 pogrom ("*Kristallnacht*") and not the war that begins less than a year later with the German attack on Poland. The pogrom is at once the peak and conclusion of mob violence against Jews and the date when what could still be considered harassment of a minority gives way to the measures that lead to the "Final Solution." It is the point at which Jews realize that there is no one and nothing to protect them. The measures that affect the Klemperers' own lives come thick and fast: the ban on Jews owning cars, on using public libraries, cinemas, swimming pools, on entering parks; the bans on telephones, radios and typewriters; the ban on Jews owning pets; the curfew for Jews; the ban on Jews buying tobacco and cigarettes, on buying flowers; reduced food rations for Jews. And so on.

In May 1940, the Klemperers are forced to rent out their home and move into a Jews' House. While in the first of several Jews' Houses, Victor Klemperer is charged with an offense against the blackout regulations. He goes to prison for a week in July 1941, and is held in solitary confinement. A trivial sentence, perhaps, compared to the sufferings of many then and of the even greater death and suffering still to come, but the reader cannot help but be in suspense as to whether he will get out. But he is lucky and is released at the end of his sentence.

The climax of the indignities to which Jews still living in Germany were forced to submit was the yellow star, the wearing of which became compulsory on September 19, 1941. Nowhere was the Jew to feel safe, she or he was to be marked out, present but already exiled in the middle of the crowd. For days Klemperer was unable to summon up the courage to leave the Jews' House and go out into the street with the yellow star displayed on his chest.

In autumn 1941, it was also made impossible for Jews to emigrate legally from Germany. But what had prevented Victor Klemperer from leaving the country before that date? Why had the 163,000 Jews still remaining in Germany not left, as the Nazis had encouraged them to do?[12] One factor was age: two thirds of those left were over forty-five, with a much higher proportion of women; then there were the restrictions on immigration imposed by potential host countries. The German state made it increasingly difficult to take assets out, and assets were required to enter other countries (legally, at least). If emigration had been delayed because a person was reluctant to abandon relatives, home, possessions, friends, or because a person regarded him or herself as German, or for all those reasons, in late 1941 there came a point at which it was too late to leave.

But every decision or set of decisions was individual, as Victor Klemperer's diary shows. First, there was the house, which gave his wife a place, a role, in that she designed and furnished it and looked after a large garden. Then there was Klemperer's fear that he would be unable to earn a living abroad, was too old to make a new start and that he would be dependent on the charity of his brother Georg, who had emigrated to the United States in 1935. Also, he never quite abandoned hope that somehow the Nazi dictatorship would fall or be overthrown. If Klemperer was subject to fits of despair at the behavior of "seventy-nine and a half million out of eighty million Germans," he never rejected his German identity. He records the step-by-step humiliation of Jewry and the abuse on the streets. However, from the diaries it is clear that many Germans, not least "ordinary" ones, shopkeepers or laborers, were not blinded by anti-Semitism and expressed their support or helped the couple in some way. It is difficult, therefore, to reconcile the evidence of I Will Bear Witness with the argument of Daniel Goldhagen in *Hitler's Willing Executioners: Ordinary Germans and the Holocaust*, which proposes the existence of an all-pervasive "eliminationist anti-Semitism" as the common sense of Nazi and pre-Nazi Germany.[13] Goldhagen's book is symptomatic of a tendency to search for simple, unambiguous, single-cause explanations for the mass murder of Jews by Nazi Germany. The corollary of this search is a reversion, more generally observable in the 1990s, to arguments, however framed, of national character and also, in the particular German case, to discredited notions of a German *Sonderweg*, a uniquely skewed course of German history.

Certainly, gestures and acts of support by non-Jewish Germans became more difficult and dangerous as Jews were increasingly subjected to shopping restrictions and were forced to wear the star. (In fact, Klemperer often found public expressions of sympathy as painful as abuse.) The marking of the Jews with the yellow star was the immediate prelude to the beginning of the deportation of German Jews to the ghettos and death camps. As noted earlier, it was thanks to his front-line service in World War I, to his wife, and to luck that Victor Klemperer escaped deportation, and survived.

Homecoming

To just once eat well again, to drink well, to drive well, to go to the seaside, to sit comfortably in the cinema ... No 20 year-old can be half as hungry for life ... And with all of that it makes me happy, that E. is working on HER HOUSE, on HER garden and is coming to life again. (June 23, 1945)[14]

In the years after 1945, anyone traveling on the commuter trains from Dresden–Plauen to Dresden Central, which remained as packed as in wartime, might have observed, among the crowds, a small, not especially conspicuous man, a little bent perhaps by decades of industrious work at his desk. This was Prof. Dr. Dr. Victor Klemperer. (Gerhard Wiesner, 1961)[15]

The last entry of the second volume of *I Will Bear Witness* ends with the beautifully simple sentence: "Am späteren Nachmittag stiegen wir nach Dölzschen hinauf"—"In the late afternoon we walked up to Dölzschen." It is Klemperer's modest confirmation of the fact that they are still alive, of the fact that their own house is still standing. That was on June 10, 1945. (The actual account of the journey from southern Germany, much of it on foot, was not completed until some weeks later.)

The German edition of the diaries Victor Klemperer kept during the last part of his life until his death in 1960 are still being prepared for publication. What has appeared in the meantime, however, is a short volume containing, virtually uncut, the entries of the period from June 1945 to the end of the year. This volume has been given the title *Und noch ist alles schwankend*—Everything is still in the balance—a phrase that is repeated and varied throughout these months.

There is no doubt that, after all he and Eva have come through, he has no intention of leaving Germany. It is hardly defiance, merely something taken for granted, even though it is during these months that the scale of the murder of the Jews finally becomes clear. Those who survived the fire-storm return, no one else. Yet once again, Klemperer is determined to pick up the threads of his work, and he soon begins reading through his diaries to compile the material for his book on Nazi language (LTI), even though he has only a vague promise of publication. Almost immediately he is worrying about the future of his academic career. He is also tentatively beginning to make a commitment to a political party. He still sees himself as a skeptic in the tradition of Voltaire *and* as a German patriot. "I am German and I'm waiting for the Germans to return," he wrote on May 30, 1942, "they have gone into hiding somewhere"—a sentence much quoted since the publication of *I Will Bear Witness*. Klemperer, one can say, was German, and had returned, with every intention of working for a better Germany.

Before the year was out, he had joined the Communist Party (KPD) and, for the first time in his life, participated in a political demonstration, for the victims of Fascism. In a general sense, this might appear unsurprising; the KPD might still be regarded as an inheritor of an enlightenment tradition; the Communists, if one disregards the period after the Hitler-Stalin pact, had been virtually the only consistent resisters during the twelve years of the Third Reich; and Klemperer himself had always felt more at ease with the "little people," as he does now with the local Communists who had spent time in prison and in camps. Furthermore, the KPD promised—although Klemperer was well aware of the limits of that promise—to make the most radical break with Nazism. What makes his decision surprising, nevertheless, is the harshness of his criticism of Russian policy and of the KPD, as revealed in his journal of these months. Not least, he is constantly alive to the continuities between Nazi and Communist discourse. (It is perhaps due to these criticisms, as well as to the hostility to Communism in *I Will Bear Witness*, that before 1989 only extracts from Klemperer's diaries and autobiography were published in East Germany.)

There are perhaps two reasons, apart from the general grounds mentioned above, that persuaded Klemperer to join the Communist Party. One was very practical. To get full recognition as a "victim of Fascism" he had to join a political party. Secondly, he was determined that those academics, notably at Dresden University, who had given intellectual support to Nazism, should be punished for their actions, and for this he needed political backing. At the very least they should not be able to continue as teachers as if nothing had happened. He had a particular animosity to his onetime friend, the historian Johannes Kühn, who had broken off contact with Klemperer in 1935, and who had penned propaganda articles. Yet, in July 1945, he had the effrontery to approach Klemperer and greet him as if they had last seen one another only the previous week. (One of the most furious outbursts in Klemperer's diaries was provoked by Johannes Kühn. In an entry dated August 16, 1936, Klemperer wrote, "If one day the situation were reversed and the fate of the vanquished lay in my hands, then I would let all the ordinary folk go and even some of the leaders, who might perhaps after all have had honorable intentions and not known what they were doing. But I would have all the intellectuals strung up, and the professors three feet higher than the rest; they would be left hanging from the lampposts for as long as was compatible with hygiene.")

By 1945 Klemperer would not and could not be as generous as he might have been in 1936. There was certainly no slackening in his anger at Kühn and his like. Nevertheless, Klemperer's campaign seems to have had little success. In 1946 Kühn was appointed to a chair at Leipzig and in 1949 he went west to Heidelberg University.

For a full understanding of the ambivalences of Klemperer's position in the Soviet zone of occupation and in the later German Democratic Republic (East Germany) we shall have to wait for the publication of the final volumes of diaries. Whatever they may reveal, Klemperer's social and scholarly engagement did not diminish. He worked in adult education, on Nazi language, and he completed the book on Voltaire and Rousseau that he had begun in the 1930s. He was made professor in Greifswald, then in Berlin and in Halle. He served in the GDR's People's Chamber and represented GDR scholarship abroad. His specific approach to the Enlightenment, however, which was at the heart of his life's work, made him something of an isolated figure, but he did not waver in his public commitment to the GDR. There is a nice illustration of the peculiarity of his position in a defense of the "classical" heritage in a short article that he wrote for the *Nationalzeitung* in Berlin in 1957.[16]

At the center of the piece is an anecdote about Lenin, which at first sight might seem like hagiography. At the time of the hardest battles (i.e., of the Revolution), Lenin sends a request to a Moscow library for a Greek dictionary, which he requires for something he is working on. Klemperer goes on to say that the Socialist October Revolution, in the person of its initiator, did not separate "old and new humanism." In other words, in Klemperer's hands the Lenin anecdote becomes a plea and an argument for the continuing worth of a classical—Latin and Greek—education in a context dominated by a practical and instrumental attitude to schooling and by the demands of industry and science.

In his final years, Victor Klemperer remained as active as ever, but he had set himself between all possible stools once again. This undoubtedly contributed to the neglect of his work after his death in 1960. For the West, he was tainted by association with the GDR and Communism, for the East, he was insufficiently "materialist."

Busy to the last, Victor Klemperer suffered a heart attack while attending a conference in Brussels. According to the editor of a memorial volume published in 1961, he had been weakened by a lengthy tour of China. Victor Klemperer died in Dresden, aged seventy-eight. He was buried in the suburb of Dölzschen where, against all the odds, he and Eva Klemperer, who had died nine years earlier, had made their home.

The Quality of the Diaries

The German edition of the diaries Victor Klemperer kept during the Third Reich appeared without fanfare in 1995. Within a very short time they had become a runaway publishing success (over 140,000 copies of the 1,500-page hardback edition have been sold). More than that, however, for the German reading public at large it has become one of the key works through which the Third Reich and the murder of the Jews is understood. There have been radio readings of the diaries, a CD, thousands of people in Austria and Germany have attended theater readings, and a television serialization is under way.

The genocide carried out by Nazi Germany has increasingly come to be seen as a defining event of European history. This process of definition was intensified between 1989 and 1995 by the fiftieth anniversary ceremonies of the Second World War and the defeat of Fascism and Nazism. In addition to the huge quantity of earlier publications, many thousands of books dealing with the Nazi period have been published, as well as numerous memoirs. What, then, are the particular qualities of Victor Klemperer's diaries that make them stand out, that make them a reference point? There is no space here to address the whole context, historiographical and otherwise, in which the diaries appeared; I shall attempt to outline only their most distinctive features.

The 1930s and 1940s were decades in which the pressure to keep a diary was especially acute. People wrote down in the privacy of their notebooks what they dared not say openly, although even in them there was circumlocution and self-censorship, the effects of the fear of denunciation and discovery. In Germany, as elsewhere, many diaries and memoirs were published in the years immediately after 1945, the number increasing once more in the 1980s and 1990s, as survivors of the earlier period were able to take stock of their lives. Among all these journals and autobiographies, Victor Klemperer's diaries are unique.

First, they were not written with publication in mind and were never reworked to iron out contradictions and repetitions, to make them stylistically more appealing, to revise judgments or to make retrospective justifications. His words and responses have a rare immediacy. The diaries primarily reflect Klemperer's own need to settle accounts with the events of the day as they affected his own life. As Klemperer grew older, they were more consciously intended to provide source material for his own autobiography, which he worked on for three years from 1939, and then for his book on Nazi language, its functions and effects, which was published shortly after the war. As already mentioned *I Will Bear Witness* is notable in being a chronicle by a Jew of all twelve years of the Nazi Reich. Perhaps more important, the chronicler himself displayed a disarming honesty and directness. His task, as he saw it, was not, in the first instance, to note the great events; there are newspapers and history books for that. Rather he wanted to set down the everyday details, because one could never tell what might later turn out to be significant, and to record his own life in all its moments of cantankerousness, suspicion, hypochondria and bad temper. Yet at the same time this chronicler and analyst of the quotidian in monstrous times never forgets his scholarly and linguistic training. Judgments are made, contradicted and revised, yet nothing is deleted to make the chronicler appear in a better light; the very lack of self-censorship gives rise to more or less involuntary comedy as with the Klemperers' troubles with their secondhand car. Oddly, and no doubt unfairly, Victor Klemperer's own self-obsession as a diarist means that his wife, while a constant presence, does not take on a substantial character of her own. On the one hand, this is the person to whom, in large part, he owes his life, on the other, Eva Klemperer often seems reduced to a bundle of whims and symptoms.

It is certainly not always the case that length, sheer volume and accumulation of detail contribute to the fascination of a text, although it is more true of a diary than of any other form. It is, however, especially true of *I Will Bear Witness*. It is an essential annotation of the criminal nightmare, which Nazi Germany was, but as a journal its power and fascination are also due to the character, Victor Klemperer, that it creates.

In 1905, Victor Klemperer had given up the chance, for a while at least, of continuing his academic career. Instead, he hoped to become a writer. This episode proved to be an interlude, both because the attraction of scholarship proved too strong, and because Klemperer did not have sufficient confidence in achieving recognition as an author. That recognition has now come posthumously both for the 1933–1945 diaries, the subsequently published 1918–1932 journals and for his marvelous autobiography, *Curriculum Vitae*, which covers the years until 1918. With these works Victor Klemperer has after all become a part not only of German but also of European and world literature.

Appendix: A Note on the Translation

The published German edition of Victor Klemperer's Diaries 1933–1945, *Ich will Zeugnis ablegen bis zum letzten* is an abridgment by its editor, Walter Nowojski, of the original German manuscript. For an English-language edition further abridgment was judged necessary to reduce the size of the work and make it accessible to a wide readership. These cuts are of three kinds: A diary which has not been kept or revised with publication in mind will inevitably include many repetitions, some of which should be retained because they are evidence of what is important to the writer, etc. Nevertheless, it was possible to scale down the number of repetitions without affecting the general tone of the work. Secondly, it was also possible to eliminate a number of incidents and reminiscences, for example, of Berlin in the 1890s, which were not central to Victor Klemperer's life during this period or at least to reduce their length. Futhermore, while the gathering of material on Nazi language, which later went under the heading "LTI" in his diaries, was increasingly important as the only intellectual project left to him (he called it his "balancing pole"), a proportion of his evidence and commentary would have been incomprehensible without lengthy explanation of context and language. So cuts were possible, indeed necessary, here too. I have tried to keep the notes as brief as possible, consistent with enlightening the reader as to persons and events. I have taken over or adapted some of the notes in the German edition, cut others (biographical data on eighteenth-century French writers, for example) and added notes on events and phenomena that are likely to be less familiar to the English-language reader. Finally, I have generally retained Victor Klemperer's own dating of the diary entries. There are obvious inconsistencies, but I felt that attempting to adjust days and dates would only cause greater problems.

Martin Chalmers
London, 1998

Notes

1. In 1933, the number of Jews registering as Jewish by confession had been 4,675. Figures in Heike Liebsch, "Ein Tier ist nicht rechtloser und gehetzter: Die Verfolgung und Vernichtung der jüdischen Bevölkerung Dresdens 1933–1937" and Nora Goldenbogen, "Man wird keinen von ihnen wiedersehen: Die Vernichtung der Dresdener Juden 1938–1945," both in Hannes Heer (ed.), *Im Herzen der Finsternis. Victor Klemperer als Chronist der NS-Zeit* (Berlin, 1997).

2. For the fates of a cross section of Dresden's Jews, including many of those mentioned in Victor Klemperer's diaries, see the letter by Heinz Mayer to Rudolf Apt, printed as "Am Beispiel Dresdens" in Gerhard Schoenberner (ed.), *Wir haben es gesehen. Augenzeugenberichte über die Judenverfolgung im 3. Reich* (Wiesbaden, 1988), pp. 413–417. The original is in the Wiener Library, London.

3. Just how relative and precarious is made clear in the diaries. Victor Klemperer, however, seems to have been unaware of the demonstrations in Berlin, in March 1943, by the "Aryan" wives of Jews who had been rounded up for deportation. Afraid of provoking further disturbances, the Nazi authorities relented on this occasion and released the menfolk. The Nazis, of course, viewed this merely as a temporary postponement of their plans to rid Germany completely of Jews. Nevertheless, the Rosenstrasse protest undoubtedly also saved Victor Klemperer's life, even if he did not know it at the time. On the Rosenstrasse protest, see Nathan Stoltzfus, *Resistance of the Heart: Intermarriage and the Rosenstrasse Protest in Nazi Germany* (New York and London, 1996).

4. Victor Klemperer, *LTI: Notizbuch eines Philologen*. The book was first published in 1947. I'm quoting from the 5th Reclam (Leipzig) edition (1978), p. 273.

5. He was well aware of this himself. In one of several remarks in his diaries that refer to his clumsiness in sociable gatherings, he notes, "I made a fool of myself in front of the Klemperers [a banking family of the same name in Dresden]. It's incomprehensible: giving speeches and at any lectern I am so sure of myself— at private parties I'm a failure. I don't know how to move, everything worries

me, I lack all calm and freedom." In Victor Klemperer, *Leben sammeln, nicht fragen wozu and warum. Tagebücher 1918–1924,* October 4, 1921 (Berlin, 1996), p. 511.

6. Auguste Lazar, "Menschliche Unmittelbarkeit" in Fritz Zschech (ed.), *Victor Klemperer zum Gedenken* (Nordhausen, 1961), p. 32.

7. Quoted in Hanns Zischler, *Kafka geht ins Kino* (Reinbek b. Hamburg, 1996), p. 159.

8. Victor Klemperer, *Curriculum Vitae. Erinnerungen 1881–1918* (Berlin, 1989), p. 167.

9. Victor Klemperer, *Leben sammeln, nicht fragen wozu und warum. Tagebücher 1918–1924* (Berlin, 1996), pp. 245 and 250.

10. See Michael Nerlich in a number of publications, esp. "Victor Klemperer Romanist oder warum soll nicht mal ein Wunder geschehen?" in Hannes Heer (ed.), as above. Nerlich has made a spirited advocacy of the importance of Victor Klemperer's contribution to literary studies. Other commentators have been more cautious, suggesting that the undoubted importance of Klemperer's autobiographical work and of his diaries should not lead to an exaggerated estimation of Klemperer as a scholar. Joseph Jurt presents a very fair summary of the case ("Michael Nerlich [ed.], Victor Klemperer—Romanist, no spécial de la revue lendemains 82/83," unpub. review ms. 1996). What is without doubt is the importance of the study of the Enlightenment to Klemperer personally. Not least, it was of crucial importance in allowing him to cope with his situation after 1933: "In the spirit of the men of the Enlightenment Klemperer found an antidote to National Socialism." (Jurt)

11. Victor Klemperer, *Leben sammeln, nicht fragen wozu und warum. Tagebücher 1925–1932,* January 6, 1931 (Berlin, 1996), p. 675.

12. For a useful summary of figures on emigration, etc. see Monika Richarz, "Einleitung" in *Bürger auf Widerruf: Lebenszeugnisse deutscher Juden 1780–1945* (Stuttgart, 1986), pp. 46–52.

13. See Daniel Jonah Goldhagen, *Hitler's Willing Executioners: Ordinary Germans and the Holocaust* (New York, 1996).

14. *Und so ist alles schwankend: Tagebücher Juni bis Dezember 1945* (Berlin, 1995), p. 30.

15. Gerhard Wiesner, Volkstümlichkeit des Erziehens, in Fritz Zschech (ed.), as above.

16. *Nationalzeitung* (15/9/57) reprinted in Fritz Zschech (ed.), as above, pp. 166–167.

CONTENTS

1933

January 14, Saturday

Rectoral election. After a great deal of plotting and scheming Reuther was elected for the second time and Gehrig was defeated. It was a dirty business; they pulled a fast one on our section. Despite my participation in the "Whispering Committee" I felt inwardly almost unmoved. It bothered me just as little that yesterday evening (section meeting) Beste became dean.

The miseries of the new year the same as before, the house, the cold, lack of time, lack of money, no hope of credit, Eva's obsession with building the house, and her desperation, still growing. This business will really be the end of us. I can see it coming and feel helpless.

The Hueber court case also plagues me greatly, robs me of time and is not going well. I should have accepted the 250M I was offered; at law the man's got the advantage over me. With all these distractions the "Image of France" is at a standstill.

Two little things have been agreed with the *Dresdener NN*. Little things (Stendhal anniversary, the new Spain), but they take up time too. Then the lectures, which are always an effort, and the domestic misery (lighting stoves, dusting, drying dishes—precious hours).

[. . .]

Yesterday afternoon Liesel Sebba was here (much aged) and the young Köhlers. From time to time our usual evening guests. Nickelchen was castrated on January 3, and now the two cats are together a lot. I sometimes have the impression that they are the only thing that is a pure joy to Eva and that give her a firm hold on life.

January 24, Tuesday

Annemarie here on Sunday, told us Fritz Köpke, the newspaperman (Harms circle) died in Leipzig. Just over forty. That shook me. I said to Annemarie: Where is his immortal soul? There are happy people who firmly believe in it. Annemarie, almost shocked, very vigorously: "But Victor! Every Christian does!" And afterward, "If there wasn't even the prospect that later things will be better!" So she, the surgeon, who has the corpse, the brain under her knife, who has a university education—and yet quite evidently for all her cynicism and lack of religiosity—is at bottom a believer, or at least hopes—

[. . .]

February 21, afternoon

[. . .]

Increasingly I fall back on reading aloud. Own work almost completely at a standstill. A review for the *Germ.-Rom. Literaturblatt,* that's all. I've put aside the "Image of France" once again. Perhaps during the holidays. On the one hand I'm tortured by lack of time: a drudge lighting stoves, washing up, shopping; on the other a sense of worthlessness. What difference does it make if I leave behind one book more or less! *Vanitas. . . .*

Lectures are coming to an end. Today is my last Tuesday because it's carnival next week. For some while I've been reading the Italy course to four, five people. Monday the conclusion of the France course—next semester the lecture theater will be even more gapingly empty. Things are throttled more and more.

For something like three weeks now the depression of the reactionary government. I am not writing a history of the times here. But I shall nevertheless record my embitterment, greater than I would have imagined I was still capable of feeling. It is a disgrace, which gets worse with every day that passes. And there's not a sound from anyone and everyone's keeping his head down, Jewry most of all and their democratic press. One week after Hitler's appointment we were (on February 5) at the Blumenfelds with Raab. Raab, busybody, political economist, chairman of the Humboldt Club, made a big speech and declared it was necessary to vote for the German Nationals, so as to strengthen the right wing of the coalition. I vehemently took issue with him. More interesting his opinion that Hitler will end in religious madness . . . what is strangest of all is how one is blind in the face of events, how no one has a clue to the real balance of power. Who will have the majority on March 5? Will the terror be tolerated and for how long? It is impossible to make predictions. Meanwhile the uncertainty of the situation affects every single thing. Every attempt to borrow money for building comes to nothing. That weighs heavily on us.

On February 14 the Thieles were here, and we were their guests in the Ratskeller. Melanie told us her husband must not know that Wolfgang, the chemistry student, a good lad, is wearing a Hitler uniform in Frankfurt. He, Thiele, was against Hitler but for banning the Communist Party. [. . .]

We spent a fine evening on the fourteenth with the Köhlers, the "respectable" ones. He wanted to celebrate after the event because he had become a probationary teacher, and because he wanted to express his gratitude to me. We very much felt the effects of excellent sparkling fruit wine.

A fortnight ago I met Wengler in Bismarckplatz, and I noticed that his mouth was twisted and hanging open. Shortly afterward I received news of his illness. A "light" stroke. The man is in his mid-forties. His father died at the same age. Inherited sclerosis or the consequence of syphilis. I visited him last Saturday. He could move, talked, made a good impression (lying down). But he's marked nevertheless. Death all about me. Young

Frau Kühn has had a serious heart attack, sixty-year-old Breit has a very weak heart. I am gripped by the thought of death and it never leaves me now even for an hour.

On the afternoon of February 4 we visited Kube, the harp maker, husband of the beautiful Maria, in his tiny workshop. Using the most primitive means and after months of labor, he has built a whole concert harp and he showed us every detail of this extraordinary work of art.

In the newspapers it is said that Baeumler had been named as candidate for the Prussian Ministry of Culture under Hitler. (Alongside Kriek!) At a section meeting he behaved as if he already *were* minister. We discussed the rescue of the seriously threatened Pedagogical Institute. The German Nationals want to do away with the academic training of schoolteachers. "You overestimate the influence of the German Nationals in the coalition," said Baeumler. — Politics everywhere and everywhere the terror of the Right.

March 10, Friday evening

January 30: Hitler Chancellor. What, up to election Sunday on March 5, I called terror, was a mild prelude. Now the business of 1918 is being exactly repeated, only under a different sign, under the swastika. Again it's astounding how easily everything collapses. What has happened to Bavaria, what has happened to the Reichsbanner etc., etc.? Eight days before the election the clumsy business of the Reichstag fire—I cannot imagine that anyone really believes in Communist perpetrators instead of paid ✠ work. Then the wild prohibitions and acts of violence. And on top of that the never ending propaganda in the street, on the radio, etc. On Saturday, the fourth, I heard a part of Hitler's speech from Königsberg. The front of a hotel at the railway station, illuminated, a torchlight procession in front of it, torchbearers and swastika flag bearers on the balconies and loudspeakers. I understood only occasional words. But the tone! The unctuous bawling, truly bawling, of a priest. — On the Sunday I voted for the Democrats, Eva for the Zentrum. In the evening around nine with the Blumenfelds to the Dembers. As a joke, because I entertained hopes of Bavaria, I wore my Bavarian Service Cross. Then the tremendous election victory of the National Socialists. Their vote doubled in Bavaria. The Horst Wessel Song between the announcements. — An indignant denial, no harm will come to loyal Jews. Directly afterward the Central Association of Jewish Citizens in Thuringia is banned because it had criticized the government in "Talmudic fashion" and disparaged it. Since then day after day commissioners appointed, provincial governments trampled underfoot, flags raised, buildings taken over, people shot, newspapers banned, etc., etc. Yesterday the dramaturge Karl Wolf dismissed "by order of the Nazi Party"—not even in the name of the government—today the whole Saxon cabinet, etc., etc. A complete revolution and party dictatorship. And all opposing forces as if vanished from the face of the earth. It is this utter collapse of a power only recently present, no, its complete disappearance (just as in 1918) that I find so staggering. Que sais-je? — On Monday evening at Frau Schaps with the Gerstles. No one dares say anything anymore, everyone is afraid [. . .] Gerstle was hobbling on crutches, he broke a leg skiing in the Alps. His wife drove her car and took us part of the way home.

How long will I keep my post?

On top of the political pressure the misery of the constant pain in my left arm, the constant thinking about death. And the distressing and always unsuccessful efforts to obtain building money. And the hours of lighting stoves, washing up, keeping house. And the constant sitting at home. And not being able to work, to think.

After cursory reading I wrote a bad newspaper piece, "The New Spain," after previously writing a bad article for *Dante* in Paris, "The Idea of Latinity in Germany." Now I want to—no, I must return to the nightmare of the "Image of France." I want to force myself to write now and catch up on the missing reading chapter by chapter.

I ordered a lot of books for my department, since it turned out there was still 100M left in my budget: Spain, eighteenth-century France and cultural history. On Tuesday I have to give a primary-school teaching candidate the now required unseen translation into French. I am so out of practice myself that I would only make a very poor translation. — [. . .]

March 17, Friday morning

Last Sunday morning in spring weather walked with Eva from the Weisseritz to Hohendölzschen, looked at our plot of land, and back down again. An expedition. In between we rested a little while at the Dembers. We found them alone at table, their children are skiing in Innsbruck. We talked about politics—cautiously, since the windows were open.

For the last two days I have been altogether stymied by a heavy, feverish cold; yesterday in particular I lay around feeling miserable or sat sluggishly in some corner. Today throat and eyes are still in a very bad state but I'm no longer feeling washed out because of the fever. We had invited people today, and were supposed to be at the young Köhlers tomorrow, but had to call off both.

But unfortunately on Tuesday evening we had the Thiemes here. That was dreadful and the end of that. Thieme—of all people—declared himself for the new regime with such fervent conviction and praise. He devoutly repeated all the phrases about unity, upwards, etc. Trude was harmless by comparison. Everything had gone wrong, now we had to try this. "Now we just have to join in this song!" He corrected her vigorously. "We do not *have* to," the right thing was truly and freely voted for. I shall not forgive him *that*. He is a poor swine and afraid for his post. So he runs with the pack. But why to me? Caution in the shape of utterly consistent hypocrisy? Or can he simply not think clearly? Probably—Eva's view— the latter. We have been mistaken in Thieme's intellect. He has a partial mathematical gift. Otherwise he is absolutely at the mercy of every influence, every advertisement, everything successful. Eva already realized that years ago. She says, "He lacks any sense of judgment." But that he would go so far . . . I am breaking with him.

The defeat in 1918 did not depress me as greatly as the present state of affairs. It is shocking how day after day naked acts of violence, breaches of the law, barbaric opinions appear quite undisguised as official decree. The Socialist papers are permanently banned. The "Liberals" tremble. The *Berliner Tageblatt* was recently banned for two days; that can't happen to the *Dresdener Neueste Nachrichten*, it is completely devoted to the government, prints verses to "the old flag," etc.

Individual items: "On the instruction of the Chancellor of the Reich the five men sentenced in the summer by a special court in Beuthen for the killing of a Communist Polish insurgent have been released." (Sentenced to death!) The Saxon Commissioner for Justice orders that the corrosive poison of Marxist and pacifist literature is to be removed from prison libraries, that the penal system must once more be punitive, improving and retributive in its effects, etc., etc. [. . .] We would be more likely to live in a state of law under French Negro occupation than under this government. [. . .] This is truly no empty phrase: I can no longer get rid of the feeling of disgust and shame. And no one stirs; everyone trembles, keeps out of sight.

Thieme told us with gleeful approval of a "punishment expedition" of SA men from the Sachsenwerk against "uppity Communists in Okrilla": castor oil and running a gauntlet of rubber truncheons. If Italians do something like that—well, illiterates, children of the South and beasts . . . but Germans. Thieme was full of enthusiasm for the strong Socialism of the Nazis, showed me their proclamation of Works Council elections in the Sachsenwerk. One day later the elections were banned by Commissioner Killinger.

Actually it's terribly frivolous to write all this in my diary.

March 20, Monday evening about midnight

At the cinema after a long gap: Hindenburg in front of troops and SA men on Sunday the twelfth, the day of the war dead. When I saw him filmed about a year ago, the President walked somewhat stiffly, his hand on the wrist of his escort, but quite firmly and not at all slowly down the Reichstag steps, an old but vigorous man. Today: the tiny, laborious steps of a cripple. Now I understand it all: that is how Father walked after his stroke at Christmas 1911, until he died on February 12, 1912. During that time he was no longer in his right mind. I am now completely certain that Hindenburg is no more than a puppet, that his hand was already being guided on January 30.

Every new government decree, announcement, etc. is more shameful than the previous one. In Dresden an Office to Combat Bolshevism. Reward for important information. Discretion assured. In Breslau Jewish lawyers forbidden to appear in court. In Munich the clumsiest sham of an attempted assassination and linked to it the threat of the "biggest pogrom" if a shot should be fired. Etc., etc. And the newspapers snivel. The *Dresdener Neueste Nachrichten* pays the government compliments. Hitler "as statesman" has always stood for a revision of the peace treaty.

Goebbels as Minister of Advertising. Tomorrow the "Act of State of March 21"! Are they going to have an emperor? The "Square of the Republic" is called Königsplatz—King's Square—again, and they've left the new name for Ebertstrasse in Berlin open. — I think it is quite immaterial whether Germany is a monarchy or a republic—but what I do not expect at all is that it will be rescued from the grip of its new government. I believe anyway that it can never wash off the ignominy of having fallen victim to it. I for my part will never again have faith in Germany.

Today at the Capitol we saw *Grand Hotel*. The film is as moving as Vicki Baum's novel. And altogether outstandingly shot and affectingly acted. Also spoken very naturally. [. . .] the performance also included (see above) March 12 and—with a good lecture—very handsome caravan pictures from Manchuria. I so enjoy going to the cinema; it takes me out of myself. But it is so difficult to persuade Eva to go. And when it doesn't appeal and she sits there miserably, then I don't get any pleasure from it after all. This time things went passably enough, although she suffers a great deal from neuralgia and muscle pain.

March 21

Day of the "Act of State" in Potsdam. Pity that we don't have a radio. — The most frightful pogrom threats in the *Freiheitskampf* together with gruesome medieval reviling of the Jews. — Jewish judges dismissed. — Appointment of a committee to "nationalize" the University of Leipzig. [. . .]

With all of that my "Image of France" crawls along a line at a time. I started writing on March 11; today there are less than seven complete pages.

Fatigue and lethargy. Weariness of life and fear of death.

March 22

Blumenfelds' maid, the honest [. . .] Wend Käthe, gave notice. She had been offered a secure post and the professor will soon no doubt not be in a position to keep a maid anymore. Fräulein Wiechmann visited us. She tells how in her school in Meissen all are bowing down to the swastika, are trembling for their jobs, watching and distrusting one another. A young man with the swastika comes into the school on some official errand or other. A class of fourteen-year-olds immediately begins singing the Horst Wessel Song. Singing in the corridor is not allowed. Fräulein Wiechmann is on duty. "You must forbid this bawling," urge her colleagues. — "*You* do it then. If I forbid *this* bawling, it'll be said that I've taken action against a national song and I'll be out on my ear!" The girls go on bawling. — In a pharmacy toothpaste with the swastika. — A mood of fear such as must have existed in France under the Jacobins. No one fears for their lives *yet*— but for bread and freedom.

March 27, evening

[. . .]

On Saturday four "respectable" Köhlers and the Dembers were here. Conversation was about politics. The Köhlers depressed and cautiously gritting their teeth. — Legal proceedings have been started against Blumenfeld; as joint owner of his brother's brick works he is a double-earner, which is incompatible with his status as a civil servant. The case is pending.

The government is in hot water. "Atrocity propaganda" from abroad because of its Jewish campaign. It is constantly issuing official denials, there are no pogroms, and has Jewish associations issue refutations. But then it openly threatens to proceed against the German Jews—if the mischief making by "World Jewry" does not stop. Meanwhile there is no bloodshed in the country, but oppression, oppression, oppression. No one breathes freely anymore, no free word, neither printed nor spoken.

Nothing by me appears anymore. I work away quietly for myself on the "Image of France."

March 30, Thursday

Yesterday evening at the Blumenfelds with the Dembers. Mood as before a pogrom in the depths of the Middle Ages or in deepest Czarist Russia. During the day the National Socialist boycott call had been announced. We are hostages. The dominant feeling (especially as the Stahlhelm revolt in Brunswick has just been played out and immediately hushed up) is that this reign of terror can hardly last long, but that its fall will bury us. Fantastic Middle Ages: "We"—threatened Jewry. In fact I feel shame more than fear, shame for Germany. I have truly always felt a German. I have always imagined: The twentieth century and Mitteleuropa was different from the fourteenth century and Romania. Mistake. — Dember describes the effects on business: Stock Exchange, setbacks for Christian industry— and then "we" would pay for all of it with our blood. Frau Dember related the case of the ill-treatment of a Communist prisoner which had leaked out: torture with castor oil, beatings, fear—attempted suicide. Frau Blumenfeld whispered to me, Dr. Salzburg's second son, a medical student, has been arrested—letters from him had been found in the home of a Communist. Our parting (after abundant good food) was like a leave-taking at the front.

Yesterday a wretched statement in the *Dresdener Neueste Nachrichten*— "on our own account." They are 92.5 percent founded on Aryan capital, Herr Wolff, owner of the remaining 7.5 percent, has resigned as chief editor, one Jewish editor has been given leave of absence (poor Fentl!), the other ten are Aryans. Terrible! — In a toy shop a children's ball with the swastika.

March 31, Friday evening

Ever more hopeless. The boycott begins tomorrow. Yellow placards, men on guard. Pressure to pay Christian employees two months salary, to dismiss Jewish ones. No reply to the impressive letter of the Jews to the President of the Reich and to the government. [. . .] No one dares make a move. The Dresden student body made a declaration today: United behind . . . and the honor of German students forbids them to come into contact with Jews. They are not allowed to enter the Student House. How much Jewish money went toward this Student House only a few years ago!

In Munich Jewish university teachers have already been prevented from setting foot in the university.

The proclamation and injunction of the boycott committee decrees "Religion is immaterial," only race matters. If, in the case of the owners of a business, the husband is Jewish, the wife Christian or the other way around, then the business counts as Jewish.

At Gusti Wieghardt's yesterday evening. The most depressed atmosphere. During the night at about three—Eva unable to sleep—Eva advised me to give notice on our apartment today, perhaps renting a part of it again. I gave notice today. The future is quite uncertain. [. . .]

On Tuesday at the new Universum cinema on Prager Strasse. Beside me a soldier of the Reichswehr, a mere boy, and his not very attractive girl. It was the evening before the boycott announcement. Conversation during an Alsberg advertisement. He: "One really shouldn't go to a Jew to shop." She: "But it's so terribly cheap." He: "Then it's bad and doesn't last." She, reflective, quite matter-of-fact, without the least pathos: "No, really, it's just as good and lasts just as long, really just like in Christian shops—and so much cheaper." He falls silent. When Hitler, Hindenburg, etc. appeared, he clapped enthusiastically. Later, during the utterly American jazz band film, clearly with a touch of Yiddish at points, he clapped even more enthusiastically.

The events of March 21 were shown, including passages from speeches, Hindenburg's proclamation laborious, his breath short, the voice of a very old man who is physically near the end. Hitler declaiming like a pastor. Goebbels looks uncommonly Jewish [. . .]. We saw a torchlight procession and a great deal of marching awakening Germany. Also Danzig with the swastika flag.

[. . .]

April 3, Monday evening

On Saturday red posters on the shops: "Recognized German-Christian enterprise." In between them closed shops, SA men in front of them with triangular boards: "Whoever buys from the Jew supports the foreign boycott and destroys the German economy." — People poured down Prager Strasse and looked at it all. That was the boycott. "For the time being only Saturday—then a pause until Wednesday." Excluding banks. Including lawyers and doctors. Called off after one day—it has been a success and Germany is "magnanimous." But in truth a wild turnaround. Evidently resistance at home and abroad and evidently from the other side pressure from the National Socialist mob. I have the impression of swiftly approaching catastrophe. That the right wing cannot go on participating much longer, cannot put up with the National Socialist dictatorship much longer, that on the other hand Hitler is no longer free and that the National Socialists are urging ever greater use of force. Today the rectors of Frankfurt University, the Technical University Brunswick; Kantorowicz, the director of the Bonn University hospital; a Christian business editor of the *Frankfurter Zeitung* were arrested. Etc. There will be an explosion—but we may pay for it with our lives, we Jews. [. . .] I am unable to work on my "Image of France." [. . .] Everything I considered un-German, brutality, injustice, hypocrisy, mass suggestion to the point of intoxication, all of it flourishes here.

On Saturday evening in Heidenau to visit Annemarie and Dr. Dressel. Both on the Right, both anti–National Socialist and dismayed. But both isolated by the mood in their St. John's Hospital. — On Sunday afternoon by myself for an hour with the deeply depressed Blumenfelds. I complain at length about Eva, whose state of health suffers in the extreme from the German catastrophe; I believe that in all the difficult years since Lugano I have never seen her in such despair. At her request I've given notice here for July 1. In order to save money, we decided to share the flat and rent only three rooms. I have directed Prätorius to fence in my plot. 635M costs out of 1,100M reserves! We are making frantic efforts to borrow 8,000 to 10,000M to build a small house or part of one. But it is now *even more* hopeless than before. For us personally, everything is also heading for catastrophe.

April 7, Friday morning

The pressure I am under is greater than in the war, and for the first time in my life I feel political hatred for a group (as I did not during the war), a deadly hatred. In the war I was subject to military law, but subject to law nevertheless; now I am at the mercy of an arbitrary power. Today (it changes) I am again less certain that the catastrophe will occur soon.

No one dares write a letter, no one dares make a telephone call, we visit one another and weigh up our chances. One civil servant at the Ministry said this, another that. But one never knows whether the one with the favorable opinion will remain in charge, or to what degree he's "in charge" at all, etc., etc. No beast has fewer rights and is less hounded. — Yesterday Albert Hirsch wrote to me from Frankfurt am Main: "leave of absence" after thirteen years service. Unsure what to live on. Is moving with wife and two children to the parents-in-law. Perhaps, at best, he'll receive a few pennies for a pension, but certainly not anywhere near enough to live on. *One* case out of thousands, thousands upon thousands. [. . .] Whether I shall keep my post will probably be settled on May 2, at my first lecture.

Meanwhile further efforts to erect a small house in Dölzschen. Last personal reserves went on fencing. The work has begun now. Yesterday the earth was plowed up. The farmer, the team of horses, eight hours work: 20M. The fence will cost 624M. Dölzschen demands the costs of laying sewer drains immediately: 340M. Total: one thousand marks—last reserves.

In between domestic work, the building business (never ending effort, deliberations, brooding) I wearily collect my thoughts for a work I hardly believe anymore will be printed or made use of in my course. Chapter II/Part One of the "Image of France" is ready at last.

Newspapers are read differently now [. . .]. Between the lines. Art of the eighteenth century, the art of reading and writing awakens again.

[. . .]

April 10, Monday

The awful feeling of "Thank God, I'm alive." The new Civil Service "law" leaves me, as a front-line veteran, in my post—at least for the time being (Dember and Blumenfeld are also spared). But all around rabble-rousing, misery, fear and trembling. A cousin of Dember, doctor in Berlin, fetched from his office in his shirtsleeves and brought to the Humboldt Hospital in a very bad state, and died there, forty-five years of age. Frau Dember whispers it to us with the door closed. By telling us she's spreading "atrocity stories," untrue ones of course.

We are often up in Dölzschen. Our "field" is now going to get its fence, we have ordered seven cherry trees and ten gooseberry bushes. I force myself to act as enthusiastically as if I believed in the building of the house, so that I even believe it a little myself and thus am able, as a kind of self-hypnosis, to shore up Eva's mood. But it does not always work, Eva is in a bad way and the political catastrophe affects her terribly. (Sometimes, for a few moments, I almost feel that the great universal hatred forces her to rise a little above the obsession with her own personal sufferings, that it strengthens her will to live. [. . .]

Man is bad. My quite involuntary feeling, when I learned that Dember and Blumenfeld were also to be allowed to escape destruction, was a kind of disappointment. As one is disappointed when someone given up for lost escapes with his life after all. But it is very probable that all of us will pay in the end. [. . .]

Annemarie Köhler was here yesterday evening. Filled with the greatest bitterness. She tells us how fanatical the male and female nurses in her hospital are. They sit around the loudspeaker. When the Horst Wessel Song is sung (every evening and at other times too), they stand up and raise their arms in the Nazi greeting.

[. . .] "Image of France" goes very very slowly. It takes too much out of me, and I have far too little hope.

I hear nothing from my relatives, nothing from the Meyerhofs. No one dares write. — No other post either.

One is an alien species or a Jew with 25 percent Jewish blood, if one grandparent was Jewish. As in fifteenth-century Spain, but then the issue was faith. Today it's zoology + business.

April 12, Wednesday evening

In the afternoon—nice walk, but heart trouble—alone to the Dölzschen council office. To ask them to divide the sewer drain costs (340M) into installments. Six installments granted. Up there the Social Democrat mayor has been suspended. I was received by the commissioner (giant of a man, Teuton with goatee) and the barrel-shaped council surveyor, both in SA uniform. The first time that I've dealt with such people. Both *very* polite, the commissioner a little reserved, visibly anxious about his dignity, the fat one a very homely Saxon, right away chatting to me about the University and the Teacher Training Institute—I must emphasize once again: both uncommonly polite. But here I saw for the first time with my own eyes that we really are entirely at the mercy of the Party dictatorship, of the "Third Reich," that the Party no longer makes any secret of its absolute power.

And every day new abominations. A Jewish lawyer in Chemnitz kidnapped and shot. "Provocateurs in SA uniform, common criminals." Provision of the Civil Service Law. Anyone who has one Jewish grandparent is a Jew. "In case of doubt the final decision lies with the Specialist for Racial Research in the Reich Interior Ministry." A worker or employee who is not nationally minded can be dismissed in any factory, [and] must be replaced by a nationally minded one. The NS plant cells must be consulted. Etc., etc.

For the moment I am still safe. But as someone on the gallows, who has the rope around his neck, is safe. At any moment a new "law" can kick away the steps on which I'm standing and then I'm hanging.

I'm constantly listening for "symptoms." A resentful speech by Hugenberg; Oberfohren, the parliamentary leader of the German Nationals, resigning his seat. Friction between SA and Stahlhelm—but what does it all amount to? Power, a tremendous power, is in the hands of the National Socialists. Half a million armed men, all offices and instruments of state, press and radio, the mood of the inebriated millions. I cannot see where salvation could come from. [. . .]

The Spanish Ministry of Education has offered Einstein a professorship at a Spanish university, he has accepted. This is the strangest joke of world history. Germany establishes limpieza de la sangre—Spain appoints the German Jew.

April 20, Thursday evening

Is it the influence of the tremendous propaganda—films, broadcasting, newspapers, flags, ever more celebrations (today is the Day of the Nation, Adolf the Leader's birthday)? Or is it the trembling, slavish fear all around? I almost believe now that I shall not see the end of this tyranny. And I am almost used to the condition of being without rights. I simply am not German and Aryan, but a Jew and must be grateful if I'm allowed to stay alive. — They are expert at advertising. The day before yesterday we saw (and heard) on film how Hitler holds his big rallies. The mass of SA men in front of him, the half-dozen microphones in front of his lectern, which transmit his words to 600,000 SA men in the whole Third Reich— one sees his omnipotence and keeps one's head down. And always the Horst Wessel Song. And everyone knuckles under. How wretched the Doctors' Congress in Wiesbaden. Gratitude to Hitler—even if the racial question has not yet been clarified, even if the "aliens" Wassermann, Ehrlich, Neisser have made important contributions to our medicine—we thank Hitler, he is saving Germany! Likewise the rest.

April 25, Tuesday

Since telephone calls are unsafe, and since everyone is depressed, we constantly have nerve-racking morning or afternoon visits. Frau Dember, Frau Wieghardt. Today, recovered, but bent over with paralysis, Wengler. Always the same conversations, the same despair, the same vacillation: Catastrophe is imminent, and things will go on like this for a long time yet, there is no salvation, always the same aversion. Eva's nerves are completely gone. The political loathing and the disastrous effect on our credit go hand in hand for her. No morning without violent weeping, no day without hysterics. I am already almost blunted in the face of all this misfortune. I no longer think about tomorrow.

Yesterday Frau Schaps and the Blumenfelds were our guests, the day before the Wieghardts, on Sunday we were invited to the "respectable" Köhlers and accompanied part of the way home by the young people. The same conversations everywhere.

At the TU Dember is now the most threatened because he was imposed on it when Fleissner was Minister [of Education]. He is suffering tremendously. A circular requested all non-Aryans to leave all committees and not to conduct examinations. God knows how that's feasible. Non-Aryans in our section, Holldack (mother), Kafka (father) . . . In Kiel the students have put un-German texts by their former and no longer acceptable teachers on the index. [. . .] Something similar is expected here. — The Prussian Minister of Education has ordered that school pupils who have had to repeat a year should, where possible, if they are members of the Hitler movement, [. . .] move up after all. — Notice on the Student House (likewise at all the universities): "When the Jew writes in German, he lies," henceforth he is to be allowed to write only in Hebrew. Jewish books must be characterized as "translations."—I only note the most ghastly things, only fragments of the madness in which we are unceasingly immersed.

Despite everything our fence is just being finished in Dölzschen, we are planning to do more—but it is quite impossible to look forward to a real dwelling, there is simply no money and credit. I really do not know what else can be done. On this point too we are facing catastrophe. We have bought gardening tools and trees; we want to go up today to do some digging.

My "Image of France" is at a standstill for days, then grows by a few lines, is at a standstill again. And yet there is no point at all in thinking of publication. And all my faith in national psychology—where has it gone? Perhaps the current madness is indeed a typically German madness. I shall write an appendix about it, which will certainly not be intended for publication.

[. . .]

The fate of the Hitler movement will undoubtedly be decided by the Jewish business. I do not understand why they have made this point of their program so central. It will sink them. But we will probably go down with them.

April 30, Sunday evening

Dember has been "given leave of absence until further notice." A statement by the student body on the bulletin board, "A Jewish professor breaks his word," pilloried him, because despite his promise he had given an examination. He says he never made this promise. He is being thrown out because he was given his chair by the Ministry against the will of rector and senate. Kafka, Holldack (50 percent Jewish) threatened, Gehrig threatened because he's a Democrat, Wilbrandt goes because he's a Socialist. — Baeumler made Professor of Political Pedagogy in Berlin, where Spranger has had to go. — But I hear from Annemarie Köhler on the telephone that Georg had to go. (I have completely lost touch with my family; no one writes to me.)

Tomorrow "the festival of labor." The Stahlhelm now subordinated to Hitler, Hugenberg about to collapse. I very much have the firm impression that the catastrophe cannot be long postponed.

[...]

In the mornings Eva often has the most violent nervous crises. "I have been going to pieces for years and no one helps me!" Then somewhat calmer during the day.

On the twenty-eighth the whole day on our plot of land. The trees were planted. She was up there with Frau Lehmann, I followed in the afternoon. Coffee in the beautifully situated Café Hohendölzschen. Afterward at the Dembers for a while. [...]

All in all I exist apathetically beyond despair and almost beyond indifference. Tomorrow another appointment with a money man; perhaps a loan can be obtained after all. But my finances are on the point of collapse. I don't earn a penny anymore aside from the 800M of my salary. And the Kirschberg swallows it up and swallows it up.

May 15, Monday evening

I'm lecturing. Old French to six, cultural history to about twenty, the seminar to ten people. All quiet. But, in compliance with the "request" from the rectorship, I don't examine. I did not attend the section meeting either. — We received sympathy visits: on the evening of the section meeting from Frau Kühn, on the Sunday after from Delekat. Delekat had just given a sermon in the Kreuzkirche—it is possible "to say more" than in a lecture. He was wearing a frock coat, had his cassock in a little case. — A visit from Frau Hirche. Gratitude and fear struggle for the soul of the Hirches. *He had to* join the National Socialist Party; the lad is serving his first weeks in the Reichswehr. He owes his acceptance as officer-cadet in very large part to *me* (reference and recommendation to Rüdiger). Beste, now dean, stands up for me, is inwardly embittered (Zentrum man). But everywhere complete helplessness, cowardice, fear.

[...]

I broke curtly and definitively with Thieme, who had declared his enthusiasm for the new regime. He phoned us with an invitation. I said, we did not want to come and I would like to end the telephone conversation, hung up.

Annemarie fears for her post because she refused to take part in the procession on May 1. She (who is a supporter of the German Nationals through and through) relates: The garden of a Communist in Heidenau is dug up, there is supposed to be a machine-gun in it. He denies it, nothing is found; to squeeze a confession out of him, he is beaten to death. The corpse brought to the hospital. Boot marks on the stomach, fist-sized holes in the back, cotton wool stuffed into them. Official post mortem result: Cause of death dysentery, which frequently causes premature "death spots."

Atrocity stories are lies and severely punished.

Jule Sebba in Dresden for a couple of days. Here one evening with Frau Schaps. The next evening we were at Frau Schaps. The Gerstles and the Salzburgs there too. Very cordial, but no new points of contact and not many of the old ones anymore. The conversations the same everywhere, the situation in Königsberg no different from here.

The next morning and for a couple of days after Eva even more shattered than usual. Neuralgia in her failing knee, severe fits of weeping and despair: cripple, "too late," she is being allowed to go to pieces without the least pity being taken on her. My heart cannot bear all this misery much longer.

Constant pain in my throat, hoarseness, pains in arm and shoulder.

On top of that the house business is more hopeless than ever. Prätorius had gotten hold of a Polish-Jewish broker called Sandel. He was going to raise—as good as certain, 99 percent probability!—15,000M in Offenbach on easy terms. I paid him 240M, almost the very last penny of my reserves. Then it all fell through, the man was even impertinent, and now I have no idea what else I can do. From time to time Eva goes up to Hohendölzschen, to varnish and paint our fence, etc. Going there and back costs 6M each time, but the expedition does not satisfy her. I cannot go on. My extra income has dried up completely, not a line by me is printed. I have given up thinking about things. I feel it's all coming to an end.

The "Image of France" creeps on. Perhaps it will be published posthumously. [. . .]

Of the National Socialists' criminal and insane acts I only make a note of what somehow touches me personally. Everything else can be looked up in the newspapers. The *mood* of the present time, the waiting, the visiting one another, the counting of days, the inhibited telephone conversations and correspondence—all of that could be recorded in memoirs one day. But my life is coming to an end, and these memoirs will never be written.

May 22, Monday

May 16 passed very gloomily this time. — Eva's nerves have now given out so completely that I too am hardly able to bear up anymore: My heart gives way more and more.

New misfortune, not to be taken lightly: Our little black tomcat has fallen ill. Wound on his stomach, the animal is suffering, the treatment by

Dr. Gross is distressing (and expensive). — On the evening of the nineteenth Herr Kaufmann was here as grass widower. His wife in Berlin with Edgar's family. They are going to Palestine next week, leaving the child with its grandparents for the present, taking 15,000M with them, want to find some kind of livelihood. Sick joke, passed on by the Dembers: An immigrant to Palestine is asked, "Are you coming from conviction or from Germany?"—Letter from Georg: He himself is retired ("they could have held on to me"); Otto, the physicist; Friedrich, the medical probationer; and the youngest, who is in the middle of his examinations in economics, want to emigrate to England or America; Hans, who has just got a son, has "up to now" not yet been dismissed by Siemens. — Three people today in my Old French lecture; cultural history and tutorial, however, better attended (about twenty and ten students).

[...]

House affair hopeless. It will send Eva and myself literally to our graves.

Since Hitler's peace speech and the easing of tension in foreign affairs I have lost all hope of living to see the end of this state of affairs.

[...]

June 17, Sunday morning

Dialectic of the soul. During the day I now forcibly cling to some relatively pleasant event or other, even the most trivial thing like the growth of a philodendron leaf or the improved condition of our little Nickelchen-Amfortas tomcat, whose stomach wound heals and then opens again (even though he was treated by Dr. Gross for some considerable time). It is really indispensable to find such support for oneself. [...]

I am content if Eva begins the morning without a weeping and screaming fit, falls asleep quite easily in the evening. I put out of my mind the fact that she does not go out, lets the harmonium, the piano gather dust, etc., etc.

I put the despair over the whole housing business out of my mind. There is no chance of finding building money. Sandel, a Polish Jew, has cheated me of 240M, does not want to pay it back, and counts on my being too afraid of the scandal to go to the police (for me to report a Jew, now! But I shall have to do it nevertheless, otherwise Prätorius and Gestein will think I'm frightened—and they are right to think so). I am now entirely without reserves, hardly know how to find the money for insurance policies, rent, etc.—and all extra income has ceased.

I had given notice here for July 1 and have withdrawn it again, but only until October 1. What is going to happen here in the winter? Eva detests the apartment, in the winter it is literally her prison. I too dread all the laying of fires. [...]

I believe my own health to be gone. Repeated heart trouble. I don't go to the doctor. He cannot tell me anything, at most forbid me to smoke.

Berthold reached the age of 59, perhaps that is how long I shall last. And sometimes my pointless horror of death is already numbed by all the sorrow and gloom. I see no way out. We are immobile in every respect. Occasionally one of Eva's little expeditions by cab to Dölzschen, where she paints our fence. Then I fetch her in the evening by cab. After intervals of months a visit to the cinema.

Recent guests: for a couple of hours (after more than two years) on his way to an NSDAP-ordered pharmacists' "coordination" day from his little town of Plauen—Scherner. Unchanged and his tubby heartiness was for me really very remote and strange. He has stopped his payments and yet is quite cheerful. One day the pharmacy will pay its way again and then he'll exchange it for one in Leipzig and will leave the small-town dump he hates. He complains, he has hopes, he is alive and kicking, he revolves in his tiny circle, is content. His friends in Leipzig. Dr. Schingnitz—he is leader of the National Socialists, their representative at the university. Scherner does not like the Nazis at all—but why hold that against Schingnitz? He really wants to get on!

Lissy Meyerhof was here on Whitsunday and Whit Monday. As optimistic as ever, modest, hard-working, yet her health obviously weakened, heart trouble. She has—so far—kept her post as social worker (war service, nurse in contagious diseases hospital). Also Martha Wiechmann and her sister, who is now living with her. Her brother, mid-forties, not a member of a party, senior district attorney at the High Court in Berlin, "placed on temporary retirement" on the grounds that a National Socialist must occupy this highest post. That same evening Fräulein Rüdiger was here, after a very long gap. Her brother, major in the old army, has a post in the National Socialist Party. "Your nerves are completely shattered, you should go somewhere where there aren't any newspapers," she said to me, when she heard my bitterness; she has no idea what is really happening.

At university my examinations have been transferred to Wengler (explicitly for my "protection," to keep me in my post). I am now lecturing on Old French literature to three students, I go through my Cultural History contortions in front of about twenty students. My most eager student is the Nazi cell leader Eva Theissig.

Also here over Whitsun was Hans Hirche, whom I—I!—helped get into the army. Looked splendid and talked very sensibly. He and his parental home evidently completely anti-Hitlerist. Hostility in the Reichswehr against the SA, attitudes more often right wing than Hitlerist, but nevertheless also a lot of National Socialism—which is compulsorily "encouraged." One never knows.

Two surprises of a more pleasant kind: Contrary to all expectations Flitner has started printing my 1931–32 education paper. [. . .] Walzel (and he has the next twelve months to decide) wrote to me, Heiss has withdrawn from his Romance literatures around 1850, whether I wanted to manage the second volume. I proposed: Schürr, French; Hatzfeld, Spanish; and myself, Italian and general introduction. I am dying to know how it will develop; deep down, however, yes or no is all the same to me. On the one hand pro Italia: God knows whether my old contracts are still worth anything, and this would be a reliable new one. It would mean a change, renewal. In addition, a subject that would also interest Eva, she would read with me. For once I would be quite outside my usual province. I have wanted to come to grips with modern Italy for a long time. — D'altra parte, a vast amount of work, for which I am not at all prepared, which thrusts me completely away from my "life's work," and I do not know how much time I still have. — And yet: Does it make any difference at all *what* I spend the remainder of my time doing? Just do something and forget oneself.

At last: On June 11, exactly three months to the day after starting, "The New German Image of France" was completed; yesterday and the day before yesterday I wrote the very peculiar "Afterword" to it and want to read it aloud this evening, as the Blumenfelds, the young Köhlers, the Wenglers are our guests.

We saw and heard the delightful Kiepura film *Be Mine Tonight* (Lugano landscape and a profusion of songs, arias) for the *third* time. (When Kiepura's concert in Berlin was banned, he was the Jew Kiepura; in the Hugenberg film he is "the famous tenor from La Scala, Milan"; in Prague recently, when his German song "Heute nacht oder nie" [Tonight or never] was booed, he was "the German singer Kiepura.")

I am corresponding with Professor I. Elbogen, Orthodox Jew and brother-in-law of the musician Otto Klemperer (the Catholic!). A relief agency for German university teachers is being set up in London, it seems to involve publication of journals above all, and he has inquired about details of people in the Romance and philological fields.

[. . .]

June 19, Monday (after lecture to three people)

On Saturday I read out my "Afterword." Shock. How could I keep something like that in the house? Köhler advised: hide it behind a picture. — But what shall I do with my diaries? I wait from one day to the next. Nothing stirs. Sometimes I lose all heart and believe that this regime will last after all and outlive me.

[. . .]

In the meantime I work up reviews. [. . .] I wrote to Hübner, asking whether he still intended to take my "Image of France." So far no reply.

The complaint to the police regarding Sandel's swindle is finished and in the envelope. I send it off with a heavy heart, God knows what kind of scandal I will be dragged into. But what will the Prätorius' say (and what will they do) if I do not take the matter to the police? They will then think that I positively want to protect the *Jew* (which Sandel is firmly counting on), or even: I *should* do so. A terrible situation.

June 29, Thursday evening

Of the 29 June 29s of our life together, this is basically the most dismal; but we have fairly successfully endeavored to get through it calmly. I read aloud. Now in the evening Karl Wieghardt is with us by chance. Since Hugenberg went yesterday without the least resistance and the German National Party "has dissolved itself," I have lost all courage.

June 30, Friday morning

There are, of course, also personal grounds for such complete loss of courage. Hübner asked me (in a very friendly, intimate—between the lines, almost in them—very depressed letter), in the name of the publisher Quelle & Meyer, not to insist on the publication of the "Image of France." There was too much supervision by not very qualified "Party cells," and after all the *good* journals must not be eliminated altogether. I withdrew, resistance would have been pointless, completely pointless—but Eva thought: Only do things under compulsion! Do not give even the appearance of voluntary renunciation.

Meanwhile for a couple of weeks I lived on Walzel's offer. [...] But I give Teubner and Quelle & Meyer excuse for termination if I do not prepare their thing in the first place for delivery on time. A dilemma, whichever way you look at it. [...] Now responsibility for saying "no" has been passed on to Walzel, who will certainly shift it on to the publishing house (both of necessity; Walzel himself has meanwhile had to resign from the management of the Kleist Society). I would not find this No, in itself, so bad. I no longer have enough energy to seriously immerse myself in a new subject, in a language that is less familiar to me; I muddle on in French. But what terrifies me is the thought of not being able to publish anything at all anymore. Quelle & Meyer and Teubner will not print anything else by me. If someone does not *want* to abide by a contract, he can always get out of it, at least as a publisher. In my case very easily; I never meet a delivery date, after all. — Now I am seriously thinking of giving up all academic scribbling for a long time and taking a stab at my life. But with that I would more or less acknowledge the complete loss of additional earnings, as is already the case, and accept it without any attempt to defend myself.

But the money difficulties—a bank balance of 40M at the moment!—worry me dreadfully. I barely manage to scrape together insurance payments, rent, etc., building is out of the question, the agreement here has been extended to October 1, and we dread the winter.

The Sandel affair is almost funny and yet also distressing. The man swindled me out of 240M, was neither in Offenbach, nor did he hand over the money, he has admitted everything to Prätorius and refused to repay anything. Since the Prätorius' know all about the business, in the end I had to report it; otherwise people would have said, one Jew protects another! But what a scandal, or at least what embarrassment I face with public proceedings. So finally, after X warnings, it has been reported to the police. On Saturday an extremely courteous call, inquiring when I would come to make a statement, Inspector Schrell, room 123 at police headquarters. Went there on Monday after my lecture. On the door: "Fraud," next door: "Serious Crimes." Large room, policemen, clattering typewriters. Schrell a very courteous, large man, plain clothes, small swastika. Puts Sandel's statement in front of me. Smiling a little pityingly, how could I be taken in by a man like that? Sandel, Polish Jew and citizen, "previous convictions," admits everything and explains that the money had gone while he was drunk. "He spent it," says the police officer. I could only confirm Sandel's statement. "What happens now?"—"Goes to the prosecuting attorney's office."—"Do I get my money?"—"*We* only punish the crime. Once Sandel has been sentenced, you can sue for your loss!"

[...]

The day before yesterday Dember here (alone) in the evening. Nothing to occupy himself with, waiting feverishly, between hope and despair. He says, we all have an "emigrant mentality," we hope for deliverance from abroad, i.e., for German defeat, invasion, etc. An evening visit by Fräulein Walter on the twenty-first tallied with that. Her father was my father's successor in Bromberg, is now rabbi in Kassel. She took her political economy examination in Leipzig, is a librarian at the State Library, is facing certain dismissal, wants to go to Palestine. She has been Zionist for some time, orthodox, kosher, flirts with Russia, nevertheless well educated and not really fanatical. But she has never really been attached to Germany, so is less vulnerable inside. Among other things she told us that observant Jews get their meat from Denmark.

I have noticed: Since June 20 government declarations no longer talk about "national awakening" (stage I) or about "national revolution" (stage II). Instead the new slogan is the desired "total state." Under the "people's chancellor." On June 29 a Reich minister (Goebbels in Stuttgart) said for the first time in a public speech: We do not tolerate any parties apart from us, Hitler is "absolute master" in Germany (Hindenburg gone).

Reviews: Schröder, *Racine und Humanität*, Burkart, *Mme. La Fayette* completed and sent off together with Appel, *Misanthrope*. Strangely enough accepted by the *Literatur Zeitung* and prospects of new ones held out. I cling to the faintest possibility of publication. Anything rather than be completely buried.

Read aloud two very affecting things. First: Nitti, *Flight* (bought for 95Pf in the Reka only a couple of weeks ago. Now of course impossible to obtain). A nephew of the former Italian Prime Minister, who escaped from Lipari to Corsica in 1928 and relates his experiences in Fascist captivity. Gripped by the exact analogies to *our* situation. The man is writing after five years of Fascism and predicting its certain end. Meanwhile Mussolini has ruled for another five years and is absolute master. And here the thing has only been going on for five months, in fact even less.

Even more affecting: Fallada, *Little Man–What Now?* Recent reading. And always the thought: For years every tenth man in Germany has been unemployed.

For my lexicon I must add to *protective custody*—the *people's chancellor.*

July 1, Saturday

Language note: Goebbels in the Political Academy on June 30 (formal lecture therefore) on Fascism (approvingly therefore): "The Fascist Party [in Italy] has brought into being a huge organization of many millions which includes everything, popular theater, popular games, sport, tourism, hiking, singing and is supported by the state with every resource." (Report *Dresdener NN*, July 1.)

At the Blumenfelds yesterday evening. Emigrant mentality. Jule Sebba and his family go to Palestine in August.

July 9, Sunday

On Friday evening at Frau Schaps; Jule Sebba there for one day. He is emigrating with his family. Lawyer since 1909, notary, teacher at the High School for Commerce, Königsberg, author of a major work on German maritime law, not among those thrown out and yet left with no alternative. With his family (little Elfriede is eleven now, she is with her grandmother here) he truly has to begin a new life. The harbor at Haifa will be opened in October; he is going to open a chandler's business there. He has found an elderly partner with experience in the Orient, he himself is providing the money. (Evidently he has assets safely abroad.) The Sebba case is not the most tragic; Sebba likes business and has a talent for it, he has never felt a special bond with Germany, his parents came from Russia— and yet his whole education and way of life make him a German. — We hear a lot about Palestine now; it does not appeal to us. Anyone who goes there exchanges nationalism and narrowness for nationalism and narrowness. Also it is a country for capitalists. It is about the size of the province of East Prussia; inhabitants: 200,000 Jews and 800,000 Arabs. — Sebba spoke very pessimistically about Germany. He said the boycott against us was very tight. The regime will maintain itself for a while with tyranny and the most extreme coercive measures like bread rationing, wage reductions, inflation, perhaps last the winter, perhaps even longer—but *then* there will be an unimaginable and bloody chaos. Because after the fall of this government there would be no "fall-back position" because it has destroyed every organization. (In the course of the last few weeks the one remaining party, the Zentrum, dissolved itself.) He makes the worst predictions for the Jews.

For my part it becomes ever more clear to me how completely useless a creature of over-refinement I am, incapable of surviving in more primitive surroundings. Sebba, Blumenfeld, Dember earn a living here and there, can somehow switch to practical things. I, on the other hand, I cannot even be a language teacher, only lecture on the history of ideas, and only in German and from a completely German perspective. I must live here and die here.

We are also continuing with our desperate efforts on behalf of our construction in Dölzschen. Now I have got in touch with a broker again, this time he is called Mendelsohn. Yet I am entirely bereft of money. Yesterday I received a supplementary demand for land transfer tax: 150M. [. . .] I can barely manage to pay it on top of the life insurance which is due now + the interest and on top of the money for the drains. Furthermore a cut in salary is likely next month or the one after.

It has been raining without a break for weeks; now it has become oppressively humid with a constant threat of thunderstorms. Yesterday we were up for the first time since Whitsun; our plot has been transformed into a prairie, grass and thistles are well past knee height. Afterward we sat in the Dembers' garden for a little while. "Emigrant" conversations.

Today, after quite a lot of work, I finished the review of Brummer's *Naigeon* for the *Literaturblatt*—of course I do not know if it will be printed. With that the pile of criticism is disposed of for the time being and now my hands are free for a new extended piece of work. For which one? I am still waiting for Walzel's decision. He suggested leaving Fascist Italy since 1918 to the "German sympathizer" Schürr, I rejected that and demanded the whole period 1850–1933. He will not be able to agree to that; in that case I shall turn to my 18e siècle and will certainly make a better decision as a result—but naturally I would be less wounded if matters took a different course.

[. . .]

July 13, Thursday evening

Eva's birthday passed tolerably. In the evening the Blumenfelds, the Kühns, Annemarie, Karl Wieghardt—in the afternoon the young Köhlers. — Kühn, who predicts a long life for the 3rd Reich, but considers it ultimately transient, made an interesting remark. He said Mussolini's regime corresponded to the tyrannies of the Italian Renaissance, it is therefore evidently compatible with the Italian psyche and will last for example like the rule of the Medici, Este, etc., it is a "southern" form of government. In Germany (and that is my opinion also after all) this form is nowhere to be found in its history, it is absolutely un-German and consequently will not have any kind of long-term duration. But for the moment it is organized with German thoroughness and therefore unlikely to be removed in the foreseeable future.

July 20, Thursday

Frau Blumenfeld's brother, the missionary preacher, was here for a visit with his wife, fell ill suddenly and died very quickly after an unsuccessful gallbladder operation, fifty-four years old. (We became acquainted with the man and his son some time ago, were supposed to spend the evening with him on Sunday—he died in the afternoon.) The funeral took place yesterday in the Chemnitzer Strasse cemetery below the Blumenfelds' windows. The Blumenfelds' friends from the intelligentsia: the Raabs, Frau Schaps, Frau Dember, etc. and the plebeian sectarian congregation the man had here in Dresden. In the hall somebody in street clothes [. . .], of the type of the thoughtful Red Indian, preached very interestingly. (Frau Schaps maintains the speaker had been a professor and engineer.) The life of the deceased: Jew + actor, then worked for a travel agency in Italy, his finger traces routes across the map. "Then God takes pity on this finger." An American Christian, to whom the man is giving Italian lessons, converts him to the Old Testament and then to the "Lamb of God." He changes his religion, he preaches. "Covenant of Christians." We know no race, no nation, only Christians and everywhere the Old Testament and the Lamb of God. And the departed has the gift of preaching in many tongues. He travels about, sometimes he supports himself with other occupations, but he preaches, he converts Jews to the Lamb of God. And he "sees Jesus," and makes him visible to others.

This address not bad, and with the equality of all Christians emphasized by a curious gesture—the palm of the hand tilted and brought down in front of the eyes like a roller blind: We do not recognize the limits of races and nations—altogether topical and bold. But then at the grave a downright comical cinema scene. An old man, white nautical beard, fat, red, blue-tinged face, preached yet again, a Bible in one hand, waving a pince-nez in the other, bawling, weeping, very long and quite childishly sectarian. 400 years before, the wise men of the Bible foretold the Savior down to the smallest detail, described his grave exactly, etc. And thus we are happy in our faith . . . Abrupt contradictions followed one another with remarkable naïveté: "He is sleeping until the Resurrection—he is not sleeping, he is already in heaven; we rejoice—we must have consolation." (I have never encountered such a muddling of the two ideas of being asleep and being on the other side and of being rewarded or atoning as yesterday.) But there are countless people who still have the strength for some kind of simple belief (or *unbelief*). I only have the quite childish horror of the grave and of nothingness—no more than that.

I was at the funeral without Eva. She is feeling very poorly again. On the telephone I heard that the first speaker was a professor at the TU, District Architect Neuffer. Lectures on reinforced concrete, on solid and wooden building and preaches that one "sees Jesus"—in addition has the courage to speak out against the limits of blood and of nation. There are happily organized people!

[...]

Political situation bleak. The only comfort or hope is when the tyranny manifests itself ever more wildly, i.e., ever more uncertain of itself: the ceremony at the grave of the "Rathenau eliminators." [...] A sound film recording of Hitler, a few sentences in front of a big meeting—clenched fists, twisted face, wild bawling—"on January 30 they were still laughing at me, they won't be laughing anymore . . ." It seems that perhaps for the moment he is all-powerful—but the voice and gestures expressed impotent rage. Doubts of his omnipotence? Does one unceasingly talk about a thousand years and enemies destroyed, if one is certain of these thousand years and this annihilation? [...]

July 28, Friday morning

Exhausting heat for days.

I ended the lecture course on Tuesday. I allowed myself a couple of half-hidden or flagrant provocations in the course of this cultural history lecture, in part deliberate, in part involuntary—it could have cost me the professorship. The oddest thing was my relationship with Eva Theissig, who is fond of me and is Party Cell Organizer or something, at any rate an adherent of the new regime. As she took her leave of me, to go to Freiburg, I gave her this advice: "Less politics and more scholarship! And don't give so much of yourself to this cause. Yours is scholarship—and one can never know what the future may bring politically. You understand me—my advice places me in your hands, I wish you well." She asked if she could continue to turn to me for advice. I believe that she and a thousand other supporters and members of the Party were disappointed long ago. I believe (or do I only hope?)—it cannot last much longer. How hysterical all the words and deeds of the government are! The endless threatening of the death sentence, the arrest of hostages, recently the interruption of all long-distance travel from noon to 12:40 P.M. "Search for subversive couriers and pamphlets throughout Germany!" In addition the ridiculous incessant articles about "the victorious battle for work in East Prussia" (where of course there are no unemployed during the harvest), about the ending of the boycott movement abroad, etc.

I met Beste, the current dean, political economist, Catholic: It cannot last! [...] The last days of the semester presented the TU with the Gesslerhut: the "Hitler greeting" made obligatory. Obligatory only within "the place of service." But: "It is expected that the greeting will also be used elsewhere in order to avoid suspicion of an attitude hostile to the state!" Until now minor employees and colleagues greeted me with a nod of the head as always, and I responded in the same way. But in offices I saw employees constantly raising their arms to one another. [. . .]

The *Polish* Jew Sandel. He has stated that he lost the 240M he received from me in the course of a drinking spree. He told Prätorius that he had been with some SA men. The attorney's office has abandoned proceedings. Really I am rather glad, why be drawn into something and yet get nothing back anyway? (The prosecution only punishes—but is not concerned with restitution.) But what course would the affair have taken if the man had been a *German* Jew and did not have some SA men up his sleeve?

Our neighbor Schmidt is building his little house and after long, in part comical, negotiations is laying his drain through our plot. We can also use this drain and are laying water and gas at the same time. That is something at least and increases the value of the plot. But what never ending misery to manage all of it with a few pennies. I have to find 300M for life insurance by August 31—how can I put by the money in August for the mains connections? I count every penny, I have never been in such straits as now. All supplementary sources of income are completely cut off.

I no longer have the peace of mind to write my diary. À quoi bon? I shall never get around to any memoirs; whether in four or five years time one notebook more or less is burned—à quoi bon? And yet the thought of the memoirs excites me ever more strongly. My very first theater review comes to mind. In the Berlin Theater I booed Wilbrandt's *Timandara*, and someone offered to box my ears. That must have been before 1900. — The first political opinion that was my own. During the Boer War, I was pro-English. I think I was instinctively against the glorification of the farmers, the old days, the old Germans.

The Schmidts showed us their little house—the roof-raising ceremony takes place today. A poor primitive stone building. The husband himself works hard during his holidays with pick and shovel. Yesterday he received us like a building worker, his shirt torn open, a handkerchief knotted on his head, perspiring. He is a minor tax officer, but was serving as a sergeant when war broke out, showed us the shot in the lungs he got on August 20, 1914, at Gumbinnen, was then in Siberia for nearly six years until 1921 and is now an officially coordinated tax official with wife and two children. A strong man, in his early forties—I was a little envious of his simple happiness.

[. . .]

I am ploddingly and hopelessly reading Crébillon for the Eighteenth Century. I do not believe that I shall once again find the youthful boldness for a grand and blind general survey, I am drowning in material and scruples. [. . .]

August 10, Thursday

[...]

The building affair makes no progress and brings us only one disappointment after another and thus slowly digs our grave. (These are not mere words.) Recently old Prätorius was completely certain—he had talked to the "manager"—that I could obtain a 6,000M loan from the Municipal Bank. Twice there in the blazing midday sun. Then the "manager" turned out to be a junior clerk, and the department boss refused us with almost pitying amusement. It really is beneath one's dignity. But *without* the building work I shall certainly be unable to pull Eva through this life for very much longer.

I have heard nothing more from Walzel and inwardly I am completely finished with the Italian plan. For about a fortnight now I have been sticking very seriously to the work on the Eighteenth Century. In my few hours of vigor it gives me real pleasure. But it seems boundless and hopeless. A few pages are already filled with notes: Crébillon, La Motte, etc. But I no longer believe that I shall manage to write this volume, still less that I shall ever see it published. One simply has to get through this time with decency. I do not feel at all well and do not believe that I have a long life ahead of me. Especially since I cannot do anything at all to recover my health.

Details from the time that is flitting past. Young Fleischhauer (after years) addressed me on the street. Probationary teacher, engaged, German National. He was with his fiancée and elegantly dressed. "Don't be surprised if you meet me in the Stahlhelm uniform and with a swastika armband. I *have to*—and as a member of the Stahlhelm I am, after all, something *better* and *different* from an SA man, and deliverance will come from the Stahlhelm." (Not from the Democrats—from the German Nationals.)—Frau Krappmann, the cleaning woman, fat "coffee sister" of Frau Lehmann, her husband a driver with the post office. She relates with tears in her eyes: one of her husband's colleagues dismissed on the spot because he did not greet with his arm raised. A friend freed from a concentration camp. There, as a man who wears spectacles, he had to answer to the name "spectacle hound," he had to fetch his food bowl crawling on all fours if he wanted to eat any food. On his release he had to sign that he would be silent about everything. — Stepun sent me a Fräulein Isakowitz for vocational guidance. She took her school-leaving certificate at Easter, father a Jewish dentist. She would like to become an interpreter. How? The institute in Mannheim has been moved to Heidelberg, Gutkind removed—who knows where—non-Aryans are not admitted. She wants to try and study here for one or two semesters. Questionable if she'll be allowed to. Fräulein Günzburger, an older student of Walzel, who came to my lectures for a while, sends me her dissertation from Paris. A part of it printed. The whole thing was supposed to be a volume in Walzel's collection. On the uses of style by the German Romantics. She received her doctorate in December '32 in Rouen. Now Hueber refuses to publish the book of a Jewish author. Her parents have emigrated to Haifa. At the moment, thanks to Lichtenberger's good offices, she herself has an award at the Cité universitaire. Future uncertain. In her curriculum vitae she names as her teachers after Walzel: Curtius, Klemperer, Rothacker, Spitzer. The first and probably also last time that I have been named as a teacher by a doctoral candidate. [. . .] Dember finally "put on the retired list." Finally—if this government is final. [. . .]

I want, even if in abbreviated form, to carry on my diary as if the time still remained for me to one day write the planned memoirs. I want to work at the Eighteenth Century as if the time still remained to me to write the book one day. Perhaps I shall after all get over my present depression and after all have a dozen years before me. Perhaps Eva will one day become a healthy and happier person again. At any rate there is no point at all in supine despair. But I await each day in greater anguish than I did when I was younger.

Astonishing and altogether cheering is the wealth of the State Library with respect to the eighteenth century. Long forgotten authors in several editions. It was European literature, and the Saxon kings were Europeans. Today I admired the abundance of voyages literature. For the time being I ordered nineteen volumes for the reading room.

[. . .]

August 19, Saturday

[. . .]

On August 12 (eight days ago today) we were the Kühns' guests in the (early) evening. Just the two of us. The trip to Weintraube, the short walk out in Lössnitz to the Kühns, afterward back to the tram at about twelve: for us that in itself was an outing and travel and a very welcome change. The evening alone with the Kühns (and their very handsome Angora cat, which once appeared gigantic to us, but now fairly small) passed very pleasantly. Kühn, whom I frequently meet at the State Library now, continues to think that Hitler's prospects are very good. He will hold on, modify his aims, but not be overthrown. The German nation, perhaps mankind, wants nothing better. — Frau Kühn talked about the difficulties of the lawyers, the Christian ones. There are no bankruptcies anymore—a National Socialist does not go bankrupt, everything like that is twisted around along with German law. A few days ago it was reported in the newspapers, forty-three percent fewer bankruptcy proceedings than under the former government! [. . .]

A novel, or too improbable for a novel. I have still not received the documents relating to my war service from Munich. It does not take much imagination to understand what is happening: Munich does not find the documents—have already received a further request—and consequently I am dismissed here. Now, around midday on Wednesday, the sixteenth, an apparently youthful SA officer addresses me on Prager Strasse. Three stars on his epaulettes, Iron Cross, First Class, and other decorations. Good-natured, friendly face, *quite* unknown to me. "Excuse me? Did you not serve with the Bavarians during the war? With the Sixth Battery of the Sixth Bavarian Field Artillery Regiment?—Zinsmeister." I pretended that I remembered him, but did not have a clue. I felt my way, what was he doing here? what was his profession? "Electrician. I have been posted here to Koch & Sterzel [. . .] after that I am to get a permanent government post" (in Baden I think). I took my leave with a few friendly words. Had he not been wearing the uniform, I would probably have invited him home. At any rate: a witness. He said he had recognized me at once. (After eighteen years!)

On Tuesday, August 15, a bus trip—a "mystery tour." *The* fashionable thing—for the petit bourgeois, for the elderly, for those who have difficulty walking. As we left the station at two, the mystery tour by tram was also just setting off (even more emphatically for the "little people," because cheaper, 1.50 against 3 or 4M in the bus). At the front a car with the conductors' band, then nine or ten full carriages. There were three buses, each with some thirty passengers (a couple on little folding chairs) and a *manager* and a master of ceremonies, who made short humorous speeches, helped when people were getting out, etc. Fortunately our (third) bus was open, and when on the return journey it rained a couple of times, our master of ceremonies, Reissmann (he had introduced himself), had constantly to wind the top up and down. We really drove zigzag into the blue to the accompaniment of a great deal of guessing. [. . .]

For coffee we were at the table of two elderly ladies "of better society," superior gossips, completely Aryan, fragments of their conversation: indignation that some Jewish doctor—such a fine man, such a good family—has been deprived of his livelihood. — After coffee there was "cabaret" in the large room. The three *managers* performed all sorts of things. Only the solemn first poem, "Michel, be German!" against foreigners. But not a shred of politics, no anti-Semitism—the most harmless comedy, animal voices, dialects, etc. [. . .] The whole leisurely excursion [. . .] probably lasted two and a half to three hours. [. . .]

From now on I want always to note briefly what occurs to me in relation to my memoirs. Do I already have my first independent political impulse? In 1899 I was for the English when everyone, the whole Jewish business of Löwenstein & Hecht, was enthusiastically for the Boers. My first impression of American music: the Sousa band in Paris in 1903. How they came in one after another and began to play. How they played "Washington Post." My first awareness of a big war: I was crossing Kantstrasse in Berlin with Eva, and the special editions were shouting about the Japanese torpedo attack at Port Arthur.

I simply cannot believe that the mood of the masses is really still behind Hitler. Too many signs of the opposite. But everyone, literally everyone cringes with fear. No letter, no telephone conversation, no word on the street is safe anymore. Everyone fears the next person may be an informer. Frau Krappmann warns against the all too National Socialist Frau Lehmann—and Frau Lehmann tells us with great bitterness that her brother has been sentenced to one year in prison because he lent a "real Communist" a copy of the *Rote Fahne* [Red Flag], but the "real Communist" had been an informer.

Eighteenth Century, first half, back and forth, always with the greatest interest and always with a sense of oceanic inexhaustibility. Travel accounts in the State Library (quartos) and at home (octavos), La Fosse, La Motte, Piron. "Over and done with": Petermann, *Vers und Prosa Streit.* Mornet, *Pensée française.* The hardest thing some day will be arrangement. Organize the thing as a whole? Disjecta membra? Currents? Types of literature? But I often believe, mostly in fact, that this "some day" will never come now. I have lost the impudent, superficial and nevertheless talented attack of my earlier years. To copy out and merely assemble in my own way does not tempt me anymore.

August 22, Tuesday, toward evening

Every day a bit of Eighteenth Century, itself, about it, and every day more discouraged. [. . .] A second mystery tour yesterday, Monday, and again very satisfactory. This time it really went through everyday Dresden, the plainer north of the city—and yet very pretty. [. . .]

August 28, Monday

On Saturday we undertook a third mystery tour. It was an exact repetition of the first. This time I saw more of the landscape than the first time. We did not bother with part of the entertainment and walked down the beautiful country road toward the Rabenauer Grund. [. . .]

The trip was doubly spoiled for me. First of all, my eyes are becoming ever more sensitive to light, severe eye pains running toward the back of my head tormented me the whole time and for the whole of the evening. And then, an exceedingly hostile and devastating expert opinion in the Hueber case had arrived in the morning. According to it I (my handwriting) must take almost all the blame and Hueber is allowed to offset 514M against my claim of 600M. If that is accepted, not only do I not get any fee, I also have to find 2,300M costs—the opinion alone costs 132M. I kept the thing to myself the whole day so as not to upset Eva, who is suffering from her nerves again. — Not until yesterday, when I was already thinking more calmly about everything and had a reply in mind, did I tell Eva as undramatically as possible—much more lightly than I see the business in fact. The effect was nevertheless catastrophic. Diesterweg had rejected my

"Image of France" two days before, because it is "purely backward looking" and neglects "national points of view." So all earnings possibilities
are cut off; and since all, absolutely all attempts to procure money for
building have come to nothing, and our financial position becomes ever
more desperate—a civil servant can provide no security, least of all a non-
Aryan one!—and since the dreaded winter is drawing closer, Eva is close
to despair once more. Even successful excursions, little walks, etc. only
bring momentary improvement. Immediately afterward there are always
the self-tormenting words, pleasures for a cripple!
    [. . .]
On one occasion, on a Sunday morning, I was up in Dölzschen alone
and went walking with Dember for half an hour; a few days later Dember
and wife came for supper. He is terribly bitter, isolated and obsessed by
his misfortune, a man completely thrown off his balance, almost broken.
    [. . .]
I am still leafing through my old travelers, the lettres édifiantes, La
Hontan, etc. I still feel very gloomy as far as my Eighteenth Century is
concerned.
    A day later: ultimatum from the government. I had to provide evidence
within four days of my hitherto "merely presumed" front-line service.
Today my "Front-line service certificate" arrived from Munich. It attests
"one engagement" and "trench warfare in French Flanders from
19.11.15–19.2.16." Eva immediately said that was not right, and indeed
going through my letters I found that I was still at the front on April 4 and
was only admitted to military hospital that day. I do not like to go through
the dusty old bundles. Besides the certificate is sufficient. I will not complain for the time being.

September 6, Wednesday morning

On Thursday, August 31, our fourth mystery tour (we do everything in series). I had eye preservers with me and for the first time avoided all
headache. Landscape especially beautiful. Through the New Town to the
"Wilder Mann." Boxdorf, Dippelsdorf—so again the heath, ponds and in
the distance Schloss Moritzburg, Weinböhla, Niederau, Meissen [. . .]
    On Saturday, September 2, at the Köhlers. Pleasant and peaceful as al-
ways. It does one good to be with "Aryans" to whom the present tyranny
is as terrible as it is to us. After twelve o'clock the young Köhlers accompanied us home on foot. We invited them up for a tot of whisky and it
began to rain. We sat up till half past two and got to bed at three.
    I write at length about pleasures; they are the exception, and in general
our life proceeds very unhappily. Eva is forever ailing and seriously depressed; I myself am constantly plagued by heart and eye trouble. And
there is the constant pointless tyranny, uncertainty and dishonorableness

of our position in the Third Reich. My hopes of a swift about-face are fading. The streets crowded with SA. The Nürnberg Party Rally has just been
raging. The press worships Hitler like God and the prophets rolled into
one. — On top of that no change in the continuing pressure of the misery
of the house business. — If only Eva could play music, everything would
not be half as bad and perhaps quite good.

I continue reading on the eighteenth century. A good book would come
out of it if I were to stay alive long enough. But I need years (plural) for it.
My eyes fail me all too often while I am working, all too often I also fall
asleep in the morning. Nevertheless my studies give me something to
hold on to and a degree of consolation.

Walter Jelski, the eternal bohemian, asked us in a pretty letter from
Basel whether he could spend the winter with us as "maid of all work."
We would really have been glad to take him in, but we had to (really: *had
to*) refuse because we do not have enough money. Our finances are hopeless. Gutkind, deprived of his post at the Interpreters' Institute in
Mannheim, wrote a letter from Paris. He is working on French sports language. I wrote to him: One has to work on the language of sports in the
way that Hettner dealt with the Enlightenment: England-America, Germany, France. This trinity would yield a very fine study in comparative
culture and idealist philology. On the situation or as comfort I merely
wrote (on a postcard): "We'll chat again ès chambres des dames, cf.
Joinville, éd. Wailly, ¶243." As in the days of the Encyclopedia!

Fräulein Günzburger asked me from Paris to recommend her to the
chairman of the Alliance israélite, the Indologist Sylvain Levi. I did so in a
German letter.

[...]

September 15, Friday afternoon

The great mystery tour, the fifth and probably the last (the first to Lübau,
second to Liegau, third to Lübau, fourth Meissen-Friedensburg) because
now it's the time for bad autumn weather and early darkness. [...]

On September 8 we ate at the Blumenfelds. Frau Dember and Herr
Gerstle were there too. Dember himself is mysteriously in Switzerland,
he is signing a contract there with Turkey and will be professor at the
University of Constantinople for a few years. Frau Gerstle was in
Königsberg helping to pack. The Sebba family is now really going to
Haifa; we shall probably see them here tomorrow. I disliked Gerstle's attitude. He seemed almost to have reconciled himself to the situation, at
least he was resigned to the will of God, declared Hitler a genius, did
"not want to underestimate" the enemy "too much," evidently considered the current situation not to be the worst of all possible bad situations, etc., etc.

On the twelfth we were up in Dölzschen, on our ill-fated plot and at Frau Dember's. These rare excursions to Dölzschen affect Eva badly—precisely because they are wearisome, because she does not get anything at all out of her land; and because she sees houses going up all around (when we bought, there were two houses on the Strasse am Kirschberg, now there are almost seven), whereas we make no progress. Hopeless. Her mood darkens repeatedly, she is often really ill, lies in bed all morning—and my own health declines more and more.

September 17, Sunday evening

Yesterday afternoon at Frau Schaps. Took leave of the Sebbas, who now really are emigrating to Haifa. Their furniture is already afloat, and they themselves are traveling to Trieste today, going on by boat from there. I exchanged a few very heartfelt words with Jule Sebba. All sentimentality was avoided, and as soon as everyone was sitting down together we talked very pleasantly. But underneath it all there was nevertheless very deep sorrow, bitterness, love and hate. It touched me greatly, Eva was hit terribly hard. Jule Sebba said he had always felt he was an Eastern Jew and therefore rootless and not attached to Germanness. But after all he is exchanging Europe and security for a new colony and uncertainty, he is leaving with wife and child and starting again as a fifty-year-old. We two, Eva and I, suffer immensely because Germany violates all justice and all culture in such a manner.

That same evening we had, for the first time in a long while, a large party here once again—the four "respectable" Köhlers, Annemarie and the Wenglers, brother and sister. All evening there was only one subject of conversation, the frightful one. We make jokes and laugh and are basically all in despair. [. . .]

September 19, Tuesday evening

Contemporary history on film! This time the Nürnberg rally of the Nazi Party. What stage direction of the crowds and what hysteria! Hitler consecrates new standards by touching them with the "blood flag" of 1923: Gunfire every time the flag cloths touch. (Eva says, "Catholic hysteria.") [. . .]

This morning State Library. I find it impossible to work there: I only study the catalog, choose things, get my bearings. I am repeatedly amazed at the wealth of 18e siècle.

A long time with my lawyer in the afternoon. My case, now almost a year old, is going very badly. Hueber's senseless counterclaim, the hostile expert opinion. We passed on to politics and since Langenhan is a sympathetic, trustworthy man, I got a chance to talk about the precariousness of

my situation, about my great bitterness. He was very shocked. He said he
and his circle had always been against Hitler's immoderate anti-Semitism,
but it was new to him, and it depressed him greatly, that so much mischief
was being caused. He said we were no longer a state based on law.

[. . .]

October 9, Monday

Birthday wishes: To see Eva healthy once again, in our own house, at her
harmonium. Not to have to tremble every morning and evening in anticipation of hysterics. To see the end of the tyranny and its bloody downfall.
See my Eighteenth Century finished and published. No pains in my side
and no thoughts of death.

I do not believe that even one of these wishes will come true for me.

The mood at home and the health of both of us became really poor
when our last hope of building money came to nothing, when there
proved to be no prospect of somehow being able to move up to Dölzschen.
We must stay here, and that means imprisonment for Eva all through the
winter and more housework for me and more blows to my literally and
not only metaphorically tired heart.

On top of that the growing tyranny, the growing misery and sinking
hope of any foreseeable end. (Although the gnashing of teeth in the most
diverse social strata is becoming ever more audible.) — Especially repugnant to us is the behavior of some Jews. They are beginning to submit inwardly and to regard the new ghetto situation atavistically as a legal
condition that has to be accepted. Gerstle, the director of the lucrative Fig
Coffee Company, brother-in-law by the way of the emigrated Jule Sebba,
says Hitler is a genius, and if only the foreign boycott of Germany ceases,
then one will be able to live; Blumenfeld thinks one must "not live on illusions" and "face facts"; Kaufmann—his son in Palestine!—says something
similar, and his wife, forever the silly goose, has got so accustomed to the
slogans of press and radio that she parrots the phrases about the "vanquished system" whose unsoundness had been proven once and for all.
Recently, on September 25, after a gap of years, we had to go to the Kaufmanns for a ghastly coffee afternoon, because the Hamburg sister, Frau
Rosenberg, was there and because we could not evade the constant invitations any longer. [. . .] Anyone who does not at every hour of the day
hope for revolt is a low dog! Eva's bitterness is even greater than mine.
National Socialism, she says, more precisely the attitude of the Jews
toward it, is making her anti-Semitic.

Dember is now certain of an invitation to the University of Constantinople and will move there in the middle of October. Actually I envy
him. We were often together recently. Once, after a meeting, which I did
not attend, Robert Wilbrandt called me, whether we would like to come

to him for tea. We had visited their then very new villa near Wachwitz some years ago, then the thing had petered out. We accepted and did not go. A week later I telephoned him to apologize and invited him here. He accepted—"but must ask us whether we wished to have a guest who was a danger to the state?"—"Why?"—He had been suddenly dismissed. He was here on Saturday, without his wife, who had a colic problem. "Politically unreliable," the business with the pacifist Gumbel, whom he had stood up for (while he was still in Marburg), had been dug up. The man is 58, in poor health, no longer well-to-do, has children from two marriages. [. . .] The Blumenfelds were here that same evening and Gusti Wieghardt, back after four months in Thurø, where she and her sister stayed with Karen Michaelis. A little émigré and Communist group seems to have gathered there. Then yesterday evening Gusti was here alone with us, and tomorrow we shall visit her. We tell one another many details, horror stories, "fairy stories" of course. Opinions on the duration of the state of affairs diverge, no one believes in a swift change, what will happen afterward no one knows. What is certain is that the terror gets worse every day.

I met Ulich in the State Library. He has been suspended on half pay. He tells me pressure is being put on him to give up his honorary professorship voluntarily. Otherwise he will be reduced to 200M. Since his first wife, Ulich-Beil, has likewise been dismissed, he has to provide for two families alone.

Holldack, the once proud Teuton (his mother is Jewish), has approached Dember to ask whether there are any possibilities for him in Constantinople; he no longer feels safe here.

Georg wrote to me today, his Otto is at the Cavendish Laboratory in Cambridge, his youngest, the economist, installed in Chicago, the fate of the two middle sons is still uncertain. Marta wrote, the three Sussmann daughters are "gone." In her muddled way she forgot to say where.

One could adapt the proverb and say, "The worse is the enemy of the bad"; I am beginning to think that Mussolini's regime is almost human and European. Eight days ago on Saturday we were guests of the Wenglers, brother and sister. They have moved into a small but pretty apartment on Weintraubenstrasse. Wengler has completely recovered from his stroke. Spaak, a drawing teacher and painter, later his wife, the actress Lotte Crusius, who—gray haired, old—could be his mother, were there as well. Both somehow "coordinated," outwardly at least. [. . .]

On her return journey Gusti Wieghardt visited her very right-wing relatives in Berlin: the widow of District Judge Mühlbach, the latter's mother, the rectoress, and her son, Lieutenant Mühlbach. Bitterness everywhere and throughout that stratum. Georg Mühlbach is supposed to have been ill literally for weeks, he had trained SA people with the greatest reluctance. — Gusti also told us a great deal about several especially bad concentration camps. About the misery the now sixty-year-old Erich Mühsam is suffering. He had already been released when a diary he had kept during his imprisonment was found and he was fetched back. I myself am constantly being warned about keeping a diary. But then so far I am not suspected of anything.

A sudden decree to make the whole of Tuesday afternoon and half of Thursday afternoon free for military sports. The Cultural Sciences Section can basically only lecture in the afternoon. A series of lectures was simply canceled. Scholarship is no longer essential.

[...]

Birthday greetings from Wally arrived in the afternoon. Her three daughters: Lotte is completing her medical training in England, the commercial Käte and Hilde in Stockholm and the USA. The parents alone.

[...]

For me slowly, interestingly and hopelessly on with the Eighteenth Century. With the minor figures, along the edges, amid the facts. Geoffroy, La Harpe. What has to be described is the absolute dissolution into one another of Enlightenment, Rococo, Early Romanticism, idea, sentiment, abstraction and positivism, the république des lettres une et indivisible, the siècle des lumières poétiques. [...] But I do not believe that I shall still manage this book. Not that and not the "Memories."

October 22, Sunday

Something from a novel. A couple of weeks ago we were infuriated by Gerstle. His brother-in-law in Palestine, and he comes to terms with the "genius" Hitler and desires only a slackening of the foreign boycott. [...] A little while ago Frau Schaps telephoned to say she wanted to visit us in the evening for coffee. Her Gerstle children have been invited to dinner at the Blumenfelds and would bring her to us in the car. At eight o'clock in the evening she called to cancel. It is not possible today, I should not be angry, another time. Depressed voice, no reasons given. Eight days later with the Blumenfelds at the Dembers' farewell coffee. That was last Thursday, and yesterday Dember left for Constantinople, his family follows him in November. Grete Blumenfeld very downcast, tearful. I inquired, she wanted to cover up, it gradually came out bit by bit. Frau Schaps—her "second mother," Toni Gerstle—her closest friend. "I shall never see them again." That evening the Gerstles had not gone to the Blumenfelds after all. Suddenly "gone away." Difficulties had been raised at his factory, they wanted to impose "changes." He required foreign currency for his Fig purchases, no doubt he did not stick to the regulations. Meanwhile the whole family—under new German law hostages are taken after all—was officially at their country house in Oberbärenburg, de facto presumably already over the border (to Czechoslovakia). Flight to the Holy Land; what property they take with them, what the genius Hitler will keep, I do not know. Neither I nor Eva nor Gusti Wieghardt could suppress our Schadenfreude. That evening I delivered a fierce speech to Blumenfeld on the duty of inner readiness, on the duty not to let hate slacken for even an hour.

October 23, Monday

Friedmann dismissed in Leipzig, Olschki in Heidelberg. — I heard today that Walter Jelski is going to Palestine. All three Sussmann daughters are abroad.

Fritz Thiele here a few days ago, with him District Attorney Fischer, whom we got to know in Leipzig. Neither of them friends of the Nazis, even if not vehement opponents. We ate at the Ratskeller with them.

Once, on the fourteenth, at the "respectable" Köhlers. Here there is particular indignation at the "German Christians." Since her return from Denmark Gusti Wieghardt is often here.

When the withdrawal from the League of Nations took place a few days ago, I believed for a moment that this could accelerate the fall of the government. I no longer believe it. The plebiscite and the splendid Reichstag "election" on November 12 are magnificent advertising. No one will dare *not* to vote, and no one will respond with a No in the vote of confidence. Because (1) Nobody believes in the secrecy of the ballot and (2) A No will be taken as a Yes anyway.

There are some things I shall hardly live to see: (1) the fall of the government, (2) the construction of our house, (3) the straightforward enjoyment of a few days. — Constant pains, and I do not know to what extent they are rheumatic in nature, to what extend to do with my heart. Always Eva's depression. Always money problems.

Twice—pleasant autumn excursions—we were out at Hauser's; a veritable estate near Tolkewitz. Choosing trees. For several days now Eva has been making everything ready for planting. She goes up at eleven, I fetch her at three. The taxi costs 5 to 6M every time. Then afterward she is very tired and even more sad than before. Now she wants to have a wall or a bit of terrace made. I shall go on saying yes down to the last penny, but I shall soon reach that last penny. My shrunken salary is further suffering from "voluntary" deductions. "Winter Aid," "National Work" one percent of total income, ten percent of income tax—that is how it is assessed. "Rector and Senate have agreed—if there is no objection, the cashier's office will deduct the sum from the salary." Who dares object? And no possibility of publishing anything. The philological journals, the journal of the university association have adopted the opinions and jargon of the Third Reich to such an extent that every page makes one feel sick. The November criminals—Hitler's iron broom—the Jewish spirit—free scholarship on National Socialist foundations, etc., etc.

[...]

October 30, Monday, toward evening

I work, I spend money as if my future were secure. Yet every hour I receive a warning from my heart, and I believe that my health is close to collapse and that either the tyranny will last for a long time yet or be superseded by chaos. *I shall* continue to behave as-if, anything else would be even more pointless.

The expenditures: Eva goes up to Dölzschen and back every day by taxi. Today was the big planting day, a whole park. That may cost 100M, a fortune for me now. Also I am raising money on my life insurance again, probably about 600M, to have a cellar, a dugout, as it were, built up there. That will mean even more interest payments. But Eva is desperate and putting pressure on me, I cannot and do not want to offer resistance—perhaps she will prove to be in the right, and the house will be built after all. And if everything goes to pieces, then at least she has had some happiness, and I have done what I could, perhaps even more.

My work: Prévost for days, notes on the *Homme de qualité*, which would yield me a very fine additional essay—subjunctive—if, that is, I knew of a journal for it. But what else should I do except anesthetize myself with my studies?—Today in an interesting émigré letter from Paris, Dr. Elsbeth Günzburger writes that a German publishing house for "us" has been established in Amsterdam. But how should I approach this publishing house? It could cost me my post, after all. Wait and see for the time being.

I now hear sometimes—moods change!—it cannot last much longer, the money will be gone in eight, nine months time, industry will break down because it has been squeezed dry. Thus Blumenfeld, who was completely pessimistic before, thus Annemarie Köhler, thus Gusti Wieghardt reporting what her Communist friends here and abroad say.

At the moment the "election" propaganda for November 12, for the plebiscite and the "unity list" for the Reichstag dominates everything. People are running around with "election badges" ("Yes") on their lapels.

November 2, Thursday

Especially depressing day. In the morning on our plot, in the afternoon with the lawyer. I am borrowing money again from the Iduna, to build a cellar. Constantly rising prices and no prospect of really carrying out the construction. But Eva clings desperately to the thing, and her desperation forces me forward step by step . . . Large expense of the planting. Additional costs of the utility connections. — The Hueber case looks extraordinarily bad for me.

The Gerstle-Schaps-Salzburg families are living in a hotel in Teplitz. A National Socialist lawyer goes across the border to them. Thus negotiations with the government are conducted safely, and no potential hostages have been left here either.

I ran into Janentzky at the bank; he told me that Holldack has converted from Protestantism to Catholicism; he does not want to be a second-class Christian because his mother was Jewish.

Walter Jelski has gone to Palestine. Perhaps he will prosper there. After all, it is like something from a novel.

I cannot help myself, I sympathize with the Arabs who are in revolt there, whose land is being "bought." A Red Indian fate, says Eva. — In recent days once at the Blumenfelds and visited Gusti Wieghardt once. In remembrance of the Gerstle case, Gusti railed against the "dirty Jews" in Palestine, capitalists falling upon the Arabs. [. . .] What shall we do on November 12? No one believes that the secrecy of the ballot will be protected, no one believes either in a *fair* counting of votes; so why be a martyr? On the other hand: say yes to this government? It is unbelievably unpleasant.

November 9, Thursday

At the first lecture Monday, French Renaissance, five people; for the exercises, Renaissance lyric poetry, four; today at Corneille, two. These two: Lore Isakowitz, yellow Jewish card—really she wants to be an interpreter, I have already been advising her for some time—and Hirschowicz, stateless, non-Aryan, father originally Turkish, blue card, the *German* students have *brown* cards. The mass of the students is uninterruptedly taken up with election propaganda; they *must* organize parades, "publicize" in every possible way—most extreme pressure; Karl Wieghardt complained bitterly to me about it; also a quite unencumbered Pedagogical Institute student said to me, "many are fed up to the back teeth" with it. It is possible, therefore, that a couple more students will come to me after the twelfth. All the same, I must now seriously, very seriously reckon with the withdrawal of my chair. [. . .] And what am I to do, if I am dismissed here? I can do *nothing* practical, not even *speak* and *write* French. I can only do literary history. I could also be a good journalist. But there is no demand for either anywhere. And yet we are putting all our financial reserves and more into the Dölzschen business. Now we have raised 900M again from the Iduna, to build a cellar or dugout. Eva is up there a great deal and gardens and "moves earth," and a laborer is regularly enlisted as well.

It is with a certain lethargy that I let everything take its course.

Last Sunday afternoon the Kaufmanns and Frau Rosenberg were here for coffee. There was a terribly heated scene, when Herr Kaufmann declared he had resolved on a "Yes" in the plebiscite. The Central Association of German Jews had after all given the same advice "with heavy heart." I completely lost my temper, thumped the table with my fist and repeatedly bellowed at him, whether he considered these rulers, to whose policies he was assenting, to be criminals or not. He refused [. . .] to reply; I had "no right to put this question." For his part he asked me mockingly why I remained in my post. I replied that I had not been appointed by *this* government and did not serve *it* and that I represented Germany's cause with a very clear conscience, that *I* was a German and *I* above all.

November 11

The extravagant propaganda for a "Yes" vote. On every commercial vehicle, post office van, mailman's bicycle, on every house and shopwindow, on broad banners, which are stretched across the street—quotations from Hitler are everywhere and always "Yes" for peace! It is the most monstrous of hypocrisies. [. . .] Demonstrations and chanting into the night, loudspeakers on the streets, vehicles (with wireless apparatus playing music mounted on top), both cars and trams.

Yesterday from one until two the "festive hour." "During the thirteenth hour Adolf Hitler will come to the workers." The language of the Gospels exactly. The Redeemer comes to the poor. And on top of that the American show style. The howl of sirens, the minute's silence . . . I was upstairs with the Dembers [. . .] In the little room sat Frau Dember, doing needlework, Emita, an elderly Wendish children's nurse and part-time maid, Frau Mark and myself. From the engine shop at Siemensstadt. For several minutes one heard the whistling, squealing, hammering, then the siren and the humming of the switched-off wheels. A very skillful, calmly delivered evocation of the atmosphere by Goebbels, then more than forty minutes of Hitler. A mostly hoarse, strained, agitated voice, long passages in the whining tone of the sectarian preacher. Content: I know no intellectuals, bourgeois, proletarians—only the people. Why have millions of my opponents remained in the country? The émigrés are "scoundrels" like the Rasser brothers. And a couple of hundred thousand rootless internationalists—interruption: "Jews!"—want to set nations of millions at one another's throats. *I* want only peace, I have risen from the common people, I want nothing for myself, I have power for another three and a half years and need no title. You should say yes for your own sake. Etc., in no proper order, impassioned; every sentence mendacious, but I almost believe: unconsciously mendacious. The man is a blinkered fanatic.

November 14

On Sunday I voted "No" in the plebiscite, and I also wrote "No" on the Reichstag ballot paper. Eva left both slips empty. That was almost a brave deed, because the whole world expects the secrecy of the ballot to be violated. [. . .] I do not believe that it really was infringed. It was anyway unnecessary for two reasons: (1) It is enough that everyone *believed* in the violation and was therefore afraid; (2) the correctness of the result as announced was already guaranteed, since the Party dominates everything without opposition. I must also acknowledge that millions were made drunk by the weeks of boundless and boundlessly mendacious "propaganda for peace," which was countered by not a single printed or spoken word. — For all that: When the triumph was published yesterday: 93 percent vote for Hitler! 40½ million "Yes," 2 million "No"—39½ million for the Reichstag, 3½ million "invalid"—I was laid low, I almost believed the figures and held them to be the truth. And since then we have been told in every possible key: this "election" is recognized abroad, "all of Germany" is seen to be behind Hitler, [the foreign powers] admire Germany's unity, will be conciliatory toward it, etc., etc. Now all of it makes me drunk, I too am beginning to believe in the power and the permanency of Hitler. It's dreadful. — On top of everything else "London says": What especially commanded admiration was that even in the concentration camps most had voted "Yes." But that is undoubtedly either a matter of falsification or compulsion. But what good is the rational "undoubtedly"? If I have no choice but to read and hear something everywhere, it is forced upon me. And if I can hardly guard against believing it—how shall millions of naive people guard against it? And if they believe, then they are indeed won by Hitler and the power and the glory are really his.

Gusti Wieghardt told me recently that an advertising brochure for some electrical goods or other had been sent to her. In the middle of the advertising text there had been a Communist article. [. . .] But what good do such pinpricks do? Less than none. Because all Germany prefers Hitler to the Communists. And I see no difference between either of the two movements; both are materialistic and lead to slavery.

November 22

Recently a great deal of socializing in our narrowed circle. At the Blumenfelds (only the two of us), at Gusti Wieghardt's, in Heidenau. There Dr. Dressel examined my heart and my blood pressure and once again found "everything objectively in good condition." For how long?—A certain depression and resignation everywhere. The government appears to be stabilized, the other countries are getting accustomed to it, allow themselves to be impressed, give way.

A philosophical letter from little Hirsch. How he employs his time profitably and guards against bitterness. I am going to collect these émigré and ghetto letters, I already have one from Mlle. Günzburger in Paris. Strange moods of waiting, hoping, resignation, finding a role for oneself, etc.

Hueber case especially distressing. A year ago it was supposed to get me my rightful 600M; now it has taken such a turn that I have to expect costs of several hundreds and must literally live in fear of the bailiffs. Because where is the money to come from? *Everything* goes into the house business. [. . .] Eva clings desperately to it. She is up there now three to X times a week—taxi there and back—often has workers to help her, it all adds up, and yet [. . .] it is simply impossible to say when we will ever be able to live up there. For the time being it is an all too expensive toy. But it makes her happy—and it is no more expensive than a sanatorium.

At the lecture I now have, and that is probably final, eight students, in the seminars three and five, i.e., I am constantly under threat of being dismissed.

Continuing studies, notes on the Eighteenth Century, but without making any progress. *Like this* I would probably have to read for another two years before getting around to writing. The attack of earlier years is quite gone, I read and take things in and make notes. I no longer quite believe I shall complete the volume. My days are completely filled. In the mornings the long sojourns with the housekeeping, then a couple of hours work, then washing the dishes, coffee, reading aloud, shopping—my only walk, unless I fetch Eva from Hohendölzschen, although I hardly leave tram and taxi; I take the taxi from Chemnitzer Platz. In the evening reading aloud again. In recent weeks *Doyen de Killerine* by Prévost.

I am pleased simply if a day passes without Eva suffering severe depression and without trouble because of the Hueber case or at the university. I have gradually become a master at suppressing all my worries, plunging "doggedly" (Hitler's favorite word) into work, any kind of work.

December 12, Tuesday

A week ago today Eva had to lie down because of a new attack of her foot ailment, and since then things have been very bad. She lies down almost the whole day, propped up in the dining room—movement always brings back the pain—and the trouble has a terrible effect on her state of mind. Since at the same time there has been a severe frost, as a result of which all the disadvantages of the apartment are brutally in evidence—rooms that cannot be heated, ice on the bottom of the bath, often impossible for Eva to climb the stairs to the bath (under the roof!)—everything is twice as bad. At moments of deepest depression Eva virtually blames me for her ruined life and wretched dying, because against her urgent wishes, her better judgment, her calculations and building plans, I had hesitated far too long with the construction, until it was too late. And even after I undertook to do it, I had done so hesitantly and reluctantly. How should I reply to this accusation? Could I know how terrible the course of events would be, doubly terrible as far as Eva's health and political developments are concerned, which drain my energy? And what have I left undone since we returned from Lugano? Still she is right: I resisted at first. The burden and the commitment seemed too great to me, my inexperience in building matters too dangerous. [. . .]

In addition to the psychological stress there is the heavy housework. I have managed, with an effort, to keep my Monday lecture going. Apart from that I have not been at my desk all week. The maid comes more often than usual, but most of it falls on me. In the morning stoke three stoves, take care of the cat "boxes," do a little dusting, prepare breakfast [. . .]— by the time I have finished all of that, it is almost twelve. And then more of the same, and a lot of reading aloud. And happy if there are no outbreaks of despair on Eva's part at the slightest thing, because they literally hammer at my heart. [. . .]

My position at the university has deteriorated. Last semester the *oral* PI examinations were handed over to Wengler. Now the secretariat is rejecting written examination topics proposed by me. The senate declared that it was unable to do anything about it. These are state examinations, and the ministry has "withdrawn me from the examining board." With that it is no longer possible for the students to choose French as an option— which is the point of the exercise—because Wengler gives only Italian instruction and is quite unfamiliar to the PI people. From Easter I will have no more students and will then be dispatched by para 6 ("superfluous").

December 15, Friday

The last few days terrible. Eva at home for one and a half weeks now, almost always confined to bed. In addition the terrible cold—today the ice burst the pipe in the bathroom under the damaged roof. Catastrophe of being unable to wash. My hands are chafed all over.

A miserable hope. The Dembers have sold their house, the money is in a blocked account. I made them the offer of borrowing perhaps 800M from it at an interest rate higher than the banks. Then we could build a "miniature" house. Frau Dember, whom I spoke to for a long time yesterday, is favorably disposed. But will her husband want to, will the state agree? Both questionable. Meanwhile work has been started on the excavation of a cellar space, but the construction of this basement will, of course, have to wait until there is a thaw.

Today I was in Dölzschen village. I handed over a letter at the town hall and visited the same "Farmer Fischer" who plowed up the land for us, to order straw for the shaft for the water pipe. The smooth, snow-covered fields, the fog in the distance and over the low-lying land, but also over the plateau, but blue sky above it was glorious. Somehow the white fields reminded me of winter walks in 1901 in Landsberg when I was a sixth former. [. . .] I do not find any time for my own work, but recently I have read a few things aloud, which are important for my Eighteenth Century. [. . .]

December 16, Saturday

Only the water supply in the kitchen is working, everything else frozen up. Living as if we were in a dugout. But Eva a little more mobile, no longer in bed, and so her mood somewhat lighter and braver. I myself yoked to the housekeeping, my hands so chapped around the finger joints that my handwriting is affected, in the seminar I tell my three to six students it's "gardening." But a little heartened and relieved by Eva's improved state of health. Once she can look after the household reasonably well again, I shall have to spend days catching up on notes. [. . .] Thank God the Christmas holidays are near.

A gray sky. Slight hope of milder weather. The nights dropped below 20 degrees. We are heating the bedroom, which never happens. We are constantly freezing.

December 23

No frost for three days and there has been a gradual alleviation in the house. But Eva continues to be depressed and not very mobile. I am still unable to think of work, the housekeeping devours me. [. . .]

In the evening the Dembers were here to take their leave. Their money from the sale of the house is in a blocked account, they have to pay 25 percent of it as Reich Flight Property Tax, for a couple of days they had to register twice a day with the police. Then at the beginning of the week Emita was arrested at ten o'clock in the evening: denounced because of reckless remarks . . . Interrogation until three in the morning, two nights in a cell at police headquarters, transferred to the court prison at Münchner Platz, there another couple of hours of uncertainty in a cell, then released. She described the psychological stress of imprisonment in great detail and very vividly.

Just heard via the Blumenfelds, that Kafka, his nerves gone, has applied for retirement. Broken down at fifty years of age.

[. . .]

December 31, Sunday

[. . .]

In the last year Gusti has repeatedly demonstrated her utter imbecility and stubbornness and extremism in political matters. Against this I have again and again emphasized that in the end I equate National Socialism and Communism: both are materialistic and tyrannical, both disregard and negate the freedom of the spirit and of the individual.

This is the characteristic fact of the year that has come to an end, that I had to break with two close friends, with Thieme because he is National Socialist, with Gusti Wieghardt because she became a Communist. With that neither has joined a political party, rather their human dignity has been forfeit.

Events of the year: the political calamity since January 30, which had an increasingly serious effect on us personally.

Eva's very poor state of health and mind.

The desperate struggle for the house.

The disappearance of any possibility of publication.

The isolation.

In June I completed my "Image of France," which was no longer published. Then a couple more reviews [. . .], no longer published; since July reading on the eighteenth century. I no longer believe that my Eighteenth Century will ever materialize. I no longer have the spirit to write something so big. My earlier books seem frivolous and superficial to me. Is it the consequence of a temporary paralysis, or am I finally finished? I really do not know.

Read aloud a great deal. Americans, Germans, recently also eighteenth century.

Much thought of death and clinging to the most general questions. Until now, Renan's "Tout est possible, même dieu" seemed to me an ironic witticism. I now take it literally and as *my* religiosity. What lack of reverence, to believe and not to believe! Both are based on an impertinent trust in the human capacity for understanding.

We shall be entirely alone this evening. I am a little afraid of that. Our two little tomcats are always a comfort and support for us. I ask myself a thousand times in all seriousness, what is the state of their immortal souls?

The historical experience of this year is infinitely more bitter and desperate than that of the war. We have sunk deeper.

After Stefan Zweig's *Marie Antoinette*—careful notes made—I read Diderot's *La Religieuse* aloud, then Goethe's *Gross-Cophta.* I constantly have in mind that my Eighteenth Century should be universal, the whole intellectual history of the age, nothing fragmentary, and should be my best work—and in resignation I repeatedly say to myself: It will not happen at all. (Vossler wrote airily to me, why do I not publish abroad, perhaps with Heiss in Strasbourg? Why? Because then I would certainly lose my post here. And anyway at the moment there is nothing to publish.)

Another greatest wish, and it will not be fulfilled either: the story of my life.

And the most desperate wish of all: the house in Dölzschen. Now we have let Prätorius place an advert for money. Only 6,000M and we will build the "miniature house." But I have no confidence in anyone. — Nor has Dember replied. But he will not want to give me any money; and if he does, the blocked account will prevent him.

[. . .]

For one month, since the recurrence of Eva's foot ailment, I have been overwhelmed by housekeeping, and managed almost no work of my own. Reading aloud from my area of study is a small compensation.

1934

January 1, Monday evening

For Christmas we had mounted fir branches bought for 20 pfennigs on the umbrella stand, together with little electric lights and colored baubles. A proper tree, not so easily transported and dismantled, is inappropriate because of the cat tribe. We turned this little tree on at twelve o'clock yesterday and drank a whisky. So it was a very quiet New Year's party. Before that I had read aloud from the charming and light Sinclair Lewis. Today again it was very quiet, and for most of the time I continued reading aloud from our entertainment book. — Making notes in between. On the "Gross-Cophta," on Zweig's *Mesmer*. But depression and worry in spite of it all. In addition to all the major misfortunes there is continually the minor and yet very distressing and increasingly expensive Hueber case. On the third there is yet another hearing, which could cost me dear.

January 9, Tuesday

Yesterday evening another meeting with Prätorius. After I don't know how many hundred. [. . .] Dember's blocked account is now our last hope. Everything has been arranged with Frau Dember, the money can be made available for creating jobs—but it is questionable whether Dember will consent. His wife will be in Constantinople on the fifteenth and will talk to him there. In the last few days she was here once more from Berlin and visited us. Yesterday she passed through (Prague-Trieste), and the dog—the sea route was chosen for his sake—was brought to the train for her.

Another adjournment in the Hueber case. The judge has fallen ill for the second time and the affair is now going to a third man. (Since October '32!)

Since a week ago and for a long time to come much time lost, torment and expense because of dental treatment. I have unfortunately had to give up old Petri, upright but Aryan, to support Israel: Dr. Isakowitz, father of my student Lore Isakowitz, who is sometimes his assistant.

January 13, Saturday

On Wednesday, after an interval of almost a year, I was at a section meeting for the first time again. The new constitution—the old senate, to which

I had pledged myself, the "self government," which was supposed to prevent my "voluntary" retirement, no longer exist. Provisional reorganization: The Ministry appoints the rector; he appoints the senate, which is only there to advise him, and which includes two students and a representative of the student SA office. The section only "advises" the section chairman, who is appointed by the rector. In it, i.e., in the more "select" section, as many non-professors as professors are represented. They are appointed by the section chairman. More interesting than these provisions were the manner and content of our deliberations. Place: the Law Department, next door one can constantly hear talking, coming and going. We *whispered,* and one participant warned the others to speak quietly. Beste, the chairman, said, I have to appoint one of the *main mudslingers,* Scheffler (political economist) or Fichtner (art historian), otherwise there will be attacks from outside. Responses: Do you not know any decent, enthusiastic National Socialists? Reply: No! Objection: Then we will not be able to talk openly here at all anymore. Beste's reply: It isn't necessary; I will not discuss anything important here. After all, I do not have to convene the section; I can nominate "committees" to advise me on anything and everything. (An example in a small way, not even the very smallest, how tyranny can be checked and undermined from the inside. Nevertheless sad enough: No one dares to resist openly; each one is always an isolated individual, who feels powerless.)

I have already often been struck by how the Encyclopedists' skills of evasion are reviving again in the face of censorship. Their satire is reviving too. Conversations in heaven are popular. The best one: Hitler to Moses: But you can tell me in confidence, Herr Moses. Is it not true that you set the bush on fire yourself?" It was for such remarks that Dr. Bergsträsser, an assistant in the mechanical engineering department—an Aryan by the way—was sentenced to ten months in prison by the special court.

[. . .]

January 16, Tuesday

Georg wrote from St. Moritz. [. . .] Two of his sons already in Cambridge and Chicago. Now he is resting with the other two in St. Moritz. They, the doctor and the engineer, are going to the USA with their wives; they have prospects and permission to immigrate, after five years they will automatically become American citizens. So Georg firmly expects our situation to be permanent. For me—without the slightest notion of my professional possibilities—he hopes I could perhaps obtain a professorship in France! (Coals to Newcastle!) If I need money to readjust and to wait for an opportunity, he will lend me a small amount at 4 percent. He himself intends to install himself somewhere in southern Germany for the summer. For all its caution and enforced calm the letter is very melancholy and somewhat pathetic. It is signed: "in fraternal devotion and in remembrance of our late father." I have not yet replied, because I do not like to write abroad.

Housework for a very large part of the day. Wearisome preparation of the Monday lecture. Next to no work at my desk, only the books read aloud now and then fit in with my 18e siècle.

[...]

Now things are like this: Every day Eva is completely depressed for a couple of hours, then I am for a couple of hours, and then for a couple of hours we both are. Eva has not got out of the apartment for weeks—black ice. Only Dölzschen could help her, but no possibility of building remains. I myself wake up every day with the intention of working and with a normal, passable degree of vigor. Then comes the battle with the stoves, the effort of shopping for the household, it is half past eleven before I sit down at my desk [...]; but by this time I am already exhausted. A similar situation in the afternoon. My getting-out-of-the-house takes me as far as the Reka; recently it has all too often taken me to the Neustadt to the dentist. That came to an end today, thank God.

Since the quarrel with Gusti Wieghardt we are quite isolated. Now Annemarie was here on Sunday afternoon after a gap of two months. As a belated Christmas present she brought *Joseph and His Brothers* by Thomas Mann. A new book by Thomas Mann—and I have not seen it announced anywhere. The press is no longer allowed to write anything about this notorious liberalistic author ("liberalistic" is now almost a more favored catchword than the already worn out "marxistic").

I am afraid after every lecture, every seminar exercise. If one of my half-dozen would betray me after all. I never raise my arm when I enter; in the seminar and in a couple of minutes of conversation afterward I easily let a dangerous word slip out. [...]

January 27

Situation unchanged, impossible to do any of my own work. Eva's health and the housekeeping prevent everything. At most an hour of reading or notes once a day. At twelve noon the morning work is at an end and so is my strength (the stoves, the "little boxes," breakfast). In the afternoon washing up and reading aloud, in the evening reading aloud again, to bed at one, happy if Eva is not prevented from sleeping by painful neuralgia.

Nothing from Constantinople. Our last hope, Dember's blocked account!

My belief in an alteration in the political situation is increasingly faint. Today the peace agreement with Poland. If a Socialist or "liberalistic" government had done that! High treason, Jewish defeatism and the mind of the shopkeeper! Now: "Adolf Hitler's magnificent new achievement." A year ago they were saying: "The shame of the Corridor will be eliminated in the summer." But instead the Stahlhelm has been finally eliminated today. Decree to discard the field-gray uniform and put on "the honorable brown one."

[. . .]

Note to Prof. Klemperer: "The Ministry has decided to cancel your appointment to the Examination Board . . . with immediate effect." The effect has been there since the spring. The question is, how much further will it go?

Note from Teubner: Do I not want to look for another publisher abroad; *he cannot* intercede for me any longer. [. . .]

Second letter from Georg. [. . .] In my reply to letter one [. . .] I wrote that I was a German through and through and intended to remain in Germany to the bitter end. — So now Georg writes from Freiburg, he has rented an apartment there and (isolated and embittered) will move in on April 1st.

[. . .]

We made a few purchases at Tietz. The big store is being wound up. Powerful impression made by the bare walls—the shelves gone—the half-empty tables, the people crowding through. A couple of months ago there were big advertisements in all the Dresden newspapers. The management of the store is overwhelmingly Aryan and it has raised Aryan capital; could the people of Dresden please take that into consideration and not throw a large number of employees out of work? Now it is being shut after all.

Yesterday afternoon in the cinema again for the first time in months: harmless and amusing film operetta *Victor and Victoria*. [. . .] The content quite unpretentiously amusing, the acting, the technical aspect quite outstanding—two hours of the most enjoyable distraction. But afterward, of course, we both felt great melancholy and bitterness. It used to be such a matter of course for us to go to the cinema two and three times a week, and how easy and fulfilled our life was! And now . . . We would have been unable to imagine how one could live with even a quarter of the troubles and miseries which constantly weigh upon us now.

Read aloud from Thomas Mann's *Joseph*. A quite brilliant achievement and absolutely new. I must make careful notes at some point. Point of view: from the Enlightenment until now, from Voltaire by way of Renan and Flaubert and Anatole France; [. . .] Really something absolutely new and very impressive (moreover less consoling and with less belief than Voltaire, Renan, France). And there is nothing about this magnificent piece of literature in any newspaper, the book is not displayed in any shop window. It bears the double curse of being by Mann and of dealing with Israel (instead of some Nordic Easter hero).

[. . .]

For myself I am leafing through Laurence Sterne. How much inspiration do I owe the old volume of essays by Frenzel, *Renaissance und Rococo*, which Father bought in 1878 from Schaeffer's book circle in Landsberg an der Warthe. And I always look at the list of notables who were members of the circle: parson, rabbi, officer, doctor, senior master . . . with emotion, and for some time past with painful envy.

[. . .]

January 31, Wednesday

On Monday the class from six to eight canceled: "solemn hour" of the student body on the anniversary of Hitler coming to power on January 30, 1933. On the very same day an announcement by Goering: He will dissolve the monarchist associations and proceed just as firmly against these enemies of the state as against the Left. That raised our spirits just a little bit yesterday. The government constantly destroys its enemies, constantly emphasizes that there is no party in Germany anymore except for the NSDAP, constantly achieves "decisive" victories. Just like Germany during the World War. The suppression of the right-wing parties is incredibly cynical, they have done nothing for Adolf Hitler's state, declares Goering implacably. Without the German Nationals, however, the National Socialists would never have got their 51 percent, their chancellor, their power. This terrible duplicity is no more than the German Nationals deserve— and yet they are my hope.

February 2, Friday

[. . .]

January 30 brought "The Law of January 30." Unitary state—no "Länder" anymore. Absolute centralization. That is what the "Jew" Preuss strove for in the Weimar constitution and was nowhere near able to achieve. I always saw it as something grand, as the great French example. Now it has been decreed by a handful of brutal state robbers. The unanimous acceptance by the Reichstag (the 600 National Socialist deputies) is a farce. [. . .] Has Germany really become so completely and fundamentally different, has its soul changed so completely that this will endure? Or is this merely temporary lethargy?

I have plowed my way right through three of the six volumes of the very average "*Lettres juives*." I can no longer summarize and write as I could years ago—the strength of purpose is missing. I cling helplessly to details. The way I work is more "scholarly," more "thorough," "deeper," more "mature"—certainly all of that; but I cannot reach a goal anymore, real success is absent, I am older and have grown too old; I no longer believe my Eighteenth Century will ever materialize. Once I would have read a dozen of these letters; now I shall go through the next three volumes as well.

February 7, Wednesday

On Saturday we went for supper to the "respectable" Köhlers in Walther-strasse. It does one good, that these completely "Aryan" people from quite different circles of society—the son a probationary grammar school teacher, the father a railway inspector—hold on to their vehement hatred of the regime and to their belief that it must fall in the foreseeable future.

On Sunday we were at the Blumenfelds for evening coffee (as the only guests). Here also (fluctuating moods!) they were no longer quite so convinced of the everlasting durability of the present state of things. Because there is a grinding of teeth throughout so many strata, professions, confessions. — But inwardly I am disheartened again and again. And my strength, all my physical and mental strength is increasingly exhausted. My work is completely at a standstill; simply preparing the Monday lecture in time is a martyrdom. So I welcome the fact that the semester is already ending on the twenty-fourth of the month. Admittedly it is ending because the students have to report for labor service, because, in fact, the regime sees education, scholarship, enlightenment as its real enemies and attacks them accordingly. [. . .]

February 15, Thursday, toward evening

At the moment Eva's health and mood are a little better, and that means a little light and a sigh of relief for me. — But the pressure of worries is undiminished. No prospect of making any progress in Dölzschen. The Dembers, whose blocked account was my last hope of money, are completely silent. The pressure of the Hueber case is also undiminished. A new expert opinion for 100M—for the time being Hueber has to pay it, but in the end the verdict will, at the very least, be partly against me and I shall lose hundreds. Nowhere any promise of an alteration of the political situation—on the contrary: The heavy fighting in Austria means that the Hitlerreich appears wrapped in the glory of peace and order, and when Dollfuss and the Social Democrats have bled one another to death, Hitler will be the heir. [. . .]

But I grasp at every little piece of comfort. That Eva is brighter again, that she gets out of the house just a little bit, recently to Dölzschen to cut trees, yesterday evening accompanies Annemarie to the station and then looks in a couple of shop windows, today into town to buy a large quantity of wool, that she finds pleasure in knitting, that she is pluckily bracing herself to advance the ill-fated construction of our house step by step—all of that is a comfort to me. And then: I read aloud for hour after hour, often late into the night. And then: One takes delight in the two little tomcats and in a camellia coming into flower and in the mildness of the weather and the approaching end of winter. And then: The hope that this state of boundless tyranny and lies must yet collapse at some time, never completely disappears.

Today was the first session of the whole faculty under "Führer" Beste. Raised right hands, a student representative, Assistant Professor Scheffler in SA uniform, Assistant Professor Fichtner with the party badge—and everything mere formality and show. But this arm raising makes me literally feel sick, and the fact that I always dodge it will cost me my neck one day. [. . .]

I now borrow books from two lending libraries. Lending libraries (without deposit) have shot up like mushrooms in the last one or two years. In my youth there were a few lending libraries, then the institution virtually disappeared completely, survived only in watering places—and now the lending libraries are everywhere, even in the poorest districts of the city, as abundant as chocolate shops, as abundant as the little pubs once were. And yet there has never been such hostility to the spirit in Germany as today.

February 16, Friday evening

Now a new ordinance has come out after all, according to which dons are allowed to lecture after February 24, if the majority of their students do not have to do Labor Service. So I shall lecture until the end of the month.

Outside lecturers and the students now sit on the faculty; in her medical journal, Annemarie showed me fierce attacks on the professors of medicine and in favor of the non-professors and lay healers. [. . .] It is all based on the same system: They look for support from those who until now felt themselves neglected, on those (really or seemingly) "without rights," on the hungry, on the mass of little people. In the past the word was: against the eggheads or against the capitalists! Now, much more appealingly, against the Jews!

Reply from Teubner to my letter. [. . .] Teubner points to "imponderables" and declines to answer my questions. The best thing for me is to write my book directly in French; he has also published Wartburg's language history directly in French!—I shall overcome my present depression. I shall write this book and shall write it in German, just as I think and feel it in German. [. . .] As I am writing there is constant singing and marching and music making outside. Buildup for the torchlight march in front of Reich Governor Mutschmann. Big advertisement in the newspaper: "German men and women! March with us! Every national comrade must be there." Etc., etc.

[. . .]

February 21, Wednesday morning

On Saturday (seventeenth), after a considerable interval, we had guests for the evening: the four "respectable" Köhlers, the Kühns and a brother of the wife, a thirty-year-old farmer without a situation, congenial, simple and engaging, good-looking, dark-eyed man with a prominent scar by his right eye (did not go to university, so from an accident). Kühn continues to predict the regime's durability. It may change, but remain. One also has to hope for it, otherwise there will be chaos. He compared it to the Jacobins, the rule of "the little people." He said, in a hundred years, when all the "mendacities" and minor abuses were forgotten, this revolution might perhaps be called "typically German," because in comparison to the French and Russian it is "so bloodless." That depressed me greatly, because Kühn after all is both an altogether unsullied character, with a feeling for legality, and a serious historian. His brother-in-law, Körner, evidently a supporter of the German Nationals, talked very interestingly about the countryside. Until a few weeks ago he was an agricultural inspector in Mecklenburg. The government demands and enforces very precisely specified deliveries for Winter Aid: so many hundredweight of potatoes of a specified size and quality, so many hundredweight of wheat of a fixed specific weight. This was absolutely the Moscow Communist system. It broke up the big estates, created peasant holdings. But in the long term it was only the big estates that fed the towns, and this is also the mistake of the present regime, because of which it must one day collapse. (Likewise, a few days before Annemarie related that in the factories the trade union, under another name, was now more mighty, the boss weaker than under "Marxist" rule.) — The impression is growing that the government is sliding ever more toward Communism. Kühn says, in one of his last speeches Goebbels, in scarcely disguised language, pointed to the danger that threatens every revolution if its radical wing is too powerful. And that is exactly why he, Kühn, thinks one virtually has to hope that the present regime maintains itself; for it can only succumb to its Communist wing. Körner, in turn, emphasized the change that had taken place in the SA. Initially an elite force—now a huge army of the most diverse, unreliable elements. He also talked about the unconcealed hostility between SA and Stahlhelm.

Johannes Köhler complained about the pressure on his conscience which, as a teacher of history and religion, he could not bear for much longer. He is already flirting with a new course of study: medicine; it would be his third, because before humanities he studied business management. (At school he had to collect signatures for the purchase of a "Luther Rose" with the legend "With Luther and Hitler.") [. . .]

Vossler, to whom I sent Teubner's letters, replied cluelessly and superficially. He knows that Athenaion took the new Italy chapter away from me, but he now advises me to offer my literary history to Athenaion. He also intends "to talk to Hueber." Is he so unaware or so uninterested? Probably the latter. Because a few weeks ago he advised me to publish abroad, and now he advises me to try in Germany first "with less timid publishers."—Today I wrote to Teubner that I am sticking to my contract. [. . .]

This evening at Frau Schaps. — Weather worse, atmosphere gloomy. Both Eva's and my nerves have gone to the dogs. Eyes badly inflamed. —

Reading all the time: Dreiser's *The Titan*. Notes on Mme. Tencin's *Mémoires du comte de Comminges*.

February 24, Saturday

[...]

Frau Schaps read out letters from Haifa. Much distress beneath plucky humor. Difficult and absurd learning of Hebrew—only the child at school learns quickly [...]. Tiny apartment (three rooms), furniture ruined by water; Jule Sebba gives cello lessons for a few pounds and takes part in conservatory concerts (program in English and Hebrew, but completely European music, Beethoven, Brahms, Tchaikovsky); his original business plan appears to have got nowhere, a new one not yet found, and the man is almost as old as I am; they are excessively grateful for 200M that Frau Schaps sent. — Nevertheless there must be some money there; some he managed to get over to Palestine, his mother-in-law has a lot, his brother-in-law Gerstle a great deal more. — Before the end of the month Frau Schaps herself will travel to Haifa for a couple of weeks. A capitalist matter: The English government does not allow any tourists into the country (because tourists have often turned into immigrants) who cannot show that they have 15,000M. I then asked her, since she had just come from Berlin and was relating how the very young Jewish generation had left the country, what people there in her circle thought about the situation. Prompt reply: They believe the worst is over; if there are agreements on tariffs, things will improve again. That means: These people are happy if they can look forward to consolidation of the Hitler regime and an end to the foreign boycott. They may be forced back into the ghetto, may be kicked and humiliated, their children may have lost their homeland—but as long as they can do business again, "the worst is over." It is so infinitely shameless and dishonorable that one could almost sympathize with the National Socialists. Afterward Eva said that some people let themselves be hit in the face with toilet brushes without taking offense. To me it seems like atavism, a return to the medieval ghetto. Frau Schaps was quite unaware of the disgracefulness of what she was reporting. She has a very cool nature, hence her unbroken vitality. The trip to Palestine: a beautiful new journey and emotion. [...]

March 2, Friday evening

I wound up this bad semester on Wednesday. I took the penultimate Corneille class with the "Jewish quota," that is, little Isakowitz, and the last one with her and a young man, who will now take his state examination with Wengler. Things did not look much different in the Monday class and even in the Monday lecture, four to five, nine to ten people. That repeatedly tempted me into subjective digressions, intimacies, unguarded remarks, but had its attractions. To some extent I was addressing people of like mind, I always had the feeling I was, as it were, inoculating a couple of the younger ones or turning them into carriers of infection. I never raised my arm. — How long shall I be forced to continue this game, how long be able to continue it?

Last Sunday a now almost customary evening at the Blumenfelds. We encouraged one another to show spirit, stoicism and skepticism; we heard beautiful Schubert gramophone records; things even got to the point that Eva *played* Schubert. Meanwhile Blumenfeld has been halfway brought down. As a teacher at the Pedagogical Institute he has "been pensioned off." That means he loses money but not the right to teach at academic institutions. It is ever more evident that the Ped. Inst. is soon likely to be completely separated from the University. Then para. 6 (reduced because surplus to requirements) can also be applied to me.

On Wednesday evening Kurt Rosenberg and his wife, the doctor, were our guests; Kaufmann's Hamburg relations, to whose marriage we ourselves lent a helping hand (and now their oldest is already over five!). Rosenberg has lost his job as a lawyer, but has earned so much he can sit back and watch for a couple of years. He now thinks that by buying out another lawyer, who wants to go abroad, he can obtain a new license to practice. With the Rosenbergs too there was endless conversation about the duration of the present regime. Rosenberg, who has an understanding of the agricultural situation, does not believe in the financial stability of the system; but he doubts whether political collapse will necessarily follow a financial one.

Blumenfelds had told me that the banker Mattersdorf would advise me in the building matter. Mattersdorf heard the story with a stupid indifference, was quite curt and almost impolite; a wooden house seemed to him something like a dog kennel. But I made the acquaintance of his partner, Councillor of Commerce Meyerhof; it turned out that he is related to my Meyerhof, he said that Leonie Meyerhof-Hildeck had died in August, we talked family and he became friendly. Result: He is going to see whether he cannot get hold of a private financial backer for me, and will let me know by phone. I am without hope and yet cling to any hope. Prätorius is optimistic once again, some bank in Hamburg is going to provide the mortgage.

The weather is becoming more springlike, and Eva has already been up twice in recent days. Two wagonloads of manure were delivered today. All the taxi drivers already know us, and a couple of times I've been told, "I drove you when your house wasn't finished yet." Then I always have to say shamefacedly, "It is not finished yet even now"; and privately I think, it's never going to be finished. Eva is bolder now and at the moment even her nerves are probably in a better state than mine. [. . .] Teubner has concluded our exchange of letters for the time being, with nothing resolved: We have to await developments.

Days that follow bank appointments (today after the Mattersdorf business) are always especially painful for me. I feel so humiliated and helpless. All the others around me have financial reserves: Blumenfeld,
Rosenberg, Dember, Edgar Kaufmann, who is fiddling a sickness insurance in Palestine, Sebba, old Kaufmann—"Hammerschuh, German-
Christian Enterprise" I read every day in Prager Strasse, and the
Kaufmanns live off Hammerschuh, the old ones here and the young ones
in Palestine, and I, "well-known" professor of Romance Languages, etc.,
etc., I cannot escape my troubles and will be completely destroyed if the
government dismisses me.

I told Commercial Councillor Meyerhof how in 1897 Leonie Hildeck
used Hans Meyerhof and myself as guinea pigs for lectures on Ibsen and
how I stayed away because I was taking cycling lessons. The last time I
heard from Leonie Hildeck was when she wrote to us a year or two ago,
asking us to look after a young sculptor. At the time I declined because we
were quite isolated and without social contacts . . . She apparently had an
honorable (editorial) obituary in the *Frankfurter Zeitung*. Nevertheless she
is completely forgotten. So, after all, is her more famous friend Anselma
Heine. — I am now constantly haunted by the idea of the "History of My
Life." That makes three ideas: the house, the Eighteenth Century, the autobiography. And behind all three so often now—Nevermore.

[. . .]

March 13, Tuesday evening

After several more passable weeks a very bad state of affairs again. Eva is
faced with protracted dental treatment. Immediately the problems with
walking start again, immediately the outbreaks of despair again. On top of
that the treatment will cost a few 100M, which of course will again be deducted from the savings for the house and get me even tighter by the
throat than is the case anyway.

March 19

Eva's condition has improved a little. The thoroughgoing treatment of her
teeth was postponed for a couple of months after the most urgent repairs
had been taken in hand and with the onset of spring she has been able to
take up her gardening in Dölzschen. Naturally this gardening costs a great
deal of money: trips by taxi, a laborer employed for days at a time, at 70
pfennigs an hour, orders from Hauber, manure, tools . . . Again and again
there are moments at which I am almost suffocated by money worries; but
partly through apathy, partly through discipline, I have reached a point at
which, in principle, I do not make arrangements for more than a day
ahead or at most a month. I force myself not to think about a bill that must

be paid in the coming month. Perhaps I shall manage it after all, perhaps there'll be a miracle, perhaps the bailiffs will be put on to me—but not till the month after next. If until then Eva has a few less fits of hysterics, if until then my heart lets me down a few times less, then something is gained too. At any rate the dull pressure weighs on me constantly.

Likewise, closely connected with the worry about money, my attitude to the worry about my post. The new semester does not begin until May 7; until then there is relative security. Then perhaps I'll have no more students and be discharged like Blumenfeld. There has already been talk of pensioning off the whole Humanities Section. But why worry about what happens after May 7? Is it so certain that we shall still have the same government on May 7? The comparison with the Jacobins is popular just now. Why should the German Jacobins last longer than the French ones?

So I live from day to day under a dull pressure. The studies on the Eighteenth Century inch forward; occasionally I see something of it clearly before me; for seconds at a time I believe that the book will be written, and it will even be my best book; but mostly I feel as if I shall never get back to writing at all. Besides, the housekeeping (heating, making breakfast, etc., the cats), Dölzschen, the dentist, to whom I accompanied Eva, all the reading aloud took up an unbelievable amount of time; if I manage one or two hours on the 18e every day, it's a lot. [. . .]

The same thing when it comes to health. Repeated heart problems. Tiredness to the point that I fall asleep at my desk, pains in my throat every time I do physical work, sore eyes and blurred sight but also hours of normal life. Sometimes I think: just another three or four years; sometimes: perhaps even twenty. [. . .]

We were at the Blumenfelds twice recently, the second time with Frau Schaps, who is going to Haifa to visit in the next few days. Once with Annemarie in Heidenau. Once—an excursion—to Hauber's market garden. Everywhere we listened for—eavesdropped in fact! very intently—symptoms of the political future. Recently there seem to have been more signs again that point to an end within the foreseeable future. National Socialism has now become completely or almost completely identical with Bolshevism; that is obvious to many who only a short time ago regarded it as a "bulwark against Bolshevism" and as a "lesser evil."

In Breslau there is a student of Neubert, a certain Kurt Jäkel, more persevering than original, but a competent and hardworking fellow. He has already got several volumes on Wagner in France and on Proust behind him; he sends me everything. Recently I wrote to thank him for something and asked him: Have you already qualified yourself as a university lecturer or when will you do so? In reply came a letter: He is no longer allowed to qualify himself, he is also losing his post as an assistant because his wife is non-Aryan, daughter of the dermatologist Jadassohn. He would like to go abroad, but has a one-and-a-half-year-old child. — The usual fate now.

Our petit bourgeois neighbors in Dölzschen "give shape" to their gardens as we do. Terraces and rock gardens (a big fashion!) are being laid out. Is there not a new classic horticulture in the making? Not a return to the seventeenth century, but perhaps even further back. Eva says, a "more formal garden design, more architectural than before." Is there not a revival of something like the pattern-card of diverse landscapes and architectural styles en miniature, which characterized the French garden in the eighteenth century before and side by side with the jardin anglais?

My 18e follows me in everything I do, see and read. Above all I am constantly occupied by the question of intellectual imagination, the fertilization of imagination and religion by reason and learning. There are X analogies with the eighteenth century throughout contemporary life. I should like to write an introductory study like a fugue about this whole relationship: the fairy tale in the eighteenth century. If I ever write it, it will be my masterpiece. *If* . . .

[. . .]

March 25, Sunday

Total exhaustion; repeatedly fall asleep at my desk. Most recently worked through Folkierski, *Entre le classicisme et le romantisme;* began Cassirer, *Philosophy of the Enlightenment.* I find my task gets ever more confusing, my belief that the book will be realized dwindles from day to day.

On Thursday we had Grete here for the afternoon and evening. Very amicable without the ill feeling of last year. The universal adversity has swept away a lot. Grete was on her way to Pressburg. Her cousin Bunzl (the love of her youth) has invited her; and since Vienna is closed to us, he is putting her up in Czech Pressburg and visiting her there. Grete spent the night in a hotel. She told us that Sussmann's eldest brother had taken his life a few weeks ago: Veronal in a hotel room; Martin and Wally were called by the police to identify the corpse. Arthur Sussmann was a good-natured human being, an optimist, dreamer and speculator. He let his brother study, often treated him condescendingly. In 1913 he visited us in Munich with Marta and Wally en route from Venice; they were his guests. I still have a postcard of all three, feeding pigeons on St. Mark's Square. I can see "Uncle Arthur's" soft, long, untidy drooping mustache. During the war he established some kind of big factory; I came from Leipzig to give the employees a couple of lectures, which were very well paid. Later things sometimes went badly for the man, sometimes very well. In his imagination he was always on top, always wanted to help the rest of his family. At the end, well into his sixties, he is supposed to have been planning a wealthy marriage. Now the breakdown. (Where do people find the courage for suicide?) Sussmanns are supposed to have lost money as a result (happy the man who still has money to lose).

[. . .]

In the last few days Eva has been in Dölzschen a lot again; the gardening has been keeping her busy. The bricks for the construction of the wonderful cellar have also been delivered. I do not know how much longer I can still find the money for all of it. If in the next few weeks, as has to be assumed, the Hueber case is decided against me, then I can only pawn the harmonium or the library or something. I do not want to think more than a day ahead; but the dreadful, wretched weight on my soul is there every morning. And my situation worsens every day.

Today in Dresden the big "Rally of the Saxon SA," 125,000 men will parade in front of the governor. Crowds, flags, garlands, pomp and an unparalleled display of power.

Para 6 of the Civil Service Law, by which any civil servant who is superfluous to requirements can be retired, has been extended for a further six months. It will be my turn in the summer.

[...]

April 1, Easter Sunday

A week ago today we were at the "respectable" Köhlers. We were supposed to celebrate their wedding day on the Saturday and were somewhat mysteriously put off. It turned out that they had not wanted to inflict "that" on us. "That"—I would in fact have liked to see it—was the arrival of the SA. The inspector had had to receive 95 trains (special trains in addition to normal traffic) at his little Friedrichstadt station. He says he had witnessed the mobilization in 1914 as a railway man; this had been a similar feat and a greater one (because then passenger traffic had been stopped, but this time was carried on simultaneously). So a practice mobilization, and the foreign powers must know that just as well as we do and even better. In the most diverse circles war is now thought to be possible, indeed almost probable.

[...]

Commercial Councillor Meyerhof of the Mattersdorf Bank recommended Tanneberg, a "business adviser," to me in the building matter. I took the ever older-looking Prätorius with me as well. Tanneberg gave me a few, not many grounds for hope; he appears to be a prudent and energetic man. To my question as to a loan (not a mortgage): "On what?—If the government wants to put in a young man tomorrow, you'll be sacked. Para 6 has been extended."

April 5, Thursday

On the evening of Easter Monday Annemarie Köhler was here with her mother. Always the same conversations, the same mood. — On Tuesday on her return journey from Pressburg: Grete, who then continued her journey on Wednesday. At the station I packed her, a little forcefully, into a taxi and drove her up to Dölzschen, where Eva was gardening furiously together with the worker and our cleaner's little Annelies. The worker had brought her two little pine trees as an Easter present and planted them. "Pinched for you, miss," says the boy in the Berlin primary school. The man had started out on his bicycle at four o'clock in the morning and cycled as far as Prussian woodland.

Blumenfeld—we were there for a coffee evening—gave me the typescript of his lecture "Religion and Philosophy." In two days I composed a twelve-point critical review in which, apart from Blumenfeld and Cassirer, Klemperer also gets a word in. It was my first productive work for ages (truly!) and this page will certainly be of central importance to my Eighteenth Century. Then Blumenfeld was here, we had a discussion, and now he has sent me his rejoinder or elaboration. The Blumenfelds are now traveling to Italy for three weeks (despite or because of his being pensioned off). [...]

It was both shocking and characteristic to see in Grete the extent to which everything German has fallen away from her and how she can only, and wants only, to look at the whole situation from a Jewish standpoint. "*You* may persuade yourself that you are German—I can no longer do so." Then the horrible ghetto oppressiveness. She relates with shining eyes as if it were something altogether special, that in Pressburg the Jews move around freely, that in the personal announcements in the newspapers there are names like Cohn and Levi next to aristocratic and Slav names, that a talk by the chief rabbi is reported respectfully, etc., etc. She is in addition all too impressed by the enforced rejoicing at government festivities in Berlin and is convinced of the unlimited duration of present conditions. All in all therefore: She has become un-German, inwardly degraded and quite resigned. *That* no doubt is how things stand with very many Jews.

[...]

April 24, Tuesday

[...]

I read aloud a great deal. And sit for hours at my Eighteenth Century, while Eva gardens in Dölzschen. There are all too many worries weighing upon me—and always the same ones—for me to make progress. I want now to wring a special study of Delille's *Gardens* out of myself. But always this paralyzing question: What for? For the drawer of the desk! And always the terrible, increasing money difficulties. The Hueber case is about to be wound up now. Two pointless expert opinions have stymied me. I sued for 600M; it is very possible that I lose that amount. Where to get it from? And where to find the money for the next life insurance payment? Everything is put into the trips by taxi to and from Dölzschen (an attempt to go on foot ended in a great many tears, fainting attack, pain, sleepless night) and into laying out the garden. The bit of cellar is now built and

stands there rough and unfinished; any hope of getting building money seems to be written off. A wooden house, a flat roof, are unacceptable and a civil service post is no longer regarded as secure. — The anxieties are always the same: money, the house, Eva's health, the political situation weighs down on us—and nowhere is there a way out. Eva is now often—not always—more hopeful than I am. She believes that she and I still have many years before us; I myself believe I have only a few years before me.
[. . .]

Rector Neumann, to whom I had recommended Johannes Köhler with such success, died unexpectedly, only 65 years old, a few months before his retirement.

On Saturday we had the Wenglers, brother and sister, here. Wengler is now examining the primary school teachers in my place. Yet Wengler inclines very strongly toward Communism. I learned for the first time that Wengler's mother was English, that in the parental home he spoke English more than German. I want to know, of everyone who comes from a different circle, what he thinks about the permanence of the present state of affairs. The Wenglers do not believe it is stable.
[. . .]

May 7, Monday

My third semester begins today. Very possible that it will also be my last. Because, as admission to the PI is blocked—where are the students to come from?

May 13, Sunday

On Monday no one at the general lecture and the seminar. A crushing experience. With a pension of perhaps 300 or 400M, as things stand, I would be facing disaster. In the evening I telephoned Beste, the section chairman, to notify him officially. He consoled me: general state of affairs in the university! He himself, a political economist, last semester still in front of eighty students, usually in front of one hundred and fifty, had six. Reasons: (a) The students were only just returning from Labor Service, not all were present yet, (b) university study in general was being throttled. — On Wednesday (French verse theory, one hour) I had two female students. (Blumenfeld, usually overflowing with students, has four students for the psychology lecture, one for the industrial psychology class.) Now I shall wait and see whether my seminar will materialize tomorrow. After that there will be another two weeks holiday. The Whitsun holidays have been extended from one to two weeks. The students are no doubt required for the new "Campaign against Fault Finders and Grumblers," and they do *not want anyone to study;* intellect, scholarship are the enemies.

This "campaign" was inaugurated by Goebbels on Friday. Speech in the Berlin Sportpalast. Gross rabble-rousing and a "last warning to the Jews." Flagrant threat of a pogrom if the foreign boycott does not cease. Promise not to harm them "if they remain quietly in their homes" and do not claim to be of "full or equal value." Europe 1934, Germany!—There is desperation behind the whole speech, a last attempt at diversion. Work on the housing projects and the Reich highways is apparently faltering already. In the same speech, addressed to foreign listeners: We cannot pay our debts, *we* made no agreements, our predecessors did. . . . The whole system is on its last legs. Who will survive the collapse, and what will happen then?

We hear more and more, especially from the "little people," on whom they rely—our petit bourgeois neighbors in Dölzschen, Kuske our shopkeeper, etc., etc.—how greatly dissatisfaction is growing. The government is increasingly drifting toward Bolshevism.

On April 25 (after an interval of years) Spamer was our guest. The sociable folklore man from Frankfurt, with his interest in primitive ways of thinking. He had been to see his publisher in Berlin. He said: In Berlin everyone was expecting an imminent collapse. Not I. The masses let themselves be talked into believing everything. If for three months all the newspapers are forced to write that there was no World War, then the masses will believe that it really did not happen. That has been my opinion for a long time. (Word for word!) Perhaps Spamer judges things too much from the perspective of his profession. A couple of years ago Eva once had to have a light ether anesthetic. The anesthetist tied her hands very loosely to the arms of the chair, he reassured her (now just start counting, nice and calm, nice and calm! and so on) as if he were talking to a child. Afterward she discovered that the man was a pediatrician. Everyone judges things from the perspective of his profession. Spamer is like that pediatrician, since he is constantly dealing with the childish side of national psychology. It is no doubt present everywhere, even among the educated. But surely not alone and not, at least *not always*, dominant. [. . .]

Constantly working on Delille. The study is turning out very well, the work of an old man, microscopic, enriched by much experience and yet squeezed past the all-embracing (the history of the whole eighteenth century). It is taking up a disproportionate amount of my time.

Every morning as I'm shaving the nightmare of the Hueber case weighs me down. Two crazy opinions against me, prospect of having to pay 600M or more, and no idea where to get this money from. Today a long, long brief arrived, in which Langenhan really did no more than make a copy (word for word) of my letter. Final appeal to the court. [. . .] The verdict appears to be imminent now.

Despite the considerable heat Eva is in Dölzschen at least every second day. I fetch her, I also spend one or two hours helping her. The garden is splendid now, the cellar finished. But no possibility of further building work and ever-increasing costs. The taxi costs 5.50M each time. If we try to walk a part of the way, then pain and a serious attack of nerves are the unfailing consequence.

Karl Wieghardt—I met him in the street [. . .]—told me that on May 1 thirty students (and the charwomen) had participated in the festive procession of university members that had been ordered. Recently there had also been open opposition at a student meeting, when a camp in Schellerhau had been ordered for the Whitsun holidays (to "encourage community feeling"). They wanted to have time to get down to work; the marches, etc. left one no time for studying. So here too a gradual awakening. But for the moment the phrase, the National Socialists are certain of the "youth" of Germany, reigns supreme.

[. . .]

As to my own memories: I see myself as a sixth former mounting the stairs to the classroom with Grimm, my fellow pupil. I want to affirm something, I no longer know what, and as I am saying that it is truly a matter of the heart for me, I strike my chest with my fist. Yet I have such a lively sense of shame, this gesture does not suit me at all and is false, that I still feel it today. It is the feeling of shame that holds me back from every theatrical expression, every rhetorical gesture on my own behalf. Which also makes weeping impossible for me. It is always embarrassing for me in the highest degree, if in the cinema or while lecturing or struck by some thought I feel tears rising. Which lately, given my shattered nerves, is all too often the case.

[. . .]

On April 27 I went with Eva to see "trustee" Tanneberg, whom Commercial Councillor Meyerhof had recommended to me. Tanneberg has not yet given up hope of procuring building money for us. But he does not seem to have any success either. Inspiring confidence, the man told us he was a front-line officer, a former member of Stahlhelm and joined the NSDAP before the "seizure of power," and still belongs to the Party. But all around he sees mismanagement, ill-feeling, catastrophe can no longer be far away. He condemned the lack of proportion of the anti-Semitism, he maintained that only the subordinate leaders were still using it for incitement, at the top they were already trying to calm things down. [. . .]

Our latest achievements on the Kirschberg: the planting of the yew tree (seven hundredweight!), which I gave Eva for Christmas, and the acquisition of a 22-yard garden hose. It was already much needed because of the constant heat and drought. One day recently I hauled over a hundred buckets of water.

May 27, Sunday

On the sixteenth we planted and worked together in our Dölzschen garden. Melancholy pleasure. The Scherners are coming for one and a half days over Whitsun.

June 13, Wednesday

All of my fairly meager free time—housekeeping! Dölzschen!—has gone into the Delille study. Begun mid-April, expanded constantly, completed at last on June 10, aside from reading through the very closely written manuscript. An excellent work—to be published when and where? I asked Wengler, if the worst comes to the worst, to look after my literary remains. Wengler has played a significant role in our life since a couple of days ago. His mother was English, he has assets in England. A law prescribes that he must realize them and transfer them to Germany. Afraid of inflation, he is looking to invest it securely. It is possible that he will give us a loan. I no longer have any real hope, we have been disappointed so often. Meanwhile Eva continues gardening fanatically, on average every second day. Taxi rides now take up around 110M of our monthly budget. I usually fetch Eva toward evening; I walk up through the park, after I have ordered the cab at Chemnitzer Platz. All the drivers already know us. I myself have been up there repeatedly for several hours at a time, to do watering, carry water, etc. (For three months there has been a hardly interrupted drought; the harvest is already said to have been badly affected. — We see everything from the point of view and heart's desire of Hitler's downfall. And so this too is not unwelcome to us, although the garden is dying of thirst. Besides watering is still *allowed* in Dölzschen, whereas there is already a ban in many places.)

[. . .]

At classes: Art poétique—Fräulein Heyne and (sometimes) Fräulein Kaltofen, prosody—both girls, principal lecture, classicism—the two of them and Herr Heintzsch. He is an SA man and says plaintively, "I am not a soldier." I cautiously-incautiously talk politics with the girls at the beginning and end of classes. Both strongly anti-National Socialist, both oppressed by the feeling of tyranny. Especially Heyne, a Catholic, who wrote me a fine letter in spring from her work camp. She said to me recently, "A kind of catechism was read out to us. 'I believe in the leader Adolf Hitler . . . I believe in Germany's mission . . .' Surely no Catholic can say that."

I have a great deal to make up; all the important things turn on the one thing that is suffocating us. But everywhere, or almost everywhere, there is nevertheless a shimmer of hope. It *cannot* last much longer.

The Scherners, fat, hearty, childish, greedy as ever. Yet their fortunes in a poor state, hating the small town and their enslavement to the pharmacy. He is disparaged as a "Jew." They came here at lunchtime on Whitsunday, directly from high mass in the Hofkirche. His first words, before any greeting, downstairs at the gate, beaming: "*That* will not perish, *that* will win, they cannot destroy *that*! Such a throng of people, such devotion, such splendor! The church, the city center, Victor! . . ." And Scherner ran away from the seminary!

He told us: In Falkenstein one is not allowed to buy from the "Jew." And so the people in Falkenstein travel to the Jew in Auerbach. And the Auerbachers in turn buy from the Falkenstein Jew. However, on bigger shopping expeditions the people from the one-horse towns travel to Plauen, where there's a larger Jewish department store. If you run into someone from the same town, no one has seen anyone else. Tacit convention.

Letter from Lotte Sussmann in Berne, where she is taking the oral examination for her doctorate. The style of the Encyclopedia, the game of hide-and-seek with the censors in full bloom. "I am so optimistic . . . I would like you to share a little in it . . . I am really not a Couéist. . . ." Embittered lines from Georg in Freiburg: He cannot agree at all with my opinion (profession of Germanness, "Germany is in my camp!," definite hope of a speedy end). In the summer he and his wife want to visit his son in England, then his children in the USA. Felix's youngest, a doctor, has now also gone to the USA. "We want to set up a Klemperer colony there."

The Jelskis here on their way to Bohemia. Trying, distressing, but in many ways interesting hours. He, 67 now, has retired and is taking a cure in Johannisbad. I had an impression of considerable senility. Out of a certain contrariness and a childish pleasure in dispassionate objectivity, he sympathizes somewhat with Hitler. After all he has achieved a great deal for the nation as a whole, he is a "demon"—of course, the racial ideology is wrong, but the Jews are not blameless. Marta for her part almost wild with hate. Wallowing in fantasies: *they* should be hanging on gallows, and we should march past and strike them as they hang there. I cannot help myself, she is hysterical, but on this point she is far from wrong. — Their house was searched once, her youngest, Willy, early twenties, is close to the Communists. She is traveling to Prague, to find out if there is any chance of a post for him and any possibility of studying political economy. Her old friend there is supposed to help her. They have repeatedly had the most dreadful quarrels about money matters, but the friendship always begins again—oh happy rabble! Freudenheim-Bloch, the dentist, already charged Eva quite shameless prices in 1904. Bloch is a self-sacrificing woman and is nursing her husband, the "Marxist" author (Revisionist), who fled to Prague. She gave up her practice, established a new one in Prague, cares for him. — Walter's fate in Palestine seems to take an almost comical shape. Through Edgar Kaufmann's good offices he got an insurance job in Jerusalem. But only provisionally, since immigrants who are not farmers or artisans must demonstrate that they have assets (about 10,000M). He has for some time had a romance with a very Aryan young lady, a Baltic German, related on her mother's side to Count Zeppelin; she is a secretary in Switzerland. (Some time ago we received a postcard from the pair of them on a trip to the south of France.) Now she has come into a fortune and bought herself a Hebrew grammar. They want to marry and share their goods in Jerusalem. But where are they to get married? He must travel to meet her somewhere, where that is possible. Because in Zion the Aryan is exactly in the position of the Jew here. Par nobile fratrum! To me the Zionists, who want to go back to the Jewish state of A.D. 70 (destruction of Jerusalem by Titus), are just as offensive as the

Nazis. With their nosing after blood, their ancient "cultural roots," their partly canting, partly obtuse winding back of the world they are altogether a match for the National Socialists. [. . .] That is the fantastic thing about the National Socialists, that they simultaneously share in a community of ideas with Soviet Russia and with Zion. — With her naive stories, Frau Schaps, who has returned from visiting her Sebba children in Haifa, confirms me in my hatred of these Zionist doings (whereas Blumenfeld sympathizes with them).

[. . .]

Marta's daughter Lilly at last married and off to Uruguay. The husband, a musician, secretary at the legation in Berlin and student of music there. Now has a post in a factory in his homeland. Was supposed to become a teacher at the state conservatory, which did not come about because of the conservatory's shortage of money. — The Jelskis were here on June 1. Shortly beforehand, Marta had the most ferocious quarrel with the Bloch woman, to whom she was now traveling as a friend, because she (Bloch) sent an excessively large dental bill, which was not paid. — Perhaps Eva and I took the world too seriously. One has to see the funny side of things. Because the majority of people are so thick-skinned that they are not really touched by disgrace of the spirit.

Fräulein Rüdiger was here on June 7 after a long gap (*one* year). We had already fallen out a little on that occasion because her only response to my bitterness was that I was overwrought and should take a rest. This time she made a wild, hysterical declaration for the "Führer," to which I gave the necessary reply (in the presence of Karl Wieghardt). She to that: "I cannot discuss it. I have faith. We have come home—we have not been at home since 1918." I asked her, assistant in the German Department, the enthusiastic student and devotee of Walzel, what Kant, Lessing, Goethe, Schiller would have said to this "home." Reply: They would have been in agreement with it, one must have "faith," for all the "tragic details and errors." And today she has written me a pathetic letter: Tragedy, pain over the friendship, everything must take second place to Fatherland and nation, the miraculous deed of the Führer, in which she believes.

Yesterday by contrast in the State Library: A collection of manuscripts belonging to the late Professor Vollmüller (Romance Languages) has been offered to it and I should take a look at it, although I do not know anything about manuscripts. (Besides it does not appear to contain anything new and valuable.) Conversation with Director Bollert, who has grown very old, and young Dr. Kästner. (I last spoke to Bollert in the courtyard of the library as he was strolling there with Ulich. A couple of months ago. Ulich is in the USA now. At the time Bollert pointed to my brown suit. Not yet brown enough, Professor. Now his letter to me was signed: With best regards, Heil Hitler! The Director, etc.) Bollert said consolingly in the presence of young Dr. Kästner: "You won't believe how few National Socialists there are. So many people come to see me. First with their arm stretched out, Hitler salute. Then they feel their way into the conversation. Then, when they've become certain, the mask falls. I too have to raise my arm. I say 'Heil'—but I cannot utter 'Heil Hitler.' I have just been in south Germany. There you very rarely hear 'Heil Hitler'—usually 'God bless!' But the Nordic race is more and more in evidence. Everyone's face has grown longer . . . The 'First of May Festival' was a failure. I had assembled forty people here. There were five left for Hitler's radio speech." (That fits with the thirty students who participated in the procession of the university "enterprise.")

[. . .]

On June 5, the young Köhlers together with Fräulein Carlo were up in Dölzschen, then for supper with us. On June 9 we ate with the Köhler parents. Exasperation and certainty that it is coming to an end. The Köhlers already knew about the decree issued immediately afterward by Rust, the Reich Education Minister, according to which all teachers are to get an annual four-week "national political overhaul" (overhaul, *again* the mechanistic terminology). The ever greater tyranny a sign of ever greater uncertainty. — Fräulein Carlo is often a visitor at the house of Kaiser, the former Saxon Education Minister. There too, they are waiting and hoping for an early end. Stahlhelm-Zentrum-Army. Köhler has heard from somewhere that nothing will happen until the death of the already more than half decomposed President of the Reich.

[. . .]

On June 8 at Hauber's, long visit, the department manager, Steffens, a man of 56, looks older, took us around. We got into conversation, he felt his way forward, complained a lot. His son, mid-twenties, unemployed, but in the SA and so without benefit. The father has a salary of 200M (two hundred marks, an expert, 35 years at his post) and must provide for son and daughter and wife. "I do not see much of my children anymore, they are always with their organization; I also have to be careful talking in front of them; mistrust has been sown in the heart of the family." The year before the same (very German, very petit bourgeois) man said with shining eyes: "the people's chancellor."

The people's chancellor was recently in Dresden for the "Reich Theater Week." For several days. As prescribed, forests of swastika flags hung in the streets all week long, newspapers printed articles: "The Thrilling Experience of Dresden" and so on. But the SA, insofar as it was not deployed on the streets, was on permanent alert (I know that from my students: "All these days in the Kugler Hostel!"), and the Leader appeared, disappeared, moved around, constantly slept in a different place and at a different time than had been officially announced. Like the Czar, like a Sultan and even more fearful.

And the signs of the approaching collapse are multiplying. For the first time, half hidden in a new victory report on the "Battle for Work": "We have discharged 100,000 emergency and a small number of permanent workers from structural and civil engineering, in order to carry on the battle above all in the cities." I.e.: work is at a standstill on the motor roads and the housing schemes, and the more dangerous loudmouths in the city must be stopped. — Then the mysterious "order" from SA chief Röhm as he went on leave to the SA as it went on leave: "We wish to grant our enemies the brief hope that we shall not come again. But on August 1 we will be back again in full force and do what is necessary . . ." What does that mean? — And on every side consistent reports about the tremendous lack of money. And the admission that the foreign boycott continues and cannot be gotten rid of. In addition the constant rumors of war. Everywhere uncertainty, ferment, secrets. We live from day to day.

An older professor, whom I had not known, Wawrziniok (car construction), shot himself. It was said: He had been very National Socialist, had emphasized that he was Aryan and of Polish extraction (Poland: our ally!). It had then come to light that he came from Breslau and not from a pure Aryan background. The truth? It is at any rate characteristic that such a rumor circulates after the death of a sixty-one-year-old man. His wife has been our honorary senator for years because of her great services on behalf of student welfare. *Her* I know personally.

Something restful at least. Once, the first time in months, we were at the cinema. We thought there was a Kiepura film we did not know, but it was the familiar *Ein Lied für dich* [A Song for You]. Tant mieux; we would gladly see and hear it a third time. So much music, humor, good acting y todo. It was a real release for me. I felt the effects for a whole day afterward.

Now for the next two or three weeks I want to deal with the reviews, which have built up for the *DLZ*, the only one to remain true to me. And then back to the Eighteenth Century. In truth, after the Delille study I feel as helpless and ignorant as before. But I have sworn to myself to begin writing by September at the latest. The Delille work is a mature and important one. It must give me the courage also to tackle the work as a whole.

Every day I expect the verdict in the Hueber case. May 15 was the deadline. Since then silence. It torments me every morning as I shave. It torments me every morning at ten as I go to the mailbox. If there is no yellow envelope inside, of the kind that Langenhan sends, then I feel I have been reprieved for another twenty-four hours.

[. . .]

I told myself recently when I finished Delille: If nothing else comes of my Eighteenth Century, then at least there now exists something complete in itself which conveys my ideas. And this study will last. At least in the sense we philologists mean by "last."

June 15, Friday

[. . .]

I have been depressed since yesterday by the meeting between Hitler and Mussolini in Venice. If he has a foreign policy success, then he *stays*. — Strange: what pleasure I gain from the report today that the Californian

Baer won the world boxing championship against the Italian giant Carnera. Baer, who recently beat Schmeling, is a Jew. Yesterday our newspaper pulled him to pieces and did not give him a chance against the Italian. — So feeling comes to the fore despite myself. Baer = Samson = David and Goliath—bellum judaicum.

Reading over Delille is ruining my eyes terribly again. My writing is even smaller than I had suspected.

June 17, Sunday

"Beautiful weather" = heat + lack of rain, abnormal lack of rain, such as has been causing havoc for three months now. A weapon against Hitler!

Yesterday afternoon and evening at the Kühns (Kötzschenbroda-Lössnitz)—walks, garden, veranda, fruit wine with resulting hangover today. Doubly, trebly interesting long conversations between Kühn and myself: (a) philological dispute. He calls the present state of affairs, which he condemns, pure democracy, and what I call by that name, Liberalism. But he already uses the word "liberalistic," such is the extent to which the terminology of the National Socialists also infects its opponents (cf. my philological notes on the movement). (b) He gave me his study of More and Rousseau, which I have just been reading. To him Rousseau is the Latin egalitarian, un-German. (Yet he sees Montesquieu as the precursor of Herder, Herder had "set Montesquieu to music," he told me. — He professed himself an opponent of anti-Semitism and yet fundamentally an anti-Semite. The German is creative, is in fact at one with nature; Luther, Meister Eckhart had creative imagination—Spinoza is not creative, a mere mathematician. The Jew is industrious, flexible, mobile, uncreative. There is no real Jewish musician nor conductor. Furtwängler "carries one away," Otto Klemperer does not. — He was surprised when I told him the National Socialists were losing or had already lost the bellum judaicum. "So you do believe in such invincibility of 'World Jewry'? Then the animosity of the convinced National Socialists is really quite understandable!" I emphasized that on the contrary I (just like the French) saw a certain relationship between Jewish and German thinking. He admitted there was something to that (Old Testament and Protestantism). But his *basic feeling* is nevertheless: the Jew uncreative, mobile, secondary—the German "creative."—Also at the Kühns were the Wiechmann sisters and the Zuchardt couple, whom we had met there once before. He is a secondary school teacher and dramatist; he and she are ardently anti–National Socialist.

July 14

I have just sent off the eight reviews to the *DLZ* (on which I have been working since June 11). [. . .]

My energy seems to have increased almost instantaneously, once the pressure of the last few years abated a little.

The actual deliverance came through the house business. About two months ago, Ellen Wengler, the sister of my Italian lecturer, saw our plot of land as she was out walking. Eva showed her the garden, the cellar, told her our troubles. A little while later this was the result: The Wenglers have property in England left to them by their late mother (who was English). A new law compels all Germans to sell their foreign assets; the government takes the foreign exchange and pays for it in Reichsmarks. Ellen Wengler did not want to leave her money unsecured and offered it to me as a long-term mortgage. From the start everything seemed so improbably favorable to us that after all the great calamities, all the hundred disappointments, we hardly dared believe in it. But things took shape swiftly and smoothly. A business talk with Heinrich Wengler, a letter, a telephone conversation, the siblings here for dinner: In two weeks we had come to an agreement. A new worry emerged: the German balance of payments difficulties, the English clearing law—would the Wenglers' assets be held back? They were not held back. On June 29 I signed the following contract with Ellen Wengler at Langenhan's chambers: She gives me as building capital an initial loan for eight years 12,000M at 6 percent, out of which I repay the present first mortgage of 2,500M to Nitzsche & Co. (My Iduna policy matures in eight years.) The corresponding contract with Nitzsche was signed yesterday. The State Bank had called me in the morning, the money was there; I had immediately transferred 2,500M by telephone to Langenhan, and on the fifth he paid the company in my presence. Meanwhile there had been planning and calculating with Prätorius. He will not be able to manage entirely with the money that is available to him now; I shall pay the rest in monthly installments. As soon as I am rid of the rent here and the tremendous taxi costs (over 100M a month) I shall be solvent. The middle section of the whole house will be built first, it is at least a self-contained little house with three large rooms and plentiful "fittings." There was an amusing difficulty: The building regulations of the Third Reich require "German" houses, and flat roofs are "un-German." Fortunately Eva quickly found that she could like a gable, and so the house will have a "German gable." If everything else comes off—and I am constantly after Prätorius—we shall have building permission in two weeks and shall start immediately. We intend to move in on October 1. What a deliverance! And how strangely ordained! All my planned efforts foundered and now this comes quite unexpectedly. And comes—the greatest irony of all!—because of a National Socialist law. Laughing, I said to Annemarie on the phone, "It is thanks to the Führer that I have got the building capital, truly thanks to the Führer!" I am becoming ever more fatalistic and am increasingly weaning myself off thinking about the end of all things. But how fortunate is he who is naive and devout. In my place he would have put his trust in God through all the bad times and now given him thanks. I can do neither.

We were given a second powerful lift by the "Röhm Revolt." (How do historical designations come about? Why Kapp *Putsch*? But Röhm Revolt? Alliteratively?) No sympathy at all for the vanquished, only delight, (a) that they are eating one another up, (b) that Hitler is now like a man after his first major heart attack. Admittedly I was depressed when everything remained calm during the days that followed. But then we told ourselves: They cannot survive this blow. Especially now with the emergency of the failed harvest just around the corner, accompanied by the complete bankruptcy of the state and the impossibility of purchasing foreign food. — Because of the fears of his mother, who is in Denmark at present, Karl Wieghardt was lured into visiting his relatives in Bohemia for a couple of days. Exchange of telegrams: "Aunt seriously ill, come immediately." Reply: "Wire whether condition really serious."—"Very serious, come immediately." On his return, he brought newspaper clippings with him, which is punishable with prison. The English: Mexican conditions. — "In the next few years we should not be afraid of Germany, but for Germany" . . . He has had his enemies killed . . . Medieval . . . etc., etc. A Prague newspaper published a picture: Hitler and Röhm in intimate conversation, and printed a letter that Hitler had written only in January to his dear friend and most loyal helper.

The confusion in the populace's ideas is shocking. A very calm and easygoing mailman and likewise old Prätorius, who is not at all National Socialist, said to me in the same words: "Well, he simply *sentenced* them." A chancellor sentences and shoots members of his own private army!

The terrible uncertainty. When there was a statement a few days later: "A German journalist in Paris was the intermediary between Schleicher and a foreign government," we immediately put two and two together: that must be Theodor Wolff, they want to divert attention to the Jews, tighten "Jewish legislation," and take away our right to live in Dölzschen on our own land. But so far there has been no move in that direction. There was even a "pro-Jewish" judgment from the Supreme Court of the Reich. A man had wanted a divorce because of a Jewish wife. The first court refused him, he won on appeal. The Supreme Court refused him again because he had known his wife's race when the marriage took place. The *Freiheitskampf* printed all this under the banner headline: "Who has to keep his Jewish wife?"

Yesterday Hitler put on a big show in front of his Reichstag. A loudspeaker was mounted on a statue in the fountain at Chemnitzer Platz; I heard a few sentences of Hitler's speech as I went to get a taxi in the evening. The voice of a fanatical preacher. Eva says: Jan von Leyden. I say: Rienzi. Today I read the whole speech in the *Freiheitskampf*. I almost feel pity for Hitler as a human being. The man is lost and *feels* it; for the first time he is speaking without hope. He does not think he is a murderer. In fact he presumably did act in self-defense and prevented a substantially worse slaughter. But after all *he* appointed these people to their posts, but after all *he* is the author of this absolutist system. [. . .] The dreadful thing is that a European nation has delivered itself up to such a gang of lunatics and criminals and still puts up with them.

Tremendously interesting were Hitler's words about the threat of "National Bolshevism." He boasts about having "exterminated" the Communists. He organized and armed them, he brutalized and poisoned them with his racial theories. What maintains Hitler now is only the fear of the chaos to follow. But we shall have to pass through that. Because: all the newspapers mentioned a small group of mutineers and seven executions. Now Hitler says he "put seventy-seven against the wall," and talks about a conspiracy that extended throughout the SA, which also involved three leaders of his praetorian guard, the SS.

And how nauseating: In the reports at the beginning of July the pederast group was pushed into the foreground. As if only they had "mutinied," as if Hitler were a moral cleanser. But after all he knew what the inclinations of his intimate friend and chief of staff were, after all he tolerated the sentencing of a large number of people accused of slandering Röhm in this respect, and this time after all it was not about ¶175 and the "revolt" did not originate only with pederasts. — But of course, Fräulein von Rüdiger and Co. will now believe with a vengeance in their heaven-sent pure Führer. Eva says, the Rüdiger woman and Thieme represent Hitler's followers: hysterical women and petit bourgeois.

On top of the building capital and the Röhm Revolt there at last came a third piece of good news yesterday, modest, but also truly a deliverance: the verdict in the Hueber case. His countercharge dismissed, 337.20M of my claim conceded; legal costs ⅗ Hueber, ⅖ me. According to that I would receive about 200M. After the terrible expert opinions I had been expecting to pay out several hundred marks. [...] How much agony and annoyance we both suffered for almost two whole years and how it weighed upon all our plans! So: At the beginning I rightly claimed 600M and was willing to accept 500, but Hueber offered 250M. Now I shall receive approximately 200M, but Hueber must fork out 700M if he wants to "stay execution," even though he has already paid for the two expert opinions which come to 250M. What foolishness! And yet, what a release. Unless Hueber were to appeal, but then I shall not worry as much as before, and then I shall also have a couple of months respite.

Building capital, Röhm Revolt, Hueber case—it is as if my life were taking a turn for the better again. And I believe I shall also be able to work again. As soon as I have caught up with my diary entries, that is, tomorrow, on to Voltaire!

Recently Jelski sent me a sermon he had preached for a deceased community leader. The heading was "To our leader . . ." I don't know, Jacobsohn or Levi or Blumenfeld . . . How tasteless and how contemptible! Observant Jews purify vessels that have become tref by burying them. In the same way the word "leader" [Führer] will have to be buried for a long time before it is pure and serviceable again.

Goebbels the advertising minister is no psychologist. He is boring, people make fun of the boring radio, etc. What is the mistake? If a factory, a single enterprise constantly tries to imprint itself on people's minds, on tramcars, with skywriters, etc., etc., that is amusing, because the aim is to capture the public in a specific and unessential respect, because it retains its freedom of choice, for example, between this or that razor blade, because this one advertisement is countered by a thousand others. Goebbels, however, does not captivate, but literally "binds" the whole person, tyrannizes him, and the one who is bound rebels against that, and he has an aversion to the utter monotony of the one thing being offered him. The progression of feelings here runs from a deadened indifference to aversion and revolt.

[...]

On June 29, delighted by the building affair, I gave Eva a lovely Japanese conifer, on July 12 a giant rhododendron bush. Karl Wieghardt had worked hard with her on the twenty-ninth, he was our guest, and there was a bottle of sparkling wine in readiness. Then the young Köhlers appeared unexpectedly after the meal to congratulate us. The bottle of wine did not go far, but was appreciated. On July 12 we were guests of the Blumenfelds, and Annemarie was there too. There was such a heavy, sweet Zion wine that my stomach is still rebelling a little against it today. But perhaps the fine roast goose is also to blame. Apart from the good food there was very beautiful phonograph music, a Mozart concerto and Bach on wonderful records. And all of us felt a little elated by the feeling of the "beginning of the end" (scilicet tertii imperii).

In my bohemian youth the name Erich Mühsam had a certain significance. I do not know whether I saw him and talked to him myself, or knew him only from Eva's and Erich Meyerhof's many stories and from the magazine Simplicissimus. He was a harmless Schwabing jester and a good-natured human being. Bad enough that his part in Councils Republic cost him several years in jail. Now it says in the Freiheitskampf—it has been sent to me during the last few days for promotional purposes—"The Jew Erich Mühsam has hanged himself while in custody."

July 27, Friday

Yesterday I ended my semester as I had begun it: i.e., I waited in vain once more for the students who had been prevented from coming. During this semester, therefore, I have given my classes before one or two people, likewise my lecture. In total I had two female students, Fräulein Heyne and Fräulein Kaltofen, one male student and SA man (of an extremely unmartial nature), Heintzsch. How will things go on? I am waiting like a junior clerk to find out whether I am given notice on October 1. But perhaps *others* will be dismissed before then. Yesterday the second blow struck the brow of the bull: Dollfuss killed and the German ambassador recalled

from Vienna because "without knowledge and instruction of the government of the Reich" he had promised the insurrectionists free passage to
Germany. Whereupon the Führer left the festival at Bayreuth because of
the "sad events" and the foreign press resumed its usual slanders. How
much longer? [. . .]

And yesterday the site was pegged out up in Dölzschen and so work
was begun.

And yesterday I arrived up there, flustered and very tired, with especially bad heart trouble and asked myself yet again very bitterly, which of
my wishes I shall live to see fulfilled: the house, the fall of Hitler, my Eighteenth Century?

[. . .]

The study on the language of the 3rd Reich also increasingly preoccupies me. To be developed through literature, for instance reading *Mein
Kampf*, in which the (partial) origins of the language of war must be evident. Eva draws attention to the language of war ("battle for work").

[. . .]

July 29, Sunday

Hardly had I rejoiced at deliverance than there was a serious crisis and assault on my nerves. Prätorius telephoned—Saturday before eight in the
evening—the required "German gable" increases the cost by 2,300M. I
shouted at him, at Eva, tears on her side, "taking advantage of a difficult
situation!" on my side, "recall of the contract"—very difficult night and
following morning. The money was available, costs 2M in interest a day,
the contract has been signed by a notary, but again: I could not get hold of
that much. Then Prätorius was here in the afternoon—desperate calculations back and forth. Result: He will raise the price by "only" 1,000M, leaving 3,000M, which I will pay off in monthly installments. I shall note the
precise costing as soon as I have the contract from Prätorius. Meanwhile a
further week has passed—we intend to move in on October 1—and as yet
there is no contract and not a single sod of earth turned. The District Office, the parish, this and that—and I am like a cat on hot bricks, all the
more so as every day can bring a state catastrophe. The second "stroke" is
undoubtedly near: foreign affairs, the economy, domestic affairs—everything is lost. Mysteriously threatening decrees from the Minister of Justice,
from the Minister of the Interior against possible sabotage by civil servants, against outside interventions in the justice system. One surely does
not write such things unless one is trembling. And a nation of 60 million
taps in the dark and scares itself.

The fate of the last few weeks: the increasingly excessive heat and sultriness; finally thunderstorms in the last couple of days—but little rain
and continuing sultry: cooking pot. Hours of sprinkling and carrying pails
to where the hose does not reach. One can start only after sundown. Went

up a couple of times before seven and watered until half past nine. Beautiful, when the lights of the city come on, but terribly exhausting. We are both sore and worn out, I am constantly tormented by painful inflammations of the eyes, on my head, at the back of the neck, on my shoulder.

Since finishing the reviews, I am reading Brandes' *Voltaire* and am stringing my thoughts for the central chapter of the Eighteenth Century to it. All kinds of things occur to me, after all I have read so much Voltaire in my life. I think it will be a very serious chapter. And the "Führer" is responsible for fundamental ideas in it.

[...]

Frau Dember here from Constantinople, to spend the holidays with her mother in Altenberg. He, Dember, is going to France, to improve his French. A few days ago Frau Dember visited us briefly in the afternoon. Yesterday evening invited with her to the Blumenfelds. The Wieghardts there too. Gusti back from Denmark. [...]

Blumenfeld, returned from Berlin, says there is an atmosphere of "mute despair" in the city. The bloodbath was worse than admitted—Frau Dember and Gusti Wieghardt say that few people abroad believe in a real "revolt," rather Hitler had organized a "St. Bartholomew's Eve"—the government was now finished in every respect and close to collapse, but that would not be followed by better times, since the economic breakdown was immense and irreparable.

Blumenfeld is particularly gloomy about the specifically Jewish future. He believes anti-Semitism is deep-rooted everywhere and in the process of spreading and intensifying. He himself is tending more and more to the side of national Zionism.

Philology of the National Socialists: Goering said in a speech in front of the Berlin City Hall: "All of us, from the simple SA man right up to the prime minister, are of Adolf Hitler and through Adolf Hitler. He is Germany." Language of the Gospels. — Something of the Encyclopedic style, somewhat modified, is now also present in the government's edicts. It hints, it warns, it threatens—whom? The public is kept in fear, individuals or groups (which?) threatened indirectly. Decree issued by Justice Minister Gürtner on July 21: "Illegitimate attempts to influence the course of the judicial process are to be most emphatically rejected and immediately reported to superior authorities . . ." Is that aimed at Colonel Hindenburg, or Papen, or a particular SS leader, or a group? Before, Eva used to say that the government's publications were distinguished by "shameless candor." I always pointed out to her the mixture of candor and lies. (First 7, then 77 "put up against the wall."—The fiction that only homosexuals were involved, that it had been an act of moral cleansing.) Now this new element of hidden threat. They say: We know everything, be careful! Yet this is also a flight into openness. And how does that fit with the constant emphasis that the people stand behind Hitler, the "revolt" is over and done with?

[...]

Five aspects so far: (1) the mechanical style, (2) the Encyclopedic style of the émigrés (Gusti Wieghardt says that in France they are called Les chez-nous), (3) the Encyclopedic style of the government, (4) the advertising style, (5) the Germanic style: Names, name changes [...], months ... Cf. the months of the French Revolution: *new ones!*

August 1, Wednesday

I do not know whether history is racing ahead or standing still. On the last day of June, the St. Bartholomew's Eve, at the end of July, the Austrian affair, the murder of Dollfuss, Italy's complete break with Germany . . . It is not my intention here to register individual historical facts. Only this feeling of holding one's breath: "Will the bull collapse this time—at the second terrible blow to his brow?" Again he does not collapse. And now this bulletin yesterday: Hindenburg's condition giving cause for concern. Surely the decision must come now. If the next few days do not see Hitler's fall, he will make himself President, i.e., he will let himself be chosen in a "free" vote by the unshakable love of his people. What I want to note is again only one point: "Language of the 3rd Reich." Yesterday's newspapers appeared with banner headlines across the front page: Execution of the Dollfuss Murderers. Underneath there were headlines about this and that. But the name Hindenburg was not to be found in any prominent position. The bulletin only came further down, amid the three or four column divisions, and no bolder than much else—and bold type is so common nowadays that it does not stand out at all (cf. celui > celuici, intensification of advertising).

In the evening at the Blumenfelds (they were supposed to eat with us, Grete Blumenfeld is on her back with a damaged knee, we went to them for evening coffee): There was a most serious discussion about the new state of affairs, in Blumenfeld's view hopeless, while I related what Johannes Köhler told me weeks ago: army dictatorship on Hindenburg's death. [...]

Reading aloud, at Annemarie's suggestion, Buck's quite Homeric *The Good Earth.*

August 2, Thursday morning

Blumenfeld telephoned, his wife had just called him from town, Hindenburg died at nine o'clock. A little like the death of old Franz Joseph. For a long time no more than a name and yet a last counterweight, which now falls away. The people may see it like that too. Only yesterday evening Schmidt, the tax official up in Dölzschen, spoke in a similar vein (the meaning was the same). He said: "After all Hitler had to deliver a report to him." I: "Rarely and only for show, in reality Hitler has been ruling alone for a long time." He: "That certainly—but the old gentleman was still there nevertheless." And his wife: "Surely he cannot be both, President and Chancellor. Two offices in one hand?" Quite simple, Aryan, petit bourgeois people. And the man, depressed: He had enough with his wound, his long imprisonment in Russia, he doesn't want another war. — But all this in a whisper, depressed, fearful, helpless. That is probably the voice of the German people.

[. . .] I find it as difficult to work on Voltaire as twenty years ago (August 2, 1914!) on Montesquieu. But then I was filled with enthusiasm and today I am very downhearted.

August 4, Saturday morning

At first, events made us extremely bitter and almost desperate, Eva almost more than myself. Hindenburg dies at nine o'clock on the 2nd of August, one hour later a "law" of the Reich Government of August 1 appears: The offices of the President and the Chancellor are united in Hitler's person, the army (Wehrmacht) will give its oath to him, and at half past six the troops in Dresden swore their oath and everything is completely calm. Our butcher says indifferently: "Why vote first? It just costs a lot of money." The people hardly notice this complete coup d'état, it all takes place in silence, drowned out by hymns to the dead Hindenburg. I would swear that millions upon millions have no idea what a monstrous thing has occurred. — Eva says, "And we belong to this band of slaves." In the evening as a tire bursts, dismissively: "It is not a shot."—We had always placed hopes in the Reichswehr; Johannes Köhler had told us long ago, as a confirmed rumor, that it was only waiting for the imminent death of Hindenburg to act. And now it calmly gives its oath to the new "Commander-in-Chief of the Wehrmacht."

But yesterday Hitler's letter to the Minister of the Reich: He had been entrusted with his offices in a "constitutionally legitimate" fashion, but all true power must come from the people, and so a plebiscite will take place. — Since when does he emphasize constitutionality? Since when does one swear in the army and have an "election" afterward? Was that the original intention? Did everything work out? And what will happen on August 19? The November mood is no longer there and Hindenburg is dead. [. . .]

August 7, Tuesday evening

The Kühns were here on Saturday. He spoke very forcefully about Hitler's "stupid demagogy." He said that it had already been obvious at the time of the Röhm Revolt that an agreement had been concluded with the Reichswehr. Hitler had undoubtedly bound himself to move his government to the "right." But that must within a short time bring him into conflict with the Communists who had been absorbed. He, Kühn, now considers civil war imminent and unavoidable.

That fits very well with the interview with General Reichenau published today amid the din of the Hindenburg-Tannenberg ceremonies [...] which cloaks everything. Who is General Reichenau? [...] He declares to the French journalist, Hitler can rely on the Reichswehr and the Reichswehr can rely on him. When has the army in Germany ever emphasized such a thing? It is making a big show of an agreement of mutual assistance with a usurping statesman. It will support him as long as he does its will. Against whom? Reichenau explains, Röhm wanted to merge "the political army of the SA" with the Reichswehr. Hitler has promised never to do that. — A pact against the mass of the National Socialist Party. [...]

It fits with the new alliance, that in the reports on the ceremonies yesterday and today the princes put in an appearance again. "The former Crown Prince, Gruppenführer Prince August Wilhelm, could be seen in the box . . ."

[...]

August 11, Saturday morning

Until the end of July we suffered from the drought. We had to water until late evening, the taxi costs were considerable. Since building started, rain is our constant fear. It can delay us, and our intention is to move in on October 1. We have been lucky until now. Last Saturday a heavy downpour began in the afternoon—work stops at one o'clock—and lasted literally until Monday morning. After that, for the whole week, the actual working time (seven until four) escaped the rain. The excavation has been almost completed, and a large part of the foundation walls are already standing. Building timber is to be delivered today. Of course, it is not certain whether we will be ready by October 1, and of course there is no lack either of worries nor awkward incidents nor unforeseen costs. [...] I put my trust in Eva, refuse to become attached to any property and am fatalistic. Aside from that, the visible progress of the house gives me pleasure, and despite poor physical condition and despite the immense uncertainty of the general situation, which affects me so severely and directly, I am on the whole more hopeful than for a long time.

After various negotiations. I signed a contract for moving [...] cost 240M. It will be covered by the glorious conclusion of the Hueber case. [...]

I discovered—which I had completely forgotten, really completely!—that in 1916 in Paderborn, Driburg and Leipzig I had carefully made extracts from all of Voltaire's important works, luckily in legible and fairly large handwriting. I read much of it through very carefully, arranged it all very precisely for reading section by section, as the writing progresses, and decided to begin today with the introductory chapter, "Voltaire and the Eighteenth Century." Yes indeed, today; this very morning, and even if it is only half a dozen lines, before I go up to Dölzschen. There is no point in reading anymore, it only makes me more uncertain. And once this structural chapter is there, then I will no doubt feel my way forward. Whatever reading is still necessary—a great deal!—must now be dealt with case by case. I will become completely giddy and slack if I go on reading and feeling so blindly around me. It was the same with all my books: There is a moment literally of aversion to the preparation, of complete confusion, of terrible despair. Double despair, because everything has already been said and because I cannot read everything. When I then begin apathetically with the order to myself: You *must* write now, whether it proves to be good or bad, fat or lean, original or imitation—until now it has never turned out so very bad and inadequate. Why should I fail this time? I am still only 53 years of age. Like a Calvinist, I must prove that I am still in a state of grace. So: Volume 4 of my Literary History begun on August 11, '34.

I believe August 11 was "Constitution Day" of the Republic. This "I believe" is characteristic; the festivities were never popular, never conducted with verve and impact. In this respect the Republic was all too Protestant; it relied far too much on the intellect and despised the senses, it overestimated the people. With the present government the opposite is the case, and it exaggerates this opposite to the point of absurdity. That speeches by ministers and by the "Führer" are put on records and repeated, that the same state occasions are time after time presented on film—wonderful. But if the funeral at Tannenberg is repeated on the radio, that is, if one acts as if Hindenburg really were being buried twice, if one does not present the evident reproduction of an act but instead creates the illusion that the event is literally taking place twice, and if this act happens to be the funeral of the "fatherly friend" and his entry "into Valhalla," then something holy is desecrated, it is automated and made ridiculous.

August 21, Tuesday

The five million No and spoiled ballots on August 19 against 38 million who voted Yes mean ethically so much more than simply a ninth of the total. It took some courage and reflection. All the voters were intimidated and intoxicated with phrases and festive noise. One third said Yes out of fear, one third out of intoxication, one third out of fear and intoxication. And Eva and I also simply put a cross at No out of a certain degree of despair and not without fear. Nevertheless, despite the moral defeat: Hitler is the undisputed victor, and there is no end in sight.

I was struck by the brevity of the propaganda barrage. It opened only a very few days before the nineteenth, but then with a frenzy of flags, appeals, radio addresses—a gamble on stupidity and primitiveness. The country lets yesterday be drowned out, the Röhm Revolt, the Dollfuss murder, etc., etc. One can only start such anesthesia immediately before the operation. — But how long does the psychosis last, and among whom? On the seventeenth Hitler gave his big election speech in Hamburg, and that was the hub of the festive jubilation that had been ordered. In fact he received the most Noes in Hamburg, 21 percent of votes cast.

Today I heard from Ellen Wengler what Kühn had recently asserted: Hitler has given the Reichswehr binding promises, he is no longer free, it is really *their* dictatorship. Can one gather hope for his fall from that? I am very much without hope at present.

The practice in the banning and permitting of foreign newspapers to be noted. Faraway places can no longer be cordoned off, too many people listen to foreign broadcasts on the radio. So as far as possible they give the impression of not being afraid of the foreign press, in the hope that the masses will not look at it anyway. Only in very serious cases is there a ban. But of course: the German press from abroad (Austrian, Swiss) is kept out.

The construction is making good progress (although we are worried about materials, varnish is already expensive and in short supply, a stop on metals and rubber is imminent); the Voltaire chapter creeps ahead line by line.

Today we will finish the *Sons* by Buck. A tremendous epic achievement.

September 1, Saturday evening

Today did not go at all according to plan. It was supposed to be the day of the roof-raising ceremony. Last week, after lengthy preparation of the individual beams, the wooden walls rose very quickly. My impression changed daily: At one moment I think I have a dog kennel in front of me, at another the thing looks more reputable. Today, however, such a heavy autumn rain began during the night and continued uninterruptedly until evening, that the men could do absolutely nothing at all. The roof will therefore be put on come Monday or Tuesday and the roof-raising ceremony will be then. I have left the arrangements to Prätorius, who has literally grown younger as building has progressed.

It was good that nothing materialized today. For the past week Eva has been suffering increasingly from a stomach bug, last night was fairly dreadful, she lay down all day.

September 2, Sunday

My own health is poor: a lot of heart trouble, constant painful inflammations on my shoulders, the back of the neck, my head, above all my eyes, minimal productivity, exhaustion. — Am I lazier than others? Others travel, go hiking, socialize, play cards, spend their lives unproductively *as well.* I spend more than half the day taking care of the household for Eva and the two cats and spend a great deal of the other half reading aloud. After a period of very serious reading, or when Eva is very exhausted, there has to be something "exciting," a detective story if possible. So now we've landed with Edgar Wallace, *The Green Archer.*

September 4, Tuesday

The roof-raising ceremony took place yesterday, September 3. Eva very fresh, and I saw indeed how close it is to her heart. I myself more an observer and very melancholy. Nine workers, among them the husband of our cleaning woman, the latter with her little girl, Prätorius and his wife, Ellen Wengler, the "blood donor." At three we came up by taxi with a mountain of cakes and a great amount of coffee.

A birch ("fetched" from the woods, of course) with white and red paper pennants at the top. The men are still working. *No* flag. I had ordained: If a flag were deemed necessary, then a black-white-red one. We clambered about on the imposed "German" roof.

It has turned out well, and the thing as a whole now makes a reputable impression. Then a table made of planks was set up in front of the house, the cakes disappeared in a flash, Ellen Wengler took pictures enthusiastically. After five we went on to the "raising feast." The Zum Kirschberg Restaurant on Altfrankener Strasse. A bare room for us. A grayish radio. Each person was supposed to get a Beffstick (= Beefsteak) with potato salad—but the restaurant had only prepared fourteen, those without got pork—there was swapping around, another Beffstick was found after all, it turned out afterward that the tall foreman-carpenter had eaten two portions, he also got the potato salad I left on my plate. Apart from that each got beer tokens, teetotalers—of whom there were several—could buy lemonade with them or exchange them for cash; two got bars of chocolate as an alternative; three leading workers also received money, two carpenters 10M each, a mason 6M. I had brought cigarettes and cigarillos with me. I had to make a short speech. I said that I was not going to make a long and beautiful speech, they could hear that every day on the radio, and here we wanted to be cheerful. But the joke was not understood. Then the tall, lively carpenter read out a speech of clichés, then the foreman haltingly uttered ponderous thanks and words about the craft of building in wood, then Frau Prätorius a little disjointed, rhetorical, but nevertheless fluent about her particular branch of construction—finally to my astonishment Eva. Fluent and spirited. Links with the Thirty Years' War. Her Nordic forebears in their wooden house arrived in Germany with Gustav Adolf. When we saw a cargo of Swedish wood on the deck of a freighter, she always thought, "There floats my house."

People's mistrust of wooden houses, no financial backer—yes, if it were built of stone!—to cap it all, her "pigheadedness." Only a miracle could save things, miraculously a friend was found as financial backer—on the very day of our thirtieth wedding anniversary. And now she hoped she would be able to celebrate many another roof-raising ceremony. The house was now a baby, it still had further to grow. — Eva also danced twice: with Frau Lehmann and with Ellen Wengler. — How often have I heard her talking about wanting to die, and what vitality there is in her! I am much more detached. Yet she has no fear of death, whereas I torment myself with thoughts of the end at every irregular heartbeat. Toward seven we drove off with Prätorius and Ellen Wengler. The workers behaved well and with subdued good cheer. Any kind of relationship with the "people" is quite impossible for me, any kind of capacity for celebration has been denied me all my life. I was glad that this had passed off without serious problems and was now behind me. At home Eva went to bed immediately, and I read aloud from *The Green Archer* for a long time.

[...]

Language of the 3rd Reich: A state secretary in the Reich Education Ministry writes, in future primary schoolteachers should no longer be "academically" trained. They should "teach German youth counting, writing and reading." Further: "A total science of people and state based on the National Socialist idea is at the heart of the non-denominational school." (From the journal *Volk im Werden*, excerpt in the *Dresdener NN* of August 22, 1934.) (a) return to the primitive (b) total science! Apart from the language study, it means the end of the PI in Dresden, that is, takes my last two students from me, so that I must expect to be retired by April at the latest. [...]

It is not merely a question of language, that a civil service oath to Hitler in person is now required of me. It was given collectively last Saturday. Those who are on holiday will swear at the beginning of the new semester. I *am* on holiday. Two months is a long time. — But I shall swear. Only now do I understand that the reservatio mentalis is necessary and self-evident. Blumenfeld, who as titular assistant professor and as retired does not need to swear, told me: "You do not give the oath to Adolf Hitler in person but to the Führer and Chancellor of the Reich Adolf Hitler for the period of his official activity." — Nevertheless: sickening.

September 6, Thursday

[...]

After an interval of almost a week because of Eva's illness and the house, I returned to Voltaire again today. With very little success.

September 9, Sunday

Yesterday housewarming coffee up at the house. Very time-consuming, bothersome, expensive—in very fine weather. Blumenfelds, the "respectable" Köhlers, Carlo, Wenglers, Frau Kaufmann (!—touching really, since we behaved so badly to her and have not seen her since the quarrel in November).

September 11

Language of the 3rd Reich: Party Rally of "loyalty" in Nürnberg. Loyalty, of all things, after the revolt. Always have the cheek to claim the opposite. The Führer: Order for a *thousand years.* Once more the fantastic number. Once more against "irresolute intellectualism." [...]

Goebbels' speech about *propaganda.* Propaganda "must not lie." It "must be creative." — "Fear of the people is the characteristic feature of the liberal conception of the state." We practice an "active influencing" of the people "complemented by a systematic long-term education of a people." "At certain times statesmen must have the courage also to do unpopular things. But the unpopular has to be prepared for in advance, and its presentation must be properly formulated, so that the people understand it ..." (September 6, '34). On the eighth: "We must speak the language the people understand. Whoever wants to talk to the people, must, as Martin Luther says, listen to what people have to say."

Once again the Führer appeals to "heroic instincts." The subordinate leaders emphasize once again: "Adolf Hitler *is Germany."*

September 12

Mussolini said at the trade fair in Bari: The Italians regard our theories with supreme pity. They had a three-thousand-year-old culture, they had Virgil, when we were still without letters to write down our fortunes!—Contempt for the barbarians! I would like to write a book: The language of the French Revolution, of Fascism, of the 3rd Reich. Basic idea: France altogether *autochthonous,* speech of Corneille's Romans, very reactionary language! Italy also almost entirely Latin, fasces! But nevertheless with American and Russian elements! Germany on the other hand: in every way entirely un-German, even in the gestural language, Romance, Russian, American. Except in the blood idea, in the animalistic therefore!

Very vigorous activity on our building. All the trades, roofers, gas fitters, electricians, plumbers, etc. are working simultaneously, the place is swarming with workers and materials. A dozen balls of peat, a mountain of slag for filling and intermediate filling, a tar kiln, the thick copper wires of the lightning conductor, boards, cement, etc. Eva is overjoyed. We are "electrifying" everything, including the kitchen. I have ordered the largest goods on an installment plan. Increases the price, but in a bearable way. Very warm, watery autumn weather. Incredible blooming of dahlias and sunflowers. Eva up at the house almost every day for half the day. Over-joyed. — Old Prätorius is, against all expectation, proving himself both in pace and prudent management. He stands smiling above the chaos and declares we will be able to move in on October 1.

The biographical Voltaire section, little biography, many ideas, is complete. Very good, but much too long. 28 extremely packed pages in manuscript, at least 40 in print. I am still pondering the arrangement of the two volumes. Preferably: Du côté de Voltaire, Du côté de Rousseau—two vertical lines, which are then brought together through (a) the mediators, (b) the Revolution. But will that be feasible? Voltaire really is part of the whole century, Rousseau comes only after so many precursors. So I would need to go back quite differently in the Rousseau book than in the Voltaire book.

September 14

Language of the 3rd Reich: When he spoke to youth in Nürnberg, Hitler also said: "You sing songs together." Everything is aimed at deafening the individual in collectivism. — In general pay attention to the role of *radio!* Not like other technical achievements: new contents, new philosophy. But: new *style.* Printed matter suppressed. *Oratorical,* oral. Primitive—at a higher level.

September 26

Incredible chaos up in Dölzschen, where we are supposed to move in on the first. Chaos beginning down here. Excessive expenditure. Everything is a "special bill," everything "has to be." Moving earth, varnishing heaters, lubricating steps, fire insurance 2.5 percent higher, fire insurance office, a drain and a water main connection not in the contract. Telephone, taxis, taxis, taxis. I shall scrape through with my last penny—*if* I scrape through. [. . .] The little house will be pretty, and when I am fresh I face up to everything with courage and even pleasure. But I am seldom fresh and often in despair. My heart often poor. — Eva on the other hand revels in plans for further construction. But she too suffers. Her right wrist is swollen every morning. But she expects to live until she is ninety, and I—warned by frequent palpitations—sometimes, often, mostly think that I have only another two, three years left.

I cling to my work. Half a manuscript page of Voltaire daily. I shall have to cut the chapter down.

But there is no point in despairing. If the Hueber case had turned out worse, I would be financially ruined already. Perhaps fate will give me a helping hand. Ultimately it is a miracle that we could build the house at all and at this time. Why should there not be further miracles?

September 27, Thursday

Last Saturday we were at the "respectable" Köhlers; it was nice as ever, but did not agree with us because of stuffy air and smoke. Father Köhler said with real feeling: How much that must mean to you, that the house you longed for is at last being completed! — I examine my feelings, they are very mixed. A blessing for Eva certainly, but a lasting one? Will not the lament about "crippling," the lack of space, the desire to continue building paralyze the blessing? Forsechè sì, forsechè no. And I? For hours at a time I am happy about it. Often I feel the financial burden, the fact of being tied down, no longer being able to travel. But I would not have been able to do that, even without a new house. Most of all I am tormented by the feeling of my approaching end. The question: What is the point now? But then I simply say to myself: for Eva, for the time that remains, be it long or short. And in the end it all balances out in the final judgment—it *matters* as little as everything else. I put the terrible memories of all the bitterness that is attached to the plan for the house to the very back of my mind. Berthold is dead, what is the point of getting even with him now? — Our friends, Karl Wieghardt, Ellen Wengler, finally (see below) Trude Öhlmann, have taken photographs of the little house, of the garden, and we have bought an album for these pictures. There one can see the bare patch of ground with the fence, then the cellar by itself, then the roof-raising party, etc.

On Sunday Trude Öhlmann was here for a day and brought her boy with her, who is now sixteen and in the lower fifth. A passionate Nazi until last year, he is now a fierce opponent and wants to dissociate himself from the HJ. I asked him what repelled him. "The leaders—fellow pupils—take more money from us for excursions than they spend. It is impossible to check, a couple of marks always go into their pockets; I know how it's done, I've been a leader myself. "Everyone must hand over 50 pfennigs for tomorrow's hike . . ." Then you write in the book: 2M surplus, and hand in the 2M. But you had a surplus of 4M. One fellow, who was really poor, a leader for some time, is now riding a motorcycle . . ." — "Don't the others notice too." — "They're so stupid," and then: "No one dares say anything or talk to the others. Everyone is afraid of everyone else!" — "Did the murders of last June not make an impression, the murder of his own people?" — "No, on the contrary! Then everyone praised his courage, it impressed them." — What manifold corruption of children! Perhaps, probably not even the majority of these class leaders embezzles money. But everyone is thought capable of it, everyone *could* do it, many will say to themselves: If I do not do it, everyone will think that I have done it anyway, so why not? The typical immoral acts of slaves are encouraged.

"*Reorganization of the student body.*" They congratulate themselves on having reduced the number from 12,000 to 4,000 ("to avoid an academic proletariat"); these 4,000 are supposed to form a "united team," live for two semesters in "comradeship houses" and wear "standard clothing" (i.e., barracks and uniform). 1,500 fraternities will no longer compete for them. (I.e., the fraternities are being dissolved.) Now the fraternities are certainly not places of liberal education, freedom and modernity; they are even to blame for the fact that the National Socialists found such large support among the students, and that they have been deceived only serves them right, as it does the German National Party. Nevertheless at this moment the fraternities, like the German National Party, stand for culture and freedom in contrast to the National Socialists. And I have the quiet hope that a new front against the National Socialists will form among the fraternity students. But such fronts reflect no more than disaffection. And it can take years until there is a proper explosion. Meanwhile the emptied universities will be "consolidated" like devalued shares. And I will be among the superfluous professors to be removed, at latest by Easter.

[...]

Write the history of the modern American novel and its relations with Europe, at the center always the problem of national psychology and what determines it! It would be such a lovely theme! If I felt healthier, I would arrange things thus: Until my mid-sixties I finish off my French literary history and "The Language of Three Revolutions" and my memoirs. Then live in America for my first year of retirement, and then *this* history of American literature. But my first year of retirement will begin in 1935, and soon after that I shall be buried.

[...]

Because we are moving I am returning mountains of books to the State Library, which have been lying here for months, hardly any of which I have read and which I shall have to order again later. It cannot be helped. As it is there will be something like fifty boxes of books, and a lot of them will end up unpacked in the loft, under the "German roof."

September 29, Saturday evening

Up since half past five. The packers did their worst here from half past seven until almost four, and now it looks a complete mess. The moving is supposed to take place on Monday—and yesterday there was chaos up at the house as well.

We moved in here in January '28. The last few years were very difficult. I bought the land on Eva's birthday in 1932, in April '33 the soil was turned up and it was fenced, in March '34 we built the cellar, which will now be furniture storage, without hope and possibility of continuing to build. On June 29, our thirtieth wedding anniversary, I signed the 12,000M contract with Ellen Wengler; construction began at the end of July.

Yesterday evening I was in such high spirits that I promised the taxi driver, who turned out to be a driving instructor, to take lessons from him in the spring (it has become very cheap now, 74M including test), this morning there was heart trouble and depression again.

This evening we are eating with Gusti Wieghardt, tomorrow with Blumenfeld.

The evening before last Walter Jelski and his "Lilo" Eggler passed through; they will return from the Saxon Switzerland in a week's time, and I will report on them after that.

[. . .]

The Voltaire chapter has advanced as far as the Pucelle poem. I am reading aloud with delight—Buck, *East Wind, West Wind*. An entirely different tone, and yet reminiscent of the eighteenth century, of *Lettres persanes*, but also of Rousseau (to suckle the child oneself!).

I let myself be carried along, rather I act in every respect, in my work and the house question, as if I definitely had at least another twenty years in front of me.

Tearing up old papers is a painful business. September '29—letter from a lieutenant colonel of the 10th Infantry Regiment, whether Hans Hirche is fit to be an officer cadet. Something from the same time: a letter from a department head in the Prussian Ministry of Education thanking me for my report in the journal *Erziehung* on the teaching of Romance Languages. And then, September '33, from the Saxon Ministry: "By submitting a certificate of award of decoration you have merely made your front-line service probable. As a non-Aryan . . . you have four days in which to produce evidence . . ."

DÖLZSCHEN, AM KIRSCHBERG 19

October 6, Saturday

The chaos, still only a little ameliorated, has now lasted one week. Still the thundering work of the carpenters everywhere, of the masons, of the electricians, etc. Great exhaustion. No more possibility of working since a week ago. Serious trouble with my heart repeatedly. Usually very despondent. People's congratulations embarrass me. Rare moments of true happiness. But despite constant fatigue and the considerable impediment of the swollen wrist Eva flourishes in all this confusion.

These are the first lines that I have dared write here. But the bustle is far too uncomfortable for me, and everything is in the greatest disorder and full of noise. Most of the time I stand around idle, worn down.

Two old packers came at seven on Saturday; by four everything already looked a complete mess in the apartment. Nevertheless, one could still find one's way around. In the evening we ate amicably at Gusti Wieghardt's, the first time since the big Christmas argument. On Sunday Eva performed tremendous feats of selection and dismantling. I could help a little. But also still read (Voltaire, *Semiramis*) and read aloud (Buck's *East Wind, West Wind*) a little. At the Blumenfelds in the evening. After the meal, the Salzburgs came, very much aged in the years since we saw them last, with their grown-up sons; the eldest studies medicine in Rome. He talked about Hitler's visit to Venice to meet Mussolini. Hitler had made a long speech, Mussolini listened icily and then said, "Now we shall drink tea." It was reported by all the newspapers and was now a household phrase in Italy. Salzburg Sr. related as absolutely vouched-for an incident at a performance of *Don Carlos* in Hamburg. At Posa's words, "Sire, allow freedom of thought!" there were several minutes of applause. The next day *Don Carlos* was dropped from every theater, including Dresden. — Then packed trunks at home until one o'clock.

On Monday I rose at half past five. The emptying of the apartment began at seven. I think eight men were working. Two large vans, a motor vehicle with trailer. Filled up at eleven, there was still enough stuff for another van. Eva went up to the house with the furniture movers. I remained with the cleaning women. While the vans were on their way, there was a thunderous downpour. When they began unloading at the house, it was over, and then the weather held. I sat on a folding chair in the empty music room. This occurred to me:

At this point, October 1, 1934, the move into our own house, whatever the circumstances, whatever my feelings, however different from what I had imagined, however bitter the memories and however great the worries—I shall one day begin my memoirs. If time is left me for them.

The furniture van came after two, to fetch the rest. Eva again cheerfully between the men at the front. A coffee, for which cups were borrowed in the house. Then up to the house again. This time I too came in the big van. Then I had to go into town again. Then the men up here were finished. Now down with Eva in a taxi. Our cats loaded. Up finally. Chaos here. Left in the lurch by the electrician. No light, no cooking facility.

October 9, Monday/Mistake! October 8, Monday

Still chaos. I am writing at a bare desk. But still unpacked, boxes everywhere, shelves not put up, workers—chaos, chaos, chaos, no chance of working. — I am 53 years old today. So far Eva has not remembered that it is my birthday. Amid all this turmoil, Walter Jelski was here again, yesterday afternoon and evening with wife and sister-in-law, alone overnight.

The first evening up here therefore alone with two cats, candlelight, a newly bought spirit stove with unpredictable emission and treacherous flame. Tea and ham. Early to bed. The bedclothes in a cupboard that could not be opened. Slept on the bare mattresses. The whole of the next day unwashed, with unbrushed teeth. The water heater in the bathroom was not and is still not installed. We were given a rough-and-ready temporary shower connection. I really do not know in any detail how this first week passed. A rude dream, shot through with a few nice moments. Nice, when one is pleased at the little house, the beautiful autumn weather, the view. But always the crippling noise of the workers, the enforced inactivity, the standing around in boundless confusion, the incredible difficulty of housekeeping in the reduced space; kitchen in the still damp cellar, the living rooms obstructed, absent cooking facility, absent crockery, bathroom unfinished, electric lighting incomplete. Money worries on top of that. The necessary new expenditures ever growing. On top of that the constant heart trouble. — Nevertheless every day sees a tiny improvement and clarification of the situation. Perhaps I shall manage to get down to work in the course of the coming week. Reading aloud is not going very well either. A brief quarter of an hour in the evenings. But the ceiling light is too bright and the proper lamp still cannot be used. — The cats cause particular difficulty. Nickelchen in particular excessively frightened. The problem of the cat boxes. First autumn rains, earth sodden, necessity of laying a firm path.

Walter Jelski's story, as I now see it overall. He put an end to his acting career a couple of years ago, found pleasure in business. He had a post in the publicity department of the *Frankfurter Zeitung,* was then in Basel. There love, cohabitation with an old friend from his acting days. "Lilo" (Charlotte Elisabeth) Eggler. Pale, blond, quite plain but sensitive creature, now 27 (he: 31), by birth a Russian German. Father was a photographer in Russia, she herself in business, an older sister is a craftswoman, a brother in Munich married to the daughter of von Geyl the conservative minister. — Walter went to Jerusalem, found a post there as an insurance agent. Then at the beginning of this year the mother died. The children came into an inheritance (war compensation in blocked accounts). Now Walter and Lilo are marrying in Berlin on the tenth as Germans living abroad, and 15,000M is released to her for Palestine. In a very complicated procedure involving some dodge, since a part of it belongs to her sister and will be given back to her in Switzerland via Palestine, where it is required as a "capitalist certificate." Walter had hinted at some of this from Basel and was supposed to be here with his Lilo in September. This visit was postponed and made almost impossible by Marta's usual tactless interference. Walter and Lilo were with us in the Hohe Strasse shortly before the move, then went to Göhrisch. There he got a dental abscess and appeared here on the second. We sent him to Isakowitz and put him up for the night in the loft, under whose "German roof" more than half our furniture is stored (waiting for further construction work!). The next day he traveled back to Göhrisch. And yesterday he appeared with Lilo and "Duding" (Estonian = "Little Dove"), the older, very refined sister-in-law. A nice afternoon and evening amid all the confusion. Meanwhile, in addition to our spirit stove, we have a little temporary cooking plate and a little plug-in shaving-water kettle, a little more electric light and a tiny little more space and are a quarter of the way to establishing order. The ladies afterward went to a hotel, Walter here until this morning.

We gave them our wedding rings (Eva's idea: I was uneasy about something so unconventional, *she* was not). They want simply to leave the

"Eva–Victor" 29.6.04 and have their names engraved beside it. The rings fit them, and they slipped them on immediately. Änny Klemperer, Berthold's widow, had sent me a check for more than a 100M so that I could buy rings for them.

I gave them the money in cash to use for something else. I like Walter's wife and sister-in-law and they speak well for him. It also speaks for him that he is extremely hostile to National Socialist tendencies and would like to return to Germany as soon as possible. His wife remains Christian. Something of this fate is related to ours. [. . .]

At the university, Gehrig and Raab, the democratic political economists, received their doctorates on October 1, Raab tainted by a Jewish wife. Spamer is to leave at Easter, he has been appointed Reich Director of German Folk Studies. So the section is gradually, or, rather, quickly being dismantled. I feel like Odysseus in Polyphemus's cave: "You will I eat last." To this Blumenfeld remarked on the telephone with a comforting quick wit: But Odysseus was not eaten, and it was Polyphemus who came to a bad end. [. . .]

Language of the Third Reich: The Jelskis have frequently heard and read as a standard abbreviation: Blubo—Blut und Boden (Blood and Soil). [. . .]

October 10, Wednesday

I have emptied a couple of drawers, put journals in boxes in the attic, in order to make space. Now that some things are standing around opened, the chaos is even more unbearable than before; but perhaps if the shelves are put up today, a degree of order will be achieved. Meanwhile never ending trouble with the electrician. He is simply unable to finish the work, there is still no cooker, and now it turns out that he provided false information about rates. I threatened I would claim compensation, he departed with his staff of apprentices, and we are still sitting in something unfinished.

How much of one's past comes to the surface when one clears up like this, but what a different aspect it all has today! A metallic identity disk, which I had to wear when I was sent to the front from Landsberg am Lech. (After that I returned to my Munich unit.) A page from the *Vossische Zeitung:* "Famous Doctors in the Field." Felix's picture. And his son is not allowed to be a doctor because his father did not fall in battle. Thanks of the bereaved at the passing away of "Doctor Wilhelm Klemperer." [. . .] Old calendar pages with fashions from the beginning of the century. Etc., etc.—I have been unable to part company with anything, everything is safe in its coffin. I shall probably never see it again. And everything lectures me about my age. And a couple of verses by Fedor Mamroth always go through my head: "What remains of it all? Ashes, ashes, ashes."
    [. . .]

October 14, Sunday evening

Never ending clearing up, unpacking, repacking, arranging, dust, dust, dust, boundless exhaustion, not out of the house all day, boxes, boxes, boxes. On weekdays a dozen (no exaggeration!) craftsmen around us, Sundays alone. Stink of paint, of new appliances, dust, dust, dust. Dragging things up to the loft, down from the loft, back up again. Down to the cellar, up from the cellar, back down to the cellar. It is still damp, the sugar is a wet lump. — Especially tired this evening. But I think: The day after tomorrow nine-tenths of the library will be on the shelves, and the last tenth will be packed away for the loft. [. . .] Just to be able to work a little again, to have a little peace. I think, I hope: on Wednesday.

The electric appliances are almost all present, the plumber almost completely finished, only painter Lehmann works and works and the costs rise and rise. God knows how I shall pay my Iduna policy this winter.

[. . .]

Georg sends congratulations from New York where he is visiting his sons. Three are now in the USA, only Otto, the physicist, is in Cambridge. How rich Georg must be to maintain this whole family, when he himself is retired. Wolfgang Klemperer, Felix's second, studying in New York, wrote to me: "The largest part of the Klemperer family is now in America." He is right: almost all the males of the next generation.

Two curious characters among our craftsmen: Trojahn the electrician, an East Prussian, but with an Austrian temperament. Always courteous, never reliable. Nothing right, everything too late. Yet he harms himself at least as much as he does me. He arrives with two little apprentices, the lads never know where the master is, the master never knows where his boys have gone off to, etc., etc. I make the most bitter complaints, he has a wealth of excuses, shakes everything off, is polite, makes promises and again breaks his word. — Master painter Lehmann, over sixty, husband of our cleaning woman. Works well, is very full of his own importance, strong ethical tendency. Good Templar, once locked up for a couple of weeks as an old Social Democrat, sees himself in charge of the work here, patronizes us, feels himself to be a teacher and artist. At present on very friendly terms with his family. But for at least two years Frau Lehmann lamented to us how badly he was treating her, and endeavored unsuccessfully to get a divorce from him at the time. [. . .]

The great and still dubious innovations of the house are the electric kitchen and the central heating. The stove is still fairly intractable—now enormous heat, now out—the hot plates take twice as long as a gas stove, perhaps even three times. — The ground in front of our house is dissolving into slippery mud; we must lay down a firm path as soon as possible, have ordered 4 cubic yards of cinders.

From time to time I have to go up to the parish rooms ("Heil Hitler!" — there's no other way). From the height of the village a quite remarkable view over the expanse of the city to the east. It is a real village, with real farms, but the "village square" is an altogether urban affair, more like the showpiece square of a spa.

[. . .]

October 17, Wednesday

Since yesterday I have my library in tolerable order. [. . .] But apart from the library: It's still chaos. The problem: squeezing seven rooms into three. The damp cellar space as kitchen—sugar, etc. always stuck together and wet. The "dining room" next to it, the first cellar, still without fittings. So forever up and down the 13 steps. Makes 600–800 steps a day. That "should" change. The craftsmen still not finished—painter, plumber, electrician. The veranda for the cats still without a railing. [. . .]

On top of all the lack of space and confusion there is the eternal desperation of lack of money. The painter in particular is eating me up at such a rate that I do not see any possibility of fulfilling all our financial obligations in the coming months. This never ending worry is terrible. In addition the constant heart problems. — But the little house is pretty and the view—in the changing light of the autumnal storms, downpours, play of the sun—is magnificent.

It is still impossible to think of work. Perhaps tomorrow or the day after tomorrow—mañana. In fact I am not much inclined to the Eighteenth Century. What really attracts me is the language of the three revolutions and my memoirs. I doubt whether I shall write either.

I hardly get around to reading aloud: We are too tired in the evenings, and the light is too poor—Trojahn is still not finished, the man will drive us to despair. [. . .]

Today Annemarie and Dressler, the "unrespectable" Köhlers, are coming for coffee and supper. We intend to put one of the two living rooms, at least to some extent and provisionally, in order. As I write, Lehmann Sr. is painting the doors, there is an immense amount of muck lying on the floor, and torn paper, pieces of furniture stand higgledy-piggledy, the settee standing on end. — The mystery of the central heating is still unsolved; now frost, now heat.

I firmly resolve to continue writing on Voltaire tomorrow, even if it is only a couple of lines.

October 21, Sunday

[. . .]

Now as before cramped conditions, chaos, hardly any lighting, craftsmen still working, excessive expenditure, constant heart trouble.

Visitors come. We had Dressel and Annemarie as guests for the evening, Blumenfelds and Frau Schaps yesterday for coffee; this afternoon we are expecting the Wieghardts, and for now (midday)—touching and terrible—the Kaufmanns, about whose meanness there was the worst gossip only yesterday, have announced themselves. — All of that keeps one back and is an effort. On the other hand it gives me heart when people like the house—but the depression is there again immediately afterward.

As for Voltaire I completed the section on epic poetry and have now faltered before drama. I am paralyzed by the certainty that after completion I shall undoubtedly have to write out this whole chapter, on which I have been working since August 11, once again, that is, reduce it by half. But I must have it completely finished before I undertake this reduction. I know too much about Voltaire, too little about the others—the impudent certainty, the recklessness of my early years is missing. We are both usually too tired in the evenings for reading aloud. [. . .]

October 24, Wednesday

[. . .]

I always face the same difficulty with my Voltaire. No matter how much I compress it, it will still be a short book instead of a chapter. I have to let it grow to its full size and then—God knows how—make a summary of it.

October 30, Tuesday

Language of the 3rd Reich: Newspaper headline (the day before yesterday, *Dresdener NN*): "Young People experience William Tell." Experience, German spirit + the American missing article, telegram soul. — I received a magazine with a swastika on the cover: "The Care of the German Cat." An essay on its usefulness by the Reich director, written in grand political style. The cat clubs are now a Reich association; only Aryans are allowed to join. So I shall no longer pay my monthly mark for the association here.

My Voltaire has advanced as far as the end of the drama.

November 4, Sunday evening

This morning the first heavy frost, during the day a wild autumn storm, several showers, thick clouds, occasional bright sunlight, the distances foreshortened In the evening I walked alone across the fields, along a blocked-off road, still in the course of construction, up to the village. From the top a tremendous view all around of the illuminated city and its surroundings. The view from here is already fine—but only a segment, whereas up there the entire surroundings twinkle. The storm howled as accompaniment. On the way up, the familiar daily heart trouble again, the ever present reminder.

Work on Voltaire laid aside since yesterday, lecture preparation. The historical introduction to Dante raises difficulties, and it no longer gives me any pleasure to compile things on which others have done the work and which I know only superficially or not at all. I also had first of all to find my way back into the French lecture course. I am beginning with Pascal and want to move swiftly to the eighteenth century. For the seminar I have prescribed a most inadequate school edition of Voltaire's little novels. The big texts are not available, the small ones are castrated. — How many students? I have put up a notice—in the office of the Romance Languages Department.

There we sit, the three of us, myself included.

On Wednesday—I was standing unshaven in the garden—the old ophthalmologist and spectacle lens researcher Professor von Pflugk greeted me from the street. He was passing by chance with his wife. We brought them in, showed off the little house. Refreshingly, he inveighed against the National Socialists. Even more refreshing was his declaration: All his patients, from the most various circles, are as incensed as he. He no longer believes it will last long. That helps for a moment, but only for a moment.

[. . .]

November 7, Wednesday

On Monday, curiously enough, six students at the French lecture and six at the class. The three from the PI were joined by three auditors. A Catholic theologian and two girls (one of them had attended last winter; she asked after Georg, who had treated a relative). It is not easy to talk about Pascal, Bossuet and Voltaire in front of a Catholic theologian. I allowed myself to be carried away by some fairly dangerous allusions. On Encyclopedic style, of the hangman of burned books, the Bastille.

Dante was supposed to begin yesterday. I fought a migraine all day, which finally became overpowering. [. . .] I began to dress at half past five and literally felt too sick to continue. I had Frau Lehmann telephone the janitor and call off the class. The first time in fourteen years in Dresden that I have canceled because of illness. I went to bed and slept till half past nine. Afterward a little slow walk with Eva and then read Hemingway aloud to the end till after twelve.

Today also, health very poor. My eyes failing. Probably a slight temperature as well. Stomach terrible.

In addition the appalling misery of money worries. Exhausted reserves, constant incidental expenses, the work on the house, visitors—every mark a torment. The cats eat 1.30M worth of veal a day. Tomorrow the young Jelskis will be here again, on their return journey. The day after tomorrow the Blumenfelds. Wine bill, butcher's bill—small sums, but they add up. And Eva does not cut down on the work being carried out in house and garden. It "must" be done; I am too anxious. Everything "has always worked out." A "voluntary" 20 percent of income tax is squeezed out of me for Winter Aid. With that my monthly salary falls below 800M. I shall have to suspend my insurance policy.

Horror and exhaustion often have me so much by the throat that they are counterbalanced only by horror of the grave.

Not a line of Voltaire since Friday.

November 9

"Day of Mourning for the fallen of the NSDAP. The Party and public buildings will fly flags at half mast. The public are called upon to do likewise." I see with pleasure that in our neighborhood a good half of the houses are without flags. So I could also hold back our flag. (Bought at the beginning of October in Reka. "Do you have any flags?" — "Yes, but only black-white-red ones." (Jews are not allowed to sell the other, holy one)— "Of course, that will do for me." — "How large?" — "On no account too large. Except not so small that it is conspicuous.")

November 20, Tuesday

Only in the French lecture am I truly in my element. I patch the Italian together without any basic knowledge. Today again on the Sicilian school of poets. — Neither the French nor the Italian lecture give me any pleasure. Yesterday the six Frenchmen were only four, and I have two Italians. How much longer?

Health very poor. Always heart trouble, often migraines, at the moment probably a bit of influenza.

Eva ill a lot, hence increased housework. — Voltaire still not finished.

On Wednesday, November 14, the swearing of the oath: "Loyalty to the Führer and Chancellor of the Reich Adolf Hitler." About 100 people; the second group. I was "not present" at the first oath-taking during the holidays, in the hope of perhaps avoiding it altogether. It was not to be. The ceremony, cold and formal as possible, lasted less than two minutes. We spoke the words in chorus after the rector, who had first of all reeled off: "You swear *eternal* loyalty; I am duty bound, to draw your attention to the *sanctity* of the oath." And afterward: "You must put your signature to the oath on a printed form." And: "I conclude with a triple Sieg Heil." He shouted "Sieg"—and the chorus bellowed "Heil!" and crowded toward the forms. Among those who swore were Janentzky, Kühn, Stepun, Beger . . . They are as good National Socialists as I am. A week before (*Lettres provinciales*) I had spoken about the reservatio mentalis and taken the part of the Jesuits. [. . .] Sickening was: A beadle calls out: "His magnificence, the Lord Rector!" Everyone stands at attention as on a barracks square. The rector, a younger man (Kirschmer, appointed by the government for two years), hurries to the lectern, stretches out his arm; everyone raises his arm. Everyone remains in this position for several seconds. Then, in a military tone: "The gentlemen may be seated." Leadership principle—"At ease!"

In my lecture (French) a theologian, a woman schoolteacher, whom I have allowed to attend as guest, since otherwise she would have to pay 25M. I had not caught the names of either. I had seen them together several times, and when the theologian was absent yesterday, I asked the teacher who the gentleman was. Answer: Baum, the former lecturer in Catholic theology, but now kicked out, who now wants to take an examination in French. The teacher spoke with dismay about the new state of affairs, *I* was fairly open and private, she said I must be very certain of my students, otherwise I was being very incautious in my lectures. Then: "Who among the professors is a National Socialist, after all? Very few, I think. My brother is in the Party, has been for a long time—but it's a battle for him." — "So he wants to get on in the world?" She retracted, a little confused: That was not what she had meant, she does not know his views. I asked her brother's name: Professor Alt, meteorologist. I was indeed somewhat dismayed. If she tells her brother . . . But how it separates brother and sister, tears families apart.

[. . .]

On Sunday there came for afternoon coffee: Trude Öhlmann from her sanatorium, Fräulein Mey, Fräulein Roth, the librarian. All embittered, all convinced that it is coming to an end, each one knows of jokes, rumors and preparations. In the open land near Hellerau the mailmen are learning how to throw hand grenades.

November 21, Wednesday

[. . .]

Walter Jelski was here from the eighth to the thirteenth. His wife was ill in Berlin, then came to join him; the pair had an argument at the railway station and she did not appear until evening, upset and tearful, regained her spirits here and remained for one day with him. I like her more than him. I think she will suffer a lot. I have no confidence in him. An unprincipled egoist. He borrowed 25M from me. "We don't need more than ten, we'll send the rest back at the border." Not a penny came, of course. They are now in Basel. Their money is in Jerusalem—their money is his wife's money—friends are expected to help out until money is transferred from Palestine. He angrily castigates the Berlin relatives, in particular Wally.

November 25, Sunday

[. . .]

Since about two months ago, at Blumenfeld's recommendation, I borrow our books for reading aloud from Jahn & Jentsch. Raab, whom I once met there, introduced me to the lender. He has rented the first floor of the bookstore, carries on his business here and in Czechoslovakia. A man probably approaching fifty, Bulgarian, resident in Germany for twenty-seven years (*not* Jewish, I believe), correspondent for Bulgarian newspapers. Like a film character with his graying goatee. Natscheff told me he had been ordered out of the country two months ago. Yet he had written no "horror stories," only sober economic reports. He had gone to his ambassador. In Bulgaria there are German secondary schools and many teachers from Germany. The Bulgarian government had threatened it would answer Natscheff's expulsion with the expulsion of 200 German teachers. Natscheff had thereupon been left in peace in Germany. [. . .]

All around us, however, there are more and more rumors and signs of an approaching outbreak of war. The Mark couple was here on the Day of Atonement (Dember's loyal friends, old Social Democrats). Mark related that his machine tool factory (saws) could not keep up with all the orders, the Döhlen plant was working three shifts producing "bottles" (shells and gas shells). Similar news on all sides.

December 4, Tuesday

My French lectures are good and also give me ideas for my book. The Italian ones are rubbish, cobbled together from Gaspary, without knowledge and without interest. That takes care of Sunday, Monday and Tuesday. I now have five students in the French lecture, three in the seminar and two auditors in the Italian lecture, of whom one was ill recently.

On Saturday I completed the penultimate Voltaire section; I shall manage the short conclusion this week. A small book in almost four months. How much of it can go into the Literary History I do not know yet.

The hope of an imminent change has been followed once more by gloomy and desperate waiting.

Eva is feeling better, she is faring remarkably well with the lengthy dental treatment. These long journeys into town are almost a stimulation, she likes Isakowitz—I am always in the treatment room. (Dentist—housework, housework, housework—lectures—is it any wonder that Voltaire is taking so long?)

My own health poor; heart trouble, eye trouble, exhaustion and the many worries, especially money worries. I shall not be able to pay my life insurance in January.

We had visitors fairly frequently (usually in the afternoon to see the house, only Gusti Wieghardt and Karl in the evening), for example, the builder and his wife, Fräulein Carlo, Fräulein Mey and Fräulein Roth, the librarian; we were out a couple of times ourselves, at the Wieghardts, at the young Köhlers. Gusti had an SPD newspaper, tissue paper, 5 pt. type dispatched in a pink oblong envelope, perfumed and addressed by hand, so that it felt, looked and smelled like publicity for a drugstore.

Eva works in the garden a great deal, and it agrees with her. I divide my day between Voltaire and the most urgent money worries.

A happy letter from Walter Jelski in Basel: They have gotten their travel money at last and are sailing for twenty-two days by freighter from Rotterdam to Haifa.

[. . .]

December 16, Sunday

For a moment it seemed as if Hitler would not last past the Saar Plebiscite (January 13), perhaps not even past Christmas. Now the tension has gone out of the Saar affair, to Germany's advantage, and Hitler is firmly in the saddle again. It is hard not to despair. But the strong, general disaffection is still there.

I call the park hill, which I climb almost every day from the city to us, my Catholic mountain. I always walk slowly, breathing heavily, often in pain, never without the question: How many times more?

The Voltaire is finished, the rest of the Eighteenth Century lies darkly before me. Money worries, domestic labors unchanged.

Very mild weather, so that Eva is constantly working in the garden. She has recently been suffering a great deal from influenza, so it was especially good for her. Her dental treatment has been interrupted for the moment, is endlessly drawn out. It will cost hundreds; I have no idea where I shall scrape the money together. [. . .]

Language of the 3rd Reich: The never ending wine offers rarely conclude with "Heil Hitler," usually "with German greeting." It is a discreet way of hinting at the German National views that they take for granted among their clients, professors and senior civil servants. On December 7 an offer by the "Ferd. Pieroth'schen Wine Estates Management Burg Lagen bei Bingen am Rhein" concludes "Yours most respectfully." That is a heroic deed and a first swallow. [. . .]

Encyclopedic style from the other side, alias pure extortion under a veil of courtesy: (a) Approximately one year ago, the Reich teachers' organization requested precise details about Aryan status, position in SA, SS, etc. That manifestly applied only to members of the organization, and the secretary's office of the TU also thought I did not need to reply to it. Now a very courteous reminder arrives. To be completed within five days, otherwise we would be grateful for reasons for non-completion. Evidently there must be some misunderstanding, "since we would not assume that you as a civil servant and educator of young people would consciously wish to set yourself against National Socialist reconstruction."—(I filled it out, and enclosed a passport photograph I had had taken. The TU secretary's office passed it on, and wrote that it assumed responsibility for my silence. That was very helpful of Lehmann and shows how seriously he took the threat.) (b) "An appeal to the inhabitants of Dölzschen" was in the mailbox a week ago. Aimed, very communistically, at the "senior civil servants" who think they have done enough if they have the Winter Aid badge (23 percent of income tax!), who on "hotpot day . . . have the maid" give 50 pfennigs, while the "smell of roast goose" comes from their kitchen, who think themselves "too smart and too good" to attend the meetings and events of the party of state, the NSDAP, and absorb at least a few crumbs of National Socialist ideology. This was contrasted with examples of the dutiful behavior of poor people. Then it continued: "National comrades of Dölzschen, those are sacrifices! The former, however, are nothing but miserable, pathetic alms! Therefore remember your duty to the national community, so that the charge of being a stranger to the people does not, for you, turn into the accusation of causing the people mischief!" Signed by the chairman of the local party group and of Winter Aid here.

December 30, Sunday

Still no snow and frost, only rarely rain all day. Eva works for hours in the garden almost every day. It's good for her, although she has become very thin. She even seems to find the endless dental treatment bearable now. (When will the man get his money?)

We have a lot of visitors, usually for afternoon coffee. Wieghardts. — After a very long interval, Hirche father and son. The lad, already a senior officer cadet, will be promoted to lieutenant in April. It sounds like a fairy tale, but *I* recommended him to the Reichswehr. I had suspected the parents of avoiding us out of fear. But it seems to have been more shame. I have known the man in his rise and glory, then in his plans to set up on his own. Now he has a minor, temporary post in some foreign exchange office and earns 280M gross a month. — Then Wengler was here. — Then Kühn and his unemployed brother-in-law Körner. Then after a gap of something like six years (the last time in Heringsdorf!) Erika Dreyfuss-Ballin turned up. Her brother Otto Ballin has got himself married in Durban; she presented his brother-in-law, Dr. Koblenz, a young chemist, lecturer at the University of Durban, father Russian Jew, mother German Jew, both emigrated first to Canada, then to South Africa. A very likable man, who has studied in Germany for two years and is now going back. It turned out that he is very interested in my field, attended many of Vossler's lectures in Munich and is very familiar with his work. He said Vossler was rather feared by his students, not much liked. He had aged considerably in the last year, and it had been thought he would have to leave.

We talk about politics to all these people. Only Eva is optimistic, *I* make an effort to be so. But everyone has the feeling that now, immediately after the Saar Plebiscite, "something is going to happen." Perhaps some government action, June 30 da capo (people say "Reich murder week"), perhaps a move from the Right or from the Left (cioè from the SA). Perhaps

Hitler will be maintained by the Reichswehr and become its tool completely. No one feels certain of his own opinion. Everyone feels a need to
exchange opinions, because nothing at all can be learned from the newspapers anymore. Most repulsive to me is the specific Jewish pessimism
with its self-satisfied composure, the ghetto spirit reawakened. They're
kicking us, that's just how it is. If we can just get on with business and if
there's no pogrom. Rather Hitler than someone worse! An evening at Frau
Schaps recently was very bad in this respect. And the Blumenfelds are in
their element here, think the same way.

[. . .]

Kühn too says: "Who will it be, if Hitler is murdered?" He simply can
no longer imagine anyone else, government without dictatorship. And of
course a dictatorship would indeed be necessary during the time that constitutional organs of government were reestablished. Too complex. The
belief in the stupidity of the people is spreading everywhere. — Kühn
said, the National Socialists had undoubtedly done some good. I: The
most terrible thing about them was that even the good they do is befouled
by their mendacity. He agreed completely with that.

[. . .]

One of the two women in the Dante lectures, a private student eager for
self-improvement: "My brother in the SS . . ." — "What is your brother's
profession?" — "None at all yet, he's a fifth former at Vitzthum Grammar
School" — "And why the SS?" — "He has to be part of something, every
Tom, Dick and Harry is in the HJ, so in his mounted section he has his own
horse and learns how to ride." — "Is his heart in it?" — "Not a bit of
it . . . but he has to. Now they have been ordered not to go to church in
groups. If at all, then individually, if they really want to."

[. . .]

It was really nice here on the twenty-fourth. The little tree had its electric lights in our own house for the first time (. . .) Eva got a black carpenter's hammer, a big pair of pliers, two angle bevels and ten hyacinth
bulbs. The Wieghardts were here, and Karl had composed some "Café
Music" for her, whose theme was made up of the sequence C.A.F.E.

On the first day of the holiday we ate at the station in the evening,
walked a little down the Prager Strasse and returned on the F bus, which,
fortunately for us, has been running between Nausslitz and the Neu-
städtische railway station since November 1. (So at least we no longer
have the inordinate cost of the taxis.) — (Coming from the dentist,
Isakowitz often takes us part of the way in his own car. We are usually
there at half past twelve, Eva then has something light to eat in town, we
perhaps do some shopping and then back for coffee. A regular arrangement, twice a week.)

Of the Eighteenth Century I completed, accompanied by many depressions, the eight pages "Paths to Voltaire: 1. Non-classical elements in the
seventeenth century." If the snail continues to crawl along like this, I shall
be working on this volume for years.

[. . .]

What did 1934 bring me?

The little house with much pleasure and many cares. — Eva's largely improved state of mind. — A stronger feeling of my own approaching death, of considerable aging. — The first 72 pages of my Eighteenth Century, before that the Delille study. — The unspeakable pressure and repulsiveness of the continuing swastika regime.

In the summer I also wrote eight reviews for the *DLZ*, of which only one was returned because its author has a post in the Ministry and must not be censured.

On the plus side of the year, I must not forget that I was rid of the burden of the Hueber case. Admittedly that meant only a pause in my money worries; at the moment I am not in a position to pay the Iduna policy in January.

As to my memoirs: How I learned to cycle, it must have been about '97, and was supposed to show Georg what I can do. How I forgot to loosen the tightly screwed handlebars and immediately fell onto the roadway. How Georg was appalled. Characteristic of my lack of presence of mind and Georg's lack of psychological sense. — Now I would so much like to learn to drive (and Eva would so much like me to do it). I will have even less presence of mind now than I did then, in addition a failing heart. On the other hand, later on I was for years quite a passable cyclist.

I see that in the summary of the previous year (which is in fact much gloomier than this one) I praised our little tomcats. That must be done here also.

1935

January 1, Tuesday, toward evening

Yesterday at Gusti Wieghardt's was nice in that she repeatedly expressed with unshakable certainty that this will be Hitler's last year. During the day I managed a successful page on the Querelle chinoise. [. . .] this afternoon I was paralyzed by tiredness and the deadly-dull visit of the Carlo woman.

Language tertii imperii: Lutze's New Year message to the SA, Encyclopedically concealed threat to the SA. — Our "fanatical will" twice in a non-pejorative sense. Emphasis on *believing without understanding.* (1) "fanatical engagement of the SA," (2) "fanatical sense of commitment."

January 9, Wednesday

Private and general situation coming to a head. On January 3 Blumenfeld asked to resign "voluntarily" from his teaching post, otherwise the authorization to teach at the university would have to be withdrawn from him. His subject is an "ideological" one, ergo . . . Blumenfeld put on record that he teaches psychology in an entirely scientific way . . . Yes, but the Reich Governor sees the matter differently and is making the decision. Blumenfeld will probably resign "voluntarily," because otherwise his pension would be reduced (which of course no one says—but . . .). Blumenfeld was already retired as lecturer and instructor of the PI a year ago. Blumenfeld always has the financial security of the family brickworks and no doubt also means of his own. I on the other hand . . .

On January 4 a decree from Reich Minister Rust: The semester ends on February 15, the next begins on the first of the fourth [April] *without* "new matriculations" and lectures for the first semesters. I still have three regular students from the PI (apart from that only, all in all, four to five auditors). The three take their final examinations at Easter. So from Easter I shall have no more students and have to retire, i.e., be reduced from 800M to 400. But even now I can hardly meet my obligations; the life insurance must remain unpaid, and when on earth Isakowitz will see his money is quite uncertain. So how to keep going with half an income? Impossible to discuss anything with Eva, to complain to her about all of it. Her nerves are failing her completely again. Warning results in hiccups, nausea, etc., etc. — Now only fate can help us.

Perhaps it will help us. While our Jewish people are completely pessimistic and in the press everything looks wonderful, we hear something very different through Annemarie and Gusti Wieghardt from Swiss and English newspapers and foreign radio. According to them SS men have been shot, there was a clash between Reichswehr and SS in Magdeburg, Hitler is completely in the hands of the Reichswehr, nor do things look particularly good for Germany in the Saar, the government, in its present form at least, will soon be finished.

I live quite fatalistically from day to day. I gave my lecture after the holidays to three people (those three), the seminar to one, the Dante lecture to the two female auditors. It is altogether wretched. Yet this business takes three full days from my writing. And then on Wednesday so much weariness and odds and ends have collected that this day too is lost. So my opus makes a listless and hopeless snail-like progress.

We had these visitors here: on the fourth, the four "respectable" Köhlers; on the fifth, Alexis Dember who is taking a doctorate in physics in Prague; on the sixth, after a very long gap, Annemarie. She spoke with particular vehemence about the compulsory sterilizations, which are also often carried out where they are unnecessary and uncalled for. — The Blumenfelds are to eat with us today.

January 15, Tuesday

In the last few days a certain improvement in mood. The situation was not "supposed" to be looking good for Hitler in the Saar, everything was "supposed" to be ready for an internal takeover by the Reichswehr. "Politiken" talked about a 40 percent vote for the status quo, Gusti was hopeful, Natscheff said "they" were "very nervous" in Berlin. The plebiscite was on the thirteenth, yesterday our press was already celebrating complete victory, and today—the result on every radio station at eight o'clock in the morning—90.5 percent of all votes, approximately 475,000, for Germany, 45,000 for the status quo, 2,000 for France. And the government here is triumphant, and we hang out our black-white-red "Jews' flag," i.e., tie it to a clothespole, which in turn is tied to the railing of the front veranda, and my Dante lecture is canceled, and once more I have been lulling myself with pipe dreams (recently to Natscheff: "Anyone who is German will vote for the status quo") and am deeply depressed. My own head is now very much on the line. The semester ends on February 15, the next, which begins on April 1, bars new matriculations. I shall have no more students and be discharged.

Even now I can no longer pay what has to be paid, the problems become greater every day—what will it be like when I receive 400M instead of 800?

The Wieghardts were here on Sunday afternoon and evening; we drank two bottles of wine, had the phonograph on—the old "hits" of free Republican days—luxuriated in hopes.

Today the man seems ineradicable again and the dirty slavery completely accords with Germany and really suits 90 percent of all Germans.

For the past week, for the first time this year, we have mild, but proper winter weather, beautiful snowy landscape, but Eva is greatly impeded.

[...]

At the moment I am most oppressed by the quite undignified lack of money. I do not know how we are to get through to the next payday.

[...]

January 16, Wednesday

Isakowitz—after the treatment it is by now usual for him to drive us in his car to the station, where Eva has soup, today after the removal of her bridge fairly toothless—again expressed the mood of Jewry, and today, in fact, my own also. Deepest depression, even deeper than in August at Hindenburg's death. The 90 percent vote in the Saar is really not only a vote for Germany, but literally for Hitler's Germany. Goebbels is surely right in that. After all there was no lack of information, counterpropaganda, free ballot. Presumably, when we talk about disaffection, we take our pipe dreams for truth and utterly overestimate the actual opposition. In the Reich too 90 percent want the Führer and servitude and the death of scholarship, of thought, of the spirit, of the Jews. *I* said: Let's wait and see, whether, now that foreign policy is no longer important, the turn to the Right begins. I shall not admit defeat before Easter. But I do not believe my own words.

And every day the money problems get worse. Today an exorbitant electricity bill. The electrical appliances are disappointing. Cooking goes at a snail's pace and costs far too much: The 15M by which my highest estimate is exceeded, can no longer be found. I have collected a few commemorative medals, five- and three-mark pieces, in the last few years. These will presumably now be put to use. And then? And how on earth, once I have retired?

February 2, Saturday evening

On Wednesday, January 30, Eva had to have a root removed under anesthetic. I find it frightful to watch as she is sent to sleep and is unconscious, whereas she prefers it and finds local anesthetic ineffective. I have to look on every couple of years and am always happy when it is over and done with. What use is the calculation that there is only one fatality per 100,000 anesthetizations? Who can give me a guarantee that the black lot will not be drawn here? — Today, on leaving, Eva smoked a cigarette to the end outside the dentist's door. So we arrived a moment later than usual at the stop on Albert Platz, where there is a flimsy wood and cardboard construction advertising Winter Aid. A strong west wind has been blowing uninterruptedly since yesterday. As we are three steps away from it, the column sways and falls. The large group of waiting people scatters, two elderly people, a man and a woman, are struck and lie beneath it. The old man, his face red, screams—perhaps a seizure, certainly shock—and is pulled out and carried away, the lady limps pitifully and is led away to a car. It could have happened to us too. The black lot can be drawn any-where. Fate? — Next week the three months of treatment and bridge work should come to an end. Deliverance for both of us. I have had to devote half a day twice a week to it. In addition the constant domestic burden and the misery of the lectures: so that this week I have been able to work un-interruptedly at my Eighteenth Century only on the Friday. I have dealt with Saint-Evremond; after more than six months writing, therefore, I am still at the beginning.

February 7, Wednesday

After three months, Eva's bridgework was completed at the dentist today and she is now in a bad way. It cost me an excessive amount of time. (About one day a week remained really free for the Eighteenth Century.) Costs: Against 600M I have promised monthly payments of 50M. I am now so weighed down by part payments that it is sheer misery getting from one salary payment to the next. I shall have to suspend the life insurance. I shall take advice from Rummel tomorrow as to how that can be managed with the least harm. But I fear the harm will be considerable. I suffer very greatly from this constantly increasing, undignified pressure of lack of money. My shirts, socks, collars are wearing out, my only suit is wearing thin—there is literally no money for replacements. Etc. for all the everyday things. And every day the burden of being a maid, every day the warning of shortage of breath and heart trouble, every day the worry of being forced into retirement. — And every day the Hitler government is more firmly established internationally and therefore more secure at home. These must be the saddest days of my life. In the past when I felt bad, I had the future to look forward to. Now I often think I am unable to go on.

The lectures have dragged on in front of two, three people and are to conclude next week. Yet they have repeatedly, especially the Dante, caused me time-consuming difficulties.

On January 28 we were at the Blumenfelds in the evening. He has an offer to go to Lima as an industrial psychologist, and will no doubt accept it. Then we shall be even lonelier here than before. I envy him. I am so ag-onizingly helpless. Because I am a modern philologist who cannot speak any foreign languages. My French is completely rusty, I am afraid to write or speak even a single sentence. My Italian never counted for much. And as for my Spanish. I can do nothing useful.

On the twenty-sixth we spent a very pleasant evening with Annemarie in Heidenau. — On the twenty-fourth (a very great rarity now) we went to the cinema. A Kiepura film (*My Heart Is Calling*), music and content poorer than his other films, nevertheless very nice. I am so starved of music. At the Blumenfelds we now always listen to good phonograph records; lately, when the Wieghardts are here, Eva sometimes even has our old hit records put on. These tangos and nigger songs and other international and exotic things from the years of the Republic now have historical value and fill me with emotion and anger. There is freedom in them, a sense of the world. In those days we were free and European and decent. Now—[. . .]

February 9, Saturday evening

Today authorization to teach at the university was withdrawn from Blumenfeld without explanation. Max Liebermann died today and gets a kick at funeral oration. Overrated rationalistic and French art. National Socialism has got rid of it.

Today Goering is on a "state visit." Instruction: All public buildings are to fly flags for three(!) days until Monday evening; the population is requested . . . That is printed only today in the *Dresdener NN*. I see many flags in the streets, but few here. If the whole street puts out flags tomorrow, I shall also have to do so.

Recent instruction, no, "advice" from the Reich Ministry to law students. Not all universities can be reformed at once. The storm troops of National Socialism in German law were the law faculties of Breslau, Königsberg and—I think—Kiel. So "advice" to study there. Apart from that a young lecturer is now allowed to hold the same lecture at the same time as the professor and the student "is free to" . . . The young lecturer is of course an NSDAP man.

[. . .]

Gusti Wieghardt's sister Maria Lazar was here for a couple of days. We were at Schrammstein Strasse last Sunday; they were our guests on Wednesday. Maria Lazar lives in Denmark in Karen Michaelis' house, her Lütti goes to school there, she herself is a respected author (of Communist-Socialist tendency); her pacifist play *The Fog of Dübeln* (a town poisoned by gas) has been performed in London and Copenhagen. Gusti Wieghardt's *Sally Pencil* and *Little Theater of the Godless* have been printed in Moscow.

February 10, Sunday evening

After five we set out for an hour at the Blumenfelds. Crowds at Löbtauer Strasse, bus stops, holdup. Street cordoned off: Goering is going to pass through. The order came by motorcycle about ten minutes ago. The traffic was jammed for about a quarter of an hour, then the road was opened again. The conductor told us: The same thing happened earlier in the afternoon, and he didn't come then either. — That is how the man is protected, in boundless fear. Presumably he takes a route that has not been announced. But in the newspaper: "unbounded joy of the populace."

The Blumenfelds were in low spirits. At all events they want to be away from here by July 1. To Berlin or Lima. They are considering what to do with their "small amount of wealth," how many thousand marks they keep as ready cash. I said, "What do you know about money worries!"

I live like a day laborer now. My salary brings in less than 800M net, almost 400 go to fixed installment payments, the remainder must last.

Began Fontenelle yesterday [. . .] Today ghastly torment with *Paradiso*.

February 13, Wednesday—yesterday anniversary of Father's death

[. . .]

The lending library man Natscheff angrily showed me a list of books that he has to hand over without compensation. Things that have been cleared by the censors but are not "for the people." For example: Hemingway, *A Farewell to Arms*, probably too pacifist; all of Wassermann, too Jewish-intellectual no doubt; Roth, the Austrian officer novel from Solferino to the World War—I can't remember the name. Maria Lazar made an amusing remark about this work. She said: The man knows his Galician ghetto, but he does not have a clue about Austrian aristocrats and officers. Proof: The General has beef for his Sunday roast. But that is an almost plebeian everyday meal and never a Sunday dish.

I have worked hard all day on a survey of the last ten cantos of *Paradiso*. I want to offer it to my two faithful girls up here on Saturday afternoon, since I have officially concluded the semester at the TU. How much study was necessary, in order to really penetrate these cantos! Study of theology. I have already written and talked about Dante so often and still know so little about him.

Now I have about six uninterrupted weeks for the Eighteenth Century in front of me. But how many hours every day? Nothing I have done has ever gone as slowly as this book.

I cannot decide whether to go into the Galsworthy trilogy here. And yet it would be well worthwhile. Somewhere inside me there is always a wild hope that some time in my later years I shall manage to get around to a proper work in the Anglo-American field. Galsworthy is so interesting for me because of his conscious and unconscious contributions to national psychology. The somewhat distanced regard for the Americans, who get on his nerves; the implicit aversion to the French, who, for him, can do too much and have too little feeling (Fleur); the repeatedly emphasized pleasure in the English feeling for landscape, in English irrationalism and in English stoicism—feelings are not expressed and evening dress for dinner is a good thing.

Also exceptionally useful to me is the second part of *Morath*, which I am now reading aloud. A discussion of National Socialism at a very high level: individual against mass, [. . .] Europe against city-state, intellect against blood. In addition the excellent description of the debased colonial Germans in Argentina and of the primitive, but in fact more decent, state of mind of the criollos. [. . .]

February 21, Thursday morning
(completely springlike since yesterday!)

[. . .]
    The work stands at Bayle.
    [. . .] I ended the semester on February 15. With my two Dante girls I started from Saturn in the *Paradiso*. I invited them out here for coffee last Saturday; after coffee they got a serious closing lecture. One of them, Winkler, humble origins (father a senior paymaster in the Reichswehr), engaged to a theologian in the "Confessional Front." — The other, Hildebrandt, I was already acquainted with from previous semesters, daughter of a very wealthy industrialist in Niedersedlitz, brother with his own horse in the SS cavalry, in order to avoid the "Communist HJ"—he is a fifth former!—sister is studying art history in Berlin and wins prizes in equestrian contests. "My" Miss Hildebrandt, who makes a very modest middle-class impression, drove here in her own car and brought the Winkler girl with her. The day before yesterday she came in her car again with her sister, who makes a somewhat more fashionable and ironical impression, and brought, as thanks for the Dante lecture, a hare that her father had shot. — The girls are completely anti-Nazi. But when the conversation turned to two young aristocratic women who have just been executed in Berlin for espionage (for Poland, our friend!), they thought there was nothing at all wrong with that. They did not ask questions about the difference between martial law and peacetime law, about the protection of a public trial, etc. The sense of justice is being lost everywhere in Germany, is being systematically destroyed.
    On Saturday evening we were at the Köhlers. The big Goering rally had taken place in their neighborhood (tram depot Waltherstrasse). It had been very quiet, they had noticed nothing of the cheering and the crowds of the newspaper reports. The Hildebrandt girl told us that Prager Strasse had been guarded by police with slung carbines; but somewhere someone had nevertheless shouted: "The Commune still lives!" Gusti Wieghardt, whom we visited on February 17, talked about arrests at the station and of the nocturnal activities of Communist "painting gangs." — But what good does it all do? Everyone keeps his head down, and the government is firmly in control and celebrates its foreign policy successes.

February 27, Wednesday

[...]

My Bayle section finished yesterday. It really is a complete success. But I am working without any hope.

[...]

Early spring days. While Eva and Karl were working in the garden, a long walk with Gusti Wieghardt, on which we went astray, out until long after dark, the city below us, somewhere up beyond Dölzschen village, ending up at Rosstal. Beautiful, almost romantic. But about three weeks ago I fell on some black ice in the park and pulled something in my left leg and since then I have been plagued and hampered by pain. The lack of money, the worry, the deep bitterness in politics unchanged.

[...]

They are trying German names of the months. Old German "Hornung" for February. The French Revolution at least invented names of its own.

Spent a long time today in the catalog room making applications for the next section. At home only the notes to Bayle. Read a little Hoche aloud. Emphatic advocate of freedom of scholarship. At the boundary of Encyclopedic and free style.

Eva has gone to bed early. Her nerves failed her once again, which manifests itself in her shivering with cold in the evenings with her teeth really chattering.

For myself the walk up through the park is always Passion and reminder.

March 4 (frost and snow, more wintry than for a long time)

[...]

I discovered Dubos on my own from the first edition of his esthetics. Typical of our State Library, it has this first edition, but not a single monograph from the nineteenth and twentieth centuries about Dubos. I shall be able to write very well about Dubos on my own and hazard a very bold comparison with Muralt. But I must nevertheless see what has already been written about Dubos. I shall order from Berlin and if necessary make additions later. Questioning fate: How long will my Eighteenth Century be? (I no longer really believe in the two volumes of the contract—in any case the contract hardly exists anymore.) When will it be finished? Who will publish it?—But in the face of all the questions: What I am writing will be good.

That I only get to know Dubos now, who publishes the whole of Montesquieu's climatic theory in 1719! Which is so important to the last books of the *Esprit des Lois*!

I feel a little ashamed of myself. But I would never have written my fine Montesquieu with such momentum if in 1914 I had already been the cunctator of 1934.

On the evening of the first at Gusti Wieghardt's. On the second at the Wenglers for the afternoon and for an evening snack until almost eight o'clock. They live comfortably. He has a receptive nature, teaches, is scholarly and has no personal ambition. They are enviably well-to-do. At Easter he is going on a trip to Italy, she is going on a guided tour of the USA. I am a little envious. A young colleague of his was there with his parents. The people obviously anti-Nazi, but infinitely timid and reserved. The general political mood: a dull yielding, a despondent waiting without hope.

Eva coined a good phrase. The program for the Saar celebration ("Homecoming" on April 1) was laid down in every detail. Then on the day itself the announcement: At such and such a time the Führer "has unexpectedly arrived at Saarbrücken city boundary." Radio let it be known, he is flying to Frankfurt, proceeding from there . . . then he landed in Mannheim and transferred to car. — So Eva said: "The Czar would have been ashamed of himself!" Of course lengthy home and foreign reports on the tremendous popular jubilation, the enthusiasm, etc. And: "Adolf Hitler in person is bringing the Saar home!" — As if without him the Saar would not as a matter of course have fallen to Germany and without anyone having a thought for the status quo. But now it is a victory for National Socialism.

Yesterday at the Blumenfelds with Frau Schaps and Annemarie Köhler. Depressed atmosphere.

For this evening we are expecting Agnes Dember, who has been visiting her eighty-year-old mother in Berlin and has invited the Blumenfelds and the Wieghardts here.

March 17, Sunday

One and a half weeks ago I had a serious bout of influenza, one afternoon I was on my back with a temperature of almost 102 degrees. I do not seem to be able to recover properly from it, constant feeling of exhaustion paralyzes me.

The long, severe cold period is now gradually coming to an end. There are still patches of snow, but Eva is working in the garden.

My work is going very badly. Last week I wrote a couple of pages on Dubos. Then I received Lombard's monograph from Berlin, worked my way through it and now have to revise everything. It is not this particular point that depresses me, but dissatisfaction and helplessness as regards the thing as a whole. I shall no longer manage this volume. And the thought increasingly obtrudes upon me that my earlier volumes, which presumably constitute my "life's work," are essentially no more than journalism. I go to sleep and get up again with the question of the purpose and value of my life. And then I do housework and boxes for the cats.

Weissberger, the chemist, who has a scholarship to Oxford, visited us. His father is in the hospital here with a stroke. He maintains he could arrange an invitation to Oxford for a "turn" for me.

[...]

The Wieghardts almost our only company. Gusti's childish Bolshevism is getting on my nerves. — Otherwise great loneliness.

Political situation hopeless, financial likewise.

March 23, Saturday

The Dubos-Muralt chapter finished, 10 written pages in about a month.

Finances so bad that I have to give up a couple of especially minted five-mark pieces, as very last reserve, to last to April 1.

Hartnacke, Minister of Education, bad enough, but still an educated man, right wing rather than a Nazi, has been "discharged." Mutschmann is his own minister of education and a wild Nazi primary schoolteacher is his commissar. For how many more weeks will I keep my post?—Hitler has proclaimed compulsory military service, the protests of the foreign powers are weak-kneed and they swallow the fait accompli. Result: Hitler's regime is more stable than ever. [...] In every aspect of the destruction of culture, Jew-baiting, internal tyranny, Hitler rules with ever worse creatures. Rust, the Reich Minister of Education, gave another speech today attacking "insipid intellectualism."

I am not recovering properly from the influenza, my heart finds everything difficult.

[...]

On Monday a really tiring evening at the Köhlers. (Their third wedding anniversary.) The only amusing part an old English aunt of young Ellen Köhler, who after decades of marriage in Germany still speaks German with a completely English accent, is very much attached to England and does not want to know about the current regime.

April 3, Wednesday evening

Fairly much tired if not of life, then of writing. Everything drags on so monotonously with the same grinding worries—an end or even a change is not in sight. What is the point of noting each and every visit we make to the Blumenfelds and the Wieghardts and the Köhlers or that they make to us? Everyone always says the same thing. Maria Lazar was here once, en route from Vienna; she did not tell us anything particularly new either. Today Chaplain Dr. Baum, who attended my French course during the winter, was our guest for coffee (Blumenfeld joined us). Baum is completely pessimistic. The Church will avoid conflict as long as it can, it is all not so important as far as the Church is concerned. It thinks everything else will pass and it will remain—so why risk trouble? An old priest had said to him recently, such an odd song had been sung at a meeting, one he had never heard before, something about Horst Wessel—what or who was that? At a meeting of priests the chairman had calmly explained, the current situation was not so important—"we have seen the Third Reich and we shall see the fourth." Lately, admittedly, the government was taking harsh measures against the Catholic Church—arrests, no conclusion to the Concordat negotiations—which might perhaps lead to firm resistance by the Church. He, Baum, did not believe so. He did not believe that the end of the regime was close, it had too much power, the country was far too enslaved and numbed by idealistic-nationalist lies—and if the end did come one day, it would come with a lot of bloodshed. — Baum, who can visit them as a clergyman, talked, like Gusti Wieghardt, of extremely overcrowded prisons.

Meanwhile I had to start my lectures on Monday, April 1, although the people at the PI do not start until the twenty-fourth. *One* student came to French, who after eight semesters at Leipzig wants to do one semester here, and stay with his parents, before the state examination. The whole of the four hours on Monday for him.

April 17

The one student in French, the two women students in Italian, the dreadful shortage of money and uncertainty, the constant heart problems, even though Dr. Dressel in Heidenau has once again diagnosed my condition as normal, the never ending rheumatic and eye complaints, the snail's pace of my Eighteenth Century—now at Lesage—nothing changes.

[...]

On the twelfth at the Kühns. Also there were Bollert, the Director of the State Library, and Frau Robert Wilbrandt, who wants to sell the villa they have here. Wilbrandt was the first who had to go, they live in Upper Bavaria. Frau Wilbrandt told us: In Munich people complain out loud when Hitler or Goebbels appear on film. But even she—economist! close to the Social Democrats!—says: "Will there not be something even worse, if Hitler is overthrown, an even worse Bolshevism?" (*That* keeps him where he is again and again.)

Bollert talked about the new tyrannical measures of the Governor and his "Commissary Minister for Popular Education," the schoolteacher Arthur Göpfert. Even the senior and academically qualified officials must now sit out office hours from half past seven until four o'clock. Göpfert often carries out inspections early in the morning and barks like a sergeant major. But he is also said to use the same tone toward ordinary employees and to have shouted abusively at the library's checkroom attendant. [...] Another guest, a secondary schoolteacher, son of Manitius, the Professor of Low Latin, said he had been in the Stahlhelm with Göpfert: "a soft, sentimental idealist, not a malicious hypocrite, but a lot of the rancor of the little man." That could also be said about Robespierre, remarked Kühn. — In any case, only personnel matters are still dealt with here; for many

weeks the circulars from the rectorate have printed only the decrees of the
Reich Minister in Berlin. In every decree for institutions of higher learning
and universities, in every speech Rust emphasizes the overcoming of "insipid intellectualism," the precedence given to "physical and character
skills," the interdiction on compensating for them with "purely intellectual accomplishments," "racial" selection. — At the psychiatric congress
recently, it was said that only now was "the Nordic child," which previously had been put at a disadvantage to the Jewish child, whose intellect
developed more rapidly, coming into its own.

Der Stürmer is displayed at many street corners; there are special bulletin boards, and each one bears a slogan in large letters: "The Jews are our
misfortune." Or: "Whoever knows the Jew, knows the devil." Etc. When
German assassins were recently sentenced to death in Kovno by the
Lithuanians there were protest meetings everywhere. The proclamation of
the Dölzschen group went: "The world must see that the international
Jewish rabble cannot provoke us to make war, but that surely we are 'a
single nation of brothers!' "

They send me the cat paper regularly, although as a non-Aryan I . . . always send it back. But here National Socialism runs riot in quite unbelievably grotesque fashion. The "German cat" :/: foreign "aristocratic" cats. In
accordance with our Führer's ideas, etc. The carnival edition of the
Münchener NN has already made fun of it.

   [. . .]

April 22, Easter Monday

The Easter weekend especially quiet up here. Eva in the garden all day;
spring weather. I wring a page a day out of myself. Short walks on the
Dölzschen plateau.

The Blumenfelds were here on Friday; I disagreed violently with him
about Zionism, which he defends and praises, which I call betrayal and
Hitlerism.

That evening our finances suffered a particular blow. Things are particularly short this month, the special five- and two-mark coins, which have
so often been under threat, must stop the gap this time. Then Eva's spectacles broke, and now the coins will not be enough either. I shall sell a couple of books to my department. On the morning after this low point a
letter from the Iduna. A couple of years ago it "revalued" my first life insurance, which went down the drain in the inflation, at 755M, payable on
my death. Now it is offering immediate repayment to the amount of
430M. We shall gratefully accept this drop in the ocean, although it may be
weeks before it arrives. It will permit me to pay the 5,000M policy in July,
which otherwise I would have had to use as collateral for a loan, as I recently did with the 10,000M policy. It will permit me a new suit, a couple
of new shirts and socks; it will permit gas fittings for the house, since

cooking with electricity has proved such a failure, and a couple of small things. What a wretched state of affairs. But I am pretty hardened by now. Eva meanwhile has got trouble with her teeth again, new expeditions to Isakowitz have begun, there will be a new bill.

[. . .]

Since the "election victory" in Danzig, since Stresa and the verdict of the League of Nations I again have a little hope that I shall live to see the fall of the government. But only a *little* hope.

The Eighteenth Century is going to be *good*. But it is turning out ever longer, ever more closely written. Who will print it? I have come to a halt at Lesage.

I would have been less fierce with Blumenfeld, had I not in the last few days received through Marta a publication of the Jewish Reform Community celebrating its ninetieth anniversary. In it was the picture of Father, and a history of its efforts on behalf of Germanness. It now appears nothing short of tragic.

April 30, Tuesday

It was a particular point of honor for me to write a page (Lesage-Marivaux) of my 18ième, today, when I do not need to give a lecture, because I received my dismissal notice through the mail.

May 2, Thursday

I was anxious about Monday to the extent that then it would be clear whether students from the PI, which had started on April 24, were coming to me. No one came. There was no need to be excessively gloomy about it, since Janentzky has apparently seen no sign of the 200 new PI students either. They have evidently been told: "The Institute is going to be detached from the University, so don't waste your time with the lectures there." So I gave the lecture to my Leipziger and to Susi Hildebrandt, her of the hare and the Dante lecture. Lore Isakowitz also appeared and asked me for books—she now wants to get a qualification at the Department of Oriental Languages in Berlin—which I promised her for Tuesday. On Tuesday morning, without any previous notification—two sheets delivered by mail: (a) On the basis of para 6 of the Law for the Restoration of the Professional Civil Service I have . . . recommended your dismissal. Notice of dismissal enclosed. The Commissary Director of the Ministry for Popular Education. (b) "In the name of the Reich" the notice itself, signed in a child's hand: Martin Mutschmann. I telephoned the university; no one there had a clue. Göpfert, the Commissioner, does not waste time asking the rector's office for advice. At first I felt alternately numb and slightly romantic; now there is only bitterness and wretchedness.

My situation will be very difficult. I shall still receive my salary, the 800M that give me so much trouble, until the end of July, and after that a pension, which will amount to approximately 400M.

On Tuesday afternoon I went to Blumenfeld, who has meanwhile finally received the offer of a professorship in Lima, and he gave me the addresses of the scholars' aid agencies. It was snowing on Wednesday, the "Day of Celebration of National Labor." I wrote correspondence for hours. Three identical letters to the "Notgemeinschaft deutscher Wissenschaftler im Ausland," Zürich, to the "Academic Assistance Council," London, to the "Emergency Committee in Aid of German Scholars," New York City. In additional cries for help (I wrote "SOS") to Dember in Istanbul and to Vossler: Spitzer is leaving Istanbul for the USA (but his comments to Dember about me were rather hostile). I emphasized everywhere that I can lecture both in German and comparative literature (my lectureship in Naples, that I deputed for Walzel at examinations, etc.), that I can lecture in French and Italian immediately(!), in Spanish within a short time(!), that I "read" English and if necessary would also speak it in a couple of months.

But what good is all this activity? For one thing the prospect of a post is very small, since the German run has been under way for a good two years and is unpopular. For another and above all: What post could I take? Eva has recently been suffering a great deal again—repeated dental treatment, root inflammation, general nervous strain—according to her, and it is true, she would be a prisoner in any pension or furnished or city apartment; she needs house and garden. And she would on no account give up this house permanently. Therefore I would only be able to accept an especially well-paid post. The likelihood of that is no greater than of winning first prize in the lottery.

With a very heavy heart, I also wrote to Georg, who offered his help last year and who is now presumably in England staying with his eldest. I sent him best wishes on his seventieth birthday and at the same time asked him if he would give me a second loan of 6,000M on my house, irredeemable until January 1, 1942; as security I would pledge him the corresponding share of my life insurance, which matures then. I am sure he will refuse me, and I shall have one more hurt to think about. But even if he agrees—how much help is that to me? I would then pay off Prätorius, and I would increase my life insurance, partly through discharging outstanding installments, partly through prepayment, so that it would be secured at a level of approximately 12,000M for about two years and that, even if later it proved impossible to continue making payments, it would still retain a value of 6,000–7,000M. So to that extent Georg really would not be taking a risk, and I could sit here unchallenged and survive on the pension. Only: All possibility of repaying the first loan would have disappeared. And we would be stuck here like petty bourgeois fallen on hard times, without any possibility of getting back on our feet again.

I now also want to see if I cannot publish abroad. I have made an appointment to see Stepun on Saturday. The ancient Remington 3 typewriter—Jule Sebba's discarded prewar present—has been brought down from the attic, and as soon as a new ribbon has been gotten hold of (35mm no longer available in the stores, has to be ordered from Hanover!) I shall begin to practice. But all of it without hope.

Yesterday evening the Wieghardts were here, a kind of visit of condolence. Blumenfeld complained to me a little while ago, what a bitter experience it was, that hardly a single one of his colleagues expressed sympathy over his being kicked out. At the time I gave him philosophical comfort. Now I shall certainly experience it personally and can give myself philosophical comfort.

May 4, Saturday morning

Changing moods. The day before yesterday, we jokingly made plans for Constantinople in the evening, the next day everything looked bleak again. I hardly do anything else except write letters. To the USA to Tillich and Ulich, today to Weissberger in Oxford. [. . .] I shall be at Stepun's in an hour. — Unable to concentrate on anything else.

Eva's condition constantly bad. Another mishap with her teeth: an arsenic burn.

This evening a lot of guests unfortunately. Unfortunately—because of the money.

Afternoon

Stepun reports that my chair will be occupied again. So I have not been kicked out to make savings. But as a Jew. Even though I served in the field, etc., etc.

He gave me two Swiss addresses for publishing and lectures: Vita Nova Verlag, Lucerne, and Dr. Liefschitz, Bern.

May 7, Tuesday

Stepun is a great playactor and delights in eloquent phrases. "Demons and Philistines populate the world, there are no saints." — "Demonism is every eccentrically different partiality, which lays claim to totality . . . that is what I have just argued in a lecture series in Switzerland."

I said: "None of my colleagues bothers about me. They think: another one gone—who will be next? I?—In Flanders we were once running through machine-gun fire, I stumbled over a rail, fell, collected myself, reached cover after the others. A comrade looked up and said indifferently: "So you're still here too? I thought, you were dead." (Ruhl, the NCO, on December 15, '15, as we were returning from the trenches.) That is what it is like today among the professors." Stepun: "You are right no doubt, war mentality, only much worse."

On Saturday evening the Kühns were here, Wengler, Annemarie and Dressel. They took my elimination very lightly. Kühn thought I should complain about the retirement, I was due emeritus status (or "loss of duties," as the new phrase has it). Yesterday afternoon I talked to Beste, the dean, about it. He said: impossible to do anything. Two "laws" coexist, the regularly extended "Law for the Restoration of the Professional Civil Service," which provides for retirement, and the new one of "Loss of Duties." The Governor chooses either as he sees fit. Para 6 states explicitly: retirement should the post be cut back for reasons of economy. "The Ministry has explicitly instructed us to make suggestions for filling your post." — "And if the University protests?" — "Evasions or 'That has nothing to do with you.' It was exactly the same in the cases of Holldack and Gehrig. There is nothing that can be done."

Yesterday evening at the Blumenfelds; a real little party. The old Kussys, Dember's industrial friends, and Breit, suffering greatly and very bitter. He said he only has 10 percent of his former income. Mood altogether gloomy. Here too people said, what I already heard from Stepun: Abroad war is regarded as imminent. I cannot believe it. The foreign powers do not need a war, and even the present government is not so stupid as to start a war itself. But Stepun says: They have overcultivated national rhetoric [. . .] they will *have to* undertake something.

In response to my many letters I have so far received an application form from England, which applies to the whole world of the unemployed and offers me no chance at all. I am faced by the distressing necessity of using the typewriter. I have obtained a ribbon and intend to start practicing tomorrow on our "ancient" ('03!) Remington. After Jule Sebba sent it to me from his office in 1909 as a castoff, it saw happy times. I dictated many essays to Eva, who typed them on this machine—I remember one night when I dictated the Jensen essay for the *Frankfurter Zeitung,* and then we took it to Anhalter Bahnhof and arrived back home near dawn, exhausted, shivering and happy; my *Montesquieu* was written on it too, then it gathered dust, and Eva's hands could no longer manage the keys. It is very painful to look back like that.

May 15

I work slowly at the Eighteenth Century, read aloud, carry on as usual, but, in the morning, above all, if there is no mail, dreadful fear grips me. What will happen? How shall we live, hold on to this house? How can I save anything, given Eva's frame of mind? Eva plants, gardens, I buy new plants, the cats need a pound of veal every day, price 1.20–1.40, debts with Prätorius, my shirts, socks, boots, my suit finished—it will truly be naked misery, when my already insufficient income is halved. — No word from

Georg. My letter of May 2 must have reached him some time ago even in England.

When he was here, Weissberger had been so full of how easy it is to get a "turn" at Oxford. Now two very polite and altogether foolish and negative letters. Cassirer says that in Oxford there is no chance at all with Romance studies. I should write to Zürich and London, best of all seek out colleagues in the same discipline.

Zürich wrote very courteously, they hoped in the foreseeable future . . . Are these just words or the truth? They requested curriculum vitae in French and English. The French tortures me, it has turned into an impossible French, completely rusty. I had Köhler do the English one and was astonished at how little it corresponded to the French original. (My opinion of Köhler's real ability has suffered greatly.) I knocked this English vita into rough shape myself. As regards English I have no need to be ashamed of myself after all. — Following consultation with Blumenfeld I very strongly emphasized my attitude to Judaism, Christianity and Germany in the first sentence. [. . .] Köhler subsequently thought this might sound too nationalistic, and I changed this: je ne peux ni ne veux être autre chose qu'allemand into: je n'ai jamais pensé d'être autre chose qu'allemand. (For a whole week now I have been worrying over whether I should not have written être instead of d'être.)

No reply from the Swiss publisher to whom I wrote at such great length. Do I have no market value at all anymore?

Letter from Agnes Dember: Spitzer is not leaving until 1936. I would "be considered as a matter of course—but along with Curtius," they had been told.

(Curtius has been my doom since 1915—the Academy in Posen; in any case, I think it is out of the question that he wants to go to Constantinople. As far as I know he still holds the chair in Bonn; and if he had to go because a democrat, then he would have many opportunities in France. Also he is reputed to be a wealthy man.)

May 30, Ascension Day

There seem to be no prospects abroad for me at all. Blumenfeld was in Zürich to discuss his Lima professorship. (Incident from a novel: On the day of his arrival, the Peruvian envoy receives a telegram, his brother in Lima has been murdered, does not keep the appointment and departs, so that Blumenfeld's business is left hanging in the air.) So Blumenfeld spoke to Privy Councillor Demuth about my case. The latter said: His letter to me had been nothing but courtesy and consolation, de facto I had no chance at all. He could find places for natural scientists—since the Notgemeinschaft had been set up he had only been able to place *three* scholars from the humanities, of whom Blumenfeld was the third. — Meanwhile I heard from Hatzfeld that Lerch has just been dismissed, that he himself has been relieved of the Bonn professorial duties that he had administered since Olschki's departure; and from a Basel newspaper I saw that Hoetzsch in Berlin had to go. So a widespread new push and with it a new demand for posts. — Opinion in Switzerland: The government is more firmly in the saddle than ever and will resort to increasingly radical measures. A letter dated the twenty-fifth from Georg in Rome, where he had traveled to see a patient, after being first in Locarno, then in Cambridge, where he had stayed with Otto Klemperer and "endured" his own seventieth birthday. He will "of course" put the 6,000M at my disposal (how rich he must be! but how fundamentally decently he has dealt with the matter!), but does not understand why I cling to my house and to Germany. If civil rights are taken from us, he will go to America, where he can still "earn a little" as a doctor; he would rather starve outside, than live in comfort and dishonor here in Germany. — Very nicely put. But how shall I get out just like that? And with what can I "earn a little" outside? He does not know my situation.

Meanwhile Eva gardens with frenetic passion and says we should be able to subsist on half an income, if the debt to Prätorius is discharged. And she already wants to use a part of this 6,000 for further construction. Perhaps she is right, because to leave money lying around or to pay off money to the Iduna is just as uncertain as anything else. I often feel as if I am being literally choked. And when I creep up through the park, I always have the agonizing feeling that my heart is going to give out.

Nevertheless, these are always only—mental and physical—passing depressions, five or six a day. Between them, curiously enough, I work well. The Eighteenth Century grows slowly: The section "Poetry besides Voltaire" should be finished the day after tomorrow; I now hope to manage the whole first volume by October. I am also slowly getting into my stride on the ancient typewriter. Karl Wieghardt has very amusingly hung a kitchen mortar from the moving part as a weight; now it works better. I type best with one finger; but I manage, and I practice diligently. I am copying out my "German Image of France," in order to show it to the Nova Vita publishing house, who have shown an interest in it. Every day one manuscript page in about two hours, there are 60 pages. I have even resolved to write the Montesquieu chapter of my Eighteenth Century directly on the machine.

A tiny little swallow, it doesn't make a summer, but is nevertheless gratifying. Sometime in the winter I am to give a lecture to the Free Student Association of Bern, perhaps also in other Swiss towns.

Otherwise very isolated, especially inwardly. Gusti Wieghardt sees everything entirely from the Soviet perspective, Blumenfelds see everything entirely from the Jewish one. And conversations with Eva usually lead to deep depressions and are best avoided.

I rarely get around to reading aloud; we are both very tired in the evenings, and my failing eyes torment me.

[. . .]

Much domestic work. Now easier, since we had gas laid. The electric stoves, which are so widely advertised and which we fell for, are a fraud: too expensive and too slow for small things.

Eva's protracted second dental treatment is over, thank God. [...] Since the treatment took a long time because of a mistake or clumsiness on the part of the dentist (arsenic burn?) we are curious to see the bill.

May 31, Friday

This afternoon I handed over the department key and the house key to Wengler. I was standing outside the door of the department, had the key in my pocket and did not want to open it myself. A beadle, whom I only know by sight, came; he was wearing an SA uniform; he shook my hand with evident warmth and then called Wengler from the side room.

June 11, Tuesday after Whitsun (oppressive heat, now at nine o'clock in the morning 82 degrees in the shade)

Heiss died on May 31. The obituary notice shook me, not because I loved him, but because the man was my generation, barely five years older. — After a long gap (two years!) letter from Hatzfeld: There is a rumor going around that I have been dismissed. Do I know why Lerch had to go? He himself has been relieved of the professorial duties that he had been carrying out since Olschki's departure from Heidelberg. (I do not know whether the devout Catholic Hatzfeld is also non-Aryan. Lerch at any rate is completely Aryan. — They are making a clean sweep and suppressing all news. Nothing but rumors. Nevertheless nothing remains secret.)

No word from Georg. I am very worried about the money. No other news. No reply from Ulich and Tillich in the USA.

After our meal on Sunday the Isakowitzes picked us up in their handsome car and drove us to the Bastei. We have not been there for years. Wonderful landscape. Incredible car and motorcycle traffic. Almost a kilometer from the hotel we had to join a long line of cars and wait. Afterward we estimated about 500 parked cars, twice as many motorcycles. The vantage points thick with people. But it is really beautiful. We climbed up to a spur, which provides a view of the magnificent amphitheater of rounded towers. Eva had no difficulty getting up and down, but then in the evening she felt serious pain and limped. We *must* stay here and scrape by, even if something is offered from outside; I cannot imprison Eva. All three of the Isakowitzes, father, daughter, mother, are very agreeable people; the wife is painted and done up like a Babylonian whore trying to hide her decline, but she has a quite simple and obliging nature. [...] After the visit to the Bastei, we rested by the forest, and had tea. Before the excursion we had shown off our little house and drunk coffee there.

I can hardly write with a pen anymore and already work quite nicely using the machine. But the old museum piece completely fails to space lines. If I get the 6,000 from Georg, I shall probably purchase a new machine.

Midday

Shopping in town. Something like 86 degrees. The way back through the park inferno and memento mori. How many years are still left? How much further with my work? I would still so dearly love to write the Eighteenth Century, my life and the language of the three revolutions. Vanitatum vanitas. — Recently a policeman was here from the district office. Whether I had a "family record" when I had been "naturalized"? I said, I'm fed up to the back teeth with it. He: "Me too . . . I have served for fifteen years. I started under the Social Democratic government. What can I do?" Then he asked me how Dember was. When he heard that I too had now been dismissed, this simple man said quite spontaneously: "Yes, but do they have someone who is right for your post, Professor?" I just looked at him. Afterward we shook hands.

[. . .]

I have begun to write the Montesquieu chapter, but have stopped, in order first of all to seriously immerse myself in the Enlightenment. At the moment I am in the middle of Helvetius. I have also hauled up La Mettrie, Holbach, Condillac.

[. . .]

The Kühns and the Blumenfelds were here this afternoon.

Since June 1 we have not read a newspaper. (Eva has not done so for a long time.) The dispatches, which one sees put up in town, do just as well. It's all the same lies anyway.

June 20, Thursday

Georg has sent me the 6,000 marks. Interest free. Repayment at my discretion. [. . .] It is very nice—and a little contemptuous of him. I am unable to be pleased about it, even if I am also a little relieved. We shall pay off the builder, perhaps extend the house a little, pay back a part to the Iduna. Then let the misery begin. I defended my remaining-in-the-country in a letter to Georg. I am absolutely tied.

Meanwhile Blumenfeld is getting ready to travel to Lima in two, three weeks. I look on with bitter envy and yet feel the envy as a betrayal of Eva. She is literally digging herself in, in her garden. Day after day.

The enormous foreign policy success of the Naval Agreement with England consolidates Hitler's position very greatly. Even before that I have recently had the impression that many otherwise well-meaning people, dulled to injustice inside the country and in particular not properly appreciating the misfortune of the Jews, have begun to halfway acquiesce to Hitler. Their opinion: If at the cost of going backward internally, he restores Germany's power externally, then this cost is worthwhile. Conditions at home can always be made good later—politics is just not a clean affair. [...]

Today Blumenfeld told me—I went there at his request, he is very harassed now—he had spoken yesterday to a Privy Councillor Oster in the Foreign Ministry in Berlin. Blumenfeld's concern is to get away without paying the Reich Flight Property Tax (25 percent!). Oster had suggested fairly openly that there was little sympathy in the Foreign Ministry for Mutschmann's latest fury against remaining Jews in the universities and there had been an approach to the Education Ministry on behalf of the dismissed Leipzig dons. Blumenfeld thereupon mentioned my case, and the Privy Councillor made a note of it. — Otherwise absolute silence all around me.

June 30, Sunday afternoon

Yesterday, for the twenty-ninth—31 years!—Eva received a delphinium for the garden; the contract for the extension of the two verandas has been signed with Prätorius for 1,300M—all as if our position were safe. Sometimes it makes me feel terrible, sometimes I am quite calm. *Like this* Eva is at least almost contented, and there is more than one way I could do things wrongly.

No post, no prospects, absolute silence.

Through Annemarie Köhler's intervention I very quickly came by an excellent typewriter. Isakowitz's "Little Erika" was (a) a loan and (b) not ideal. Now for 40M I have bought a massive, completely intact "Ideal," which really is ideal, from Dr. Schümann, head physician at St. John's Hospital. On Saturday, June 22, we were out in Heidenau—nice supper, inspection of the object and of the head physician's vegetable garden; on Sunday, Lange, the carpenter, fetched the heavy piece on his motorcycle, and from Monday until today I have really made the whole Montesquieu chapter good enough to go to press, not only copied onto 25 pages in duplicate, but also completely polished. This is how I now want to continue working: sketch out section by section by hand or set it out in abbreviated form and then type the final version. But the next section: Condillac, etc. is raising the greatest difficulties. What repeatedly worries me here is the question of the limits of literary history, of its actual content.

The last week has been difficult because of the terrible heat. Yesterday somewhat cooler, today beginning to be humid again. If I had not been able to cling to the typewriter, the whole time would have been wasted.
[...]

July 21, Sunday

Condillac and Helvetius finished et in machina. I cling to this work—ready for press and in typescript it is independent of me and can survive. Vanitas! I ask myself again and again, what is new and original about it and my own. These philosophical chapters require quite new studies, a large monograph each time and a lot of reading of the texts. Lately I have also been availing myself of the library in Berlin.

I must hold on to the book; because worries are increasing to such a degree that I no longer can or should allow myself to think about them; it is just like being in the dugout: If one is forever thinking about the next shell, then one goes mad. [. . .] Today is July 21, and I still do not know what I am going to be paid from August 1.

The Jew-baiting and the pogrom atmosphere grow day by day. *Der Stürmer*, Goebbels' speeches ("exterminate like fleas and bedbugs!"), acts of violence in Berlin, Breslau, yesterday also here in Prager Strasse. The struggle against Catholics, "enemies of the state," both reactionary and Communist, is increasing. It is as if the Nazis were being driven toward and prepared to go to any extreme, as if a catastrophe were imminent.

Prätorius, with whom we had an argument because the roof was leaking and who is now to extend the hall and to glaze the veranda for us—1,300M of Georg's 6,000, God knows if I am doing the right thing, but what is sure?—Prätorius said the District Chairman "is not well disposed to me," he had raised objections to the new roof and spoken contemptuously of me and my "front-line experience," he is "just a Nazi." I think I've already written that recently a policeman wanted to know since when I have been "naturalized"; they had to be informed about non-Aryans in their district. I truly expect that one day our little house will be set alight and I shall be beaten to death.

On August 11, we took our leave of the Blumenfelds amid the chests in their already emptied apartment. They traveled to Paris on the thirteenth, yesterday their ship departed from La Rochelle. They left us a great many things: a bronze tub, flowers and a window box, cigars . . . I gave him the first edition of Hegel's *Phenomenology* (which Father left me, my most valuable book), for her: Quevedo's *Vida del Buscón*.

Gusti Wieghardt was here for Eva's birthday (and also frequently apart from that). She is far too simplistic. [. . .]

I gave Eva a couple of plants—we are literally digging ourselves in here, as in the trenches.

After an interval of a year, we *had* to go to the old Kaufmanns once; they stick to us like burrs, pathetic and ghastly. They were with their children in Palestine for three months. They received and entertained us extravagantly (despite their stinginess), grateful for our visit; they talked very interestingly about their journey, while we, after the hot day, sat on their balcony and looked out toward Borsberg—but, radiating evident pride, they also told us that Fräulein Mey still came to see them every week, as "liaison officer," since she is on visiting terms with the mayor and is even received by the Governor! Eva said the latest Jewish snobbery was to sympathize with the Nazis. They spoke "without hate" in fond memory of Thieme. I said, if I had the power, I would have him shot. Kaufmann said of someone or other in Jerusalem: he feels at home and yet previously "had been as assimilated as you *were,* Herr Professor." I replied: "Were? I am German forever, German 'nationalist.' "—"The Nazis would not concede that."—"The Nazis are un-German." That was on July 17, we felt ill all day on the eighteenth.

[...]

Grete was dangerously ill and is still in a *Catholic* hospital in Berlin (St. Norbert). I wrote to her at length (but inwardly cold and estranged). My dismissal makes no impression at all on her and Marta, etc. I have never made an impression on my family. What a celebration there usually is for a school graduation, doctorate, a professorship, etc.! Whenever I got that far, it was already nothing out of the ordinary in my family. Now in being dismissed—it's the same: m'ont devancé mes neveux.

Vossler (a new Spanish book from him!) wrote to me, Lerch had to go, denounced by an enemy, because "he had been living in concubinage with a non-Aryan." With the "nebbish" Pietrkowska! Vossler also wrote—he can afford to!—that at this time one must set most store by lasting values and not complain that one is no longer allowed to lecture to 20 or 30 Saxon lads and lasses toeing the Party line. He is now traveling to Spain again. But he also said he had put in a word for me to Spitzer several times, and Curtius is secure in Bonn and is not competing for Istanbul.

"I said" (as Montesquieu puts it in his diaries when an aperçu follows): Let Blumenfeld travel happily to Lima, we are sitting here as *in a besieged fortress, within which the plague is raging.* — If one day things get going against this government, a special *professors' assault force* should be formed. — My principles about Germany and the various nations are beginning to wobble like an old man's teeth.

[...]

I have never, in fact, worked harder, never been busier than now "in retirement." I never get around to reading aloud during the day. In two weeks we have managed only 200 pages of Reymont's magnificent epic *The Peasants* (1,400 pages). But every page is a pleasure, and every scene a work of art. [...]

August 11, Sunday

On August 1 there was still no news about my "retirement pay." I telephoned the Ministry; the first official on the line, somewhat incautiously no doubt, said, "Berlin has raised an objection—we don't know anything yet." After that they expressed themselves more carefully, the personal file is still in Berlin. Then they wrote to me, until further notice I would receive an estimated payment at the "probable level." I was credited with 480M (after tax deductions, the salary was 800M). A small hope, that "Berlin" will do something in my favor, remains open. At the moment both of us are as calm as during the war. There is something in reserve from Georg, and things are coming to a head.

The Jew-baiting has become so extreme, far worse than during the first boycott, there are the beginnings of a pogrom here and there, and we expect to be beaten to death at any moment. Not by neighbors, but by purgers who are deployed now here, now there as the "soul of the people." On the tram stop signs on Prager Strasse: "Who buys from the Jew, is a traitor to the nation," in the windows of small stores in Plauen sayings and verses from every century, pen and context (Maria Theresa, Goethe! etc.) full of abuse, in addition, "No Jews do we want, in our fair suburb Plauen," the *Stürmer* everywhere with the most ghastly race defilement stories, wild speeches by Goebbels—acts of violence in many different places. — Almost as wild, agitation against "political" Catholicism, which is allying itself with Communism, befouls churches and maintains that it was the Nazis. — Everywhere dissolution of the Stahlhelm. The feeling stronger every day for weeks now, it cannot go on like *this* much longer. And yet it does go on and on.

I went to see old von Pflugk, since my eyes are completely failing me. He received me very warmly—blood pressure measurement with the scale on the anesthetized naked eye, pressure too high—and also said, it was close to the end. He treats a lot of workers, they were in a state of ferment. Gusti Wieghardt has it that strikes have taken place.

Meanwhile despite constant serious eye and heart problems I have for several weeks worked through five books of minor figures, which I had from Berlin and had to give back in time. I now hope to get back to writing in the next few days: Holbach. But my health is giving way more and more every day. Today, August 11, it is exactly one year since I began the volume.

A friendly but gloomy letter from Ulich in Cambridge, USA. There are no prospects there. — Frau Dember here once again, with her mother in Altenberg: Spitzer has a relationship with his assistant Rosemarie Burkart, his wife has gone to Austria; he cannot go to the USA with the mistress, thus remains in Istanbul. So that faint hope too is gone.

After many months to the cinema, Prinzesstheater; *The Cossack and the Nightingale;* such awful trashy rubbish that it is not worth making any note of it. But in it the role of a gunrunning Levantine monster. Immediately a girl beside me whispers: "The Jew!"

The three Isakowitzes were here once in the evening for coffee. He touchingly offered me money, if my pension should not arrive. He said his nerves were finished, and he is thinking of emigrating.

Pflugk told me: People say they have broken their word to everyone, except to the Jews!

September 15, Sunday, toward evening

I have never in my life worked with such concentration as since my dismissal. As if I wanted to prove to myself that I can still do something, and that it does not matter if my book is late in coming. It is no doubt also the blessing of the typewriter: Everything becomes clear, completely detached from me and finished, I polish it down to the last detail, it is so much ready to go to press that it can be published *without me.* The book will be very good—but it is getting ever longer and taking ever longer. After d'Alembert, Buffon has now been completely finished. Perhaps I shall manage the volume by the end of the year. It will run to about 500 pages. [. . .] (The broken contract with Teubner provided for 300.)

My situation and the general situation remains entirely unchanged. I still receive my "provisional" 480M, the government still stands firm as a rock above all discontent, the Jew-baiting gets even worse, the *Stürmer*—"race defiler," "murderer"—even crazier.

The correction of Blumenfeld's book, *Puberty as a Conflict Situation,* which he left behind, takes up a lot of time. There are stylistic lapses, a drawing doesn't correspond with the text, everything is written in haste and not fully ready to go to press—and I bear the responsibility. The book is worthy, but does not contain anything that I did not know anyway. For myself the attention to polishing is gradually becoming an obsession.

[. . .]

Enclosed here Teubner's letter on the decision in principle of the High Court in Munich: Contracts with non-Aryan authors are not valid. — Also Hueber's letter, which reached me with some delay.

September 16, Monday

Before I start on the essential chapter, "Political Economists," a few words to catch up. We had conversion work for a full four weeks until last Saturday, now the painting (Lehmann) remains to be done, and Lange is working on the cat compound. The little house is now a proper house, in fact a "villa." The large hallway, which has been created by putting a roof on the terrace facing the city, is very elegant, even more elegant is the "winter garden," which is the result of giving the previously useless veranda by the music room a glass roof and walls (together with a solid floor). Eva's particular joy here are the three narrow strips of colored window. — The whole undertaking, including the painting, comes to around 1,600M, which I took from Georg's 6,000. I am left with an emergency reserve of about 600M. — Have I done the right thing? There was at least as much to be said in favor as against. Everything is completely uncertain and is in the hands of fate.

For a couple of days the *Dresdener Nachrichten* was sent to us free of charge, I thought one had to make an attempt at reading the newspaper again—it was impossible, it makes me physically sick. Later—if I last that long and am working on the "Language of the 3rd Reich" or on the "Language of the Three Revolutions." But my heart will give out before then.

I read only the newspaper telegrams and inflammatory placards and verses on the streets. But I ask every visitor and every person I meet his opinion, his news. All vacillate or have contrary views.

On August 30 the Wenglers were here with their English cousin, Mr. Otto, a pleasant forty-year-old headmaster and teacher of Romance Languages. (We have found all the English whom we have ever met to be congenial, not one, man or woman, was *stiff*. Opinion on how long: Question mark.)

[. . .]

On September 10 we were at Frau Schaps for supper, together with her children, the Gerstles. The last time, a year and a day ago no doubt, we had found Gerstle very disagreeable; an opportunist, who hoped to do business even under this government, had little time to spare for the victims, although Sebba. . . . Now quite different. Bitter and bitterly *German*. We agreed on the sentence: "Germany is in *our* camp." As an officer, he had just been to his annual regimental day. He had asked the commander beforehand whether he should *really* come. Reply: *Yes,* unreservedly, welcome from comrades, rank and file and active Reichswehr officers *very warm*. But the young army officers "a different type" from our day. They feel they have a political responsibility and role, they are all "like a sphinx." Gerstle's opinion constantly vacillating. The economy—he has 300 workers in his coffee additives factory—completely ruined, the mood resentful, one sometimes thinks it cannot go on like this much longer. But then again: the terror, the power of the government, and where is there an opponent capable of taking action? The Reichswehr altogether opaque: Blomberg and Reichenau are reputed to be loyal to Hitler, but not Fritsch. Gusti Wieghardt had told us about a Reichswehr order given to a Jewish cap manufacturer, also of Jews being accepted for the army. Gerstle said his travelers meet with considerable difficulties. Most frequent response of the paymasters: "Personally we would gladly place an order—but it could cost us our position, we cannot take the risk."

[. . .]

Gusti Wieghardt, whom we see every week on reciprocal visits, reports the Communist Party view: another 6 to 12 months. This Party thinking and feeling makes her ever more stupid. She talks about her "faith in Marx, faith in Lenin." Their dogmas have unqualified validity for her. As soon as she talks about these things, a phonetic indication of her frame of mind appears: she begins to roll her Rs. Recently she read out a little poème en prose by Brecht smuggled in from Denmark in shorthand. [. . .] A prisoner writes "Long live Lenin" on the wall of his cell. Painters are supposed to get rid of it, again and again the writing shows through:

"Long live Lenin!" A few more prose verses. Then: "Tear down the wall! ordered the soldier." Very nice, but one could allow oneself the joke of transferring the poem word for word to the Nazis after the 1923 Munich putsch. The prisoner only needs to write "Heil Hitler!" on the wall.

One afternoon Fräulein Papesch visited us; brave of her to come. Her Protestantism keeps her at a distance from the regime; but she is of course cautious to an extreme. I read the La Mettrie and d'Alembert sections to her.

[...]

Yesterday a characteristic scene: Traffic jam on Prager Strasse. Crowd of people, cars. A young man, pale, rigid, mad in appearance, shouts without stopping at someone else whom I could not see: "Whoever buys from the Jew, is a traitor to the nation! . . . I said . . ." and so on and so on ad infinitum. Everyone is disturbed, embarrassed, no one interferes. No police in sight, the traffic is building up and the man keeps on shouting: "I said . . . I can say that: Whoever buys from the Jew, is a traitor to the nation, a traitor to the nation, I said . . ." After a while I walked on.

The Blumenfelds sent a postcard from Bermuda, in which they complained about seasickness. [...]

I work at and polish my Eighteenth Century as with no other book. All reservations have fallen by the wayside—whether it will be too long, whether critics will like it—there is no externally imposed impediment anymore, the book is being written for me alone. Sometimes I believe it to be good and unique, sometimes only cobbled together. During the last few weeks I had to open the door for one worker as early as half past six every morning. So I accustomed myself to getting up very early. Apart from going shopping or to the library, I sit at my work all day—apart from the large amount of time spent on the cat boxes and making tea and coffee, etc. — An altogether secluded life. Quieter, more enclosed than it ever was before. If there were not health troubles and the memento every day, then it would not be unhappy.

September 17, Tuesday

While I was writing yesterday, the Reichstag in Nürnberg had already passed the laws on German blood and German honor: Prison for marriage and extra-marital intercourse between Jews and "Germans," prohibition on "German" maids under 45 years of age, permission to show the "Jewish flag," withdrawal of civil rights. And with what justification and what threats! Disgust makes one ill. Gusti Wieghardt came here in the evening; to give vent to her feelings, she said: "Schiwe sizn." But she is not interested in the Jews. Hitler has threatened Lithuania, Germany in league with England will defeat the Russians, exterminate Communism.

September 29, Sunday

The économistes finished, the littérateurs under way. Slow and exhausted. Sometimes I believe it will be my best book, sometimes a useless compilation and transcription. This continuing absolute concentration exhausts me greatly; but it is the only antidote against the desperateness of the situation. I have the impression that an explosion is imminent, I am reckoning on a pogrom, the ghetto, money and house to be taken away, anything. Rather: I am reckoning on nothing. I wait gloomy and helpless.

October 5, Saturday

God in history: Gusti Wieghardt says: Hitler has accelerated developments by at least thirty years, he is working for the victory of Communism. — Isakowitz says: In fifty years people will probably recognize that he had to appear, so that the Jews became a nation again (Zion!).

It so happened that on two occasions in the last few weeks we were with the Isakowitzes twice in one day. Eva unexpectedly required a supplementary repair; in the evenings of the two days the three Isakowitzes were first of all our guests for coffee, the second time our hosts, for supper (which unfortunately demands a return match) and that on the Jewish New Year. It turned out that the Isakowitzes are more orthodox than we had known; the man came from the "temple" (I have not heard the word for thirty years), his head covered he read from the Torah, a hat was put on my head too, candles burned. I found it quite painful. Where do I belong? To the "Jewish nation" decrees Hitler. And *I* feel the Jewish nation recognized by Isakowitz is a comedy and am nothing but a German or German European. — The mood on both evenings was one of extreme depression. Isakowitz fears that at any moment he will no longer be allowed to treat insured patients and thus be deprived of a living. He has been considering emigration to Palestine for some time. An Aryan has long wanted to buy his practice from him for 15,000M. He at last decides on this sale—with the heaviest of hearts, because in Palestine there is said to be at least one doctor in every house—when at the last moment such sales of Jewish practices are forbidden. For what reason? is not yet known. Isakowitz fears the worst and is left in uncertainty. — His wife had gone to Berlin to make inquiries at the "Jewish town hall in Meineckestrasse," i.e., the advice center of the Zionists, which now represents all German-Jewish interests. Mood of panic, crowds of people, broken windows from the last rampage, which are ostentatiously left unrepaired, strongly advised to emigrate, more and more people fleeing. — At the service (the New Year celebration, the time of joy!) the rabbi's words had been deeply depressing, had spoken a prayer for the dead, there had been many tears.

[. . .]

The loyal and the brave, for now this is brave: On September 23, Fräulein Mey was here for coffee. She and Lehmann, the rectorial secretary, whom I always supported, alone of the whole administrative staff of the TU, do *not* belong to the Party. The cashier's office is the worst. There one's arm can be raised by force, if one does not give the Fascist greeting.

On October 2 for coffee: Ursula Winkler and Susi Hildebrandt, whose sick mother has meanwhile died of cancer. The opinion of her father, the big industrialist: untenable situation: extreme tension among the workers—but no one knows what is going to happen and how things look in the Reichswehr.

In the stocks: Frau Fischer writes from Giessen to Gusti Wieghardt (we were there the day before yesterday): she would like to accompany her husband to the Philologists' Congress in Dresden, it is impossible for her to stay with the Kaufmanns, she has been forbidden to socialize with the "dear, good Kaufmanns," although she herself is still "the same person," could she stay with Gusti, she is too poor to pay for a hotel. This dirty hybrid of sheep and pig, who used to sponge like a beggar on the Kaufmanns, has no idea that Gusti is not Aryan, nor of her political opinions. Gusti curtly wrote her off. (This philologists' meeting fills me with the greatest bitterness.)

The tepid: Frau Kühn unexpectedly here for a friendly visit. Preaches an "unembittered" serenity of heart to me . . . Even today one can still be a Nazi for idealistic reasons, without being a criminal or an idiot. I told her: She does not know what dreadful things are happening. I changed Lessing's words—Anyone who does not lose his reason over certain things, has no reason—into: Anyone whose heart remains calm today, has no heart. She departed stricken, she is truly a good person.

The evening on which we had to invite the tepid Kaufmanns did not go as badly as feared (a) because the pressure of events also hardens these jellyfish a little, (b) because young Frau Rosenberg had an agreeably mitigating effect. Kaufmann talked about the hostility of French Jews toward the German-Jewish émigrés. He said: To them we are the dreaded "Eastern Jews." He told us of a nasty incident in Tunis, where a German-Jewish doctor was allowed to practice by the government, but his position made impossible by his Jewish colleagues.

Now Janentzky has been dismissed. I long ago found him too light as a human being and dropped him for lacking character; I now feel a little malicious pleasure—but the business itself is wretched. Our whole Humanities Section destroyed. [. . .]

Meanwhile the situation is more and more coming to a head. Food shortage. — Memel. — Beginning of the Abyssinian War. If England relies on Germany for support, if the government receives a loan from England, then there is no end in sight of the ignominy. The loan negotiations are said to have failed for the moment. "Said." One is forever tapping in the dark, a thousand times worse than in the war. The day after tomorrow, Germany's unity and triumph will be celebrated on the Bückeberg with a huge hullabaloo. Harvest festival with 10,000 special trains. [. . .]

Once, as relaxation, a nice Kiepura film with a doppelgänger role: He acts and sings as a famous tenor and as salesclerk. Harmless slapstick with every part excellently played: *Ich liebe alle Frauen* [I Love Every Woman]. But beforehand a bit of Nürnberg Party Rally with the Jewish laws read out, at least the ban on marriages.

[. . .]

My book eats me up and keeps me alive and gives me balance. Blessing of the typewriter. Marmontel and Raynal finished.

My eyes bad, my heart bad. Eva also complained about problems with her eyes (curved ceiling!). I went with her to see Best (since I feel embarrassed to be treated gratis by von Pflugk); because the symptom is serious, he examined her twice very carefully and found nothing.

For a mortal two months now there have been workers in the house. The painter expects to be finished today.

My financial situation still undecided. Berlin says nothing, and the Pensions Office pays 480M "until further notice." How long will my reserves last?

After a gap of several months I have subscribed to a newspaper (*Dresdener NN*) once again. Every time I read it I feel sick; but the tension is now so great one must at least know what lies are being told.

October 19, Saturday

"The Opponents" finished; "Encyclopedia" and Diderot remain.

My heart ever worse, I fear and hate the path up through the park.

The situation in general unchanged.

The Modern Philologists' Congress met here this week. One of them spoke about the religion of the ancient Germans, another about modern language teaching from the National Socialist perspective, not for "intellect" and "culture," but for "the German man and woman." E. von Jan about France's "national symbols." Not one of all my Romance Language colleagues called on me; I am like a plague corpse. [. . .]

I met Gehrig. Completely convinced of the permanence of Nazi rule. He told me that Janentzky's dismissal had been withdrawn for the present; but the Humanities Section would be wound up entirely in 1936; its professors would be retired or transferred. So the absolute end.

[. . .]

Georg wrote [. . .] he is going to emigrate. It will cost him three-quarters of what he has saved, but after Nürnberg he does not want to live "under the guillotine." What do I intend?—But he is in a better position. How could I "practice" in the USA? That was Georg's birthday letter.

[. . .]

On the eighth we had the Wieghardts and the Isakowitzes for supper. He is now trying to find a living in England. His wife is there at the moment to make inquiries. *We* are prisoners without hope of rescue.

The Bishop of Meissen was arrested on the tenth. For currency speculation. I place my hopes on that, really. But this government can risk anything.

A new aspect of the language of the 3rd Reich to be considered: the character sketches of schoolchildren now being introduced, which contain an assessment of their suitability for the national community. Gusti Wieghardt tells us a teacher is said to have written of a seven-year-old Jewish boy, he "shows all the characteristics of his race." On the other hand a Catholic teacher at the Benno Grammar School is said to have credited a small Jewish boy with "especially fitted for the community." I have asked Johannes Köhler for material.

Annemarie Köhler tells us in despair that the hospitals are overcrowded with fifteen-year-old girls, some pregnant, some with gonorrhea. The BDM. Her brother has vehemently refused to allow his daughter to join.

Superstition: Jehovah's Witnesses are now frequently being sentenced by special courts. Mostly people of modest circumstances or old women (they are very attached to the Old Testament and are pacifists). I asked Lange, the carpenter, whose mother is one of them, what all this intensive study led to. He gave as an example that it says the Last Judgment is near "when carriages shall move without horses." This is read as meaning automobiles and therefore the present. — People believe this sort of thing, and for such a belief one is sentenced to prison in Germany for up to one year!

[...]

October 26, Saturday

An abscess developed very suddenly in Eva's mouth and had to be lanced today. Unpleasant intermezzo. — The trouble with my heart continues unchanged.

[...]

Karl Wieghardt here with his mother yesterday. Farewell visit. He is going to study in Göttingen. He really wanted to go to Berlin. Only those students with NSDAP membership numbers below one million are being allowed to matriculate there.

It made a deep impression on me that today on Löbtauer Strasse, for the first time since the war, I saw two "butter lines" snaking out of the shops. Perhaps they could choke Laocoön-Hitler.

October 31, Thursday

"Encyclopedia" completely finished, typed. Now at least a month's reading for Diderot. Have begun Rosenkranz. If the machine did not, to some extent, allow me to compensate for the pressure, and if the resulting complete detachment and objectivity did not give me the hope that this completely finished and readable text can also be published without me and after me—then I believe I would be unable to bear this time, would at any rate be unable to summon up the concentration to write. My opinion of the value and originality of the work fluctuates several times daily between the entirely positive and the entirely negative.

My heart problems while walking become ever more serious. Not a day on which I do not see death staring me in the face.

On Sunday afternoon the three Isakowitzes were here. Frau Isakowitz was in London for a week; there is a possibility that her husband will be allowed to practice as a dentist in England without sitting for an examination. She relates that the rabbis preached the boycott of German goods from the pulpit; they addressed the women: It is natural that your husbands do not order machines from Germany for their factories; but *you* must not buy any German Odol mouthwash or other toilet or domestic things! Her Christian landlady said to her with reference to Hitler: "And there is nobody who kills this big swine?" People say we are ruled by madmen, are completely bankrupt—it *cannot* last much longer. People are paying 20M:£1—officially the rate is 14M.

But on Tuesday we were at the station to see Marta for twenty minutes, who was on her way to Prague: the mood of the Berlin Jews is wretched: "We shall not live to see the end of this tyranny, the populace is enthusiastically devoted to Hitler." — At the same time wild rumors: Marta's youngest was off to Prague at a moment's notice because word was going around that the borders would be closed in the next few days, there was going to be war. Against whom—uncertain, but certainly war! (And *that's* how a European nation lives in 1935!) Further: Hitler undoubtedly has cancer of the larynx, he can only whisper, the thunder of his speeches is produced by the loudspeakers.

Yesterday evening—it did neither of us any good—at the "respectable" Köhlers. Here absolute uncertainty given as the popular mood: it could collapse overnight, it could last for years yet. But tendency to pessimism.
[...]

Clipping, saved for a long time, from the *Dresdener NN* of September 29. "Watchword for Workplace Meetings on September 20": "Blood determines character and soul, / For your soul rests in your blood! / Once the Jew has spoiled your blood and soul, / Then you are dead for race and Fatherland."

The Jew-baiting had subsided for a few weeks. Now *Der Stürmer* is presenting ritual murders once again.
[...]

November 9, Saturday

Hitler said of those who fell at the Feldherrnhalle in 1923: "My apostles." Today at the triumphal and burial ceremonies, the word is: "You have risen again in the Third Reich." — Further: The buildings in the "capital city of the movement" are only a beginning. We are building "a hall for 60,000 (thousand!) people" and "the biggest opera house on the globe." And all this in a bankrupt state. — Religious madness and advertising madness. And always the lies accompanying everything. Hitler's thanks to the Stahlhelm, which has just been dissolved, Seldte's thanks to Hitler.

[. . .]

On the 2nd we were at the Wenglers in the afternoon. It once again made an enormous impression on me when they put on the radio and leaped from London to Rome, from Rome to Moscow, etc. The concepts of time and space are annihilated. One must become a mystic. For me radio destroys every form of religion and at the same time gives rise to religion. Gives rise to it twice over: (a) because such a miracle exists, (b) because the human intellect invents, explains, makes use of it. But this same human intellect puts up with the Hitler government.

November 11, Monday

Marta, coming from Prague, was with us from yesterday at 3:35 until today at 12:45. Very trying and complicated, not least because of the need to make arrangements for the cats, of whom she is afraid. Nickelchen still ailing, in the music room, Muschel, very understanding, overnight in our bed, Marta in my room.

She was more amicable than usual, she liked our house. She gives the impression of a woman whose health is failing badly: walks laboriously on swollen misshapen legs, talks laboriously and has ruined teeth, excessively nervous, frail. Only 61—Grave's Disease—*our* heart.

She told us in strict confidence that her youngest, Willy, who has just fled to Prague, has prospects of a position in Moscow, is evidently a member of the Communist Party. She told us that her husband, that Lotte Sussmann sympathize with Hitler, told us about the Naumann Jews who in defiance of all the kicks repeatedly beg to be admitted into the NSDAP. A stepbrother and the stepmother of Heinz Machol are with these people. — The NSDAP is quite obviously even more a party of the mentally ill than it is of criminals.

[. . .]

Diderot studies. I want to bring out the impressionist, the forerunner of the nineteenth and twentieth centuries, the experimental psychologist, etc. It is costing me a great deal of reading, perhaps once again more time than I provided for, but it will be my Diderot.

[. . .]

November 19, Tuesday

We are to a tragicomically great degree dependent on our cats. Whenever Nickelchen is unwell, Eva lapses into downright depression. The veterinary surgeon helped for a while; now both beast and Eva are poorly again. Sometimes I think: Drastic measures with poison would be best for all concerned, sometimes I chide myself as heartless, feel sorry for the little animals and ourselves. The terrible untidiness of the house, the constant loss of time through the removal of the excrement are unpleasant additions to the principal evil. Meanwhile a stray little tomcat has turned up in the garden; Eva has been feeding it for days now and keeps it in the builders' hut. Should no owner be found for the "Bartholo-Mäus" (and none will be found), then the cat nuisance will be even greater.

A few days ago a "law" was published, according to which Jewish front-line veterans are to be retired on full pay. If that applies to me, then my troubles are at an end.

December 2

The waiting really gets on my nerves. In fact everything suggests that they will give me my full salary and even have to backdate it from August. Because so far I have always received the 480M as "part payment" and "until further notice," and I am, after all, a front-line veteran and was, indeed, dismissed as a Jew. Also, I have heard that the whole Humanities Section is to be wound up by April 1, '36, the professors are to be in part transferred, in part retired. I too am one of them. But given the arbitrariness and malice of the government, who can answer for the interpretation and execution of its "laws"? They can say that I was dismissed on May 1, and not as a non-Aryan, but as superfluous (para 6!), and the law applies only to those who have to go after January 1, '36. They do not need to explain anything at all, since they are accountable to no one.

Today it occurred to me: Never has the tension between human power and powerlessness, human knowledge and human stupidity been so overwhelmingly great as now. Radio, airplane—and the Führer and Reich Chancellor, the racial laws, *Der Stürmer,* etc. Also our powerlessness to help our little black Nickelchen, who is slowly dying, an apathetic, thin little stick.

Two serious depressions, which have lasted for several weeks now on top of my uninterrupted heart problems: (a) the Diderot chapter is unexpectedly presenting me with excruciating problems. I have again and again made alterations to the first section (Paradox and Hardouin), now, as I am typing, I am still perfecting it and am still dissatisfied. I cannot "put across" the Petrarch-Goncourt comparison, which seemed and still seems so important to me. I should really like to complete the volume by Christmas. (b) The torments of driving a car, senseless in every respect and contrary to nature.

December 31, Tuesday afternoon, New Year's Eve

On December 29, at seven o'clock in the evening, I completed the first volume of my Eighteenth Century, *Du côté de Voltaire* or *From Voltaire to Diderot*. I started writing it on August 11, '34, I started work on it in spring '33. During the last few weeks I have so fixedly spent every possible hour on it that I pushed everything else into the background. It was a state of obsession and exhaustion; the obsessiveness held even when of necessity I was occupied with something else. Typing and polishing it will now last until March. But the book is finished and it is indeed good. However— who will publish it? It will come to about 500 printed pages.

As second main point I place here the death of our little Nickelchen, which really affected me like the death of a very dear human being and which gave rise to all the "corresponding" bitter questions in me and which still haunt me today. The animal, friendly to me and everyone else, was attached to Eva with a touchingly ardent affection. It faded away in the last ten, twelve days only half conscious, even completely unconscious; when Eva lifted it up and put it on the table in front of her, it recovered a little and nestled against her. During the last few weeks he was very dirty, the music room, in which we kept him, smelled dreadful, looked dreadful; but we always thought, the little tomcat will recover. On December 9 we took him to Dr. Gross. He was already lying quite still in his box. There he was examined once more, was then given a prussic acid injection. — Sentimental? But where is the difference as compared to the death of a human being? — Nickelchen had come to us as a tiny baby stray on July 31, '32.

Very disappointing was the settlement of my "retirement pension." The shopwindow paragraph by which Jewish front-line veterans are to be discharged on full pay was not applied—it exists for foreign opinion, is a lie like every single thing this government does—not a professorial pensioning off, but the supererogatory paragraph 6. They calculated 61 percent and gave me back pay of 59M for 6 months on top of the 480 "provisional" marks. I must therefore make do with approximately 490M. Others live on less money, but it is all the more disappointing since for quite a few weeks we lulled ourselves in the hope of the full salary. However, this money business must by no means drive us to despair.

The false hope had a very real consequence. We had so often talked about driving, Eva's difficulties with walking, the bad money situation on top of that, which forces us to economize on taxis and does not even allow us to think of traveling, cars all around, nearly all the quite ordinary people on our new streets have their garage, though admittedly they are business people—in short: I booked a driving course at Strobach, paid 60M for 12 hours, and after two hours of theory began driving on November 22.

At first it went terribly badly, I came home completely shattered and soaked through, then much better—the high point of my pride: a drive through the whole city (without feeling any fear!) almost as far as Pillnitz and back (Luthe, the driver, mechanic, forty years old, simple man: "You'll be a little racing driver yet, Professor!"), and then a short drive up here with Eva in the car (a few minutes), the last time terrible again ("I don't know, Professor, you always accelerate when you should be releasing the accelerator, you drive into every obstacle, you can't turn" . . . etc., etc.). Responsible for this relapse was: (a) Luthe's mistake in hounding me through the tangle of the city center, corner after corner, which exhausted me dreadfully, (b) the depression about the money business. — The course ended shortly before Christmas, without my being able to take the test. Then I was seized by a mood of defiance. I also heard from various parties that the test is not especially difficult and that at the beginning no one drives confidently in the city, that after acquiring a driver's license one still practices a long time for one's own benefit—various parties, id est: the Isakowitzes, carpenter Lange, Fuhrmann, who delivered the cinders, etc. [. . .]. . . . On examining my inner self, I also believe that the initial feeling of fear is actually gone. So a couple of days ago I went to Strobach (the showroom in Sidonienstrasse, the big garage, from which we drove, is in Polierstrasse) and booked a second course, this time for 40M. It is to start next Monday at the latest and after this second course I want to—I want to and must!—take the test. And once I get the driver's license, then I want to take some money from the life insurance and buy a secondhand car and, not having a garage, keep it in the garden under a tarpaulin. The car will give us a little bit of life and of the world again. I have an income of 490M; I assume it is 400, and that the car will cost 90M a month. I should not allow borrowing against the insurance policy to depress me. This year I have to borrow the annual contribution from it anyway, so I borrow a couple of hundred marks more. At a time like this, what point is there in thinking about next year? Perhaps by then I shall be murdered, perhaps have my post back, perhaps the insurance will be destroyed by inflation again, as before, perhaps—I *want* to be frivolous, I want to be so quite deliberately. When I die, there must be a small pension there for Eva and in that event she also gets a few thousand more from the insurance. The mortgage of 12,000? Because of the extensions the house has risen in value. Should the Wenglers foreclose after eight years, another mortgage may be obtainable. The debt of 6,000 to Georg or his heirs? It can wait until the policy matures and will not be foreclosed. I intend to be frivolous to the utmost—I believe that is in Eva's interest. There is something like an inner voice inside me, which drives me forward.

The *pension*, the *car*, *Nickelchen*, those were the big things of these last diary-less one or two months. In between there were all kinds of lesser or more everyday things: people, reading, cinema, "Uncle"—I shall have to jot it down as a postscript tomorrow.

For today just the somber summary of the year 1935.

Dismissed on May 1, '35. Foreign hopes come to nothing. House extension. Eighteenth Century, volume I completed [. . .]. Driving lessons. —

Death of our little tomcat. Blumenfelds to Lima. Work at editing his *Psychology of Puberty.* [...]

Still the Third Reich and hopes of living to see the fourth greatly diminished. — Very little hope of living to see much more at all: constant heart trouble, the path up through the park my daily memento. Have abandoned limiting my smoking and other precautions, in this too I want to be frivolous. Less attachment to a long life. Frequent feeling that it is coming to an end anyway. It was our most sedentary year, the longest journey took us to Heidenau. — The most important thing however: I learned to type!

POSTSCRIPTS TO 1935, NOTED DOWN ON JANUARY 1, 1936

People: The final break came with the Kaufmanns, who are now leaving Dresden and emigrating to Palestine. Their nauseous trimming and crawling up everyone's arse and show of education and tolerance, and continual meanness and tactlessness. Fischer and the Modern Philologists' Congress put the lid on it. Frau Fischer, lavished with kindness by the Kaufmanns, was "not allowed" to stay with Jews, but came to Dresden and visited the Kaufmanns. Fischer, the so-called man of the family, thought it inopportune, like all the other Congress participants, even to get in touch with me by telephone. [...] Frau Kaufmann thought it necessary to phone and inform me of the Fischers' presence, and seemed to want to invite us together. I was very blunt and that was the end of an almost fifteen-year (long since tarnished) friendship.

The Blumenfelds went to Lima. On her last visit here Frau Kühn preached calm to me and was herself all too calm with respect to National Socialism. So there too: an end. — Spamer came to visit me once in November and was too mild for me. He closes his eyes to everything terrible and is a beneficiary. An important man as an ethnologist, director of some national organization, publisher, speaker at a congress in Edinburgh, proposed for the chair in Berlin. He wears his gray hair in nicely coiffured locks hanging down to his shoulders. Jesus from Oberammergau. *Der Stürmer* is a "little yellow press rag," such as there have always been, Gertrud von Rüdiger overwrought and not to be taken seriously. (In Upper Bavaria she was fortunate enough to photograph Hitler's dog!) On the other hand, it does not seem to him out of the question that, as master painter Lehmann maintains, Stepun is a police spy. He has been assured that he will keep his post, whereas the rest of the TU Humanities Section is being wound up. And Janentzky is a coward and is clinging to his income. He himself, Spamer, would gladly leave, the Bibliographical Institute is offering him a post with 500M a month; that would leave him time for scholarly work. I no longer quite trust the honest and easygoing Spamer, he is playing a role of complete innocence, and it both suits him and leaves everything open to him.

The Wenglers have remained loyal to us, Anna Mey, the secretary, Irene Papesch, the teaching assistant, Susi Hildebrandt and the paymaster's daughter Ursula Winkler.

On December 10 we were invited to Frau Schaps. The old warmth, and we liked her Gerstle children better than before.

In the course of this year we won as new friends the Isakowitz family. That has turned into a really warm friendship with father, mother and daughter. They will probably emigrate to England, and that would be a real loss for us.

On December 1 and 3 Berthold Meyerhof—in Dresden on business— was our guest, and it was the old good friendship.

Gusti Wieghardt emerged from her absence in Czechoslovakia, Karl Wieghardt from his semester in Göttingen. They were here at Christmas, yesterday—a lot of alcohol!—we were their guests. [. . .]

To be able to believe! Hatzfeld sent some printed matter with a penciled note: "Ex-professor! 75 percent" I do not know whether 75 percent Aryan or non-Aryan; the effect is the same. When I wrote to him warmly and at length, he replied that I was too bitter, cats were a "poor way to repress things," "only the faith in a personal God" could do anything to help, I was "too much of a rationalist." I responded to his New Year's card: There was a great deal to be said about repression and nothing to argue about. Walter Jelski wrote an intelligent and contented letter from Jerusalem, where he is an insurance agent.

Lion, the engineer and technical journalist, an in-law and friend of Berthold Meyerhof, was here one afternoon. He is emigrating to the USA—could I recommend him to my nephew. I could not, but we were very hospitable to him. An altogether likable man of 40 years of age. Firmly convinced that the 3rd Reich will last into "double figures." Gusti Wieghardt on the other hand, usually well informed through the Party and from abroad, believes with certainty in a collapse in the next few months. But it will not be followed by anything good (i.e., nothing Communist).

Michel Scholze, the husband of Agnes, peasant in Piskowitz, came as he does every Christmas, sold us a goose, gave us a sausage as a present and received presents for Agnes. The year before he had still reported a passable degree of contentment. Now he talks of widespread resentment, partly of an economic, partly of a religious nature. The Sorbs around Kamenz are strictly Catholic. "We shall not let God be taken from us. We would rather die!" Language of the twentieth century! But I no longer quite believe in the actual outbreak of a crusade.

Scholze took "Uncle" with him in a little box and wrote a few days ago in his laborious German: "The health of Uncle is very well." "Uncle" is a strong wild tomcat, not castrated. He used to come here very occasionally. About two months ago we noticed that he was constantly on our piece of land, shy yet friendly. He seemed to be turned out and homeless. It grew colder, the mice probably disappeared. He regularly spent the night on the mat in front of the hallway door, let himself be fed, became more trusting, but belligerently put the Schmidts' Peter to flight, was at daggers drawn with Muschel, startled unsuspecting visitors with sudden wild flight or by spitting. It grew even colder. Eva put out a box with straw for him. We fed him, but he became thinner, dirtier, was also very cold, made us feel very sorry for him, had no one besides us. Now he is in good hands in Piskowitz.

The cat's name "Uncle" comes from Annemarie in Heidenau. We see her rarely, but she is one of the most loyal to us (and like us counts the days of the tyranny). On every birthday and festival she gives us expensive modern books, chosen with the best of taste. (It no longer gives me any pleasure to own such books. I would like dictionaries, reference works of every kind, only such things now. Mater Schaps has given me a complete Rousseau, as well as the works of Eugen Hirschberg on D'Alembert and the opera wars of the eighteenth century, from the library of her deceased brother. Curious coincidence: My attention was drawn to these things through my work during the last few months; I could not get hold of the opera monograph. The author was, I believe, a distant relative of hers, a wealthy banker, who in his later days discovered his love of the Romance languages and took his doctorate in Leipzig. I had found the *Discours préliminaire* in the State Library; the opera book will do service with Rousseau.)

Among the most loyal I must of course not forget the four "respectable" Köhlers. In the last few weeks we were there and they here.

[...]

After a mild early winter and a few frosty days the weather is now almost springlike. It could be March.

I still have three wishes as an author: Volume II of the Eighteenth Century, the Language of the Third Reich (or of the Three Revolutions) and "My Life." What will be fulfilled? My heart and my eyes are failing me. But I shall work, my quota daily, comme si de rien n'était. And shall not ask what the point of it all is and what the prospects of success.

Yesterday and the day before yesterday there was a host of letters to answer, yesterday and today the diary.

First work in the new year: the Cacouac supplement. It took weeks and a lot of bother until I was able to get hold of the two copies extant in Germany from Bonn and Göttingen.

1936

January 24, Friday evening

My first Strobach receipt dates from November 16, my registration for driving lessons; on November 22 my first time at the wheel. Then weeks of despair. On December 28 registration for the second course. It started on January 2 and lasted for thirteen hours, all in all I have driven 25 times. I passed the test yesterday morning. This business is really two things for me, a victory over my own nature, achieved with great difficulty, and a matter of the utmost importance. The preliminary work for building the garage is already under way with Lange, the carpenter, feelers have already been put out to buy a car, an application has already been made to the Iduna. I want to take 3,000M from my policy, out of that cover the insurance itself for one year (about 800M), build and buy with the rest. Desperado actions—appropriate to the times. Who guarantees the security of the policy? The garage raises the value of the property. I would like to relate all this in more epic fashion. But I am still much too tired to do so.

During this driving-lesson time I have made Diderot good enough to print. Copied, provided footnotes, collated. An hour ago I dotted the last "i." On Sunday or Monday I shall begin making a typewritten copy (reworking certain points) of the first three books of the volume. The completed Book IV, however, makes up a good third of the whole.

All of this despite a bad heart. Pains in my throat every day when I'm climbing up here. They were also very bad yesterday during the test. [. . .]

January 25, Saturday

After overcoming a serious depression, because the first driving course had been in vain and my "retirement pay" assessment so low (480M), on December 28 I registered for the second course in a mood of defiance. It began agreeably on January 2. Luthe had to drive the tenant of the Zauckerode Crown Estate to his farm via Freital, and so by chance I had a practice drive in the country (the road along the Weisseritz below Dölzschen). That went very well. It was also very interesting out in the country. The tenant, an elderly man with the Party badge [. . .] showed me his stalls, in particular his pig breeding, and complained bitterly: Previously he had twelve-year tenancy agreements, and said he could work only with long agreements. Now, however, there was a gentleman in the Ministry who was concluding only one-year agreements, he was all-powerful, it was impossible to get to him by writing, still less to talk to him. I played the innocent: How could that be reconciled with the NSDAP principle of safeguarding agriculture, the farmers? Exasperated reply: Not at all, it was not at all "what the Führer wanted"—but what could one do? There was a man sitting there, against whom one was powerless . . . I said nothing and was glad.

On the fourteenth I had another nice driving lesson. We drove through the city after dusk, between five and six, up to Dölzschen village and back to Polierstrasse. It was my one and only night drive, it went not badly and I came home in rather high spirits. But for all of the rest of the eleven lessons (almost daily) we always drove in the city. Sometimes it went really well, sometimes wretchedly. I had overcome the terrible fear and helplessness of the first few times, but I nevertheless came home covered in sweat every time; very often Luthe grabbed the wheel and maintained that without him I would have done some mischief or other, I was driving straight at obstacles, accelerating where I should be braking, etc., etc. After a while I felt really miserable and somewhat overtrained. I told myself I should now be practicing alone, in a quiet location to begin with. Luthe, however, had the test in mind and repeatedly forced me into the heaviest traffic and narrowest streets. [. . .] On Wednesday we drove for the last time. I took the splendid porticus of Portikusstrasse, with its terrible bottleneck and problems, I did very well crossing over and driving down Pragerstrasse—but "turning" and "reversing"! I always confused right and left. Luthe's final instruction: corners as slowly as possible, if I nudge you with the tip of my shoe, let go of the accelerator pedal!—On Wednesday afternoon I once again had a little look at the engine, which is still fairly mysterious to me; I thought I knew the traffic regulations. I was required to be at 2 Kulmstrasse at quarter to eight on Thursday morning.

The Thursday began badly. I have been having dental treatment for a while, a disgusting root infection. Against all habit I spent the night lying awake with the pain; I had to get up at half past five. I lit the stove, attended to Muschel, to Eva's breakfast, trotted off at quarter past seven and lost my way. Up Bernhardstrasse to the top of the hill, experiencing severe difficulties with my heart, pains in my throat. Up there at quarter to eight. And Kulm Strasse was down by the District Court! (15 years a professor of the TU, and I have never been in the new buildings on Mommsenstrasse!) I arrived down there at eight, completely shattered, bathed in sweat, in pain—there was plenty of time. A dozen people were sitting in the waiting room next to the cashier's office, gradually we increased to fifteen. Mostly young people, a girl among them, all younger than I, most of them working class or the like. Only one gentleman from my driving school, early forties, a war invalid who drives a specially constructed car. (Hand accelerator, brakes and clutch all close together, since he is missing one leg.)

We paid 10M at the counter and were allocated to examination rooms. I was with five people, including the one-legged man. A proper classroom, a lectern (splendid view of the heights on the other side of the Elbe!), a gray-haired engineer, so Austrian that he did not seem Aryan at all. Herr

Doctor Klemperer—what is on the rear axle? I, proudly: the differential gear, around the wheels . . . I also knew something about engine-cooling, about dipping headlights, about green and yellow lights on city squares. But I did not know the new "No Waiting" sign, the one-legged man whispered it to me, and engineer Kroh said, "But no prompting!" Had I been asked about the ignition, things would have gone badly. But it went quite well, I knew just as much and as little as the others, the examiner was very nice, gave a helping hand all the time, explained things—this hour from half past eight to half past nine passed very cheerfully. It was very funny that I, a professor and senator of the TU, was sitting there as an examinee: I had thought that the oral in 1914 was the last examination I would take and in the subsequent twenty years I myself have so often been an examiner. The "oral," therefore, was behind me. Then someone called out, "Strobach Driving School leaves at 10:30."

Now we stood around outside the building for an hour. The weather was fine, about 34 degrees, I was very cold, but chatted with the others. [. . .]

Then Luthe arrived with the invalid's special car. I was squeezed into the back, next to me came the examiner—not the one who had tested us orally—a fat man, about forty, rather overbearing and brutal in disposition. He complained about the car; he found fault with the driver from the start, when Luthe tried to intervene, he said authoritatively: "I'm speaking." He had the man drive into the city, down to the Elbe embankment, stop, reverse, drive on. I felt as if someone were being guillotined in front of me and I was next. It ended at Strobach in Polierstrasse. Long palaver, the engineer required a modification to the brake.

Now at last it was my turn. Luthe had drilled me to be easy on the accelerator and then even easier than that, to start up gently. I started up so gently that the car did not move from the spot. "That is not the way to do it," said the examiner behind me. Then the car started moving. Postplatz, Altmarkt, Johannstrasse, right, toward Pragerstrasse, across it, another loop, out towards the station, Bismarckplatz, Werderstrasse. It really did not go badly. But I had a pain above my chest, and Luthe was all the time secretly knocking my foot off the accelerator, and from behind Lindner was shouting: "You're standing still, do step on it!" At Werderstrasse, when I believed myself to be already out of danger: "Stop, turn!" Naturally I confused right and left again. But then I got around, and the examiner was quite gentle. He seemed to feel pity for my advanced years. Back to Kulmstrasse, I stopped well, had also managed a good start from a last halt with the hand brake on an uphill street. "It was not a brilliant performance—I am giving you the driving license!"—I was in such a state that I was quite unable to be pleased. I asked Luthe why he had constantly stopped me accelerating. "Professor—I was sweating blood—I never once took my hand off the clutch (teaching car with two clutches)—you were driving too fast all the time. You would not have managed a single corner. Just let the examiner complain. No one fails because of driving too slowly; but bump against the curb and you're finished." Then Luthe drove me over to Isakowitz (I was glad to let myself be driven!). After the treatment I went to Postplatz and bought a bottle of Haute Sauternes. In the evening we both celebrated. Con amore. — But I am still shattered today.

And today Isandro, the Strobach representative, was here. The young man is indeed right: A new car would be the most sensible thing. But the money. We are quite undecided.

On January 3 we were invited to the Isakowitzes together with Gusti. It was very pleasant—but unfortunately Friday evening, hats were brought in again, also for the unsuspecting Karl Wieghardt, and Dr. Berlowitz, likewise a dentist, and a younger brother-in-law of Isakowitz, sang a long prayer—fabulously authentic and eastern. It got a bit on my nerves. On another evening we had Gusti Wieghardt and Frau Schaps here, and we were at Gusti's once. We are to be there again this evening. On Monday she is traveling to Denmark for several months.

January 31, Friday evening

[. . .]

My health is very poor. My heart, my eyes. In addition, painful inflammations on head, shoulders. Weeks of torment at the dentist. Tomorrow he wants to carry out an operation, a resection: I am not looking forward to it. (And the expense!)

The car business has been tiresome so far. The district authority is bullying me because of the planned garage. A shed with a flat roof "disfigures" the neighborhood. But the garages all around have flat roofs! But this is an opportunity to annoy "the Jews." So a roof with a pitch of 45 degrees. A dog kennel, says Eva. The negotiation up in the District Office upset me very greatly. My helplessness and lack of rights weighed upon me. — Nor has a suitable car—a new one costs too much—turned up yet. Again and again I have doubts about whether the whole business is sensible and right. We are poor, our future is quite uncertain, I believe ever more frequently that I have only a short, very short time left to me, and I want to spend 2,000M of my life insurance on this luxury. But perhaps it is after all not as senseless as it appears to me.

The political situation is increasingly depressing. I have hardly any hope of living to see a change. Everyone knuckles under—baseness triumphs over all. Yesterday the pompous celebrations of January 30. *Three years!* It may turn out to be a hundred.

[. . .]

February 11, Tuesday

After mild springlike weather suddenly, for the last two days, severe cold, 14 degrees in the mornings.

The situation ever darker. In Davos a Jewish student has shot the German Party agent of the NSDAP. For the moment, as the Olympic Games are taking place here, everything is being hushed up. They will turn on the hostages, on the German Jews later. That is how it is on the whole. And in my own case: I am the only Jew in Dölzschen Rural District, at least the only "prominent" one. Kalix, the mayor, has already raised difficulties and complained to Prätorius about me, when we built the extension in the summer. I was "disfiguring" the neighborhood with a wooden house and tar-board roofing. It is worse now with the garage. A few weeks ago, a garage, the usual shed with a flat roof, was completed here on Kirschberg. But *I* am not allowed to build one. *This* year there must be no more *disfigurement;* they are demanding a pointed decorative roof, which would take space and view from us. At the District Office I told a clerk: "I am not disfiguring anything. Then there will simply be no construction and no work." He: "You can perhaps talk to the mayor, but I don't think . . ." I: "I am not begging for anything that appears to me a matter of course. Good-bye."—The next day the master mason and the carpenter go to the mayor and ask him [to reconsider] for the sake of their work. He gives them a message for me: I did not seem to know the way things were, I was a guest here, and he had a mind to take me into custody for a night. Reported by Lange, the carpenter (who had his house searched a few weeks ago and was threatened at the police station: denunciation, a scientific book was found, which the "fugitive Jew Blumenfeld" had left for him—after Lange had helped him pack and so on). I am very well aware that my life really is in danger. — The whole business with the car seems ever more absurd.

A gentleman addressed me on Postplatz. "Do you not recognize me? Dr. Kleinstück, rector of Vitzthum Grammar School. I passed you recently, you saw me and looked away. I was afraid you looked away because you thought I would not greet you. That is why I am addressing you today. How are you?" His behavior moved me, I told him about my situation and added: "Furthermore, I have been told that you, Rector, are a big Nazi." He: "Oh God, one can never do everything right for people, I do not know from one day to the next whether I shall still have my post the next day. My sister . . ." What is wrong with her? "She was private secretary to Chairman Sommer, a Jewish industrialist. She was in custody for six weeks." — That is the big Nazi rector of Vitzthum Grammar School.

On top of the worries and the constant heart problems I went through great torments with my teeth. I could not make up my mind to undergo a doubtful resection and had the bad tooth taken out. It could not be done without my heart letting me down a little and without the injection having unpleasant aftereffects.

Last Sunday the Isakowitzes were our guests in the evening. The man is much worn down by worry and uncertainty; despite his despair he told terribly smutty jokes, he himself said: "Out of despair." Dressel and Annemarie were here about two weeks before. Otherwise quite isolated.

I type and revise Voltaire, Eva paints the music room. And again and again car offers and garage building plans. Isandro, the salesman, whose Florentine family was called Isidoro, is amusing. Italian on his father's side, Greek on his mother's, we suspect a strong dose of Jewishness. He is employed at Strobach, is making an effort on our behalf, is a likable man. His father is in the tobacco trade here; the son did military service in Italy and learned Italian only then. In other respects, too, looking for a car gives one a view of a different world. But the business is pure madness and desperation, like Isakowitz's smutty jokes.

[...]

No news from Georg since October. He wanted to emigrate and speak to me in person before that.

March 6

In October Georg wrote that he was emigrating, but would see me beforehand. I wrote back, I sent him good wishes for the New Year, I wrote to Freiburg two weeks ago. No reply.

On the third, after a gap of several months, Susi Hildebrandt and Ursula Winkler (my last students) were here for coffee. Susi Hildebrandt told us she had heard from her aunt that Georg was in the USA.

Yesterday I spoke to Marta at the station; she was traveling to see her boy in Prague; he is still waiting for an entry permit to the Soviet Union. She told me, Georg has emigrated to Boston where his son has a hospital medical post. He visited the Sussmanns in Cologne beforehand, he at least wrote Marta a farewell letter. Me he left alms of 6,000M in the summer (because he had promised Father!) and then he brushed me aside. He evidently considers me dishonorable because I am staying in Germany. I shall probably never see him again. He is over seventy, and I have a poor heart. — Marta went on to tell me: Felix's eldest has gone to Brazil, Betty Klemperer wants to go to the USA, the Sussmanns and the Jelskis themselves also want to get away—even before the Olympics. I shall be the last of our family here and shall perish here. I can do nothing else.

We are literally digging ourselves in. It is madness, but perhaps this madness will be victorious and the best investment. We have now got to the point of excavating the garage. After an endless amount of trouble it is now to be built into the terrace at the front. That will cost at least 900 to 1,000M. The car was bought on March 2. 850M—but 19M a month tax on top of that. Opel 32hp, 6 cylinders, built in 1932, completely open. The grocer had recommended a reliable mechanic, Michael, to us, and he drove us from dealer to dealer. We first saw "our car" through a window, but behind locked doors (at Meyer's in Friedrichstrasse). Its appearance captivated us. It was here in the afternoon, it was bought in the evening. I have not seen it since. It is lodged with Michael, who is to give it an overhaul. I can only drive it once the papers have been obtained from Brandenburg district. Will I be able to drive? How will my nerves, how will my money bear up? 19M tax, 33M insurance a month! The whole thing a desperado adventure. — On our sightseeing tour in Vogel the grocer's car (in return he takes care of the insurance) we saw a vast garage building on Arnhold-strasse, a whole casemate system as it were, hardly noticeable from the road. What a commercial item the car, and everything that goes with it, has become! A world.

After many false starts, Lange, the carpenter, skillful but unreliable, intelligent, but like a twelve-year-old boy, has placed the whole garage business under the formal aegis of his master builder, Grosche. A curious fellow, whose folksy talkativeness has already cost me two afternoons. [. . .]

The "respectable" Köhlers were here on the evening of February 28. Köhler Sr. told us that Poland (our ally!) has blocked all freight traffic on the railway through the Corridor because of debts, because we paid in marks instead of zlotys. The most important foodstuffs—and corpses—were coming from East Prussia by sea.

Isakowitz informed me by telephone that he has permission to practice in England and wants to leave in April. We shall soon be quite alone.

I type and polish my book every hour I can. I am at Fontenelle. Perhaps I shall manage it by the end of April.

I am always tired, always have shoulder pains and breathing difficulties, smoke a lot, type, have to lie down on the sofa, sleep for a quarter of an hour, continue typing. The days slip away. I live in a state of constant dull anxiety, I am all the time waiting for *the* end, for *my* end, for something. There is not a moment's time for boredom. A lot of housework, a lot of typing, on top of that the constant distraction caused by the building of the garage and the attendant hitches.

[. . .]

On February 29, 4,500 bricks from the demolition of a nursery garden were delivered. Price including transport 105M; new they would have cost 156. We formed a chain and unloaded and stacked. My heart gave me trouble occasionally, on the whole it was all right, but the following day I had bad muscle pains. The heavy physical work is no problem for Eva. She works all day in the garden helping to move earth, etc. In rainy weather she paints the music room and does carpentry in it.

March 8

Yesterday on Bismarckplatz I ran into the middle of Hitler's Reichstag speech. [. . .] I could not get away from it for an hour. First from an open shop, then in the bank, then from a shop again. He spoke in a completely healthy voice, most of it was well formulated, read, not overladen with pathos. The speech on the occupation of the Rhineland ("breaking the Locarno Treaty"). Three months ago I would have been convinced there would be war the same evening. Today, vox populi (my butcher): "They won't risk anything." General conviction, and ours too, that everything will remain quiet. Hitler's new "act of liberation," the nation rejoices— what does internal freedom mean, what do we care about the Jews? His position is secured for an indefinite period. He has also dissolved the Reichstag—no one knows the names of those "elected"—and "asks" the people to [confirm] him through a new election on March 29, etc.

I am infinitely depressed, I shall not live to see any change.

March 23

It will be a tremendous triumph for the government. It will receive millions upon millions of votes for "peace and freedom." It will not need to fake a single vote. Internal policies are forgotten. — Exemplum: Martha Wiechmann, who visited us recently, previously completely democratic. Now: "Nothing has impressed me so much as rearmament and marching into the Rhineland." And then: "I heard a lecture about Russia, that is too dreadful, we are much better off." (a) The horror stories about Russia are believed; (b) only the alternative Bolshevism–National Socialism is recognized, nothing in between; (c) in the intoxication of foreign policy everything else has been forgotten. — It all impresses the foreign powers and, despite condemnation by the League of Nations and the proposal of a supranational police authority for the Rhine zone, will also be a tremendous victory for Hitler. He flies from place to place and gives triumphal speeches. The whole thing is called an "election campaign." The Kroll Opera is called the Reichstag. Typical. Those elected are chorus, extras, the claque. Hitler said recently: "I am not a dictator, I have only simplified democracy." Napoleon's coins at first bore the words "République française." [...] Ursula Winkler introduces her fiancé, Greiner, to us, Bavarian through and through, Protestant theologian, prospective clergyman. He told us about a circular from the Minister of the Interior on National Socialist festivity: "Liturgy," "Singing together," "Reading out the text" (from Hitler's writings), etc. [...] The election rules refer to Aryans, Jews and "half-breeds."

Marta on her return journey from Prague expressed uncommon optimism. Then came Martha Wiechmann as vox populi. Then came the never ending "election propaganda" and England's deal making. My basic mood at every hour of the day: I shall not live to see the tide turn.

Friendly letter from Georg in Boston—but from Boston. I am dismissed, paid off.

Today the third week of the construction of the garage. The hall itself (truly a hall 22 × 9 feet) is up. But the earth-moving, digging and access raise the cost of everything immeasurably (given my circumstances). Afterward we shall be left without any reserve. This causes me increased anxiety with every day that passes. Even the car itself only gives me real pleasure for minutes at a time. A double worry outweighs it. (1) The cost.

It has turned out that we need 4 not 3 gallons of gasoline per 62 miles. So cheated after all. Tax, insurance and a single wash already amount to approximately 66M monthly. And I have 484M "retirement pay!" (2) The constant worry that I as a driver must not cause any mischief. On March 19, the car with all the documents was finally at our disposal. Since then I have been driving with Michael every day, who is not as careful as Luthe—visited us recently!—but does his job quite well. At first after the long gap of two months and with the fast car, to which I was not accustomed, I drove very badly, now it is going substantially better. But I am afraid of driving alone and of the responsibility for Eva. She comes on the drives now. The first longer one was to Niederwartha. When I am driving I see *nothing* of the landscape, my eyes are fixed on the road. Returning from Niederwartha I fell asleep for a moment on Habsburgerstrasse [. . .] The day before yesterday a trip up hill and down dale along narrow village streets around Gorbitz went better. I saw a tremendous setting sun, otherwise only road; yesterday the drive to Edle Krone, on a road with many curves, went very well. But I do not feel absolutely confident by any means. Driving in reverse is hard work for me, I cannot imagine direction. Long straight country roads often disconcert me more than curves. The trees flicker, I draw closer to them, correction, on the other hand, throws me too far over to the left. I must force myself to drive slowly. With all these worries and distractions the typing of the Eighteenth Century moves forward at a snail's pace.

And always the inflammation or rheumatic pains on my head, in my eyes, on neck, shoulders and arms, always the heart problems.

Now I have the driving license, the car, the garage—and feel even more depressed than before.

When I took the car over, the odometer stood at 18,673 miles. Yesterday afternoon I unfortunately had to let Michael have it for a trip to Kamenz, etc.; he drove 80 miles. I myself already have 62 miles behind me. Yesterday I tanked up for the first time, had air put into the spare tire. All of them experiences for the present.

Because of the workers I have to rise before six, Eva also starts early. I always feel sorry for her because I plague her with my money worries, I am always in despair because the estimates of costs are so greatly exceeded and continue to be ever more so. The removal of earth and rubble, the digging, etc. Again and again an extra man, more working hours, etc.

[. . .]

March 31, Tuesday

The whole complex, garage construction–car is for the moment causing endless worry, trouble and annoyance. Perhaps later on it will all appear tragicomical, and we shall be amused by it; perhaps also everything will go to pieces. There is too much that aggravates the situation: (1) The lack of money. The terrible digging, the rock, the deep excavation for the access, the removal of rubble, have cost much more than foreseen. My reserves are completely exhausted, and nothing is quite finished yet, a huge amount of earth and stone [. . .] is piling up in the devastated garden, the construction of the veranda has come to a halt. I am beginning to face the altogether desperate idea of taking even the last possible 1,000M from the life insurance. Then we could probably manage the construction and would not go short in the summer, but would have pretty much nothing at all in January '37. And how can I count on any change in the situation, after the plebiscite of the day before yesterday, the 99 percent for Hitler? (2) and this was knocked into me on Sunday in the most painful way: Is a Jewish professor allowed to have a car, to be "noticeable" in any way? There was work being done in the gardens all around, strollers and voters were streaming past, Lange, the carpenter (whom I had warned, this time as so very often!) was hammering on the veranda, Eva was hoeing at the side of the path. In the afternoon the policeman appeared, the same one who has already several times recited his woes and shared his opinions with me.

April 5, Sunday

In retrospect it is comical how the aforesaid policeman vacillated between the roughness he had been ordered to display and respect and sympathy. At the time it was dreadful, and objectively it is a terrible symptom of my situation. He shouted at Eva, "he" (Kalix, mayor) had said, he should lock her up, lock us all up. Prohibited work, "National Holiday," an SS man had lodged a complaint against us at the polling station. I: "But it's our garden, constable, there is work going on all around." He, quietly, courteously, regretfully: "No complaint has been lodged against the others." The carpenter was in a difficult position. He established that he had to secure a wobbly veranda pillar, and this despite my warning about prohibited Sunday work. So everything turned out well, or at least not too badly, but the bitterness and uncertainty remained. Lange meanwhile is constantly employed building air force barracks in Lausa (working day and night for peace), and garage and arbor remain mere shells, unfinished. There is also still a lot of work to be done on the driveway, the rubble is piled up mountain high, a further 1,000M has been requested from the Iduna, final reserve which can be drawn upon has shrunk to 350M, value of the policy to 6,000M. But I am calmer again. Head down and keep going!

Meanwhile I, or we—because Eva bravely suffers with me—have all kinds of driving experiences behind us. [. . .] The worst: The car does not start, so far all the checking and repairing has not really helped; we are already thinking of exchanging the six-cylinder for a four-cylinder. On Monday evening we wanted to go to the Köhlers; the car stood in the garden and would not move; at the last moment we had to order a taxi. This morning we were supposed to go to the confirmation of Annelies Lehmann, daughter of our maid: Once more the car stands in the garage and does not move. (In this case the trouble is not altogether unwelcome.) Sometimes the engine is too cold, sometimes it is supposed to be the battery, sometimes the starter, sometimes the gaskets on the carburetor filter. The result is always the same: it doesn't go; always expenses.

Aside from car and garage: (1) serious depression and hopelessness of the general situation. (2) Heart problems. (3) Increasing indifference. (4) Finished copying Volume I of the Eighteenth Century yesterday; there remain footnotes and reading through, about another few weeks. All in all this volume (typed—close spacing!—330 printed pages against 400) will have cost me three years pure writing time since summer 1934. (5) Last Sunday the Isakowitzes, man and wife, were here, ready to depart for London, very nervous and low in spirit. [. . .]

I find writing by hand ever more difficult. It is probably also weakened by the driving. So: typewritten letter to Gusti.

April 12, Easter Sunday morning

The car eats me up, heart, nerves, time, money. It is not so much my wretched driving and the occasional agitation it gives rise to, not even the effort of driving in and out of our property; but the car never works properly, something is always failing, I have lost all confidence in it, in the mechanics, in Michael, my chief nurse and adviser. I am always assured (with receipt) that now everything is in perfect working order, and yet something goes wrong every time I drive it. Fuel pump, starter, battery, brakes, tires. Most harrowing of all is the starter. I have now learned how to use fuel injection and crank—yesterday I was my own mechanic on Bismarckplatz. The worst was last week; we wanted to get to a timber dealer between Nausslitz and Wölfnitz. Just beyond the terminus of the Nausslitz bus, *before* the hill: gasoline gone. (I thought empty, but no.) I went through the village: no filling station. An old man and his son pushed the car up to the crest of the hill. I let it roll, without the engine, down busy Saalhausener Strasse. A filling station at last. Took 3 gallons. The car stalls. A repair shop a little distance away. A mechanic from there works in vain from five until seven. He fetches a car from his shop, tows ours away, drives us home, brings the car at ten o'clock in the evening, under its own power. Next morning I get the thing in front of the door, no further. It then went on for days like that until Michael got "everything" in working order (receipt!). Yesterday I simply went to Gesch, Feldschlösschenstrasse, from whom I have a new battery (32M), for a little extra checkup. It lasted an hour, then we had to go to a workshop: to mend the brakes. And so on day after day. Exhaustion and misery. Today I have promised to pick up the

Isakowitzes at eleven, so that we can go for a drive together. The question is, will I get the car to start? Yesterday evening the rear light came on and could not be switched off; we had to unscrew the bulb. What now? It sounds comical, but drives me to despair. And always heart complaints and always expenses.

It is already certain that the Voltaire volume will not be quite perfect by May 1.

[...]

As for politics I am completely apathetic and without hope.

April 24, Friday

The most difficult part of the corrections, the still quite virgin sections II, III finished. Now just the footnotes to Part IV and revision of *Zaïre*. And then at last on to something new, Rousseau.

On the thirtieth it will be exactly one year since I lost my post. Then I was at Marivaux. Since then the volume has been finished, I have had extensions built to the house, I have learned typing and driving, my heart has got worse, my skin thicker, the political situation has remained unchanged, I have not found a post abroad.

The car still rules me. On the whole I drive adequately. But the car vexes me with two great weaknesses. The starter fails again and again; thanks to an inconceivable consumption of gasoline, the tank is again and again empty at impossible moments. Result: excessive costs, a great deal of annoyance and upset, hardly a single drive accomplished without incident yet. Sometimes it is impossible to get the car out of its stable two days in a row. — Our biggest runs so far: Grillenburg, where we visited Fräulein Carlo in the Gopfert hostel, Kesselsdorff-Wilsdruff, where we bought two handsome broom shrubs in a nursery. Yesterday proudly to the dentist by car. On the return journey on Bismarckplatz gasoline runs out, push it close to the filling station, fetched gasoline in a can. The only time I got into real danger was also on Bismarckplatz. I was coming from the bank alone, wanted to drive off, rammed an empty DKW in front of me, reversed, forgot, in my panic, to indicate, and narrowly missed being caught by a bus. God, how the driver swore!—I still do not dare drive faster than 30 miles an hour. — We must try to exchange the car as soon as possible for a four-cylinder one that consumes less gasoline and costs less to insure. I still find the most difficult thing is driving in and out here at home. I repeatedly dent the mudguard, damage the gate and the little garden wall. One has to persevere; perhaps the pleasure is still to come. — Work on garage and veranda advances very slowly; Lange has regular work and finds little time for us. — I lifted money from the Iduna once again; our last reserve has now been committed.

[...]

The Garden Show, for which we have bought season tickets, opens today. This flower show is a major reason for my decision to learn to drive. Eva so much wanted to see just this show. To take a taxi there every time would be prohibitive; but if she has to go on foot as far as the tram, then she is already completely worn out by the time she gets there. The second motive was that Heiss, as Vossler wrote, had "died of heart failure beside his little car." I thought: Heiss was my predecessor here in Dresden in this respect also. The third reason: that as a dismissed non-Aryan front-line veteran I expected to get my full salary. That hope came to nothing, and so there was the fourth motive: dawke or proprio!

We become ever more lonely, I become ever more mistrustful. Especially since Martha Wiechmann swung over to the Hitler front. Why has there been not a word from Annemarie Köhler for months? Why has Johannes Köhler not phoned, as agreed, to arrange an excursion by car together?—The Isakowitzes are getting ready to emigrate to London, after that we shall be quite alone.

Today I had a dream that is characteristic of the general situation. A government declaration in bold print covered many pages of the newspaper: an ultimatum, "failing this" war would begin in 24 hours. And I could not find out who the enemy was. It seemed to be Turkey, but I really could not understand it properly. I wanted to ask Eva and woke up.

The whole foreign policy situation is entirely opaque. The play of interests England-France-Italy-Russia is too tangled up. But what is clear is that tremendous arming is going on in this country, which is in an extremely powerful position. And that Hitler has never been more firmly established. On his birthday, April 20, he made Blomberg a field marshal. Wilhelm II is a novice compared to the present masters.

Evening

From six until quarter to seven we waded through the garden show, which was opened today, in pouring rain, the ground sodden; I got my way and drove Eva there in the car. I maneuvered wretchedly on Stübelplatz and had to go up a side street—but I got my way. So far there was little to see at the show, the main thing a hall with pictures and words in the advertising style of the 3rd Reich, for Hitler, Blood and Soil, productive work, peasants, etc. — but I got my way and drove Eva to the first day of her show.

April 28, Tuesday

The driving is gradually becoming more enjoyable. The garden gate is still torture, but the starter works, I am driving better, and we use the car a lot—Eva really has become more mobile. We have already been four times to the flower show, from which she gets a great deal, and which in the main gives me pleasure for her sake; we combine these visits with other things, the dentist, today the railway station, where we greeted Maria Strindberg, who was passing through. We were at the Wenglers one afternoon, before that at the exhibition again, and then also in Radeberg with them. I do not see much when I am driving, but the driving itself is a pleasure and a distraction, and Eva is no longer as trapped and bound to the house as she was previously. — D'altra parte: Tiredness, heart problems, expenses.

And hopelessness of the situation. A decree for civil servants: They are prohibited from "consorting with Jews, including so-called decent Jews, and disreputable elements." We are completely isolated. We have heard nothing from Annemarie Köhler, nothing from Johannes Köhler for weeks.

[. . .]

May 3, Sunday evening

Yesterday, May 2, I completely finished the first volume of the Eighteenth Century, bundled up the whole manuscript, which is ready to go to press, and laid it to rest, without particular hope of its resurrection. Today I began, with considerable reluctance, to read the *Contrat social.*

[. . .]

May 10, Sunday—drive to Piskowitz

Agnes our first Wend maid, go-between for the subsequent ones, seven years married, lives in Piskowitz by Kamenz. We had promised that the first excursion by car would be to her, and we were invited there yesterday. On Saturday evening we had come back from the show with a boiling and dripping radiator, and Lange (he and his wife have been busy for weeks now in the evening with the never-ending work on garage, veranda and path), enthusiastic motorcyclist, jack of all mechanical trades, who has straightened out my bent bumper X times, has piloted me into the entry X times, Lange found nothing. So skepticism on Sunday morning. The first two points of doubt, whether the engine would start and whether I would get the car on to the road with a straight bumper, were resolved happily. Now I drove to Opel-Harlan in Tharandter Strasse, who recently towed us away, and had checked the brakes meanwhile—but the rattling remains— and whom I owe 60M. Only a nut on the radiator outlet needed to be tightened, in a couple of minutes and for a dime and a cigar I was in running order. But always this uncertainty, anxiety and mechanical helplessness! I now picked up Eva and at half past eleven, in humid, unsettled weather, we began our first "tour." I was wearing new, very dark goggles. Proudly across the Altmarkt to the Neustadt, the same fine route that we recently drove with the Wenglers, to Radeberg, then on to just before Pulsnitz. There a bare hilltop, large, imposing black wooden cross with the inscription "Versailles!," beside it a memorial stone to Schlageter. Wonderful view all around and into the distance: a kind of round, green bowl, framed by chains of low, forested mountains. [...] Continued after a quarter of an hour. The little town of Pulsnitz seemed altogether insignificant. After that a very straight road, rising steeply and falling just as abruptly, in the distance, curiously, three exactly identical hills, as a child would draw three green hills. At half past twelve we stopped in the market square of Kamenz. We had put 28 miles precisely behind us, at points I had reached a speed of over 30 mph. In the Golden Stag [...] a proper menu for Eva and a forbidden kümmel for me. We continued at two: the town did not seem to present anything especially Wendish or anything else of special note, a small town with a central marketplace, where cars park now, and where *Der Stürmer* with its nice headlines adorns a pillar. [...] I drove into a difficult gas station at a dashing angle and out of it again; after that another 4½ miles on a poor road—the warning sign "Potholes!" was quite unnecessary, one noticed them anyway—through a couple of villages to Piskowitz. We stopped there as the first raindrops were falling and looked around. As we did so Agnes' husband appeared and we drove onto his farm. He helped us right away to pull up the top; a heavy thunderstorm began. Emotional greeting: Agnes bore a stillborn girl at Christmas; she has a good-looking four-year-old boy who cannot speak a word of German yet, and a healthy stepson of about ten years, various relatives in the house as well. It is a half-timbered house, somewhat in need of patching up, but rather spacious and easy to live in, the house her husband was born in. A large, low room downstairs, pictures of saints, Hindenburg and Hitler (although the Wendish Catholics are not at all Nazi supporters—nevertheless: "It may not be deliberate intention that so many injustices are taking place," says Scholze), five tiny windows. Behind the house a solidly built stall: two cows, one sow, goat with young, hens, pigeons, behind that a large orchard and meadow, vegetable plots, in front of it a little bit of garden and beehives. We drank coffee, we were supposed to wait until the rain stopped, but it did not stop completely, so the outside inspection took place in the wet. Then with a bit of effort, I got the car through the gate, and the four of us drove more than half a mile along a bad road to the Scholzes' more distant farmland. They have a long, broad strip of grain, a long potato field and a bit of woodland. Apart from that the husband works in a quarry. These people are completely content and live on their own produce.

The little village is entirely Wendish, the children learn German only at school. The female dress is Wendish. The distinctive nationality of the people, however, is as little evident in the appearance of the village as in the appearance of Kamenz.

Back from the fields we ate bread and sausage and drank coffee, were also given a little sack of potatoes as a present. Then in solemn phrases Agnes expressed her thanks for the visit of her "master and mistress" and for "the words of comfort." Very genuine feelings and tears accompanied by stiff, memorized, conventional words. (No doubt it is just the same with the Catholic prayers.)

Set out for home at half past six. [. . .]

Today of course very tired. During the day slogged away at Ducros' *Rousseau* as far as I could.

Writing with a pen becomes ever harder for me, my hand is unsteady, my eyes fatigued. [. . .] This is my first attempt to switch to typing the diary.

May 16, Saturday afternoon

Motorized wedding anniversary: yesterday evening after a very long gap, to the cinema: left here at quarter past eight, parked on Freiberger Platz at half past eight, back home at half past eleven, a quarter of an hour after it ended. It was a great pleasure, and on this occasion the car really provided what we had so much hoped it would. And this morning alone in the car I did all the shopping in town—I now drive quite confidently in the city— then at half past eleven to the tree nursery at Wilsdruff with Eva, almost two hours there, loaded eight conifers (3 cwt—34M) into the car, and back, occasionally up to 30 mph. That was nice and pleasant, but in the last few days I have paid Harlan 75M for checkups and small repairs, the gasoline consumption is still excessive, my belief in the permanent health of the car is small, my doubts of financial survival very great. All the greater as work on the garage and—above all—on the driveway is never ending: "Dirt" has to be carted away again and again, the evening work of the Langes goes on and on, an old uncle of the wife is now in action all day, digging away—it all costs money, and even the second and final Iduna reserve will soon be eaten up.

The mood of the wedding anniversary? I feel old, I have no confidence in my heart, I do not believe that I have much time left to me, I do not believe that I shall live to see the end of the Third Reich, and I let myself drift along fatalistically without especial despair and cannot give up hope. Eva's stubborn attachment to extending the house is a support to me. I cannot imagine how I would bear the pressure, the humiliation, the uncertainty, the loneliness without Eva. Things really are getting worse all the time. Yesterday a farewell greeting from Betty Klemperer from Bremen (and Felix was one of the first doctors to receive the Iron Cross, First Class, he took part in the Hindenburg offensive against the Russians, bound wounds in the trenches); now the women in our family are also leaving Germany, and sometimes my staying here seems dishonorable to me—but what should I, who could not even be a language teacher, do elsewhere?

Isakowitz, whom Eva is seeing a lot of again (further financial deterioration), is emigrating to London in a couple of weeks; there is not a word from the Köhlers, decentes et indecentes: A civil servant is not allowed to consort "with Jews and disreputable elements." The foreign affairs situation is completely confused, but it undoubtedly presents the Hitler government with the greatest opportunities. The huge German army is feared and used by every party: perhaps Germany will do a deal with England, perhaps with Italy, but a deal will certainly be done and to the advantage of the present government. And I certainly no longer believe that it has enemies inside Germany. The majority of the people is content, a small group accepts Hitler as the lesser evil, no one really wants to be rid of him, all see in him the liberator in foreign affairs, fear Russian conditions, as a child fears the bogeyman, believe, insofar as they are not honestly carried away, that it is inopportune, in terms of Realpolitik, to be outraged at such details as the suppression of civil liberties, the persecution of the Jews, the falsification of all scholarly truths, the systematic destruction of all morality. And all are afraid for their livelihood, their life, all are such terrible cowards. (Can I reproach them with it? During my last year in my post I swore an oath to Hitler, I have remained in the country—I am no better than my Aryan fellow creatures.)

The work on Rousseau makes very slow progress: The man literally sends me to sleep. I have now worked my way through the first two *Discours* and can in no way understand what is original about them. So many empty phrases, superficialities, contradictions! And I cannot even discover the famous poetic or oratorical force and passion: For every thrilling sentence there are ten tortuous, obscure, ponderous ones. And I find the *Contrat social* no different.

I have to lie down three or four times in morning and afternoon, and immediately fall asleep for several minutes. God knows if the second volume of my Eighteenth Century will ever materialize. [...]

May 21, Thursday morning, Ascension Day

Yesterday (as a couple of times already) nothing but a taxi driver: in the morning took Eva to a nursery garden in Nausslitz, drove to the bank on Bismarckplatz, back to Eva, in the afternoon went to fetch Annemarie Köhler from Heidenau, I was alone and so lost my way, but on the return journey uninterrupted conversation, at the same time hampered by extremely dazzling sunshine; in the evening took Annemarie to the station; in a very weary state by now and once again bent the bumper on the garden gate, damaged the wall of a flower bed. From the railway right away to a filling station to have the bumper straightened, at home Eva immediately patched up the little wall with the headlights switched on. And today we want to go to Rochlitz. Car, car over all, it has taken a terrible hold of us, d'une passion dévorante.

We had heard almost nothing from Annemarie for almost three months and had already given her up for lost; finally I phoned her up, she should tell us openly whether there was a ban on her seeing us. Reply: No, there had simply been so many hindrances. Then we agreed to meet the next day, and here everything was as it had always been, the old intimacy, the old medical and political conversations, the old continual alternation between optimism and pessimism.

[. . .] My Rousseau-Ducros reading creeps along, nor is there much reading aloud. Car, car over all, first and last thought.

[. . .]

May 24, Sunday evening eight o'clock

Yesterday the Isakowitzes announced their farewell visit for this evening at nine o'clock (the ladies are leaving at the end of next week, he two weeks later). I drove to Fürstenstrasse in a terrible cloudburst, to invite Frau Lehmann for today. — This morning to the garden show with Eva: the magnificent rhododendron displays mostly from Seidel in Grüngräbchen. Then immediately after coffee away again, to Kipsdorf. Departure here: quarter to four, arrival there, quarter to five; stayed an hour or so, managed the return trip in 55 minutes. And now very tired and the guests still to be faced. The car eats me up, Rousseau is a mere counterweight now.

Kipsdorf gave us considerable, somewhat melancholy pleasure. How many memories it has for us. Old Nitzsche and his daughter dead, Georg, who was with us there after his return from Lenin, in Boston. Etc. We ourselves have not been there for years because Eva's feet fail her. Now the very nice excursion in our own car. It was cloudy hazy weather, and the landscape displayed itself to especially good effect. We walked part of the way up toward Oberkipsdorf; nowhere around Dresden does one get such a strong feeling of being completely shut in by hills and forests, of being literally sealed off from the plain, the city, the world [. . .]. In the village a new railway station with a place for cars to turn in front of it, a new post office, otherwise little change. The beautiful road to Oberkips is now called Adolf Hitler Strasse, and at the station *Der Stürmer* has its box and there are Hitler Youths with collecting cans. — And now we are waiting for guests who are fleeing Germany, while we stay here. And Eva is just planting forest flowers which she dug up by hand in Kipsdorf.

May 27, Wednesday evening

A couple of weeks ago a small building plan of the garage had to be reproduced, and it turned out the owner of the copy office was a brother-in-law of Frau Hirche. I passed on kindest regards to our old neighbor. Then Frau Hirche telephoned, and yesterday afternoon she was here for coffee.

Her husband was unemployed and receiving dole for a year—the Director of the Eschebach factory, the owner of a Packard, the father of a lieutenant—now he is traveler for a sheet metal company and on the road for weeks. They are not well-disposed to the Nazis, but even they repeat the nonsense that is hammered into everyone and is current among Jews as well: But after them there would be the Communists and that would be even worse! I fetched Frau Hirche from her apartment in Reichenbach-strasse in the car, just as in their heyday the Hirches picked up Eva and took her back in the evening. (Naturally there are plaques of Hitler and Hindenburg in the living room.) In the late afternoon we went for a wonderful drive. Pesterwitz, Wurgwitz, Kesselsdorf, Grumbach, Tharandt. We stopped for a little while at an especially beautiful view of meadows and woods. [...]

May 30, Saturday evening

Very resigned letter from Georg in response to my congratulations, Harvard University maintains an age-limit of 65, and he is 71; he no longer feels fresh enough for the very brisk competition among doctors; hence he has completely withdrawn from active life, awaits the end with equanimity and is occupying himself with writing, including an attempt to describe his life, for which, however, he probably lacks the literary ability. He hopes with all his heart that I obtain a post abroad and a foreign publisher. It touched me very greatly that Georg too is thinking of memoirs. Ultimately, after all, he and I are the real bearers of our name. If I could only make up my mind to work at my Life. Instead of that I am endlessly reading Ducros' *Rousseau*, am constantly falling asleep over it and cannot get a grip on any of it.

The Isakowitzes' farewell visit last Sunday was fairly depressing, and the leave-taking today at the station was very depressing. It was from the women; over Whitsun the family is staying with relatives in Landeck, while he is returning to his surgery for one more week, will also complete Eva's treatment; mother and daughter are traveling to London via Berlin. The day before yesterday I fetched flowers, which have been left to us, from their liquidated apartment. A repetition of the Blumenfelds' departure. Nothing has changed in the meantime, the power of the Third Reich has only grown ever greater and more secure.

[...]

June 3, Wednesday

[...]

I read the third volume of Ducros to the end and feel just as empty with respect to Rousseau as before. I do not know what will come of it.

In the morning I had an unpleasant and costly experience. Michael, who "ran me in," whom I have long known to be a hysteric and probably also a drinker, but a decent human being nonetheless, who was a pilot during the war, then unemployed for years, and now works as a fitter with the army air units, a man 39 years old, came and immediately burst into violent sobbing. He wanted only "to get things off his chest and say good-bye," he was "finished," he wanted to die, he had his razor with him, he could pay off 15M a week but not raise 150 all at once, word of honor, he wanted to die, he could not bear it anymore, his girl, an illegal abortion, 350 had been paid, the rest now due in May, he wanted to die, his life insurance, and tears and razor and good-bye and 15M a week, and so on for an exhausting hour. I told him that he was the victim of a shady extortion and that he had nothing to fear, but nothing would calm him. I fetched Eva to help me. Finally he got a check for 75M from us, maintained that he and his "bride" would clear the rest of the debt to the man, whom he could not name, by the end of the month, thereafter repay the money to me in weekly installments, had to be given another 22 pfennigs for the tram and left for work consoled—presumably first of all to his favorite drink, a "warm schnapps." Only today I had made a gloomy estimation of my finances, I have almost used up the reserve money from the Iduna and do not know how I can keep the car on my pension alone. And now another 75M, which I shall no doubt never see again. It is always said that "good deeds" are their own reward—I do not feel very rewarded at all. I was certainly the sucker in this affair. But one never knows what a hysteric will think of. If I had kept saying no, he would probably have done no more than drink two warm schnapps to strengthen his nerves. But only probably. There was a little—and not such a little—fear of a madman involved as well. In any case I am rid of my 75M. But I no longer get as upset about money as I did in former years. With the constant uncertainty I have become exceedingly hardened. I merely imagine how many liters of gasoline or apple trees for the garden could have been had for this money. And the man doesn't thank me for it; he thinks I am rich, after all I have a checkbook.

June 9, Tuesday

On Thursday the young Köhlers came to us in tears. His mother has died of a weak heart after an operation, only 52 years old, a good, simple, very generous woman. His father faces instant dismissal if they associate with us, minor railway official living in a company apartment block shared with many other parties. I cannot find it in myself to blame their Johannes so very much, conflict of conscience, tears of nervous exhaustion. (Twice on consecutive days this spectacle of weeping men.) We could not go to the funeral, that could also have been risky for them. I sent a wreath and a letter of condolence.

June 10, Wednesday

If only I could get a handle on Rousseau. I have read my fill of monographs and biographies, I now want to get further into my own reading of
the texts. No doubt everything has already been said. But perhaps some
things look different in the light of contemporary experiences. Except I
lack all confidence and all impetus.

A couple of days ago Rector Kleinstück (courageous!) sent his son, in
the upper fifth at Vitzthum, to me. The boy is interested in French literature, he has read my *Corneille*. I am to advise him further. A quite innocent
lad, moreover without any knowledge of French as a language, because in
Vitzthum they only begin French in the second half of the upper fifth
(which is educational nonsense). I found what he had to say about the
opinions of his class extremely interesting, also his use of language in
doing so. "We are all in the HJ; most of us would dearly like not to be in
it . . . They are 60, 80, 100 percent against the Nazis, only the three stupidest boys, whom no one respects, are entirely for it." To my question,
whether the others were German National (as they were in Vitzthum before 1933), came the serious and immediate response: "No, liberalistic!"
Laughing, I explained to him what a pejorative was and that he had evidently wanted to say liberal. Yes, certainly, but nowadays one always
hears the form "liberalistic." — The next generation will not belong to the
Party, but I shall no longer be here to see the reversal.

June 11, Thursday

The Rousseau torture continues. Now I am sitting in front of the *Confessions*,
with which I am completely familiar through the monographs (and my own
reading in earlier years). With regard to Spiegelberg's visit [. . .] I shall note
what he told me. Delekat, the theologian, has been suspended from his post.
Mutschmann sent for him personally and demanded that his lectures be
more in the spirit of National Socialism. Delekat replied that he could not
consult a Party program for guidance and must follow his conscience.
Thereupon the Governor brought the audience to an end with the three
words: "You are impertinent!"—which was followed by the suspension. The
whole Humanities Section was now being wound up; however a Political
Science Section remained, and prominent and secure within it, Stepun. [. . .]

June 12, Friday

I am now forcing myself further into the *Confessions*, want to keep strictly
to reading the texts for the next one or two months, take notes and then try
my luck. I absolutely must bring the History of the Eighteenth Century to
a conclusion.

[...]

Isakowitz was with us—for the last time—yesterday evening. As well as the imperturbable Frau Schaps, just back from Italy.

[...]

June 14, Sunday midday

[...]

Yesterday we were invited to Heidenau to eat asparagus, which has already become something of a tradition. Beforehand we spent a brief half-hour at the garden show, which was packed; all the stands selling and advertising the most diverse things lent it something of the atmosphere of a fairground. When I see the mass of the people happy and peaceful like this, then I believe less than ever in any change in our political situation. Since the car was waiting in the hospital courtyard, we were not dependent on the last bus and stayed late. Although I was strongly under the influence of alcohol and large sections of the route were pitch dark I got us home very smoothly. I only struggled a little with the entry. It was almost two when we got to bed, and today of course we are very much the worse for wear.

June 20, Saturday, toward evening

Back from Frauenstein, Frau Lehmann phoned us with the news: the Jelskis ante portas. It turned into a difficult week, made doubly exhausting by great heat, and naturally ended with fraying nerves and domestic ill feeling. I fetched both Jelskis from the station at midday; Marta had to go on to Prague in the afternoon, Julius was to wait one or two days for her here. I took Marta to the station in the afternoon, then we went for a drive with Julius to Freiberg and looked a little at the town and the cathedral (from the outside). Nevertheless another 50-mile drive and great weariness in the evening and no opportunity for proper rest. A bed was made up for Julius in my room, he rose early, wanted to be entertained and provided with breakfast, then disappeared into town, but was back after lunch. This time we took him for a drive, via Kipsdorf, to Oberbärenburg and went for a short walk there. Again 50 miles, again the strain of the evening, of the next morning. Again a brief respite. I took him to the station on the Wednesday afternoon. He has become a frail old man, too frail, really, for 69 years of age, walks with difficulty using a cane. He is not unpleasant and unaffectedly grateful for any friendliness. The fondness for Hitler, which Marta maintained he had, has evidently disappeared completely. He cannot help the fact that he was such a strain on our nerves.

Thursday was a day of rest as it were, and for the first time I felt that I shall get something out of Rousseau after all. But Marta arrived in Dresden at midday on Friday, en route from Prague, and, of course, given the blazing heat, immediately allowed herself to be persuaded to spend the night. I picked her up from the station at half past five, shortly before seven we went for a drive toward Meissen, took the Nossen turning, because the sun was dazzling, found ourselves on a bad road, had to turn around and somehow got home via Wilsdruff and Tharandt. On this stretch, Eva and I had an argument, for the most trivial reason, simply because our nerves were strained. An unpleasant evening; then today I had to get up at five, maneuver the car out by myself, take Marta to the seven o'clock train, and afterward make our breakfast. I slept for the rest of the morning, often on the settee, otherwise while attempting to read. Not until the afternoon did I come to grips with the Reveries of the Solitary Walker; but the wretched, pointless ill feeling with Eva remained, the exhaustion and the many painful inflammations remained too. My pleasure in driving is somewhat subdued for the moment. Marta's report from Prague is very gloomy. No one any longer believes in a change in the situation. Her son Willy cannot get into Russia despite his Communism, has neither work nor sufficient assistance in Prague, can no longer be supported from Germany, since all export of money has been stopped, sells bedbug powder and studies the flute. [. . .]

June 26, Friday

Since we went to Oybin on Sunday, [. . .] I have not driven at all until today, and today only to make an essential trip into town. The reason is the great lack of money; I hardly know how to keep going until next payday. And today when I at last wanted to have a tire patched, it transpired (at Schlecht's, the big specialist repair shop in Trompeterstrasse) that it was necessary to change one tire immediately, a second "after a couple of hundred miles." That means 34M twice over. I do not know how we'll pull through, the more so since work on garage and driveway is still not finished. This ever increasing pressure, in addition the ever more painful eye problems, drain my spirits. In earlier years too I was frequently short of money; but then I was, so to speak, an honorable poor devil. This time my situation is infinitely more unpleasant. A house, a car and yet I do not know how to pay for the simplest and most essential things. It looks like a fraudulent bankruptcy. But getting rid of the car would make hardly any difference either. It would fetch less than 300M, and I have to pay the big insurance policy by the end of the year. Above all I miscalculated the costs of constructing garage and driveway, and above all the running costs of the car.

A couple of days ago Railway Inspector Köhler turned up unannounced after nine o'clock in the evening and under cover of darkness to thank us for our expression of sympathy. His son collapsed at his mother's grave, and is resting with relatives in the country, Ellen Köhler has joined him, and the father, the one who is most affected, sits here alone and does his duty. He is a good, simple and courageous man, whom we both like very much. He remained for a long time, drank coffee with us and evidently left in a somewhat better frame of mind than he had arrived in. "In the course of my work I see so many bad marriages, where people would so like to be free of one another—and we got on so well together, and then we . . ." At the same time the man obviously has a very firm Christian faith. And apart from that, traditional petty bourgeois custom provides him with support, comfort and things to do.

[. . .]

June 28, Sunday

Isakowitz finally took his leave of us on Thursday evening; he was very tired and nervous—a new tablecloth suffered the consequences, in a single movement he poured a whole cup of coffee over it—but nevertheless in high spirits. Because at 45 years of age he is once again making a new start, because he is moving from servitude and lawlessness to humane and civilized conditions. Yet it was visibly hard for him to leave Germany. He philosophized a great deal and talked about art, with somewhat limited knowledge and clarity, but with much interest and an evident moral foundation. I heard with satisfaction, that despite the "customs examination," he has still managed to get some property safely abroad, and that other émigrés evidently also repeatedly find opportunities to do so. The most curious comic feature of the present political situation is that at this very moment France is ruled by a Jew. And that Blum expresses himself very courteously toward Hitler (not without sous-entendus), and that the German press has to be very courteous toward him and passes over his Jewishness in silence since he has come to power (whereas the Russian Litvinov is regularly called Litvinov-Finkelstein).

Ever more frequent desire to write Memoirs, individual details rise to the surface more and more. On a very hot day recently we were reluctantly waiting for "Uncle," the old workman who is Frau Lange's uncle; cementing the walls of the garage access is an incredible strain on Eva, and a cooler day would have been more suitable. Uncle had not arrived by nine. "Perhaps he won't come—it looks very hazy down in the city and the weather might turn." But he did come at nine, and cement had to be brought up from Zwickauer Strasse in the car, and Eva had to toil away again until late in the evening, and it was beastly. [. . .]

A modest excursion to the Müglitztal is planned for today; on the twenty-ninth we shall give ourselves the new wheel and a visit to the cinema as presents. We want to save on food and on the maid, in order to keep the car.

Emile for the past week. Everything looks different if one reads it oneself. I do not find Rousseau more likable, but certainly more interesting.

July 2, Thursday

[...]

On Monday, the twenty-ninth, the heat was very great, and we spent the day peacefully at home, Eva in the garden, I, as far as I could, with *Emile*. But I just had to take a look at a couple of pages of my diary for 1904. I simply cannot get it into my head that I am already so old. — We wanted to have a quiet evening at the cinema.

But in the afternoon, Anna, the last and most intelligent of our Wends, visited us unexpectedly with her carpenter brother. She now has a situation in Bautzen and has not been to see us for several years. It is nice how these girls remain loyal. The Wends are all good Catholics, and so there is a comforting community of political despair.

Then there was a telephone call to say that Gusti and Karl Wieghardt were back for a few hours; we should come to them in the evening for coffee.

July 5

We had not seen the Wieghardts since February—Karl in Göttingen, Gusti in Copenhagen—but nothing in the situation, conversations, cordiality had changed, it was as if we had last been sitting down together only yesterday. In Copenhagen Gusti had looked up the writer Karl Federn, whose beautifully illustrated but otherwise worthless *Dante* Father gave me as a present some thirty years ago, with the remark that we were in some way related to the Federns. The old gentleman sent me the address of a London agency, Curtis Brown Ltd., which would surely find me a foreign publishing house. I sent a detailed letter and received a reply today by return of post: ". . . *too specialized . . . afraid there is nothing we can do to help you.*" That hit me very hard and doubly so. For one thing: I find it ever harder to work without hope and only for myself; I am not confident that these books—unprinted and their scholarship out-of-date—will retain their interest. For another: It is becoming ever more essential for me to earn money. Quite without warning there arrived a demand for payment of arrears: local property tax 1934–36: 42M. I hardly know where to scrape it together. And an unexpected expense like that comes again and again and is added to the rest. I do not dare undertake any further excursions with the car; 3 gallons of gasoline, 3.60M, are too great an expenditure. I asked Ellen Wengler, who visited us, whether she could increase the mortgage on the house, so that it would certainly fall to her if ghettoization is introduced once the Olympics are over. She has no cash available. On July 1 we went for a drive with the Wieghardts and then they ate with us in the evening. [...]

Every day my depressed study of Rousseau is interrupted by sleep, every day serious pains in my eyes. Once to the garden show with Eva.

In the evenings Eva works very late in the garden, so we rarely get around to reading aloud. [...]

Ellen Wengler said recently: "If the regime falls—will things be any different for us? Perhaps a little less false—but otherwise?" — The saddest thing about it is that everyone now reckons only with extreme governments: NSDAP or Communism—as if there were nothing in between.

July 8, Wednesday

For days now very great sultry heat. The work on Rousseau crawls forward even more slowly than usual. *Emile*—notes.

On Sunday evening at the Wieghardts; we see each other a lot, since it is only a matter of a month.

[...]

After a long silence a long letter from Blumenfeld in Lima; I envy them, and they feel like exiles. With Grete Blumenfeld's reflections and descriptions of nature, I always feel that they have come out of a book. Everything is cultured cliché, but still a cliché. Perhaps I am doing her an injustice; probably I would be unable to write any differently. He, Blumenfeld, is always succinct and matter-of-fact.

This afternoon I returned all the books belonging to the Romance Languages Department, two briefcases full, which I shall sorely miss and which will now lie around unused. The department has been finally wound up, Papesch given notice. Wengler appears to be keeping his post for the time being, presumably because Italy is politically friendly. Written on the door of my office now: History Department. The Romance Languages library room next door still bears the old sign, and it was here that I found Wengler and Fräulein Papesch. I said to Papesch: "You will find it odd at this moment, but things can change, and if I ever return to my post, I shall call upon you again." In such tragicomical fashion I kept my authority. It was not a very pleasant half hour for me. Papesch and Fräulein Mey want to visit us; I said to Fräulein Papesch: "I shall be very pleased if you come, but I do not expect anyone to sacrifice themselves and am not inviting anyone."

July 16, Thursday

A "Property Tax Re-Assessment Notice," going back to April 1934, demands 41M 95Pf, a sewerage charge comes to 10M 80Pf. These sums, which in themselves are small, are almost a catastrophe for us. As Frau Lehmann is on holiday, we have not taken on any other part-time help and wash up ourselves, we are careful with every penny and with every pint of gasoline; it would be tragicomical—a man with a house and car of his own!—if it were not so wretchedly depressing and therefore tragic after all and if it were not getting worse month by month. A kind of stoicism, apathy in a word, has befallen me: perhaps some kind of change will take place; and if not, then we will simply perish. We are both 54 and have had quite a full life—if it ends sooner or later, makes very little difference [. . .]. And absurdity or disgrace? Those are ideas from a bygone age. We were respected people. What are we now? And what will we be in two months time, once the Olympics are over and it is open season on the Jews and once the Swiss trial against the Gustloff murderer is under way?

Spitzer's post in Istanbul has finally been given to Auerbach. On the other hand a tiny possibility of publishing the Voltaire volume and of receiving a small amount for it has arisen, which would then postpone the financial catastrophe for a couple of weeks or months. And in these few weeks, after all, I might be saved by a miracle in my personal circumstances, or in the general situation to which it is linked. [. . .]

I am working very little, more precisely not at all. In 1927, in the Deutsche Bücherei in Leipzig, I made very detailed notes, on about 50 typewritten pages, on *Nouvelle Héloïse*. But I have gotten stuck rereading the novel. It will take many weeks before I begin to write the Rousseau section. I have lost faith in the meaning and value of my activity. Question as above: What was I, what am I?

A postcard greeting on Eva's birthday from Frau Schaps on Lago Maggiore. The stamp shows the Capitol in Rome and bears the words: Dimillenario Orazione. Stet Capitolium fulgens. Likewise in this country every little dump celebrates the 300, 600, 900, 1000 years of its existence. And the publisher Markus, my new Voltaire hope, has a list for "German Customs and Traditions" (formerly under German or at the outside Folk Studies). But with the Italians it sounds more natural and has more de quoi. A little while ago, when Mussolini was Germany's enemy, he said: We had a tremendous literature, when the Germans did not have an alphabet yet. — Admittedly today the Duce is Germany's great friend, and since the day before yesterday (peace with Vienna) there is something like a Triple Alliance again, and England courts it, and Hitler is more powerful than Kaiser Wilhelm II was before the war.

No doubt Italian Fascism is no less reprehensible than National Socialism and I only find it less repugnant because it does not ask questions about blood and does not persecute the Jews. We are reading a German translation (borrowed from Gusti Wieghardt) of Ignazio Silone's *Fontamara*. Published in Zürich, the novel is denunciation and satire. The Fascist government's deception of and sins against the "Cafoni" in the Fucino, exploited peasants and rural laborers in southern Italy. Mutatis mutandis horribly similar to the methods of the NSDAP. The unscrupulous rule of a party supported by big business, petty bourgeoisie and criminal elements and which mendaciously stimulates and enforces popular assent and popular enthusiasm. The most grotesque scene in the book is an interrogation of opinions that Blackshirts impose on the unsuspecting peasants. "Who should live?" goes the question, and the Cafoni know nothing about the Duce and Fascism. One replies: "All should live!" and is listed as a "Liberal." Another says: "Down with the thieves!" and is marked down as an "Anarchist." All of them are "refractory," which in this country would probably be called "subversive" or Jewish.

[...]

Again and again I feel that the most terrible thing about our situation is that one appears to be stuck with the alternative Communism-Fascism. What are France, England, USA doing?

A card from Betty Klemperer, who has settled in Cleveland (Ohio); Wolfgang, her youngest, has passed his medical examination there and is working in a hospital in Cleveland.

There was no money to buy Eva something for her birthday. We celebrated by driving to the cinema the evening before and by going for a long drive on the Sunday itself. As the Wieghardts were going halves on the trip, we could be ambitious in our goal and afford 8 gallons of gasoline and a half-gallon of oil.

[...]

The Birthday Excursion to Torgau on July 12

Uncertain weather, which held up well all day, the car always open. At the Wieghardts in Schrammsteinstrasse at eleven. Through the city by way of Kötzschenbroda, Coswig to Meissen, over the Elbe bridge and the same fine view of the river and back to the cathedral as on our Leipzig trip. Gusti needs the Elbe and the life of the bargees for a children's book; so the watchword was: as much of the Elbe as possible! We continued to Riesa at a little distance from the river. We have often crossed the big Elbe bridge there on the train; this time we stood on it and allowed river and ships to make an impression on us. A pretty, calm, simple landscape, river meadows, no hills at all. A couple of barges, but we could not discern the river harbor. After taking a wrong turn we found ourselves on the road to Leipzig and followed it as far as Oschatz, where we had liked the Café Zierold so much once before. We sat here for an hour very cheerfully and in terms of our mood this was the high point of the day. After that an uneventful drive to Torgau. A middling town, like dozens of others we have seen. But with a surprisingly huge and beautiful castle. [...] We left Torgau at around four, and now it was probably Gusti's Elbe mania that led us astray and ultimately added bitterness to what otherwise had been sweet. We drove over the river bridge and a little way upstream beside the Elbe, which here looked fairly insignificant. After that we found ourselves on increasingly bad village roads: mud, potholes, virtual shell craters, out of which dirty water splashed over us like a heavy sea. The car bumped, turned at an angle to the road, jumped, skidded: The engine or the tires could have been damaged or the car could have turned over. Then a few miles farther on the road was closed, we turned with difficulty and had to crawl back the whole hellish way. We had wasted an hour and a lot of nerves. As soon as we were on a good road, at five, and not very far at all from Torgau, I let the car go, almost without a break, for a good two hours at 35 and often even at 45 mph. That was pleasant, but very exhausting. Woods cared for like a park, villas, a spa hotel: Bad Liebenwerda. The next larger place: Elsterwerda; the next: Grossenhain; the next: Radeberg—now it was only a matter of driving and making headway. Finally at Moritzburg the price for placing myself under too great a strain: in front of me a very slow car, I hesitate to overtake it for a long time, then finally when I risk it, I find myself at the top of a steep gradient, I brake too quickly, and am too quickly on the right-hand side again in front of the overtaken car and evidently put the man at considerable risk. Nothing worse happens, but now the other driver races past me, shakes his fist, shouts something, and stays in front of me in the middle of the road, going at a crawl, until we get to Dresden. There he rushes up to a policeman and reports me. The policeman comes up: "Have you been drinking beer?" Fortunately for me, my accuser behaves so wildly, insults me, claims I had been going at 60 mph, my companion had been asleep, my brakes were broken, he had driven into the back of my car—and yet for all that cannot point to the least damage. I defend myself energetically, the other driver should have braked on the gradient, and reject all his accusations, if the police officer is talking about cautioning anybody, then he should caution the other too. It is obvious that I make a better impression on the policeman and public than the enraged, thick-set accuser; he says something about "Jew talk," against which you can't win an argument, and drives off; I am also allowed to continue, and until today, Friday, nothing further has ensued. (The policeman said right away, if nothing has happened, then the police can at most issue a caution.) Nevertheless the evening was completely ruined for me. We reached Gusti's toward nine; I was so tired I was able to eat very little of her very nice supper, and I found the journey home an effort. We were in bed shortly before twelve, we had driven 156 miles exactly. The next day we were both quite knocked out and left the car in the garage.

[...]

July 17, Friday

Susi Hildebrandt got in touch after quite a few months. She had been traveling for a while; did we want to visit her? I said she should hear the reason for our refusal in person and come to us. She arrived for coffee yesterday in her vast old-fashioned 6-foot-high touring car and stayed until evening. Her father was in Münchner Platz for ten weeks and then released. He is a Stahlhelm man and out of favor, embezzlement by a company employee appears to have been the pretext for an act of revenge. He was interrogated once, after he had been held for ten weeks. His daughters are in despair over his imprudent expressions of outrage. Susi Hildebrandt came from the golf club; she said there was hardly a single member who had not already been in prison. For her, the daughter of a big industrialist and of an aristocratic mother, there is no difference between National Socialism and Bolshevism. She says that opinions among the officers of the army are completely divided, there are the most enthusiastic supporters and the most decided opponents of Hitler. But she had also encountered fierce hostility to Hitler among SS officers. She no longer believes in a turn for the better.

This morning, with a recommendation from "Vosslaiir," I was visited by Edmondo Cione, a little librarian from Florence, amico del Croce, antifascista. Would like to be a lecturer in Germany, did not know that I had lost my post. I recommended him to Gelzer in Jena. He will see if he can be of assistance to me in Italy. He told me how Auerbach came to the Istanbul appointment. He had already been in Florence for a year, and Croce provided an opinion on him. [. . .] Now Auerbach is brushing up his French in Geneva. And Spitzer had been saying in Italy that only someone who could really speak French would get the appointment! If I go off to Geneva for a couple of months then I too could "really speak French" again. — Cione says people had been very anti-Fascist in Italy, but the League of Nations sanctions and then the victory in Abyssinia had greatly strengthened the Duce's position.

July 18, Saturday

The Wieghardts here yesterday evening. I talked about the Hildebrandts. Gusti, fairly self-satisfied: "Do they occasionally arrest an industrialist? That goes down well with the workers. In any case, they only put the posh people, who have it easy, in Münchner Platz, they don't get beaten there." She cannot think like a human being anymore, but only in the Communist Party mold. I am almost pleased that she is going back to Denmark in August.

Syntax of the Third Reich? Trude Öhlmann writes that she is arriving tomorrow on a "KDF"—Strength Through Joy—train. [. . .]

The heat at the moment is extraordinary, 89 degrees in the shade, did dishes from half past eleven till half past two; Eva washed up, I dried, and polished the knives. We are, in fact, completely proletarianized, substantially more proletarianized than Gusti—but we do not feel ourselves to be proletarians and keep our freedom of thought.

July 20, Monday

[. . .]

The KDF train arrived at Neustädter station at ten; we waited at both exits. The people poured out in dense crowds and were met by SA stewards: Zittau to the left!—Bautzen this way!—Leipzig straight ahead! Trude tells us: For 4.50M her Leipzigers get a return ticket, lunch and a conducted tour of the town and of an exhibition. She had also been to Norway (for 55M) on a ship of the Hamburg-Süd line; more precisely she saw the Norwegian coast, since there was no disembarking, whether because of shortage of foreign currency or to avoid contact with foreigners. At any rate these KDF undertakings are prodigious circuses.

July 26, Sunday . . . No, July 27, Monday

Meanwhile eight particularly disagreeable days have gone by, and yesterday, Sunday, on which there was as little writing as there was driving, was especially prominent in this respect.

A week ago on Sunday we went for a very nice and successful 60-mile drive.

[. . .]

I would have put all this down in greater detail, had not all kinds of unpleasantness occurred in the meantime. Lange, the chatterbox, whose wife cleans for Gusti Wieghardt, reported at length how many nasty and truly defamatory statements Gusti had made about my driving, while to my face she was very much in favor of the Torgau tour. Karl had vomited, he had been so seasick because of my bumpy driving, he had several times wanted to grab the steering wheel from me, I had been making such bad mistakes, it was irresponsible that driving licenses are handed out so carelessly, etc. Because of such falseness I have once again broken off all relations with Gusti Wieghardt. Anyway her narrow-minded Communism had already been getting on our nerves.

For two weeks Eva has been plagued by headaches, for one week by pains in her mouth, she has developed a nasty abscess on her gums.

July 30, Thursday

That resulted in a couple of very distressing days. Finally a dentist had to be consulted. Isakowitz had recommended a Jewish dentist to us but the recommendation had been so lukewarm and hesitant that it almost amounted to a warning. Heidenau gave us an address: Dr. Kunstmann, Reichsstrasse. I made an appointment for midday on Monday. Before that I had to go to the bank. As I am coming back and gently turning into Adolf Hitler Strasse from Residenzstrasse in second gear, the car suddenly jolts forward several yards onto the pavement, whereupon I brake violently. Now it loses gasoline and is immovable. First Weller, the gardener, helped me get it onto the road, then I fetched Eva, and instead of being driven gently to the dentist, she pushed the car, until I could let it roll as far as our front door. I was doubly lucky despite the accident: Her abscess had burst

in the meantime, and I had caused no harm on the pavement, nor had anyone seen me. Through Vogel, a mechanic was quickly sent up, and in a
quarter of an hour the mischief had been dealt with. Float wires had got
stuck—it happens sometimes—then the car shoots forward a bit, and then
the engine floods. "Is there anything one can do to prevent it happening?"—"No."—"And if I do any harm because of it?"—"You are to blame
because the car was not in proper working order, and you should have
known that."—"Can one know before it happens?"—"No!"—Sometimes I
feel the miseries of driving very strongly, and in recent days I have been
very nervous; but then again and again it also becomes obvious what a
wonderful thing it is.

In the afternoon we drove to the dentist; an elderly, very taciturn, very
careful gentleman, in every respect almost comically the opposite of the
animated Isakowitz; but clearly an extremely painstaking man, also to our
liking in another respect—a picture of Hitler is nowhere to be seen. He
carefully cleaned the wound and brought Eva relief. (Meanwhile we have
been there today for the second time, and the treatment will be further
drawn out—which will do nothing to lessen our money worries.)

[. . .]

Yesterday shortly before evening at the flower show for a while, today
we went there again from the dentist (. . .), this time to the special section
for related industrial products: greenhouses, sprinklers, etc. While we
were there we heard the closing session of the Leisure Congress in Hamburg, expressions of thanks in very broken German, one in unpleasantly
hissed and nasal-sounding Chinese, then a long speech by Goebbels. I
heard the most poisonous and mendacious of all Nazis for the first time
and was doubly surprised at his bass and at the pastoral unctuousness
and heartfelt tone of his delivery. Going by his face and opinions I had believed he must speak in a high, sharp and brash voice. But he must have
been speaking in his usual manner because a woman who was passing
said to her companion: But that's Goebbels! [. . .]

Last week Gehrig was here for an afternoon; to discuss a planned South
American trip. We have not been in contact for a very long time. He made
a very good impression on both of us; calmer and less authoritarian than
before. He too is no longer interested in prophecies: It can still last a very
long time, it can come to an end very suddenly. He told me that at the beginning of November '18 the Crown Prince of Saxony had asked him what
he thought of the situation on the home front; he, Gehrig, had replied, the
workers were no doubt discontented, but he thought a revolution was out
of the question.

Yesterday and today I worked through Rousseau's Encyclopedia article
Economie politique; whole passages could be from Hitler's speeches.

The essential features of my study are clear to me: the flight from the
present and from oneself in three divergent directions: to Nature, to God,
to the Spartan state, the prostitution of reason in the service of subjective
feeling, Romantic longing, the shaping of judgment in the spirit of the

eighteenth century, both formally and substantially, rococo voluptuous-
ness accompanied by a pathologically overwrought sexuality, the obsession with virtue as antidote and self-deception. I shall read for many more
weeks yet, before I get around to writing.

August 7, Friday

Yesterday the heaviest blow since my dismissal: Markus, Breslau with
whom I had been involved in promising negotiations, has now rejected
the Voltaire book after all, and, what is more—and this is the really
wretched thing about it—entirely for reasons to do with the book trade,
which are undoubtedly correct and which must be equally valid for every
other publisher: In more favorable times, not enough buyers had been
found in the space of eleven years to sell out the first edition of the more
marketable nineteenth century—who would now summon up enough interest for a scholarly tome about the eighteenth century? Commercially it
was an impossibility. It is hardly a question of vanity. After all this is my
life's work which has been deprived of influence and even existence, and
I now feel as if I really am buried alive. At the same time I am also tormented by the financial aspect of the matter. I had been hoping for a couple of hundred marks at least; but nothing and less than nothing; the
certainty of being cut off from all means of earning money. We do not have
the 50M to put cement down on the veranda above the garage, we literally
have to count every penny, and we are no longer young enough to accept
such privation easily.

In accordance with the law of inertia I still continue poring over the
Contrat social.
[...]

August 13, Thursday

[...]
The Olympics will end next Sunday, the NSDAP Party Rally is being
heralded, an explosion is imminent, and naturally, they will first of all take
things out on the Jews. So much pressure has built up. The Gustloff trial is
coming up in September; the Danzig business has only been postponed,
our Polish "allies" have made the French general Gamelin a marshal,
Mussolini has pocketed Abbyssinia scot-free—and the Spanish Civil War
has been under way for a couple of weeks. In Barcelona four Germans
have been "murdered" as martyrs of National Socialism by a revolutionary court, and even before that, they were saying the German-Jewish émigrés were stirring up hatred against Germany there. God knows, what
will come of it all, but surely and as always a new measure against the
Jews. I do not believe that we shall keep our house. Marta tells us from

Prague that there and in England they are expecting war as early as autumn—but how often have they believed that in Prague. The political aspect changes almost daily, it would be tremendously interesting, if it were not so dismal. The third Napoleon began his war of desperation over Spain—but how much of an analogy is there? I hear repeatedly, the last time from Forbrig, the teacher: Hitler really wants peace for another one or two years, because our armaments will not be ready before then. But: Mr. Léon Blum cannot be ignorant of what every child in Germany knows. Are they so stupid in France that they're just waiting to be led to the slaughter? But: Why have they taken everything lying down so far? In France from Germany, in England from Italy? Everything is completely opaque and dark. Probably no one, not even in government, knows the real strengths, checks and moods.

The Olympics, which are now ending, are doubly repugnant to me. (1) as an absurd overestimation of sport; the honor of a nation depends on whether a fellow citizen can jump four inches higher than all the rest. In any case, a Negro from the United States jumped the highest of all and the Jewess Helene Meyer won the fencing silver medal for Germany (I don't know which is more shameless, her participating as a German of the Third Reich, or the fact that her achievement is claimed for the Third Reich). In the *Berliner Illustrierte* of August 6, a Doctor Kurt Zentner writes a serious and, so to speak, educational article: "Outsiders Without a Chance (Only Hard Training Gets Results)." He relates that many sports heroes have begun with "pitiful initial results," but then by training to the utmost achieved the greatest success, for example, "the world's most brilliant tennis player, Borotra," and he concludes his article (in the style of the moralizing weekly, the *Spectator*), once an unknown young Corsican sat in the military school at Brienne and told himself every day, he wanted to be a field marshal, and became the Emperor Napoleon. No doubt in England and America sports have always been uncommonly and perhaps excessively valued, but probably never so one-sidedly, and at the same time with such a disparaging of the intellectual aspect as in this country now [. . .]; it must also be borne in mind that these sporting countries do not have universal compulsory military service. And (2) I find the Olympics so odious because they are not about sports—in this country I mean—but are an entirely political enterprise. "German renaissance through Hitler" I read recently. It's constantly being drummed into the country and into foreigners that here one is witnessing the revival, the flowering, the new spirit, the unity, steadfastness and magnificence, pacific too, of course, spirit of the Third Reich, which lovingly embraces the whole world. The chanted slogans on the streets have been banned (for the duration of the Olympics), Jew-baiting, bellicose sentiments, everything offensive has disappeared from the papers until August 16, and the swastika flags are hanging everywhere day and night until then too. In articles written in English, the attention of "our guests" is repeatedly drawn to how peaceably and pleasantly things are proceeding here, while in Spain "Communist hordes" are committing pillage and murder. And we have everything in abundance. But the butcher here and the greengrocer complain about shortages and price rises because everything has to be sent to Berlin. And the "hundreds of thousands" in Berlin are brought in by "Kraft durch Freude"; the foreigners, before whom Germany is supposed to be "like an open book"—but who chose and prepared the passages at which the book lies open?—are not very numerous and the landlords in Berlin are complaining.

A new phrase has appeared in the papers and presumably comes from France. The French Popular Front is starting a "crusade of ideas," for the Spanish Communists and against Fascism. That is quite shocking, our press responds, scandalized, National Socialism doesn't do anything like that, it wants every nation to be happy in its own way, it doesn't carry on any propaganda outside Germany. This is the most loathsome feature of the swastika crusade, that it is conducted hypocritically and in secret. "We" are not conducting a crusade, "we" do not shed blood either, we are completely peaceable people and only want to be left in peace! And at the same time not the smallest opportunity for propaganda is missed. At the Reich garden show there is a pretty display of mark coins and notes. The cases showing the inflation period bear the inscription: "Documents of an insane time." Everyone can draw his own conclusions about the health and flowering of economic life today.

[. . .]

On Monday we were visited by Fräulein Papesch, who has in the meantime also received her dismissal notice from the university. The period of her quiet sympathy for the Third Reich is evidently completely over, she too knows about the general discontent, but she too is unable to answer the question How much longer?—She knows the Schwartenberg and wants to take us there; i.e., we have to take her with us on a car trip.

I learned from Frau Schaps that Raab has died suddenly (embolism after operation), in Berlin, 47 years old. He always gave me an impression of great liveliness and youthful agility. I very much envied the way that after his dismissal he immediately managed to create a different job and life for himself—he was an economist, quite far to the right. I once had a fierce argument with him at the Blumenfelds because he wanted support for the German Nationals, who were allied to the Nazis. I felt ancient compared to him. In one of Schnitzler's plays, a very old man feels a kind of triumph when he learns of the death of a younger man. I thought of it despite myself and while experiencing genuine sorrow. Raab was married three times, the last wife is Jewish. The picture of an officer killed in the war is supposed to have hung over his desk. When asked, he explained candidly, "the first husband of my second wife." I think also of his silent and amiably boring Angora tomcat Eilhart, who was once boarded with the Blumenfelds.

On her return from Prague Marta stayed with us from Tuesday until Wednesday afternoon. A considerable strain, since of course there is no domestic help, since in the great heat I always had to be in *full dress*, since

Marta constantly wanted to be entertained and taken for drives. [. . .]
Apart from that Marta gives the impression of suffering greatly. Excessively aged, sluggish, gone to seed. She says that Wally has been ill in bed
for a month. Gallbladder and evidently suspected cancer. She talks about
the Sussmanns' dire predicament. She envies us because things are still
going very well for us (everyone believes that about everyone else). Her
youngest, Willy, is leading a precarious existence in Prague. He plays and
studies the oboe, he is unable to earn anything, given the present currency
regulations it is hardly possible to support him from Berlin; he cannot
come back, since he is at risk as a Communist.

[. . .]

August 16, Sunday

Yesterday afternoon—we had just returned very tired and hot from the
flower show, I had peeled off and was making coffee—there appeared in
cycling clothes, with sandals and shorts, gray with green cuffs, a yodeling
lad, Wengler, and stayed for hours. Everything spoke against him, but he
is such a thoroughly decent fellow that one finds him likable even at the
most catastrophic moment. He had spent several weeks on holiday in
Italy. He thinks Fascism or rather the Italian Fascists more human than the
Nazis. He relates as vouched-for, that a few weeks before the beginning of
the Spanish counterrevolution, General San Jurjo, who was later killed,
had discussions in the Adlon Hotel in Berlin and that there are German officers with Franco's Moroccan troops. He believes the victory or defeat of
the Spanish Popular Front decisive for the whole of Europe and says quite
seriously, thoughtfully, without any pathos, as with a weighed-down conscience: "One should really go there and help them; but I can't even
shoot." Later he complained how disagreeable it is for him to start teaching again on Tuesday.

That is Wengler. Johannes Kühn, however, whom I always took to be a
man of integrity and a genuine thinker, professor of history Johannes
Kühn has written a short article in the Sunday edition of the *Dresdener NN*
(August 16) on the one-hundred-fiftieth anniversary of the death of Frederick the Great. In a hundred lines he twice calls him emphatically "a
Nordic-Germanic man." His philosophy is out-of-date and unimportant;
behind it stands the Germanic belief in things higher and beyond this
world; his inclination toward French culture is the northern German's typical longing for form and the south. — If one day the situation were reversed and the fate of the vanquished lay in my hands, then I would let all
the ordinary folk go and even some of the leaders, who might perhaps
after all have had honorable intentions and not know what they were
doing. But I would have all the intellectuals strung up, and the professors
three feet higher than the rest; they would be left hanging from the lampposts for as long as was compatible with hygiene.

August 20, Thursday

There is some kind of analogy in the current European situation to Machiavelli's thesis that the unification of Italy foundered because of the Papal State, which was too weak to achieve this unification by its own efforts, but also too strong for any other power to accomplish unification against it. The powers of Liberalism, i.e., basically of reflective reason—France and England—are too weak to ward off both radicalisms, Bolshevism and National Socialism, by their own efforts; they have to gain the support of one of the two, in order to stand firm against the other, and must at every moment ask themselves, which of the two is the lesser evil. England and France do not at every moment give the same answer to the question, and that, in turn, leads to frictions between the two powers. So there is a constant guessing game as to what is going to happen, which alliances are being formed. In 1914 the situation was clear and unambiguous, the present one is very complex.

August 24, Monday

The Spanish hate campaign has taken second place to the Russian hate campaign agitation. Every day more disturbing news about Russian preparations for war with Germany. Does our side want war, have things got to the point that they must have it, as a diversion, a way out? In recent days I have heard expressions of extreme hostility, unrest and alarm from very diverse circles: Natscheff, the lending-library man, who until now believed in peace and the durability of the present regime, talked of widespread disaffection, of the possibility of war. Ulbrich, the worthy butcher, complained bitterly. "Instead of people who know what they are doing, there are Party veterans everywhere, a barber and a cucumber dealer are in charge of the abbatoir—and the farmers are uncooperative, and at 35 Herr Darré is too young to be the farmers' leader—and the expense of the Olympic buildings in Berlin, as if we were made of money—and the meat shortage . . ." I asked him: "Are you a National Socialist?" He, carefully, as he no doubt thought: "Under compulsion, yes."—Michael, the mechanic, employed at the military airfield and having sworn loyalty: "I would jump out with a parachute, to go over to the Russians; I would make a red flag, even if I had to cut open my veins to dye the cloth!"

Yesterday evening Annemarie and Dressel were here after a very long gap. Their frame of mind unchanged; nor do they know anyone who is contented; they admittedly are fairly much without hope.

More news from Marta about Wally's illness. Very gloomy, almost hopeless. I find my own involuntary coldness loathsome. Always the ghastly "Hurrah, I'm still alive," and then the calculation, how much time may still be granted me. And in addition as the latest problem, the question whether and how one would drive to Berlin to the funeral. I see it all in front of me in every detail, it is a kind of obsession which I cannot get rid of. Yet I really feel for Wally, although for many years she has been a complete stranger to me.

[...]

August 29, Saturday

The fighting in Spain has become ever more intense and ever more clearly rather more than a Spanish conflict. A couple of days ago a conscription period of two years was announced. So the tension grows from day to day—but this is the fourth year it has been increasing like this or in a similar way—why should it not continue for another dozen years without an explosion? Besides in Kriebstein recently I was thinking about the German army. As everyone knows, the Republic left Germany defenseless and Adolf Hitler created the new army. Except that in the Republic the Reichswehr trained every private to be an NCO and every NCO to be a lieutenant and thereby created the framework of the future army and made it possible; except that beyond the permitted 100,000 men, the Republic uninterruptedly trained men and thereby accomplished the most difficult part: the beginning of the military revival. I was able to follow it all in the directives to the universities, secret documents that as a senator I read for five years, and in the confidential oral reports during senate sittings. Who will testify to that one day? (If only I could still manage to write my Memoirs!)

On Wednesday we were at Frau Schaps for supper and met the Gerstles there; he was about to go on a business trip to Paris. What I find unfortunate about the Gerstles, is that given the alternative National Socialism–Bolshevism they prefer National Socialism. Both are repellent to me, I see their close relationship (which Gerstle does too by the way), but the racial idea of National Socialism seems to me the most bestial (in the literal sense of the word).—[...] A fairly contented airmail letter from the Blumenfelds in Lima was read out. We heard of a friend of Grete Blumenfeld—with whom we are acquainted—that she has opened a salon de beauté in Johannesburg. Of Erika Ballin-Dreyfuss, it was reported that she too is already making a living in South Africa, while her husband is still in London preparing for the test that allows him to practice as a doctor. So many people are building a new life for themselves somewhere, and we are waiting here, with our hands tied. Streicher is speaking in the city today. The preparation for this "major event" has been preceded by all the features of an election campaign: posters, broad banners stretched across streets, processions, drummers and slogans chanted in chorus in the streets. [...] Today the newspaper prints his own words: "Who fights the Jew, wrestles with the devil." I often very much doubt whether we shall actually survive the Third Reich. And yet we go on living in the same old way. Despite the terrible money problems that have us ever more by the throat, we have now also given Lange the job of laying cement on the terrace above the garage. That will cost another 50M. My fears as to how I shall get by grow ever stronger; but the building cannot simply be left for the winter in such an unfinished state. If the worst comes to the worst the dentist will just have to wait.

Because of lack of money we only rarely go for a drive now, every tiny bit of damage to the car is a cause for despair. [. . .]

We have promised to drive tomorrow to the village of Bucha by Oschatz, where Trude Öhlmann is holidaying with her boy. That may turn out to be nice, but will cost about ten marks.

After many months, Anna Mey, the secretary at the TU, telephoned to ask whether she could visit us. I said I was aware of the regulations, she should not put herself at risk, I did not want any sacrifices made for me.

We were at the cinema. Kiepura: *Im Sonnenschein* [In the Sunshine] [. . .] That same evening we saw fighting in Spain in the newsreel; it made a great impression on me, to see Popular Front troops ("red hordes") advancing in line without helmets, without cover.

I have now been studying Rousseau since April and read more or less all of him. I feel that I can get nothing more from reading; I must now start writing and repress all questions as to the point of the effort.

[. . .]

September 2, Wednesday

Today I began to write the Rousseau chapter, the second volume of my Eighteenth Century. A hopeless and wretched beginning; but to put it aside would depress me even more, and after all there is nothing more worthwhile on which I can spend my time. If I had any possibility at all of earning money, then I would turn it to good account; but I do not see any. I began the first volume August 11, '34; the real work on it was over on December 29, '35 with the completion of the Diderot chapter; but transcription and polishing lasted until well into March. Then I embarked upon reading Rousseau. In the meantime the Markus affair has given my hopes the coup de grâce: Even if the regime and the Aryan paragraph were to fall, I would not be able to publish the work at its present length. But I cannot condense it, without taking from it precisely what is my contribution. So I continue. [. . .]

September 5, Saturday

Yesterday at last to Trude Öhlmann's summer place. On the drive there the beast behaved abominably and thought up new tricks. Hardly had we left completely congested Radebeul behind us and were on the less crowded road to Meissen, than the engine began to race, without my being able to stop it. I constantly had to brake, and the radiator was boiling. We stopped beside a quarry; three workers on their midday break, one with an open pocketknife, came out and, friendly and knowledgeable, immediately helped us. [. . .] The spring between the accelerator and the carburetor was worn out and jammed. First aid: but we should get the spring changed in a garage in Meissen. 50Pf and three cigarillos and the pleasant feeling of having met friendly people. Just before the Elbe bridge at Meissen a garage. Large business on the main road. A South German mechanic, a woman owner. The spring was good, it only had to be adjusted. Another stop of half an hour, 1.20M costs. Now the pleasure of driving. The wonderful view by the river above Meissen, the splendid road to Oschatz. For a while the greatest enjoyment, then the racing started again, worse than before. I used a curious technique, pushed the accelerator down, until the car gained some momentum, took my foot off and let it roll forward. That was hair-raising of course, soon ruined the brake lining (and my nerves) and could by no means be accomplished in town traffic. In Oschatz, near Zierold's—but it had to be reversed into a side street, and in that condition!—an "Opel Service." There was another check-up and adjustment, another half hour and 50 pfennigs. From then on the engine held up excellently. But it was three o'clock when we finally stopped in Bucha, and the Öhlmanns were waiting for us until two every day. I left Eva by the car and looked for master tailor Hessel in the strung-out village. It was always supposed to be a corner house on the left, but I walked for more than half a mile, and it never was. Finally I found a vacationer with a child; by chance she had got to know the Öhlmanns only today; [. . .] they had certainly gone out, but she knew where. I brought the talkative woman back to the car, and we drove off on our search. All over the place; then Eva and the woman got out, and after a while the Öhlmanns were really found and their master tailor's house likewise. Trude was running around voluptuous and unlovely in silk trousers and a clinging blouse, but one swiftly forgot the Rubenesque bulges because of her great warmth and genuine delight. Her boy, just 18, trainee in the Deutsche Bücherei, is extremely good-looking, a disturbingly perfect image of his pederast father, still half a child, but a good and studious one. HJ of course, but (also by now of course) very reluctantly. The Öhlmanns also reported what one hears everywhere, absolute discontent in all circles, in the village too. Interesting to me and characteristic of the petit bourgeois was the fear of Russia. They believe Bolshevism—perhaps rightly—to be the greater evil. They see through the Jew-baiting and do not like it, but they put up with everything out of fear of Russia. We drank very strong coffee, prepared on the spirit burner in accordance with our instructions, on the lawn, the view was fairly nondescript, but nevertheless of a country village. It was terribly sultry and thundery, I had long ago become wet through with sweat. We then took a few steps through the village, drove the Öhlmanns a couple of miles on narrow field and forest tracks and then very fast on a wide road to Dahlen. From there to Bucha it's 2 or 3 miles, to Dresden a little under 40 miles. As we took our leave it began to rain heavily and the top had to be put up. Sweatbox. The drive back began just before six. Now the car just bowled along, I often drove at 45 mph. [. . .]

The evening before (Thursday) to a much-praised film in the Universum: *Allotria* [Skylarking]. Disappointment. [. . .] At the beginning of the century, in the Residenztheater, my father laughed himself into rude health at the very same kinds of things that derive from French formulas of around 1860. The Third Reich called things like that Jewish and immoral non-Art. But now it is a German film masterpiece. — Again we saw pictures of the red terror [. . .].

September 9, Wednesday, toward evening

Sat fruitlessly all day over the first chapter of Rousseau. My head hot and completely depressed. All the worse because I constantly have to tell myself that all this effort is pointless. What does it matter whether I have one manuscript bundle more or less in my drawer. The Nazi regime is more firmly in the saddle than ever; even now they are triumphant in Nürnberg: the "Party Rally of Honor," and making plans for eternity. And the whole world inside and outside Germany is keeping its head down. The Jewish Cultural Leagues (they should be hanged) have issued a statement, saying they had nothing to do with sensational foreign news reports about the situation of German Jews. Next they will certify that *Der Stürmer* publishes nothing but the truth in fondest fashion—Bolshevism rages in Spain, while here there is peace, order, justice, true democracy.

On Sunday we went for a longer drive again. [. . .]

Home by quarter to seven, very, very tired. Eva was in bed at half past eight, I not much later. — Completely knocked out the next day. We did not even have to resolve to make less arduous excursions in future; extreme shortage of money in any case forces us to be sparing with gasoline. Besides the weather has meanwhile turned unpleasantly stormy and rainy.

Today we sat at home all day like prisoners; perhaps we shall drive to the cinema after our meal.

September 14, Monday

We did not go to the cinema; car use for the whole week amounted to 18 miles, the Sunday drive yesterday was limited to 32 miles. 60 miles = 3 gallons of gasoline + ¾ of a quart of oil = approx. 5.20M. We are at such a low ebb and so miserably weighed down by large bills (insurance with 108M is the worst, in addition the exasperating church taxes, the dentist, etc.)

that we have to count every penny and count it ever more gloomily. I shall try to obtain another mortgage of 1,000–2,000M. That would save the life insurance, allow the terrace construction to be carried out and remove the worst financial embarrassment and constraint. Only: for how long?—And who will consider our little house is worth enough to bear it?

On top of the money problems there is ever again and ever more sharply (not blunted) the ghastliness of the political situation. What the "Party Rally of Honor" produced in paroxysms and insane Jew-baiting lies in the speeches of Hitler, Goebbels and Rosenberg beggars all imagination. One always thinks that surely somewhere in Germany voices of shame and fear must be raised, protests must come from abroad, where everywhere (even in Italy, our ally!) there are Jews in the highest positions—nothing! Admiration for the Third Reich, for its culture, trembling fear of its army and its threats.

Despite everything and despite our terrible abandonment by all friends, yesterday, Sunday, was consoling. In the morning I managed the very difficult "essential features" section of my Rousseau, that is, the dreaded curtain-raiser of the second volume. Certainly bitterness at the hopelessness of the work was immediately there too; but nevertheless I have managed this again, something has been completed, which is waiting; perhaps there will be a miracle. [. . .] And at all events: I have proved to myself once again that I can still produce. And once again I solemnly swear to myself to continue working in the face of every challenge. (Today and tomorrow I shall make a typed copy and polish it at the same time.) [. . .]

Read aloud for a long time in the evening. [. . .]

September 27, Sunday

The mayor's latest effort: "Causing a Public Nuisance" through the condition of my garden. [. . .] The matter has incensed and alarmed me since yesterday to such a degree that everything else fades into the background by comparison. We are so medievally helplessly powerless.

When I woke up early this morning I thought with dismay of my own coldness of heart, that this blow affects and preoccupies me much more than Wally's wretched condition. After four months of grievous suffering and fevers—recently the talk was always of a liver problem—her gall-bladder has now been removed. I thought Wally lost beyond all doubt, expected news of her death with every post and merely asked myself every time, whether there would be enough money to drive to Berlin. It had already become an obsession for me, I saw the car at the cemetery gate, just as at Felix's funeral the car of the widowed Frau Klemperer stood there. — Now this morning Marta writes, the operation has gone well, and there is every hope. Admittedly in the last few months first Mother Köhler and then Professor Raab have died after operations that went well, both much younger than Wally.

We had Lilly Jelski de Gandolfo, here on September 17 and 24 on her journey to and from Prague. What I wrote in a letter to her brother Walter yesterday is no polite lie. We used to call Lilly "the sea cow" and after her Uruguay marriage, "the overseas cow." [...] Now we were both very surprised and pleased at her simultaneously modest and confident character, introspective and with wide interests. We got on from the first moment. She complained how very miserable her childhood had been, because of her parents' constant quarreling. Her husband studied music in Berlin with a stipend from his government, they presumably had an affair for several years. She herself was employed as a secretary in the Uruguayan legation. In his homeland he found a provisional resting-place as an office worker and had her follow after a year. They have now been married for three years, and Lilly is back to see her parents for the first time. What a mixing of blood, once she has children! The man Italian on his father's side, Spanish on his mother's side—it is not quite certain whether with or without some drops of Indio. She wears a Uruguayan flag on the lapel of her dress: That way she does not look Jewish but South American and so is spared trouble (especially as Uruguay has broken with the "red" Spanish government).

The two excursions into the Erzgebirge and the Saxon Switzerland really went very well. A little before that, on Sunday September 20, we had been on the Bastei by ourselves and had—car owner's pride!—reversed into the very same parking place among all the other cars, in which Isakowitz's car stood on Whitsunday last year. On both occasions the view through the thick and yet still transparent autumn fog was truly fantastically beautiful. "Fantastic" is now evidently a fashionable word, just like "colossal" in the days of the Imperial Guards lieutenant. With Isakowitz and Jelski it was in every third sentence and with Lilly in every second. [...]

I went to see Trustee Tanneberg, whom we saw in vain in 1934. He immediately said a mortgage of 2,000M could not be obtained: people are afraid of not getting their money back because the government protects debtors in every way. When he heard I was non-Aryan: "Then it is completely out of the question." Apart from that we had a long and friendly conversation. The man, in his early forties, member of the Nazi Party since '29, formerly in the Stahlhelm, anti-Semitic as regards the immigrant Eastern Jews, is nonetheless a vehement opponent of the government, not only of its Jewish policy. His most interesting words: "I laugh every evening when I listen to Radio Moscow. One only needs to substitute Stalin for Hitler every time and Bolshevist for National Socialist, then the speeches are identical." He said it was a puzzle to him how the regime managed to carry on, above all an economic puzzle, but he saw no prospect of an end to it. If there were peace, it would be years before the thing petered out. He did not think much of German war readiness. Rearmament was incomplete, the troops had been trained too quickly, the young people—the generation born during the war—were lacking in robustness. He had seen them in the exercise area only recently, completely exhausted. He too seemed to regard war and defeat as deliverance. But he said: The young (not the old!) officers are completely loyal to Hitler: "They always say, things could not be better for them than they are now." His anti-Semitism: "Why did they let in the Galicians during the war? Why did the Police Commissioner of Berlin have to be a Jew, why a Jew in every prominent position?" From which one may conclude that the NSDAP has assessed the popular mood quite accurately and that the Jewish dream of being German has been a dream after all. That is the most bitter truth for me. On the other hand, Tanneberg quite rightly said: For propaganda they simply have to have an enemy. First it was the Jews, now Bolshevism is the scapegoat. — For all that I have no mortgage, and the money shortage is even greater as a result of the mayor's latest threat, because I must now immediately hire a gardener. Also Lilly's visit was expensive (and terribly exhausting—I was busy in the kitchen the whole time, had to converse the whole time, never got out of collar and boots).

A "Herr Doctor Helm" presented himself on Wengler's recommendation. Good-looking intellectual. Lawyer, counsel for workers, was locked up for nine months, sells car polish at 2.50M a bottle, his wife makes clothes. We conversed as colleagues, so to speak, he got a cigarette, I did not buy anything.

When collecting stamps [. . .] I now pay attention to the postmark. Before they only used to say, for example: "Visit the Leipzig Fair!" or perhaps "Drivers! Show consideration for others"; today, on a card from Berlin: "Without a newspaper one is a man in the moon," and beside it a man sitting on a crescent moon, his legs dangling. In our newspaper (and therefore in all of them) they have been writing for days that one has to read a newspaper. Recently in a speech by a Reich Press Leader (or something, I think the name was Dietrich) statistics were presented, according to which the Third Reich, by amalgamating and de-Liberalizing and removing all Jews and those "intermarried with Jews," has reduced the number of German newspapers from around 3,500 to around 2,500: now there are not enough readers even for these, even though a subscription to *Der Stürmer* and similar excrement is compulsory in many places. I do not at all believe that it is only the competition of the radio that is to blame. People have had enough of always hearing the same thing and of knowing that they are not getting the truth anyway. There remains only a psychological puzzle, which I encountered for the first time in 1914 in Italy. Then someone from some newspaper or other said to me: Everyone knows and everyone repeatedly says, è pagato, and yet they allow themselves to be influenced and to believe! In those days I thought: the illiterate mentality of childlike nations! That would be impossible here in Germany! And now? Martha Wiechmann, ed-

ucated, a teacher, a democrat, the sister of a dismissed Prussian public prosecutor: "I heard a lecture about Russia . . . Terrible! We're really better off,"
etc., etc.

[. . .]

Since making a fair copy of the "Essential Features" the work on
Rousseau has been considerably interrupted. First of all I do not like the
Life section at all, because I have to copy it all, after that I struggled
through the tome: Jansen, *Jean-Jacques Rousseau as Musician,* then there
were the days of Lilly's visit and their aftermath, then I absolutely had to
write for once to Walter and to Lissy Meyerhof [. . .], then yesterday there
was the shock of the public nuisance, then I spent the first half of today on
the diary and am still unshaven, and if the weather holds we shall probably go for a little drive in the afternoon. But I want to continue with it tomorrow at the latest. [. . .]

We talked with Lilly several times about having children. She does not
want to, at least not yet, she too is of the opinion that it is not the essential
and important thing in a marriage. ("One does not need to marry for
that.") She told us how strange she had found it that her father asked her
about it, that he regarded it as her duty, but above all that he had mentioned the subject at all. Once he would not have done so at any price.
[. . .]

October 4, Sunday

Financial straits to the point of despair; a number of essential bills had to
be put off until October, which is now overburdened in turn. I am left with
about 160M for everyday needs for 31 days. Gasoline included.

I have not taken the car out of the garage at all for a whole week, today
admittedly because of the ghastly rainy and stormy weather [. . .].

Last Sunday too only a very short drive for reasons of economy, but peculiarly interesting. Half by chance we found ourselves on the new Reich
autobahn from Wilsdruff to Dresden, less than an hour after it was
opened. There were still flags and flowers from the ceremony in the morning, a mass of cars moved slowly forward at a sightseeing pace, only occasionally did anyone attempt a greater speed. This straight road,
consisting of four broad lanes, each direction separated by a strip of grass,
is magnificent. And bridges for people to cross over it. Spectators crowded
onto these bridges and the sides of the road. A procession. And a glorious
view as we were driving straight toward the Elbe and the Lössnitz Hills in
the evening sun. We drove the whole stretch and back again (two times 7½
miles), and twice I risked a speed of 50 mph. A great pleasure, but what a
luxury, and how much sand in the eyes of the people. There are constantly
accidents at hundreds of railway level crossings, thousands of roads are in
the worst condition, everywhere there is a lack of cycle paths, which

would do more to prevent accidents than all the tightening up of the law. None of it is done because of course it would not catch the eye. On the other hand "THE ROADS OF THE FÜHRER"!

All week I have been writing the short section "Rousseau the Musician" and have completed it today. Never has a work of mine turned out so well as this Dix-huitième. And I shall never be able to publish it.

October 9, Friday

This is probably the worst birthday of my life.

In the morning Martha informed me that Wally, who was thought to be saved after a serious operation—supposedly removal of her gallbladder, but no doubt it was cancer after all—is considered beyond help; she has been packed off home from the hospital; Lotte, the doctor, recalled from Switzerland, will care for her till the end.

In the morning at the library I was told gently, that as a non-Aryan I was no longer allowed to use the reading room. They will let me take everything home or give it to me in the catalog room, but an official ban has been issued for the reading room.

In the afternoon we were in Tolkewitz for the cremation of Breit, of whose death we learned quite by chance: Frau Lehmann had heard of it at another Jewish cleaning job. At this funeral ceremony which was attended by a very large number of people, most wearing top hats, only a very few bare-headed brave Christians, like Gehrig (incidentally Frau Kühn was also there), so here I had a firsthand survey. Instead of a cleric, a friend, a Berlin lawyer called Magnus, spoke first of all (he kept his hat on and so I did too, although Breit was a Protestant, as I am).

The beginning was an imitation of a whining clerical tone, but then the man got into his stride and spoke in his own fashion. He spoke in such a way that none of his words would have been of any use to an informer, and yet in such a way that Gerstle, who was standing beside me, whispered to me afterward: "For once someone who spoke from the heart!" An instruction had been issued the day before, removing all legal works by non-Aryan authors from the libraries and forbidding any new editions. Breit, however, a former examiner of candidates for the bench, published many important texts. The speaker repeatedly emphasized how much he had given *German* law, and how he had constantly argued for living German law and against formalism, and how that had been acknowledged everywhere and how influential it had been, and how the *future* will value it. [. . .] So it turned out to be a peculiarly "good funeral." [. . .]

We took Frau Kühn a part of the way back in our car. Deeply moved she tearfully flung her arms around Eva's neck and made a true declaration of love and loyalty (some months ago she had responded somewhat coolly to our political embitterment and after her husband had discovered the Nordic soul of Frederick the Great).

October 10, Saturday

A couple of days ago there were birthday greetings from Ilse Klemperer. Divorced from her mentally ill husband, she is going to Rio de Janeiro, to her brother Kurt, with her son, and taking the ashes of her father Felix. He "must not be left here alone." She can also take his Iron Cross, First Class.

Berthold Meyerhof visited us. The Meyerhofs always float to the top in the strangest way. He has just been sacked from his job as representative of a factory because he is not Aryan; so he is rid of debts that he owed the factory. In Berlin, which as the capital is open to the eyes of the world, anti-Semitism does not appear to be quite as rampant as here. Streicher in Franconia and Mutschmann in Saxony are probably the non plus ultras. For example, Berthold told us that Landsberg had been retired from his railway post on full pay. Only recently we heard from his wife Idy-Bussy (cf. the happy times of 1906!) in the oddest way. Cione, an Italian librarian, visited me here; he sent a greeting card from Florence con gli amici the Landsbergs, mother and daughter. Bussy's lines began: "It's a small world."

A letter from Georg, who has gone into retirement in Newtonville and travels back and forth between the growing families of his sons. They are all in good positions (as young men and in practical professions) and have all escaped the inferno germanico. I replied at considerable length today, also wrote about the car and how I would hardly be able to maintain it.

[...]

We were at the flower show for the twenty-sixth and last time; it made a melancholy dying impression and will be closed on Sunday. Among the sculptures there a pretentious-looking group always annoyed me: a young man, balancing on the toes of one foot as he runs, holds a young girl by the waist, who, gripped at just that moment, arches backward coquettishly with the upper part of her body and has more support at the waist than on the ground. The whole thing is evidently meant to embody the great movement of youth, but is only a wobbly bluff of difficulté vaincue. This sculpture suddenly seemed to me a symbol of the new Reich, and I called it Stabilitas. The private historical significance of the show for me is that it was almost the main reason why I started driving. I wanted to make frequent visits possible for Eva and made the purchase of the season tickets dependent on learning to drive.

I read the third volume of Buck's China trilogy, *The Divided House*, aloud; it is the richest and most interesting. The development of China between old and new. A very great writer.

October 14, Wednesday

The manuscript of the second Rousseau chapter is finished at last. For whom? The simple fact that I give the long quotations in French would be a major obstacle to publication even in a Germany with a different government; because this whole generation no longer learns French anymore.

After a long gap we went for a little drive on Sunday afternoon. As far as Kipsdorf and back after stopping for a brief walk. It was really our first winter drive, and my hands became numb at the wheel. I was twice alarmed by my eyes when the low sun flickered in my face. I have often been troubled by glare before, but this time there was something new. In the hazy sunshine I see a cyclist in front of me on the right and want to pass him, when suddenly he disappears, as if blotted out—not there indistinctly, but literally gone. The same thing happened a few minutes later with a whole troop of walkers. I realized afterward that I must have been affected by a momentary blindness.

This evening we are supposed to be at Frau Schaps', together with the Spiegelbergs—whose wife we do not know yet.

Language of the Third Reich: The day before yesterday in the newspaper: "Eight *national comrades* were injured . . . when the trams collided." — The *Querschnitt* was banned until further notice, because it published a series of *intellectualist and almost subversive* comments.

Eva's state of health has been rather indifferent again recently. In the evenings she has to lie down immediately after our meal because of nervous shuddering, I read aloud in the bedroom. Her powers of resistance in the face of ever-increasing poverty and oppression are fairly exhausted.

[. . .]

October 18, Sunday

Wally died on the evening of October 14 while we were with Frau Schaps. 59 years old, she was cremated yesterday afternoon. Cancer of the pancreas—all the other information was untrue, so as to deceive her. They had tried some new injections, in vain. About two weeks ago when they made another attempt to operate, they simply opened her up and stitched her together again, without doing anything, because it was completely hopeless. In the end she was given a lot of morphine—"otherwise it would have taken longer," Lotte told me.

I set out for the cremation yesterday at midday and was in Dresden again at ten. Considerate of poor Wally to make a weekend ticket possible; even those twelve marks were almost beyond my means. 1931, 1932, 1936: To the funerals of Berthold, Felix, Wally, each time for a few hours, these have been my visits to Berlin in recent years. It was the most dreadful funeral I have ever attended. At Wally's request the time had not been announced and all fuss avoided. But then one should have been consistent and not organized a ceremony at all. So sitting in the absolutely empty big hall in Berliner Strasse (where Felix had also been cremated) there were only Sussmann, Lotte, Hilde (a good-natured, plump young creature with full lips, her face swollen from weeping, come from Stockholm for a few days, but too late to see her mother alive), Änny, Berthold's widow, Marta, Lilly and I. And Jelski, whom no one in this circle takes seriously or even respects, spoke (without vestments) a few words, incidentally neither tactless nor bad. Before and after a couple of paltry bars on the organ. The coffin slid smartly down, the flap closed like the door of a railway station lift, not even a few flowers thrown after it as a substitute for earth. Before and after the very dry businesslike words of an official: "Sussmann? . . . Is no one else coming? . . . Who's speaking? . . . Then we can begin . . . Please sign here." I saw the clock above the entrance: 6 o'clock till 6:20. Marta and Lilly had picked me up at half past three at Anhalter Station in Änny's car; we were driven to her small, pretty apartment in Kudowastrasse. A whole new residential quarter has been built there at Roseneck. At the Jelskis a tense atmosphere as always. He does not want to hear anything about politics, I think he still sympathizes with the Nazis a little; Marta extremely bitter. Marta, Lilly and I walked to the crematorium, which was fairly close, arrived very early, sat down on a bench in the outer hall and talked while a very animated assembly of mourners poured out, conspicuous among them two cheerful, laughing old men (hurrah, we're alive!). Marta told us that the Sussmanns had long been dissenters, but that Wally had for many years and not just since her illness firmly believed in God and the immortal soul, and under the influence of a woman friend, had done so in a specifically Protestant form with Bible reading. She had also not feared death as such, only she would have so much wanted to live another couple of years and see the end of the Third Reich. . . . Sussmann is an old and broken man. Lotte told me she fears so much for him because depressions and suicide have occurred frequently in his family. She has given up her post in a Swiss mental hospital and wants to do theoretical work and journalism and stay with her father. All private suffering is multiplied and poisoned a thousand times over by the political circumstances; Sussmann's two other daughters have to live abroad. . . . Sussmann kept a tight hold of himself. He asked me about my work. On the subject of language he said I should pay attention to the word *dynamic*. As a doctor, he said, he had quite a lot to do. The harassment had lessened now, yes, they were even supposed to be encouraging some émigré doctors to return because there were not enough doctors for the coming war. And Marta talked about Milch, the air force general, who had a Jewish father and an Aryan mother: he claims he was the offspring of his mother's adultery with an Aryan.

I could not refuse the embarrassment of returning with Änny, whose car was this time ceded to the Sussmanns, and who herself had a taxi waiting. She took me as far as her old apartment and then paid the driver to go on to Anhalter Station. It was terribly unpleasant for me, but how could I have avoided it? There was no time for explanations. Änny herself had aged, was hard of hearing, very emotional, in addition suffering from influenza, restrained, but her voice sullenly tearful so to speak. Her oldest is studying technology in the USA, her Peter, whom I have never seen, is now eight, she herself fifty-one. "If he had not been bestowed upon me so late, I would no doubt have put an end to it all . . ." She asked about my work. "Why don't you publish anything in America?" I said: "I am waiting." She: "What for?" Somewhat agitated, my voice and expression perhaps overtheatrical, I said: "For my Fatherland, I have no other!" She, rather surprised and almost pleased: "Oh, so you still think . . . ?" And: "I do not want to emigrate either." And Georg, her eldest, thinks likewise, thank God. On the whole I had the impression that none of us dares hope for change anymore. "It" has already lasted so long in Russia and Italy, said Sussmann, and the juxtaposition did honor to his reason . . . On the journey to Berlin and back I clung to Janet's *Fénelon* monograph. I would so very much like to complete my book and the Language of the Third Reich and my memoirs. And so very much like to survive this time. But my heart is very poor. And Eva's nerves are deteriorating very badly. But it was a great joy to come home and to love each other very much.

I asked Lilly to approach the Japanese legation through her friends at the Uruguayan legation and find a contact for me. The Japanese are supposed to be attracting all kinds of German scholars to their universities or colleges. That takes me to the evening at Frau Schaps on the day of Wally's death. There was a small party. I talked a lot to Spiegelberg and his young (second) wife, who is Swiss and a student of Mary Wigman. Spiegelberg wants to go to India, makes many applications and to this end has frequently been abroad and attended conferences. He said: Only connections, only making yourself known to people personally procures a position. He put me on to Japan. He also passed on a greeting from Tillich, who did not reply to my letter last year. Tillich does not write to anyone. He is established in America. He says written applications are pointless, one must arrive in the USA penniless, if possible starving and in rags, best of all just out of prison (or at least act as if one were). Only then, but then with certainty, would one get a post. Spiegelberg, who has no idea in what financial difficulties I find myself—how should he? after all our car is outside—repeated his message to me again and again: Travel to Italy, travel to the USA, it does not cost much, sell a few securities, why wait until it is too late? He does not know that I do not have "a few securities." Also for both of us, it remains an open question whether we should not after all hang on here to the very last, even till it is "too late." Spiegelberg says that in Switzerland they do not believe there will be any change in Germany without war. But the war will be a long time in coming, because the international arms industry is still making too much money from the general rearmament. . . . An old District Court Judge told us that Goebbels had just published an essay in the *Europäische Revue*. He said the NSDAP knows that a political system, which is in the least degree dependent on lies, cannot be a lasting one; consequently they, the Nazis, had never made use of even the smallest lie . . . Then also of great and melancholy interest to me, to discover that Toni Gerstle, whom I had always believed to have a cool head, is a firm believer in astrology. She believes in star positions, "it" has always proved right so far. She was half offended and half contemptuous that my shallow rationalism should doubt these things. Reason was impotent after all, the influence of the constellations, perhaps on the hour of our conception, was absolutely certain. Should I be surprised if Hitler assails "intellectualism" and swears by blood? What else is the daughter of a Jewish Supreme Court judge doing? And in what way are the Zionists different from the Nazis? People treat reason as if it were the most minor and harmful aspect of a whole human being. It is as if a soldier standing guard were to say to himself: What good would my rifle be, if I were now to be attacked by a dozen enemies? I shall therefore lay it aside and smoke opium cigarettes until I doze off.

Fräulein Roth, the librarian, was here on Friday afternoon and evening. Vehemently opposed to the Nazis—but: "If they had expelled the Eastern Jews or had excluded Jews from the bench, *that* at least would have been comprehensible." So *that* would not have seemed absolutely evil to her. So here too Hitler is not without a base.

I love my Dix-huitième more than ever. Besides, Fräulein Roth was very taken with my first Rousseau chapter and pleased at the contemporary references. The fact is, that the Nazi doctrine is in part not really alien to the people, in part is gradually polluting the healthy section of the population. Neither Christian nor Jew is safe from infection. — Roth further told me that my books have been removed from the library reading room.

October 30, Friday

Very bad days. There is a demand for church tax of 121M to be paid by November 10 (that it happens to be a church tax is a particular mockery), and in December I am supposed to pay 108M insurance. We are virtually destitute. I still had five of the three-mark coins that had been taken out of circulation. [. . .] A coin dealer did not want them but curiously enough the Reich Bank still redeemed them. So an extra 15M. Then Frau Lehmann was cut back: only once a week and from November 1 "on leave for a couple of months." Then the telephone was canceled. Then I gave up my cigarillos and went back to the short pipe (which is a considerable torment for me—dirtiness, tobacco juice in my mouth, inflamed tongue and lips— but it only costs 12 pfennigs a day). All that depresses me horribly. And the car stands unused and is expensive even when it is not moving. There is no money to adapt it properly for the winter, and the starter is on strike. — Particularly bad, that Eva's powers of resistance are fairly much exhausted: bouts of trembling in the evenings, deep melancholy and so on. — And nowhere any prospect of change. Goering's speech yesterday on the "Four-Year Plan" sounded gratifyingly desperate, and that was a ray of hope; but I no longer quite believe that the end is really near; there is no

one who is really resisting, neither here nor abroad. And this government
has all the trumps. As now in the Spanish game. Sometimes I am dead-
tired. But again and again I force myself to go on working. The third
Rousseau chapter crawls forward.

I read aloud a great deal in the evening.

November 24, Tuesday

We were delivered from the worst of the situation by a quite unexpected
and truly very moving present of 500M from Georg [. . .]. With that we
got out of the tax difficulty, we could finally have cement laid on the terrace above the garage—last Saturday Lange worked on it until midnight,
now old carpets have been laid over it to ward off the frost, there have
been 4 to 6 degrees of frost at night—in Wilsdruff we bought Eva's longed-
for fruit trees and bushes, we also bought a little heater for the car and had
some small repairs done to the old thing, but there is not much that can be
done, the pistons are loosening, and the money will just not stretch to a
general repair. In any case the weather and the early darkness keep us
from driving. Apart from Wilsdruff we were only in Dippoldiswalde once
(on the open road I managed 50 mph) and a couple of times in town. Once
on a Sunday morning to a free publicity film produced by the Aral Works.
Magnificent pictures from mines and industry, information that interests
me very much now, about combustion in the pistons, test stands, etc.; in
between there were amusing pictures and scenes of driving. [. . .]

During the financially most critical days I turned to Trude Öhlmann, to
ask her if she could help me sell a number of books. She took on the task
with friendly enthusiasm. In fact Fock in Leipzig gave me 40M for the
Creizenach; on the other hand I could not get rid of my *Handbook of Literary History.* An antiquarian offered 100M for the 200 or more parts (value
when new 440M), not in cash, but as a credit against further orders; he appeared to think I still had my post, and of course I used to buy this and
that for the department library.

Anyhow: Georg was of very great help, we are back on our feet again for
a couple of months, perhaps we can even raise the January installment for
the Iduna—and who can think further ahead than that? I now have the impression that war is unavoidable; every day brings it closer, the Spanish affair can hardly continue to be restricted to Spain, we follow the news with
the most desperate interest and talk about it for hours. But here I do not
want to keep a note of what, after all, is general history, the German-Italian
alliance, the recognized Franco regime that champions the Spanish-
national and European cause with Moroccans, Madrid still unconquered,
the tension with England, etc., etc. We have learned patience and were
quite without hope and are still only halfway hopeful, but the pitcher has
truly been going to the well for a very long time now, and every day with a
greater (perhaps desperate?) foolhardiness.

On the language of the Third Reich: [. . .] The Führer must be followed blindly, *blindly!* — Systematic use of quotation marks as a means of rendering contemptible: In the Spanish business the newspaper has for weeks only been allowed to write "government," "cabinet," "minister," when the talk is of the "Reds" (mild version) or the red hordes. [. . .] Indirectly characteristic: Helmut Lehmann, in the fourth year of an apprenticeship at Horch, is working on the car. Whenever he is considering whether a screw should be unscrewed or a nozzle checked or even the smallest manual action, he does not say: I want to do or attempt this or that or use some other verb, but always (even though he is entirely alone) repeats again and again (a dozen times at least): "That can be *organized.*" (Mechanized catchword.) — I must relate my Rousseau observations to this study of language.

Spamer, who had spoken so contemptuously about national psychology and is now in charge of the Reich Office for Folk Studies, is the editor of an anthology, *German Folk Studies.* The publishing house has just announced a second edition after five months! How can this work fit with Spamer's basic ideas? As much as the Nordic Frederick the Great with Kühn's ideas. And *they* are the most human among my former colleagues! Truly: Fiamme dal ciel!

I must also pay attention to the Congress on Research on Jewry, which has just met, and its opinions of Jewish and German natural science—not with a completely clear conscience because I myself went astray a little because of my cultural history.

A card from Grete, who feels in need of contact, she is old, suffering, can no longer leave house or garden. Perhaps half of it is true. [. . .] A lengthy and contented letter from Betty Klemperer in Cleveland. She is settling down and feels at home. She has had her first driving lesson. Betty is living with her youngest (Wolfgang), who is a doctor in the hospital there.

A young man hurries past me in the crowd on Prager Strasse, a complete stranger, half turns and says with a beaming face: "I've got work— the first time in three years—and good work—at Renner's—they pay well!—for four weeks!"—and runs on.

I wrote a few lines to Martin Sussmann on his birthday. It was embarrassing because of a poverty of language. [. . .]

Meanwhile the third Rousseau chapter is finished, half of it already typed.

[. . .]

December 8, Tuesday

The last few days marked by influenza or something like it. Eva has a stomach complaint, is knocked out, lies down a lot; my usual rheumatic pains have got so much worse that I spent almost all of one night out of bed, could hardly use my left shoulder, my left arm, am still much impeded now (in addition the usual reminder of my heart in the park). Our housekeeping came to a halt; today we brought Frau Lehmann here in the car, and as I drove in I collided with the garden gate again for the first time in months. Bent bumper and a great blow to my pride, since [. . .] in recent weeks [. . .] I had felt very sure of myself and believed I had now finally outgrown my swaddling clothes as a driver. [. . .]

One day war seems imminent and the next completely remote. Today is one of the latter. And tomorrow the trial of the Gustloff murderer, the "Jew Frankfurter," begins in Chur.

Last Sunday Berthold Meyerhof was here for a couple of hours. Affected by a kidney problem, sacked as the Jewish representative of a local engineering factory and always Meyerhofianly indestructible. [. . .]

Otherwise completely alone, absolutely alone. [. . .]

Rousseau, Chapter 3, is completely finished, typed, corrected, read out to Eva. Today I started the *Contrat social*. At the moment I believe *this* will be the hardest part, and here everything has already been chewed over for me by Ducros. But things always look like that at the beginning.

Our telephone was removed on December 1. An almost symbolic act. Completely impoverished and completely isolated.

[. . .]

December 10, Thursday

[. . .]

Began to write the fourth Rousseau chapter, but so utterly tired today that I cannot write a single line.

I shall write the necessary Christmas letter to Betty Klemperer. And in the evening perhaps at last to the cinema again.

December 13, Sunday evening

At the cinema on Thursday, *Der Bettelstudent* [The Poor Student]. [. . .]

Today around noon a little winter drive to Kipsdorf. Skidded for the first time on an icy road near Schmiedeberg. Horrible feeling.

In the Gustloff trial in Chur, the murderer, Frankfurter, said he hesitated when Frau Gustloff opened the door to him, for the first time he had the thought, a married man, a human being . . . Then he heard Gustloff talking on the phone: "These Jewish swine!" and he fired. [. . .]

Language of the Third Reich: Last summer battle of production. — Now in the Christmas advertisements: battle of customers. [. . .]

In the film paper bought recently I was struck by the appalling degree of toadying to the government. An actress gives a brief account of her life. It had to have the sentence: I was fortunate to see the Führer as he drove to the stadium.

New Year's Eve 1936, Thursday

Johanna Krüger, the student friend of our Munich days, whom we had not seen for years, spent three of the evenings since Christmas with us. Aged a great deal (older looking than sixty), very nervous, but still nimble. She teaches at a private school in Limburg, friends with a number of Jews, once an intimate of Fritz Mauthner, free thinking, an opponent of the Third Reich, but nevertheless imbued with a fairly lukewarm opposition and without the aversion that is necessary to a genuinely thoughtful person. We did not exactly argue, but we did not come to a real understanding either. I am quite pleased that she is spending the second part of her holidays in Berlin. The old common points of interest (Muncker, Hermann Paul, Albert Hirsch, from whom a letter just arrived—he has managed to find a post at a Jewish school in Frankfurt) no longer bound us closely enough. Whoever is not a mortal enemy of the Nazis, cannot be my friend.

We passed Christmas very quietly. We drove to Wilsdruff and bought a fir at the nursery there for delivery in the spring, we also took a little Christmas tree with root bales away in the car; the lights will burn in the room for the last time today and after that it will be bedded out. Unfortunately the buggy has recently been more a cause of worry than of pleasure once again; hardship simply leads to poverty; it was bought secondhand, now it needs to be repaired again and again, Georg's financial help did not go very far. (It is doubtful whether we shall be able to pay the Iduna in January.)

Very irksome in recent weeks and very much at the expense of my Eighteenth Century has been the large amount of work in the kitchen. I wanted to manage the fourth Rousseau chapter by Christmas and yesterday wearily finished the *Contrat social.* So the work on Rousseau will drag on into March. Getting rid of Frau Lehmann hits me hard.

There were Christmas letters from the Isakowitzes, who are getting on tolerably well, from Georg's eldest, who is about to be naturalized in England and has two sons of seven and nine at English schools, from Hatzfeld, who like me is endeavoring in vain to find a post abroad—who wants a Romance scholar from Germany?

The fifteen-year-old daughter of Lange, the Communist carpenter, came home from work camp, won over to National Socialism, alienated from her parents. The group leader gathered the girls around her on the railway platform and delivered an invocation in the form of a farewell speech: "You are independent human beings, act according to what you have heard from me, do not let your parents lead you astray!" When Frau Lange tried to have a serious talk with her daughter, she was told: "You are insulting my leader!" I think of this case multiplied a hundred thousand times and am very depressed.

After my dismissal in the summer of '35, when I still had foreign hopes, Eva, whose intuition has always been very good, thought that Japan might offer an opportunity. Since then we have been reminded of Japan a couple of times, even if at long intervals. Spiegelberg talked about it, and Marta's Lilly believed she would be able to find contacts in the Japanese legation. Today Marta sends an article from a Jewish newspaper: The director of the (Tokyo) Music Academy, Professor Pringsheim, has given a speech. Pringsheim (brother-in-law of the expatriated Thomas Mann) is a friend of Georg's, I should immediately try to make contact through Georg. And so I immediately sent an urgently worded letter to Newtonville.

[...]

The Dresden Lord Mayor has decreed that the "Judenhof" ("Jews' Yard") is to be called Neumarkt (New Market). There is no need to be reminded that a synagogue once stood here. (Funny really—because "Jews' Yard" sounds very ghettolike and not philo-Semitic at all.)

I can sum up the year very briefly.

The joys and sorrows of driving, the test in January, the car in March, drove 3,750 miles.

Constant impoverishment and increasing financial woes; in October Georg saved us from the worst embarrassment, but saved us only for the moment. Increasingly isolated. No hope at all anymore of a post abroad, very little—I do not want to say none at all, it changes from hour to hour— very little of an end to the Third Reich.

The first volume of the Eighteenth Century completely finished (and not placed with the Breslau publisher); Rousseau since May (and still not finished).

In October to Wally's cremation in Berlin for a couple of hours.

1937

January 10, Sunday, toward evening

In the morning the Langes brought an old craftsman, who will perhaps transplant part of my heating here in the study to the garage. The man began to talk philosophy and politics in an intelligent and moderate way, [. . .] and so the time passed until midday and then I was utterly tired. [. . .]

The *Contrat social* part is finished and typed, I am now at the beginning of *Emile*. Again and again and ever more clearly: This will be my best book and the best section of the literary history.

On New Year's Day we went for a pretty little midday drive: Wilsdruff—autobahn (it was quite deserted and the beautiful view of the heights above the river was hidden by fog), back right through the whole of Dresden . . . Otherwise in recent days only short trips into town, unfortunately usually to the dentist, where we are both patients, unfortunately in the piston-rattling car. There is not enough for repairs—Michael wants to do it in February during his holiday to discharge his debt—also there is not enough money for the Iduna. I am quite fatalistic about it. Perhaps there will be war, the threat of which comes closer every day—Spain and thrice Spain, then Poland-Danzig, then Czechoslovakia, and eternally the predatory cry for colonies and the raving against "Russia-Judah" (as I saw it recently in the *Freiheitskampf*), and perhaps it will bring revolution and aid or death, at any rate a conclusion, and perhaps something will come of Tokyo and at all events: *I cannot help.*
[. . .]

I think it was '23, in any case the year of the Ruhr occupation, that I was prevented from holding the speech on January 18. Afterward Ulich, the department head, came to my lecture to console me—but the republican government did nothing about the fact that I had been prevented from speaking. That is how weak it was, and National Socialism already so powerful and popular. Except that at the time I did not yet see it like that. How comforting and depressing that is! Depressing: Hitler really was in line with the will of the German people. Comforting: One never really knows what is going on. Then the Republic seemed secure, today the Third Reich appears secure.
[. . .]

How much I would like to write my memoirs one day! But first the Eighteenth Century and then the Language of the Third Reich or even of three revolutions and then, "and then you are dead."

January 11, Monday

In the last Sunday summary of the *Dresdener NN*, Theodor Schulze writes: "Liberalism is the cradle of Anarchy." Schulze was already editorial writer of the paper when it was still liberal and belonged to the Jew Wolff. Shoulder against the same wall with Kühn, the historian of the Nordic Frederick the Great.

[...]

Then I read from Pearl Buck, *The Exile*. [...]

Annemarie Köhler sent the book to us at Christmas with a puzzling note: she had had to cut short her holiday at home in September, since then "not had a minute's peace," she would visit us soon. I wrote her a cordial, but very serious letter, I had thought that I had to "write her off," like so many others, not out of sensitivity but of necessity. She should let us hear from her. I also sent greetings to Dressel, inasmuch as he had not yet recalled the duties of a true German. There has been no reply yet.

Nor has there been any word from the Wenglers for many months.

January 18, Monday

For a moment last week I thought matters had come to a head, war was about to break out over Spanish Morocco. The next day peace talks between Hitler and France. No one believes in them, the tension is just as great as before and everything is as it was.

This week I hope to complete the manuscript of the *Emile* section. The whole work on Rousseau will turn out well, my best and most mature altogether. But in every respect I work without hope. It advances so slowly, not only because the kitchen, etc. takes up half the day, but also because I tire so quickly, neither my head nor my eternally inflamed eyes get me very far anymore.

Again, with the Rousseau more general thoughts are constantly and simultaneously going through my mind. On the Language of the Third Reich and beyond that. That national literatures or the national element in the literatures have declined into insignificance and into the small-mindedness and danger of mendacity of "locally rooted art." That radio, film, airplane underlie the intellectual fusion of the world. That here one can no longer separate technological and spiritual, body and soul. [...] Then the eternal mission, the eternally avant-garde Jewish spirit. Now Hitler, the scourge of God, has ensured another worldwide diaspora. Georg writes from Newtonville, Betty and Wolfgang describe their experiences (and the same joys and sorrows of driving) in Cleveland, Ohio; I ask Georg for a recommendation to Tokyo, Frau Schaps tells me about her nephew in Sacramento, she tells me that Blumenfeld in Lima is conducting aptitude tests for pilots ... Who wants to halt the course of the International (not in the political sense and yet again *also* in the political sense)? On top of that the international elements in the Language of the Third Reich. As I am talking about that, Eva also adds the USA and ghetto, and the ideas associated with them, which have so often gone through my and our heads. All of that would have to find a place in the introduction to the Language of the Third Reich. All of that could at some point lead me away from French to American literary history. But I am so infinitely depressed with respect to the general situation and to my own health. For the most part I believe that it will all remain unwritten and not even my Eighteenth Century will be completed.

[. . .]

January 24, Sunday

People are dying all around. In the last few days: first Prätorius, the honest little master builder cum craftsman with his insufferable wife, who built our house and was going to finish building it in better times. He was old for as long as we knew him, but until last summer vigorous and indestructible. Then he became obviously senile. He reached the age of 71, we had known him for a good dozen years. Then yesterday we heard the news that Kalix had shot himself. I never saw the dog, but felt his dirty persecution for years. He was mayor here, well known as a depraved fellow, widely hated and feared. He twice threatened me with arrest. Cause of death is likely to be venereal disease or graft or both. The typical minor dignitary of the Third Reich. We took his end as a good omen.

We heard the news from the "vegetable peel woman" (collector of scraps for her rabbits) on the twenty-third, that is, the first anniversary of my driving test. That day as I was waiting in Mommsenstrasse between the theoretical and practical parts of the test, Trefftz happened to leave his nearby apartment and we chatted. I had for a long time disapproved of Trefftz, professor of engineering and aviation, Rhinelander, seven years younger than I, close friend of the Wieghardts despite emphatically national opinions, because of his boyish character, but later I learned to appreciate him because of his human decency. He told me that day: "The Nazis are fighting with their backs to the wall; they will fight desperately, but they will fall; only that won't help you, because where will the next government get the money for such a luxury subject?" — Then I met him three months ago, I think in front of the State Bank; he was walking with a cane, but was very cheerful. He said he felt as he did in the field, when he left the trenches: blood poisoning caused by something quite insignificant, several operations, almost given up for lost, but now saved and almost completely recovered. Yesterday his obituary was in the *Dresdener NN* †21.1.37, * '88. I had often envied the man. He leaves five young children.

January 28, Thursday

The *Kalix* case (whatever the actual circumstances may be) is extraordinarily characteristic of the Third Reich. In a little place like Dölzschen, which is quite separate from Dresden, the inhabitants certainly know all about their local notables. The mayor, previously a traveler in leather goods, was already out of office for some time last year. At the time people said with an ominous grin: "Sick—probably won't come back"; sexual offenses were supposed to be involved. Now, at his sudden demise, the word immediately is: suicide or coerced suicide. Then in the newspaper there was the most honorable obituary for the very "old warrior" ("old warrior": Language of the Third Reich!), who had been shot in a tragic accident; he had handed(!!) a revolver to two policemen as they were going on duty, the weapon had gone off and killed him immediately. The whole population attended the funeral. He was solemnly taken from the Begerburg (now the Party House) to the cemetery. Zörner, the mayor of Dresden, was there with other Party bigwigs, the minister of Pesterwitz gave a pious sermon—a long report about it all in the *Dresdener NN:* "Taking Leave of Mayor Kalix." Just imagine how it will have looked in the *Freiheitskampf!* — Then the vegetable peel woman came by: "My husband (railway worker) says the two policemen forced him to shoot himself. And the funeral procession! It was as if they were at a baptism!" Then came Vogel, the grocer, who makes deliveries to about fifty people up here every Wednesday and so of course knows Dölzschen's happenings and vox populi inside out: "It was definitely suicide, in all probability he was forced to do it—sexual offenses—I told you last year, didn't I, he won't be around much longer."

The new Civil Service Law of the Third Reich is published in the same number as "Taking Leave of Mayor Kalix": Previously civil servants had to swear an oath to the Weimar Constitution; now "the new law establishes a relationship of loyalty to the Führer in the true German sense of personal loyalty and allegiance." Furthermore "the law expresses the indissoluble unity of Party and State." [. . .]

Lange told us different sources had confirmed that a whole SA unit has been sent to Spain, that several families had been informed of the heroic Spanish death of their sons. But *we* are neutral, and only Moscow and France . . .

[. . .]

Fräulein Carlo visited us after a long gap. She told us that SA men often complained to her; there is very great embitterment in their circles, and the revolution will come from that side.

[. . .]

The *Emile* chapter finished.

On Saturday (January 30, fourth anniversary of the seizure of power): Reichstag and government declaration, shops closed, "everyone listens to the Führer." The butter seller has just been up to our "lighthouse" and reports, people say that this time there is going to be a colony—leased from Portugal for 90 years. — If that is true and goes through without a war [. . .] then the 3rd Reich will last for decades yet. I am deeply depressed.

February 5, Friday

Nothing seems to have come of the colony, an official denial of the "rumors" was issued on the morning of January 30, in the big speech there was a solemn assurance that one only wanted to have the "stolen colonies" back. Aside from that the speech was less pacific than the previous ones. But when will war break out? My hopes have again sunk below zero. On the thirtieth, on the other hand, I was very happy that at least the big success had failed to materialize. I asked first a tram conductor, then the man at the lending library about the content of the speech.

The speech again was grist to my Rousseau mill: "Sole bearer of sovereignty is the people." — Goering slipped up once again: the Reichstag does *after all* have a significance. The after all significant Reichstag voted to give Hitler discretionary power for a further four years.

Yesterday anniversary of the death of Gustloff, shot by the "cowardly Jew." SA boss Lutze in a commemorative speech: the unfathomable hatred of the lower race. — The Reichstag continues to be played in the Kroll Opera House. Bad conscience in the face of the proper building?

Again a completely wretched lack of money, and the car in a completely wretched state. The pistons are failing to such a degree that yesterday I steered the car only with difficulty, and today it had to be laid up. Michael owes me money and wants instead to carry out the expensive repairs (otherwise beyond my means) in February, when he is here on leave from his air force camp. February has another 23 days, and Michael has never kept his word to me yet.

Yesterday—after a long interval, and after Eva had, literally for days on end, cleaned out the completely greasy and oily engine space and had fitted a new ventilator belt, and after we had previously had the worst luck several times over: Once when we wanted to drive out the radiator water boiled over, that was the old belt finished, once after repairs the gasoline was finished, the car was standing in Goeringstrasse at half past eight, I fetched a gallon from Bienertstrasse in a can, then I could not open the gasoline tank cap, then we were back in our shed at half past ten (and that was supposed to have been a cinema evening)—in any case after all that we ventured out yesterday, largely making use of first gear and with a lot of noise. Still: We did many of our errands over lunchtime: the obligatory new "automobile certificate" at the county office (military stock-taking?), oil in the New Town, the unfortunately necessary new gas stove. And in the evening the long planned cinema visit.

San Francisco. All too American. [. . .]

February 11, Thursday

Emile chapter completely finished. I wrote to ask Wengler, from whom I have heard nothing for months, whether he could borrow the critical edition of *Héloïse* (and a number of other things) from the department library. He came here with his sister on Sunday afternoon: he did not dare do so, the new Civil Service Law is too strict . . . people of German blood . . . and so on. It was brave of him to visit me at all. Thus the sense of being cut off gets worse every day. Wengler told us he had been sent for a course in a "camp" at Königs Wusterhausen. Teachers between forty and fifty. They slept six to a room, wore uniforms, did digging and sports, were given educative lectures. A headmaster talked about the character of the French; they were similar to the Jews, they did not love animals. [. . .]

March 5, Friday

I have at last just written the final line of the *Héloïse* chapter and so ended the manuscript of the Rousseau. Typing the remainder, plowing through the work as a whole once again will certainly take up all of March; I began the reading at the beginning of May, the writing at the beginning of September: so the little book (more a monograph than a chapter) has taken me eleven months.

Wengler wrote to me in the last few days, his lectureship ceases to exist from April 1, the TU now only retains an English lectureship.

[. . .]

March 27, Saturday—Easter tomorrow, probably a white one

The Rousseau was completely finished yesterday, fit to print with all the notes, all 104 pages checked, corrected, harmonized once again. Now it can be bundled up and grow moldy. It is a desperately sad business: my best book and altogether useless, a quixotic effort. To what extent was emphatically demonstrated to me once again only yesterday. The senseless relegation of French as a school subject began in 1919. Now the culturally destructive schools program, the Third Reich's "reform," has been issued with immediate effect. All secondary schools lose the upper sixth, and French will basically only still be taught at some girls' schools. Even if at some point in the future a publisher should be found (unreal if!)—who in Germany would still be able to read my book? It abounds in French quotations, and if I were to translate them into German, all the comments on style would be left hanging in the air. Whatever, whether I think of the Rousseau as a monograph or as a part of my far too lengthy literary history, it has in either case no prospect of ever seeing the light of day. But if I wanted to abbreviate the Rousseau or the whole Eighteenth Century, that would leave a compendium, of a kind that has already been written by others a hundred times, and my very own contribution would be lost. It is wretched, and yet there is nothing left for me to do except continue my work, now already in its fifth year, because I have been at it now since '33.

In addition to the wretchedness of this matter there are the ever increasing money difficulties. Bolts were changed for 20M and from that arose the necessity of changing all six connecting rods and cleaning the valves. In one workshop that would have cost almost 300M; through Vogel I found a reliable mechanic, who would come to the house. He worked here for a full three and a half days, it "only" came to 140M, of which I paid 110 immediately and put off the rest until April. But one mudguard is as tattered as it was at the beginning and a superannuated tire can give out any day, and changing oil and this and that. On top of that the dentist's bill of 74M, and one of the fillings that has not been paid for yet has fallen out again. Week by week we find ourselves in worse straits, my suit is fraying, our home is thick with dirt, neither house nor garden is finished, and I count every penny. We are so proletarianized and constrained, that I often wish not to wake up again. But I am afraid of death, and I also do not want to capitulate. I do not see any way out. To give up the car would be to imprison Eva. Yet our use of the car bears no relation to the costs incurred. We so much wanted to drive to Berlin at Easter—we have promised Grete and Marta dozens of times that we would do it, and they invite us again and again and do not understand why we decline; [. . .] I have a villa and a car, I have a monthly pension of 492M, and we are poorer, more bound down, proletarianized than in our most miserable bohemian and destitute days. We eat as poorly and simply as possible to save money and time—always this washing up, cooking, cleaning—I spend half the day in the kitchen, Eva does the dirtiest jobs, it is unspeakably horrid. And saving the pennies does not help—the jalopy, the house, the dentist, a tax demand at the moment eat up many times the amount in marks that we have agonizingly saved in pennies. I smoke the cheapest cigarillo, 4 pfennigs. Occasionally, to bring down costs even further, I smoke a pipe—I do not like the taste at all anymore and it saves only pennies. Show heroic willpower, and not smoke at all anymore? But my nerves and spirit have already gone so much to the dogs, and if I deteriorate even more, Eva will break down completely, I've noticed that so often. I really see no way out and let everything slide. Somehow there may be a turn for the better or we shall perish.

Our life insurance is completely lost; I do not know what Eva will do if I bite the dust. She has lost a lot of weight in the last few months, wasted away, aged, sunk into poverty, so to speak. I myself am fat and plump, but as soon as I walk or crank up the car or make some kind of physical effort or have the least upset I am forever brought up short by throat and heart problems. And after Berthold and Wally it has been engraved on my mind: 59 years.

I am slowly giving up hope of politics; Hitler is after all the Chosen One of his people. I do not believe that he is in the least bit shaky, I am slowly beginning to think that his regime can really still last for decades. There is so much lethargy in the German people and so much immorality and above all so much stupidity.

Nevertheless, what Johanna Krüger wrote to us after her visit in January is right: "You still have so much." In our great loneliness we are perhaps even closer to one another than in former years. For myself the feeling of How much longer? also no doubt plays a part.

We now only rarely go for a drive, shopping or for a short walk. The jalopy can only slowly get used to its renovated limbs, 60 miles not over 25 mph, 60 miles not over 30, 60 miles not over 35. It feels as if we are crawling along, and since we drive so little (and the weather is so bad) we find it very hard. [...]

The best part of the day is reading aloud in the evening, if—there are three ifs: if Eva is not too exhausted and falls asleep while I am reading (she often lies down immediately after the meal, and the critical point is then the quarter of an hour in which I see to the stove); if I am not so tired that I no longer grasp what I am reading; and if my eternally inflamed eyes do not hurt too much. But in the end these three conditions are very often completely or halfway fulfilled.

[...]

April 15, Thursday

Annemarie Köhler, together with Dr. Dressel (to whom she is a little in thrall and who exploits her a little), is going to open a private clinic in Pirna. Both have been assistant doctors in Heidenau for about twelve years, which inevitably gives rise to frictions with the head physician, and now everything is exacerbated by politics; the head physician over-anxiously knuckles under, Dressel practices passive resistance and Annemarie active resistance; she has been harassed by the local rag ("Anyone who says Heil Hitler, gets poor treatment from Doctor Köhler"), there was a row. Among other things, an intelligent, high-class (as it were) maid is required for the clinic. Eva suggested our second Wendish girl, Anna Dürrlich, who at the moment has a position in the "Sozietät," a Catholic association in Bautzen, and who visited us here last year. Yesterday morning Annemarie wrote that she liked the suggestion very much; so in the morning we did some shopping in town, after that, making a sudden decision, we left the car standing outside and after coffee set off for Bautzen just before four. This was our first longer drive for a very long time, and I took pride in treating it not as some big excursion, but as a simple afternoon drive. [...] At half past five we drove through a gate into the town square; there Eva ate a little snack we had brought with us, in the car, then we asked the way to the "Sozietät." A couple of minutes later we came upon Anna in the middle of her kitchen and work, and everything was settled very quickly. The drive back in the twilight and into the darkness was very fast for some time, but toward the end somewhat checked and made difficult by the darkness and dazzling lights. At the station by eight; nourishing and cheap pork ribs with horseradish sauce and dumplings; at home Eva lay down immediately, and I read aloud for almost an hour. In all about 80 miles, the exact distance from our house to Bautzen Town Hall: 37½ miles. — If only we had the money for longer trips! But our predicament grows more desperate day by day.

[. . .] The odometer now shows 23,750, in the autumn it was 23,125. For these 625 miles we have paid out hundreds in taxis and for repairs and suffered so much hardship. Madness really, and yet whenever we reflect on it, the conclusion is to keep it and hold on. It is, in the fullest sense of the word, tragicomic.

The Gehrigs visited us, they are thinking of building a house out here. He said he is writing his reminiscences now. Like Georg. Presumably every second dismissed professor is doing the same thing. I drew two divergent conclusions for myself, (a) what Georg or even Gehrig can do, I too shall surely accomplish, so why such fear with respect to my Life? (b) what is left of the originality of my enterprise?

Besides I will probably not get around to it because my Eighteenth Century grips me again and again, although there is virtually no hope of publication anymore.

[. . .]

Who records the most wretched everyday miseries in his memoirs? Until my fortieth year or so I always had neatly cut newspaper in the smallest room. The toilet roll was a luxury enjoyed in hotels. Then I got used to the little rolls at home. I can no longer do without them anymore. But the few pennies they cost, add up and are a burden. I used to smoke a pipe. I became accustomed to cigars, then to cigarillos. I paid six and eight pfennigs each. The cheapest cigarillos are now the ones at four pfennigs (and then only in a few shops, usually the minimum price is five pfennigs). I reproach myself for not going back to the pipe: it inflames my gums and tongue, it does not satisfy me; I carry on with my four-pfennig luxury with a bad conscience. And likewise in everything and with everyone. The ripped suit I wear at home—and people come to me and beg for an old pair of trousers! But I have a villa and a car. The tragicomic will have a section to itself in my memoirs.

[. . .]

April 25, Sunday

On the twentieth the special postmarks and most of the newspaper headlines said: "The Führer's Birthday." The *Dresdener Anzeiger* or the *Dresdener Nachrichten* are supposed to have printed "Führer's Birthday." The *Dresdener NN* published an article, or rather a religious meditation by a certain Kilian Koll, which in form and content would have perfectly fitted Jeanne d'Arc. [. . .]

An always recurring word: "Experience." Whenever some Gauleiter or SS leader, one of the minor and most minor subordinate gods speaks, then one does not hear his speech, but "experiences" it. Eva rightly says it was already there before National Socialism. Certainly, it is to be found in the currents that created it.

In a strange letter Sussmann inquires about my language study. I wrote that its motto will be: In lingua veritas. [. . .] Sussmann has joined the believers and asks as to my opinion. Sussmann's case is symptomatic three times over: religious in old age, in misfortune and loneliness and probably also carried along by the current of the times.

[. . .]

A psychologically comprehensible, but very silly effect, just like the one already produced by Georg's gift of money in October: communication from the Tax Office about the "adjustment of my retirement income" backdated to April 1, '36. I receive 12M a month more and 173M in arrears. Instead of being pleased at this small relief, I am quite painfully reminded of the countless holes that I *cannot* plug with it (especially the lapsed life insurance). Nevertheless: It is a small help, at least the terrace over the garage can be completed and perhaps the disgraceful mudguard can be patched up, and Eva gets the longed-for roses for the garden, and the excessive dentist's bill, which I complained about, is a little less of a burden.

Very little of the day at home. At eleven o'clock in the morning to the Capitol in Freital: a free film made by the Shell company: *Germany is Beautiful!* All their advertising is based on their touring maps. Wonderful pictures. (Close to the Capitol, on open ground by the Weisseritz, there is a youth club; I was there on the morning of the day before yesterday for the jalopy's "army medical." In the evening at eight to the Sophienkirche (in which the Köhlers were married) for a serenade of music composed by Dietrich Buxtehude (300th birthday). Wonderful, really quite secular music (peasant dances, minuets, etc.). All these trips—even the medical— in pouring rain. Cold, rain, having to keep the heating on all through April. Yesterday I fetched a sack of coal in the jalopy, since our supply exhausted.

April 29, Thursday

[. . .]

For a couple of days now I have been coming to grips with Fénelon. Doubly disappointed: (1) everything has been said about him, I can only repeat it, and (2) it seems to me he does not quite deserve his reputation.

May 12, Wednesday

In the American magazine an advertisement for a laxative snaked its way right through the middle of my article: "A human being has thirty feet of intestines." [. . .]

I am only getting around to noting that today, because in the meantime I got my teeth into Wilbrandt. Robert Wilbrandt sent me two addresses, a periodical in Los Angeles and one in Vienna. After thirty years I found the two articles hard, but they turned out really well and proved to me that I can still manage journalistically as well. "Perhaps you'll even earn some money!" And if I have very good luck, then I also have a contact for further journalism. At any rate I spent one and a half weeks on it. Tomorrow I want to plunge back into Fénelon. [. . .]

What absorbs us most at the moment is the trip to Berlin. Grete has begged us again and again, the last time literally with a quotation from the New Testament. And the 170M which fell from heaven would not have sufficed for the insurance anyway. So we made up our minds. Gratifying preparation or outfitting for the trip: I bought a very ordinary pair of trousers and a light jacket, which will do service over the summer; Wolf, the better successor to the dubious Michael, has just patched up the disgraceful mudguard for me for 15M and put metal bands on the ragged strip of running board.

Our plan is this: on Monday to drive via Frankfurt to Grete in Strausberg, on Tuesday to go with her to Landsberg, then on Wednesday we want to be with Marta, and go for an excursion with her, on Thursday see something of Berlin and drive back. Unfortunately I have been hampered for weeks by some mysterious pulled muscle or inflammation in my right arm, which seems to get worse rather than better. Perhaps Sussmann will know what to do. I am as excited as a child about this first journey (*journey*, not excursion) by car; not since our South American trip have I so yearningly counted the days before a departure. Everything about it is exciting, the journey itself, unfamiliar Berlin, my relatives; it can all turn out equally nice or equally horrible. It will certainly be very exhausting, but has gradually become unavoidable and we must now see it through.

[. . .]

Agnes and her husband cycled here from Piskowitz to visit us. The usually calm Scholze, now very embittered politically, maintained that the Catholic Wends were "seething." The newspaper has also been full of indecency trials against priests; it seems to me to be the barrage preceding a blow against the Catholic Church. When the zeppelin was destroyed I felt sad: Poor people! But everything that weakens this government's prestige is to the benefit of Germany.

Agnes told us that the Thiemes had visited them in their own car, he is now chief engineer and a very important person, apart from that he has already turned gray. Perhaps he has backed the wrong horse after all; his forsaking of me is one of the saddest things among the many bitter experiences of this kind. (In your Memoirs do not forget those who made it easy for themselves and those who were cautious on both sides! and not the philistine Spamer, who visited us and called the *Stürmer* an insignificant scandal sheet, such as have always existed, and is now a big ethnologist with the Nazis and so betrays his discipline; who talked to me so openly about the stupidity of the people, whom anything can be drummed into.)

May 21, Friday

Drive to Berlin, Strausberg, Landsberg a.d. Warthe, May 17–20, Whit Monday–Thursday.
    [. . .]

May 22

Lange came on Monday morning and brought the dashboard clock, which he had repaired. We drove off a little before ten and took him with us as far as Klotzsche. Upsetting, time-consuming incident at the Neustadt station: A boy coming at right angles to me went into my car and fell off his cycle, he was unharmed, the bicycle twisted. Long interrogation of the boy and of a witness at the railway station police office, the boy was solely to blame, had to have bicycle repaired and pay a one mark fine; afterward I gave him 50 pfennigs as a present. At last we got going just before eleven. The stretch through Königsbruck Forest is always lovely, being able to pick up speed on long flat sections always gives me great pleasure. Eva's lunch had been scheduled for Cottbus, but the road took us past the edge of the town. Well Guben then—but the road branched before that. We finally stopped at a proper village inn at Sembten. Lunchtime over, all the rooms empty, radio music, occasionally a soldier or a village lad. There are still dumplings, at most a little meat with it. There appeared a plate of soup, a giant plate of roast veal, a bowl with five dumplings, stewed fruit and jelly and it all cost one mark, and my kümmel cost thirty pfennigs. Then on to Frankfurt. Urban and elegant, mighty church, but the best the bridge across the Oder. Truly a broad river [. . .], splendid with its green and sandy white islands. We had a break for coffee on the terrace of a handsome hotel in the town center, walked through the streets a little, were in the Marienkirche church for a couple of minutes. Departed at five—the time at which Grete was expecting us. [. . .] Müncheberg, finally Strausberg. A strung-out place, then road through woodland, then suburb "Strausberg II." Grete lives at 4 Moltkestrasse, in the little house of a small farm, by the "Threshing Mill," a tram stop between Strausberg and Strausberg II. There at half past seven.

Grete considerably aged (69), walking slowly with a cane but actually very vigorous and lively nevertheless. Probably really suffering from a heart condition and needing a lot of digitalis. But since she has been hysterical and affected all her life, she gets little credence from Sussmann-Jelski. [. . .] Grete, with whom we did not get on very well a couple of years ago in Dresden, could not have been more welcoming. Her landlord and landlady, old smallholders, positively cherish her, admittedly they also appear to live off her to a great extent. Grete plays at or lives (who can separate the two?) being one with nature and the last pleasures of an old woman who is half a cripple and entirely a hermit. Frau Kemlein, the motherly landlady, says last year she really was close to death, the doctor had almost given up hope.

A vegetable garden and an orchard, a henhouse, all of it only separated by wire netting from the pine forest, which Grete and the hens are free to roam. All of it several degrees more natural and less parklike than in the allotment settlements closer to Berlin. Then there is the landlady's mother, something of a forest witch, 88 years old, deaf, garrulous, idiotic, inquisitive, stealing and hiding food, roughly treated by her children. "Me old mother," physically robust, was in Buch alcoholics asylum, was taken out a little while ago because of the cost. On the last election day SA men turned up, to get her to the ballot box. She thought they were going to forcibly take her back to Buch, screamed and struggled, was seized by the arms and dragged into the car. At the polling booth she was shown where to draw her cross, given a glass of wine and then taken home in a state of bliss. Thus she was one of the 99 percent of Germans who voted for the Führer . . . We were put up in Grete's living room, it was very simple and makeshift, but all done with the greatest affection. We breakfasted in a summerhouse, the jalopy spent the night in the street in front of the house.

The next morning, at about ten, to Landsberg, good smooth drive—we had great luck with the weather throughout the trip. The only really annoying thing for me was that later Grete asked, in all seriousness, whether I was also able to drive when I was alone and Eva did not constantly direct me, "Watch out, bend!" or "More to the right!" etc. "I thought you might have arranged it like that so that you drive according to her instructions and not by yourself like a chauffeur!" . . . In Küstrin we stopped at the Warthe bridge, [. . .] we stood by the water and listened to the frogs croaking. After that long straight roads, frequently with a view of the river. For long sections I went at 40, 45 mph, even then it still took almost three hours to reach Landsberg. I have not been there for 35 years, it was a completely unfamiliar, ordinary middling town. Only a few names of suburbs, the big red market church, the grammar school and the river behind it, as well as the low ground around the Hopfenbruch tavern (where we played skittles) brought back memories; everything else left me cold and indifferent. There is a large modern official building opposite the grammar school, town hall I think; instead of the suspension bridge, which we crossed to reach the playing field on the other side of the Warthe, there is

a solid new bridge; the Rathauskeller, in which we ate at lunchtime, is
new, as is the big café beside the grammar school. Grete knew this coffee-
house as the Confectioner Kadoch of her childhood, she showed me a
house in Bergstrasse, where I was born, a corner nearby, where the nurse-
maid sat on a bench with me; she wallowed unceasingly in memories. We
were already thinking of driving back when [. . .] an old lady asked us
where our car came from. Grete got into a conversation; Böhm, her father,
had been a well-known town architect, her twin sister a friend of Grete's—
the lady got into our car, we had to drive down several streets, in which I
found nothing of interest, unlike Grete. To me it was embarrassing that
Grete held back her name, which the old girl must ascertain very quickly
from what we said. And what if we are non-Aryans! We, who put Landsberg in the Brockhaus Encyclopedia, are not the ones who need to be
ashamed! The old girl, piano teacher for 50 years, told us she had "received 200 marks from Goebbels." We left Landsberg at half past four.
[. . .] Back at our quarters at half past seven. On Wednesday we breakfasted in the summerhouse once again [. . .] A short drive through the
town, parked the car [. . .], walked a little by the shore of the lake, while
Grete sat on a bench. A large expanse of water, completely surrounded by
woods. One part of the town on a hill protruding into the lake looks Italian (from a distance of course). A ferry, villas along the wooded lakeside
road, jetties, trees at the water's edge, fishermen, a croaking frog, silence.
Back for an early lunch, Eva got a beautiful piece of jewelry as a present,
we had to swear to come again. Departure two o'clock. In my cold heart I
was actually pleased to have put this behind me. The feeling of being a
stranger did not leave me for a single moment.

Now the 22 miles to Berlin, first still the countryside of the Mark Brandenburg, another large lake, then gradually the suburbs and suburban
traffic; we drove slowly down Frankfurter Allee, and then the great bustle
began at Alexanderplatz. I got past the Palace and into Unter den Linden
without difficulty. It made an enormous impression, not the street—I only
saw the "little limes," nothing else—but the huge amount of traffic, such
as I had previously only seen in Paris and Buenos Aires. The vehicles in
each direction four abreast, one has to calculate distances down to the last
centimeter. I got through safely, but sweat was pouring down me. Constantly forward at speed a little bit, then stop. I could not see the traffic
lights at first, which are small and hidden away to the side. Once I stopped
at the last moment. A policeman in a white jacket (like Russian students,
says Eva) came up to give me a warning, very polite and paternally ad-
monishing, when he saw the out-of-town number plate. Throughout both
days I was repeatedly very much taken with the friendly and humorous
manner of the policemen; the same was true of the "people" of Berlin,
with whom I came in contact again after so many years. We drove through
the Brandenburg Gate, along Charlottenburger Chaussee and into the unfamiliar western expanses, we were at the radio tower, we drove over
Halensee Bridge twice, before we eventually found Kudowastrasse.

Everywhere streets of fine villas, everywhere streets with big apartment blocks and yet streets with greenery along and around them. Certainly it is not so different from what existed before, certainly it is not so different from what we have in Dresden—but this huge expanse! Truly, a metropolis. I don't know: Has Berlin really grown so much, or have I become such a bumpkin? At any rate I was literally fascinated, and the enormous impression made by the city grew ever greater. Between coffee and evening meal I went for a short walk with Jelski, saw a vast open sports field, on which a couple of girls were practicing the discus, a couple running, boys playing ball, saw the huge lawn that serves the block of houses at Kudowastrasse as a communal garden.

Sussmann had been there for coffee; after the meal Heinz Machol—now grown unnaturally fat and thickset—appeared with his second wife. Naturally and unavoidably a lot of politics was talked, and since Jelski still stands up for the Nazis to some degree and fears Communism, without seeing how identical they are, we became very heated. But I discovered with pleasure that the temper of Jewry, which had once been so pessimistic, is now hopeful. Things are said to be very bad for the government both economically and as far as the mood in the country is concerned: Heinz Machol, an automobile engineer, virtually maintained that the end must come before the year is out. The night before, Marta had copied out a handwritten letter circulating in Berlin, which Thomas Mann had sent from Küsnacht to a Swiss newspaper at New Year: a response to the withdrawal of his doctoral diploma and of his citizenship, addressed to the dean of Bonn University. I read the letter next morning: terribly brusque and contemptuous. But what excited me more than the content was the fact that the letter circulates "everywhere" in this way. It is supposed to be exactly the same with the banned papal pastoral letter, "everyone" has already read it. (In Strausberg Grete found a chain letter to everyone in the mailbox, the scandalous trials of churchmen are based on lies.) There was a "People's Asparagus Day" in Berlin recently, so that the populace could buy the delicacy cheaply; the well-known reason is the shortage of tin cans. Many factories are said to be in ferment and the workers very open in their speech. On Friday, when I told Vogel, the grocer here, the mood in Berlin was bad, he had already heard about it long ago, and he added that in Munich things were boiling up even more. That lifted and encouraged me immensely . . . Machol tested my squealing engine and said it could only be the slip ring of the clutch. He lectured me fairly arrogantly, I did not understand anything about driving yet, I was far too nervous and opened the throttle far too much when I started. Nevertheless, with this trip I have acquired a license for long-distance journeys. . . . The jalopy once again spent the night safely in the street, and we spent it in Marta's living room. In the morning I heard a cuckoo clock, but it kept on striking, it was a real cuckoo. As we were sitting at breakfast, there was an almighty crash outside (no, it was on Wednesday evening during dinner): a gentleman from the house next door had bumped into my car, but only dented his mudguard without damaging me.... On Thursday morning we went for a drive with the Jelskis. It was very exhausting, because whenever Marta said "Left," Jelski said "Right." The road to Potsdam as far as Wannsee. Extremely impressive; broad straight highway between marvelous rows of trees, villas or big similar-looking apartment blocks, behind them the forest, pines and oaks, all of it simultaneously nature and symmetrical order, all of it elegant and wealthy and in endless succession. From Kudowastrasse, which itself is already in the Grunewald Forest district, we had driven 10 miles without the buildings—now a group of villas, now a housing development, a bit of main street, but always surrounded by greenery—being interrupted for even a yard. Again the impression of the endless and endlessly well-kept city. At Wannsee railway station we turned slowly, had a view of a corner of the lake (yacht harbor) and drove back the same way. [...] Back at the Jelskis at twelve, swift leave-taking and now to déjeuner at Sussmann's, i.e., via Kurfürstendamm and Wittenbergplatz to Bayreutherstrasse. Just as crowded as on the Linden on Wednesday, but I was already more practiced. When we stopped at Sussmann's, we saw a broken bottle behind our car and immediately had dark forebodings.

Sussmann received us with great friendliness, entertained us, examined my right arm, which has been strained for weeks, in fact months (without being able to help), showed off his stamp album, gave me a large number and a pair of tweezers as a present. He believes he is creating a valuable asset with his collection, buys and arranges systematically, it probably helps him get through empty evenings. Afterward I said with relief to Eva that one must be widowed to be a proper stamp collector. Departed at half past one. Just at the corner of Kurfürstenstrasse a policeman called out: "There's no air in your wheel!" (It then turned out that the tire had not got a puncture at all, but rather that a stud inside had rubbed through the tube.) My jack was too high for the level of the car, the policeman pointed out a repair shop in the next street. There was a young man there who seemed somehow disabled, because his wife joined him and solicitously took his arm during the wheel changing. In a quarter of an hour the spare wheel had been fitted; I asked him how much it cost, he looked at his wife, she said: "50 pfennigs." He got a cigar as well, and both went off thanking us. I moved off slowly [...]. Now Bülowstrasse, Yorckstrasse [...], then into Belle Alliance Strasse, past the airport (there was a huge machine on the grass), past a complex of half-finished buildings and out of Berlin on a smooth road. Problem: Is all of it real or only apparent prosperity? ... In Wusterhausen a forest of radio masts. Eva counted 15 at one spot, immediately afterward a similar circle with probably the same number of masts. The way the perforated steel constructions rose up into the haze and seemed to disappear in it was very extraordinary. [...] In the nineties, when Eva lived in nearby Niederlehme, Königs Wusterhausen was *the town* for her. Our jalopy was parked by the road to the side of the castle: There was a shoe shop here, and in the window Eva discovered a pair of linen shoes that fit her and which she bought immediately. I must also add that shortly before this stop we had come across yet another huge transmitter facility, close to a military training area. We also passed mobile antiaircraft guns that looked like very large brigands' rifles in old Italian pictures: long narrow barrels, widening into funnels at the muzzle. Everything around Wusterhausen made a military impression, aviation and radio very much in the service of war. Then it was a matter of driving as fast as possible, I tried to keep to a regular speed of 40, 45 mph. All the time straight, fine smooth, almost empty roads through forest. If the road was shut off on both sides, the effect was almost dangerously soporific, when a view over meadows or plantations appeared, I became more wide awake. [. . .] No stop until Lübben just before six. Gasoline and water for the jalopy. Grape juice, soda water, cheese and bread for us on a hotel terrace. We set off again at half past six, in order to cover as much ground as possible before darkness. Now I saw hardly anything else except the side of the road, but again driving in itself was a pleasure, but of course also tiring. Through Cottbus and Spremberg, then lights became necessary. Now the romance and the strain of bends and forest driving with headlights. In Königsbruck and after, the continual problem of approaching lights and of constantly having to dip my lights. Naturally I had to reduce speed, but I made good and safe progress. (The only thing that is dangerous is always the second after passing a car with powerful lights; at the next moment it is impossible to see whether one has a pedestrian or a cyclist in front of one on the right.) From time to time the jalopy squealed shrilly and mysteriously, but otherwise it ran well. After ten in Dresden; the jalopy squealed terribly again in Pragerstrasse, of all places. [. . .] Home at half past ten; Frau Lehmann had slept here the past few days and taken care of house and tomcat very well.

All in all therefore a completely successful trip and full of interest as regards countryside, driving, relations, likewise politics. Principal impression remains: Berlin and the handwritten Thomas Mann.

May 23, Sunday

Vacation week until tomorow; then back to the opus.

I have been typing the diary since Friday, seeing to the jalopy. Wolf was here, I took the tire to him in Freital, we brought back the patched tire together, oil experiments were carried out everywhere to track down the squealing. I read aloud, I made an effort to return to normal life. [. . .]

A great wealth of blooms in our garden. Rhododendron, azaleas, tulips, iris, cornflowers, first roses, thrift, the herbs of the rock garden, in particular pale blue soapwort, a viburnum, a hawthorn, masses of buttercups, red, yellow, blue, white, confusion of tulips, extraordinary variety. A recurring problem, however, is the final cementing of the terrace above the garage. After we had frost damage at the beginning of the winter, we (i.e.,

Lange, Eva and myself) are very anxious, and since there is a constant threat of thunderstorms, the work is postponed again and again.

[...]

June 2, Wednesday

I began to familiarize myself with Fénelon at the end of April. Then there was the Wilbrandt episode until May 12, then, with effects felt long after, the Berlin trip. Only today, with a great deal of effort, have I written the first lines of the Fénelon section. I find it immensely difficult, first of all because he has been so thoroughly "done," secondly because I want to slip in Saint-Simon at the same time. And with all this struggle always the feeling that I am probably working for the desk drawer and the worms.

The encouragement of Berlin has not held up. That the bombardment of Almería is once again calmly tolerated, is proof to me of the power of the government. In today's newspapers the struggle against the Catholic Church takes precedence again. What a gift, by the way, for a future satirist, when the Nazis and the monastery people accuse each other of homosexuality and buggery.

Eva made the most pertinent remark on the Almería business. She pointed to the deep indifference, indeed evident apathy with which the whole thing was received. Neither in front of the newspaper display boxes nor in any way in the traffic on the street or in people's behavior or in fragments of conversation was the least degree of any kind of concern to be detected. No patriotic excitement, no fear of war, no sympathy with the sailors of the *Deutschland*—nothing at all. The never ending alarms, the never ending phrases, the never ending hanging out of flags, now in triumph, now in mourning—it all produces apathy. And everyone feels helpless, and everyone knows he is being lied to, and everyone is told what he has to believe. Whether one gets a quarter pound of butter tomorrow or not, is much more important than all the problems with Spain and the Vatican. And probably no one expects war anymore; people have gotten used to the foreign powers putting up with everything.

June 11, Friday evening

For days really enervating heat, over 30 degrees in the shade. On top of that today again, as last autumn, harassment by the local council because of the unkempt garden, the risk of weeds, etc. Three-mark fine, threat of legal action. I am quite helpless in the face of this deliberate malice. When the letter came, the grass had already been partly cut and the "Uncle" was continuing the work. In addition the lack of movement in the political atmosphere. Almería smoothed out, the glorious indecency trials against the monasteries continued day after day, day after day articles and speeches about happy, united Germany freed from unemployment, peace day after day. — Helmut Lehmann doing his Labor Service in East Prussia has already been withdrawn from the shared work, along with other especially strapping lads, for special parade-ground drill for the Party Rally in September. [...] These people are simply confident that they will still be in power and at peace in September. So far their certainty has never been proved wrong, no matter how they have provoked Germany and the world.

Besides, under the pressure of the council harassment, my mood has of course relapsed. The last few days were better. I made infinitely slow progress, but made progress nevertheless in the difficult Fénelon–Saint-Simon chapter, and the manuscript will probably be finished on Sunday. And yesterday I was very pleased at Grete's invitation to a car trip to be worked out by us. [...] Of course it was Eva who immediately suggested Cuxhaven and drew up the plan. [...]

June 14, Monday morning

At last a little cooler and at last (after two and a half months, counting all the interruptions and preparatory reading) the manuscript of Fénelon–Saint-Simon is complete. Only yesterday! If possible I want to type the piece before starting on the new journey, that is before Monday.

June 20, Sunday

The journey to the North Sea is to begin tomorrow, and just half of Fénelon has been typed. The whole of yesterday was swallowed up by shopping and having the car lubricated; today I am hampered by a bad migraine, have only copied one page (copying means: reading my tiny writing and turning each sentence inside out again and writing out the quotations!) and then proceeded to accumulated correspondence, above all a handwritten birthday letter for Blumenfeld. The migraine is probably the result of visiting Frau Schaps yesterday evening; her widowed sister-in-law was there, a Frau Lemberg from Berlin, whose husband had been a barrister (she gave me the Rousseau from her husband's library as a present). She related how her husband had retired from his profession at the age of fifty and lived entirely for his interests, languages, literatures, music, his own singing, Bayreuth, travel.

I noted for myself, type: Herr Karl Kaufmann, shoe manufacturer of Dresden, now Tel Aviv. Something similar had gone through my head in the morning. A letter arrived from some sixth-form girl in Mülheim/Ruhr who is enraptured by literature. My *Romanische Sonderart* [Romance Peculiarities] had stimulated her to ask questions ... there followed esthetic and bibliographic questions, only a very small number of which I answered immediately. Once the writer would have interested me, now she is nothing more than a first-semester type (before it begins). Such instant categorization and classification is a sign of age. Another, no doubt general sign of age: When I came to Dresden at 38, and for a long time after that, I inwardly distanced myself from colleagues, from a great many other people likewise; I felt: They are old, it is impossible for them to feel as you do. Now the same feeling of distance a hundred times over: They are young, they do not feel as you do. I think every person quite instinctively and naively divides the whole of humankind into old and young and up to some moment reckons himself to be in one half and then in the other. I do not know when I changed over. Nor do I know when I first had the feeling of age in eroticis (which is no way to be confused with a lessening of desire, nor with impotence).

It was a pleasant evening at Frau Schaps; there was a garden party in the villa garden next door with a big fireworks display, we were the enchanted lookers-on from the hallway. On Frau Schaps' radio we listened to a live broadcast of *Götterdämmerung* from the Vienna Opera, I found the recitatives curiously stiff and 300 years away; on an electric phonograph we heard splendid songs by Richard Tauber and from *La Traviata*. [. . .]

The constant rumors throughout the populace about Mayor Zörner. People always only say as an afterthought that he is implicated in an embezzlement or bribery case, which is linked to last year's garden show (Linke). All the little people (Lange, butter dealer, Wolf, the car man, Frau Lehmann, Vogel) always first of all come out with the expression, He is "infected." Everyone always says his wife left him long ago. Which is because his wedding here was staged as a kind of government ceremony and as propaganda for National Socialist population policy and morality. In a single day three people came independently to us: "Zörner has shot himself." (Wolf: "An official told me.") Later: He has been suspended and is in Berlin with Hitler, his personal friend. There is not a word in the newspaper. They *must* know that the rumors are going around everywhere, and yet nothing is repudiated. . . . Also important to me is that I several times heard from ordinary people: There should be an "educated" man in a post like that, why did they give it to a shopkeeper, a Party man? Thus I listen out for anything stirring, but ultimately it is probably always the singing in my own ear in the midst of great silence.

Zaunick, grammar school teacher and honorary professor of something to do with physics at the TU, man around fifty, once indebted to me, recently came up to the car as we were parked at Bismarckplatz. Party badge. Could easily walk past without acknowledging us, could at the most greet us. But comes up with evident heartfelt pleasure. How am I, whether I have stayed in Dresden, how sorry he is . . . What I had published recently? "Wait and work!" — "For posterity?" — "One has to wait and see." Hearty handshake and sorrowful withdrawal. A Party member!

I have received proofs of my Wilbrandt article for Vienna. It was at once a pleasant and very melancholy feeling to see myself in print once again.

The cads had not even acknowledged receipt of my article, and not replied at all to my inquiry whether occasional further contributions were welcome. I first had to turn to Robert Wilbrandt, who complained. That is how small I have become; and yet I was pleased. [...]

Betty writes from Cleveland (Ohio) that she is coming to Europe in the summer—invitation from her sister Grete Rebenwurzel-Goldschmidt, who has been living in Paris for years. We invited her to stay with us. . . . Considerable jealousy between Marta and Grete because of our Whitsun trip. How much worse will it be after we have been to the North Sea! I am really concerned, would not want to offend Marta, but what is to be done? [...]

June 28, Monday

On Monday morning, June 21, we were making final preparations for the Strausberg–North Sea trip. Then at eight o'clock the council gardener turned up: inspection to see whether the garden has been weeded. I show him that everything has been cut; he reaches for something on the ground: "There are still weeds here—and here and here. I have to report that, they will send workers here compulsorily"—Forest law, etc. I: "What is it that you require?" — "You have to pay a couple of hundred marks for the garden to be worked on by professional gardeners." — I: "Where shall I get the money from? I have been thrown out of my post." — He, a good-natured, simple man, who now realizes what is going on: "Oh, then you are a non-Aryan?" Now the context and the inescapability of the situation were clear to him. He is sorry, but if he reports anything other than that weeds are still growing here, then a senior inspector will come and he loses his job. — Under these circumstances I could not risk leaving. Telegram to Grete. Went to see Weller. He was here at midday, and in the evening I signed a contract with him: The whole garden will be worked on and a lawn sown, price: 400 to 500M at most. Monthly installments 50M. That means many months of the greatest privation for us, means that it is impossible to pay anything at all to the Iduna, with that the final surrender of the life insurance, a loss of thousands, and the loss of cover for the mortgage (the Wengler mortgage runs for another four years). And it does not at all mean that I am now safe from further harassment. They can always find something if they want to. And they want to. The next thing is likely to be the roof. A building law against "unrestrained liberalism" has just been published, houses must all without exception fit in with street and landscape; so they will demand slate instead of my tar board. Etc., etc. It is curious how apathetically I endure it all: Perhaps we shall soon perish, perhaps the other will perish, perhaps a way out will be found somehow, as it already has been a couple of times in the past. It cannot be helped, one cannot live normally in an abnormal time. I am no longer going to worry about what happens after tomorrow, it is all so pointless.

— So we have remained at home, so two men have been working in the garden since Thursday, so I have covered the first two garden installments with the money set aside for the Iduna.

Meanwhile Eva's teeth are acting up again, luckily only the technical ones that do not hurt; but that too is a financial burden. After a quite shameless bill from Dr. Kunstmann we have changed to Eichler, the young and congenial successor to Dr. Isakowitz and so drive to Königsbrücker Strasse again, where everything (except the dentist), everything, nurse included, is unchanged.

Is it idiocy, philosophy, age, or is it the feeling of living in an age which is absolutely without rules? I now only have fits of depression, otherwise let things take their course and have for hours at a time a quite cheerful feeling of being alive. So now our garden will be luxuriant. Who is going to fear what will happen in four years' time? — And likewise with my Dix-huitième. I forcibly repress the thought that there is no prospect of publication and am happy that my work is making progress. If the worst comes to the worst I shall bequeath the completed manuscript to a Swiss library.

And so in this not–North Sea week, the Fénelon–Saint-Simon section was finally completed, after almost two months, right down to the last dot on the "i," and now I have embarked on the study of Vauvenargues. (Thus far his reputation seems exaggerated. [. . .].)

My Life. Recently I suddenly saw before me and heard: I have got out of reading aloud (Graetz, *History of the Jews* or something like it), I am tired. It is about half past eight. My bed, that is the sofa in Father's room, beside me the tall bookcases. Now Wally is sitting at the desk and goes on reading. It was probably still in Albrechtstrasse, opposite the Grenadiers' barracks, Wally was 17, I was 12, Father (to me the ageless old man) much younger than I am today. Father dead, Wally dead, and so many pictures crowd in on me. I would so much like to write it down. But first the Dix-huitième, then the Language of the Third Reich and then, as Father said, on Sirius. How I played marbles downstairs with street Arabs, while upstairs they were weeping over Hedwig's death, how I ran as far as Potsdamer Platz with my hoop and was proud of it and then left it lying, because it had rolled through sh . . . and disgusted me, how the soldiers drilled, how Georg came to dinner from the Charite and had free tickets for the adults, from a patient, for the Deutsches Theater, where Naturalism was in its heyday, how Grete went into raptures about *Hannele,* how in floods of tears I explained that I *could never* learn the French school prayer: Notre commencement soit au nom du Père qui a fait le ciel et la terre . . . If I only think for ten minutes, X things occur to me.

The biscuit tin, out of which only Georg was given Father's apple cake (which Grete also recently mentioned with resentment) . . .

Language of the Third Reich: Rust, the Education Minister at a Heidelberg University ceremony: Now scholarship had a National Socialist orientation, and students were political soldiers. — Today a Hitler speech in

Würzburg once again pure religious madness. Only that he did not say I, but we. "Providence guides us, we act according to the will of the Almighty. No one can make national or world history without the blessing of this Providence."

Letter from Hatzfeld in Heidelberg. He feels, he says, almost word for word what is going through my head; he has never worked more intensively and with greater interest than now; and yet he cannot conceal how much he longs to be out of Germany.

[. . .]

July 13, Tuesday

On the 29th of June the weather was too bad for an excursion. But at least we could go to the cinema in the evening. On July 12, on the other hand, a storm was raging (for the second, in fact the third day) with unceasing cloudbursts, such as we have never ever experienced in Dresden, and we sat confined at home; except in the evening Eva set about draining the flooded garage and I carried out water by the bucketful (almost as I had emptied the battery emplacement in Aubers). So a birthday entirely without celebration. I read aloud a lot—during the day, which I only do very rarely now—and in between completed the manuscript of the Vauvenargues section.

[. . .]

The garden work, delayed by the continuing bad weather after excessive heat, is coming to an end. Recently a conversation with Weller brought both of us almost to the brink of despair. The man, discriminated against by the Nazis, a bitter enemy of Kalix, of Zörner and many others, not unintelligent, not a Jew hater, expresses ideas that in form and content are pure National Socialism. About the necessity of the community of the people, of distinct races, of the identity of law and power, of the unquestionable superiority of the new German army over all attackers (since *we* do not want to attack, of course, and only want peace), of the need to fight off Communism (without realizing that here we have a more hypocritical form of Communism), etc. I said to Eva, the man is quite unaware how much of a National Socialist he is, and Eva compared the Weller case to that of Martha Wiechmann. And I said to myself once again, that Hitlerism is after all more deeply and firmly rooted in the nation and corresponds more to the German nature than I would like to admit.

On Eva's birthday there also came a joint card from Frau Schaps, Liesel and Elfriede Sebba, sent from the Dolomites. (They met in Venice, while Jule Sebba is setting up a branch of his chandlery in Tel Aviv.) Jule and Liesel Sebba married on September 21, 1921, as I was giving the speech for the Dante commemoration. The child was born exactly one year later

[. . .] Little Elfriede Sebba was completely German and a European soul and with ideas about humanity self-evident in the twentieth century. When she was twelve years old, her parents had to go to Palestine. What view of life will the young girl have today? Can it bear even the remotest similarity to my view of life? The psychologists of the next generation will find a great deal to interest them there: for me, however, it is not a subject for scholarship, but a matter of failure and despair.

July 19, Monday

[. . .]

When politicians idealize rural labor, they are always being hypocritical. Rousseau has never triumphed to such a degree nor been taken ad absurdum to such a degree as today. The posthumous unmasking of Rousseau is called Hitler.

We have rediscovered the cinema at Freiberger Platz: It has the most naive (truly proletarian and enthusiastic) audience, it is cheaper than the other cinemas (80Pf for a seat in the stalls against 1.50M or 1.30 elsewhere), it has a good program, good projection, and the most spacious parking lot, a real harbor. We saw a revival of *Maskerade* there, Paula Wessely's earliest and most famous film. [. . .] In the supporting program the opening of the Dresden-Meerane autobahn and a part of Hitler's speech. Without the least exaggeration: The man shouts in a strained voice like a drunken and paranoid laborer. The choice of words and the content corresponds to the tone: This is the greatest feat that has ever been accomplished. A couple of foreigners come to our country and in time more, and in the end they have to accept us after all and no longer believe the Jewish lies of the foreign press (sic!). The mixture of absence of dignity, megalomania, impotent fear is frightful. The only thing more frightful is that Germany allows itself to be governed by that.

[. . .]

On the fifteenth in Hirschsprung over lunchtime—the glorious stretch Kipsdorf to Altenberg—to visit Riese-Dember. The mother, 83, up there again after yet another, the umpteenth, light stroke, as lively as last year, Frau Dember with her again. Unchanged. — Abroad no one believes war is coming. England doesn't want it. And Hitler carries on. — In Istanbul Auerbach is generally judged a flop, but is now firmly established; Spitzer had come over from the USA to see his assistant, whom he had bequeathed to Auerbach.

[. . .]

I leafed through *Nathan*. It was not the (questionable) philo-Semitism that touched me—questionable because *Nathan* is emphatically an exception—but the sentence: "What does nation mean after all?" — I myself have had too much nationalism inside me and am now punished for it.

July 26, Monday

On Saturday, without advance notification from Georg or the bank (as the first time) a mysterious note from the Diskontobank: A sum of money is ready for you on proof of identity, etc. I thought it was a Wilbrandt fee from Los Angeles or Vienna—I have received a copy of *Theater der Welt* [Theater of the World] from there with my article. Again it was 500M from Georg's blocked account and so again a couple of big and beneficent drops of water on a very hot stone. Again we do not really get out of our difficulties, the Iduna question remains unsolved, and again we are to some extent released from great worries and again more mobile. I wrote to Georg, he puts me greatly to shame, but along with other concepts, the sense of shame has probably also undergone a change, and the best thanks is probably if I tell him how much he has helped me out of my difficulties, and that the first thing I did was to put 6 gallons of gasoline in my tank and to drive to the Scherners. — So now the garden business has immediately become less of a tragedy, and I also immediately ordered fifty hundredweight of coke as winter store. [. . .]

August 6, Friday

My Dix-huitième is stuck for three reasons. (1) The *Vauvenargues* by Lanson and the Monglond I ordered from Berlin arrived. Lanson forces me to make a partial revision (not far-reaching, but it means a delay), Monglond needs to be read for my later chapters and must be returned by the end of August; on the other hand I am in the middle of the Prévost section, and so I am always vacillating between reading and continuing to write and wanting to improve and do not really make progress with any of it. (2) The appalling stagnation of the political situation, the maneuvering of England, etc. robs me of all spirit; once again I believe that the Third Reich can last for decades yet, that it really corresponds to the national will and national character of Germany, and in this state of depression what I do seems so completely pointless and it seems a matter of complete indifference to me whether a couple of dozen manuscript pages more or less are lying around when I die. (3) The money from Georg which is unable to stuff any of the larger holes and runs through my hands (I have nevertheless saved the small Iduna policy for six months with 150, but perhaps it would have been more sensible to spend this 150M also on amusements—and I ordered 90M worth of coal, and there is a little reserve for the dental bill, which is increasing dreadfully again), the money therefore makes larger gasoline expenditure possible for a couple of weeks, and so again and again we simply trundle away from the heat and the kitchen duty and the misery of the gloomiest thoughts, for just as long as the reserve lasts.

On Saturday, July 24, we were in Hirschsprung once more. This time Frau Riese had greatly deteriorated and was for the first time an old woman with a failing memory. [. . .]

The very next morning, Sunday, July 25, making a sudden decision, we set out for Falkenstein to see the Scherners. Partly because I drive better now than last year, partly because we made full use of the Dresden-Meerane motorway, we covered the distance more rapidly than the last time. Halfway between leaving the autobahn and Falkenstein, in Ebersbrunn, a little tourist café, Eva ate lunch and I telephoned the Scherners. He was on duty, and the bookkeeper, who brought us greetings from him a couple of weeks ago, was with him; we later took her back with us on the return journey, she was no trouble. We got a good coffee in Scherner's pharmacy, we took the Scherners (and their dachshund) for a drive of a couple of kilometers to a little dam in the forest, we drove back at seven and reached the autobahn at Glauchau as darkness fell. Now a very fast, but nevertheless exhausting night drive—the approaching headlamps make it more difficult to see, but are also fantastically beautiful. (In addition a very large moon hung over forest and road.) At the central railway station after ten, where we set down the girl, who comes from the Meissen district, and ate a snack as well. Day's performance 209 miles.

Scherner has become excessively fat, a little sickly, probably also mentally aged. Nothing remains of the aspiring scholar, nor of the hatred of the small town of earlier years. He is the slave of his pharmacy, he sells like a greengrocer, he has problems with his eyes and with walking, he turns over 60,000M per annum, but works only for his creditors, cannot purchase a car because they would take it amiss, he raises chickens and pigeons in the garden behind the pharmacy, occasionally also sells eggs; like him his wife is very fat, is in the pharmacy during the day and like him content with that. They are not Nazis, are very fond of us, but the Führer's picture hangs in the pharmacy, and they seem quite indifferent to politics. They vegetate bourgeoislike and are all in all contented old fat good people. [. . .]

August 8, Sunday

In between only a very short tour (12 miles), Coschütz–Bannewitz, in order to escape the terrible stifling heat and get a little air. But tomorrow we want to fetch Frau Lehmann from Thuringia, and today a letter came from Grete, full of enthusiasm for travel, to which I replied immediately. Grand combinations are being planned—God knows how our finances will cope with it, especially as the dental bill mounts and mounts and I have now after all flung 150M into the jaws of Iduna.

The philologist registers a momentary lifting of mood in his style: Today I brought the manuscript of the Prévost to a very nice conclusion— it really is too good for the worms and yet probably written only for them.

Plan for the coming week: tomorrow Haardorf, near Naumburg. Then revise Vauvenargues, then plow through the Berlin books, before I type Prévost. [. . .] The beginning of the trip to Strausberg and the seaside has provisionally been set for Wednesday, August 18.

There are cinema evenings to be caught up with, very enjoyable ones— if only there were not each time the bitterness of the Third Reich's self-adulation and triumphalism. The renewal of German art—recent German history as reflected in postage stamps, youth camp, enthusiastic welcome for the Führer in X or Y. Goebbels' speech on culture to the Germanized theater people, the biggest lecture theater in the world, the biggest auto-bahn in the world, etc., etc.—the biggest lie in the world, the biggest disgrace in the world. It can't be helped. . . . So in the Fü-Li *Ramona*, the best color film so far. [. . .] In the Freiberger Platz cinema *Gordian the Tyrant*. [. . .]

August 17, Tuesday

[. . .]

Today now practically ready to set out—i.e., Eva is packing, which always makes her extremely ill-humored; but after the trip came to grief the first time, I am, if not superstitious, then at least very skeptical, on top of that much too depressed by the general situation, to have felt any kind of pleasure so far.

I have worked through the larger part of the Monglond borrowed from Berlin, but not yet taken notes; I shall apply for an extension. I am also ever more skeptical with respect to my opus.

[. . .]

In the *Stürmer* (which is displayed at every corner) I recently saw a picture: two girls in swimming costumes at a seaside resort. Above it: "Prohibited for Jews," underneath it: "How nice that it's just us now!" Then I remembered a long forgotten incident. September 1900 or 1901 in Landsberg. In the lower sixth we were 4 Jews among 16, in the upper sixth 3 among 8 pupils. There was little trace of anti-Semitism among either the teachers or the pupils. More precisely none at all. The agitation of Ahlwardt and Stoecker is no more than historical fact to me. I knew only that a Jew could become neither a fraternity member as a student nor an officer. [. . .] So on the Day of Atonement—Yom Kippur—the Jews did not attend classes. The next day our comrades told us, laughing and without the least malice (just as the words themselves were also only uttered jokingly by the altogether humane teacher), Kufahl, the mathematician, had said to the reduced class: "Today it's *just us*." In my memory these words took on a quite horrible significance: to me it confirms the claim of the NSDAP to express the true opinion of the German people. And I believe ever more strongly that Hitler really does embody the soul of the German people, that he really stands for "Germany" and that he will consequently maintain himself and justifiably maintain himself. Whereby I have not only outwardly lost my Fatherland. And even if the government should change one day: my inner sense of belonging is gone.

In the newspaper the relevant supplement is no longer called "The Car" or "Motor Vehicles" or the like, but "Motor Vehicles in the Third Reich." The swastika must be prominent everywhere. Everything has to be related to it and only to it. — In Monglond I encountered for the first time the language of the orators, journalists, preachers, etc. of the French Revolution: precisely the same thing!

I hear from Marta (who is offended that we are going to Grete) that Georg is in Switzerland. He does not treat me with much affection. I believe he gives me all the money because 25 years ago he promised Father to help me. I believe that he is guided neither by fraternal love nor by any kind of respect for my work, convinced that I am not congenial to him and am to some extent contemptible. . . . But I have become a little thick-skinned and cynical and as things stand, I have much more use for cash support than for fraternal respect and love. As I have already often observed, there is very little feeling for people left in me. Eva—and then comes Mujel, the tomcat.

August 29, Sunday–September 5, Sunday

The coast and Hanseatic trip with Grete (August 18–27) and the trip to the Riesengebirge (August 31–September 1). [. . .]

At last, on Friday, September 3, I took Grete to the morning fast train, had her whisked up to the platform on the baggage elevator, saw her to her compartment and made sure that she disappeared toward Brünn at 10:41 to her cousin and friend of her youth Gustl Bunzl (Assekuranz-Bunzl, Vienna). She will appear again in about six days, in order then to be conveyed back to Strausberg in the car.

[. . .]

September 5, Sunday morning

Returned from the station on Friday, I picked up Eva and drove her to the dentist. The consultation had the anticipated unpleasant result; removal of loose teeth and replacement by dentures are necessary, lengthy torment, expense, stuttering, uncertain end result. Nevertheless: There are worse illnesses, and this business is more embarrassment than misfortune.

We attempted to get over it, Eva in the garden, I at the typewriter. In the evening I read a little from the very charming Holtei (*Die Vagabunden*). Yesterday, Saturday, we were invited to dinner at Annemarie's, from whom we had heard nothing for months. The journey there rather slow and difficult with an uncommon amount of approaching traffic (a whole torchlight procession of cycling workers from the dreadful stinking Küttner artificial fiber factory in Pirna, etc., etc.) on the narrow, twisting road to Pirna. Afterward the drive back in the quieter night was better. The clinic and the private apartment now furnished and elegant. We had to admire everything, especially the impressive X-ray apparatus. Strange, how completely Dressel dominates. Annemarie is merely general practitioner, medical and technical assistant—financial backer. For a dozen years surgery was everything to her, and now she is quite happy to be a subordinate and forget about the knife. Just as Scherner no longer thinks about philosophy and big city and is content in his small-town pharmacy. [. . .]

A full supper at Annemarie's with a lot of alcohol, wine, champagne, liqueur. I became dangerously tired, but a strong coffee revived me, and I got the car safely home. In bed at two.

Welcome, given our financial situation, which is again very stretched, is that Annemarie paid 100M for the three cabinets passed on to her. In the matter of money I have become very fatalistic and thick-skinned and quite unbourgeois.

September 11

Conclusion of the days of restlessness and travel.

Grete was supposed to return from Brünn on Wednesday; early on Monday morning (September 6) she announced by telegram that she was coming the same evening. That morning I had to go to see Wolf in Freital: The patched tire had not held. With Wolf to the car dump (the first I have ever set foot in, interesting enough!) in Schandauerstrasse. Neither an old nor a new tire to be had, a new one—by chance—promised for next week, normally one now waits six weeks—signum temporis. From there to a specialist shop on Freiberger Platz, where at least an inner tube could be found; from there back to Freital, where Wolf fitted the inner tube inside the defective tire. There was at least one good thing about the inadequate state of the spare wheel; it provided a plausible reason for calling off the visit to Marta and Sussmann. We were both far too tired to endure another visit to relations, and longed for some rest, less from driving itself than from the misery of relatives. This hunt for the fifth wheel cost me the first 25 miles on Monday. Then off to Oberbärenburg after lunch. Immediately back to us with the Frankes and had coffee here. Walter Franke, now over fifty, has become a stout gentleman, otherwise very like his father, good-natured, friendly, as inconsequential as his wife, head clerk of a nitrogen company with 450M a month gross, modest, satisfied, unpolitical, as a half-breed has kept his job, member of the Labor Front and citizen of the Reich. After coffee I drove them both through the city to the equestrian statue on the other side of the Brühl Terrace and back. After that we both took the two of them back to Oberbärenburg and drove home again. Then, after a hurried meal, I fetched Grete from the station. That meant that in one day I had driven 144 miles in aggravating circumstances (always in company!); I was completely shattered. Then there were still long conversations with Grete; Eva was also finished.

I would have been very pleased if we had immediately been able to send Grete on her way the next day, but she rested here, and for us that meant further endless disruption and strain on the nerves. [. . .]

On Wednesday all four of us were in fact "knocked out." Eva trembled and shivered with exhaustion, Grete had overdone things long ago, the jalopy only had four wheels and I had "had 'nuff."

Eva had very little room in the car beside the thickly wrapped Grete, I was hampered by the big suitcase beside me. Despite all of that a large part of the drive passed off quite pleasantly. Tolerable weather, we revived. Away just before eleven. [. . .]

In Strausberg at half past seven. Grete got out, even before we turned the car, let herself be put to bed immediately after the meal and stayed there the next morning; her doctor was supposed to come in the course of the day, she was obviously very much afraid. We ourselves took a couple of steps along the country road and retired early and exhausted.

The next morning (September 9) not very pleasant. Eva really worn out. As for Grete, I did not know and do not know to what extent she is a malade imaginaire, to what extent she is really ill. But certainly she is old, helpless, unworldly and dependent on strangers and at the same time tyrannical, much more tyrannical than she realizes. Also she does not pay as well as she imagines. The Kemleins, decent people, but nevertheless dependent on earnings and customers, told me a little of their problems with Grete, and in the light of my experiences, they were neither unjust nor did they exaggerate. I said that to my sister I was still her little brother and so without any influence on her. My heart was fairly heavy when we quickly said our farewells at half past ten. [. . .] On this concluding drive I covered exactly 315 miles door to door, but it was not just the miles that had worn me out so badly.

September 12, Sunday

Exhaustion and depression persist of course; the diary entry is just finished, the second volume of Monglond has just been worked through, and now I am going to make the briefest possible notes—but there is not yet any kind of liberation from the general disgust and feeling of the uselessness of all things. Pity that I have one screw too few or too many to be a good Catholic. Eva lies down a lot and reads (while the weather has been very bad and thoroughly autumnal since immediately after our return); I am very much occupied with the household, domestic errands (on foot, since I do not dare drive the car out of the garage alone), with typing, reading and reading aloud, but my much nourished disgust will not lift.

Eva's dental business is horribly before me: I do not like this anesthetic. [. . .] I lack the confidence that my opus, (1) has real value, (2) can ever achieve success, (3) that I shall bring it to a conclusion. Grete's fear of extinction has had a very bad effect on me and the constant heart problems while I am walking repeatedly forces the thought of idiotic nothingness into my mind also. — And then the political disgust. Everywhere on my way I see the sign "Jews Unwelcome!" and now, during the Fifth Party Rally, hatred of Jews is being whipped up again. The Jews are murdering Spain, the Jews are the criminal people, *all* crimes can be traced back to *the Jew* (the official *Stürmer* and the minister Goebbels). And the people are so stupid that they believe everything. Certainly, in a fit of rage Frau Güntzel, the baker's wife, waves a roll under my nose: "*That* is the muck we have to bake!" Certainly, everybody grumbles; but nobody makes a move, and in the end the masses believe everything. The very decent, intelligent and far from innocent Frau Kemlein in Strausberg says to me: "Starvation is better than Communism! When we built this here, before the Third Reich, someone shouted over the fence: You're building—but we'll live in it! . . . And there is so much starvation and murder in Russia—after all less blood is spilled in this country . . ." There is no doubt that 99 out of a hundred think like that. And the intelligentsia and the scholars prostitute themselves.

The Party Rally is in every respect a poor copy of the last one. The Americanism of the language has increased even further. Speech by the head of the press: The *Völkische Beobachter* is building "the biggest publishing house in the world"; the daily print run of the German press, placed one on top of the other, would stretch 12½ miles into the stratosphere, the Party press makes up 70 percent of it—and abroad they tell lies about the decline of our press. And the Führer warns against and protects Europe from the Jewish-Bolshevist world enemy.

September 20, Monday evening

Prévost-Aisse typed, another two or three days for corrections, and then I can go on; but my spirits sink ever deeper, as the manuscript pages mount up. Basically the whole thing is self-deception and killing time. In the present situation I see nothing at all on which one could pin hope of a change. Hitler's speech in Nürnberg about the morally and intellectually inferior Jewish race—no matter how thick my skin has gradually become and how lunatic the accusation (and the assertion that Bolshevism is purely Jewish), I nevertheless find it painful to have to spend the rest of my life here. And I am ever more convinced that Hitler truly speaks for more or less all Germans.

September 24, Friday

Dreadful autumn weather, dreadfully depressed about everything, still muddling along.

Prévost filed away apart from the footnotes; I am intending to start Morelly today. Held back during the last few days by a great deal of reading aloud, since Eva, who is very poorly, has been lying in bed a lot. (Dentist has been halted now and postponed indefinitely—but the entirely dreadful business of the bigger operation and of the possibly useless dentures still lies before us and weighs on us.) [. . .]

September 25, Saturday

After a gap of several months we were at Frau Schaps yesterday (turned 70 meanwhile and yet going by disposition and appearance 60 at the outside) together with the Gerstles. I always find their mood and judgment very valuable as an expression of the group. On the whole I was not dissatisfied: (1) even they have by now realized that they no longer need to fear Bolshevism because it is already here (Gerstle said the Bolshevist tendency within the NSDAP is constantly increasing), (2) for all his pessimism, Gerstle does not expect the regime to last that much longer, (3) he talked of considerable dissatisfaction among the workers, of the government's great financial difficulties, of the completely dismissive attitude of the English with respect to colonies (he read from the *Economist*). [. . .] The Gerstles also told us [. . .] that in Munich Vossler, just turned 65, has been retired. (I am no longer in contact with him, since his evident support for Auerbach's candidacy in Istanbul.)
[. . .]
In recent weeks two very pleasant film evenings. *Show Boat,* thoroughly American in music, dance, humor, fights, gum chewing; *The Voice of the Heart,* Gigli film, thoroughly Italian singing.
Today I began reading the terribly boring Morelly.
[. . .]

October 9, Saturday afternoon

For a good week now we have been plagued by every kind of influenza symptom. Eva is extremely handicapped and worn down by lumbago, I myself have been more badly troubled by sniffles, coughing and probably also a temperature than for many years; for a couple of days I was properly ill and completely incapable of work, today I still feel wretched enough, but at least I can actually exist again and have until now, five o'clock, read from the life story of Fanny Lewald at Eva's bedside. A big step forward because during the last few days I was so hoarse that reading aloud was impossible.
We repeatedly got through the evenings by going to the cinema. The most interesting things were the support programs, the Nürnberg Party Rally and Mussolini's visit—various excerpts from all of that, but above

all the whole of Hitler's and Mussolini's speeches on the Maifeld. Mussolini's gesticulation and facial expressions and his broken, barely comprehensible German were very amusing. The spectacular staging was terrific—but in the end it is exactly the same staging again and again: militarized masses and goose-stepping and war games in support of peace and laying wreaths. In the long run the effect is deadening—provided one is not aroused by it.

[. . .]

Reka, the most reputable, the best department store in Dresden, was Aryanized last year or the year before. Now it is advertising its "Anniversary Sale: 25 Years." At the same time a notice has been painted on all the entrances: "Aryan Store."

[. . .]

It goes without saying that I am spending my birthday in fairly subdued fashion.

October 27, Tuesday, toward evening

I returned books to the State Library, the "Pre-Rousseauism" section has now finally come to a conclusion with Haller. I have worked on these sixty typewritten pages since the beginning of April. The whole undertaking seems ever more pointless to me, I shall continue but only by the law of inertia and without any illusions. How?—that is also obscure to me. The dubiousness of the basic structure is becoming increasingly evident. In the last few weeks the work has been and is being slowed down by Eva's still quite wretched state of health. I have sometimes read aloud literally day and night (once from two till half past four in the morning), I read by her bedside every morning. That not only takes up the hours of reading themselves, but has a very tiring and paralyzing effect far beyond that. But I do not really mind doing it, I can no longer get rid of the thought that it makes no difference at all how I pass the rest of my life: I no longer believe in any political change, nor do I believe that a change would be of any help to me. Neither in my circumstances nor in my feelings. — Contempt and disgust and deepest mistrust with respect to Germany can never leave me now. And yet in 1933 I was so convinced of my Germanness.

[. . .]

On October 18 Georg's wife Maria died in Merano in the middle of their European trip, in her early sixties at most. It is dreadful how cold deaths like this leave me—and what fine letters of condolence I write. Now when I receive a letter from Georg, the only question I ask myself is: Will it contain a notification of money?

Pity that I do not have time to make notes on what I read out. I shall set down a few key words at least. The memoirs of Fanny Lewald, written around 1860, are by far the most important for me. The relationship of her parents (Napoleonic period and after) to Germanness. One so much wants to submerge oneself in German and Christian society, feels German by education, but sees oneself rejected, has a lot of time for France and nevertheless commits oneself to Germany. Fanny Lewald herself, unbaptized, feels completely German, portrays Börne as the national German, sees Auerbach as the German author. Seen from the present state of affairs, this Jewish penetration of German society, the part they played in Liberalism, in Young Germany is deeply moving. If I should after all write my Life, then I shall have to remember Fanny Lewald, also her father and his half German, half Old Testament views. [...]

October 29

[...]

Eva's health continues to be very poor, politics stagnating and gloomy, makes one want to throw up every day—today another race defilement trial: ten years in prison for a 56-year-old Hamburg lawyer. The report on it literally stinks of nauseating lies.

I am very depressed because I cannot think what structure to give the remainder of my book. I increasingly believe the basic structure to be unworkable and doubt the intrinsic value of the whole thing. I want to give up the search for a while now and work stubbornly at the little Gessner chapter.

November 11, Thursday

The manuscript of the Gessner-Werther section is now finished, library preparations for the English, who come next, either made or under way. Everything proceeds infinitely slowly and without any pleasure. First of all half and whole days are taken up with reading aloud because of Eva's continuing bad health—on top of the rheumatism there is now a dental problem as well, periodontitis or an abscess—then I am not sure how to continue with the book, the basic idea on which it is based (the possibility of separating sensibilité and Rousseauism) appears dubious and the meaning and value of the whole work more than dubious. I "muddle" on so as to pass the time and the rest of my life—my opus probably came to a conclusion in 1933 with the Corneille. That was made distressingly clear to me today by a double letter: I asked Hatzfeld if he could find out the date of the first publication of Haller's *The Alps* in France, he had passed the question on to van Thiegham, who gives me a friendly and detailed response, in the belief that I am writing a specialist study along the lines of "comparative" literature. Hatzfeld, who always combines a serious, upright Catholic piety with a great deal of worldliness, advises me to thank Thiegham politely, as he could perhaps find a place for part or even all of my book in one of his publications. So then once again I felt a weight on my soul: What would this scholarly specialist think of my work? It is not research after all, for him and his kind it is not a scholarly work. And it is far too scholarly for the general public. So no hope anywhere.

In politics always the same thing, continuing triumph of the National Socialist cause, at home and abroad. It is as if the rest of the world were paralyzed. — An exhibition in Munich, called "The Eternal Jew," informs about the Jewish "blood rite."

November 28, Sunday

The day before yesterday a speech by Goebbels: We have weeded out the Jews, and the *layout* of our newspapers is better than ever before! Mocks himself without knowing it. . . . Yesterday a striking example of this layout: banner headline, "The Rebuilding of Berlin Begins" (with the laying of the foundation stone of the "defense engineering" faculty of the TU in Charlottenburg) and noted in very small print below and then hidden somewhere inside the newspaper, that Schacht has given up the Economics Ministry, has given it up to a National Socialist journalist. But it is nevertheless possible that future historians will describe this little point as the beginning of the end. Only: How many years separate this beginning from the final end?

I cannot wait much longer. The complete exhaustion of my determination and of my capacity for work shows me how worn down I am. For weeks now I have been reading about the English influence (Thomson, Ossian, etc.), cannot get hold of enough material, hesitate again and again, do not write a single line. All confidence in my work is gone, I merely keep myself busy and pass the time. Besides, not so much of it goes on the book at all, fortunately perhaps. Daily routine: rise at seven in darkness, the stove, make breakfast, no time to shower. Eva still lies in bed for half the morning. Once I have provided for Eva and myself, I read aloud until almost eleven. Then she gets up, and I am so tired that I fall asleep for twenty or thirty minutes. Then from around half past eleven until half past two I sit at my reading smoking countless cigarillos. Then I dress, then I make coffee, then I clear up, then I am dead tired again, then I am "floored" again, and then I have just two more working hours, provided that we do not drive into town or I do not creep down through the park and back up again with my heart trouble, in order to go shopping. Eva lies down immediately after the evening meal, I read aloud, replenish the stove, read again, until she falls asleep, browse through this and that until half past eleven and go to bed. The tomcat is also fed and usually some hungry feline turns up outside as well.

[. . .]

Quite a few weeks ago now two films with half-decent content but outstanding acting: *Die Warschauer Zitadelle* [The Warsaw Citadel] and *Zu neuen Ufern* [To New Shores] with Zarah Leander.

I repeatedly catch myself thinking about my Memoirs. They will remain unwritten.

December 28, Tuesday

On the twenty-fourth after several days of frost, there was a sudden thaw. So we drove to Wilsdruff, as we did last year, to buy a living tree, which will afterward be planted here, just like its predecessor. At twelve there was not a soul at the nursery, we sat in the Weisser Adler [White Eagle] until one, again no one at the nursery. I fetched Weber, the old head gardener, whom we know, although he has meanwhile retired, and he dug up a tree for us. So in the evening we had quite a tolerable Christmas; Eva had got a window for the dining cellar, we drank a little bottle of schnapps and we both felt quite reasonable. On the first day of the holiday, with rain pouring down uninterruptedly, at home, each doing his work, Eva paints the music room, I correct the "Antique Elements" section. In the evening read out *The Avenger,* a very wild Edgar Wallace (the mad guillotine murderer). On the second day of the holiday went for a drive along the beautiful road to Meissen on the left bank of the Elbe.

I had been very afraid of these days because things are going very badly. Money worries are again especially oppressive, we count every penny, we can no longer keep up the life insurance. And the hope of political change is hardly a hope anymore.

It hit us particularly hard that the Gerstle-Salzburgs are also emigrating now. The Weber Flavored Coffee Factory was sold to Kathreiner. Gerstle inherited it from his father and managed it for 28 years, he served as an officer during the war. From the breakup of the household we got many flowers (as from the Blumenfelds and the Isakowitzes), including a monstrous rubber tree. I could have had books by the hundred; I did not take many, I already have so many moldering away, partly in boxes, partly also on the bookshelves, since without any service there is no thorough cleaning. A handsome old greyhound, which the Gerstles themselves had already taken over from emigrants, is being poisoned. Even after the huge loss of the breakup of the household, Flight Tax, etc. the Gerstles are probably still rich. They are going to England "by way of a world cruise." The seventy-year-old Frau Schaps is accompanying them on this cruise, but she wants to return here. She will then be completely alone.

Gerstle gave me the address of a London banker called Bacharach who might be interested in helping me; I wrote to him. [. . .] But I shall not get away, and it is also certainly contrary to Eva's innermost desire to leave— see the planted Christmas tree, the new window, the painted music room . . . we are digging ourselves in here and shall perish here.

The loneliness weighs ever more heavily. Berthold Meyerhof has to leave Berlin. Johannes Köhler did not send me greetings on my birthday nor for Christmas (as he otherwise has done for years).

With all the pressure my work makes ever slower progress. Admittedly my age is probably also to blame: the nonchalance is no longer there, I often read for months, only to write a dozen pages. This year exactly 95 typewritten pages have been completed: Rousseau, Chapter V—"Antique Elements." But it is not age alone, the external encouragement is lacking, this just-writing-for-oneself is so depressing. Also all of Eva's lying down has meant that in the last few months I not only read aloud in the evenings, but in the mornings as well. God, how much! [. . .] Most recently, as I said, the Wallace from the Gerstle stock. (In addition I took a great deal of Bismarck literature, Ziegler's *Geistige und soziale Strömungen in 19. Jahrhundert* [Intellectual and Social Currents in the Nineteenth Century], several Heinrich Manns, a Sholem Asch, a volume of Ossian and the reply of the Diocese of Cologne to Rosenberg.)

[. . .]

Fräulein Carlo's visit was certainly some kind of relief. Under the auspices of KDF she toured the small towns of Saxony with four other people, acting in *Till Eulenspiegel*, a play for children. Modern players, they drive by car, the trailer carries the properties, they play in secondary schools, public houses, etc., each person takes six different parts, the schoolmaster, the old woman, the donkey, the dressing rooms are not heated, the pay is 20M for each performance, which has to cover food, they help one another with the rapid costume changes. [. . .]

Vossler, with whom I broke some time ago (after he did nothing against, presumably a great deal for, Auerbach's appointment to the Istanbul chair), sends me a page from the *Frankfurter Zeitung*. Under "Approaches to Dante" it reports on a new translation and on a talk that Manacorda gave in the Harnackhaus. He begins: In 1921 after all the anniversary fuss was over, one critical thinker wrote, with some justification, about "Dante the Stranger." But the name of the critical thinker can no longer be mentioned in an Aryan newspaper. I wrote to thank Vossler, half amicably, half ironically and emphatically d'outretombe.

I now find it just as hard to force myself to the diary as to private correspondence. But often I am overtaken by some scene from my planned memoirs. But I always think that I must remain loyal to the ill-fated XVIII-ième. And at the same time my heart problems while walking are getting worse every day.

A summary of the year '37 is probably unnecessary. The famous 95 pages of the Rousseau volume; the summer trip to Berlin, to the sea and to the Riesengebirge; the terrible standstill of time, the hopeless vegetating.

1938

January 8, Saturday

The determining influence on the first week was the weather. Tremendous snowfalls, constant effort to keep a footpath clear, impossible to get the car out. In the mornings I went along our front fence with the snow sweeper a couple of times; it caused me such heart problems that I had to leave the real work of cleaning (hours of heavy work!) to Eva. A big thaw set in yesterday, but there are still masses of snow outside and the car still shut in: I went into town by tram and on foot and came back exhausted. Worry about my heart is with me constantly, at the same time I grow ever fatter and smoke ever more. And this month there really is no way that I can keep up the life insurance. Eva went to bed early on New Year's Eve, I read [. . .] to her, at twelve Eva got up for a little while, and we drank three schnapps. On New Year's Day we went about our work, I began the Colardeau. (Which is now followed by the Dorat—it is going far too slowly.) Johannes Köhler, from whom I have heard nothing more since the summer, did not send New Year's greetings either. On the fourth *we* sent him greetings; there was no reply. — The Jew-baiting has increased again in recent weeks. The reason is the new Fascism in Romania; Germany plays the accompaniment to the anti-Semitism there and celebrates it. The letter to Bacharach, the banker, had fairly embarrassing consequences; instead of giving a private reply to a private letter, the man passed it on to the Warburg Institute (what is it?); there a Fräulein Dr. Gertrud Bing made two copies and sent them to my old friend Demuth and a *Society for the Protection of Science and Learning.* Now today a letter comes from Demuth again: Send three curriculum vitae, etc. to us once again, we shall go on looking. Just scribblings, waste of time, annoyance, hopelessness. However, Fräulein Bing also wrote to me, she will try to arrange a lecture for me in London, and whether I knew Dr. Gutkind, who is now Italian lecturer in London. I wrote back that we had almost been friends, he can provide any information about me. — But what is the point of it all? It is not only that there are no prospects, but that I am afraid of the prospects. Eva and house and garden and I myself without knowledge of the languages—how could it work out? But what is going to happen here?

January 11, Tuesday

So I have written curriculum vitae and publications list once again and sent them off. Among the documents I have kept here there is now the new curriculum next to the French version of May '35; it is less emotional by several degrees, I am no longer capable of underlining my Germanness, the whole national ideology has quite gone to pieces for me. — The scribbling took up an annoying amount of time. The rest of the time today was taken up with a shopping trip. The worst of the snow trouble is over, but driving is still very difficult and exhausting. I wanted to get cigarettes from Weinstein, the old Jewish dealer [. . .]; he had died four weeks ago, his wife has already moved away from Polierstrasse. The man was killed by heart trouble, my commiseration no doubt consists for the larger part of egoistical fears.

January 18, Tuesday

Berthold Meyerhof was here on Friday; he had to settle accounts with a manufacturer whom he used to represent, and took his leave of us: at the beginning of March he goes to the USA with his wife, from complete hope-lessness into uncertainty. He said, everywhere he goes, he thinks of 1918, the atmosphere is the same as then. But he cannot wait and does not want to either; his earlier ardent patriotism, which he inherited from his father, has been rooted out, he longs to become an American. — I feel exactly the same. Whatever happens, I shall never again be capable of trust, never again have a sense of belonging. It has been knocked out of me, retrospec-tively so to speak; too much of what, in the past, I took lightly, viewed as an embarrassing minor phenomenon, I now consider to be German and typical. The superlativism, which is a special hallmark of the language of the Third Reich, is different from the American one. The people in the USA talk big in a childlike and fresh manner, the Nazis do it in a way that is half megalomania, half frantic autosuggestion. One of their favorite words is "eternal." We have, says Ley yesterday, at the official opening of a number of Hitler schools, "the way to eternity." — A particular example, in recent weeks, of clumsy lying and suppression and distortion were the reports of the fighting around Teruel. First Bolshevik hordes had entered the in-significant place, then the heroic garrison of the citadel was relieved, the "general staff" of the Reds taken prisoner, their new army bled to death. Then "pockets of Bolsheviks" were still holding out in the town, then the Nationalist troops were withdrawn from the unimportant position, prob-ably because of the section commander's incompetence, insofar as they had not been taken prisoner as a result of the commander's treachery, he had surrendered so as not to face a court-martial; then there had been an agreement to allow the Red Cross to evacuate 300 dead and 700 wounded from the citadel-like seminary, but the Bolsheviks had broken their word and murdered the garrison as soon as the gates were opened. And the reader is supposed to believe all of it, whatever it is that is printed in *all* the newspapers each day, because all the papers are only allowed to print the *one* thing they have been ordered to.

Very quiet and yet quieter living-for-ourselves. Johannes Köhler did not reply to my greeting. Bad weather—after the snowfall there were föhn winds and downpours, in addition shortage of money, which makes every purchase of gasoline distressing, keeps us at home. Eva paints cupboards, does carpentry and other manual work, as if we were established in our little house for all eternity; I sit brooding over the Dix-huitième all day, always with the old doubts, always with the same slow progress, and yet also with a certain success. Today the Colardeau-Dorat section is typed and finished (going from the manuscript to the typed version still involves revision). The typescript has still to be corrected and the footnotes written: about four days. So then eight typewritten pages of text will have taken a good three weeks. But *I can't help:* They are good and not copied from other people.

The only drive recently, aside from a few trips to the library, was to Frau Schaps: belated New Year greeting. We are to eat with her on Thursday. Departure; after that she goes around the world with her children, who have emigrated once and for all and are in Switzerland. For weeks I have been reading aloud from Körmendy, *Farewell to Yesterday*, in the evenings. Basically the tragedy of a Jew disappointed in his desire for assimilation. In addition an elegy to Liberalism. The book has remained in the lending libraries by mistake, a barely comprehensible mistake, probably protected by its thickness—who plows through a thousand pages?

January 31, Monday evening

I add here the letter that I received today from the normally so calm Martin Sebba, about the expulsion, without a reason given and without delay, of his sick daughter Käthe. At the same time he sent the commemorative postage stamps for January 30, '38 (five years of the Third Reich). In the newspaper: symbol: A youth carries the torch of honor and truth through the Brandenburg Gate.

I had already been seriously depressed by yesterday's celebration: I no longer really believe I shall live to see a change; now this letter. Note in it also the sudden exclusion of non-Aryan doctors from the private insurance schemes. Apart from that in recent weeks anti-Semitism has once again been very much in the foreground (it rotates: now the Jews, now the Catholics, now the Protestant ministers). [...]

In the cinema newsreels one sees: Japanese artillery mopping up last-ditch resistance in conquered Chinese territory. And, sentimentally, feeding of returned Chinese refugees by the Japanese in Shanghai, where iron discipline now prevails. (Happy idyllic faces of Chinese children eating.) The propaganda operates on the principle of the chivalric romance with the Japanese as hero and as benevolent helper and bringer of peace. For a while the pictures from the National Spanish side looked exactly the same.

And the Chinese too are now gradually being turned into Bolsheviks. The only thing that surprises me is that they have not yet become Jews.

[...]

And with every day that passes I am again and ever more strongly disturbed by the trite antithesis: such tremendous things are being created, radio, airplane, sound film, and the most insane stupidity, primitiveness and bestiality cannot be eradicated—all invention results in murder and war. Terrible shortage of money, literally ragged (my jacket is coming apart), my gloves are nothing but holes barely hanging together, my socks likewise), on the first of the month more than half the money I get immediately goes on current bills. Despite that, we were at the cinema twice in recent days after a long gap. The Gigli-Cebotari opera film *Mother's Song*, very sentimental, very pretty, a little boring. But yesterday afternoon in the Schauburg way out on Königsbrücker Strasse (at the same time one of our very rare drives, besides the jalopy went seriously on strike on the way to Frau Schaps, we had to leave it at the gas station and arrived late by tram)—anyway yesterday the *Habañera* with Zarah Leander, altogether impressively good. (...)

Léonard finished and perfect, so the achievement of January '38: 13 typewritten pages, Colardeau, Dorat, Léonard.

February 19, Saturday

[...]

"Reichstag" again tomorrow. Which as before meets in Berlin's second-class opera house, the Kroll. Symbolic. The Führer—"The world awaits the Führer's speech!"—will probably talk about the fact that since February 4 he is his own Minister of War and has dismissed Blomberg and Fritsch and that Austria is now halfway incorporated. And everything in Germany and the world is calm. — Yesterday, when he opened the car show in Berlin and spoke about the economic upturn and the "mistakes and crimes" of the previous government, the basic principle of the whole language of the Third Reich became apparent to me: a bad conscience; its triad: defending oneself, praising oneself, accusing—never a moment of calm testimony.

[...]

February 23, Wednesday

Terrible hopelessness of the situation. Hitler's Reichstag speech like a threat of war (increases in the armed forces), he said not a word about his military coup d'état; National Socialism holds sway in Austria, and it is not only that everything remains quiet, but that English national policy is being turned around, Eden is going, Chamberlain is negotiating with the triumphant Italians, has announced negotiations with Germany, kicks the League of Nations in the backside and for this valor gets 330 votes against 168 in the lower house of Parliament. But sometimes I tell myself: What would be different for me in the fourth Reich, whatever form it took? Probably I would only then face the very greatest loneliness. Because I could never again trust anyone in Germany, never again feel myself uninhibitedly to be German. There is nothing I would like more than to move abroad, best of all to the USA, where I would be a stranger as a matter of course; it is impossible, I am tied to this country and this house for the rest of my life. A recent promotional report of a private security company: Enumeration of its deeds in the last year: X burglaries prevented, X fires prevented, X crimes brought to court, one race defilement.

In the Dix-huitième: Parny completely finished; preparatory work on the ghastly Lebrun-Pindare, which I eventually tracked down in Berlin (no edition either here or in Göttingen). Everything turns out too long, and I have just as little belief in the end of this opus as in the end of the Third Reich. But the end of my money, I believe in that. In the last few weeks every day has been more unbearable than the last, and in March things will be even tighter for us.

[...]

The greatest isolation.

March 1

Today on Carnival Tuesday as part of the Berlin carnival celebrations Hitler presented General Field Marshal Goering with his marshal's baton in a great ceremony. They have no sense of the comic impression they make. [...] Their conscious humor is spite against the defenseless: There is a carnival parade here in Dresden today: "Exodus of the Children of Israel." Presumably as a prelude to the propaganda week (meetings and marches) that begins on March 4: "Peace between the nations or Jewish dictatorship." — On Sunday, for the first time in months, we went for a short drive, in the direction of the Versailles cross and out beyond Radeberg; those words were on a banner stretched across the road there. (Apart from that it was still wintry, cold and bare.)

[...]

March 20, Sunday

The last few weeks have been the most wretched of our life so far.

The immense act of violence of the annexation of Austria, the immense increase in power both internally and externally, the defenseless trembling fear of England, France, etc. We shall not live to see the end of the Third Reich. The flags have been waving for eight days, since yesterday a broad yellow handbill with the Star of David has been stuck to every post of our fence: *Jew*. Warning against the unflagged plague barracks. *Der Stürmer* has dug up its usual ritual murder; I would truly not be surprised if next I were to find the body of a child in the garden.

A couple of days before the annexation, a letter came from the Wengler woman, from whom I have the 12,000M mortgage until July '42. Due to a mistake at the bank the payment for this month was one week late. The letter, without a greeting, threatened legal action and included "precautionary notice of foreclosure." The policy that covered it is used up. There are still four years to go, but I do not believe I will be left in peace here for another four years. Publishing contracts with non-Aryans have been canceled—so why should a mortgage contract not be set aside as well?

March 30, Wednesday evening

Sometimes I draw a certain comfort precisely from the terrible hopelessness of the situation. This is a peak; nothing, neither good nor evil, can remain in a state of superlatives. The hubris, the brutality, the cynicism of the victors in their "election speeches" is so monstrous, the threats and abuse of other countries assumes such lunatic forms, that the counterstroke must come some time. And we two have got so used to our poverty and troubles, that again and again there are nevertheless hours that are bearable. Reading aloud in the evenings, the work on the Dix-huitième, no matter how pointless it is. Today the short theory section on didactic and descriptive poetry was finished. A compilation or my own ideas? Valuable, valueless? At any rate written, worked.

The creation of legends in the middle of the twentieth century: Vogel, the grocer, in all seriousness and quite shocked tells me something that is "certainly true and vouched for" and is circulating secretly, because dissemination carries the threat of prison: A man in Berlin takes his wife to the hospital so that she can give birth. A picture of Christ hangs over the bed. The man: "Nurse, that picture must go, I don't want the Jewboy to be the first thing my child sees." The nurse: She herself could not do anything about it, she will report it. In the evening he gets a telegram from the doctor: "You have a son. The picture did not need to be removed, the child is blind."

Frau Lehmann, our cleaning woman, showed me her daughter's vocational school-leaving certificate: Conduct very good. *Ready for action.*

Less than a week after the occupation of Austria the map of the new "Greater Germany" was hanging in a shop window on the Altmarkt. It must have been printed long before the business.

[. . .]

April 5, Tuesday

Yesterday the announcement of the death of Felician Gess at the age of 78. His life's work appears to have consisted of a publication on the Saxon duke Ludwig the Bearded and his relations with Luther. But he was always an upright Teuton and in 1920 objected to my appointment. Now my most intimate enemies at the university, the two Försters with their three eyes and Don Quixote Gess, are in Valhalla, and I hope I shall never see them again. But on the one hand: How petty and comical my battles and troubles of those days seem to me now; and on the other: How deeply Hitler's attitudes are rooted in the German people, how good the preparations were for his Aryan doctrine, how unbelievably I have deceived myself my whole life long, when I imagined myself to belong to Germany, and how completely homeless I am.

[...]

Yesterday Baldur von Schirach declared Braunau the place of pilgrimage of German youth. Today Goebbels' instructions for the Sunday before the "election." One always thinks the spectacle has reached a peak, and then an even higher peak emerges. This time all traffic will stop for two minutes, and the locomotives will howl along with the sirens, and squadrons of aircraft will circle in the air "over all of Germany."

Roucher complete [...]. Now I want to type the finished pages of the chapter on epic poetry and then start on Delille. Just don't think about the pointlessness of the enterprise.

Grete is yet again inviting us to come and sent 50M; it is very touching and very humiliating.

April 10, Sunday afternoon

The "election" today, the "Day of the Greater German Reich." Yesterday evening pealing bells for a whole hour, mixed in with them a roaring sound, evidently the radio transmission of the Vienna or Berlin bells. In addition the smoky red of the torchlight processions over the city, lights in windows even up here in our lonely place.

For some days now divine right has been given ever more prominence. Again and again in the newspaper: *He* is the instrument of Providence—the hand that writes "no" will wither—the sacred election. ... Large facsimile copies everywhere of the assent of the Austrian bishops. We think he will have himself crowned Emperor. In Christian fashion as the Anointed of the Lord. That made me for the first time ask myself the question, why the proclamation of the Emperor in Versailles (since Wilhelm I was truly a believer after all) took a completely secular form, as a purely political act. It's not the answer (Wilhelm only felt himself to be King of Prussia by God's grace, for him the Imperial title was an embarrassing po-

litical matter), that's not what I find interesting here, but the question sur-
facing after I had taken the fact for granted for almost fifty years. I now so
often ask myself questions about things (e.g., of a linguistic nature) that I
took for granted for fifty years. The main thing for tyrannies of any kind is
the suppression of the urge to ask questions. And it is so easy to do. If *I*, a
professor, schooled in thinking all my life, have not asked myself so many
and such obvious questions in the course of fifty years, how should the
people hit on asking questions? One hardly even needs to force them to do
the opposite.

On Thursday we had our spectacles checked by old Professor von
Pflugk. We had not been to see him for a long time because he never sends
a bill. He always receives us with cordial friendliness. It was the day after
a Goebbels speech in Dresden ("The Conqueror of Berlin—our doctor—
addresses 20,000 comrades of the people—tumultuous reception." That
and similar in the headlines). Pflugk glanced into the empty waiting
room, took each of us by the arm, bent down and whispered, before anything else had been mentioned: "There was a patient here who saw
Goebbels yesterday. In the midst of the silent, listening crowd someone
shouted "Do you know what you are? You are scoundrels, all of you are
scoundrels!" Then two men seized him by the throat and dragged him
out. For God's sake don't pass it on!" — In the evening I passed it on, of
course, and, of course, told Natscheff in the lending library in just the
same whisper. "We are a center of agitation here," he told me, "you can't
imagine all the things people say here!" And immediately thereupon to a
customer entering: "Heil Hitler!" — Pflugk then grumbled and complained vigorously. He had not been allowed to accept an invitation to the
ophthalmologists' congress in Cairo, he's not trusted. He hears and sees so
much that is dreadful and so much dissatisfaction. I said: "And on Sunday
you'll get your fifty million votes." He, with emotion: "But I *have* to."
That's just it: Everyone has to; half of them have been made stupid, and no
one believes the ballot is secret, and everyone trembles.

April 18, Easter Monday

After a very long interval two excursions. Both of them half pleasure, half,
almost three-quarters, duty and effort. On Good Friday, on the first and
only sunny spring day, to Piskowitz, there at midday, back at seven for our
evening meal. The pretty little girl, born in January; rabbits, pigeons, hens,
eight piglets, three kids, two cows, beehives, fruit trees. But I do not
greatly care for the rural love of animals which has half an eye on the
butcher's knife. The husband terribly worn out, eight or nine hours a day
in the quarry, the farm work on top of that, Agnes just as thin, but the children clean and well behaved and content and the whole family probably
the happiest people I know, secure in this world and in a well-vouched-for
world beyond. Hearty welcome. [. . .]

Then cold weather set in again, more snow than rain. Despite that we decided yesterday to undertake the repeatedly postponed trip to Leipzig to visit Trude Öhlmann. Luckily the two chairs intended for her even fitted in the car with the roof up. [. . .] Trude Öhlmann now has a tiny apartment of her own. Complains about her twenty-year-old boy. Eva says: American tragedy; he wants to be "elegant," "go out," etc., does not appreciate how very poor his mother is. (He was on a cycling tour.) Trude reported to us what she had been told in the library under the seal of official secrecy. Some time before the occupation of Austria there were careful investigations (books and periodicals) on behalf of the Gestapo as to who among the Austrian professors and writers had published anti-Fascist work. These people were then immediately arrested. *Now* the same investigation is being carried out for the Czech territory. What they say is: First of all the Czech lands. Then the Corridor, but in amicable agreement, as *we* shall give the Poles a part of Lithuania.

Today, as already mentioned, very tired. In the morning (with constant driving snow) I read from Sayers for a long time. [. . .]

In the afternoon I salved my conscience by writing the first half-page of the Delille section. This whole book of minor writers has turned out far too long and an opus in itself. But what is the point of rewriting it now? I must keep on going and bring the whole thing to a conclusion. It's good that I don't have a choice. If I could do more immediately useful paid work, then I would probably do it. As things stand, the question as to the internal value and external success—I doubt the former every second day, the latter every day and every hour—is completely superfluous. I have nothing better to do. I cannot remain idle: therefore I do this. — If only enough time remains to me. There is not a day on which my heart does not make itself felt. But what is the point of staring at the End? So I continue. And then if there is still time—my Life. And then Lingua tertii imperii. And then learn English and American literature! And before that to be able to drive all over England and the USA! Probably none of it will come to pass. But the most sensible thing is always to tell oneself: Maybe yes! — and act accordingly. And if one has no choice, then one simply does this most sensible thing.

[. . .]

April 28

Trip to see Grete: Strausberg, Berlin, Frankfurt (Oder), April 23–27. 500 miles in all. [. . .] Grete in good health, affectionate but tyrannical, full of family quarrels, dragged me into her affair with the Sussmanns. Monday, twenty-fifth, [. . .] to Berlin with Grete. [. . .] At the Sussmanns at half past four, he and Lotte have become very ugly. Extremely friendly welcome and coffee. [. . .] At six in the café in Güntzelstrasse again and return. Tuesday, twenty-sixth, [. . .] the very successful excursion to

Frankfurt (Oder). We took Frau Kemlein with us as reward and as nurse for the incredibly spoiled Grete. [...]

About Sussmann I only want to report today that he asserted most emphatically that the recent election results had been falsified. Hitler had not received even 50 percent, in a particular case in the province of Brandenburg 83 Yes votes had been counted and 583 declared. I don't believe it. Most of them write Yes out of fear that the secrecy of the ballot is not respected. [...]

May 3, Tuesday

Hitler traveled to Italy yesterday with a large entourage. [...] At the same time the scale of the Italian reception is reported. Again and again, with ever greater intensity the components Americanism, Technicism, Automatism and deification. Apart from that, this is a meeting of the two men "who have created the new Europe." (Poveretto d'un re d'Italia!)

Yesterday we had 74M net winnings in the first class of the lottery. We immediately laid plans to blow the money on alcohol and gasoline.

Finished typing Delille today. For the moment hesitation and depression again.

[...]

May 10, Tuesday

Yesterday we still had the stove on, today it's warmer, but still cool enough.

A somewhat more extravagant life following the big lottery win. Frivolous? It does not in any case allow us to save enough to maintain the life insurance, to cover the mortgage. For a long time now we have fatalistically taken things as they come and tried to make the best of every day that passes. Only in my work do I have my eyes set doggedly on the future. [...]

The Führer returns from Italy this evening. A summons by Goering, to prepare a triumphal welcome for him, to show the profound happiness, the deepest gratitude (I am quoting pretty much word for word), order to put out the flags "until further notice." It has been going on like this for many weeks now: Vienna, return from Vienna, birthday, May Day, departure for Italy. How can they heighten things any further, what are they planning? — Yesterday (I am even fatalistic with respect to these notes, I doubt they will search the house—and if they do, not read every manuscript), so yesterday Berger, the greengrocer in Hermann Goering Strasse: "Tonight at half past seven I'll be trying to find the secret German radio station, I get it on short wave." — ?? — "Yes, a friend of mine heard it yesterday. There is a secret German radio station in operation. It actually said: 'The scoundrel is in Italy now.' " There are certainly X Bergers in Germany. All these quite ordinary people are technologically accomplished, more accomplished than I am. And Berger, a front-line veteran and a peaceful man of almost forty, is certainly no Communist. Beside that I place: There is an attendant at the State Library who has been very friendly to me for years, who gripped my hand when he saw me for the first time after the reading room ban, who is most certainly not a Nazi. Yesterday our greeting was very friendly once again. But yesterday he was wearing the Party badge. There are certainly millions of such Party members.

During the Führer's visit the little king and emperor played the most pitiful role (I would not have expected something so tastelessly pitiful from the Italians). He had to stand around at the railway stations in Rome and Naples like a porter. If they are going to play at empires, then they should also let their emperor represent them in an imperial fashion. Instead he walks beside the two greatest men of the new Europe like a well-behaved dog on a leash. Film confirms it and records it forever.

[. . .]

It remains to be said that recently my heart is particularly troublesome when I am walking, that I force myself not to think about it, smoke like a chimney and intend to be fatalistic on this point also. Georg will be 73 today. The real talent in our family has fallen upon the two of us, the oldest and the youngest. We are both in the Brockhaus, the siblings in between are not. Of the ones in between three are dead, and Marta is moribund. Perhaps I shall keep pace with Georg's longevity. I should so much want to, there is still something to be said, but I do not believe it.

May 14, Saturday evening

[. . .]

I am stuffing myself with weak and badly printed epigonal tragedies. Up to ten acts a day. And with every day that passes I am less confident of completing my Dix-huitième. Surely I am no more lacking in ideas or resolution than I used to be; but my relationship to the history of literature has changed fundamentally. In the past I wanted to clearly mark out a general summary of a period; now I am interested only in the details, the particular, the complex. Everyone says: Tragedy in the second half of the century: c'est du Voltaire. But the interesting thing about it is precisely the ways in which here and there it is just not du Voltaire. Only: What is the point of drawing out these details? For whom? Vossler recently sent me the third part of his *Poesie der Einsamkeit in Spanien* [Poetry of Solitude in Spain], published by the Bavarian Academy of Sciences. The works of other academics are listed on the back: *On the Lists of Bishops of the Synods of Chalcedon, Nicaea and Constantinople—Biton's Construction of Siege Engines,* etc., etc., things I have never heard of. Who is interested in them?

And why should Saurin and Lemierre, etc. be more interesting to other people than these things to me? Vanitatum vanitas.

May 18, Wednesday

Trip to Breslau, May 15 and 16, Sunday/Monday, about 375 miles. [. . .]

May 23, Monday

Frau Lehmann appeared on Thursday evening. She had been summoned to an official: It was known that she was a cleaner for a Jewish professor and a Jewish lawyer. — She was over 46, therefore permitted. — "Certainly, but your son will not get his promotion in the Labor Service, and your daughter—I have heard that you took the young girl with you to Dölzschen!—will lose her post, if you do not give up this work." — So the woman was rid of two of her three jobs, and we are alone. On Friday we washed dishes for almost three hours, and our travel plans were abandoned, since house and tomcat cannot be left alone. Frau Lehmann was in our service for eleven years—a confidential post.

Eva stubborn as ever. She goes on planting, planning, hoping.

Meanwhile the big events also slowly roll on; the Czech business is close to an explosion. Germany is going to march in, that seems certain, and the Austrian success will presumably be repeated. I once wrote in my review of Jolles [. . .] that one should not separate intellectuals from the general population, but the popular stratum in the soul of each person, what is instinctive and in thrall to suggestion, from the thinking stratum. I now add to that: The aim of education in the Third Reich and of the language of the Third Reich, is to expand the popular stratum in everyone to such an extent that the thinking stratum is suffocated. (Festivals, meetings, press, national emotions, *Stürmer*, etc., etc.) [. . .]

May 25, Wednesday

[. . .]

The Czech conflict continues, every day we are provoked, we are peace loving, the whole world slanders us and tells lies about us, especially England. I have been waiting for five years now—but since the German bluff has worked so often before now, it will no doubt work yet again this time. Recently Heckmann, the gardener, and today Vogel, the grocer, in complete unanimity: "I have no idea what's happening, I don't read a newspaper." People are apathetic and indifferent. In addition Vogel said: "It all seems like cinema to me." People simply regard it all as a theatrical sham, take nothing seriously and will be very surprised when the theater turns into bloody reality one day.

June 1, Wednesday

At the laying of the foundation stone of the Volkswagenwerk (the car for 990M) the Führer said that, previously, political economists had believed that a nation that did not produce sufficient foodstuffs for itself must spend all its money on foodstuffs. Thus panem et circenses has been outdone: Pro pane circenses. [. . .]

On Ascension Day (May 26) we drove the magnificent stretch up to Zinnwald, to see if there were any signs of martial activity on the border. It was all utterly peaceful, only on the Czech side little concrete walls had been erected to right and left of the barrier. On the way back we ate in the little village inn at Naundorf. [. . .]

I suspect there is a tragedy behind the printed announcement of May 26: Dr. med. Dressel–Katharina Roth, née Roth: married. We had thought he would marry Annemarie Köhler, and that is certainly what she thought too, when she—*she*—set up the clinic for him, whereas she now plays more the role of a matron and at best junior doctor. We have heard nothing from her for months. I have long thought that she tends to submissiveness and he is inclined to play Louis XIV.

The threat of war seems to have passed, and the Greater Germany continues to flourish happily.

June 16, Thursday

The final version, with all the corrections, of the wretched little chapter on tragedy was not completed until today; at the end I was handicapped by my failing eyes. I continue to lose hope of seeing the end of this work. And yet I would so much like to get around to the other subject as well. [. . .]

The newspapers declare the suggestion that troop movements aimed at Czechoslovakia had taken place around Dresden to be the most outrageous lie. We hear the opposite from three quite different sources (Wolf: the men in the barracks have been fitted out; Annemarie: troops moving through Pirna all night; Vogel: aunt reports the same as Annemarie from Rathen). So the whole of Saxony knows how things stand, (a) with the truth and (b) with the newspaper. But Vogel says, and that is vox populi: "Ach, it's all stuff and nonsense, nothing's going to happen." People are deadened and take everything to be just "stuff and nonsense." Annemarie Köhler was here the day before yesterday, quite incensed with the married Dressel and quite self-assured as the financial mistress of her clinic. Dressel has married a former nurse at the Heidenau Hospital. Otherwise completely isolated. Many worries, expenses, hindrances, vexations because of the car, which is in most urgent need of general repair, and treacherously breaks down when it is most urgently needed—as today. Yet also very pleasant drives again, some especially successful.

[. . .]

Since the loss of Frau Lehmann time spent on the kitchen, etc. has doubled. But even when I have the whole day to myself, then my eyes give out. And every day when I drag myself up through the park here, I think: Dead at 59, like Berthold and Wally.

News from Frau Schaps in London, where her children are settling after completion of the trip around the world.

News from Marta in Soprabolzano. (No mistreatment of the Sudeten Germans there, the Tirolese were simply sent to the Abyssinian front.)

News from the Blumenfelds in Lima. — Long woeful letter from Lissy Meyerhof. (Berthold in New York without a job.) I want to answer all of them before beginning the new chapter.

June 29, Wednesday

34 years—we could have a twelve-year-old grandson; we said to each other: Thank God, at least not that! And I think of the line from some modern French writer: Les enfants, c'est pour les femmes malheureuses. And add: et pour les hommes malheureux.

We had a very quiet day, since the car had to be put in for general repairs after all (which means at least three months of installments and corresponding hardship). But it is our last little piece of freedom. We spent the morning filling out forms: Inventory of Assets of Jews. We had nothing to declare. The house at 22,000M, of which 12,000 is the mortgage, the Iduna at 15,000M, which is encumbered by debts of 9,000 (and how we shall go on paying is a mystery). What is the point of this inventory? We are so accustomed to living without rights and to waiting apathetically for further disgraceful acts, that it hardly upsets us anymore.

June 30, Thursday

The last longer excursion before the jalopy gave out completely was on June 19 to Augustusburg near Chemnitz, there via Freiberg, Flöha, back via Frankenberg, autobahn, about 90 miles, left the house at three, back at nine for supper. Augustusburg, to which we have been tempted to go for years by a picture at Central station, is downright imposing. A mighty fortress high above a wide plain, visible from far off, partly reminiscent of Frauenstein, partly of Nossen. At the foot of the hill an old small town, itself still high enough above the plain. Fairground bustle again of course. It is noticeable that, everywhere and always—we have passed through so many places in the last few months—again and again and not only on Sundays: festivals and flags. Fairs, marksmen's and regimental meetings, sports meeting of an SA unit, 600th, 625th, 650th, etc., etc. anniversary of a town, mining anniversary (in Freiberg recently with traditional costumes), etc., etc. Always festivals, community of the people, Third Reich, flags, flags, flags. Apathy, revulsion, *thought* must come. Always the exact analogy with Rousseau and the conditions at that time. — Maria Kube, the Wendish maid, the wife of the harp maker, visited us. A gentle, very pretty, very good-natured creature. She talked very calmly, but passionately about Catholic affairs. Complete mood of martyrdom, things as if from other centuries and distant lands, here in Dresden and around Dresden. Priests imprisoned, priests expelled from the pulpit, the congregation—"except for two"—follows him, he celebrates mass in his garden. Catholic schools closed, it is forbidden to give children's names to the parish office. [. . .]

I recently jotted down: Hitler, National Socialism *despise* the "intelligentsia," scholarship, insofar as they do not produce any technological benefits. — Vossler, Kroner, Janentzky despise the whole of the natural sciences and technology. How incredibly easy it is for these simplistic natures. But whoever is not simplistic and not "fanatical"—is "liberalistic."

For the last two weeks continual reading for the chapter "A Less Restrained Theater."

July 12, Tuesday, Eva's birthday

I find it very difficult to display the requisite festive mood: The day reminds us all too strongly of the wretchedness of our situation, and I am sorely in need of the tenacity of hope, which I postulated yesterday in the birthday letter to the Blumenfelds. Lissy Meyerhof writes that Berthold has found work in the United States; Frau Schaps writes of her children settling down in London and of contact made with Isakowitz the dentist. All these people have made new lives for themselves—but I have not succeeded in doing so, we have been left behind in disgrace and penury, in some degree buried alive, buried up to the neck so to speak and waiting from day to day for the last shovelfuls.

But whining, to say nothing of entering my complaints in the diary, is a waste of time. The first overview section of the "Less Restrained Theater" section (now the beginning of the fourth volume, after I have at last found a way of structuring the book: Volume III, The Influence of Rousseau: Growth and Connections; Volume IV, The Influence of Rousseau: The Central Literature—I could hardly call Volume III "Marginal Literature" when it contains André Chenier and the studies of English, German and Ancient literature and only now did I really have the feeling of getting to the heart of the matter, and I was reluctant to present the whole mass of material as a single book)—so this little part is finished, and now I see that I have ended up repeatedly and flagrantly contradicting the first volume.

I have simply been working on the whole thing for too many years now, have learned more and have forgotten much that I wrote more carelessly and mechanically at first. If I really do ever finish the whole thing one day, I think it will need weeks, months of touching up and harmonization. In the first volume I still find grand words to acknowledge that tragedy dies with Voltaire; in the second volume my scholarship solemnly demonstrates the opposite!

[. . .]

Anti-Semitism again greatly increased. I wrote to the Blumenfelds about the declaration of Jewish assets. In addition to the ban on practicing certain trades, yellow visitor's cards for baths. The ideology also rages with a more scientific touch. The Academic Society for Research into Jewry is meeting in Munich; a professor (German university professor) identifies the traits eternels of Jews: cruelty, hatred, violent emotion, adaptability—another sees "ancient Asiatic hate flickering in Harden's and Rathenau's eyes." The Psychological Association is meeting somewhere else, and Jaensch condemns the materialistic psychology of the Jews, especially of Freud, and contrasts it with the spirituality of the new theory. And it goes without saying that, at the opening of exhibitions of German art in Munich, Hitler, etc. recite their familiar slogans.

[. . .] On Sunday a slow drive, with many stops, along the right bank of the Elbe to Meissen. There for the first time the new Elbe road outside the town and below the castle. Here a curious (monastery?) ruin, in which there is now a nursery garden. Much life on the river: rowing competitions, a police motorboat, a speedboat racing along, steamers, Elbe barges. On the way back, a friendly young man, so tired he was swaying on his feet, asked me to give him a lift to Dresden. He was from Tetschen, "Sudeten German," showed a Sudeten Deutsche Partei membership card, he had wanted to go to Hamburg, to find work on merchant ships; had not been successful, got neither lodgings nor food. He was going back to his mother in Tetschen. We were in a real quandary; as I said, the boy made a good impression and we felt sorry for him. On the other hand: whatever we gave him, we were giving it to the most merciless deadly enemy. We chose a middle course, drove him to Dresden railway station, the Travelers' Aid or the Frauenschaft or some other organization of the *National Community* can take care of him there. On the way he told us in all innocence how his deceased father and even his grandfather had been National Socialists, and how not a single Social Democrat works in their German factory, and how the "Heller yid" (that was the owner of the large clothes shop) had spat and said: "Someone should put a bullet through Hitler's head!"

[. . .]

We are expecting Annemarie tonight. Yesterday the cinema and a sack of cement, today a tongue for the evening—that is all there is to the birthday celebration. Our finances will be in a somewhat better state in August, and we want to have a belated celebration then.

I wrote to Grete [. . .] telling her about the unfortunate repairs and today she offered me 200M; I declined, I would turn to her if "the worst came to the worst," we were "struggling" at the moment, but still getting by. Perhaps this feeling of shame was a foolish and untimely luxury.

July 27, Wednesday

Rock-bottom days. It is absurd to go on hoping for a change. They are so firmly in the saddle, in Germany people are content, abroad they're keeping their heads down. Now England is intervening in Czechoslovakia on behalf of the Sudeten Germans. Today the *Stürmer* carries the headline: "Synagogues are dens of thieves." Underneath: "The Shame of Nürnberg" and a picture of the synagogue there. 1938 in the middle of Europe. — In the course of the last few days racial theory and anti-Semitism have been officially instituted in Italy as well.

[. . .]

We had planned to go to Bautzen last Sunday, the twenty-fourth: Past the Weisser Hirsch, a couple of hundred yards from a gas station but far below it, the car breaks down [. . .]. A lot of fiddling around, gasoline injections in the carburetor. Brisk pace after that (overheating). A good two hours lost, so only a little excursion, side roads to Radeberg, back via Heidemühle. Again and again: the beautiful landscape around Dresden. But the loathsome figures at the Weisser Hirsch [literally, White Stag]: "The Stag chases away the Jews." And here the most friendly assistance, and any payment declined.

August 10, Wednesday

Frau Lehmann announced she was coming to visit on Friday evening, July 15: She just had to convey birthday wishes to Eva. She came late in the evening, all worked up. She had wanted to wait for complete darkness and slip in unnoticed, but there had still been someone or other on the street and she had been afraid. She did not realize how terribly that depressed us; her fear was undoubtedly the fear of all "comrades of the people." In recent days I have been very bitterly reminded of Frau Lehmann's visit. Grete wants to go to Kudowa next Sunday; she invited us to pick her up in Strausberg, drive to Kudowa, and take her back to Strausberg four weeks later. Such an extended trip would have done us both so much good. But it was impossible: We now have no one to look after house and cat, we are completely isolated. Vogel, the grocer, suggested we should use a private security company. And if the people look at my notes? There is spying everywhere. In their advertisements the company takes pride, inter alia, in having uncovered a number of cases of "racial shame."

The enforced no to Grete hit us all the harder because we are very much *down* for a combination of reasons. For something like three weeks constant wearying sticky heat. For weeks now, and with no foreseeable end in sight, lack of money, which makes everything more difficult. For weeks intensified Jew-baiting again and drastic new measures all the time. From October 1 all Jewish doctors have been struck from the Medical Register, nor are they allowed to practice as "healers"; so they can starve. An identity card for Jews is being introduced at the same time. One will certainly not be allowed to stay in a hotel with one. Prisoners therefore. [. . .] In foreign policy everything remains unchanged. Extreme tension everywhere and fear of war everywhere.

That I view my Dix-huitième with ever greater despondency and boredom is no doubt related to the general feeling of disgust. For about two weeks I have been reading for the Beaumarchais section. I find the man less significant literarily than I had expected, but must nevertheless give him a prominent place.

After we had worked our way through the four volumes of the very important and very uneven *War and Peace* in eighty days, I read out Fallada's inflation novel, *Wolf unter Wölfen* [Wolf among Wolves] in a very short time. [. . .]

August 24, Wednesday

The Beaumarchais section, almost eight manuscript pages, was not finished until midday today. It gives me very little satisfaction. The factors impeding me, which I mentioned two weeks ago, continue to have their effect. Only the heat has turned into wet, cold weather, and the money difficulties are a little worse than before.

The excursions of recent weeks, only rarely undertaken, usually on Sundays, were first of all to Bautzen. We headed there no less than four times, varying the route slightly. [. . .] Then two drives to Hinterhermsdorf, on August 14 and 22. The landscape was simply magnificent. Hinterhermsdorf, Vogel's summer retreat, 13 miles beyond Schandau, close by the border with Bohemia, high above the Kirnitzschtal. The Königstein–Schandau stretch; the Kirnitzschtal itself, the impressive panoramic view from high up in Hinterhermsdorf are quite unforgettably beautiful, the newly improved wide road from Pirna to Königstein makes for splendid driving, the view of the fortress of Königstein from a wide crossroads in the forest in itself makes the drive worthwhile. How beautiful Germany would be if one could still feel German and feel proud as a German. (Only five minutes ago I read the just published law on Jewish forenames. It would make one laugh, if it were not enough to make one lose one's reason. Most of the new names are not Old Testament ones, but curious-sounding Yiddish or ghetto ones. [. . .] I myself have to notify the registry offices in Landsberg and Berlin, as well as the town hall in Dölzschen, that my name is Victor-Israel, and have to sign business letters accordingly. I still have to establish whether Eva-Sara is a possibility for Eva.) It was only the second drive, the day before yesterday, begun following afternoon coffee, ending with supper in the restaurant of the central market halls, that provided complete pleasure; the first was marred because we lost our way between Pirna and Königstein, strayed up and down very difficult and really quite dangerous tracks, wasted time and strained our nerves and were offered a coffee in Schandau that was as revolting as it was expensive. But what does "complete pleasure" mean now? One constantly has the pressure and the feeling of disgust in one's soul and escapes it only for minutes at a time. And new baseness is being devised all the time. [. . .]

Wolf entrusted our speedometer for repair to Bronnetz in the narrow Palm Strasse, close by Freiberger Platz, and I, or we, have been there countless times. Bronnetz is a precision engineer and a specialist in these things, a Bavarian of about 50 years of age. He is rarely at home, usually in one of the three small nearby pubs. He speaks in dialect, is very engaging and not at all grasping, he acts up "the original Bavarian," he rails against the government, in every register: He had stood by his "fellow countryman," Hitler, from the very start, his SA membership number was 2000, and now he had been thrown out of the Party because there had been "a Jew in his family 400 years ago." [. . .] there was no justice anymore, etc., etc. All very interesting, but with all of that I finally had to give up getting the instrument repaired by him. When I drive at 40 mph the speedometer invariably indicates 14, and it has stayed that way despite all the fiddling around.

[. . .]

For Eva's birthday, Annemarie Köhler gave her *The Barrings*, a novel of an East Prussian family set in Bismarck's time (I would have preferred the money, but one cannot say that to her). I only read out the beginning. [. . .]

But whatever I work at, do, think, the terrible pressure of the situation is always there. So very often a verse goes through my head, which I heard Father say a thousand times: "I would that it were time to sleep and everything were done." I always laughed about it, because Father clung so very fearfully to life. Now I know that it is possible to cling so very fearfully to life and simultaneously quote the verse with complete conviction and honesty. Only, I have more reason to quote it than Father ever could have had. He may have suffered from financial difficulties in his early days (but hardly at all in the last twenty years of his life), but he never experienced such a fall and such a depression as I do now.

A little while ago I noted down: To write classically means to write simply. Without affectation, so not *too* simply either, because that is an affectation. Also not to deviate from the use of language of one's own time, for example write today in the German of Goethe, because that would again be an affectation. But also not to confuse the language of the time with "topical" language, because everything topical is already out of date tomorrow. Here I am always reminded of the pointed booths opposite the Great Garden at the beginning of the twenties. In the first year their Expressionism impressed me, the next year they already looked awful. One always has a choice between what is topical and what is enduring; one cannot have both together.

I so rarely set aside a couple of hours for the diary now that as a result everything has to be got down on paper jumbled together and as briefly as possible.

Tomorrow the typed copy of the Beaumarchais. I go on working at the Dix-huitième out of pure obstinacy and without any hope or illusion. I, Victor-Israel Klemperer.

A couple of weeks ago the Nürnberg synagogue, on which I reported on July 27, was "solemnly" demolished under Streicher's supervision.

I have heard nothing for weeks from Marta, from Grete, from Sussmann—the silence around me is frightening.

September 2, Friday

Eva's "Little Russians," the handmade cigarettes. Isakowitz had recommended Weinstein, the ghetto man to us; after his death a Jewish shop in the city center wrote to me; after it was "Aryanized" I got the cigarettes in a little shop in the Plauenschen Gasse, then the woman there told me she could no longer obtain them. Vogel, the grocer, ferreted out "Factory Beresin's Widow" for me, and I went there. Flat three flights up in a tenement house, but a proper little business. An ancient woman, who speaks only a few broken scraps of German, a man in his forties (son? employee?), intelligent, agreeable. He said some firms were still being supplied and hoped to pull through. Russian Jews. A few days ago he brought me 500, and will now do that every four weeks; we talked for a very long time, i.e., he talked, mainly politics, not entirely uneducated, evidently with a great deal of knowledge from foreign newspapers and radio stations. He was at once optimistic and pessimistic. There would be no war now, Germany and Italy could not wage it, they lacked money, they lacked gasoline. It was inevitable that there would be internal collapse here this winter, the Stock Exchange was in a constant state of panic, by October industry will be unable to pay wages—and then that would be followed by chaos, and the situation for Jews was desperate under any circumstances.

I no longer believe in these predictions of collapse. I see how much the foreign powers court Germany, how they try to conciliate it in the Sudeten affair, everywhere here I see pomp, amusement, people eating their fill, complete calm. The man also said that Mussolini had been forced to take action against the Jews by Germany, which finances him. Yet another proof of Germany's power, because it is inconceivable that Mussolini feels at ease with this new—new for Italy—business. He would not join in if he did not rely on Germany and therefore had to, whereas even a short time ago, Germany seemed to be dependent on him. I am gradually beginning to believe as firmly in the unshakability of the NSDAP as if I were a sworn supporter . . . Thus are our hearts very dejected, each day a little more.

Monotonous life. Few excursions; partly lack of money, partly the car frequently breaking down.

September 11, Sunday

For the third time Georg has remitted 500M to me from the blocked account "of the deceased Frau Maria Kl." My joy is already no longer as great as the first two times. Because this time I was almost counting on the sum. Also it is only a very partial help; also I feel more humiliated than before, since he has not written me a single line since October and replied neither to my letter of condolence nor to my birthday greetings. Nevertheless the sum (which by the way I do not yet have in my hands, and no one knows what is going to happen tomorrow, everything is uncertain and every hour may bring new coercive measures and war), so nevertheless the money is a great relief to me at the moment. Eva was always preaching: Let the Öhlmanns come here during their holiday, then we can go for a trip with Grete. I had vacillated, the Öhlmanns' holiday came to an end, and Grete took the train to Kudowa. In view of the 500M we announced our visit to the Öhlmanns and drove to Leipzig yesterday. Luck with the weather and a very successful drive via Niederwartha, Meissen [. . .]. New rest house in Lonnewitz. Village just before Oschatz, "Long Distance Lorry Drivers' Restaurant." The huge vehicles outside, the huge portions inside. The Party Rally was coming over the loudspeaker. Announcement, the arrival of Field Marshal Goering. Introductory march, roars of triumph, then Goering's speech, about the tremendous rise, affluence, peace and workers' good fortune in Germany, about the absurd lies and hopes of its enemies, constantly interrupted by well-drilled roars of applause. But the most interesting thing about it all was the behavior of the customers, who all came and went, greeting and taking their leave with "Heil Hitler." But no one was listening. I could barely understand the broadcast because a couple of people were playing cards, striking the table with loud thumps, talking very loudly. It was quieter at other tables. One man was writing a postcard, one was writing in his order book, one was reading the newspaper. And landlady and waitress were talking to each other or to the cardplayers. Truly: Not one of a dozen people paid attention to the radio for even a single second, it could just as well have been transmitting silence or a foxtrot from Leipzig.

At the Öhlmanns' by two and then like the last time in early spring coffee and conversation in her little room until six. According to Trude Öhlmann's stories from the Deutsche Bücherei, where they get a great deal of official information, war is virtually certain. The air-raid precautions (we too have just had several practices, blackout, sirens), the preparations for mobilization all point to it. Mood of the public, of the workers in particular, is bad. If I talk to the butcher or the butter man here in Dresden, then there will certainly be peace, but if (as the day before yesterday) I listen to Wolf, the car man, then so many of his mates have been fetched straight from work to the army again: "Things are coming to a head now!" If I read the newspaper, see and hear the film reports, then we're doing soooo well, we love the Führer soo much and sooo unanimously—what is real, what is happening? That's how one experiences history. We know even less about today than about yesterday and no more than about tomorrow. [...]

September 20, Tuesday

The Third Reich will win again—whether by bluff or by force. Perhaps so overwhelming that it does not even need to fight? Chamberlain flies to Hitler for the second time tomorrow. England and France remain calm, in Dresden the Sudeten German "Freikorps" is almost ready to invade. And the populace here is convinced that the Czechs alone are to blame and that Hitler loves peace [...].

Don't think about it, live one's life, bury oneself in the most private matters! Fine resolution, but so difficult to keep. Nevertheless: the manuscript of Bernardin Saint-Pierre was finished today after disproportionately long and difficult work. — A little bit of driving, unfortunately repeatedly interrupted by a whole mass of necessary repairs. Recently we were in Freital for three hours with Wolf, who fitted a new (secondhand) mudguard. It then turned out that the spare wheel is completely useless; it was quite certainly deceitfully switched at Kleemann's repair shop, but that can no longer be proved. A large part of the money Georg gave us is spent on these repairs and yet the car runs more badly every day. [...]

October 2, Sunday

Yet again extreme excitement and hope of an end. Godesberg appeared futile, ultimatum to Czechoslovakia for October 1, expectation of war in France and England. At midday on the thirtieth we drove to the dentist. Machine guns at the Elbe bridge. I thought: War this evening. Perhaps our death in a pogrom—but the end. I dropped Eva at Eichler's and drove to Bismarckplatz, where I usually park, to do some shopping. A gentleman called out to me. Aron. "We saw you in the car recently, we thought you had left long ago, you are neither in the telephone book nor in the directory. My wife and Neumann would like to drop in on you some time." (???) Then of course politics. I: Now there would probably be a terrible end to things, for us and *them*. He: Did I not have a radio? — ? — After a second threatening telegram from Roosevelt, after full mobilization of France and England, *he* had given way. Four-power meeting today [September 29] at three in Munich. Czechoslovakia continues to exist, Germany gets the Sudetenland, probably a colony as well. — Everything else will be in the history books. For my diary only this is interesting: For the populace on the front pages of the German press it is of course the absolute success of Hitler, the prince of peace and brilliant diplomat. And truly it is indeed an unimaginably huge success. No shot is fired, and the troops have been marching in since yesterday. Wishes for peace and friendship have been exchanged with England and France, Russia is cowering and silent, a zero. Hitler is being acclaimed even more extravagantly than in the Austria business. Yesterday's headline in the *Dresdener NN:* "The nation of eighty million greets its great Leader." And something tremendous really has been achieved. But *we* are now condemned to be Negro slaves, to be literally pariahs until our end. For half a day I thought, now one must find the courage for suicide. Then the old state of mind returned: apathy, waiting to see what happens, Johanna Krüger's observation: "You still have so much, the will to live, and hope too once again. Every hour can bring change, every hour in which one is still alive." But when little Muschel wakes me up in the night and I cannot fall asleep again immediately, then it's terrible. Nevertheless: on I go, and no thought of the next morning.

Bernardin de Saint-Pierre is completely over and done with. After a whole month. On I go.

500M have come from Georg. That will make the winter easier. It is impossible and pointless to carry on with the life insurance; we shall spend nothing of this 500 on it. The mortgage runs for another three and a half years. Don't think about what happens then. And what will happen to Eva when I die—with a widow's pension of perhaps 200M? And what would happen to her if she received the still remaining 4,700, instead of the 1,000 or so if we stop paying now? I think that either way her fate will be that of the Indian widow. Am I without a conscience, should we rather do without every kind of relaxation and keep up the insurance? Or are we doing the right thing to make life more agreeable now? Don't think about it—on I go.

During the last few weeks we twice saw Doctor Margarete Gump, a likeable Swabian woman, employed at the Philanthropin, visiting her sister here and recommended to us by Albert Hirsch. We went for a drive with her: Edle Krone, Dippoldiswalde (the beautiful view from the top!), Kipsdorf, took her back to Blasewitz, where she is staying, ate at the central market hall. On her first visit she said: "Why don't you learn English? You've got the time!" I spent two mornings reading the old Gesenius English grammar, my opus was at a standstill. Then it looked as if war were imminent: I threw myself at the book again (correcting the Bernardin, reading *Florian* by Saillard, which I received from Göttingen). Then the German triumph. Until now I have stuck with the Dix-huitième. Whatever I do, my conscience is troubled. What is the value of my opus? What value does learning English have? I could always brush it up in six weeks if any prospect of being able to get away turns up. But perhaps I am making excuses to myself. Then again—I could go back and forth over things for hours.

I sometimes think my heart is in such a poor state that it makes no difference at all how I spend the rest of my time. Sometimes: perhaps it's just neuralgia. Sometimes: the book is just thrown together and crap, sometimes: my best work, my God-given task. On I go.

[. . .]

I have just brought my diary entries up to date because tomorrow—difficult decision, horrible back and forth, for and against—we are driving to see Grete in Strausberg. We get away from here for a couple of days—but where do we end up? Klaus Öhlmann was not allowed to leave Leipzig because of the risk of war, the Wolf family (the mechanic in Freital) will now look after the house and cat here.

October 5, Wednesday, toward evening

On Sunday, as I was dusting, I was overcome by horror at the trip to Strausberg. That we should let the Wolfs in here, into this very bohemianized household (the inches of dust), the intimacy that would inevitably follow, then inevitably come to an end à la Lange (who disappeared at Christmas with 5M and a last broken promise): That did it for me. I wrote a note. In the afternoon we drove to the Wolfs in order, as had been arranged, to let them know our plans. They were not at home, *contrary* to the agreed arrangement. Thus our decision was confirmed as the right one.

Then a pathetic postcard arrived from Grete. Bitterness, no more invitations, forbidden "on pain of a heavy punishment to send birthday greetings." She will be seventy tomorrow. Thereupon we both spontaneously, each on his own, made a new plan. Muschel can be provided with food for 36 hours. We shall drive to Strausberg tomorrow and back on Friday. An evening, one morning with Grete, two days driving: so everyone will be happy, and unpleasantness can be largely avoided. [. . .]

On Monday at the Capitol Sudermann's *Heimat*. [. . .] In the newsreel the meeting in Munich, Marseillaise as Daladier's aircraft lands, part of Hitler's latest bellicose speech, Sudetenland scenes. Very loud applause again. A burden has evidently been lifted from everyone's soul. It is impossible to say what still threatens the Third Reich internally or externally. Munich is Hitler's Austerlitz.

October 9, Sunday

My birthday. Naturally the most awful mood, made worse by the letters received, which are without exception gloomy. The most tragic one from

Sussmann: without a job since October 1, Käthe in an American sanatorium for months without any improvement; Lotte in Switzerland, not as
an assistant doctor, but suffering a nervous breakdown and pneumonia
and admitted as a patient to the very hospital in which she was supposed
to take up a post. But the man has his faith; he thanks me for my criticism
of his text; it helped him to remove a final logical mistake! If he now sends
me the "corrected" version, I shall probably agree with it, I shall have this
lie on my scholarly conscience. — Every person's thinking faculty becomes detached on some point or other: Marta, otherwise quite discerning
in literary matters, thinks her youngest son's travel letter is accomplished;
Sussmann, with his education in philosophy, thinks his study of religion is
good and convincing. When shall I reach that point of self-delusion, or in
which respect am I already at that point? (How at ease I would be, if I were
at that point with respect to my Dix-huitième!)

All the Judeans write delightedly about the peace that has been preserved (Frau Schaps, Lissy Meyerhof); they do not see that *our* fate is
thereby sealed. Otherwise it would perhaps have been the death of us; *this
way* our Negro slavery has been made eternal. Only Grete thinks the way
we do.

So we were in Strausberg with Grete. [. . .] The surprise went off well.
Grete was in bed with bad myositis, suffering considerable pain, but was
evidently very delighted to see us, did not look all that poorly and was
soon very animated. We got supper and talked with her for hours. Her political judgment speaks for her intellectual alertness; likewise her literary
interests. (We brought her a consignment of books again and took the previous one back.) But Grete's age is noticeable nevertheless. She tells the
same story in the same words for the umpteenth time [. . .]. Every person
probably has a few details in his mind, emotionally loaded trifles, which
overshadow everything else. With Grete it is the story of how on a journey
Father ordered a chocolate for himself and only a glass of beer for her, a girl
of about fifteen. The antipathy to Father gradually intensifying into hate increasingly preoccupies her. (I also remember the apple cake, which he ate
by himself, to accompany his pills, while everyone else watched.) The
chapter "Father, Daughter, Sons" will be a very important one in my Life.

Grete had a very world-weary letter from Georg. (He has not yet written to me; I shall have to thank him for the 500M, which has been tossed to
me like an unwrapped bone—and are unfortunately much more important than the wrapping.) The Kemleins continue to be very friendly to
Grete, take the Jew-baiting as something given, do not allow themselves to
be upset by it, are quite unpolitical and yet evidently delighted with conditions in Germany: pomp, order, peace. The old man, a war veteran, is
completely convinced that, if it had come to it, Germany would have been
victorious against the whole world (the biggest army in the world, the best
air defense in the world, the best fortifications in the world, etc., etc.), that
Hitler is the greatest statesman and has saved Germany from Russia. And

that is certainly the opinion of 79½ million Germans. — Grete told us ghastly things about the treatment of Jews in Bad Kudowa. — The next morning breakfast, afterward lunch in her room, by her bed, in between only a few minutes on the road outside. I took 20M from Grete "for gasoline," and so my travel costs are only a couple of marks.

Set out on the return trip at one o'clock very exhausted. [. . .] Home at ten. Grete had given me her favorite Jeremias Gotthelf, and I read out a few pages [. . .]. On the whole this 36-hour excursion went well, also helped by the weather. So that was October 6–7. [. . .]

Whatever may happen politically, inwardly I am definitively changed. No one can take my Germanness away from me, but my nationalism and patriotism are gone forever. My thinking is now completely a Voltairean cosmopolitanism. Every national circumscription appears barbarous to me. A united states of the world, a united world economy. This has nothing to do with cultural uniformity and certainly nothing at all to do with Communism. Voltaire and Montesquieu are more than ever my essential guides.

November 22

First of all it was probably the desire to get a little bit further with my work before I made another diary entry, and then misfortune followed misfortune, one could say: catastrophe. First illness, then the car accident, then, following the Grünspan shooting business in Paris, there came persecution, and since then the struggle to emigrate. So first of all in the middle of October an ordinary influenza. Following that a quite unfamiliar bladder complaint, ever more horrid aneurysm, and no doctor here to whom I could turn. On October 26, when it had become completely unbearable, I wrote two brief postcards to Marta and Sussmann, and on the twenty-seventh we drove to Berlin again.

November 25

(I completely lack the peace of mind to write.) The journey there in beautiful foggy autumn weather with stops in Elsterwerda and Jüterbog was uneventful. This time we found a straight road from the south through the suburbs—Zehlendorf was probably the last stage, everything runs into everything else, villas, parklike bits of woodland, wide avenues—and reached Kudowastrasse in the suburb of Grunewald without touching Berlin itself. In addition to the Jelskis, Sussmann himself was waiting for us. His house is being watched so that no one can go to him during consulting hours (but the Spanish lessons he gives seem to be dispensed to his old patients). He examined me after coffee and was rather shocked. He came again after supper and brought a catheter with him, secretly, as priests brought the sacrament during the French Revolution. I was catheterized for the first time in my life; it was not nice, and what was brought to light looked altogether unlovely and pretty bloody. Sussman explained that I was in urgent need of longer treatment, possibly in a hospital bed. We spent the night at the Jelskis in a very depressed mood, especially as the evening before very unpleasant things had been reported from the concentration camp near Weimar (Buchenwald, I think). The next morning, Friday, the twenty-eighth, Sussmann appeared again. We agreed that I should drive back immediately and see Dressel for treatment at the Pirna clinic that very afternoon. But I must at all costs say nothing about Sussmann having treated me already, if necessary I should mention Jakob, the licensed Jewish medical assessor. At ten therefore a hurried drive straight back, again in fine autumn weather. (Sussmann, for whom things are going badly enough, had offered financial help if the need arose.) In Jüterbog we ate lunch together, my first lunch for a long time, and also had our coffee quickly in Café Blomberg; I was feeling a little better, our mood was quite elated, we wanted to be in Dölzschen by five, after that I would drive to Pirna immediately. A few miles past Elsterwerda at the village of Weinberge, smooth road, a side road intersecting, a motorcyclist wants to cross and does not stop. I become nervous, brake, the car immediately skids sideways. A second less of fear than an irritating and fatalistic anticipation (fortunately the braking got no harder). Behind me I hear only Eva's likewise somewhat irritated "Well!," the car rolls over the embankment, and with a jolt I am lying on my back in the field close by the car, my face stinging. Quite instinctively—vile Nature—I call out: I am not injured! and jump up. I see Eva standing on the other side of the car, bent over, her hands covering her face, blood running down. I run to her, a couple of women are there already: Lie down! She, completely calm in voice and manner, demurs, it is only a nosebleed, she had bumped against the front headrest. The motorcyclist is there, shouting defensively: You braked quite unnecessarily. Someone asks: Shall I call a doctor?—Yes—Just then a car halts, a young man gets out, immediately stretches out his hand to feel Eva's nose. Are you a doctor?—Yes, nothing is broken. It doesn't appear to be anything more than a nosebleed. — A friendly first aid woman has turned up and dabs at my grazed chin. I to the doctor: I'm ill, I must be catheterized today. — I'll take you in my car, I have only one more visit to make here. — His chauffeur helps us into his car, our belongings are left lying there. In Elsterwerda a large clinic, a nurse, the young man is substituting for the doctor who had been called, but who is on holiday. The nurse takes over Eva; I have to get on the operating table for the catheter. I tell the doctor I am not Aryan—medical assessor in Berlin. He deals with me quickly and is already gone. The nurse writes out a bill: Professor Klemm (sic), Dresden, car accident and catheterization: 8M. Half an hour later—the doctor had told me: Take the train, don't drive yourself. You are badly shaken—we are at a repair shop. The man takes his tow truck and two assistants, we drive to the scene of the accident. A little knot of people, no police, darkness. The car has literally to be dug out of the field. The engine is intact. But some oil has run out, the steering wheel has been torn away—the spokes are still there—the hood is stuck, one door is hanging loose. The door is secured with string, the hood is half open, half shut. Will I get to Dresden like this? (A little less than 40 miles. — If you think you are capable of it, drive slowly and don't run into any police, perhaps, it's hardly something I would advise you to do. — It is pitch dark, about six o'clock, it's raining, we drive off. A little filling station beside a lonely inn. I drive past the point that's lit up, leave the car in the dark, ask for a quart of oil inside. — Can't you move back into the light? — There's no need to go backward. Here's my pocket lamp, pour it in. — Drove on, feeling at once half dazed and half gripped by convulsive energy. We get safely through Grossenhain, reach Meissen at last, park the car in a dark spot with the parking light on, eat in the station waiting room, continue on the left bank, where there is less traffic, and where we do not need to go through Dresden first. Very difficult to steer with the spokes alone. Really at home at ten, in bed an hour later. The next morning Eva very swollen, including the left eye, otherwise quite cheerful, myself in a very bad way. Telegram to Wolf. He appears that same evening and brings back the patched car on Tuesday. He gets 35M, the recovery man got 10M—thus far we got off quite lightly or appeared to do so. But two weeks later Eva has trouble with her eyes. Old von Pflugk is away; to Best who meanwhile wears the Party badge, but examines carefully. Slight damage to the vitreous body, no movement of the head for three weeks, little reading, drops, then come again.

That was on November 15. Since then the eye has not got worse, but also only marginally better. And Eva needs the physical work, and the house needs her labor, and I have a great deal of housework, and I read to her for hours during the day as well. And the other disaster came in the middle of all this.

My bladder problem has almost cleared up, but not entirely. On the Saturday I went by bus to see Dressel (Annemarie was in Leipzig), told him everything. He is sympathetic—but he is evidently afraid, and that is probably the state of mind of most intellectuals. He gave me a thorough examination and gave me some medicine. After that my condition gradually improved up to a certain point; the inflammation is not completely gone, but at least the functional disorder has not come back.

By the time I returned to Pirna about a week and a half later the Grünspan affair had supervened. Before I went I had just heard from Natscheff that the night before the synagogue here had been "spontaneously" burned to the ground and Jewish windows smashed. I do not need to describe the historic events of the following days, the acts of violence, our depression. Only the immediately personal and what concretely affected us.

November 27

On the morning of the eleventh two policemen accompanied by a "resident of Dölzschen." Did I have any weapons? — Certainly my saber, perhaps even my bayonet as a war memento, but I wouldn't know where. — We have to help you find it. — The house was searched for hours. At the beginning Eva made the mistake of quite innocently telling one of the policemen he should not go through the clean linen cupboard without washing his hands. The man, considerably affronted, could hardly be calmed down. A second, younger policeman was more friendly, the civilian was the worst. Pigsty, etc. We said we had been without domestic help for months, many things were dusty and still unpacked. They rummaged through everything, chests and wooden constructions Eva had made were broken open with an ax. The saber was found in a suitcase in the attic, the bayonet was not found. Among the books they found a copy of the *Sozialistische Monatshefte* (Socialist Monthly Magazine—an SPD theoretical journal) [. . .] this was also confiscated. At one point when Eva wanted to fetch one of her tools, the young policeman ran after her; the older one called out: You are making us suspicious, you are making your situation worse. At about one o'clock the civilian and the older policeman left the house, the young one remained and took a statement. He was good-natured and courteous, I had the feeling he himself found the thing embarrassing. In addition he complained about an upset stomach and we offered him a schnapps, which he declined. Then the three of them appeared to hold a conference in the garden. The young policeman returned: You must dress and come to the court building at Münchner Platz with me. There's nothing to fear, you will probably(!) be back by evening. I asked whether I was now under arrest. His reply was good-natured and noncommittal, it was only a war memento after all, I would probably be released right away. I was allowed to shave (with the door half open), I slipped Eva some money, and we made our way down to the tram. I was allowed to walk through the park alone while the policeman wheeled his bicycle at a distance behind me. We got onto the platform of the number 16, and got off at Münchner Platz; the policeman kindly covered up the fact that I was being taken into custody. A wing in the court building: Public Prosecutor. A room with clerks and policemen. Sit down. The policeman had to copy the statement. He took me to a room with a typewriter. He led me back to the first room. I sat there apathetically. The policeman said: Perhaps you'll even be home in time for afternoon coffee. A clerk said: The Public Prosecutor's Office makes the decision. The policeman disappeared, I continued to sit there apathetically. Then someone called: Take the man to relieve himself, and someone took me to the lavatory. Then: To Room X. There: This is the new committals room! More waiting. After a while a young man with a Party badge appeared, evidently the examining magistrate. You are Professor Klemperer? You can go. But first of all a certificate of discharge has to be made out, otherwise the police in

Freital will think you have escaped and arrest you again. He returned immediately, he had telephoned, I could go. At the exit of the wing, by the first room into which I had been led, a clerk rushed toward me: Where do you think you're going? I said: Home, and calmly stood there. They telephoned, to verify that I had been released. The examining magistrate had also replied to my inquiry, that the matter was not being passed on to the Public Prosecutor. At four o'clock I was on the street again with the curious feeling, free—but for how long? Since then we have both been unceasingly tormented by the question, go or stay? To go too early, to stay too late? To go where we have nothing, to remain in this corruption? We are constantly trying to shed all subjective feelings of disgust, of injured pride, of frame of mind and only weigh up the concrete facts of the situation. In the end we shall literally be able to throw dice for pro and contra. Our first response to events was to think it absolutely necessary to leave and we started making preparations and inquiries. On Sunday, November 12, the day after my arrest, I wrote urgent SOS letters to Frau Schaps and Georg. The short letter to Georg began: With a heavy heart, in a quite altered situation, pushed right to the edge, no details: Can you stand surety for my wife and myself, can you help the two of us over there for a couple of months? By my own efforts I would surely find some post as a teacher or in an office. — I telephoned the Arons—the husband had spoken to me on Bismarckplatz on the day of the Munich Agreement. Herr Aron was not at home, Frau Aron would receive me at eight in the evening. I drove there: a wealthy villa in Bernhardstrasse. I learned that he and very many others with him had been arrested and taken away; at present we still don't know whether they are in the camp at Weimar or are working on the fortifications in the West as convicts and hostages.

November 28

Frau Aron advised us in the strongest terms to take immediate steps to emigrate and to sell the house; everything here is lost, German money is almost valueless abroad, the mark is worth sixpence halfpenny sterling. The next day, on Frau Aron's advice, went to the Public Information Office for Emigrants (the man in charge, a Major Stübel, is a very decent gentleman). In the waiting room a voluptuous, blond Eastern Jewess to a girl: At police headquarters they sent us away, they didn't know where the men had been taken. . . . The old major said to me: Within these four walls you can speak your mind. In recent days I have heard a great deal that is very distressing, in my free moments I walk in the Great Garden in order to calm myself down. — I set out my situation. I said, a regime that espouses banditry with such openness, must be in a desperate plight. — He: That is what every decent German thinks. — What did he advise me to do? — He could not advise me. — Were the situation to change tomorrow (which I do not believe), then you would be sorry to have gone. — From his explanations it emerged that they really would let us out stripped and naked and with seven and a half percent of the proceeds of the house.

December 2

On Sunday, November 13, we drove to Leipzig to see Trude Öhlmann. Would she be able to take Mujel? — No, he would hardly be able to adapt, it would be more humane to have him put down. She told us how the SA had mounted the attack in Leipzig, poured gasoline into the synagogue and into a Jewish department store, how the fire brigade was allowed to protect only the surrounding buildings but not fight the fire itself, how the owner of the department store was then arrested for arson and insurance fraud. In Leipzig we also learned about the billion-mark fine the German nation had imposed on the Jews ... Trude pointed out an open bay window on the other side of the street. It has been open for days; the people have been taken away. She wept as we drove off. On the way Eva's nerves gave way; supper in Meissen did little to help, at home she had a screaming fit.

Then letters came from London, from Frau Schaps and from Friedrich Salzburg, who, driven out of Italy, is now applying to the USA from England. One would so much like to help but cannot. They approach Demuth again and again, who has failed to be of any help to me for three years. Salzburg wrote, only my brother in the USA could help me.

December 3, Saturday

Today is the Day of German Solidarity. Curfew for Jews from 12 noon until eight. When at exactly half past eleven I went to the mailbox and to the grocer, where I had to wait, I really felt as if I could not breathe. I cannot bear it anymore. Yesterday evening an order from the Minister of the Interior: local authorities are henceforth at liberty to restrict the movement of Jewish drivers both as to time and place. Yesterday afternoon at the library, Striege or Striegel, who is in charge of the lending section, an old Stahlhelm man of middling position and years [...]: I should come into the back room with him. Just as he had announced the reading room ban a year ago, so he now showed me the complete ban on using the library. The absolute end. But it was different from a year ago. The man was distressed beyond words, I had to calm him. He stroked my hand the whole time, he could not hold back the tears, he stammered: I am boiling over inside ... If only something would happen tomorrow ... — Why tomorrow? — It's the Day of Solidarity ... They're collecting ... One could get at them ... But not just kill them—torture, torture, torture ... They should first of all be made to feel

what they've done . . . Could I not give my manuscripts to one of the con-
sulates for safekeeping . . . Could I not get out . . . And could I write a line
for him. — Even before that (I knew nothing about the ban yet) Fräulein
Roth, very pale, had gripped my hand in the catalog room: Could I not get
away, it was the end here, for us too—St. Mark's was set alight even before
the synagogue and the Zion Church was threatened, if it does not change its
name . . . She spoke to me as to a dying man, she took leave of me as if forever. . . . But these few, sympathizing and in despair, are isolated, and they
too are afraid. The developments of the last few days have at least rid us of
inner uncertainty; there is no longer any choice: We must leave. But I have
run ahead in my report. The most important event was Georg's cable on the
twenty-sixth: Assume surety help letter follows Georg. The letter can be expected about the tenth of December and will be decisive. But with the constant worsening of the situation I want to go to the American consulate with
the telegram as early as Monday (the day after tomorrow).

Frau Schaps had drawn my attention to Edith Aulhorn, who works for
the Quakers. I called on her in the beautiful family villa in Liebigstrasse.
[. . .] She had already been summoned to the Gestapo and given a warning many times: Aryan friends of the Jews are always treated worse than
Jews themselves. She wrote to Elsbeth Günzburger for me, who is a
teacher at the Ecole normale in Sèvres. The latter then replied to me immediately [. . .]. Edith Aulhorn believes that a coup d'état is relatively
near and that the government is completely finished. But she is very intimidated, feels she is being watched. I have heard nothing more from her
directly; Elsbeth Günzburger refers to her as "Our common friend." [. . .]

The Wengler business is extremely mysterious. Last February, when the
bank dawdled in transferring my mortgage payment, a curt and nervous
letter arrived from Ellen Wengler in Leipzig: She threatened, she gave notice of foreclosure as a precaution, she did not address me by name and
signed with German greeting; she justified herself, saying that she now
needed the money because she had been forced to separate from her
brother. At the time I let the bank reply. A few days ago, I wrote to Heinrich Wengler to see if he could give me English lessons, after I had repeatedly telephoned in vain: There was no ring at the other end. The letter
came back: address unknown; opened by the Reich Post Office in order to
ascertain sender. I imagine: Wengler, always a Communist and idealist
could no longer bear it in the teaching profession; half English on his
mother's side and still in touch with relations there, he will have made for
England. Every day brings new restrictions. Only today, Saturday, December 3, the newspaper reports ghettoization and limitations on the free
movement of Jews in Berlin. Further stringent measures are promised.
What for? Pure madness? I almost believe, rather, that they want to sub-
due opposition abroad by outdoing themselves with acts of terror.

The terrible thing about the last few weeks is that they have been at
once empty and overcrowded. No possibility of concentrating on any
work. Waiting for terrible news, which always comes. Being kept busy.

Writing to government offices, my Israel (three departments), my identity card with mug shot, proof of Eva's Aryan identity (X letters to registry offices, churches in East Prussia), consultation with the moving company, repeated discussions with Annemarie who came here many times (heroism!), who may buy the house, list of published works, eight copies, for Fräulein Günzburger. Endless reading aloud by day and by night, since Eva sleeps badly—her nerves are failing, my heart—and since she must rest her eye and since reading aloud is still most likely to distract her (admittedly it is the condemned cats who always keep her company, and that is dreadful). I think we have never gone through such a hellish time, even during the war.

December 6, Tuesday

[. . .]

The last films that we were still allowed to see—the programs have been lying around here for something like two months or even longer, were the circus film *Fahredes Volk* [Wandering Folk] and *Die vier Gesellen* [The Four Journeymen], which was meritorious both from the literary and the acting aspect. [. . .]

Now I note only the ever more frequent phrase: It is in accordance with the healthy sense of justice of the people, which is always printed when some new atrocity is initiated. And that disposes of the contemplative intermezzo.

The healthy sense of justice of every German manifested itself yesterday in a decree from Police Minister Himmler with immediate effect: withdrawal of driving license from all Jews. Justification: Because of the Grünspan murder Jews are unreliable, are therefore not allowed to sit at the wheel, also their being permitted to drive offends the German traffic community, especially as they have presumptuously made use of the Reich highways built by German workers' hands. This prohibition hits us terribly hard. It is now three years exactly since I learned to drive, my driving license is dated 1/26/36.

I had already heard about the ban on the afternoon of the day before yesterday from the Arons, who in turn had heard it announced as imminent on Swiss radio. I was at the Arons a second time, to get information about emigration possibilities and about my property assessment (which no one at the Tax Office could enlighten me about). It has been announced that the first installment must be paid on December 15 without waiting for a bill, and no one can tell me how large my property—purtroppo!—is. Aron, detained in Buchenwald for several weeks with 11,000 others, come back sick, prevented from emigrating to Palestine at the last moment, customs has already put its seal on the furniture, and he cannot raise the 1,000 pounds sterling that is required, even though he is offering 175,000 marks in German money, is extremely overwrought and pessimistic. He says

Georg's surety would be no help at all to me, thousands upon thousands were applying to immigrate, had already put their names down, I could wait three years. In Berlin crowds of applicants were camping in front of the American consulate from six o'clock in the morning until evening just to be admitted. — We shall just have to wait for Georg's letter, but our spirits have now sunk even further, and since new Jewish laws come out nearly every—no, really every day, so our nerves have gone to the dogs. As for the property assessment, on the other hand, we appear to benefit from our poverty. According to what Aron and today Rummel from the Iduna told me, I shall probably be under the 5,000M limit, since the repurchase value of the life insurance will now only amount to a couple of hundred marks, and the present value of the house is less than 17,000, of which 12,000 is the mortgage.

The frightful hints and fragmentary stories from Buchenwald—pledge of secrecy, and: no one comes back from there a second time, between ten and twenty people die every day anyway—are awful.

With the library ban I am now literally without work. I have resolved to really make an attempt at my memoirs. Because I cannot just cram the *Little Yankee* all day either. But for the present all peace of mind is lacking: errands, correspondence, reading aloud, brooding and reading aloud again.

December 15, Thursday

We continue in this simultaneously crushing and stupefying chaos, this empty and breathless busyness, this absolute uncertainty.

My letter to Georg sets out the facts of the USA—Havana possibility. The visit to the American consul very amusing. Large, elegantly furnished offices in Schlossstrasse. After some back and forth received by a younger black-haired gentleman. Handshake, courtesy. He could not speak a word of German, called a blond Dr. Dietrich (introduction, handshake) as interpreter; then it turned out that the consul spoke Italian—(Maltese, says Natscheff, whose wife is American)—so there was a curious mixture of languages. Result: no hope, it is not even possible to register me as a professor because for that I would have to have been dismissed for two years at most, but not as long ago as 1935. I told the story of my saber, etc. Finally Dr. Dietrich said: Go to Haessel's Travel Agency with a recommendation from the American Consulate and ask to see Herr Haessel in person; he can probably tell you more than we can! Afterward I realized that they were suggesting an unofficial way. As soon as I entered the agency on the Altmarkt, I had the definite impression from the physiognomy of a customer and from a fragment of conversation I caught (You must not lose heart. You must wait in Hamburg . . .) that I was in the right place. Two young people, brothers. As soon as I opened my mouth: The American consul . . . , I was interrupted: You have the affidavit and can't do anything with it. . . . All you get in Berlin is trouble and cold feet! And then I was advised to take the Cuba route. I asked myself and still ask myself: Just business or really good advice? — Today I received a letter from the agency: Please call; I shall hear more then.

Toward evening

The Havana possibility is virtually settled. I now have to decide by January 1 at latest whether to book two berths for June, everything before that is sold out, even though the number of sailings has been doubled; after that there are no more places to be had until 1940.

Rush on Haessel by fleeing Jews. The recent impression considerably strengthened. Meanwhile another mysterious possibility has turned up. Without any explanation a Sydney newspaper arrived from London, in all probability from Demuth. First riddle: Has an application on my behalf been made from London, or should I take steps myself? Second riddle: What is Sydney (New England)? The Sydney in Australia or one in the USA, or a Sydney in Canada? No one can answer these questions. After long, passionate discussions, I sent an application in German by airmail to Australia. I thought the counter clerk in our little post office would be astonished and not know exactly what to do. Instead he was in the picture immediately and said disapprovingly, the letter would take some time to arrive, perhaps a whole week. Piccolo mondo moderno.

I went to see Edith Aulhorn, in order to have the Sydney riddle interpreted. She too was uncertain. She had been about to write to me, to give me the address of an English woman who is working as inconspicuously and secretly as possible for the Quakers to help those non-Aryans whom the Jewish aid organizations turn away. I wrote to Miss Livingstone in Berlin-Charlottenburg [. . .]. The desire to go to the colonies is Eva's favorite idea. Plans repeatedly surface, according to which some colonies or other are supposed to be earmarked for mass emigration. First they said Alaska, now Rhodesia. Eva thinks a schoolteacher will always be needed, and she can be an organist, draw building plans, perform agricultural work. Her latest plan is a mineral water factory in Rhodesia. The times are so crazy that no plan is too fantastic. And in any case these plans sustain her. I assume that what is most probable is that we shall be forced to stay here. Sometimes we think we could never be happy here again or feel at home, even if things were to change; but sometimes we also cling to this place.

In April, when, in wise anticipation of the Grünspan murder and its atonement, Jewish assets had to be declared, I innocently gave the rebuild value of the house and the value of the Iduna policies on which money had been borrowed. As a consequence I was called on to pay a property assessment of 1,600M. Enlightened meanwhile, I inquired as to the repurchase value of the policies and had the current sale value of the house estimated (which all in all has cost us 26,000M). Result: Iduna surrender value 240M, house estimated at 16,500, of which 12,000 mortgage. I do not therefore have 5,000M assets, the level at which the assessment begins. I went to the Tax Office in Sidonienstrasse. They were not unfriendly. I had to submit an appeal immediately, and the first 400M installment due today is in abeyance until it is dealt with. We did and do feel quite indifferent to this business: because one way or another all our property will be lost anyway. The house will certainly be expropriated in the next few months; they have also begun to encroach on pensions, for the time being of those dismissed on full salary (of whom I should really have been one). In my case it has been calculated that I have mistakenly been paid 6M a month too much, so that I owe the state about 280, which will be deducted in monthly installments of 20M. (That is precisely the amount of my now superfluous car tax.) We responded just as apathetically to the fact that one thousand marks were transferred to us from Georg's blocked account as we did to the business of the property assessment. What am I supposed to do with it? I cannot take anything out of the country, and here—what is certain here, and what pleasant things can one do? We can no longer go for drives, we can no longer make purchases for house and garden. Still, for the moment the 1,000M saves me from petty miseries. But what pleasure it would have given us only a few weeks ago. — District Judge Moral, whose acquaintance we made at Frau Schaps', visited us. The man looks very old, but is only sixty. We hatched Rhodesia plans together, half jokingly, half in earnest; we puzzled over the future together.

Beresin recommended a Frau Bonheim to us for housework (since Eva's eyes continue to be affected, both eyes now). Latvian Jew, young divorced woman, her husband, German and Aryan, wanted to be free of her, gymnastics teacher, grammar school education, real lady. A pretty, obligingly hardworking person. We treat her as a friend, she has coffee with us, and she does the heavy work of scrubbing well and without squeamishness for 50 pfennigs an hour. I told her about Rhodesia and Sydney. She said, I have a relative in Rhodesia, a woman friend in Sydney. Piccolo mondo moderno. Curious: At the very moment modern technology annuls all frontiers and distances (flying, radio, television, economic interdependence), the most extreme nationalism is raging. Perhaps a last convulsive uprising of what is already a thing of the past. And another oddity: The National Socialists have always talked about World Jewry; it was an idée fixe and a phantom. They have gone on talking about this phantom for so long until it has become reality.

I now take learning English more seriously, much more seriously. Sometimes a chapter in *Little Yankee* and sometimes a section of grammar. And from half past three till five I have just had my first arduous and not quite unsuccessful lesson with Mrs. Meyer. Natscheff recommended her to me. His wife is American and a friend of hers. Fifty-seven years of age and actually a musician and organist at the American Church. But the church is a German charity, and Meyer is of Jewish descent and has therefore lost her post and is also not allowed to teach Aryans. She is English, her husband an unbelievably vigorous eighty-two-year-old, looks sixty-five at most; German, retired opera chorus singer. I went to see them on the fourth floor of a good house on Feldherrenstrasse, was cordially received in the kitchen-parlor; a large birdcage and the little budgerigars treated tenderly, taken out and kissed, at the same time tears because of the situation and thoughts of emigration and fear for the pension and fear at giving lessons at home. So today she came out here. One and a half hours for three marks with 30 pfennigs tram fare on top of that. I intend to carry it on assiduously.

Shattering letters—more exactly and honestly: letters, which would be shattering without the present deadening and the fact that our fate is identical—from Sussmann and the Jelskis. Both letters in part the same word for word: We go as beggars, dependent on the support of our children, Sussmann to Stockholm, to his youngest daughter who has married there, Jelskis to Lilly in Montevideo. The Reform Community has been wound up, the pension has stopped, a lump sum will be paid as compensation, out of which the passage can be paid. A little while ago Constable Radke was here from the local council, I should come up to the council office because of the identity card. We had a friendly conversation, the man shook my hand, told me to keep my spirits up. We know from before that he is certainly no Nazi, that his sister is in difficulties, because her husband, a gardener, has a grandmother who is not Aryan. But then the next day, when I was up there, he happened to come through the room; he stared ahead as he went past, as much a stranger as possible. In his behavior the man probably represents 79 million Germans, perhaps half a million more than that rather than less.

December 23

Everything continues with such deadening wretchedness. The days are as if wasted. I take quite frequent lessons from Mrs. Meyer, I work at a little bit of English by myself—I don't make much progress, and often I do not get around to it either. The housework, again and again the useless SOS correspondence, errands *without the car*, all the reading aloud during the day. Eva's eyes are not improving, her general state of health weakens all the time.

[. . .]

Yesterday Natscheff maintained with great certainty that a new Röhm affair was imminent in Berlin, which would lead to a general catastrophe: Himmler, Ley, Streicher, Goebbels, the ideologists, against Goering and Schacht, the men of business. For a moment that gave us hope. But we have experienced disappointment so often.

December 25, Sunday

Eva cut a few branches from a fir tree in our garden and arranged them into a tree on the frame of a table lamp; we drank a bottle of Graves with the tongue, and the dreaded Christmas Eve passed more pleasantly than I had dared hope.

A friendly letter arrived from Walter Jelski in Jerusalem, asking if there was any way he could help. I shall at any rate send him as usual my list of published works—a torment to type it out again and again—I cannot produce more than three copies at a time—perhaps he'll meet the High Commissioner or some other VIP in the Café Europa (his permanent address). And the affidavit from my nephew Georg E. Klemperer in Chicago arrived. I shall at any rate pass it on to the Consul General in Berlin.

Yesterday for the first time in the Third Reich the Thought for Christmas in the newspaper was completely dechristianized. Greater German Christmas—the rebirth of light of the German soul, signifying the resurrection of the German Reich. The Jew Jesus and everything relating to the spirit and humanity in general excluded. It has undoubtedly been ordered for *all* newspapers.

New Year's Eve '38, Saturday

Yesterday I cursorily read through the diary for 1938. The résumé of '37 maintained that the peak of wretchedness and intolerableness had been reached. And yet compared to the present state of things the year still contains so much that is good, so much (everything is relative!) freedom.

Until the beginning of December I could use the library, and up to that time I wrote one hundred and twelve good pages of the Dix-huitième (from Retour à l'antique to Rétif). And until December more or less I still had use of the car and we were mobile. Piskowitz, Leipzig, the Schwartenberg, Rochlitz, Augustusburg, Bautzen, Hinterhermsdorf, Strausberg and Frankfurt on the Oder in April. Beautiful Breslau on May 16, Strausberg again on October 6 for Grete's seventieth birthday, the trip to Berlin because of my illness and then the accident, Leipzig once again. And so many short trips and the ease of shopping. — And then from time to time the cinema, eating out. It was a little bit of freedom and life after all—no matter how pitiable it may have been, no matter how it may have rightly appeared to us as imprisonment.

Certainly things were getting manifestly worse and worse in the course of the year. First the Austrian triumph. Then from the end of May the absence of Frau Lehmann. (More serious for us personally than the carry-on about Greater Germany.) Then in September the frustrated hope of a war that would deliver us. And then the decisive blow. Since the Grünspan affair the inferno.

But I do not want to assert prematurely that we have already reached the last circle of hell, for uncertainty is not the worst thing, because in uncertainty there is still hope. Also we still have pension and house. But the pensions are already being tampered with (no special arrangements any more, i.e., the promised full salaries, which I never received, are being cut), and I have already had to provide the Office for the Liquidation of Jewish Assets with all particulars relating to the house. We must not let ourselves be deceived by the relative calm of recent weeks: In a couple of months either we are finished here or "they" are.

Recently I have really been doing everything humanly possible to get out of here: The list of my publications and my SOS calls have gone everywhere: to Lima, to Jerusalem, to Sydney, to the Quakers via Miss Livingstone. I gave the affidavit sent by Georg's youngest to the US Consulate in Berlin, confirmed by telephone that the Mr. Geist named by Georg is still there and will be available after the New Year, and wrote a letter requesting a personal audience. But that any of it will do any good at all, is more than doubtful.

Moral was here again on Thursday afternoon: feeling of friendship and isolation and the same irresolution. He thinks and hesitates as we do. Away and into absolute nothingness? Give up the pension one still has? But precisely: still! And afterward, if it is too late? But where can we go now? etc., etc., ad infinitum. Moral is a District Court Judge, is 61 and looks, also behaves a little as if he were 71—it is therefore even harder for him than for me. He thinks it possible that war and collapse are near. A St. Bartholomew's Eve—such a pogrom would surely be the beginning of the end, there would, he argues, be only one night of blood, because then the army would restore order—he therefore wants to escape the night of blood by lying low in Berlin in a neutral and Aryan pension. He has already provided for that eventuality.

The *News Review* London of December 8, which I have from Frau Meyer, claims that there was a military plot to kill Hitler at the Berghof recently. Himmler had uncovered the plot, executions had been carried out. Truth? Rumor? To go by this newspaper, we must be close to the end here. But here we read just such reports about Moscow. And Stalin remains, and Hitler remains.

To the extent that I have worked at all since the catastrophe, it has been a haphazard courting of English. Now grammar, now vocabulary, now the translation of a short text; since December 15 one and a half hours (with dictation) two or three times a week with Mrs. Meyer. Perhaps I have learned a tiny amount more, at least with respect to reading and understanding the spoken language; but I continue to be quite unable to speak it and I am increasingly alienated from the syntax, indeed regard it with helpless dismay. And in the long term I am unable to bear this fumbling around, this complete lack of productive work. If January passes without bringing any certainty about emigration, then I shall concentrate on my Vita, of which I recently wrote down the first tentative lines.

1939

New Year's Day, Sunday

Yesterday afternoon we were invited to Fräulein Dr. Gump and her sister Hirschel in Prinzenstrasse. She was in Dresden one last time. The way there, through a great deal of half-thawed snow, extremely difficult and expensive. As before '36 we took a taxi from Chemnitzer Platz. The driver still remembered me—Now you can't drive anymore, Professor?—commiserated, complained (they all do that, but they all say Heil Hitler! — How long will it go on? Now they want to put a tax on our tips—can you not go abroad? etc., etc.). Fräulein Gump told us terrible things from Frankfurt and her hometown Ulm. All the male teachers from the Philanthropin were sent to Buchenwald. Hirsch was lucky because he broke his ankle and was admitted to the infirmary; however the ankle was so badly set there that afterward in Frankfurt it had to be broken once again. He is still in bed. After two weeks the female teachers were forced to resume teaching alone. Fräulein Gump was jostled and abused by the mob, the police stood by and did nothing. When there was vandalism and also looting everywhere, the local army general enquired in Berlin whether he was allowed to intervene—but then just did nothing. — In Ulm the rabbi was chased (by the mob, that is, by the people, and not just by SA carrying out orders!) around the market fountain with his beard alight and was hit on the hands when he tried to touch his beard; afterward he was in hospital with burns. — On that very night Herr Hirschel was on the train to Paris. They wanted to pull him off the train; unaware of what was going on, he defended himself vigorously, the sleeping car attendant took his side against the SS hooligans, so they let him go on. The next morning in Paris he read the special editions; he would never have summoned up the courage for such dauntless resistance if he had known what was going on. He does not yet have a position in Paris, and his family does not yet have final entry and exit permits. But Frau Hirschel speaks with great warmth of Aryan friends who are looking after both her and also her husband in Paris. [. . .] Eva was intensely annoyed because Fräulein Gump said nothing would get any better until we had a Jewish state somewhere in the world. Certainly that is pure Nazism and just as odious to me as it is to her. But as things stand, I would nevertheless like to grant Fräulein Gump extenuating circumstances. She is very attached to German culture and passionately felt herself to be German.

At seven we went by tram to Central railway station, ate there, then took a taxi again. Eva soon lay down, I read aloud, at twelve she got up, we lit the little tree and drank a number of schnappses.

January 2, Monday

I had an English lesson on the afternoon of New Year's Day, but was too tired to take anything in. Only the faithful Wends, Agnes and the beautiful Maria, the wife of the harp maker, sent greetings. Johannes Köhler had already dropped out last year, this time Fräulein Carlo was also missing. But she came in person at six under cover of darkness and stayed for dinner. She told us that on the day of the catastrophe she had been on the street and involuntarily said Shame! Had been arrested, had explained she had not meant the government, had been released, but was now being watched. She was very intimidated and very resentful.

Later I finished reading our novel of the last few days: Howard Spring, *Geliebte Söhne*—Beloved Sons. The original title is *O Absalom!*—evidently far too much of an Old Testament title to be allowed to remain in the German. Strange that such a vehemently pacifist and anti-nationalist work, in addition one with the sympathetic figure of the Jewish theater director Wertheim, has slipped past the censors. No doubt because the rebellious Irish say God punish England. [. . .]

January 8, Sunday

All the working hours of the day (there are not many of them) taken up with the sheets *of particulars* and the accompanying letter to Otto Klemperer in Iver. How many such sheets, vitae and lists of publications I have already sent all over the world.

[. . .]

I am reading aloud a great deal, partly because of Eva's eyes, partly because of my own emptiness and restlessness. I do far too little English. Perhaps because I do not really believe that I shall get away from here (and am still waiting for the miracle that one day we shall wake up without the Führer).

[. . .]

On Wednesday afternoon Fräulein Gump and her niece, sixteen-year-old little Hirschel, were here. Always the same conversation. — The day before yesterday Frau Lehmann came under cover of darkness, full of goodwill but very inconveniently and catastrophically for Eva's nerves; she wanted to see how we were and to bring us some of her Christmas stollen. If one adds Frau Bonheim, who comes twice a week, then we now have more company than for months. But there is not much joy in it; it always means wallowing in the same misery—and extra washing up.

A very cordial and very depressed letter from Frau Schaps. (Sebi Sebba from Danzig has turned up in London and wants to emigrate to somewhere in the world.) A very woeful letter from Lissy Meyerhof. On a picture of a fancy dress party in 1906 there is a young girl called Otti Steinhardt, distantly related to the Meyerhofs, whom Erich Meyerhof had a crush on. Lissy writes quite matter-of-factly: A member of Otti's family committed suicide because a hope of emigration came to nothing; Otti Steinhardt died of shock, of a heart attack, both were cremated at Christmas. She also writes of one of Erich's sons, who as a half Jew is permitted to serve in the army and even to become a corporal (but no more than that). In September his unit was sent to Upper Silesia on maneuvers, they were marching along when to their great astonishment they were suddenly welcomed in a village with flowers, wine and sausage, they had no idea what was going on. That was the occupation of the district of Hultschin. The clueless lads would have marched just as cluelessly into shell fire. Self-determination of a people.

January 10, Tuesday

Marta sent me the *Jüdische Nachrichtenblatt* [Jewish Newspaper], and a number of fundamental ideas, which had long been on my mind, came to me or rather became more defined.

There is no German or West European Jewish question. Whoever recognizes one, only adopts or confirms the false thesis of the NSDAP and serves its cause. Until 1933 and for at least a good century before that, the German Jews were entirely German and nothing else. Proof: the thousands upon thousands of half and quarter, etc. Jews and of Jewish descent, proof that Jews and Germans lived and worked together without friction in all spheres of life. The anti-Semitism, which was always present, is not at all evidence to the contrary. Because the friction between Jews and Aryans was not half as great as that between Protestants and Catholics, or between employers and employees or between East Prussians for example and southern Bavarians or Rhinelanders and Bavarians. The German Jews were part of the German nation, as the French Jews were a part of the French nation, etc. They had their place in German life, and were in no way a burden on the whole. Their place was very rarely that of the worker, still less of the agricultural laborer. They were and remain (even if now they no longer wish to remain so) Germans, in the main intellectuals and educated people. If the intention is now to expatriate them en masse and to transplant them into agrarian professions, then that will inevitably fail and cause unrest everywhere. Because they will remain Germans and intellectuals everywhere. There is only one solution to the German or West European Jewish question: the defeat of its inventors. — What must be treated separately is the matter of the Eastern Jews, which again, however, I do not regard as a specifically Jewish question. Because for a long time those who are too poor or hungry for culture or both have been pouring from the East into western countries and forming an underclass there, out of which vital forces crowd upward. Which does no harm to any nation, because race, in the sense of pure blood, is a zoological concept, and a concept that long ago ceased to correspond to any reality, is at any rate even less a reality than the old strict distinction between the spheres of man and wife. The pure or the religious Zionist cause is something for sectarians and of no importance to the majority, very private and backward like all sectarian matters, a kind of open-air museum, like the Old Dutch Village near Amsterdam. — It seems complete madness to me, if specifically Jewish states are now to be set up in Rhodesia or somewhere. That would be letting the Nazis throw us back thousands of years. The German Jews concerned are committing a crime—admittedly one must grant them extenuating circumstances—if they agree to this game. It is part of the Lingua tertii imperii that the expression "Jewish people" appears repeatedly in the *Jüdische Nachrichtenblatt*, that there are repeated references to Jewish states or Jewish colonies to be founded as dependencies of an ideal Palestine. And it is absurd and a crime against nature and culture, if the West European emigrants are now to be completely transformed into agricultural laborers. The movement back to nature proves itself contrary to nature a thousand times over, because development is part of nature and turning back is against nature. The solution of the Jewish question can only be found in the deliverance from those who have invented it. And the world—because now this really does concern the world—will be forced to act accordingly.

January 17, Tuesday

During the last week all time not taken up with housework and reading aloud has been spent writing letters of application, even at the cost of neglecting the English (with the exception of Mrs. Meyer), though I am not spurred on by optimism [. . .]. It is forever the same thing, and yet forever different, so-called intellectual work and yet deadening to the intellect. [. . .] Georg gave me addresses, Fräulein Günzburger in Sèvres, Walter from Jerusalem. Assistant Secretary and Prefect (retd.) von Loeben, pillar of the non-Aryan Christians, to whose attention I had been drawn by Miss Livingstone, announced his visit in Christian solidarity—in those very words!—[. . .] came and revealed himself to be an amiable, good-natured windbag, busybody and caretaker of Jewish souls. I was directed by him to Spiero in Berlin. Our mood is most succinctly expressed in the letter to Georg: the vacillation between too soon and the fear of too late. It is clear from Georg's letters that he has no idea of the difficulties here. Obtain a visitor's visa immediately—how easy he thinks it is!

In the paper a couple of days ago on Himmler's birthday, an article about his blood order; the SS is an order of Nordic blood, not like the Christian orders an order against blood. The SS people have to obtain permission to marry; Nordic blood is being raised. — The solution of the Jewish question is increasingly and ever more openly emphasized as the principal duty of the NSDAP (and not just by the *Stürmer*). Since the last catastrophe nothing else exists for them.

January 22, Sunday

[. . .] All that interests me in the English lessons are the newspapers Mrs. Meyer smuggles in and brings with her, the *Manchester Guardian* and a quite sensational magazine, the *News Review*. Deeply anti-Nazi, always biting, often witty, but naturally laced with rumors and dependent on speculation.

No one, whether inside or outside, can fathom the true mood of the people—probably, no, certainly there is no general true mood, but always only moods of several groups—one dominates, and the mass is apathetic or is subject to changing influences—neither can anyone know with certainty the relative strength of the parties. I read the report of a debate as to whether the German people approve of the persecution of the Jews. Some of the English deny it vehemently; Schroeder, a Cambridge professor of German, maintains the opposite: The Germans were relativists, did not acknowledge one beauty, one morality, distinguished between state and private morality. (A line of thought that the French, in their hostility, have often advanced.)

On language: Do the words "cold weather front" in the weather report reflect the militarization of language in the Third Reich? I almost believe it. [. . .]

Annemarie came for supper on Thursday, brought three bottles of Burgundy, a bottle of champagne and a bottle of cognac as Christmas presents—under the present circumstances we had declined a book, also brought Dressel with her, who has not been here for a very long time. There was no mention of Dressel's wife, even though he had sent us his wedding notice. The most curious social situations are emerging now.

A postcard to Eva from Johanna Krüger, signed only Jo and recognizable from the handwriting, saying we should set her mind at rest, let her know how we were. I wrote her a few fairly sharp words.

February 5, Sunday

In two weeks not the least alteration in situation and mood. The same dreadful emptiness of the days, the same fruitless effort at English, lessons, reading, grammar—nothing helps. Eva's nerves are bad, I read to her for many hours of the day and night. Eye problems, heart problems. Parts of the Vita go through my head—I write nothing.—No reply to the many applications. — Politically everything the same. Germany all-powerful, Spain will soon be finished. Campaign against the Jews further intensified. In his Reichstag speech of January 30 Hitler once again turned all his enemies into Jews and threatened the annihilation of the Jews in Europe if they were to bring about war against Germany. He presented himself as a man of peace and a few days later expansion of the submarine fleet and of the air force was announced.

[. . .]

Prof. Best has declared Eva's eyes are restored to health, but the problems are not entirely cleared up. No excitement! Trips into town, to the doctor, to do shopping, are always depressing, difficult and very expensive. We ate at the station a couple of times. Once we went as far as the wholesale markets restaurant, which we liked so much last year; when we got there tired and hungry, there was a new sign: Jews not welcome. So we got the tram back to the station.

February 24, Friday

I had already hesitantly sat down to write the introduction to the Memoirs a couple of times, without doing so; in order to convince myself that I was actually able to write, I began the first chapter on February 12—the anniversary of Father's death—stuck to it and finished it yesterday. I shall now type it and then read it to Eva; she can decide whether it is worth continuing. My English lessons naturally suffered because of this work, which got a grip on me, but were not quite abandoned. Apart from that the writing did me good, the dreadful idleness was interrupted. Otherwise no change whatsoever; prospects of getting out are zero, and since for us personally nothing has taken a turn for the worse in the last few weeks—at the bank I now sign Victor Israel Klemperer, but I still get my pension and no date has yet been set for me to give up the house—we just go on living fatalistically. Except that Eva's nerves continue to deteriorate.

Frau Hirschel and her daughter visited us on February 7; in a few weeks they hope to be able to go to France, where her husband lives but has not yet established himself. — On the nineteenth, after an interruption of two and a half years, a new Gusti Wieghardt chapter began, about which I shall report in context. Now I want to copy the Memoirs chapter.

In the *Jüdische Nachrichtenblatt*, which Grete sometimes sends, Shanghai is very prominent among the small ads. Wanted: boat tickets to buy or exchange. Wanted: marriage partner with affidavit. — Moral was here, having the same thought as we were, as unsure as we were, also talked about Shanghai and shuddered at the thought.

March 6, Monday

On February 19 Gusti Wieghardt—I knew from Fräulein Roth, the librarian, that she had moved to Vienna to stay with her impoverished sisters—wrote a moving letter from Loschwitz. She was here in order to arrange her emigration to England, she wanted "to be reconciled to all her enemies before she died," as the Russians say; in the present tragic situation everything that one had previously considered important, appeared trivial. I called her immediately very cordially [. . .]. Gusti promptly came here, there was no talk of the past. It was a meeting of great warmth. That is all the easier since her love for Russia seems to have cooled greatly. If I had been able to go to Russia then, she says, I would probably already have been shot as a Trotskyist. She explained the opposition Trotsky (World Revolution)—Stalin (internal consolidation, betrayal of Czechoslovakia and Red Spain) to us and since then Eva has seen Stalin as Hitler's future ally. — Gusti talked about the sufferings of the Jews in Vienna; she says the pensions of Jewish civil servants would be stopped in the near future because there were far too many of them in Austria. (Meanwhile, as an intermezzo restriction, the surrender of silver and a tax rise has been imposed on us: the Jew is always in tax group I.) Gusti herself is taking a post as cook with two elderly philanthropic ladies in England. On March 2 she cooked here, so well that I got an upset stomach and afterward we had a terribly increased amount of washing up. This cooking business was going to be repeated today, but Gusti came yesterday by mistake, just as we were washing up, and had to share our tomato soup.

In the afternoon I had just read Eva the conclusion of the first Memoirs chapter (all typed now, but still to be corrected) and met with her strong approval; now I read the whole thing once again in one go to Eva and Gusti, and once again it was very well received. Naturally I am now passionately full of thoughts of continuing to write; but whereas previously I believed that the first chapter must be the most difficult, it now seems to me to be the easiest, and the difficulties lie before me.

Because of the writing I have completely neglected English for at least a week, especially as I have stopped Frau Meyer since March 1 under a pretext and supposedly only for six weeks: She was getting far too boring for me and far too expensive, also it is impossible to know if and when I shall turn my knowledge of English to account. But now I do want to study some English, so as to be prepared for whatever happens. I read a few lines with Gusti; I do not think I know much less than her, but that is very little. [...]

On the fourth we were at the Hirschels, who are still waiting for an entry permit to France. — Moral will come here again the day after tomorrow and report on a trip to Berlin. But we don't hear anything new. Only ever this: Economically things are going so very badly for them that they must collapse, but no one knows when, and we shall hardly survive it. Everyone is making enormous efforts to get out, but it is getting ever harder. We personally do not appear to be having any success. Silence all around. From the American Consulate in Berlin we received Waiting List Registration Numbers 56,429 and 30.

And so everything remains unchanged for us: Eva's nerves in poor condition, I gloomily fatalistic. Endless reading aloud by day and night, lately all kinds of visitors, a great deal of household stuff, a little work, now English, now Memoirs. And forever waiting.

[...]

District Judge Moral writes to us with stiff, old-fashioned courtesy: Herr Professor ... and so on; he is extremely cautious, never gives his name and address as sender. But his hatred breaks through the caution and decorum: Bandits are stealing my silver. [. . .]

March 14, Tuesday

Work on the second chapter of the Memoirs very slow. English completely at a standstill, since there is no prospect at all of getting out; instead, after a very long interval, French, indeed modern French, came to the fore in the strangest way. Natscheff did not have any more translations of English and American writers, I took a translation from French [. . .]. We possess, with a personal dedication by Jules Romains, vols 3–8 of his *Les Hommes de bonne volonté*. It transpired that Natscheff has all the parts of this huge work (16 volumes). I therefore borrowed the beginning from him and early this morning we finished off volume 1. I already feel quite at home in the language once more.

In recent days I had some hopes of the Slovakian business. It is so obviously stage-managed from Berlin, in order to destroy Czechoslovakia completely and to open the way to the Ukraine. I told myself, even if England and France once again stand idly by, it would nevertheless be one more step in Germany's policy of aggression and so one more step toward the catastrophe. But now that according to today's evening paper the fixed game appears to have been so very swiftly and smoothly and completely won by Germany, while England and France take it all lying down, I feel as sick as a dog again.

Moral was here on the afternoon of the eighth: the same old conversations and fears, nothing new. We asked Annemarie to come here the day before yesterday: We gave her our silver things; if she cannot return it to us in better times, then she can have it; if the confiscation of silver is also extended to Aryans, she must throw it into the Elbe. But it must not fall into the hands of the Nazis. Annemarie thinks as we do. Among the silver cutlery are Eva's historical pieces with the stamp of the Wars of Liberation (1812 and Prussian crown [. . .]).

On the tenth I collected my identity [. . .]: a big J on the front, prints of both index fingers, Victor Israel.

[. . .]

April 7, Good Friday

Cool spring and fairly long days. How much I would have looked forward to it and welcomed it, if I were still allowed to drive! Now it only makes me more bitter and, even more than before, I try to bury myself. I think it is exactly the same for Eva. She tidies up, puts in order, weeds out, sews a lot, so as to be ready. But ready for what? There is no out for us.

The swallowing up of Czechoslovakia (and of Memel) is now having its effect, and if we had not been disappointed a hundred times, we would think war imminent. But it will not come, and if it does come we two have little prospect of surviving it. — I try to think of nothing contemporary. Curriculum Vitae (which has got as far as the end of the French grammar school) and *Les Hommes de bonne volonté* (the middle of volume 5). Otherwise housework, shopping errands, which I find very exhausting, a great deal of Gusti Wieghardt and nothing else. — I could not make up my mind to take leave of Marta in person. She invited us to come to Berlin or Hamburg at her expense. I declined, it would have been too dreadful. The Jelskis left for Montevideo on April 3. — Heinz Machol passed a servants' examination and he and his wife have found a post in England as housekeepers. That is serious, whereas Gusti Wieghardt's post as a cook appears to be as spurious as her Communism. She is being taken in as a writer and is already planning a book, "The Diary of a Cook." Sussmann is already in Stockholm. — The Hirschels, who visited us and bought our washing machine and with whom we shall have coffee tomorrow—the sister, Margarete Gump, is in town again—the Hirschels are waiting from day to day for permission to enter France. We alone . . .

On March 28, at the pawnbroker's at Neustädter Markt, I handed over a small golden clock and a little golden chain, which I had foolishly described as my belongings in the property assessment. (The things actually belonged to Eva and would have been released to her because she is Aryan.) There were separate booths at the table where the objects were handed over, so I could not see who was next to me. On the table there were two heavy shabbat lights and a charmingly delicate Chanukah menorah with the Star of David over it. The official said: You may keep one piece. A woman's voice replied, that was no good to her. Whereupon the official good-naturedly comforted her: The Lord is satisfied even with one flame. They pay, without regard for artistic value, 3 pfennigs for each gram of silver and then even deduct 10 percent from the total. I received 15M 70pf. for my gold things.

The day before yesterday at Grimm and Lederer (all new names, all expropriated Jewish companies in clothing, shoes, department stores), Wettinerstrasse, corner of Grosse Zwingerstrasse. After long deliberation, I bought a loden coat and a suit—extremely necessary. (I always carry Georg's 1,000M in my wallet in case of an emergency, always top it up from the bank.) An elderly man served me and was very friendly. I gave my address. Shall I spell it? — No, I am pleased to meet you, Professor.— ?—My daughter has told me a great deal about you and always with affection. One of your last students. We so much deplored . . . Since January she has been teaching at the German school in . . . Indian name . . . Chile. We shook hands. Community of the people. — I cannot remember anyone by the name of Heynen; but the very few who still came to me from the PI had long been chosen swimmers-against-the-current. The bulk went to study English. And to the Aryan.

Walter Jelski sent me half a pound of coffee from Jerusalem for Easter. Very touching. He knows what coffee means to us, and has no doubt read about the coffee shortage in Germany. In fact people here have to make do with an eighth of a pound a week. Walter cannot know that my jack-of-all-trades in Chemnitzer Platz has a secret stock and supplies us with one and a half pounds a week. (For how much longer?)

[...]

At every corner, in a hundred shop windows the repulsive poster for the political touring exhibition: "The Eternal Jew." In the newspaper daily references to the need to visit this exhibition: the most odious race, the most odious bastard mixture.

April 9, Easter Sunday

Yesterday afternoon at Hirschels. [...] There was much talk of the most recent aggression of the Axis, the bloody attack on Albania—the Hirschels have a radio. I said: one step closer to the inevitable catastrophe. A friend of the family was there, Günther, once arts and literature editor of the *Dresdener Neuesten,* editor at Reclam's Universum publishing house, writer himself, author of a monograph on Shakespeare, man of 54, Aryan, but expelled from the Literature Chamber and therefore completely without prospects because his wife was Jewish (friend of Frau Hirschel). Was—she died last year, and now they should really let him earn a living again, but they don't. The man states with complete resignation and conviction: Hitler is the victor, the Western powers are impotent, they will never risk anything, it will all be too late—we shall not live to see any change—I was so incensed that I jumped down his throat. Afterward I was sorry that I had done so; we sat alone together in a side room for quite a while and had a friendly conversation about literature and politics. He said quite simply, he wished from the bottom of his heart that I would turn out to be right, but could no longer believe and hope in anything, he had been disappointed far too often.

This morning, in reply to our Easter greetings with an invitation for Wednesday, a letter from Moral: just as gloomy; he is lonely, without hope, he will gladly come, if he is still alive on Wednesday—there is no other way of accepting an invitation now. That is how this most punctilious man writes! Also from Lissy Meyerhof a much more depressed letter than is usually her nature. (Things are going very badly for Berthold Meyerhof in New York; he is working as a laborer in his wealthy relatives' brewery.)— Everywhere this awful hopelessness. And I believe it has taken hold of the foreign governments as well. They all tremble, they think Hitler is invincible—and consequently he is invincible—Gusti Wieghardt told us recently, Hitler has fits of raving madness, there is always a psychiatrist with him. I thought it was Russian tittle-tattle; but Günther related something not so different; he says: fits of rage—inability to tolerate the least contradiction;

only Goering and Himmler could really contradict him. However de facto Hitler was the real leader—What is the truth?—Goering and Himmler are supposed to be complete enemies.

April 20, Führer's birthday

The fiftieth birthday of the creator of Greater Germany. Two days of flags, pomp and special editions of the newspapers, boundless deification. In the *Berliner Illustrierte* a half-page picture: The Führer's Hands. The theme everywhere: We celebrate in peace, the world rages around us. — It really does seem to rage now, after Bohemia and Albania. But will it once again be no more than unceasing silent rage, given the naval concentration at Malta, given Roosevelt's message, to which Hitler intends to reply on the twenty-eighth in the Kroll Opera Reichstag? And what will war mean for us, us?—Each day as wearing as the next. We are dulled by so much tension. Just as yesterday in the special birthday edition amid all the hymns of peace, happiness, jubilation, contempt for the poor lunatics who question the general Führer, we follow you! atmosphere, there is in small print the almost daily notice: Two traitors to their country executed (it is usually two poor devils, workers, 20, 30 years old)—so the small print runs daily through my head: Will they beat us to death? But really only in small print and by the way.

People often here with whom conversations always run along the same track. On the twelfth Moral, completely depressed because they have blocked his assets; very old and gone to seed. There is some secret about the man, something broken inside him. Why his whole life long, in 40 years of service, never more than District Court Judge in small places? He said, that as a safeguard he had made a bequest to his housekeeper, who has been with him for 28 years. Hinc impedimentum? [...]—On the thirteenth at the Hirschels; leave-taking; they [...] have their visa for France. — Gusti, who was in Vienna over Easter and will probably be able to go to England in the next few days. She says in the government offices here, tax, police, etc., all except the Gestapo, they were courteous to Jews in a way that was almost a mark of opposition, but can nevertheless do nothing to alter the prescribed harassment and robbery. — Frau Bonheim, despite the fact that she scrubs, etc. for two marks twice a week, is also a visitor, has coffee with us, tells us about the midday meals at the Jewish Community; she too is on the point of leaving, returns to Riga in a few weeks.

Through all of this we quietly pursue our everyday tasks, Eva mending, tidying up, making ready—what for?—I the Curriculum and *Les Hommes de bonne volonté*. English still completely put to the side, although Georg wrote from London a few days ago that he has made a very promising contact, will be able to say something definite in June after his return to the USA, hopes to see me over there before the year is out. I do not know if that is what I want. As I said: I am burying myself in Curriculum and Romains.

May 3, Wednesday, toward evening

Gusti Wieghardt has just left; she unexpectedly succeeded in suddenly getting out; she travels to London tomorrow, where she takes up her (fictitious or semi-fictitious) salon kitchen post. Strangely she has not been treated as an emigrant but as the widow of a German professor, who is going abroad for a year and during this time continues to receive her widow's pension, paid into a special account—she is free to dispose of it within Germany. Curious and yet quite natural psychological observation: Until now Gusti was passionately interested in political developments, desperately waiting for war to break out at last, was full to the brim of radio reports, etc. Today it was as if it had all been blown away, she had not listened to the radio, she was indifferent to the situation—no matter what happens to Germany, no matter what happens to the prisoners here: all that lies behind me, is all the same to me, I am getting out! Of course she did not say it in so many words, but yet something like it, and it was so very evident from her whole behavior. Her last remark: I won't get cross anymore when I walk past a cinema! In London I can go in! (in fact she is not going to London, but to some little place near Bristol to some charitable old ladies, who have already engaged several women emigrants). [...]

Last Wednesday afternoon we visited Moral for coffee in, or rather over Pillnitzer Landstrasse. A costly and difficult trip for us. Landscape wonderful: the house high up a hillside, a view right down to the river, the big Blasewitz Bridge to the right, on the other side the city and ranges of hills, below, trees in blossom everywhere. Moral grows his tulips in the little garden in front of the house, lettuce and potatoes in the allotment ground that rises behind it. In his parlor an already moth-eaten tiger skin: He shot the beast in a trap in Java; native stuff on the walls: the year in Java the high point and the glory of his life. On his desk the Toussaint-Langenscheidt English dictionary and a Bible commentary. He lives all alone with an old cook cum factotum, his mother died only a year ago, must have been in her eighties. He received us very hospitably and with evident great pleasure, but spoke with the deepest pessimism—(I consider him a suicide candidate). I went at him in a tone of extreme optimism, and I believe with some success. But I did not and do not fool myself.

The Polish business will also be peacefully decided in Germany's favor.

I received a second demand and an advance demand from the Tax Office amounting to more than 300M: The new tax law places a heavy burden on Jews. I can simply pay that out of our reserves—but once these reserves are finished. . . . But all ifs and thinking about the future are pointless now.

Eva gave Gusti an old cookbook of her grandmother's from the 1850s. [...]

June 7, Wednesday evening

For weeks I have been unable to settle down to make any diary entries. Always buried in my third chapter (apprenticeship years finished, is now being typed up) and in *Les Hommes de bonne volonté* (at the fourteenth volume).

I do not know if time is standing still or rushing on. Sometimes, in fact every day, it seems to me that this time he is speeding toward his doom: The Polish business is developing in the same way as the Czech one, the encirclement proceeds. But I have been deceived so often.

How perfidious the people consider him to be: Generally it is said that he will divide Poland between himself and Russia. And how little it concerns him that he betrays his own lies: We had never supported Spain (Franco), and now the newspapers have for days devoted whole pages to celebrating the Condor Legion and its guns and aircraft. And every day a speech and a parade or a military exercise as demonstration of our invincibility and our desire for peace. And women conductors are being hired on the trams. And great shortages in the butcher shops and in the greengrocers, because everything is being stored for the army. — But the people really do believe in peace. He will take Poland (or divide it), the democracies will not dare to intervene. Moral has visited us three times in the last few weeks. The man is utterly depressed and in a panic, is having thoughts of suicide, and finds solace with us like a child. He is always particularly afraid that his home will be taken away from him. Now he wants to move into the Jews' House as a precaution. We strongly advised him against it. [. . .]

June 20, Tuesday

Slow and stubborn work on the fourth chapter: the sixth form in Landsberg. Just don't think about the point of the whole undertaking! Constant reading aloud: the sixteenth and for the time being final volume of *Les Hommes de bonne volonté*. At least I brush up my French and my relationship to modern French literature. In good moments I am once again playing with the possibility of a supplement to my Nineteenth and Twentieth Century. But the good moments are rare; I have a lot of problems with my heart and my eyes.

The political situation unchanged and yet *sourdement s'aggravant*.

Every day I hold forth to Eva, who no longer reads a newspaper, that war is inevitable and will break out by autumn at the latest, I hold forth about it every Tuesday and Friday to little Bonheim, and sometimes I also really believe it, but only sometimes.

Ulbrich, the butcher's wife, recently said to me: Every week the allocations we and all the others get are smaller; but Noack and Jacob in Prager Strasse have had big increases. The foreigners buy there, they're not supposed to notice anything.

Is it really a mark of strength, if literally every day a minister or the Führer himself declares, we have the strongest army in the world? Does it inspire confidence, if every day the newspapers declare, England is helpless and defenseless?

The garden blooms as it has never bloomed. Now roses and more roses, jasmine, carnations, sunflowers. At the same time usually a damp sultriness, when it is not pouring: And it did pour until a few days ago, though it was freezing cold; we lit the stove again on the seventeenth no more than three days after we had stopped heating.

Absolute silence on the part of all relatives and friends. Absolute isolation. In the last two weeks only expensive taxi rides to the dentist.

June 27, Tuesday

The manuscript of the sixth-form chapter is complete; the next 10 or 12 days set aside for typewritten copy. I will not ask how far I can take the Curriculum, nor what its fate will be. Only keep going—Poetry and Truth; I respect the inner truth completely, writing is not much more than shaping and arranging, sometimes condensing, sometimes leaving out. The work is much harder than might have been assumed, my diaries often let me down.

The 16 brilliant Romains volumes finished. Began the more classical and weaker *Thibaults*. Unfortunately only the German translation to hand for the earlier parts. [. . .]

The propaganda against England more vociferous every day, even more vociferous than against Poland; every day new emphasis on the absolute defenselessness and helplessness of England, its humiliation by Japan, its prostrations before Russia, its songs of hate against Germany. I absolutely want to believe, I really do 75 percent believe, that the catastrophe will come before autumn, but everyone (Natscheff and all of Juda) around me doubts it. Either England will back down, or Germany will back down, or the hostile powers will calmly sit back and watch Germany partition Poland. Always with the same arguments, the references to everything that has already happened.

Yesterday I received a very nice letter from Max Sebba in London, to which I want to reply today. A type of emigrant letter is taking shape: Our relatives are in Uruguay, in New York, in Sydney, etc., our eighty-year-old mother remained in Germany . . . And always: I can't complain, things are much worse for so many others . . . And always the helpless pity for those still in Germany.

July 4, Wednesday

June 29 was especially moving for us this time. 35 years, and now this situation, this loneliness, this enormous tension. But on the whole we were cheerful and almost optimistic. In the evening we drank a whole bottle of Haut Sauternes.

Today I said to Vogel, who collects his orders in Dölzschen on Wednesday morning: One always hears three things at once: First there are those who say, he will not dare do anything. Then there are those who say, there have been such tremendous preparations that he will overrun Poland in the next few weeks, it will happen as quickly and smoothly as with Czechoslovakia. Finally those who say, this time it will be the big war. What is your opinion? Vogel, a calm man, not at all a Nazi, answered immediately and with conviction: He'll probably bring it off again. And that is the most widespread opinion, the true vox populi. Yesterday Frau Bonheim, she had spoken to her divorced husband (which only takes place in secret and at the risk of prison). He said: Only Jews and Communists believe in war, Poland will be swallowed up as quickly and bloodlessly as Czechoslovakia; the Western powers will not raise a finger. Beresin, the cigarette man and stateless, was here yesterday. He dug for six weeks as a laborer, with very many others he is being expelled from August 2 and has no idea where to go. He is learning photography, his hopes are pinned on Shanghai. A civil servant told him: Don't worry about August 2—by that time there will be war. I can no longer believe it. Disappointed too often. It will all go smoothly for him this time too. The newspapers ever more excited, even though one would think any further increase impossible. Hess, the Führer's deputy, in a speech at the West Wall: Everything that comes from the Führer cannot be surpassed by anything in the world, this Wall is his work, it would mean suicide for any nation that attacked it.

July 14

We wanted to celebrate Eva's birthday as we had celebrated June 29. In the afternoon her nerves failed her; it was not nice, it is not nice. The self-induced optimism of recent weeks can no longer hold up. It is increasingly evident that Germany is negotiating with Russia.

Language: An article recently bore the headline: Heartland Bulgaria (state visit of a Bulgarian to Berlin, the usual courting of the Balkans, the usual crooked double game of the Balkanese). What is interesting about it: In itself heartland is a geographical expression referring to a central location and does not correspond to Bulgaria's position; but it becomes infected in National Socialist language, its original emotional meaning is restored, becomes the country in which the heart of the Balkans beats, in which Balkanese heroism, nobility, etc. has its home. In which no usually hook-nosed intellectualism rules. (Hook-nosed intellectualism from an article yesterday about art in Germany and Munich before the seizure of power and now.)

Max Sebba wrote to us from London, where things are going badly for him and his family. [...]

Curriculum: Sixth form in good. Student chapter very difficult. Despite looking everywhere I can find nothing about the Sorbonne in 1903. Nothing in my diary, no memories, no lecture notes, no document. For the other semesters everything is there. Puzzling.

July 25

Time stands still: nothing changes; always the same deadly, lethargic uncertainty and imprisonment.

[. . .] Georg has been silent for months. — At the beginning of August Grete leaves Strausberg for an old people's home in Friedrichshagen (Berlin).

A young tram driver, at first I thought him in his early twenties, but he must have been a couple of years older: Do you know why they made the changes at Bismarckplatz?—?—The lawns were divided differently before. — ? — The paths marked out the lines of the English flag, the diagonals. — Are you joking or serious? — Serious and really true. My mother-in-law told me. She's English. She has gone back to England; she doesn't like it here anymore. — You should not say that out loud. — There are many things one should not say out loud. — Are you in trouble? — My two boys have English first names, I'm supposed to change them. — Here a man with a Party badge got on. End of the conversation. And I got off at the corner of Waisenhausstrasse. Such little incidents always give me hope for a quarter of an hour. No more.

August 14, Monday

The same tension for weeks, always growing and always unchanged. Vox populi: He attacks in September, partitions Poland with Russia, England-France are impotent. Natscheff and some others: He does not dare attack, keeps the peace and stays in power for years. Jewish opinion: bloody pogrom on the first day of the war. Whichever of these three things may happen: Our situation is desperate.

We go on living, reading, working, but in an ever more depressed state. [. . .]

Yesterday afternoon a Herr Schroeter, whom we do not know, was here. From Leipzig for the Naval Day, with greetings from Trude Öhlmann, who asks us to write to her—she herself dare not get in touch with us. The man had a fixed, gloomy stare, sat there as if made of stone, had difficulty speaking, long gaps—he had suffered greatly. We were glad when he was gone. [. . .] Then there was a letter from the Confessing Christians, Pastor Grüber's Office. I should inform the National Association of Jews, they would deal with it. So today I went to their office in Johann Georgen Allee. I no longer need to pay the church tax, without thereby losing my Protestantism: But I shall have to pay twice as much to the National Association as I previously paid to the Church. [...]

August 29, Tuesday

It has become tremendously difficult for me to finish the section Paris 1903, these last few days pulled and still pull too much at my nerves. The unconcealed mobilization without any mobilization being announced (people, cars, horses), the pact with the Russians and the incredible turnabout, confusion, the incalculable situation, the balance of forces after this volte-face. (Where does popular opinion stand? to what effect? what is the mood? etc., etc. Endless, agonizing conversations.) Incalculable danger for all Jews here. From Friday to Monday constantly increasing tension. Masses of people called up for military service during the night, horses gone from the market hall. Moral came unexpectedly on Sunday morning: He wanted to go underground in the home of an Aryan friend in Berlin, he is expecting the outbreak of war and in that case being shot down, perhaps not in some wild pogrom, but properly rounded up and put up against a barracks wall. Then in the afternoon food ration cards were distributed; that prevented him leaving and going underground. In the evening I went to the station, the people there looked considerably depressed (later Eva told me that up here too, all the people streaming home from the open-air swimming pool had spoken quietly, without laughing and fooling around as usual). There was a crowd around the notice announcing the reduction in rail traffic. The ten-day postal ban for all troops out of garrison was already published on Saturday. What particularly depressed us on Sunday was the suggestion that we should give our little tomcat an easy death by injection, since he eats only meat and we really need a quarter pound for him every day, for him alone, and all three of us are now supposed to get one pound per week. Since then we have switched him to fish and accustomed ourselves to the never ending crisis. The prospects of war and peace, the prospects and groupings in a possible war appear to fluctuate from hour to hour. Everyone guesses, waits, the tension is too great and is already giving way to apathy once more. At the moment what seems most likely to me is that Hitler wins the game yet again, through sheer pressure and without a battle. But how long can he then remain an ally of the Bolshevists . . . , etc., etc.?

Leave the broad lines to history, note down my own little observations for the Curriculum. Memories of the last war coming to the surface: the ration card. The way it fell upon people on Sunday afternoon, it must have had a terrible effect on their mood. A joke had just been going around: The war will last three days, begin after the Tannenberg celebrations, that is, on the twenty-eighth, and the Poles (they alone) will fight to the last. The celebrations, already announced on a postmark, are canceled, likewise the Party Rally. It's possible that optimism is already on the rise again. Or just indifference. Who can judge the mood of 80 million people, with the press bound and everyone afraid of opening their mouth? The maddest thing was the hand-in-hand picture of Ribbentrop and Stalin. Machiavelli is a babe in arms by comparison. It is always said that the separation of morality and politics was his discovery. But a politics that is too immoral turns into political stupidity.

[...]

It had been a difficult decision, but we had decided to travel to Friedrichshagen to see Grete last Sunday; then she wrote to cancel: heart attack, in the Jewish Hospital, Berlin N, Iranische Strasse, 20 people in the ward, no conversation possible. According to Trude Scherk, Grete is not seriously ill, only wanted to get away from the home, which she does not like. But do they have room in the Jewish Hospital nowadays for people who are not seriously ill? My conscience is not quite clear. Then again: Travel now, when there is no certainty of getting a train back? To chat for a couple of minutes in the general ward? And perhaps make Grete feel that things must really be looking bad for her, if we come all that way to see her for half an hour?

Lingua: [...] There is now no longer any talk of Bolshevists, but instead of the Russian people. However, in his last speech Hess said: Jews and freemasons want war against us. — In the newspaper just now: Nothing decided, but no matter how hardened one is, it does seem as if war must begin in the next few hours, all measures in Germany, France and Britain point to it. A relaxation had been expected as a result of the visit of the British ambassador. Not a word about it and new war measures everywhere.

Especially exciting and kept under a cloak of secrecy the news of the guarantees of neutrality to Holland and Belgium. [...]

September 3, Sunday afternoon

This torture of one's nerves ever more unbearable. On Friday morning blackout ordered until further notice. We sit in the tiny cellar, the terrible damp closeness, the constant sweating and shivering, the smell of mold, the food shortage, makes everything even more miserable. I try to save butter and meat for Eva and Muschel, to make do myself as far as possible with still unrationed bread and fish. This in itself would all be trivial, but it is all only by the way. What will happen? From hour to hour we tell ourselves, now is the moment when everything is decided, whether Hitler is all-powerful, whether his rule will last indefinitely, or whether it falls now, *now*.

On Friday morning, September 1, the young butcher's lad came and told us: There had been a radio announcement, we already held Danzig and the Corridor, the war with Poland was under way, England and France remained neutral. I said to Eva, then a morphine injection or something similar was the best thing for us, our life was over. But then we said to one another, *that* could not possibly be the way things were, the boy had often reported absurd things (he was a perfect example of the way in which people take in news reports). A little later we heard Hitler's agitated voice, then the usual roaring, but could not make anything out. We said to ourselves, if the report were even only half true they must already be putting out the flags Then down in town the dispatch of the outbreak of war. I asked several people whether English neutrality had already been declared. Only an intelligent salesgirl in a cigar shop on Chemnitzer Platz said: No—that would really be a joke! At the baker's, at Vogel's, they all said, as good as declared, all over in a few days! A young man in front of the newspaper display: The English are cowards, they won't do anything! And thus with variations the general mood, vox populi (butter seller, newspaper man, bill collector of the gas company etc., etc.). In the afternoon read the Führer's speech. It seemed to me pessimistic as far as the external and the internal position was concerned. Also all the regulations pointed and still point to more than a mere punitive expedition against Poland. And now this is the third day like this, it feels as if it has been three years: the waiting, the despairing, hoping, weighing up, not knowing. The newspaper yesterday, Saturday, vague and in fact anticipating a general outbreak of war: England, the attacker—English mobilization, French mobilization, they will bleed to death! etc., etc. But still no declaration of war on their side. Is it coming or will they fail to resist and merely demonstrate weakness?

The military bulletin is also unclear. Talks of successes everywhere, reports no serious opposition anywhere and yet also shows that German troops have nowhere advanced far beyond the frontiers. How does it all fit together? All in all: Reports and measures taken are serious, popular opinion absolutely certain of victory, ten thousand times more arrogant than in '14. The consequence will either be an overwhelming, almost unchallenged victory, and England and France are castrated minor states, or a catastrophe ten thousand times worse than '18. And the two of us right in the middle, helpless and probably lost in either case . . . And yet we force ourselves, and sometimes it even succeeds for a couple of hours, to go on with our everyday life: reading aloud, eating (as best we can), writing, garden. But as I lie down to sleep I think: Will they come for me tonight? Will I be shot, will I be put in a concentration camp?

Waiting in peaceful Dölzschen, cut off from the world, is particularly bad. One listens to every sound, watches every face, pays attention to everything. One learns nothing. One waits for the newspaper and can make nothing of it. At the moment I do tend to think that there will be war with the great powers.

At the butcher an old dear puts her hand on my shoulder and says in a voice full of tears: *He* has said that he will put on a soldier's coat again and be a soldier himself, and if he falls, then Goering. . . . A young lady brings me my ration card, looks at me with a friendly expression: Do you still remember me? I studied under you, I've married into the family here. — An old gentleman, very friendly, brings the blackout order: Terrible, that it's war again—but yet one is so patriotic, when I saw a battery leaving yesterday, I wanted more than anything to go with them! No one is outraged by the Russian alliance, people think it is brilliant or an excellent joke— Vogel's optimism (yesterday: We've almost finished off the Poles, the others won't stir themselves!) is to our benefit in coffee, sausage, tea, soap etc. — Is this the general mood in Germany? Is it founded on facts or on hubris? [. . .]

The Jewish Community in Dresden inquires whether I want to join it, since it represents the National Association of Jews locally; the Confessing Christians inquire whether I shall remain with them. I replied to the Grüber people that I was and will remain Protestant, I would not reply to the Jewish Community at all.

Note how on September 1 the Führer declared lasting friendship with Russia in two words. Is there really no one in Germany who does not feel a pang of conscience? Once more: Machiavelli was mistaken; there is a line beyond which the separation of morality and politics is unpolitical and has to be paid for. Sooner or later. But can *we* wait until the later?

We invited Moral for a discussion of the situation and received no reply. Evidently he really has left for his Berlin mousehole.

On Thursday Natscheff claimed that Himmler is against war because he mistrusts the mood at home. Despite the pact with Russia Hitler is lost in a general war. — ??

September 4, Monday afternoon

Yesterday, Sunday, September 3, after a big washing up, went to the Plauen station. I bought a bar of chocolate and asked the elderly assistant about broadcast news. She reported the English-French ultimatum. I asked: Rejected? She smiled, as if I were a bit simple, shrugged her shoulders: But of course. I could ask the two gentlemen there, if I liked, they had heard it themselves. They were two fitters. They confirmed it. I asked: France too?—Reply: Yes, but now Italy will get involved too. At home we were doubtful again. — This morning we got confirmation from the mailman. The man was dismayed: I was buried alive in 1914, and now I have to serve again as a reservist. Was it necessary, is it human? You should see the gloomy faces on the troop transports—different from '14. And did we start off with food shortages in '14? We will be defeated, it can't last four years again. — In Bienert Park, Berger, the grocer, a soldier in '14, now a radio operator: You've got it easy now!—I? I expect to be beaten to death. — You're well out of it—it's us poor swine who have to do it all again!— Notices and newspapers in town, likewise the *Dresdener NN* which has just arrived, trivialize, virtually *suppress* the fact that France has been at war with us since five o'clock, and talk only of French support for Poland, are full of the successes on all fronts (i.e., Poland), report on approval of the German victories in the Italian press and do not *once* mention Italian neutrality. Only in the *Basler Zeitung*, which curiously enough was also displayed, did I see the headline: Italy neutral for the time being. Striking in Hitler's three proclamations: (1) Now the enemy is the *Jewish plutocracy* instead of Jewish Bolshevism, and it battles against the government of the German people. (2) The constant insistence: Traitors will be exterminated. (That is, they are expecting there will be traitors. As in the speech on September 1.) (3) Not a word about Italy. (4) Friendship with the Russian people. (5) Poland will be defeated in a few weeks, and *then* we shall turn on the West, the West Wall will hold that long. — The mailman said, Dresden and the whole of Germany was under military dictatorship. If that is the case, then we probably do not need to fear a pogrom.

Annemarie brought two bottles of sparkling wine for Eva's birthday. We drank one, and decided to save the other for the day of the English declaration of war. So today it's the turn of the second one. During the day I was full of hope, now I am depressed again.

Little peace of mind, but not much time to work either. Increasing difficulties with food supply. I try to leave meat and butter for Eva and the cat, but eating so much bread and fish gives me stomach pains, and now preserved meats are also increasingly in short supply. Everywhere: Only one tin! Or: No longer available! E.g., smoked herrings have disappeared. — Hampered by constant blackout. The last two days I killed time. (We can only black out the kitchen and the dining cellar and so have the light on there.) Today I intend to choose a Florian volume and read it. After our meal I read aloud downstairs. Early to bed. Until now the moonlight has helped up here. But only for a few more days. Lack of air downstairs, to smoke I have to sit in the dark behind the study door. Eva's cigarette glows less conspicuously.

Half of the Paris chapter copied and read out. Eva says, the page about the enmity with Georg should be left in autumn '03 where it actually belongs. I shall change it.

England has already violated Dutch neutrality.

September 10, Sunday morning

Eva says: The war is being covered up. That is true in all respects. *And is a mistake.* There was no mobilization, people were fetched individually from their beds. No casualty lists are being issued. The flags are not being put out, even though Warsaw has already been reached in this first week. Nothing is said about the front in the West. The butchers' shops have to shut on the side facing the street: people line up in the courtyard. — This is the view that has to be maintained: war only with Poland and the quickest possible victory. But at the same time constantly intensified measures, which point to a long war. Income tax raised by 50 percent, permanent blackout, yesterday warning of punishment since blackout discipline was slackening. Yesterday *flour* was added to the list of restricted foodstuffs. Since there is less and less in the fish shops, since frequently not enough meat is delivered to make up even the rationed amount, then everyone *has to* turn to food made with flour. Therefore each person *has to* ask himself how long bread will remain unrationed. And each person *has to* ask himself how all these orders accord with the view of a short war with Poland alone. The whole business is very dubious and must appear dubious—all universities closed down except for Berlin, Vienna, Munich, Leipzig, Jena, all technical universities apart from Berlin, Munich. — [. . .] Gasoline shortage, rationing, yesterday threat to punish driving for pleasure. — Ban on listening to foreign broadcasting stations. But they don't seem able to block them and have to rely on the fear of denunciation. Natscheff listens to England and France, passes it on to us. There will be many Natscheffs. Yesterday for the first time in the military bulletin: Two French aircraft shot down in the West. Until now France has not been mentioned at all as a belligerent. — 20 percent war tax in the cigar shops and for the time being a maximum of only five cigarettes. Yesterday I was able to grab two boxes, I hoard cigarettes, buy tobacco. — What has happened to the tremendous and annihilating air attack on England, which was expected? What has happened to our absolute air security, if the whole country has to be permanently blacked out? What has happened to our ally Italy, to Spain's attack on Gibraltar, to the defection of the Dominions, to Japan, to the Arab war of annihilation? All the world neutral and full of admiration for Germany's successes in Poland.

On Friday Moral, the hero, reemerged. He was hidden for a week by Aryan friends in Lichterfelde (Berlin), for fear of pogroms. (But Jew-baiting appears to be suspended for the moment. Perhaps because of the alliance with Russia, perhaps because too many Germans interned in South Africa.) He was in high spirits as never before. In Berlin people feared for their winter coal: going by the ration cards they were calculating six briquettes per day and household. — A doctor, who treats him here in Dresden, told him: Military hospitals around Dresden already very full, heavy losses. But the military bulletin says: Very light losses, 4 dead and 25 wounded for every 10,000 men.

And yet: What is the popular mood? Schmidt, our neighbor, just brought me a card that had to be filled out (some kind of card, y en a x). The man is sober and certainly no Nazi. But now wears the survival badge. Says quite calmly: "We're winning. Our U-boats will starve England out before they wear us down! Italy will knock out France, it isn't neutral, Italian troops are fighting in Poland. We are not being attacked in the West, but just let them take a run at us. If the man believes only half of what he is told and what he has to say, and perhaps many millions believe it all . . .

The situation looks darkest for our little tomcat.

Where is Goebbels? He has been silent since the outbreak of war, no, since the Russian alliance.

[...]

Chapter V of the Curriculum completely finished. [...]

September 13, Wednesday

On Monday, September 11, *house search* again. For a radio. Amiable child's play for 30 minutes, but nevertheless house search. A fat country police lieutenant from Gittersee and *our* police constable. Friendly, sympathetic people. "And why aren't you abroad yet?"! — Today demand for a new statement of assets. Which means? — The Polish army finished, skirmishes in the West. Very widespread certainty of victory. They're not doing anything in the West, they can't do anything!!

September 14, Thursday

Yesterday afternoon Fräulein Kayser, a lady unknown to us. Acting on behalf of Grüber-Richter. Government order to be passed on *orally* to all Jews: Forbidden to leave the house after eight P.M., forbidden to put up Jewish relatives as guests. In addition a questionnaire to be filled out for the *Gestapo*, how far progressed with emigration? Do they want to expel and exchange us? Do they want to force the non-Aryan Christians to join the Jewish Community?

Vox populi Master Haubold, who is supposed to replace the rusty stovepipe. Frequent employment of "shitty" to describe the situation. But everything blamed on England. They want everything, talk big, our U-boats will give it to them all right, things won't get bad in the West. Poland was messed around by England. On the other hand: It will last through the winter and even longer, we certainly have more dead than officially stated (four for every 10,000 men, no casualty lists are published, death notices only rarely, so far here in Dresden only a motorized squadron commander and an editor of the *Dresdener NN*, otherwise no one!). And poor people have to carry the can for all the shit.

Handed in the questionnaire to Feder, Eisenstuckstrasse. The same District Judge whom I met at Richter's (Grüber). He says, in addition to me, a further 36 families are looked after from here.

He made me fear for our little house: Several owner-occupied houses had been taken away in the last few days. But there is no point in being especially afraid: one has to expect the end at any moment.

My daily route now: grabbing a couple of cigarettes, cigarillos, mackerels and shrimps. Managing to get a little bit of something forbidden from Vogel, an end of sausage or butter or margarine.

After days of reading my diary I want to make a start on Chapter VI today. . . . Much time is lost in the evenings because of the permanent blackout. We sit in the dining cellar and go to bed in the dark shortly after ten.

Reading aloud (German unfortunately): Pourtalès, *La Pêche miraculeuse*. Very good.

September 18, Monday

Friday and Saturday spoiled by Moral. He wrote, was in a state of excitement, didn't come, wrote again, he had a temperature, wanted to come after all, didn't come again, I wanted to go to him, ran into him here at the door; then, a picture of misery, he spent the whole of Saturday afternoon with us, allowed himself to be talked out of thoughts of suicide. His home has been taken from him as of October 15, he will have only one room, part from his housekeeper (Kathl) after 28 years.

On Sunday morning desperate letter from Grete: discharged from hospital as recovered, starving in her old people's home, deprived of her diet, in the same room as a sick, foul-smelling old woman. In the evening a friendly policeman: I had to sign that I know of the eight o'clock curfew. — In the morning my spirits had been raised a little at the baker's: There they said that it was certain that bread rationing would come before the end of the month. Immediately afterward I wrote to Grete: Take this comfort absolutely seriously and literally and understand it properly: God is closest, where need is the greatest. [. . .] Then today catastrophic: Russians march into Eastern Poland, Polish campaign over, Jews and convicts murder Germans in Warsaw. What will become of us now??? [. . .]

Politically now quite at a loss. Peace in a couple of weeks and Hitler all-powerful? Or will England-France fight? But how, where and with what chance of success? On the one hand Germany now appeared to have all the trumps, really all of them in its hand. On the other: why the ever greater shortage of foodstuffs? And has England ever admitted defeat without a fight? Ever blindly taken up a lost cause??? [. . .]

September 20, Wednesday

Our situation grows daily more catastrophic. Order yesterday: restricted access to bank account, surrender of all ready cash; today police inquiry as to our suppliers; it therefore looks as if we are to be more strictly rationed than the general populace. I was in Pirna in the morning.

Yesterday afternoon I heard the greater part of the Führer's speech over the loudspeaker at the *Freiheitskampf* office on Bismarckplatz. Some of it rhetorically very effective. The Polish soldiers fought very bravely, the junior officers did their duty, the middle ranks lacked intelligence, the commanding officers were all bad, the organization was Polish . . . We do not have a kept government as in 1918, we are a nation in the tradition of Frederick the Great, we shall not capitulate even after three years, even after five years, even after six years. Etc., etc. At the same time France is courted, it should abandon England. The English are bunglers at propaganda, they need to take lessons from us. Peace with Russia, they remain Bolshevists and we remain National Socialists! . . . I had the impression that all the bystanders were completely satisfied, sure of victory, sure even of imminent peace. — But every single measure points to a long war. Today reduction of bus services . . . Natscheff has had all English books and translations from English withdrawn from circulation. I obtained a very last one . . . Eva's nerves and my heart are completely finished. One of two things will happen: either Hitler will conclude victorious peace in a week—then we shall perish. Or the war only really starts now and lasts for a long time—in that case we shall also perish. — The political future is completely dark. I do not see in what way England can fight, but I do not see how it can give in.

September 22, Friday

In the newspaper yesterday (naturally therefore in all newspapers) triumphant report about the end of the Polish campaign and a touching article, "At the Soldier's Grave of Paul Deschanel." French First Lieutenant, son of the former Prime Minister (I think) of the Republic [. . .]. Tricolor over the bier—I once had a comrade—the Marseillaise—address by a battalion commander: nothing but compliments to France, with whom we want *only peace*, of whom we make no demands at all . . .

Is that a sign of strength on the German side? Is it merely a ploy? Will the French rise to the bait? Vox populi (at Berger, the grocer): . . . He is in the West. — In the West yet again?—Well, it won't last very long. — Everyone thinks: England will give way. Perhaps they will turn out to be right about that, as with the German-Russian partition of Poland. But if not, the mood would shift tremendously. For the moment people are still intoxicated by the destruction of Poland and do not know what the losses are.

When I went to the Deutsche Bank yesterday to open my restricted account and wanted to pay in 300M, they were astonished (What for? You can freely dispose of 400!). I should first of all go to the Currency Office today in person, in case there is some error.

Errand upon errand, Eva's nerves and mine are completely shattered; for several days now not a word of the Curriculum.

[. . .]

September 25, Monday

I *had to* open the restricted account. Running around, expenses, obstructions. A blessing to be able to stay at home all day yesterday, Sunday.

After an interruption of many days able to write a page of the Curriculum again.

From today cards for bread. Chocolate confiscated.

Colonel-General Fritsch, until a few months ago commander-in-chief of the army, fell outside Warsaw on September 22. A few lines of obituary, tiny little picture, details merely in passing and trivialized. Eva and I placed the same question mark independently of one another.

September 27, Wednesday

Yesterday on top of the other misfortunes a very heavy cold, sneezing and temperature and all the unpleasantness that goes with it. Curriculum creeps forward a line at a time.

Grete asked me to inquire about a Jewish boarding house. I went to the Jewish Community at Zeughausstrasse 3. The house is adjacent to the empty square on which the destroyed synagogue stood. It was no pleasant errand for me: I am Protestant, my sister is Jewish. And it was an errand in vain, as I had foreseen: There is a ban on Jews moving to the city and district of Dresden.

To the extent that there is nothing more of interest to be reported on Poland, the newspaper is drained of content. Polemics against English lies. Confirmation from a newspaper in Manila or somewhere that Germany is invincible, that a continuation of war is pointless. — Meanwhile ration cards, blackout, imprisonment. Impossible to tell when and how it will end.

September 29, Friday

Vogel, the grocer: I don't believe it will last three years, the English will give in, or they will be destroyed. Vox populi communis opinio. It has proved in the right with the Russian alliance and the partition of Poland, it could prove in the right now too. There is absolute confidence and intoxication in victory everywhere here. There seems to be no war at all any more. Nothing is happening in the West. In the East, Modlin and Warsaw have surrendered now too, 600,000 prisoners of war already. In Moscow Ribbentrop and Molotov are negotiating with the Balts and Turks. The tremendous victory pushes all internal dissatisfactions into the background; Germany rules the world—what do a few blemishes matter?

But who is playing this game, and who is outplaying the other? Hitler? Stalin? — I am just reading the first few pages of the Tocqueville, which Frau Schaps gave me in 1924. No one, not even the most significant and knowledgeable contemporaries, anticipated the course of the Revolution. Every page of the book surprises me with analogies to the present. (It is my blackout reading. It's dark at six, and I cannot write downstairs. Though I shall soon have to get over this I cannot.)

October 6, Friday

The day before yesterday, October 4, another house search: library. Two Gestapo men (very polite) looked for books to be confiscated, catalog in hand; a lady (from the State Library—she afterward secretly passed on greetings from Fräulein Roth, but I then regretted having shaken her hand—certainly: forced into carrying out this duty, but what a duty!), so this lady was searching for cultural treasures to be safeguarded, i.e., valuable first editions and the like. She didn't find anything, the other two got six or seven volumes of Emil Ludwig, which had been overlooked, among them the *Cruises of the Goeben,* one of the little patriotic volumes from the last war—now Jew literature. Otherwise nothing . . . censorship gap . . .

Safeguard and *cultural treasures* belong in the Lingua tertii. Likewise *world.* Today at twelve once again: The world listens to the Führer. Then tomorrow: The world responds to the *act of peace.* We are always in a state of peace, we don't shoot, but since 5:45 A.M. on September 1, '39, we are shooting back. *World* can be compared to the universe of the century of Louis XIV. It would make sense, if the world did not also listen to a speech by Chamberlain and this and similar things were not kept from us.

I would not make any progress with the Curriculum even if the Eva '04 section were not causing me problems. Always errands in town, always the kitchen. Feeding ourselves, shopping, cooking, washing up (more vegetables, more dishes)—everything has become more difficult and time-consuming. Today I shall catch a bit of Hitler speech at the *Freiheitskampf* again. The peace offer with the splendid justification: Poland does not exist anymore.

October 9, Monday

Moral †. Suicide in the night of October 1–2. A card from us arrived on the second and we waited for a reply. Yesterday the letter from his Emma [. . .]. Yesterday morning—I was unshaven and without a collar—the Feder couple (District Judge, who looks after the Jewish families) paid us a visit. He had already known about the Moral case for days. Despite his Protestantism, the man had been refused burial in a Protestant cemetery because he was a full Jew. [. . .] yes and apart from that it's my birthday today. We do our best to be cheerful. And to hope for the next birthday.

October 12

In the Webergasse ("gluttons' alley"): in the fishmongers', confectioners' etc. the goods are often replaced by the picture of the Führer with flag cloth and victory green. In one candy shop all their excellencies in the window; above them: We cannot guarantee that all the goods displayed here are available. In the Reka I asked for five little handbrushes at 7Pf each. Stern reply: I'll give you three. Shaving soap (for ration coupons!) nowhere to be had. Hasn't arrived yet. When it does, one piece will have to last three months. In the fishmongers' the constant reply: You must come at ten or three. Everything's gone after that. One elbows one's way into confectioners' and receives 7 or 12 pfennigs' worth of sweets. Chocolate has been confiscated. — But there is *no* real shortage as in 1917–18, and it is hard to see how it should happen, since supplies are coming from Russia. On the other hand, England-France appear to believe in the prospects of a long war, since the peace offer seems to have been rejected. At the same time day after day: light artillery fire in the West, otherwise nothing. But military trains are supposed to be rolling westward day and night. So we remain in the dark about everything.

[. . .]

The Pension Office had not transferred the money for October. I went there. Hours of calculation. We have made a mistake, not enough retrospectively deducted for the increased Jewish tax, an additional amount, which other civil servants have been receiving since July, has been paid, you *must* pay it back! Result: Instead of the 480M of recent months, I shall receive 300M until January, then 350 until April, after that 400. That's what they say now; but more likely is that I sink below even the 300.

[. . .]

A long family report from Lissy Meyerhof. Erich himself managed to escape to England, but two of his sons are in the army; as half-Jews they have the honor of fighting for the 3rd Reich, they can even rise to the rank of corporal (no higher).

October 18, Wednesday

The manuscript of Curriculum VI "Secret Drawer" finished at last. A full month's work, admittedly with constant encroachments [. . .]: housework, blackout, shopping.

The Webergasse is the perfect illustration of the hollow phrase of our command of the North Sea (because of a few U-boat successes). Ever more pictures of Hitler and fewer goods. Every day to Paschky in Zwickauer Strasse and to the Fischhalle and the Nordseefischerei [North Sea Fisheries]. Usually quite in vain. All tins of preserves gone. I always ask about shrimps first, which the *three* of us eat and which are not much in demand by people in Dresden (ignorance and mistrust). Yesterday—a feast day!— I obtained altogether three-quarters of a pound in the two shops in the Webergasse. The first time in many days. Yesterday in the Nordsee shop an interesting occurrence as well. A line, several abreast, through the whole length of the large room; dozens more immediately joined the line behind me. I could not see what was happening at the shop counter. After a while I asked a young worker in front of me: What have they got?—First it was sprats, now the packets are longer. Then I saw the issuing counter. A girl was standing at the head of the line and giving out receipts. Another girl rang these receipts up at the cash register according to a list in her hand: 20, 25, 27, 20, 25, 25 . . . always tiny, approximately similar amounts. A lad brought a wooden box, from which identical little white packages were laid on the table.

Whenever one had received a receipt, one went to the cash register (line 2) and paid, then went back to the girl at the head of line 1. I received a receipt for 20Pf; as I handed it over I asked what I had bought. Smoked herrings. There were two small herrings and two baby sprats. I had stood in line fifteen minutes for that. Whenever a box was finished, there was a pause and alarm in the line. But one did not (*yet*) hear any word of dissatisfaction. People laughed with one another. Half ironically, half (and three-quarters) to emphasize their plucky confidence and positive mood. People let off steam only in private. We command the North Sea, England's naval position is badly shaken by our U-boats and Stukas (Sturzkampfflieger— [i.e., dive bombers]), we are invincible. It's in the newspaper every day, it is confirmed from Spanish, Italian, etc., etc. newspapers. At another counter I really did get shrimps as well.

[. . .] but we are not really starving yet either, things are simply tight— and so can continue like this ad infinitum.

A battery for the flashlight (blackout!) *nowhere* to be found. Matches no longer in packs, at most five boxes.

Natscheff completely confident of English victory. Russia has concluded a trade agreement with England, is at heart hostile to Germany, has enforced the emigration of all Germans from the Baltic States [. . .]. Italy is making deals on every side, Germany must attack and bleed to death or collapse economically. I am not firmly convinced of the correctness of his view of the situation. The adversity is not yet great enough for rebellion against the tremendous power, organization and ruthlessness of the government, the flush of victory is still there; Chamberlain's words, There can be no peace with this government! simply strengthens this government, people remember 1918. Nor can the Communists complain, and the Stahlhelm people, etc. will not make a revolution in the face of and at the request of the enemy.

Did I already note on language: The opposite of a democratic press is the *disciplined press* (Hitler speech in Danzig after the Polish victory). Bolshevism used to be *World enemy no. 1* (Americanism!); now England is *Enemy of peace no.1.* [. . .]

Today I want to start the typescript of the sixth chapter of the Curriculum.

November 1, Wednesday

The "Secret Drawer" completely typed at last. Tomorrow begin the preparatory work for Chapter VII. Too much hindrance and lack of time because of the blackout, which confines me to the kitchen where writing and typing are impossible. Eva is now working on blacking out the music room, which is very difficult because of the many panes of glass. That will be a help.

War at a standstill. In the newspaper we are ever more victorious. Catchphrase *"secure against blockade"* is out of date. Lately: *"German blockade more effective than English."* Growing distress in England—75 percent of all losses at sea on the English side—Every day new proof of German invincibility from Italian and Russian newspapers. Every day friendship and common peaceful goals with Russia, speeches by Molotov to the Supreme Soviet, every day condemnation of the shared interests of the Jews and the English, every day the poor French people.

As to security against blockade: One gets one, at most two rolls of toilet paper. Transportation difficulties. When an English minister recently mentioned transportation difficulties for wooden boxes there was an exclamation mark in brackets after the words. (Pay attention to the *punctuation* of the Third Reich, exclamation and quotation marks.) One only gets two boxes of matches.

A cigarette dealer said to me recently, he was pessimistic, he no longer understood German policy. Russia! He didn't trust it. Look how the man laughs! He means the picture of Stalin and Ribbentrop, in which Stalin is shaking with laughter. (Was in all the papers after the conclusion of the pact.)

[. . .]

November 12, Sunday

On November 8 the attempt to assassinate Hitler with a bomb in the Munich Bürgerbräu. [. . .]

In the night after news of the attempt (We know the culprits: England and behind it Jewry) I was reckoning with arrest, concentration camp, perhaps also the bullet. On the morning of the ninth when the cigarette dealer was the first to tell me about it, for all my philosophy I had problems with my heart and pains in my chest. Untouched until now. Which means nothing of course.

On Saturday, November 4, at the Feders for simple afternoon tea. Friendly people. He is dealing with my tax business. Either 25 percent of income tax has to be paid to the National Association of Jews or 13 percent to it and 12 percent to the church. So in accordance with my confessional bigamy [. . .] I gave 12 percent = 56M (as much as that, since I had to declare 1,500M from Georg for tax) to the Confessing Protestant Church.

Herr Richter, in Johann Georgen Allee, the treasurer of the Confessing Church (friendly, gray-haired, fat, looked like Uncle Eduard Franke), complains bitterly about particularly severe recent persecution, but was above all optimistic (just like Hans Feder). Eva said: One more step toward the concentration camp; but I nevertheless believe I have acted rightly. The Jewish communities in Germany today are all extremely inclined to Zionism; I shall go along with that just as little as I do with National Socialism or with Bolshevism. Liberal and German *forever.*

[...]

For all of the past week I have been working through my diaries (and letters from the lecture tours). Now shall spend another two days looking through my journalistic publications from these years from 1905 to 1912. And then I must try to order this huge mass. I shall be content if I manage this Chapter 7, "Half a Profession," by the end of the year. No idea how long the section will be, sometimes it seems to shrivel up (same old things!), sometimes to expand greatly.

Circular from the Jewish Community: The new telephone book must immediately be informed of the supplementary name Israel on pain of punishment. — I haven't had a telephone for a long time, thank God. The levy on Jewish assets has been increased from 20 to 25 percent (but only for assets above 10,000M). Affects me as little as the telephone. Poverty also has its advantages. Apart from that the increase took place several weeks before the assassination attempt.

November 21

Semper idem. Virtually nothing is happening at the Front. Natscheff maintains that all foreign and neutral reports present it as an open secret that Hitler wants to attack and the army command is opposed. — Bread and potatoes are available, everything else in depressingly short supply. No opportunity to get a clear idea of the mood of the people. Every day absolute certainty of victory in the newspaper.

[...]

I am now paying Jewish Winter Aid, small (door-to-door collection) 5M, large 16M a month. It is unbelievable how many taxes can still be paid out of our few pennies (this month I received 298M from the Pensions Office). [...] I paid the large contribution in person at the Jewish Community House in Zeughausstrasse. I was already there once before recently, on account of Grete's impossible move. I am so upset and preoccupied there that I stutter as if after a second heart attack. I find the situation all too painful and beastly. Aside from that there is lively activity in the place, quite a few people are working in various offices, there is no outward sign of low spirits. Yet each one of them has certainly already been inside, and each one is hourly in danger of rearrest. Brave people.

[...]

November 28, Tuesday

Last Tuesday the Feders were here for tea. Their calm optimism did us a great deal of good. [...]

November 29, Wednesday

Yesterday the sinking of an armed English steamer (auxiliary cruiser with eight 2" guns) by German cruisers patrolling off Iceland was announced. The headlines (very large letters) read: "German naval victory off Iceland—Germany commands the North Atlantic—England's fleet is further decimated." I know how much is behind that, or how little. But on the other hand I do not know whether the mass of the people knows it too, and I really cannot quite see how the English blockade is supposed to overcome Germany. My mood is very changeable and on the whole I am greatly depressed. The ever increasing food difficulties are slowly getting on my nerves. This state of affairs—light harassing fire in the West, usually quiet—can, almost certainly will drag on for years yet, and it is just as difficult to see how England can deal with Hitler as how Hitler can deal with England.

The Curriculum progresses ever more slowly. Partly inner, partly external difficulties. Another dental epoch begins with Eva today. Increasing difficulties and expense, since there are no taxis at Chemnitzer Platz anymore and one has to phone for them from Nürnberger Platz. (Gasoline shortage: Several bus routes have been stopped altogether, there are fewer cabs, and these few are constantly engaged. Especially so, as with a very few exceptions private cars have been laid up since the beginning of the war or handed over to the army.)

[...]

In order to get us to Dr. Eichler in the Königsbrücker Strasse, the taxi had to come from the Wettin station in the morning. Eichler, trained as a naval pilot, did not display very great confidence. As yet we do not have enough planes to mount a major attack. They're producing at a frantic pace—there is often very good flying weather in the winter months. — But they always used to talk about Germany's superiority in the air.

December 9, Saturday

Immediately after the first trip to the dentist Eva got a bad abscess in her jaw. The worst pains quickly passed, but she was still very much affected after that, and even now has considerable difficulty chewing, and is physically weakened by the guaio. Right in the middle of this misery came the long-expected blow, which nevertheless had a dreadful effect.

On Monday I was in the Jewish Community House, 3 Zeughausstrasse, beside the burned-down and leveled synagogue, to pay my tax and Winter Aid. Considerable activity: The coupons for gingerbread and chocolate were being cut from the food ration cards: in favor of those who have family members in the field. The clothing cards had to be surrendered as well: Jews receive clothing only on special application to the Community. Those were the kinds of small unpleasantnesses that no longer count. Then the Party official present wanted to talk to me: We would in any case have informed you in the next few days, you must leave your house by April 1; you can sell it, rent it out, leave it empty: that's your business, only you have to be out; you are entitled to a room. Since your wife is Aryan, you will be allocated two rooms if possible. The man was not at all uncivil, he also completely appreciated the difficulties we shall face, without anyone at all benefiting as a result—the sadistic machine simply rolls over us. Then on Thursday he was here with Estreicher, the responsible Jewish Community official, to inspect the place. Again friendly and helpful: You will find it impossible anyway to carry on here, from January 1 you will have to fetch all provisions from one specified place in the city. Estreicher told me I should discuss the details with him. Eva much more collected than I, although she will be hit so much harder. *Her* house, *her* garden, *her* activity. She will be like a prisoner. We also lose the last bit of property, because to rent the house out would leave us open to harassment, and if we sell it, once the mortgage has been deducted we are left with a tiny amount that will go into a blocked account and we shall never be able to put our hands on it again. And what to do with our furniture, etc.? And our little tomcat will have to be poisoned. But Eva is holding up and is already making plans for the future. A log cabin in Lebbin!—Yesterday discussion with Estreicher, who was very friendly and accommodating, in the Community House. I went away heartened, but the boost did not last long. In essence Estreicher said: Don't lift a finger, wait and see what happens. He will keep the matter in his hands, defer it as long as possible, almost certainly until May, perhaps until June, then he can provide two rooms for us immediately—and *it's such a long time until May. We all hope.* . . . It is this mood at the Community House that gives me heart. All of those working there have already suffered more than we have. Most have already been in concentration camps, and all of them do their duty with the calmest tenacity, and all are optimistic. I must make more detailed notes about these people soon, only I am too tired. Today and in recent days I have made two shopping trips, housekeeping becomes ever more difficult, takes up ever more of my day. *Poor* Curriculum.

At least I am managing a little reading aloud. [. . .]

On the Language of the 3rd Reich [. . .]. If I feel that I no longer have time for this book, it could be sketched in the last chapter of the Curriculum. But there will probably not be time for that either. My heart is used up, it protests at every walk into town, at every bit of physical labor (yesterday while clearing snow). [. . .]

December 16, Saturday

Last Sunday evening Berger, who has a grocery shop round the corner, came to see us, very decent man, no Nazi, soldier and NCO in the World War. I had told his wife that we have to give up the house. He wants to rent it, for 100M—that is how much it costs us every month, and that is its taxable rental value—set up his shop in our music room. I said in essence: Agreed, if nothing has changed by April 1, and if he rents it *only* for the period of time that the regime lasts—(He: perhaps until tomorrow, there is a great sense of outrage everywhere—but perhaps another 20 years)—and if he keeps the garden in decent condition. We left it at that.

All special allowances have been cut out of our new food ration cards. But these special allowances are entirely counterbalanced by reductions in other rations. (E.g., more butter = less margarine.) We are very greatly depressed as a result. Vogel slips me one bar of chocolate after another, and the butcher writes on the back of a receipt: For Christmas we have put by a tongue for you. [. . .]

For my Curriculum even more than for my Eighteenth Century I am forced to reflect again and again: No victorious revolution without an idea. Certainly! But just as certainly: It is not the idea that makes a revolution, but privation that causes it to break out. And once under way, it deviates from the idea.

December 24, Sunday afternoon

Eva is decorating the tree, which I dragged up here with very great difficulty—three shopping trips in one day! But she is even more depressed than I am. We are simply, so to speak, in extremis. If there is no upheaval, before we are forced out of the house, then we are pretty much lost. And whether by April 1 . . . ? Nevertheless this Christmas is not as gloomy as the last one. Then there was peace, the West seemed to have capitulated finally, Hitler secure for an indefinite period. But now the decision has been made and *must* go against Hitler. For us the only question is When. Despite the constant newspaper victories recent weeks have obviously been very bad for Hitler. First the naval victory and immediately afterward the self-destruction of the *Graf Spee*, then the scuttling of the Lloyd ship *Columbus*. But above all: the repeated warnings not to listen to the seditious poisonous lies of the foreign broadcasting stations, together with the deterrent sentences: 2½ years prison for a whole family in Danzig, 15 months prison for people in Württemberg and the Rhineland. And the terrible ignominy of Hitler's congratulatory telegram on Stalin's sixtieth birthday. And the outbursts and protests of neutral countries, which were previously friendly and whom we were supposed to protect against England. — We also had signs of growing disaffection from several sides; I cannot put any faith in them, but they add up. Eichler, the dentist, tells us everything had been ready for the offensive, it had been called off at the last moment. The Feders, here for tea the day before yesterday, report disaffection in the army. Yesterday Michel Scholze from Piskowitz was here: all of the Wends listen to foreign broadcasting stations (in the villages!!), mood in the army and in the navy was bad, a seizure of power by the military was expected in the spring, it was widely said that Fritsch had *not* been killed by a *Polish* bullet before Warsaw. (But warning to myself: the Wends are Catholic and Slav and therefore oppositional, and Michel Scholze already counted on the army in vain years ago. — Popular feeling: Yesterday Berger, the shopkeeper: Look, you don't have any coupons for sweets—here's a box of chocolates! Of course, Berger sells me the box and is reckoning on our house. Nevertheless . . . And today, completely disinterested, brave and truly kind: Frau Maria Haeselbarth—I no longer remember her maiden name—once my student from the Pedagogical Institute, now married to a lawyer, they have a house on the Kirschberg, she has brought us our food ration cards since September, knows our situation, we have talked frequently. So today she turns up: because we didn't get a number of coupons, and because she was in a better position because of her three children, she was bringing us a couple of Christmas gifts. Namely: two big scallops of veal, an egg, a tin of ersatz honey, a bar of chocolate, two gingerbreads, a pair of socks, two tins of milk and half a liter of opened skimmed milk. On top of all that a book by Reinhold Schneider, which has just appeared: *Corneille's Ethos.* We were both deeply moved. These extraordinary times. These are presents one gives a professor! It is an expression of courage and a profession of opposition. It is a most significant symptom of the general mood. — In return I gave her *Germinal* and, with the dedication "with sincere thanks," the Wilbrandt. She had never heard of him. I wanted to give her my *Corneille;* but she already had it. For New Year Eva is going to crochet a cardigan and send it over, and I shall add another book. I spoke quite openly to the woman: "He is lost and beyond hope, he has been delivered into the hands of his enemies." But for us: Either this is our last bad Christmas or our last Christmas altogether. All the details of the Haeselbarth business are to be used in the last chapter of the Curriculum. Perhaps in it I shall be distributor gloriae. I must also note how people scrambled for alcohol, mostly in vain. Thanks to Vogel and other efforts I myself managed to assemble quite an amount of things. 73M from Natscheff was very helpful.

New Year's Eve '39, Sunday evening

This Christmas and New Year's Eve we are decidedly worse off than last year, we are threatened with the confiscation of the house—despite that I feel better than I did then; there is movement now, and then everything was stagnating. I am now convinced that National Socialism will collapse in the coming year. Perhaps we shall perish with it—but it will certainly end, and with it, one way or another, the terror. Shall we manage to save house and tomcat, however? — We have lit our nice Christmas tree every night and intend to do so again today.

As far as writing is concerned I can actually be pleased with 1939: close to 200 very closely typed pages of the Curriculum are finished, 6¾ chapters.

I force myself to hope but not to think about it. Each day has to be got out of the way bit by bit: the housework, food for us and the cat, reading aloud and a little writing.

By way of thanks Eva sent Frau Haeselbarth a cardigan she had crocheted herself, I enclosed Keller's novellas *Sinngedicht*. Frau Haeselbarth gave our stuttering cleaning woman a mysterious message for us: We should not be too anxious about the house, perhaps—she had it from a reliable source—"it would not happen at all." Likewise Vogel said to me recently: It's a long time until April, *soo* much can happen before then. Is it just talk, or are people expecting a revolution? At any rate a Christmas like those in the dugout. Di doman . . .

[. . .]

I believe the pogroms of November '38 made less impression on the nation than cutting the bar of chocolate for Christmas.

1940

January 13, Saturday evening

[. . .] Yesterday the SA official at the Jewish Community was here for the second time because of our house. If I want to rent, the Party supplies the tenant, for example from among those being repatriated—we are not entitled to propose anyone. That means things are even more unfavorable for us than we previously assumed. Also from February 15 we are forced to fetch our rationed goods from one particular shop in the city. — Greatly depressed, especially Eva. We try desperately to believe that a reversal will occur in time, but it is not a very firm belief. The war will make no progress before spring, and God alone knows how it will develop then. Natscheff was very pessimistic today: England reckons on three years, and England has never yet miscalculated.

[. . .]

Every day only a dozen lines of the Curriculum: from morning till night household errands and kitchen, in the late afternoon and evening reading aloud and always tiredness and the desire to think of nothing, to keep one's nerve, to give Eva a good example. The situation is made infinitely more difficult by the unsuspecting tomcat, whom we keep alive with almost the whole of our meat ration and for whom our moving out will be a death sentence. Eva is passionately fond of the poor creature, which is basically better off than we are. At Paschky's they had crayfish in tins at 1.20M unrationed for a while, I feed the cat with that, when there is no meat. Reserve 14 tins; how long will they last?

Rumors going around; Frau Haeselbarth recently: They will get troops to England in airplanes. Madness; but people still believe in England's guilt and Germany's victory. And by the time that changes, *we* shall be done for. Yesterday Natscheff slipped me the *Stampa;* very interesting, but also no more than hypotheses, about Russia, Finland, Sweden. Everything remains in the dark.

January 21, Sunday evening

The frost stopped for only two days, then continuously 15 degrees below at night, 11 at midday. We now place hopes on the frost. Daily in the military bulletin: English reconnaissance planes entering Germany from Holland. They want to put the blame for the breach of neutrality at England's door. Natscheff says there are 40 German divisions at the Dutch border. It is protected by flooded fens, and this floodwater is now frozen. So we daily expect the invasion. Natscheff says it nearly happened recently, and then the risk had once more not been taken and would not be taken either. I said: *He* will have to. Internal pressure drives him to it, the cold is against him. There is a shortage of potatoes, there is a shortage of coal. (We were lucky: a few days ago Schinke delivered 65 hundredweight of coke.) The sooner the battle begins, the sooner the outcome will be decided. Perhaps still in time for us after all. We talk about it day after day. But the waiting gets harder every day.

Nevertheless I go on working at the Curriculum. [...]

Meat and foodstuffs coupons have been taken away from us again; the policeman came to fetch them. Butter shortage increasingly a problem for all three of us. In Paschky's, the fishmonger, I was given a small bag of potatoes as a present.

[...]

February 11, Sunday

Today I finished the typewritten manuscript of Chapter VII and with it Volume I of the Curriculum. About 70 typewritten pages. Worked on it since November 14. I counted it out today. This whole Volume I until Father's death should [...] come to around 450 printed pages. It will be about four weeks work to make a copy of Chapter VII, then go over the whole volume. Till about the middle of April. Vanitas vanitatum: My opus will probably never appear. — What will happen after the middle of April? Go on with the Curriculum or not go on at all? Dios dirà.

It is still uncertain whether we shall be allowed to keep the house beyond April 1. They may perhaps close their eyes until June 1. And then?

Everything continues unchanged, the inactivity in the West, the war against shipping at sea. The question whether the offensive will begin in the spring and how it will turn out. It is impossible to assess anything.

The heavy frost stopped for two days and then started again. Instead of the missing potatoes the Aryans have been given an extra 3½ pounds of bread, the Jews 2 pounds. Also parts of the meat and foodstuffs cards have again been stopped for Jews. I now receive the cards from the Jewish Community. I also had to fetch the potato coupon (contingency coupon) from there, it was refused me in Dölzschen. On the other hand the threatened Jewish shop has not been set up yet, and I can buy from my old suppliers until March 10. They give me especially plentiful amounts of marked-down goods. Moral's imagination was always with the Colorado beetle. The frost is said to have penetrated 30 inches below the surface and destroyed many potatoes in the pits. Colorado beetle substitute.

Everyday there are prison sentences for listening to enemy broadcasts. Reason: The nation must be protected from the subversive poison of lies.

In the *Freiheitskampf* they are now threatening the death sentence for listening illegally.

On January 30 Hitler spoke very combatively. But was it really notice of an offensive?

[. . .]

March 17, Sunday evening

More than a month without a diary entry, I can no longer rouse myself to keep it up. I spend whatever time is not taken up with domestic chores on the fair copy (and revision) of the Curriculum. The piece is now called Book II and is slowly being finished.

Apart from that the waiting, which wears one down. It appears (no certainty) that we will be allowed to go on living here until May or June. Yesterday I had to see the mayor: young man in SA uniform, not discourteous, not even excessively dislikable. A tenant was interested in my house; if he does not like it, then they will perhaps not put me under pressure. The interested party came and found the house unsuitable. So another reprieve probably. So not a single hour of certainty.

Situation absolutely obscure. Will Hitler attack? Sometimes I think: He must. The food shortage is ever more serious. The frost has abated recently, but it is still very cold, we have to heat, there is a shortage of coal, of potatoes, of fat, of fish, etc., etc. For a while everything seemed to point to an offensive; now they seem to be backing away: Our successes have already been sooo great, we can wait, we can hold out for seven years. The most insoluble and yet decisive riddle is the mood of the people. What does it believe? All the world curses and complains. But I believe most are patient and trust what is drummed into them. A couple of weeks ago a trade agreement (yet another one) with Russia was published: Vogel Sr., who should after all have some idea about transportation matters, was beaming as he told me, now everything will improve. Two weeks ago Italy gave way to the English: It will no longer import German coal by sea. Proof, first of all, of the effectiveness of the English blockade, secondly of the sincerity of Italian friendship and of Italy's will to go to war. Here this was immediately turned into a triumph of German-Italian friendship over English blackmail: Germany will get 12 million tons of coal to Italy by land!!! How many millions take that at face value, how many millions do not? Who believes that the blockade is ineffective, that England is suffering more than Germany? Who believes that the Russo-Finnish peace treaty is a serious defeat for the English and French? Rumors and mood change from day to day, from person to person. Whom do I see, to whom do I listen? Natscheff, Berger, the grocer; the cigar dealer in Chemnitzer Strasse, who is a freemason, the charwoman, whose forty-year-old son is stationed in the West and who is on leave just now, the coal heavers. Vox populi disintegrates into voces populi. [. . .]—I often ask myself where all the wild anti-Semitism is. For my part I encounter much sympathy, people help me out, but fearfully of course. The women in the fishmonger's, Vogel, Berger, Frau Haeselbarth. [...] Yesterday I met Moses, the green-grocer, up in the village; he only rarely comes by now—lack of goods. "If you're not ashamed to carry a sack?" I was not ashamed and was given an unfrozen cabbage, a rutabaga and carrots—all rare delicacies. In addition a present of a bread coupon. Moses has repeatedly given Eva potatoes. It is well known that we are allocated fewer coupons than "comrades of the people."

Hitler's speeches have become pious recently. First he talked about his belief in Providence. On the Day of Commemoration of Heroes he "humbly" hoped "for the grace of Providence."

Eye pains and sensitivity to light very frequent, in addition Eva, who has a great deal of cooking to do, tires quickly. Thus there is relatively lit-tle reading aloud. Also we had little luck with reading matter recently (es-pecially as Natscheff's choice is becoming ever poorer). [...]

And all day and every day the pressure: What is going to happen?

March 31, Sunday morning before seven

Every day I think an entry is important with respect to the future Curricu-lum chapter and then omit it after all, because nothing changes. Con-stantly and destructively left hanging in the air, and that is as true of private as of general matters. Is the offensive coming? When? And when do we have to be out of here?

For weeks they've been collecting a "voluntary metal donation" (al-though they say the blockade is ineffective) for the occasion of the Führer's birthday with every sentimental trick (old dears making sacri-fices and the like) in the book. Yesterday decree with immediate effect: Anyone profiting by the metal collection will be sentenced to death for committing a crime against the Great German War of Liberation. — I have the impression that the war in the air is not going according to expecta-tions. Rare and minor successes against convoys. No matter how much they make out of it in the press, it's not much. Visit from the Feders, other-wise quite alone. The Feders came on the day I had just completed the draft notes so I read aloud from them. I shall have to spend another month making corrections to the volume, I have not worked through Book I at all, I manage no more than seven pages daily. [...] Neumann, "the small Winter Aid," formerly cigarette company secretary, now with the Jewish Community, mid-fifties, Hungarian Jew, a friend of ours since the begin-ning of the winter, came to make his farewell visit: was suddenly added to a group that is going to Palestine (Vienna–Danube steamer). The man is fortunate: someone is already looking out for him there (the "Comité"), finding him some kind of work. His wife goes with him, his son long ago in the USA. One of the common fates. — The Lublin business must have made a terrible impression abroad (sudden deportation of the Stettin Jews), about which there are only rumors here: in the newspaper an article about German civilizing work on the Lublin Ghetto. — Grete has moved from Friedrichshagen to stay with Heinz Machol in Charlottenburg.

April 10, Wednesday

Situation ever more dismal. The house compulsorily rented out from June 1, to Berger, who will set up shop in our music room, our own home still unsettled. — Meeting with the emigration adviser of the Jewish Community, result less than zero: You *really must* get out—we see *no possibility.* American-Jewish committees support only observant Jews. The office responsible for you is Pastor Grüber, who lacks funds. Yesterday, April 9, occupation of Denmark and Norway. Estreicher: "Don't you think that they will land in England in four weeks?" I acted as if I did not believe it; but in truth I begin to believe a German final victory probable, something I had at first considered impossible.

Both Eva and I in very poor health, the bottom has been reached. Revision of the Curriculum wrested with ever greater effort from eyes that are increasingly failing me. Busy with that until the end of the month.

Yet another farewell visit from "small Winter Aid," this time with still youthful wife. [. . .]

April 13

A big English newspaper headlines its appeal to the whole Empire: "Israel arise!" Puritan of course. Our press responded to that without comment: "altogether characteristic" (i.e., for Judaization). [. . .]

April 19

I arranged a short tenancy agreement with Berger; Dölzschen parish forced a different agreement on me through the district headquarters of the NSDAP. According to it the house is rented out for two years, I am not allowed to enter it without permission from the local authority, I am not allowed to make any demand of the tenant without its permission, I grant him first right of purchase at the fixed price of 16,600M through entry of this paragraph in the land register. The contract is such a piece of extortion and instrument of future harassment that we wanted to sell the house to Berger right away. But we would thereby lose everything: 4,600M would go into our blocked account, and even if we ever saw it again—the mark is worth just 3 pfennigs, Estreicher told me. So I signed (reservatio not only mentalis, but also oralis to Berger: "Extortion," right of appeal reserved), applied to have the entry made in the Land Register, accepted the potential harassment, retained a last small hope of salvaging a little money. Eva says that she too is now so disgusted with Dölzschen, she is weaving plans for a future new start somewhere on the Baltic.

At the moment utter uncertainty. Estreicher says he will find something as good as possible for us, perhaps two rooms and kitchen; but as yet he has not, and we must clear this house by May 25. The question of cost is also a burden: The cost of moving, renting storage space, and the agreement even forces me to have the fence here painted. All of it now out of a pension of 400M without any reserve whatsoever. I am overcome by fear, but only intermittently; I cannot lose more than the house and my last penny; and as a beggar, like countless others who have been turned into beggars, I avail myself of public assistance, i.e., the assistance of the Jewish Community.

Estreicher is a curious fellow. A Jew and in charge of allocating accommodation. Feder, Neumann, etc. warn against him: spy, informer, takes bribes. But so far the man has been very friendly to me, and his advice *not* to sell the house certainly contradicts his Nazi instructions; because they want Jewish private houses sold "voluntarily," in order to avoid the odium of expropriation. Perhaps I shall also be deceived by Estreicher; but what difference does it make? I am under any circumstances helpless and without rights.

Politically I no longer see the situation as gloomily as on the day of the occupation of Norway. "Israel" really does seem to have arisen, and Norway seems to have been too big and indigestible a mouthful. We follow the battles for Narvik with desperate interest. Big German victory reports, among them guarded admissions of difficult situation and heavy losses; in addition the news via Natscheff. (Yesterday another series of prison sentences for people listening to foreign broadcasts!) Most of all we speculate on the role of the German air force; much suggests its great effectiveness and superiority, much also suggests the opposite. It is impossible to make sense of it. The military bulletin always reports English cruisers destroyed but never says anything about German losses. Three cruisers in one day: that is tremendous; but if the German bombers are so absolutely irresistible, why is a fleet still blockading Narvik at all, how could English troops get to Norway, why is there still a single ship unharmed in Scapa Flow??? I cannot type enough question marks.

The constant trips to the Jewish Community, the nuisance of housework, the pressure on one's soul: my poor work! Book I has now been corrected, which took about five weeks. Perhaps Book II, more painstakingly polished, will go more quickly.

I am reading aloud: Maurois' *Edouard VII et son temps* (in the original).

Grete is now living with Heinz Machol. She seems to be in danger of going blind. Perhaps we can visit her for a couple of hours in June after the move. Eva has not left the garden plot for months now; she needs to have her hair cut; she cannot, since it is next to impossible to get hold of a taxi.

April 29

On the twenty-seventh I was at last able to consider the first volume of the Curriculum finished. Whether there will be a second and how it will come about is very much open to question. Leafing through the Munich period has so far been utterly unproductive. At least until my doctorate, indeed up to the stay in Paris there is a complete lack of material.

Awfulness of the housing business. On Saturday, Estreicher, so far quite courteous, showed us two rooms in a villa on Caspar David Friedrich Strasse (formerly Josephstrasse). Very nice, but also with great drawbacks. I was supposed to meet the co-tenant, a Frau Voss, in his office on Monday, and then discuss the matter further. I looked at the rooms with Eva (taxi, her first into town for months, her terrible mane cut). It was self-evident that a number of questions still had to be settled with Frau Voss, etc. on Monday; also we had not yet seen *anything* but these two rooms. At my first question Estreicher became extremely presumptuous, I was ungrateful, I should be throwing my arms around him, I had to decide immediately, etc., etc. He began to shout and threatened that in his omnipotence he would allocate me an impossible single room. I was enraged, I jumped up, struck the desk with my fist and bellowed at him, to behave like a gentleman. It was a frightful scene, I paid for it with real heart trouble and am still shattered today. After we had both raved at each other for a long time I took the rooms, Frau Voss will come at twelve so that we can discuss things further together. — I had been repeatedly warned about Estreicher, by Neumann, by Feder, he took bribes, he was a spy for the NSDAP. I had always hoped to be able to curb him with friendliness. Yesterday, partly in the presence of the woman, partly between the two of us, the man said a couple of things that belong in the chapter on the 3rd Reich. In her presence: I should be particularly grateful, he could have given this paradise to an Orthodox Jew and was giving it to me, who was only now coming to the Community. Afterward in private: "People have already been begging me on their knees here and offering me two and three hundred marks and I threw them out and you, for whom I do so much, are ungrateful!" Then his injured vanity showed itself: "The mayor of Dölzschen was right in his judgment of you on the telephone—he did not know that I am a Jew. You want to be the great man, you are the famous scholar, and I am only little Estreicher!—But I am an official, and if I had not made allowances for your unworldliness, when I reported to Party District Headquarters . . ." Admittedly I had replied in the presence of the woman: "Why do you give a single woman two rooms?" Ultimately I did not want to continue the quarrel. I said I was certainly indebted to him, only I simply could not tolerate his tone. He played the offended innocent, who is used to ingratitude, the decent man, who despite everything makes allowances for the "unworldliness" of the scholar (for the third time). He signed the apartment over to me, we even shook hands. He said majestically, this business was over and done with, our paths would not cross again. My response was very friendly but he may have detected something else in it: One can never be sure of that. — The man is worse than any real Nazi. Eva says he made an unpleasant impression on her from the start because of the pinched look around his eyes and forehead. — Of course I am once again most dissatisfied of all with my own stance. Too brusque at first and then far too ready to give way. [...]

German victories over the English in Norway; I now firmly believe that the war will be won by Germany after all. But it will have to hurry with the victory. Latest cutback in foodstuffs: Cake will now only be provided against bread coupons.

[...]

May 3, Friday

Very gloomy days, and my heart is causing me such problems that I do not give myself much more time. I am convinced I am suffering from the beginnings of angina pectoris. Partly reassuring was the visit by Frau Voss the day before yesterday, with whom we must henceforth live. Unaffected, rather, as Eva rightly says, possessing a Berlin bluntness, seemingly sensible and not uneducated. Vedremo—there will be more to write about her. For the time being: She likes animals and raises no objection to Muschel. Meanwhile, however, the meat ration is so low that we shall not be able to save him anyway. That is our main worry today. On top of that there is the heavy defeat of the English at Åndalsnse. What will become of the world, if Germany wins? And of us? Voces populi: Berger: "They say Gibraltar and the Suez Canal will be taken now."—Today a teller at the bank to a messenger: "Now we'll get the English. The Jews are already fleeing England. We'll put them where we can make use of them. And now the Italians will take Gibraltar."

I met Feder at the Jewish Community (where I had to wait an hour and a quarter for our ration cards). He also: "I do not think it impossible that the Italians and Spanish will together take Gibraltar."—Vogel, the grocer: "In six weeks England will be completely finished!" Whispered: "Not because of our planes, but because of our new artillery."—So everyone here is convinced of German final victory. I was out and about for hours. Aside from bank and Community: moving company. The one recommended to me by "small Winter Aid" did not have any storage space. I contacted our old moving firm by telephone. Tomorrow to the Land Registry. Because of the entry granting first right of purchase to Berger, which was forced on me. Read aloud a great deal recently. [...]

No one will help us. To the Jews I am apostate. I should be informed in writing about emigration consultation; this did not happen. They say I belong with Pastor Grüber's group. But this group is quite without funds.

May 8, Wednesday

Unable to work. Only diaries up to Naples and reading Paléologue aloud (with complete loss of enthusiasm for Napoleon).

Constantly running errands. I had to pay the Land Registry 54M for the entry. Today I signed to settle the final details of the move by the moving company. The packers on the twenty-third, out on the twenty-fourth. Cost 250–260M. Agreement on four installments. I shall not be able to afford everything from the pension (storage rent 30M, two rooms in Caspar David Friedrich Strasse 65M, in addition water and light also paid separately there, laundry given out). I have to see that I get some money from Annemarie Köhler. I had wanted to break with her completely, since she has not been here since autumn (pleaded heart trouble, as if she had not taken a taxi before); I can no longer afford to be sensitive. So I telephoned her today, and tomorrow afternoon we shall be in Pirna. — Today called for emigration consultation at the Jewish Community in the morning. A slightly overbearing, not discourteous gentleman from Leipzig. Quite hopeless. Only "reality" Shanghai, one can wait there to be allowed into the United States if a member of one's family advances the passage and 400 dollars, and as long as the 400 dollars last. But I have had no word from Georg since April '39. I wrote him a card as a greeting for May 10, a kind of "message in a bottle."

Berger, the shopkeeper, who will get our house and is building a flight of steps for access to the terrace, is here at least once a day. An altogether good-natured man, helps us out with ersatz honey, etc., is completely anti-Hitlerist, but is of course pleased at the good exchange.

The Feders visited us on Sunday. Not great minds, but cheering optimists. Maintain there is an internal crisis looming, protest attacks, like the harmless bomb at the Technical University here in Dresden (broken windowpanes), had occurred in various cities, there had been an attempt to assassinate Himmler, there existed a group with the motto: "Everything for Germany, nothing for Hitler," the government will fall, even if Germany were victorious.

Will it be victorious? Long discussion with Natscheff and his young man Minkwitz. Natscheff still does not really believe that Italy will intervene, still believes that Chamberlain will turn out to be right with his "Three years of war!" but has of course begun to waver. The English defeat in Norway puzzles everyone. He talked about the mood in Italy: the Royal House, the Vatican, also the people against war, Mussolini for, but will only strike if he is convinced that the war will not last longer than three months, the decisive blitzkrieg (the latest catchphrase) of the Germans certain. Is he convinced after the Norwegian catastrophe? That is the question. Bulgaria (Natscheff is Bulgarian) has declared that it will not resist a Turkish invasion if Germany does not deliver tanks and airplanes, but Germany short of material, cannot deliver. It has promised Romania

100 Messerschmitts in exchange for oil and not yet delivered a single one.
— Natscheff does *not* believe in a reversal inside Germany, people are patient, cowardly and loyal to Hitler.

I find many an analogy to the present in the Paléologue. Napoleon's megalomania, the unscrupulous offer to leave Poland to the Russians if he is given the hand of a sister of the Czar in marriage, how Talleyrand and Caulaincourt betray him, how people reckon on his certain fall because his power is overextended, his gobbling up of Europe unsustainable in the long term.

Toward evening

Berger. He has given us some ersatz honey (officially only available with children's coupons), sees the cartons in the hall, is horrified. "In another container please, don't leave them *here*, *destroy* the boxes. Otherwise I could be in a hell of a lot of trouble."—Yet illegal deals are going on everywhere. [Berger says:] The price of lettuce is fixed. That's what goes on to the invoice. But if I don't give the market gardener 2M on top of that, I don't get any lettuce. — There is *no* asparagus to be had at the fruit and vegetable market today. People drive into the country, buy privately, take a bit of butter or margarine or a bottle of oil with them. — Today I stood in for an acquaintance and took a load for him. (Berger was a driver during the war.) The whole car full of chocolates. [. . .] Where were they going? Of course it was illegal. Yet there are "informers" everywhere.

May 9

At two by taxi to Caspar David Friedrich Strasse. Frau Voss just moving in. Tremendously talkative. Eva measured out walls. — Then by bus to Pirna. Cordially received by Annemarie, who with her puffy face really does look ailing. Perhaps her staying away really was not intended as a slight to us. At any rate she was warm and open, and we arranged to meet as planned. The whole district covered in fruit blossom. — In our garden Berger and his mason took apart what Eva had so elaborately and laboriously laid out.

Frau Voss talked about Estreicher: "Apart from money I had to give him a wardrobe and opera glasses as a present 'for his boy.' He didn't want to keep his word to you and put other people in with me. Estreicher's position is unassailable; *you* are more likely to be put in a camp than get him put in one. Faulstich (the representative of the local Party, whom the Jews call Müller, the man who inspected my house) needs and supports him."

After Paléologue, whom we shall finish today, I shall read *Talleyrand* by Duff Cooper. Today Annemarie lent me *Haig* by the same author.

Only a bare typewritten page of Curriculum. I am not making progress with the second part.

May 11, Saturday morning

Yesterday, May 10 (Georg's seventy-fifth birthday), the offensive through Holland and Belgium began "at dawn." Naturally a "counterattack" to "ward off the hostile invasion at the last moment." The whole "staging," Hitler's proclamation with the famous "thousand years," his assumption of command of the operation(!) shows that *everything* will be decided now. If he does not win (even if he is fought to draw), he will fall. In terms of the philosophy of history Montesquieu is right: "The Republic would have fallen, even if Caesar had *not* crossed the Rubicon." True—but *when* would it have fallen? Historical development takes more time than an individual human being has. And I fear Hitler's halo of invincibility.

[. . .]

May 14

After the initial successes (Liège, Northern Holland) I no longer think it impossible that Hitler will enter London on August 1. (The "new weapon" in the storming of Liège—the parachutists. Perhaps *more* than mere bluff.) I am reading Duff Cooper's *Talleyrand* aloud. What parallels to the present! But once again: The historical balance sheet is no comfort for the individual. It all takes too long. — Frau Voss here yesterday afternoon. — Today alarming letter from Heinz Machol, Grete's mental condition appears to have suffered, as Trude Scherk already indicated a couple of days ago. Where can she go?

May 16, Thursday evening

Perhaps the gloomiest wedding anniversary we have ever celebrated. The chaos of the move has begun, nine tenths of our furniture has to go into storage, much written and printed matter, which we had preserved for so long, is being destroyed as ballast. Berger is building the steps to his shop in the garden and destroying what took Eva years to make. And with all of that the wretched feeling that a favorable change in our situation can by no means be assumed. The successes in the West are prodigious, and the nation is intoxicated. All Holland, half Belgium taken, the superiority of the pilots, etc. Berger today: "In the market hall they're saying Hitler will speak in London on May 26." And further: "And then Gibraltar and Suez will fall." Moral concepts have also become completely confused. "Hitler only wants what belongs to Germany, and besides he has always promised to keep the peace." And Poland?—"We're leaving most of it to Russia and are really only taking what was German before, at most Warsaw as well." And Czechoslovakia? "Well, it's not viable as a separate state anyway." Hitler's about-face from anti-Bolshevism to friend of Russia and everything else is forgotten: "He only wants peace, that's what he's always promised."—It is impossible or almost impossible to avoid the general influence and not reckon on the "lightning victory" (note *lightning victory* and *counterattack* for the Language tertii imperii!) and the fantastic landing in England. And yet we simply cannot believe that England and France will allow themselves to be destroyed. Today the first small pause, the first small damping in the triumphal reports since May 10: "The enemy has taken up battle positions between Antwerp and Namur." Hitler is like a boxer who must win in the first round; he cannot last two rounds. Will England and France be able to take the punishment?

May 21, Tuesday

Since Friday in the midst of the chaos of the move and myself more actively involved in it than ever before. It's a matter of getting rid of all ballast. We can take very little with us, most has to go into storage. Every day the French collapse makes a bigger impact on the move. The victory of Hitler's Germany seems certain. And since that means every prospect of us returning to our old hearth disappears, I should like to extend the concept of ballast to almost everything I own and am virtually ravaging my past. Whole piles of books [. . .] have been removed, e.g., all poetry by Adler, Salus, Brod, long runs of picture newspapers by the box load. (Only the handsome-looking Uhu is left. It is not only handsome, there is a breath of a freer time in them, a kind of dix-huitième spirit.) *Every one* of the reprints I collected in twenty years as a university teacher, all the reviews of my work 1904–1933; I am keeping two copies of each of my studies, so a mountain of reprints is staying here. All handwritten copies of printed things remain here; likewise theater programs, letters and similar mementos (but the big cinema programs with their amusing pictures will be preserved). All old lecture notes. [. . .] Berger will be surprised at his inheritance. To C.D.F. Strasse goes everything that is important to the Curriculum: a great amount of paper from the time of the war and the revolution. To Annemarie goes one copy each of the completed parts of the Curriculum and of the Eighteenth Century.

We are both most deeply depressed by the incomprehensible course of events. It destroys our future. Eva, already badly worn down by all the moving work, has quite wasted away in recent days. I myself am suffering greatly from heart and bladder complaints, am very apathetic. [. . .]

The unordered, but undoubtedly valuable stamp collection also goes to Annemarie together with a suitcase of linen. Instruction with respect to my manuscripts: Should anything befall me they are to be given to Dresden State Library, *after* a change of circumstances.

May 22, Wednesday evening

Principal activity of this day: burning, burning, burning for hours on end: heaps of letters, manuscripts. Irritates the eyes, the stuff has to be turned again and again, otherwise the manuscript pages, all on top of one another, only burn at the edges.

French defeat is becoming a catastrophe. Latest propaganda tenet: The true military genius, to whom everything is owed, is Hitler himself. [. . .]

Berger is building steps as an entrance to our terrace. Today he removed stretches of fencing in front of our garden. Now there are yawning gaps.

Breakthrough on our front. — Reynaud, the French Prime Minister, is supposed to have said in the Senate, he still believes a miracle will come as deliverance.

We try hard not to despair.

JEWS' HOUSE, 15B CASPAR DAVID FRIEDRICH STRASSE

May 26, Sunday morning

A handsome villa, too cramped, too "modern" in style, stuffed full of people, who all share the same fate. Wonderfully situated amid greenery. Old parkland divided into lots, meadow and fields behind the strip of trees and gardens; when we stand on the balcony, which does not face the street, then our view is cut off on the right by a rock-dash wall, on the left by a hospital. The street fairly narrow, on the other side also villas, gardens, sanatoria, villas. The nearest thoroughfare leading to the city (also a parkway, not an unbroken street): Teplitzer Strasse (bus to Pirna and through bus). Wasaplatz, large and green, is a few hundred yards farther along C.D.F. Strasse. Next to it is the older Strehlen development with a few shops. All of it amid an abundance of lilac, chestnut blossom, spring in all its forms. Really splendid the magnificent gardens on wide Waterloostrasse with the police station and the very modern building (each floor a kind of filebox) of post office A 20. In short Dresden at its best. So far so good: otherwise a most terrible state of affairs; there are many moments in the day when one would wish to be dead and buried. And meanwhile Calais will probably fall today, and the Third Reich's prospects of victory are very high, to say the least.

On Thursday, the twenty-third, the packer played havoc in Dölzschen, on Friday, the twenty-fourth, loading up took until one. Arrived here in a taxi with remaining pieces and with Muschel. Everything was unloaded by five. I washed myself properly for the last time at half past five on Friday morning, since then day and night in the same sweaty shirt, teeth not brushed, shaved once in città. Two rooms, the larger, more elegant one with a parquet floor (unfortunately) and a balcony is the bedroom, the other the living room. The two do *not* have a connecting door. Hallway in between. Even today still a tangled chaos in both. Muschel's box, garden peat, bread, crockery, beds, suitcases, furniture—all inextricable. The misfortune was, that large, packed wardrobes had to be taken apart here because the stairs were too narrow. Now Eva is putting things back in them, and since we haven't made room to breathe, we can't get any further. In between we had and have to wash dishes. I went up to our old district, did the shopping at Vogel's and Janik, the butcher, at Pashky's, "our" fishmonger—they had flounder—at "my" little cigar shop. On Friday evening, for the first time since the beginning of the war, we went to the railway station and ate what was available without coupons. (Too expensive for us to do often, more than 4M.) Jews are now allowed to be out until nine o'clock.

The greatest loss of time is caused by the constant fussing interference of strangers. Frau Voss, fifties, very well-to-do non-Aryan widow of the Aryan director of the Public Insurance Institute of Saxon Savings Banks (formerly a Catholic priest), is a somewhat childish, barely educated, somewhat petty bourgeois woman, good-natured, helpful, very much in need of company, tremendously talkative. She appears when Eva is still lying in bed, she breakfasts on the balcony. On the day we moved in she twice invited us for real tea, yesterday she prepared our flounder—we in turn had to help wash her crockery. Thus there is very great promiscuity, which hopefully will not lead to friction, but of course strains the nerves even without friction. Best about Frau Voss is her great affection for Muschel, an immediately reciprocated affection. That makes many things a great deal easier. It is not easy for the poor animal to get used to the small space, and of course the business with the box is a very great difficulty for us. — Frau Voss is not the only fussbudget, even if she is the principal one. The house is really a community, all of whose members truly share the same fate, and we shall have to make visits. Kreidl, the owner, lives above us, early sixties, originally head clerk of a bank, below us his widowed sister-in-law, who also had to leave her own house, all kinds of people with her besides. So far only conversations on the landing. The subject of course always: what there was and what I had *before;* further: which way will the war go?

On this alternating hope and hopelessness. Yesterday a visitor for Frau Voss: a gray-haired Frau Aronade, who knew Moral well; she talked about her sons abroad, one a Zionist, "retraining" in Holland, after he was forced to abandon his interpreting studies in Heidelberg. The usual conversations for and against Zionism, which I equated with Hitlerism. Frau Feder was here for a moment to console and welcome us with flowers and a packet of tea. — So our whole lifestyle has suddenly been transformed. But it is still quite impossible to know whether a tolerable existence can be established here. Between writing individual lines I carry every kind of thing to Eva, the morning is gone, and as yet there are still only small clearings to be seen in the bedroom, whereas here complete chaos is rampant, crockery on my desk, the piano piled high, chests, etc. everywhere on the floor. It will go on like this for another two, three days. The Curriculum came to a standstill in Dölzschen after ten pages of the second volume (summer semester Munich 1912).

Today shocking letter from Trude Scherk about Grete. I was prepared for it by news in recent weeks, but not for something as bad as this. She has been in a mental asylum in Bernau for a week now. Persecution mania due to sclerosis of the brain. For a long time she believed that the Machols were stealing from her, then she imagined the wife wanted to poison her, and fled to Trude Scherk. She was already very difficult when she last stayed with us in Dölzschen, that is more than two years ago. But Frau Kemlein in Strausberg knew how to deal with her. After she had to leave there everything took a turn for the worse; first she was in a home in Friedrichshagen, then in a hospital, then in a private pension. Everywhere it was tolerable at first, then after a few days hell. [. . .] We had long ago made up our minds to visit Grete, I always shied away from it—the difficulties such as lack of money, Muschel, the evening curfew, fear of the impressions we would get in Berlin, our own helplessness in the face of Grete's complaints. Now I feel emotionally completely cold again. What I can muster in real love is entirely limited to Eva alone.

The first thing I found waiting for me here was a letter from the Jewish Community: personal details for the Labor Service; to all Jews from sixteen to sixty. If I am enlisted for digging, my heart will be the death of me.

Well over half of our furniture went into storage, the rest came here; of my books *only* the dictionaries, Lanson and Scherer and Meyer, grammars of the modern languages and my own scholarly works. A few of the papers, which I need for the Curriculum, I did not burn, and brought here, further all letters from wartime and the revolution, finally the handwritten verses of the Talmud, of which I want to make a typewritten copy when opportunity arises. Everything else, books and magazines, insofar as not burned or left lying for Berger, was put in storage, probably never to be seen again. [. . .]

Since the move began, there has been heavy, sultry heat, after the preceding cold. There was one thunderstorm, repetition threatens at any moment.

With these notes amid chaos and dreary standing around I have regained a little bit of strength.

May 30, Thursday

Instead of lifting, the chaos is getting ever worse. At the same time the ever more wretched position of the Entente, the almost certain final victory tertii imperii. I envy Moral a hundred times a day. I have now already wasted a week in mess and busy inactivity. Two failed attempts to get on with the Curriculum. Standing around, going shopping and having to change at Chemnitzer Platz—here, if one wants to buy a box of matches: "Are you registered as a customer with me?"—repeatedly washing up the crockery, far too little of which is available for use and which cannot be put away anywhere. And the cat. With its box, with its imprisonment. And Frau Voss, from morning to midnight Frau Voss. Early in the morning she's sitting by Eva's bed, she is there at every meal, she never stops talking.

May 31, Friday

A few gaps in the chaos, a few boxes in the cellar, but still a wasteland, restlessness. Own work impossible. The terrible lack of space means constant clearing up and washing dishes, on top of that the many errands and Frau Voss. Who by the by is very good-natured and helpful. Often afternoon meals together, we help one another out, she prepares some meals for us, we wash up for her, etc. In the evening tea together, till half past twelve, "Blessing at Cohns," 2 pfennigs a point. Completely unintellectual life, many attacks of despair, Eva much braver than I.

The Jews' House: Above us Kreidl, the owner, citizen of the Protectorate, to that extent somewhat freer. His wife, early forties, probably fifteen years younger than he, Aryan. Below us, his widowed sister-in-law.

Her husband owned a large sporting goods shop, which their son (thirty-five years of age) then managed. Competitive fencer with prizes for foil. Was in a concentration camp for three weeks, his mother in custody for a week. Foils with the points missing were found behind her stove. Public prosecutor decided: sports gear, not weapon. Permit for England. Frau Kreidl Jr. came over five days before the outbreak of war, Kreidl Jr. detained here. *Everybody* in the house *absolutely certain* of German victory. Then downstairs, related by marriage in some way, a fat, brutal-looking Herr Katz, businessman, served as an officer during the war, is a monomaniac of the German soldierly spirit, his talk is more nationalist than any Nazi, is happy at German victories, contemptuous of the Entente. "We" shall starve England out, "we are irresistible, invincible."— The English blockade? "Nebbish the blockade!" — With the others of course, for all their pessimism, again and again hopes, rumors, secret news. (American intervention seems more probable, German stocks and shares fell a few days ago.)

Yesterday evening Kreidl Jr. brought us our ration cards, which he fetches from the Community for the whole house, and stayed to talk. He now does nine hours labor service every day with the spade.

Letter from Trude reporting on Grete's condition. She is now allowed to move freely around the asylum, but she is irremediably mentally ill.

[...]

June 6

Lack of space, promiscuity, chaos virtually unchanged, never ending
washing up made utterly difficult by the lack of space, constantly doing
shopping over in Dölzschen. Unable to concentrate, a few lines of Curriculum, no reading aloud or reading for myself. Always busy with trifles,
every day the same wretchedness, the same conversations—at the same
time tremendous German victories accompanied by frenzied triumphal
language. Yesterday "countless divisions" left "defensive positions" to
begin new operations to "destroy" our opponents. Every day a torment. In
the evenings calming one's nerves with the card game lottery—in the
mornings the whole miserable situation.

Superior concentration camp.

June 11

Italy in the war since yesterday. Coup-de-grâce for England-France?

Yesterday in the newspaper the puzzling withdrawal of the English
from Narvik and the capitulation of Norway. A couple of hours later I read
a note in red pencil on a shop on Wasaplatz. "At 6:45 P.M. the Duce will
speak on all German radio stations." I knew then that the vulture Italy was
joining in. Miserable evening in the Jews' House. Kreidl Sr. said to me:
"We live in a world that has gone. We still believe in England's strength. It
is weak; it will become a very small island state. Italy with its air force will
take everything it wants. Afterward we Jews will be put up against the
wall." Today I heard: A woman comes to see her wounded husband in the
military hospital here; on entering the room she sees a completely mutilated person, an ear, one half of the face, an arm have been torn off. She
starts screaming and doesn't stop: It's the Jews' fault! It's the Jews' fault!
— They really will put us up against the wall yet. Frau Voss said: "We'll all
be sent to Lublin!" — This morning in town I was reading the news of
Italy's entry into the war. A respectable-looking woman turned to me:
"The French government has fled Paris. Will they be handed over?"
Sancta Simplicitas. I think there are now 79 million such simplicitates in
Germany. — My absolute despair lasted until the afternoon. Then, al-
though France seems lost, the newspaper gave me new courage. From the
small print, the euphemisms and trivialization I think I can conclude that
England is far from thinking itself beaten and—above all—that American
intervention appears probable.

Nevertheless we are going through the most miserable time. Eva looks
very pale and ill. Getting these far too small rooms in order is proceeding
at the same snail's pace as work on the Curriculum. We have been here almost three weeks. I am ten manuscript pages further on (Paris 1913, Uni-
versité populaire). I still do not have anywhere in the house where I can
shave. Reading aloud is an impossibility. Frau Voss comes into our bed-

room in the morning and onto the balcony; in the evening she sits here with us and we play "Blessing at Cohns." Rare that a day passes on which I am spared the long shopping trip to Plauen.

June 23, Sunday

This morning finished the draft manuscript (in parts very rough) of the "Summa cum laude" chapter. Actually a respectable achievement in view of the situation. But then again not, because it would destroy me completely if I were unable to muddle on a little. — Meanwhile everything has become even gloomier. France! The boundless German triumph. And in France they are hunting down the "*guilty men.*" Synagogues are said to have been set on fire in Toulouse and a number of other places, French soldiers have fired on English. How does England intend to continue the fight? And the USA doesn't make a move! The language, the gestures in the Forest of Compiègne. Foch's Pullman car brought to Berlin (cf. Napoleon's traveling coach), the memorial of 1918 brought to Berlin (cf. the journey of the quadriga of the Brandenburg Gate). On language I note: the ruthless, lightning-fast changes of tone. In autumn France was a chivalrous nation, only led astray by England, and it was courted. Then, during the offensive, in ever increasing measure "Jew ridden," "nigger ridden," "decadent," "sadistic" . . . Pictures of bestialized Negroes, reports of stomachs slit open, mutilated corpses etc., and while the newspaper is still full of atrocity stories and open letters of accusation by individual correspondents and while in an interview Hitler talks about the wretched leadership and pitiful generalship of our enemies, the "Preamble" to the (not yet published) armistice conditions has fine words about preserving the honor of the foe, who had offered heroic resistance. And a day later the old lack of moderation again, intensified by the frenzied arrogance of the victor.

Privately and psychically hardly any change. Sometimes we eat or try to eat at the station. If we're lucky, we catch a dish which is coupon free. But such a supper is meager, fairly expensive (between three and four marks), and once we even came back without having eaten because nothing was to be had without quarter-pound fat coupons, and all our coupons are in Plauen with Vogel and the butcher (which is worthwhile). Once at the Feders. Good people—but were they not affected as Jews, they would be Nazis. He said: "Perhaps there will be a relaxation after the war. If they would only leave the non-Aryan Christians alone, then that would be a help to us, after all."—Between evening tea and cards I now read out a couple of pages of Louis Bromfield's *The Rains Came* but I never get very far. Frau Voss, who deserves a couple of lines to herself at some point, is always present. Eva read the book herself some months ago, and has long wanted to hear it once again. It is indeed excellent.

June 29, Saturday

Very difficult to give the day even the slightest trace of a festive air. We bought a flower box for the balcony and a couple of flowerpots. Otherwise everything the same as every day now. We await the attack on England with a certain degree of apathy. Among the populace the absolute certainty of speedy final success even before autumn. Constantly in the paper: the war criminals—liberated Europe—the *young* nations—France ruined by England. Meanwhile the Russians have taken Latvia and Bessarabia for themselves. The expression Bolshevism no longer exists. Now there's only plutocracy. Recently Frau Voss asked me: "What does plutocracy really mean?" How many "comrades of the people" will know that?

July 6, Saturday

New prohibition for Jews: Not allowed to enter the Great Garden and other parks. Effect in the Jews' House. Katz, the fat old man with the officer's monomania, brings it to us to sign. He has formed a curious affection for us, although I argue against him. Because I like listening to him. Because he hopes that I will turn out to be right. Because recently he is no longer so sure of victory—the difficulties of a landing! He has a particular liking for Eva. Because she did not take offense at a "Jew's card," which was sent up to her by mistake instead of the "Aryan" one to which she is entitled. (Cards are now fetched for the whole house.) There are differences in the house.

Frau Kreidl Sr. is also "Aryan" and bitter at being stuck in the Jewish schlamassel. In Eva's case she made a scene about the J. She says: "What's it got to do with me?" "Let her get a divorce," says Katz. Kreidl Sr. is also in a class of his own. Has the J, but as a German from the Protectorate (born in Bohemia) is allowed to be on the street after nine, is allowed to walk in the Great Garden. His wife goes to the Opera. Allowed. Tensions because of all that. — I test my own heart. I always declare: "One day the J will be my alibi." But it is always horrible for me to show the J card. There are shops (I have not come across any, but, e.g., Kraus, the chocolate shop) that refuse to accept the cards. There are always people standing beside me who see the J. If possible I use Eva's "Aryan" card in shops that are unfamiliar to me. Apart from that Eva is now on a wearisome hunt (via identity card and diverse official bodies) for clothing points cards, in order to get something by way of exchange for me for my raggedness. — We go for short walks after our evening meal [. . .], make use of the minutes until nine on the dot. How anxious I was, in case we got home too late! Katz maintains we should not be eating at the station either. No one knows exactly what is allowed, one feels threatened everywhere. Every animal is more free and has more protection from the law. — Recently the Kreidls Sr. were here until half past one at night. Until blackout with Frau Voss, then with us. He is a friendly man (over sixty), good storyteller, she (much younger) is unpleasant (somewhat overdressed and taciturn in a somewhat insidious way). — Situation tense to the point of producing apathy. Churchill ("greatest, loathsome, etc. criminal") has taken the French fleet. Dr. Carratsch, the Swiss correspondent, has been expelled because he spread poisonous lies about German-Russian relations and so "endangered Switzerland." Day after day English aircraft cause "insignificant damage to non-military targets" and kill only civilians, mostly women and children, and Germany will take terrible revenge for these crimes— when will the Germans land? And what will happen to us in the case of a German victory? And what in the case of German defeat? Katz says: "In Berlin the Jews are praying for Hitler's victory."

Vogel, the father, goes into raptures about German organization and power. England will be destroyed in a few days, "out of the question, that there will still be war by winter! But we are prepared for everything. There is an unimaginable number of pigs stored in the Felsenkeller!" At the same time, the wife of Janik the butcher explains: "So much livestock has been brought to Dresden, because everything has been moved here from Hamburg." Cf. the non-military damage by air attack. Cf. the new deterrent sentences for "moral traitors" who listen to foreign broadcasting stations—eight years imprisonment, whole families in prison. — I should note all these details and moods of everyday life (or what is called everyday life now). It always makes me feel sick, and I stick to the Curriculum.

July 7, Sunday

Yesterday Frau Haeselbarth came to see us in the late morning, in black: her husband fallen near St. Quentin, he 35, she 33, married for five years— "four and a half really, then he was called up for service"—three children. She brought me socks and shirt and briefs. "You need it, it's of no use to me anymore." We really did accept the things. Sympathy? Very great. But with it the dreadful "Hurrah, we're still alive!" And the sympathy limited to the woman. The husband, whom I had not known, had first been a lawyer on his own account, and then for the Regional Farmers' Association, in the direct service of the Party therefore.

On the way into town, two women at the bus stop here: "Heil Hitler!"—"What have you heard from your boy?"—"Good news a week ago, they're looking forward to England." Telegrams in town: Hitler in Berlin today. Triumphal entry. Count Ciano guest of the government. Then at the butcher: It's just been on the radio: "The English government has fallen." Now there'll be peace. Very good, why should they let themselves be shot to pieces first? — Then at Fishmonger Paschky: The English government has fled. A woman: Drop a bomb on the whole lot of them! — Then at Vogel's: The English government has "bolted." First the swine shoot at their allies and now they run away! — There was nothing about England in the newspaper. Frau Voss came in the evening: "My friend heard on the radio that the English government has resigned. Now they'll make peace and we'll be packed off to Madagascar." We puzzled over it. We cannot think through the English giving way, and its consequences for England, for the world, for ourselves; we cannot say anything is impossible anymore, but we still hope. This morning Frau Voss came from telephoning with another "Aryan," therefore radio-owning friend: Up to yesterday afternoon at five o'clock there had certainly been no news about England on the radio. But Janik had heard it before her, and the others likewise: the one "fallen," the other "bolted," the third "resigned." And what about Hitler and Ciano in Berlin? Merely an exchange of pleasantries?—We are groping in the dark, are fatalistic, hope again and again.

Dreadful: The Haeselbarth case has given us a lift. We embraced after she left: *I* returned from the field, *we* have so far always managed to get through in the face of all adversity, at the moment we still have, under the given circumstances, all kinds of possibilities of happiness. And even if it is only the little evening stroll up to the nine o'clock limit. And that the cat is still alive. And that in the evening I read little drops of *The Rains Came* aloud, and that we get on with Frau Voss, and that I am working on the Curriculum. [. . .]

July 9, Tuesday

Becoming skeptical of big ideas, like Fatherland, national honor, heroism, etc., may be a general feature of growing old. But the truths, which I held to be certain and on which I essentially built my life's work, have now completely collapsed. My idea of Germany was lost years ago, and now France! As if it were Czechoslovakia or a small state in the Balkans. First giving up militarily: Two million surrender, Metz is captured by a handful, Belfort does not defend itself at all, whole stretches of the Maginot Line, the same. And now they are convening a general assembly, in order to make their constitution "totalitarian," are fighting against England, which they had already harmed by accepting the conditions of the armistice, threaten death for anyone who as a Frenchman goes on fighting in the English army, turn themselves into a German protectorate. What is left of my idea of France?

The copy of "Summa cum laude," begun on May 2, is completed today. But correcting the manuscript will no doubt take another week. Too much distraction by domestic duties. — No one can say how the rumor that the English government had fallen or fled, and which spread throughout Dresden, arose.

July 14, Sunday

Eva's birthday celebrated on a scale which it has not been for many years. That was thanks to Frau Voss. First thing in the morning she baked a strawberry flan and brought flowers and wine. Then in cool, rainy weather (interrupting hot, thundery days) a proper outing. At half past one in the crowded bus to Pirna, from there on the steamer to Rathen. It is certainly a dozen years since we have undertaken such a trip on the Elbe. [. . .] I myself had given Eva flowers for the balcony. Buying the flowers in the morning, followed by the outing and the party in the evening were a little too much for her. The next day she was really knocked out, and now that naturally expresses itself as gloom and hopelessness.

So we were very depressed on the thirteenth, and washing up in the stifling heat did not make anything better either. Then Herr Kreidl Sr. appeared. After his first words I called Eva in, she came reluctantly, but a moment later the depression was gone. Kreidl related as coming from the most reliable source (an "Aryan banker friend" and eyewitness): Train upon train with troops, guns, tanks was rolling eastward. To "protect" Hungary and probably also Romania against Russia, which was negotiating with the English. Since yesterday we have been speculating on and raising our spirits with this piece of news, which has since been confirmed from several sides—rumors and bits of news in the Jews' House. It can mean *the* reversal and moment of decision. Especially as Kreidl has heard "from officers' circles," that a large-scale landing in England is impossible.

[. . .]

July 18, Thursday

Recently while Kreidl Sr. was bringing us the news of the eastward movement—everyone in Dresden is still talking about it, and no one knows exactly what is behind it, and the newspaper writes as if the landing in a *defenseless* and *desperate* England were to be expected any day—on the ground floor an old lady, the mother of Frau Katz, was dying of a stroke and died while we were chatting up here. The Gestapo had made it difficult for the Jewish nurse to get permission for night duty. I had the impression that the death was less important to the whole house, including her nearest and dearest, who by the way, stand to inherit nicely, than the political situation. On Tuesday afternoon the three of us went to the funeral. It was the first time that I had been to the Jewish cemetery here (Fiedlerstrasse), probably the first time in my life at an Orthodox Jewish funeral. A teacher in a gown spoke briefly. Then the coffin was carried out of the hall into the side room, the men stepped forward, the rabbi read a long Hebrew prayer, the men broke in with many Omeins, the women stood by their benches. Before that, those who had carried in the coffin washed their hands. No music. The deceased, who will in fact be cremated in Berlin, is supposed to have been very rich. It was noticeable how shabbily the males among the fairly large number of mourners were dressed. — My own need of clothing has gradually become grotesque. I have to save my "good" suit and what I have is literally fraying away, I could at most try to buy worn items from the clothes store of the Jewish Community. Feder told us recently that even before a corpse is cold the Jewish Community is already asking for the things. Frau Voss is concocting a plan to obtain one of Moral's suits for me. But the man was much slighter than I am, socks from the fallen Haeselbarth, perhaps a suit from Moral, who killed himself—Jewish clothing in the 3rd Reich.

[. . .]

July 24, Wednesday

Last Friday Reichstag suddenly called. We and presumably everyone else were expecting the occupation of Romania. Instead the "peace offer" to England. Weakness? Bluff? Preparation for a gas attack? England rejected it, and now our headlines say: England throws itself into the abyss, and the like. The populace is certain of landing, destruction of London, peace in a few weeks. — In the Jews' House I always play the role of the optimist. But I am not quite sure of my position at all. The language of the charlatan certainly, but so far every charlatanlike announcement has been realized. Even Natscheff is now in very low spirits and says: "I cannot imagine how he can succeed—but so far he has succeeded with everything."

Yesterday Kreidl Sr. and his very unpleasant wife sat here all evening over tea. It was very unwelcome. The same subject was chewed over again and again without anything new being added until we were completely exhausted. I have the feeling that one hour after the death of her husband, his stiff, cold wife ("Aryan") would ask to be admitted to the NSDAP. (Frau Feder is not *quite* as bad.) Two days before, the Katzes were here in the evening to thank us for attending the funeral. He is a military obsessive, this time with the twist of equestrian successes—his father had him trained, before he entered the Horse Guards, richest boy, sole ambition of father and son: to shine as a Jew in the army, curious mixture of snobbery and honest endeavor—so equestrian successes as recruit, in the field and at horse shows, childish (disarmingly childish) boasting about it. Apart from that passionate enemy of the common enemy and lately not quite without hope, because he considers the landing of an army to be almost impossible. — Peculiarity of the Jews' House that each one of us wants to fathom the mood of the people and is dependent on the last remark picked up from the barber or butcher, etc. *(I am too!)* Yesterday a philosophical piano tuner was here doing his job: It will last a long time, England is a world empire—even if there were to be a landing . . . immediately my heart felt lighter.

The final expulsion from the house in Dölzschen has begun. Demand from the parish, delivered to me yesterday by Berger: to make the roof fit in with the surroundings, that is to cover it with red bricks or red imitation slate instead of the tar board. Cost about 600M. I am rejecting it as financially impossible at the moment.

We have to see Annemarie tomorrow because of money difficulties, paying the installments of the moving is a very heavy burden.

I have been reading the Naples diaries for the last couple of days. Everything about landscape in them absolutely worthless, everything else good.

July 26, Friday

Yesterday afternoon in Pirna. Annemarie—handed over manuscripts, also diary, borrowed some money—much and very depressingly changed. Swollen face, both eyes infected like a bulldog's, constant cough. She evidently has serious heart disease. The inner change is worse. Usually talkative, lively. Now almost apathetic. Faltering conversation. Indifferent or fearful in politics? Did not enter into any discussion. Also little about private matters. She was all alone. Dressel was deputizing for the head of the Heidenau Hospital, who is sick, his family away, the clinic itself closed, but a great deal of duty work for Annemarie. We were there for only an hour, we were received very cordially and hospitably—only corn coffee! —but with reserve, a kind of seclusion from the world, to put it in medieval terms. Does she feel she is dying? Has she been struck so badly by Dressel's behavior? Mystery.

Afterward at Dresden station a watery soup, which called itself cabbage and potato. At home real tea and a curd cake baked by Frau Voss. Food has become *terrible* in recent weeks. *Very* little meat, very poor preserved meat (the small quantities of sausage almost inedible), no fruit, no fat, the worst ersatz butter. But very many eggs from Denmark. Are they preparing for winter?

Natscheff says: *One* of them is deceiving himself. — *Which?* The Germans declare, England will unquestionably be destroyed; the English: The German attack will certainly fail. Both parties evidently believe what they say. Who will be right in the end?

The tension seems to be enormous everywhere. If I can draw conclusions from the butcher and from Vogel, then confidence in Germany has perhaps abated a little. Janik: "Why are they waiting so long with the landing?" Vogel Sr., only a week ago: England's stupid, in four weeks, perhaps in a few days, it will be destroyed. Now: Perhaps it will take longer after all? — In addition everyone is puzzling over Russia, over America.

I recently found in the telephone directory: Robert Israel Bruck, Professor. (Once Rector with the most German National wife.) Frau Voss is not in the telephone directory. She told me today: Disconnected before the new edition of the directory, reconnected again afterward—I do not want to be listed as Sara.

Finished reading the diaries of the first annoscolare; tomorrow or the day after I shall start to write.

Hitler's enormous prestige. He is considered invincible, no one knows how he will land, everyone is convinced *that he* is going to land. Tanks are already said to have been transported across in aircraft (!!), Annemarie tells us as rumor. But also as fact: East Prussia is crowded with troops.

[. . .]

August 3, Saturday, toward evening

[. . .] Changing moods in the house. Kreidl Sr. full of hope recently. The vouched-for rumor was going around that the Russians had invaded Hungary. Yesterday a speech by Molotov about Russia's friendly relations with Germany, and Kreidl was deeply pessimistic again. Apart from that no doubt tremendous tension everywhere. The English are over Germany every night, hitting "non-military targets," murdering civilians and spreading "hair-raising lies" about pulverized Hamburg, etc. in the Jewish-American press; every day our newspaper declares, the real main attack, the frightful revenge, the destruction of England is imminent. Only once, about three or four days ago, was there a different tone. Then it said, victory was certain, but it could not come as quickly and easily as the arm-chair strategist assumed, because England was a world power, which until now had resisted every enemy. But after that everything was full of England's desperate fear, which was driving it to crimes like the "cow-ardly night attacks" on Cologne, Hanover, peaceful farmhouses, etc., of England's approaching hour of death.

[. . .]

August 11, Sunday afternoon

The Sunday page of the Curriculum written: Read Manacorda; otherwise it's no more than lines at a time. Washed dishes with Eva, and now we want to find out whether, as Frau Voss maintains, the ersatz coffee in Mockritzer Brewery is drinkable.

[. . .]

Jews' House: Terrible argument with Kreidl Sr., who accuses us of using too much water and demands an extra payment. Trifling amount of 1.50, but characteristic vehemence, I have to say, on both sides. Everyone's nerves fray in this ghastly situation. Yesterday, invited by both Frau Voss and ourselves, the Katzes were here for a long time for tea. He sees every-thing from the military viewpoint, considers England useless. Since the Italian successes in Somaliland I am irresolute and depressed again. The war appears to be continuing into the winter and *yet* to be won by Germany. — Connections: Frau Katz told us, they had been neighbors of the Sussmanns in Berlin for years, their daughters had gone to school together.

Frau Voss deeply depressed today. All Jews have been given notice that they are forbidden to have a telephone (she talks endlessly on the telephone every day to friends and relatives). We are ever more closely confined. — Measures against Jews in Romania and Slovakia, more closely attached to Germany. Triumphal entry of homecoming troops (in the middle of a war). Latest slogan (also used on welcoming signs): Our Führer "Creator of a New Europe." — A ghetto has been set up in the General-gouvernement Poland and the Jews have been ordered to wear Zion armbands; they are doing forced labor. — Mutschmann as he greeted the troops: The Jews are to blame for the war.

[...]

Last Tuesday we were invited to the Feders with Frau Voss. Fairly boring. He had had some business with Pastor Grüber in Berlin and told us there was tension between Hitler and Mussolini because Hitler was playing the dictator at the moment. Further: Those of mixed race had been withdrawn from the front because while the army wanted to promote able men, the Party did not permit it. Finally: Children of mixed race were also no longer being admitted to secondary schools. Officially it was still allowed; but a rector who permitted a mixed-race child among his pupils would earn a complaint to the Party from Hitler Youth and parents: Thus one rector had been dismissed for being "pro-Jewish," as a result of which no headmaster accepted a mixed-race child anymore. — Everything points to a constant worsening of the situation for Jews. [...]

August 12, Monday

Thus do our moods change in the Jews' House. Frau Voss continues to be bitter about the notice given on telephones. She has to go to an "Aryan" birthday, she would prefer not to go, she cannot bear to see any Aryans anymore. As we are sitting at our evening meal, she returns, extremely happy and excited. A lady from western Germany was there; she said that Saxony and Silesia were full of west Germans "who cannot stand it anymore," who want to get a good night's sleep. Air raid shelter every night, destruction and dead everywhere. And no one believes it will end before winter. "And there was another woman there, I thought a National Socialist, and I was careful, and she could not possibly have known that I am not Aryan. She talked with tears in her eyes about a Jewish friend who had suffered so much. It all made me feel so much better." And today Frau Voss comes in upset again: Her dentist said that England will be destroyed in four weeks at the latest. Because a report is out that German planes have destroyed Portland harbor and shot down 90 English bombers for the loss of only 17 of their own airplanes. I am just as much depressed by this as the childish Frau Voss. Until I read in the newspaper, the English were lying again and turning the battle at Portland into an English victory, maintaining they had shot down 50 German craft for the loss of only 26 of their own, further, that Portland had suffered only very minor damage.

[...]

August 30, Saturday

[...]

For *weeks* autumn weather with wind and rain and usually cold. That hampers the German air offensive. But which anyway despite all the victory announcements—enemy losses always five times the German ones—does not seem to make any progress. In any case the English air raids, which "cause no significant damage," and always hit only "non-military targets," are getting more numerous by the day and extending further into the country. We had heard many times, by letter and word of mouth, of aircraft over Berlin; then about four days ago—we have no sense of time anymore, everything is an undifferentiated viscous endlessness—the military bulletin reported the "first attack" on Berlin, with leaflets, about which "the whole of Berlin is laughing," and ineffectual incendiary bombs at the edge of the city (a summer house hit). But then yesterday (night of August 28 to 29) "systematic and cowardly attack on Berlin residential areas" from midnight until after three o'clock with "numerous dead and wounded among the civilian population" and only one of the enemy planes shot down on the flight home. And that very same night we had our first air raid warning here in Dresden. It woke me up at half past two, we dressed and went down to the "air raid shelter," to see it for ourselves; Eva smoked a cigarette first. Hall leading to the cellar itself, more open and unprotected than our own rooms, an absurdity. Only the landlord Kreidls were down there—embarrassing after the violent water dispute—the ground floor did not come. After a quarter of an hour, without anything happening, the all clear. Before falling asleep again we heard a distant artillery shot. That was all. The next day Vogel Jr. claimed to have seen the English airplane from Chemnitzer Platz caught by the searchlights and flying at a great height. There are supposed to have been a dozen. God knows where they were coming from, where they were going, the military bulletin now only mentions a number of "towns in the territory of the Reich," at most it singles out a church somewhere or a farmhouse or a hospital or Goethe's house in Weimar or the Bismarck Monument in the Sachsenwald, the English never bomb or hit anything else. — The never ending rain is said to be damaging an already poor harvest before it is brought in and to be endangering the potatoes. What is the mood of the populace? The insoluble riddle. At any rate everyone is now reckoning on the winter, and everyone fears it.

It is actually a miracle that I still manage to do any work on the Curriculum at all: because a series of extended walks have been added to the usual activities. Eva's foot has improved considerably (after years of lonely gardening), it is now only sensitive to pavements. We take the D and E buses (to Torna and Mockritz), also the long-distance bus to Possendorf, and walk for up to three hours. Always nearby to the southwest. Leubnitz, Mockritz, Torna, Prohlis, Nickern, Gostritz, Bannewitz, Possendorf. Always a village nucleus with handsome farmhouses, old manor houses and porches, small new housing estates and groups of villas. [. . .] I see a great deal, which I did not see when I was driving. A district is really only revealed to the walker. [. . .] Being of a pious nature, I almost have to thank God for Hitler's last, I mean most recent piece of harassment, the limitation of shopping hours; now that I am allowed to go shopping only between three and four (Saturday eleven and twelve), I am indeed forced to rush around during this hour, but usually gain the morning for the Curriculum. [. . .] but the glass of wheat beer on the way and the daily half-page of the Curriculum and the occasional minute of hope are all too little in the face of the ever stronger pressure of slavery and the wretchedness of everyday life.

[. . .] The misery gets more lamentable and hideous in every way. An application had to be made to the Jewish Community to receive 20 pfennigs worth of thread. I did not want to meet the corrupt tyrant Estreicher, who deals with the application. A whole conspiracy, a week of plotting (Feder and Pionkowski) was necessary to get hold of the permission in Estreicher's absence. I needed new paper collars from Mey & Edlich: There are only paper collars without a cloth covering now.

[. . .]

When shall I ever get around to the description of Frau Voss and of her mysterious late husband, who slipped out of the cassock and became a banker?

Two closely written sheets from Sussmann. He describes how he clears land all day. His son-in-law has bought a little summer house with a bit of woodland near Stockholm; it is supposed to be turned into farmland. Lotte Sussmann is working as a doctor in Switzerland, in the same mental asylum in which she was an almost hopeless case for years; tubercular Käte has been restored to health and advanced from seamstress to "pinning up"; she has invited her father, her earnings are sufficient for two—I think to New York. Georg seems to have given up all contact with Europe, Sussmann has not had any direct news since January either, Betty Klemperer had written to Änny Klemperer that after an operation he was feeling better than before. Not a word about Marta. I am more irretrievably isolated than all other members of the Jews' House and of the Jewish Community: Everyone has support, a connection, a hope abroad—we are alone, absolutely alone.

Every day there are rumors about new torments, and so far most have come to pass. The latest said: Yellow armbands to distinguish the Jews (they have already been introduced in the factories), further the confiscation of Jewish sewing machines and typewriters. But there is also another rumor that turns up again and again, which is very likely true: An attempted landing has been repelled and a military transport with many soldiers sunk. — I am so far not suffering any privation despite all the taxes on my money; the reserve at Annemarie Köhler's has hardly been broken into and only by the installments for the moving. But I am now wearing the unfashionably tight black trousers of a suit from about 1922, my carpet slippers are nearing their end, the situation with socks is very bad—Frau Voss has parted with several pairs from the estate of her late husband, in return she makes use of the Aryan clothing card that Eva eventually managed to get hold of—it is impossible to see how I can continue to get by with respect to clothing. But we have strictly accustomed ourselves not to think beyond tomorrow. It also leaves us cold, when the Jews' House continually reckons on massacre in the case of German defeat.

[...]

September 12, Thursday

Has there been a turn for the better? For three weeks now the Berliners have been sitting in their cellars night after night; yesterday they were hit very hard ("entire streets in the diplomatic quarter evacuated"), triumph and fear alternate in the Jews' House. Germany "retaliates" on London; England carries out "cowardly pirate attacks." Rumor or truth: They are supposed to have aircraft that can climb 12,000 feet higher than the German ones. Whose statements are true, who will be able to hold out longer? Will there still be a landing? What is the mood here? [...]

An evening with the Kreidls and the Katzes downstairs. Boring. But young Kreidl is a bridge partner at the Breits; through him we were put in contact with Frau Breit after several years, and at the last moment: She is leaving on December 17. For the USA, Denver, via Moscow and Japan. We visited her the day before yesterday (we last saw her at the funeral of her husband about four years ago). Very affecting: a deaf old lady with a large ear trumpet. The villa in Prellerstrasse, in which we attended the most spectacular parties, in disrepair. Tenants, empty rooms, the curtains of windows facing a neighboring military hospital must be drawn. Wealth lost. Two sons, one was co-owner of the Mattersdorf Bank, moving from one minor position to another in Denver; their mother is going to them "as a dependent," as she said to me; the journey is costing her the remainder of her money: 44,000M, since the mark is calculated at around 4 pfennigs. One twenty-seven-year-old daughter, fresh-faced, modest, unmarried, remains here—no entry permit for her. How rich these people were! Frau Breit tells us how brutally she was treated by the Gestapo. Reichenbach, the lawyer, who gave me friendly advice on emigration matters at the Jewish Community, was also there with his wife. He was in Buchenwald for weeks, she in solitary confinement at police headquarters for five days. Eva offered Frau

Breit her clothing card to buy a woolen dress. Most touching gratitude—
and then embitterment, which was difficult to dispel, on the part of Frau
Voss, who had believed this card destined *entirely* for herself. I am always
uncertain as to how much of my time I should spend on these details, and
how much on the current chapter of my Curriculum; every day my heart
tells me that I do not have *much* more time at my disposal. Sometimes I
think: This present misery constantly impresses itself upon my mind even
without notes; then I see from my diary how I have forgotten things from
the World War, in part how I remember them differently from then. Sometimes I think: The mood and the conversations are the same every day; then
again: The nuances change from day to day. Yesterday on all my errands in
town, how strong the impression of the Berlin disaster was: Everyone was
talking about it. Once again I typed an English curriculum vitae with car-
bon copies, as Frau Breit wants to take it with her. How many of these
sheets have already been sent off. For years now. And all without success.
   [...]

September 15, Sunday

[...]
   Today Frau Breit paid us a farewell visit and thanked us, brought 3 bottles of wine as a present in return for 40 clothing points and her likable,
unaffected daughter Lotte, who looks like twenty and is twenty-seven.
The daughter stays here, is going to a nursing course in Berlin, has hopes
of Shanghai and of going on from there.
   [...]

September 23, Monday afternoon

A church has been advertising on the advertising pillars recently: "A Nation's Hero," Oratorio by Händel. Underneath in small print: "(Judas
Maccabeus. New version of the text)."
   On an envelope from Berlin the postmark says: "Fight the Colorado
beetle" with a beetle printed beside it. Recently there was an item in the
newspaper: "English aircraft drop Colorado beetles on Holland." Moral's
last wish: He committed suicide last year. Before that he was always fan-
tasizing: "If it were only possible to import Colorado beetles!"
   [...]

September 27

I have been "called" [typed above the crossed-out printed word: "invited"] before the mayor in Dölzschen at half past four this afternoon. It's

about the expulsion from my house, they are demanding a brick roof in the style of the village. This, and Eva's rebellious nerves and her foot, which is failing her, in addition heart problems, has a very depressing effect.

Frau Voss' brother-in-law has been visiting her for the past week, and occasionally we are also in his company. Retired secondary school headmaster from Cologne, late sixties, was mainly in administrative posts, very Catholic, papal order in his buttonhole, sister a nun, forced to go in '33. A level-headed, calm, educated man, unquestionably an enemy of Hitler, but also an enemy of England. He wants Hitler's downfall, but he also wants a German victory over England, even admits himself to be contradictory, apart from that believes Germany will be victorious and considers Hitler's position unassailable for a long time (not forever) to come. Had no notion of all the restrictions placed on non-Aryans.

Yesterday I saw this same lack of awareness in another place. A friendly, obliging senior official at the Pensions Office, where I had to make some complicated inquiries about church and Jewish taxes. We got into conversation, I unburdened myself a little incautiously, afterward asked for my remarks to be treated as a matter of confidence. That my house had been taken away from me, that I cannot leave Dresden, that I had been arrested, etc., etc. — He did not know any of it. "I thought, you as a veteran . . . Can you not live in another town, where you can forget more easily? . . . Can you not receive your pension abroad?" He was genuinely shocked. At the same time stamped by National Socialism. "That it hits you like this! But you must admit that *the* Jew did us tremendous harm . . . We had made a mistake calculating your tax, we did not know that you are a Jew—I beg your pardon!" I told him, I could not live abroad even if I were to receive my pension there, because the mark stood at four pfennigs. "But that will change now. You surely cannot have doubts about our victory." I intimated a quiet doubt, and this too was evidently a shock and very incautious on my part.

[. . .]

Today I want to write to my sister-in-law Änny and ask her what is happening to Grete, since Trude Scherk's cards are far too muddled and lacking in objectivity.

October 5, Saturday

Political conversation with Voss, the Cologne headmaster (who left today) always ended the same way: *I* believe it is necessary for Germany to start from the bottom again and learn the ABC of morality and culture and humanity anew. *He* hates the regime as I do, believes, however, that it will fall from the inside, after the war has been won, believes this military victory to be *necessary*, because otherwise Germany will be destroyed forever. (Resentment against England dating from the time of the occupation of the Rhineland also plays a part.) Millions will think as he does, and *that* shores Hitler up, *only that*.

[. . .]

The house in Dölzschen is to get a new board roof for about 240M.

Grete accommodated privately in Charlottenburg, since non-Aryans are no longer allowed in the asylum. Änny's letter friendly, but not very informative. Trude Scherk urged me to visit Grete in person, Änny advised against, and I was *very glad* to be advised against. I sent a couple of lines on Grete's birthday—wretched [. . .]. I emphasized to Trude and Änny that the Gestapo would not give me permission to travel to Berlin (which in all probability is the truth).

October 14, Monday

I pulled myself together and got through October 9 without an eruption. In the evening a semolina pudding in the Bräustubl of the Monopol by the station, as a bonus and birthday treat—50 grams of bread coupons.

The days are getting shorter in every respect. Summer time has been retained, and so the early darkness is all the more irritating. In addition house arrest from eight o'clock again. Since the first of [October]. We did not know about it until there was a police check at a quarter past eight the day before yesterday; in the days before that we had come home later without suspecting anything; I could have been put in a concentration camp because of it. On top of that, bitterness over the imprisonment afterward led to an argument with Eva. One's nerves give way. So now Eva has to cook more often at home again and very soon all the time. Since she is very attached to the long afternoon walks—again and again emphasizing this is "the only thing she has left" (which subjectively at least is true, and here the subjective is all that counts), so she tires herself out very badly, and that leads to miserable evenings and unhappy mornings. And since in the mornings the light in bed is poor, I read aloud a great deal. Thus the Curriculum comes to a complete standstill for days on end. Sometimes I am depressed by this standstill, sometimes I am depressed by my egotism, sometimes I find my melancholy over the Curriculum pointless. The few people to whom I have read from it so far, Moral, Feder, Lissy, did not find it interesting at any rate, and sometimes I almost believe that Eva does not either.

An offer by Reichenbach, the lawyer with Jewish Economic Aid, whom I got to know better at Frau Breit's, to write to Chile about a position for me, cost me a whole day. I shall never get this position, neither of us *wants* to have it, and yet I feel duty bound to do what I can. This consisted of the hispanicization of my curriculum vitae. Without any knowledge and without any tools to help me apart from the Spanish-German volume of Tolhausen it was an unpleasant and tormenting business. I also have to let myself be photographed. I tell myself again and again: Either I survive the war, then I do not need to leave, or I do not survive it, then I do not need to leave either, and during the war I cannot get out. So why torment myself? But on the other hand: Is it not perhaps autosuggestion, if I keep on knocking it into my head: Hitler is losing the game? The present state of play could not be more opaque, all the time the often described air battles, the business of Japan–America–Russia still undecided, the Balkans, Egypt, Gibraltar threatening, mood of the people and food situation unclear.

I am reading from Theodor Lücke, *Wellington.* Very good, very interesting, also with respect to the English character and to English military strategy. There are parallels with the present. [...]

I am failing to finish the Curriculum, I did not complete the Dixhuitième, and I am making notes on the "Language tertii imperii," which I shall never write. Day and night (literally) I am dogged by thoughts of death and futility and am so obsessed by these things that all my knowledge of languages is beginning to go rusty, all (literally). Only its ending will show how I have spent the last part of my life, whether I shall be considered irresponsibly indolent and unprincipled or tenacious and selfassured or whether nobody will give a hoot, myself included. The last is 99 percent likely.

On the ninth I became aware not only of my age, but also of my terrible isolation. Cool lines from Annemarie Köhler, who has not come to see us for at least one and a half years. Johannes Köhler, Fräulein Carlo, my former colleagues—where are they? "When all become unfaithful," one would need to be able to believe in a bon dieu. Georg has been mysteriously silent since April '39, Grete is mentally ill. *Only* Sussmann wrote a nice letter. He wished me "freedom." [...] We also go walking in the Lockwitzgrund [...] with its beautiful autumn colours.

October 21

Depreciation of the superlative: Day after day London is destroyed, day after day the Londoners spend a longer time sitting in their cellars. But a day has no more than twenty-four hours, and a city cannot be any more than destroyed. Three days ago it was "the greatest bombardment in the history of the world," two days ago "St. Bartholomew's Eve for London." Now they have to pause, the "unceasing retaliatory attacks" take second place in the reports, U-boat successes move back into first place. Meanwhile England is over Germany every day, over Berlin every second or third. Yesterday, already at half past ten, we had an air raid warning *here* for the third time, a couple of anti-aircraft guns even fired, but the all clear came even before we had gone down to the cellar. In England (for the moment) they are not interested in Dresden.

New coercive measure in judaeos: Use of lending libraries also forbidden. Two years after the prohibition on using public libraries. Why, in fact? I believe: out of fear, to prevent any contact between the populace and critical minds. From now on Eva, Aryan, must go to Natscheff.

October 25, Friday

Yesterday evening eighty "mass rallies": "Everything for victory. Slogan of the Home Front" (stimulus very necessary therefore). Air raid warning at three at night. The fourth in Dresden, again without anything further happening and only of short duration (about thirty minutes). But Frau Voss unwittingly put it in the right perspective: "Six hundred thousand people have got no sleep." And each one of those six hundred thousand knows that the aircraft flying past overhead have got down to serious business somewhere else . . .

Morale must be very low. Young Kreidl relates rumors that are circulating among the workers, with whom he is forced to lay railway sleepers: The senior managers and employees in the big companies and banks have been armed because of fear of revolts. Almost certainly only a rumor, but it is interesting that such rumors can arise. The wife of Janik, the butcher: It is said that the English drop bombs on buildings marked with the red cross because there are munitions factories under red-cross roofs.

Real coffee has been completely stopped for a full year. This month 1½ ounces for Aryans, none for Jews. In Cologne and Berlin 2½ ounces, because they spend their nights in the cellar more often. We received 1½ ounces for Eva; we had a cup each once, it was almost comical. The ration will stretch to a second.

[. . .]

Demand for synagogue and church tax, 30 percent of income tax (12 percent for Aryans), some 220M are a great burden for me. In addition the roof, estimated at around 230M. Last reserves melting away.

November 2

Two days of snowfall, frost, muck, awful paths, foretaste of the winter cold with shortage of coal, of hauling coal up from the cellar. Weather improved now. Too much shopping to be done and limited because of the prescribed hour, Eva has to help out. I do not have gloves—she wants to obtain a large pair of ladies' gloves for me on her clothing card. But when can we manage it? — I now telephone Paschky's in Zwickauer Strasse every day to find out if fish is available. (In the right-hand shopwindow: "No saltwater fish today," in the left-hand one "No smoked goods today.") Yesterday all of a sudden: a heap of flounder and a real carp. Feast, but embarras de richesse. And where shall we get the butter that is needed?

On the day of the worst weather [. . .] walk near Coschütz. There over a wheat beer news of war with Greece.

Section "On Outbreak of War in Munich" complete. But still several days to correct it.

November 7, Thursday

[...]

For a few days now a Berlin plan has been hanging in the balance with some things for and some against. The idea came to us because of Katz. Much perturbed by brutal evacuation of Jews from Württemberg. The people had been expelled naked and empty-handed at two hours notice, to the south of France, put in the barracks of the Spanish Communists. Katz held forth: 1,000 Jews from Dresden are easier to evacuate than 120,000 from Berlin, where there is in any case greater freedom (very relative!). Moving there is permitted, he had ascertained that (showed us the relevant letter) and is definitely going there with his wife in February. Frau Voss came to us the same evening with similar plans and ideas, independently of Katz. This is evidently the latest Jewish fear and intention. We are thinking it over back and forth, much attracts us, much cautions against it. It almost seems to me that it is best not to tempt fate, destruction threatens everywhere.

But I increasingly feel that it is five to twelve. Only—shall *we* live to see twelve o'clock? The mood of the people seems very low, every day Frau Voss reports curiously significant conversations, she even maintains that people are saying "Heil Hitler" less and "Good morning" more frequently. — Roosevelt's election became known yesterday. Greece at any rate will not be an Italian lightning victory, and Crete has been occupied by the English, and the reprisal victories over London don't really seem to be making any progress.

[...]

November 11, Monday

The 6th air raid warning yesterday was not without its comic side. Sunday at about quarter to ten. Nothing happened, but the all clear did not come for a good two hours, and everyone who was at the cinema or cabaret had to go down to the city cellars. I felt it was some kind of revenge. The restaurants had been terribly crowded and we had been held up having our (ever more tasteless, expensive, unpleasant) meal in the Monopol and had missed our last bus. Taxis without exception occupied. I felt as if I were a hunted animal, had awful problems with my heart. I wanted to telephone the police, my wife has sprained her foot, could the infringement of the curfew please be excused—then we caught a taxi after all (shared with another party), and were here at eight. Deeply depressed by the wretchedness of being without rights. Then came the air raid warning. We did not go down to the cellar.

Today severe depression because of Molotov's Berlin visit. If a real alliance with Russia materializes . . .

November 21, Thursday

Night of November 18–19 warning 8: twelve until one, nothing to report. Night of November 19–20 warning 9: quarter to eleven until quarter past senza niente. Warning 10: four until half past five with flares, anti-aircraft fire and some dull thuds, people said incendiary bombs. The main attack is supposed to have been on Chemnitz. Evident impression on the people of Dresden. In addition to that there is the failure of the Italians in Greece (war there began on October 28), a speech by Mussolini in which there was a note of depression between the boastful words, the obscurity around Molotov's quickly concluded Berlin visit.

I paid the church tax in installments. Richter, white-haired, calm man: "It is to be *hoped* that they will lose the war. But it will take a long time yet. In the meantime we shall increasingly starve."

November 26, Tuesday

Bread: Vogel now has a sales assistant. I ask Vogel Sr. for half a loaf without coupons. He whispers: "For God's sake never ask the girl for that." The girl (in place of the boy who has been taken away for Labor Service) is standing in the back room. Old Vogel very loud: "So the coupons first." Takes my cards and the scissors, cuts the air. Gives them back to me, fetches the bread, whispers: "You could get my shop closed down." — *Coffee:* Eva's Aryan 2 ounces a constant source of envy on the part of Frau Voss. We give her less than an ounce as a present. Bliss. We invite the Reichenbachs for genuine Aryan coffee. He, lawyer, foreign consultant of the Jewish Community has tried to help me; we were at Frau Breit's (who has now reached the USA via Japan) with the two of them. Very pleasant people. — *The trousers:* I had badgered Lissy Meyerhof into it. She had an Aryan friend in Hamm. She bought a new pair of trousers, sent them to Berlin, from there they came to me. Enchantment here. My first new piece for I don't know how long. 14.75M.

November 30

Eva has not been very well for more than a week. Stomach, intestines, shivering, nerves. I am reading aloud a great deal. The household on top of that. Curriculum completely at a standstill. [. . .] We had to change our lending library, since Natscheff, threatened by informers, is causing problems. Paulig. Made friends with Fräulein Paulig. She offered me a couple of points of her clothing card. "If you need a tie, for example."

Farewell conversation with a very depressed Natscheff. I: Morale is poor, this is Hitler's last winter. He: "Illusions! Another three years!" [. . .]

December 10, Tuesday

The worst thing is Eva's declining powers of resistance. Her state of health is approaching that of the genuine melancholy, which overcame her before and after the last Lugano trip ('32?). "I am so bored." A couple of months ago Frau Voss got her on to solitaire, a couple of weeks ago, perhaps unfortunately, I gave her a new pack of cards for solitaire—now she is playing one game after another. Virtually non-stop. "Such a nice objective activity and one doesn't think about anything else." Not a note is played, hardly a book and no newspaper opened. The bad weather, the early darkness stop us from going for walks, the shivering in the unheated apartment, the terribly meager food add the finishing touches. She looks very pale, has lost weight. I am deeply depressed.

Two letters written yesterday to Sussmann and Lissy Meyerhof indicate what has preoccupied us lately. (1) Plan, to move to Berlin. The whole world, i.e., the Jewish world, wants to go there. ("They all want to," said Pionkowski, "but I do not know of anyone who has actually got there.") One is supposed to be "more free" there, one is supposed to be in less danger of evacuation or deportation there. (Jews from Württemberg and Alsace have been sent to the Pyrenees, that is to concentration camps set up for the Spanish, before that Jews from Stettin were sent to Poland.) One is free to move to Berlin. But apartments, i.e,. rooms are very expensive, people have problems with the Gestapo, and the business of the greater freedom and security is unproven at the least, it will be like the fable of the town mouse and the country mouse. We asked Lissy Meyerhof for advice, her reply was very cool, also fearful that the movement from the provinces could lead to the evacuation of the whole of Berlin Jewry (which is evidently altogether the fear of the community there). (2) USA. Once again after a long gap. At Reichenbach's urging. In a new pamphlet it says, the paragraph by which a professor is *only* allowed to enter outside the quota if no more than two years have elapsed since he stopped teaching, is usually not applied to dismissed Jews. In the course of discussion it emerged that it must be our turn soon even *within* the quota (admittedly there is a block on visas at the moment). Reichenbach wrote to some Jewish Central Committee again, wanted a letter written to Georg; I rejected that—hence the letter to Sussmann. Behind it there are of course a hundred fruitless, very ill-humored, repetitive conversations and reflections with Eva. What can I do over there? Who will want me? My English . . .

On Sunday downstairs for tea with Katz-Kreidl. Half the Jewish Community. A pharmacist, in the Labor Service and carrying loads in Donath's Wine Cellars; an elderly former army doctor, who has been removed from his post as medical assessor with an insurance company. Everyone says:

Get over there, no matter how great the uncertainty! They don't let anyone starve, and here one's life is increasingly at risk. Apart from that everyone was in high spirits because things are going badly for the Italians in Albania and the English are obviously masters of the entrance to the Adriatic and of the Mediterranean. But always the fear: They will abduct or slaughter us. — Public Jew-baiting is rising again. Film propaganda *Jud Süss* and the *Eternal Jew*. This second film, evidently very nasty and launched with the greatest ballyhoo, has incidentally disappeared here again after less than a week. Why? Weariness and disgust of the public?

Our evening racetrack: along the promenade of Teplitzer Strasse beside the cycle track to the 14 at Horst Wessel Platz. Back along the same stretch if we got the meal at the station over with quickly and we can be back before eight. Romantic: the darkness, the lights, the moon, the open fields.

[...]

Lingua tertii imperii: the Jew, *the* Englishman—nothing but collectives, no individual counts. [...] Katz says: Herzl's racial theory is the Nazi's source, not the other way around. [...]

Constant dilemma: I find so very little time for the Curriculum, that I devote hardly any time to the diary. But this, after all, is the basis of one of the most important chapters of the Curriculum. At times I only note down a catchword. But the next day it appears unimportant, the fact and the mood already overtaken. But the changing details of everyday life are precisely what is most important. — Every evening, when Frau Voss is back from her many errands and visits: "Tell me, what have you heard?" I know she blathers on without rhyme and reason, and [I] again and again want to hear what rumors and moods there are, who is talking about evacuations, who has set his hopes on England, whether a worker has been grumbling, etc.

[...]

December 20, Friday

Severe frost for days, 5 to -1 degrees at night. Apartment cannot be heated, 15 to 7 degrees in the room. Dispute with the landlord, a hole found in the stovepipe, it is "supposed" to be better now—supposed. I have got chilblains on my fingers, of course also chapped hands and feet. Eva suffers greatly, also because of the diminished possibility of getting out into the open air, is pale, thin, deeply depressed. — When the moon is shining, we eat out, so that she gets some distraction. Monopol or railway station (which is supposed to be prohibited and always makes me anxious). Expensive and bad. We then shiver through the rest of the evening (I fill myself with apple tea and bread).

New intensification of Jewish harassment: After eight o'clock confined in the apartment itself. Visiting other residents of the house, spending time in the entrance hall or on the stairs is prohibited.

Without any explanation my tenant Berger sent me a bill of 38M for removal of rubble last summer and deducted the amount from the rent. God knows what alterations the man undertook that produced the rubble. I telephoned. No explanation: The parish says, *I* had to pay. I am defenseless. The house is to be taken from me. Our finances are ever more wretched.

Yesterday the rough draft of "Naples in Wartime" completed at last, after almost six weeks. I hardly ever get down to work anymore. The last part written by hand. Something impeding the typewriter. Who will repair it? There is no mechanic of any kind to be had now.

Only comfort: the failure of the Italians in Albania (no longer in Greece!) and Africa, the English offensive. Εσσεται' Ημαρ. [The day will come.]

[. . .]

December 26, Thursday, toward evening

Christmas, at least the twenty-fourth, passed more tolerably than feared. A little tree for 60 pfennigs from Leubnitz (Eva's favorite place), Frau Voss companionable, abundant alcohol, before that in the station a proper venison goulash without meat coupons (my first bits of meat for months). A package from Lissy Meyerhof with unexpected treasures: coffee, tea, cocoa. (The day after a further more humble packet from Frau Haeselbarth, a couple of gingerbreads and apples, a little pearl barley, a blancmange powder. The accompanying card "Christmas greetings from the Kirschberg" unsigned!) From Vogel I obtained a pound of curd cheese without coupons, begged a little sausage from Janik as well: We were rich. I was also pleased that Seidel & Naumann had picked up my typewriter in the morning. "Only one van now, not much gasoline, even less from January 1. If we don't manage it tomorrow, the twenty-fourth, we certainly won't manage it all—we can't promise anything." It was managed, and that was all the more pleasing because meanwhile young Kreidl had, with good humor and a big mouth — "I can do it!" — fiddled around with it and made the damage worse. — So the twenty-fourth passed tolerably. But our spirits sank on the twenty-fifth. Eva became overfatigued on a walk to the Moreau Tavern—the frost has abated, but snow and ice outside, and at home we continue to freeze with very little alleviation—and collapsed. Today also on shorter walk to the churchyard of Leubnitz Church Eva broke down again. Her health is very poor. She will not be able to bear the situation for much longer.

In pen (unfamiliar) I am writing tiny amounts of the beginning of the "Soldier" chapter, have just stopped at Lerch. I am slowly finishing reading Fontane's *Stechlin* aloud. My feet are chapped, I have chilblains on my hands, frequent problems with my heart while walking—at any rate I ascribe it to angina.

On the Language tertii imperii. Trajectory of a word. Kin (Sippe). In the Middle Ages the usual word for family. Pejorative in modern times. Now with a sentimental halo. "Christmas the festival of kin folk." (In Leubnitz there are street names like Römchenstrasse, under which they then have: Councillor or family of councillors in the fourteenth century. Or: Author of a local chronicle in the fifteenth century. — In *Stechlin*, chapter 33, I find: "Now instead of real men they have established so-called supermen; but in fact there are really only subhumans left . . ." Most new words are to be found here and there long before they become new. (I also assume that Fontane did not invent "subhumans," the counterpart to superman was in the air.) But that does not detract from their novelty. They are new at the moment where they emerge as expression of a new way of thinking or a new idea. To that extent the subhuman is indeed a new and specific word in the language of the Third Reich.

December 31, Tuesday afternoon

The *résumé of 1940* to be kept brief: On May 24 expelled to the Jews' House. There was one good thing about it: for the first time in years Eva learned to walk again, even to go for long walks. In summer when France collapsed we were without hope. Then gradually our spirits rose a little. Every day did a little more work on the Curriculum. The second volume has almost reached July 15, my entry into the army, around 175 pages in the format of my history of literature. Not much, but rebus sic stantibus a bit at any rate. — The year of summer rambles.

Language tertii imperii: In Hitler's New Year Order of the Day to the troops again the "victories of *unparalleled dimensions,*" again the American superlative: *"The year of 1941 will see the accomplishment of the greatest victory in our history."*

1941

January 5, Sunday afternoon

Yesterday to the Reichenbachs to have tea, "real" tea. Reichsstrasse 7 (first floor), it had no doubt constituted a single grand apartment; now half a dozen Jewish families live there. Cooking stoves in the corridor. The Reichenbachs have two rooms, one as parlor, one as *kitchen*-parlor. Oil paintings, original engravings, bronzes, valuable furniture, the man was a lawyer with a good position, now lives in poverty as an official (foreign adviser) of the Jewish Community. Was in a concentration camp, his wife was also imprisoned. A couch in each room, they sleep separately. Next door one can hear a man's voice praying loudly in Hebrew. It goes on all day, he's a devout old man. "If it consoles him . . ." — Reichenbach told us the latest news, which is a catastrophe for us: From January 1 a new Jewish tax: 15 percent of income. That means my 400 shrink to 340M. I again and again resolve not to worry about money. We are coming to the bitter end—but not just for the Jews.

Cold again with lots of snow.

[. . .]

January 20, Monday morning

Manuscript of Soldier I section finished. Meanwhile the typewriter is back from Winkler after four weeks (first complete stripping and cleaning it's had after all these years, but it also cost 20M! Apart from that the worst thing—I had to plead for it—was the transportation, there is such a shortage of people and gasoline): So now I want to start the fair copy. Since Naples III also has to be added, it will take several weeks. — Vanitas vanitatum. When I began the Curriculum, Georg wrote to me that he too was working on his memoirs. Then I met Gehrig: He was writing his memoirs. — A couple of weeks ago at the Jewish tea downstairs with the Katzes and Kreidls, Leipziger, an elderly medical officer and insurance doctor garrulously and somewhat boastfully and conceitedly monopolized the conversation; recently Frau Voss comes back enchanted from one of her bridge parties: The medical officer had read so interestingly from a book about the doctor, it is his own life. So now all the Jews who have been thrown out are writing their autobiography, and I am one of twenty thousand . . . And yet: The book will be good, and it helps *me* pass the time. But then the old doubt also revived again, whether it would not have been better for me to learn English. Now on the one hand the new reduction in our money is in the offing, on the other the block on American visas has been lifted and it will soon be the turn of our quota number, and Sussmann [. . .] has passed on my documents by airmail to Georg. Wait and see—stick with the Curriculum.

It continues to be cold with snow (without interruption since December), apartment difficult to heat, bad chilblains on my chapped and swollen hands.

Reading aloud continues [. . .] Now a very good novel about artists by Buck, whom we only knew as an author of China novels. [. . .]

January 21

Recently on the platform of the tram. Through the window I see a young man inside reading a booklet. By his appearance he could be a Party member with the swastika on his coat, I take the booklet to be an order book. I decipher: *What is that? — That is a . . . I know* at once, the man is a Jew and is waiting for his quota number to be called.

The naïveté of American literature. Naïve in the best sense, even where it is kitsch. Even Hollywood is naïve. Naïve Buck's Biblical style (*Proud Heart*). They are a new nation, and they are *one nation, one* although mixed from a hundred races, tribes, cultures; they utterly contradict the *racial* theory of the Nazis. I must amplify that in the Curriculum, in the last book on the Third Reich. I would so much like to go deeper into American literature. If I could only speak English. Impossible wish: To criss-cross the USA for a whole year in my own car. To speak English during this time, only read newspapers, magazines, go to talkies. Then study and write about American literature in my own house on the American East Coast. After (*after*) I have finished the Eighteenth Century, the Curriculum and the Language tertii imperii. But I am going to be sixty and my heart rebels every day.

January 31

On language: Pay attention to: *Seizure of power,* not taking office or taking over the government, but *power. —* Since when Marxism instead of Social Democracy? From the Russian? (Cf. the book by Krasnow, *Endless Hate.*) I am considering whether my Lingua tertii imperii should not become a proper lexicon, Dictionnaire philosophique in individual articles.

Pharmacist Weisbach, Planettastrasse, sometimes gives me rationed war soap without coupons: "People get fine soaps from the soldiers in France."

Eva not in very good shape, awfully thin, very pale, upset stomach for the last couple of days. I am very concerned.

After a few mild days severe frost and a strong east wind again. Rooms cannot be heated, my hands literally full of chilblains. Every errand, everything I do is hampered by pain.

When Eva here in the room (playing solitaire!), the banging of the typewriter is torture to her. Then I read the 500 pages of letters from the field. So both the copying and the further preparatory work creep forward at a snail's pace. And the household (carrying up coal, shopping, washing up) always robs me of time.

[. . .]

February 8

Lissy Meyerhof sent six pairs of secondhand socks, presumably originally belonging to Erich's sons—a mercy, since I am running around with holes and sore, dirty feet. The package and the letter was accompanied by a note, translated from the Italian, from Hans Meyerhof, I was able to establish his concentration camp, on the Deserto [. . .].

Cohn, congenial Winter Aid man of the Jewish Community, whom I was this time unable to grant any additional donation, saw my completely torn carpet slippers and supported my application for a pair from the Jewish clothing store; I am to fetch them there on Monday. Yet another mercy.

On the evening of the fifth almost friendly contact with the corrupt and powerful Estreicher, with whom I clashed so violently in May because of the accommodation business. It was about reorganizing the billets, though we are spared. The Katzes on the ground floor are going to Berlin, in their place comes a homo novus, who appears to have given a very good bribe: He is not only to get two rooms just for himself, but a third one as well for his Aryan housekeeper. It was the third room that was at issue. Through the ceiling we could hear the screaming and weeping fits of the very unpleasant Frau Ernst Kreidl, from whom an attic room is to be wrested. The whole house in commotion. — How similar to our situation the conditions described by Krasnow in his pitiful, one-sided and trashy book. In Russia everything seems to proceed in more Asiatic, even more uncivilized and more openly bloody and cruel fashion than here, but all in all (housing, corruption, inquisition) it seems to be exactly the same as here.

On the fourth to Frau Kronheim for a touchingly nice short visit (real coffee, cake, a cigar). We had made her acquaintance at the Kaufmanns many years ago, she approached us a few months ago while we were eating at the Monopol, we did not know her name, she visited us with her daughter (who is now completing a "retraining course" in Berlin), we still did not know her name. Then young Kreidl put us on the scent. A woman of about sixty, widow of a straw hat manufacturer, evidently once affluent, probably a little even now. Large room in Bautzener Strasse, of course bed and washstand y todo in the same room, most furniture in storage. Conversations naturally always the same: Affidavit—will America enter the

war? — Recently: What is going to happen to Italy? — Here the English recovery is tremendous. Only yesterday I saw the December issue of *The
Twentieth Century* at the dentist's [. . .]: There the Italian offensive against
and in (*in!*) Egypt was discussed and there was a big map, and today
Benghazi has already been taken. Will England succeed in defeating Italy?
Hitler's speech on January 30 ("I shall force a decision this year") had a
different tone from all the previous ones. Nothing more about a seven
years' war, nothing more about friendship with Russia and the Balkans—
now only: We are prepared for *every* eventuality, and submarine threat
against the USA. The speech is supposed to have sounded like a cry of
rage, his voice breaking. True security or despair? — Rumors everywhere
of new levies and troops sent eastward and motorization.

I had to fetch money from Annemarie Köhler. (I can deal with the 15
percent reduction for about six months—who can think or worry further
than that?) Her welcome was very friendly, she maintained that she really
was not able to come to Dresden, as long as Dressel had to work in Heidenau; her conversation was very anti-Nazi and very defeatist. The workers
had had enough.

[. . .]

February 12, Wednesday afternoon

Anniversary of Father's death, and began the Curriculum exactly two
years ago today. Yesterday evening reading for the Front chapter completed, the first line written today.

Early spring weather since yesterday. Grateful for every additional
minute of daylight, for each degree of warmth, for each yard of ground
that can be walked (this last especially for Eva's sake). Eva has declined,
lost weight, aged so very much—and yet, as my own body declines, I love
her ever more ardently, d'amour say the French. — Yesterday for the first
time in ages a somewhat longer walk: Südhöhe, Toll House, from there the
E bus to station grub. Today we want to go to Lockwitz.

Hopeful, although threatened by catastrophe. Charge because room
not blacked out. That can mean a fine of so many 100M that I am forced to
sell the house; it can also be disposed off with 20M. There are examples of
both; I assumed the worst for a whole day, I am calmer now.

It was truly a misfortune, liability through negligence, as can happen
with a car. We are usually both extremely careful with regard to the blackout, on our evening walks we often grumble about illuminated windows,
say the police should really do something. And now we ourselves are
caught in the act. On the Monday (the tenth) all kinds of things came together, which made me lose the thread. During the day I usually return
from shopping at about half past four. Unpacking, hauling coal, a glance
at the newspaper, *blackout*, going out for supper. On Monday I found Frau
Kreidl, whom both of us greatly dislike, here. She wanted to be consoled:

The whole house had been inspected by the Gestapo—new tenants? Confiscation of the house? (Cupboards opened in our rooms also—there was rather too much tobacco in the house! But they saw only five packets, as a precaution four others are already with Frau Voss.) It grew late. So blackout after the meal. In the Monopol the food so bad that Eva didn't eat it. I wanted to get her something else at the station. Nothing there either. So I was very out of humor and distracted when we returned, immediately hurried into the kitchen to make tea. Against the night sky, once the light has been switched on, it is impossible to tell whether the shutters have been closed. When the policeman rang the doorbell at nine, we were quite unsuspecting, we led him to the window so that he could see for himself that it was blacked out. The man was courteous and sympathetic; he had to charge me because neighbors had reported the light. I had to state income and property: Afterward "the chief of police" will determine the level of the penalty. Until yesterday I was *only* expecting the worst; yesterday Frau Voss told me of a case in which someone had only paid 12M; admittedly the someone was the Aryan wife of a general, and I have a J on my identity card. Now I must wait, my mood going up and down.

February 13, Thursday

The little walk in the Lockwitzgrund yesterday was nice, the first for months. — In Lockwitz as here, posters had been stuck up everywhere: "1000 rallies. The year 1941." It is supposed to become the naturally victorious year of decision, αὐτὸς ἔφη [he says it himself], because really no one is willing to hold out for seven years, as *He* at first promised, and morale seems bad. An ominous novelty: a small *printed* (thus necessary and widely used) note was stuck on top of the posters: "*Anyone found tearing down or damaging this poster, will without exception be called to account.*" Symptom!
[. . .]
On the Monday, which then brought the catastrophe—I am still in suspense—I was at the Jewish clothes store in the morning. Bautzener Strasse, wretched back house, one crosses an empty hall into a little room. There a man, a woman and a boy of Galician appearance work at three sewing machines. Immediately adjoining is an elongated storeroom, like a secondhand shop: hats, piles of shirts, worn clothing on tables, on shelves, hanging from racks. A thin elderly man, hat on head, pipe in mouth, serves me. I was very lucky. There were some brand-new carpet slippers there, and when I revealed my much darned thin socks, brand-new socks also turned up—although I had no slip for them, I believe the "professor" did a good turn. I received all of three pairs and paid 6.60M for all these splendors.
[. . .]
Curriculum at a standstill. Very depressed mood. Shopping, food at home and in town ever more difficult. The day is overloaded with trifles and dwindles away.

February 20, Sunday

Since Friday morning upset and completely taken up with a letter from Dölzschen parish, the car must be sold within a week. I was at the Jewish Community, they were unaware of any ordinance, at the Traffic Police on Sachsenplatz: "not responsible," twice in Schiessgasse at the county prefecture, where I surrendered my driving license in '38. Compulsory sale had been in force for one year, they were under no obligation to show me the ordinance. Wearily after a great deal of toing and froing, they looked at my vehicle registration document which I had handed in then. Luckily I took it to the local Opel man in Prager Strasse. A good looking, confidence-inspiring man, early forties, it turned out that he was a nephew of my former colleague Barkhausen (communications engineer and once a democrat—now—still has his post). I think his advice was good, I was in any case too *down* to do anything else. Result: Because taxes are owed on it, the car would not find a buyer who would pay more than a junkyard. He, Barkhausen, has a friend who is a secondhand dealer, trustworthy and decent-thinking, who will not exploit my predicament and the fact that I am not Aryan. Agreement by phone: Meincke, the dealer, Schandauer Strasse, will take possession of our jalopy, as junk, for 170M. Tomorrow morning we will drive up to Dölzschen together, he will tow it away. How much running from place to place and how much standing around, how much extreme bitterness is contained in this entry, what robbery and what an irreparable loss. When will I ever have a car again? To make matters worse an agitated recriminatory conversation with Eva. Her old complaint: that I hadn't listened to her and had built too late, that I had been the cause of "years of torture" for her, that I had not signed the house over to her in time to give us security. It hurts me greatly to be accused like this. And yet she is no doubt partly justified. Building the house was completely against my nature, education, family *pressure,* advice of everyone around me, I did not at all feel equal to it. Perhaps during all these years I have had no less sorrow than Eva, but I always believed that I was putting her interests before mine and doing what was humanly possible for her. She seems to think differently. Discussions are of no help at all, they only make Eva even more miserable and myself also. I often say to myself now: Why all this offense over what is past? We are so close to the end. — With all of that and simply because of the never ending morning and afternoon errands and the great amount of domestic work the already faltering wartime chapter of the Curriculum has come to a complete standstill.

The next blow to be expected is the confiscation of the typewriter. There is one way of safeguarding it. It would have to be lent to me by an Aryan owner. There is Frau Voss' curious friend Frau Paul. Her second marriage was a very happy one to a Jewish businessman, she is now having a very unpleasant divorce trial with her third husband, an Aryan teacher. She would very much like to help me; she is *afraid* because of the trial. Everyone is afraid of arousing the least suspicion of being friendly to Jews, the fear seems to grow all the time.

Fragments of conversation picked up while eating at the Monopol: A girl who had been working for a year in some kind of administration office in Poland, on leave here, to her girlfriends, shootings were going on constantly, it was rarely in the papers. There was no blackout because of the many attacks. Another girl about a third: She had been frozen out, "because too friendly with the Jews."

Yesterday the Reichenbachs here for tea with us. He (62 years old) let me feel a scar on his skull. Hit on the head with a cudgel "when we had to get out at Buchenwald." After a while a first-aid attendant gave him a dirty towel. There for six weeks. Ten thousand people herded together. Nothing at all to do. Resting places, wooden bunks without any blankets so close above one another that one could not sit, only lie. Lack of drinking water, no water for washing. Later there was soda water at 1M a bottle. People collected rainwater to drink. No medical help. Some needed to be catheterized—it wasn't done.

On language: I am thinking more and more about the idea of the Dictionnaire philosophique. The Reichenbachs said that the expensive novelty of "frozen" vegetables is called *"plutocrat* vegetables." Foreign words [. . .] are used like church language. Halo of what is not understood. The mockery linked with it. — Article on *Jokes:* [. . .] The tour of inspection of devastated London: "We've arrived." — "Not yet. That's Bremen." *Adaptation of World War Jokes.* Question, how long will the war last? Reply 1917–18: "Till the officers have to eat the same food as the men." Answer today: "Until Goering fits into Goebbels' trousers." [. . .] On the article *Jew:* The *Jewish people* created by Hitler. We now stand in the same relation to Palestine as the Swiss Italians to Italy. — *"Looking through Jewish spectacles"* means: optimism and pipe dreams, also applicable to black pessimism. Are simply the spectacles of an overheated, overthreatened state of mind. — *"Please not in the Jewish mailbox"* means: Please don't leave the letter in your pocket. Is supposed to be an old expression, but is now widespread. Based on what? On "Jewish haste"? But how does it fit with Jewish business sense or craftiness? Pay attention to Hitler's words about the Jews as the "stupidest nation" in the world. — Article *race:* the invented Aryan, Nordic race (Gobineau) romanticism. Oldest, the chosen tribe, combined with modern (pseudo-) science. [. . .]

Sudermann in his story "The Mad Professor" describes the breakdown of a scholar. The man manages only to scribble on slips of paper. Is that how far I am now?

A Frau Banasch came to see me and demanded (demanded, did not ask) very importunately a contribution for the Association to Aid Jewish Emigration. It would not be a problem for me, only a banker's order necessary, charitable donations were not debited from the monthly account allowance. She did not believe that I am completely without assets, thought me callous, hard-hearted, when literally from sheer necessity I refused.

The police penalty for failing to black out is still hanging over me—now I shall be able to pay for it with the money for the car. — Growing money worries, food ever worse, Eva's appearance and health ever more wretched, little mobility for her with wet roads under a new covering of snow, frozen smooth again, now the grief, real grief at the theft of the car. I once again suffer from the terrible feeling of looking forward to going to sleep and fearing to wake up.

The SOS letter to Georg via Sussmann has remained unanswered. (Although it was sent on by airmail from Stockholm on January 6, '41.) I do not want any help at all from Georg, and yet his silence wounds me. Reichenbach, the official adviser on emigration, said to me yesterday, our quota number, 56,400, will certainly be called up even before the end of the year. (Provided that the USA does not enter the war.) I often compare the present with Leipzig 1916–17. Which is worse? Today no doubt.

February 25, Tuesday evening

Eva is sleeping, the last few days have greatly weakened her; the car and house business, on top of that the lack of fresh air because of the miserable conditions on the roads (thawing snow, night frost, ice). This afternoon a few steps in Lockwitz, a liqueur in the Scharfe Eck, which we have already sought out a number of times, then a luxurious, for present circumstances, supper in the Pschorrbräu by the Reformed Church—it only cheered her up a little.

Yesterday morning to Automobile Salvage Meincke in Schandauer Strasse. Wooden shed, inside a not inelegant office for an automobile junkyard. Meincke, a hearty younger man, confidence-inspiring, attempted to console me. More money was not to be made on it at the moment, I would not have been able to maintain the laid-up car anyway, one could always find a good secondhand car. We drove up to Dölzschen in his car; I did not want to enter my house, which looked good with the new red roof that had been extorted from me. But afterward I helped push the jalopy out of the garage. A very laborious task, in which Berger also participated. The car had suffered badly: rust, mold, the wooden ring of the steering wheel fell apart. A couple of small boys were standing around outside as the jalopy was fastened by rope and they repeated again and again: "The Jew's car, the Jew's car." Berger, who helped to push it out, stressed his innocence in this matter and the earlier demands for money. The parish wanted to bully me, they really wanted to expel me from the house. "Your car was discovered recently when they inspected the house again. They will send you a new demand soon: The whole house and the big veranda must be painted and completely renovated to prevent them from falling into disrepair."

The last time, over the roof, the mayor had already declared: "Sell the house, you will not be able to bear the costs that will arise." To his surprise

I did after all take on the costs of the roofing. But this new demand? Now that I am poorer by the new 15 percent tax. And if I still manage even this payment—when will the next demand come? They will torture me until I give up the house, and Eva will grieve.

Towing the jalopy, we drove slowly down the snow-covered streets. I got out at Teplitzer, corner of Josephstrasse. The jalopy still looked good as it rolled away; it wounded me dreadfully that it was being driven to the slaughter.

Meincke, the dealer, loosened up quite a lot. Quite obviously anti-Nazi, philo-Semite, far from convinced of victory, anzi (he asked my opinion, which I expressed fairly incautiously). At the same time: "I am an old Party member. I have to stay in the Party, if I leave now, I'm finished."

The day before yesterday speech by the Duce, yesterday speech by the Führer. Both talked in superlatives, despite the Italian defeats in Africa, of victory this spring. I laughed at Mussolini's speech, Hitler's made me stop short with fear. He has so often proclaimed like a charlatan, and yet things always turned out well for him.

Yesterday evening we arrived at the Monopol as Hitler was raving the last few sentences into the radio in his paranoid, screaming voice. We went out and waited until he and the Horst Wessel Song were finished.

March 1, Saturday evening

In the morning the milkmaid refused to come up. She is no longer allowed to deliver to Jews' Houses.

At midday at the bank only 178M had been transferred from the pension office instead of the 409M of previous months: the new "social deduction" from Jews, 15 percent of income, deducted all at once for the three months January to March. — After that the butcher declared he would have to give less from now on because deliveries were so poor.

In the afternoon the news that Bulgaria had joined the Tripartite Pact. So Greece is lost, so Russia looks calmly on, so the route to Egypt through Turkey-in-Asia is open, so Germany appears to be winning the war.

In the evening we wanted to eat something at the Pschorrbräu and found nothing edible without meat coupons, went to the Monopol and found only turnips, went to the station and found nothing at all, went back to the Monopol and ate the turnips. (All in spring weather and slush.) As soon as we were home there was a police check.

One day in my life in the Third Reich.

March 4, Tuesday evening

Since yesterday—entry into Bulgaria—very depressed again. Yesterday news from Änny Klemperer, who also heard only in a roundabout way, and without any details, that Georg has had a stroke. Emotion? Hardly any. Consequences for me? Emigration to the USA *even* more difficult than before. But then did I want to live there on his charity? [. . .]

Today there is supposed to be a report in the *Dresdener NN:* "Yid Klemperer, who yiddified the Berlin Opera" has escaped from the mental asylum in Hollywood and been caught again. In his last letter about two years ago, Georg wrote that he had treated Otto Klemperer for serious brain disease. — I am now outliving those whom I envied, feared, sometimes hated—but in what a position and for how long? Stupid, mean, pointless feeling of triumph and yet despite all self-knowledge undoubtedly present. Perhaps a feeling of relief. No one there anymore whose rejection of me could cause me any offense.

On language: 100 Percent. Certainly American. Title of a novel by Upton Sinclair translated into German. Constantly used in Nazi German.

March 11, Tuesday

Georg's letter came on Thursday, March 6, doubly surprising after such a long time and Änny's news. About that and about Sussmann's two letters and our considerable reservations because of the 3,000M—"only" about 1,000M is deducted directly from the sum, but the rest is added to total income and this total is taxed at 25–30 percent—see enclosures, copies of the letters to Änny and Sussmann, Georg's letter itself. All of Jewry congratulates us; our own feelings are very mixed.

The Balkan business is undecided and weighs on us.

[. . .]

March 13, evening

[. . .]

Official notice in the newspaper: "Cards of prisoners of war and J cards are not to be supplied with oranges." We and the prisoners of war. Almost half of our most recent ration card was cut off.

Language: Irrepressible will.

March 14, evening

For a long time I feared a large fine because of the failure to black out on February 15. When nothing happened, I thought I had not been charged. This morning summons of a *prison sentence* of eight days, and to present myself at police headquarters within two weeks. I am dreadfully afraid of it, and my heart is very, very heavy at leaving Eva alone. But I must force myself to be calm, simply for her sake.

By comparison my stored-up little notes seem futile.

I now fetch our milk from Chemnitzer Platz. It is forbidden to deliver anything to Jews' Houses, our shop was far away, and the shops nearby are not taking any new customers. I have old friends at Chemnitzer Platz. That is where Eva must now go.

The Jewish world today. A lady who was downstairs visiting the Kreidls conveys greetings from my niece Käte Sussmann (in Switzerland). Käte was in a tuberculosis sanatorium there, is now employed there (as dressmaker), [. . .]. — Cohn, an honest man, who often collects donations for the Jewish Community and to whom I have been unable to give anything recently, brought me (with anxious secretiveness—he could be punished for it) two pairs of socks. The Community board refused my request for a reduction of the enormously high tax (279M); there were no grounds for a reduction, I should sell my house to alleviate my situation. These people have no time for a baptized Jew. Especially when, as I do, he gives one third of this tax to the Confessing Church.

It was Frau Voss' birthday on March 11. She spent half the night in the kitchen and made four cakes; homemade cakes are de rigueur for her on such occasions. Petit bourgeois proper thing to do. Later ten ladies came for tea. We had to be there too.

It's less the lack of space, dirt, bad food, etc. of these days that I dread than the anticipated complete lack of activity and emptiness of those 192 hours.

March 24, Monday evening

I have so much accustomed myself to the idea of imprisonment that it no longer disturbs me in my work and I see the matter in an almost humorous way. Besides there is still a degree of hope. I went to police headquarters to inquire. Courteous response: I was advised to make a plea in writing. [. . .] (I sent it off handwritten, so as not to draw attention to my typewriter.)

On language: On the printed arrest warrant "Police Headquarters" has been replaced by "The Chief of Police." Likewise: ". . . you will be . . . sentenced" by: ". . . I order you to be imprisoned." Leadership principle! [. . .]

At police headquarters I was told I would be allowed to read and write (in pencil).

March 27, Thursday evening

I should have reported for my sentence today. I went there (to Police Headquarters), but I was told, my petition was "being considered," it had been "passed on with a positive recommendation," the decision lay with a department head, I should wait and see what happens. At the police station they are very courteous, but since in the end some senior Party members make the decision and my name is Victor Israel . . .

My mood and view of the situation as a whole change from day to day. Conclusion of the Tripartite Pact with Yugoslavia: low point. Our troops do not march in, so Russia objects after all: upswing. Some tiny place in North Africa reconquered by German motorized troops—how did they get across the sea? — new low. Etc., etc.

[. . .]

There was an unpleasant argument with the impossible Kätchen Sara Voss, and from the Deutsche Bank I learned that the 3,000M that Georg is transferring to me from his blocked account will almost certainly be released and not taxed until next year. From these two roots there grows once more, and this time with considerable force, a desire to move to Berlin. It would be stimulating, a new cool place for one's pillow, to use the French image, and there is very little here that still binds us. Also Eva is better on her feet than before, more mobile. And the idea of emigrating has after all become more tangible. In Berlin we could find out more and make preparations more easily than here.

Some time ago I inquired of Lissy Meyerhof about it. Her response was negative, and at the time we had no money whatsoever. Now I have written a couple of lines to Heinz Machol, who runs a kind of pension. Perhaps Eva, who as an Aryan can move freely, will go up there to get a sense of things.

On language: The *young* nations of Europe. When is a nation young? When Mussolini was still opposed to Germany, he once said in a speech: We already had a great culture, when the Germans did not yet have an alphabet. Now Germany and Italy are the "young nations" of Europe. (Cf, The Young Germany—the Young Italy of Gutzkow and Mazzini.)

April 10, Thursday

Non-Aryans are to be completely barred from settling in Berlin. So our plans of moving have again come to naught.

[. . .]

On language: Heinz Machol wrote of the occupancy of empty apartments by *demolition tenants,* that is people from houses destroyed by bombing. — Pay attention to the now ever more frequent "European New Order"; no longer the freedom of Germany, but a euphemistically circumscribed European supremacy. — Have I already noted *ready for action?* In my diaries I note in the summer of 1916 how military language is penetrating non-military spheres. Draw on Bergson's psychology for this expansion. In my diary for 1916 or '17 also a remark on the racialist element in the Wandervögel. That would be a separate article for my Dictionnaire: Scouts [Wandervögel] Hitler Youth.

[. . .]

I interrupted the Curriculum, which is proceeding at a snail's pace, for one and a half days, to deal with the most pressing Easter correspondence.

April 14, Easter Monday

Russian Easter: Eva is lying down a lot—neuralgia in her right arm, suffering greatly—I have interrupted the Curriculum and have been reading from Goncharov's *Oblomov* for hours. Fräulein Paulig in her old-fashioned lending library suggested the book as something amusing, I had no idea that we were taking on board such a classical and significant tome.

Only to the Pschorr yesterday evening and afterward walked back in the rain for a bit past the Great Garden.

On the way to the Pschorr we read of the fall of Belgrade and Baria. — Today I called old Kreidl up from downstairs, to "strengthen his backbone." I told him, even if Egypt were to be conquered now, even if Turkey were to open the way through Asia, Hitler *must* lose the war, neither Russia nor the USA could accept the risk of his final victory. Do I believe what I am saying? About 50 percent. But I am calmer now. I can face the course of history more coolheadedly. What are ten, twenty years in the history of a nation? In the *long term* Hitler cannot remain victorious, all world conquests fall apart at some point. All I am interested in now is our temporally very limited particular fate. And I am fatalistic about that. — Naturally accompanied by many hours of severe depression. I dread the thought of the USA. Dependent on Georg or his sons, not knowing the language, completely out of practice as a teacher and 60 years old. But perhaps this cup will pass from me, perhaps it will not taste quite so bitter, perhaps I shall die first. I often say to myself now: After all I have a long, interesting, not even so unsuccessful life behind me, and, whatever happens, only a remnant before me—why does it matter so much? But Eva . . . sterile speculations, it would also be sterile if I wanted to plunge into English grammar once again. I am sticking to the Curriculum, I shall bury myself in it, as often as household and Eva's illness leave me time. Tomorrow or the day after the handwritten manuscript of the "Front and Military Hospital" section will be finished.

April 16

On the situation: Serbia, Greece destroyed, English expeditionary force being evacuated, whole of Cyrenaica reconquered, Egyptian frontier crossed. Turkey does nothing, Russia does nothing: (1) Why do the others allow themselves to be butchered *one at a time*? England has miscalculated repeatedly since '39. Russia must know that an all-powerful Hitler Germany will take the Baltic States, smash the Soviet Union. (2) The National Socialists are the only ones who have learned from the World War and its aftermath and avoid the mistakes of that period. (Food supply, brutal rule, concentration of power.) They do not lack greatness. But their greatness is coupled with pettiness. (3) Every conqueror, every nation goes to war with *ostensible* altruism, *conscious* egotism. But behind the subjectively egotistical aim, behind the feigned humanitarianism there is an unconscious objective one. The conqueror Napoleon is in the service of progress, the conqueror Hitler in the service of repression, of backward movement, egotistical England in the service of the freedom of mankind. (4) Once I would have said: I do not judge as a Jew . . . Now: Yes, I judge as a Jew, because as such I am particularly affected by the Jewish business in Hitlerism, and because it is central to the whole structure, to the whole character of National Socialism and is uncharacteristic of everything else.

April 20 ("Führer's Birthday"), Sunday–April 21, Monday

Lissy Meyerhof here since Friday evening, staying until Monday evening. (As last autumn.) Extremely exhausting, especially as Eva is suffering badly from her neuritis, is lying down a great deal and is quite incapable of working. Washing up, housework ad infinitum. In the intervals endless talking. Main meal out, everything else at home. Also coupon and money pressure; I paid Lissy's train journey—Georg's 3,000M not yet here, transfer questionable.

But Lissy tells us many interesting things. (1) "Demolition tenants" are not only those from bomb-damaged houses. Rather whole housing estates of the "system period" are being pulled down to make way for new buildings. People say Hitler is more concerned with his building plans than with the war. They say he has his astrologer (Hess ditto) and is completely dominated by him. In addition to the demolition tenants there is also a demand for housing (which is satisfied at the expense of the Jews—Lissy too has now had to leave her apartment and has been given *one* room) from: (a) Civil service families that are recalled from the Gouvernement Poland. The idea is to give Poland to the Russians in exchange for the Ukraine. If they do not agree: war. We must have a granary. A broad strip of land has been evacuated in East Prussia, a strip of no man's land, masses of troops. (b) Corner houses at important traffic junctions are also cleared of Aryan tenants and SS quartered in them. As fortifications in case of an uprising. (I also heard both, [a] and [b], confirmed from another source.) (2) Lissy talks about and shows letters from the many branches of her scattered family. Erich was in England, is now interned in Australia. His family: The two sons were soldiers, were discharged as corporals. Are *not* especially anti-Nazi. Their mother, always treated as inferior by the Meyerhofs, daughter of a Christian petit bourgeois family, brought up the children to be anti-Semitic. Apart from that the boys are more interested in sports than anything else. Only now, now that they themselves are feeling the pressure, now that the woman is separated from her husband, are mother and sons drawing back from the Third Reich. — There has been no direct news for years from Albert, whose family is now also in South Africa. Berthold in New York is employed as a beer-truck driver in the family firm of his benefactors; his wife makes home visits as a dressmaker. Hans is in an internment camp on the Deserto near Sorrento. [. . .] Our joint letter to him did not get through; Lissy had an unpleasant interrogation at the Berlin Gestapo because of it.

April 22, Tuesday

Lissy went off yesterday evening at seven o'clock; we were really exhausted. Eva's health not very good, we shall have to go to a doctor.

On Saturday, as we were eating at the Monopol, we heard Goebbels' congratulatory address to the Führer. Clerical pathos in a confident bass. Nuance: "Our victory is as good as certain." (Until now it was always: We have already won, the English just haven't noticed yet.) Most characteristic expression: We do not need to know what the Führer wants to do, we *believe* in him. Always and everywhere: National Socialism does not want to know, to think, *only believe.* Eva heard a sentence, which I missed and which is not in the newspaper either: The English "sow mistrust in the army."

Frau Kreidl Sr. just been to see me. She only wanted to hear what people were saying in Berlin. Immediately afterward unrestrained weeping: She could not bear it any longer, she wanted to die, she was 66, too tired, a burden on everyone, she would never live to see the end of the tyranny. Hitler would be victorious over everyone, over Russia too. . . .

[. . .]

Language: [. . .] Since when *bunker?*

For a while we were buying wheat beer. Now it is only being dispensed in tiny quantities. A new decree reduces beer production as a whole by 50 percent: shortage of barley.

We shall be finished with *Oblomov* today. Great classic—very Russian.

April 24

Impossible to work on a single line. Eva lies down a great deal, I read aloud a great deal, the rest is housework and shopping. And still hauling up coal.

Eva now receiving treatment with diathermy. Dr. Gottreich Mehnert, Oskarstrasse. Gray-haired, good-looking man. In his waiting room, in the bookcase below the obligatory picture of Hitler, the complete Heine, Remarque, *All Quiet on the Western Front,* muster roll of his student fraternity, several World War histories and that of an infantry regiment. Certainly no Nazi. Frau Voss, who recommended him to us, assured us of that in advance. But I wish he would give Eva, whose loss of weight alarms me, a *complete* examination. That is still outstanding.

The 3,000M from Georg, which I now need very urgently, not yet there. If the Foreign Exchange Office forbids transfer, then I shall be rid of my house before autumn.

[...]

I am now often depressed by the thought that my work on the 18ième will be for nothing, because I shall be unable to find my way into it again, and because everything will already be out of date—research has not stood still. A work of literary history must emerge in its own time, it may age afterward and thereby remain young. But it must not be born out of date. Then again I say to myself in resignation: And if I had died in 1933? Then my *Corneille* would simply have been my last work. What does one book more or less matter?

[...]

April 25

The renewed affidavit that was requested has already arrived today from my nephew George E. Klemperer. Its arrival was announced a few days before in a letter from "Georg Klemperer Sr." How Georg's style always unconsciously adjusts to prevailing convention. [...] He himself is only "a worn-out old tub in a quiet harbor, without influence. But Gog is very much a respected citizen, who has already established himself."

Today, after a typing gap of about four months, I began a copy of the Curriculum. Rest of "Naples in Wartime," army chapters 1 and 2. That will take many weeks, especially as I get around to it for only a few minutes a day.

[...]

May 15, Thursday

Hess affair (Deputy of the Führer, to England in a plane), three days ago on the radio, as we were sitting in the Pschorr, the day before yesterday confused "explanation," now not a word, appears to have caused a great sensation among the whole population. Should one place any hopes in it? In my war diaries I come upon facts that I only allude to, because they seemed to me incredibly momentous and imprinted on me forever—and today I no longer know what they were about, they were unimportant after all and slipped away. Will it be the same with Hess?

Last Saturday at the Neumanns in Winckelmannstrasse for tea. A niece of Arthur Finks, with whom we are acquainted through Grete, her husband (65, at least 20 years older than she) once manufacturer, now working in the Jewish Community, vehemently anti-German (with Iron Cross from the World War) and Zionist. Despite everything I emphatically declared my commitment to Germanness. ("No one will believe you." — "It is not a question of what others believe of me, my conscience alone is the judge of my Germanness.") They lent me Sammy Gronemann, *Hawdoloh und Zapfenstreich* [Havdalah and Last Post] with drawings by Magnus Zeller. Fits in exactly with my present diary reading for Supreme Command East.

Surprise today, after about five years Karl Wieghardt here from the Göttingen Kaiser Wilhelm Institute. On his honeymoon trip with plain young woman, secretary there. Outwardly unchanged, inwardly, for all the old cordiality, disappointing. Nothing but fear and determination to remain undisturbed. Without any contact with Gusti since the beginning of the war. Yet it would be an easy matter for him to reach her via Maria Strindberg. Does not even know Maria's address. ("Are you still keeping a diary? You surely haven't been noting my name?!" — "Write to you? Why? One cannot say anything anyway.") Extenuating circumstance: He is in an exposed position, experiments on effects of flying on pilots. His non-Aryan stepmother. The dubiousness of his own Aryan ID. — His wife East Frisian, therefore unobjectionable. Church wedding. — Little Karl, the anticlerical Bolshevist! — On the other hand brave and touching that he came to see us.

Typewritten copy making very slow progress. — Yesterday first day without heating, today cold and damp again.

[...]

May 21, Wednesday

At Annemarie's in Pirna for money. With heavy heart—she has not come to see us for two years. Fear? Disloyalty? — But she was completely unaffected, warm, passionately anti . . . She really cannot get away, Dressel is standing in as head of the Heidenau Hospital, all the work of the clinic is on her shoulders, also she has serious heart problems. (She has an unnaturally thick, swollen head, a constant dry cough.) A number of her remarks encouraged me. "What are you going to do with the American affidavit? You cannot use it while the war is on, and afterward you won't need it anymore." — "I always knew that the war is going to be lost, this absurd underestimation of England!" — "In the last few weeks ten thousand people have been called up here in Pirna district alone. Everything is being sent east. Russia! And America will come too." — "Why does the Führer not say a word about the Hess affair? He really *ought* to say something. What excuse will he use—Hess has been sick for years? But then he shouldn't be Hitler's deputy. He flew in a Messerschmitt plane, so high that the antiaircraft guns could not reach him." — "Sonnenstein has long ceased to be the regional mental asylum. The SS is in charge. They have built a special crematorium. Those who are not wanted are taken up in a kind of police van.

People here all call it 'the whispering coach.' Afterward the relatives receive the urn. Recently one family here received two urns at once. — We now have pure Communism. But Communism murders more honestly."
  [. . .]

May 24, Saturday

Today we have been in the Jews' House for one year. Eva, in the midst of tolerable cheerfulness, was irritated when I reminded her. — We have resumed the walks of last year.

Yesterday on the radio in the evening—it starts at eight, we listen while we are eating (Pschorr and/or Tögel, Monopol has become unusable)— warning against illegal *broadcasting*, not against listening. High treason, prison or death sentence! So some things must have been broadcast, I suppose in connection with Hess. So the joke is widespread—I have also heard of leaflets stuck up in Löbtau: "Brown budgie flown away. Return to Reich Chancellery." I have just found diary notice September 5, '18: General Headquarters Berlin threatens one year in prison for spreading rumors, even if at the same time one casts doubt on the rumor. Is the situation now, mutatis mutandis, analogous? Is the analogy a pipe dream? Yesterday in the Scharfe Eck in Lockwitz I for the first time heard people talking with genuine enthusiasm about Hitler and National Socialism. Two draymen: "Our Adolf will pull it off all right. — 1918? That ass, Wilhelm betrayed us, the Jews were in charge—but now! They should be even tougher though, we're still being too decent . . ." The sinking of Prien's U-boat had just been announced. "Shame—but for every boat sunk we've got five new ones." And a soldier: "We'll be home at Christmas." — Always the question: What is the mood of the people, who can account for it?

Latest rumor: The vast quantity of troops is not going E, but N, to Norway. From there in the near future a landing in England.

May 27, Tuesday

Ups and downs. Two days of deepest depression: the parachute landing on Crete, the tremendous cruiser losses of the English there—I took it all as a successful dress rehearsal for the landing in England—the sinking of the *Hood* (the "biggest battleship in the world") in the naval battle off Iceland. I was even more firmly convinced that Hitler would be the final victor than last year after France's defeat. But yesterday evening the usually pessimistic Kreidl Sr. told me, (1) the action on Crete was far from decided, the Germans did not have a firm front line yet, nor any heavy artillery, and (2) "Crete was not England." [. . .]

I am now working through the diary pages Vilna '18, reading them first of all. How much I had forgotten, how immensely important are precisely the details of such a time! For the sake of my Curriculum I must make notes even now, I *must,* no matter how dangerous it is. That is my professional courage. Certainly I also put other people at risk. But there is nothing else I can do.

Sussmann writes that Lotte has lost her position because the native who formerly held it has turned up. Now the Police Aliens' Department is threatening her with deportation or concentration camp. *In free Switzerland!* Which is not free and fears occupation.

May 29

The most miserable thing for us in the last war was having to eat separately. What then arose from lack of money, appears this time to come from lack of coupons. The day before yesterday—extreme shortage of coupons at the end of the four-week cards—the "regular," the dish one could have without coupons, in the Pschorr was off. I left Eva there (since I polish off %₀ of our common bread ration at home, I have to leave her the necessary fat and bread coupons for the restaurant); recently there has been hardly anything without bread coupons, frequently not without "cake coupons" (that is, bread coupons not stamped R, i.e., for rye) and went to Jakob in Prager Strasse, big sausage shop and "snack bar." I was already sitting in the back room when I saw the sign "No Jews allowed" —not just the sign usual elsewhere: "Jews not welcome." I remained nevertheless. There was black pudding soup and vegetables and black pudding soup again—all without any coupons and I only paid one mark. But there were also conversations at my table. A young man with Party badge, a family. The young man talked about the latest bulletin, sinking of the *Bismarck.* Which had destroyed the *Hood* the day before. The German loss was more serious than the English, was irreplaceable. Our most modern battleship. The daughter of the family said literally: "It's a sad week for us. First Hess, then Prien, now the *Bismarck.*"

June 3, Tuesday after Whitsun

Of Georg's 3,000M present the Foreign Currency Office, Freiburg im Breisgau, has "provisionally" allowed "1,200M in monthly installments of 200M." That is not much help because only doctor and taxes and expenditure on the house (mortgage, repairs etc. = "maintenance of inland assets") are outside the tax-free limit of 320M. The reserve at Annemarie's has shrunk to 400M—so we shall hardly be able to continue the luxury of eating out beyond the autumn. [. . .]

But I do not believe that the situation will last the year. Crete has been conquered and is being played up as a great victory and the prelude to the conquest of England from the air. But Iraq has been taken by the English

(Baghdad!), and morale here is in part poor, in part apathetic. — Today when I paid my storage rent at Thamm's one of the moving men from last year greeted me heartily and gave me encouragement in a bellowing voice. — "It's getting better, the war is going well for us." — "What do you mean 'for us'?" — "Well, not for the Nazis!"

[. . .]

June 9, Monday

It is now a game (only a Jewish game?) to fathom the popular mood. In restaurants, in shops. Today Hochgemuth, cigar dealer, lottery agent, freemason, told me: "There are rumors everywhere that we've been marching through Russia for three weeks. I don't think there is anything to it. — The mood is very poor. The workers are switching off (sic). They used to say 'Heil Hitler,' now they say 'Good morning.' I have been warned, there are 'professional grumblers' going around, they provoke citizens into speaking their mind, by grumbling themselves. *They* are allowed to, they're covered by their Party cards. — I think it'll go wrong." — Yesterday in the Pschorr a fresh young woman at our table exclaimed after her headcheese: "God knows, that has not filled me up." She ordered a bockwurst as well, gave a quarter-pound's worth of meat coupons for it. I asked if she was full up now. She became affable: There wasn't even enough for four such sausages every week. "And next month we'll be cut by another 1½ ounces a week, I saw the new card in Magdeburg. The cake coupons are to be dropped as well. And my husband has been called up now. Our good young blood. And there's nothing but foreigners running around the streets, Belgians, Italians, Serbs in the armaments factories . . ."

Today the news that the De Gaulle troops have marched into Syria. Hourly we quote Frau Voss's favorite phrase: "I wonder what will happen next."

For a whole hour today very dispirited with all my old doubts. I had to invite the Reichenbachs by telephone. (Very unwillingly. No tea, no cake coupons.) He declined; they have suddenly been expelled from their apartment, must be out by June 20, and do not know where to go. Their apartment was already two makeshift rooms like ours here. Now they will probably have one room. He lamented: London, the lawyer, his colleague in Emigration Advice left early this morning—for the USA. "One after the other. We shall remain quite alone. Our own affidavit rendered invalid by the death of the issuer. The widow has refused by telegram." There I asked myself again: Shall I expedite our emigration? By sending in the new affidavit and adding, Passage can be guaranteed to me by telegram? (It is supposed to help.) Long painful consultation with Eva. She said, over there she would have no hope of ever again finding a life of her own, there she would only be able to sit around and go to the cinema, nothing else. *Here* at least she still retained some hope. I myself fear dependence on relatives—[. . .]—and impotence with regard to the language. We shall do nothing to speed it up and continue to wait and see as "obstinately" as before. It wounds me so much to hear Eva say that "for many years she has had nothing from life." Since she took up the organ in 1917, our mutual bonds alone have not been enough to give her fulfilment. Everything starts here. The desperate longing for a house began when she could no longer play the organ.

June 14, Saturday

After three months and against all expectation my plea of March 18 has been rejected, and so there remains a prison sentence of a full eight days, which I must begin on June 23. Reading and writing in *pencil* are supposed to be permitted. Keep smiling—I shall try.

After years (I think decades) Eva feels a desire and the skill in her fingers to start typing again. She's getting practice through my dictating parts of the front-line chapter to her. Apart from this copy, which whether made by myself alone or by both of us, will take weeks, no work at all on the Curriculum. But before the sentence I want to make summary notes on "Book Examination Sup. Com. East"—only the first Kovno page has been completed—perhaps I can write something in vinculis.

[. . .]

Yesterday it became clear to us how the rumor—it has been doing the rounds for weeks—"we've already been marching through Russia for a long time," probably comes about. A woman said to Voss: "My son has written to me from Russia." — "From Russia? From where then?" — "Beyond Warsaw." For these people Poland and Russia merge into each another.

June 18, Wednesday

I am counting the days until the beginning of the sentence; the waiting is the worst. — I want to add after the event, that Wilhelm II died in Doorn a few days ago, in his eighty-third year. It touched me, because it brought my age home to me. The Emperor of my youth, in my mind always the young Emperor of the nineties. I feel a hundred years old.

Language 3rd R. The symbols: (⚡) expressionist. Y for born, ⅄ deceased. Cross frowned on. A few days ago decree from the Minister of Culture to delete the subject of religion from school reports. "Where confessional religious teaching is given: mark on a separate sheet." — The life rune Y on Bienert's wholemeal bread. — The extravagantly abusive and offensive tone of the newspapers. The day before yesterday an article against the Biesterfeld man, the Dutch prince consort who is making propaganda in the USA for Holland :/: H. "Scoundrel," "degenerate," etc. Churchill and Roosevelt every day: Criminals, liars, murderers. [. . .]

I read a Stevenson story aloud. [. . .] Now we are going to start another great Goncharov: *The Precipice.* But we do not have much time for reading. [. . .]

Yesterday evening on Südhöhe a convoy of dusty, battered military vehicles (troops, canvas rolled back); chalked inscriptions like: Athens–home, Corinth–mummy–Balkans; flat, ugly English helmets stuck onto the radiators. The convoy stopped for a while at the little Toll House, a crowd of passersby gathered. *No* demonstration of sympathy—indifference.

June 22, Sunday afternoon

The worst part, having it draw nearer, is almost over. Tomorrow.

Today the most tremendous distraction. *Russia.* Kreidl Sr. came by in the morning. "It's starting with Russia." Fräulein Ludwig (Friedheim's housekeeper) heard Goebbels on the radio, "Russia's treachery"—Jewish-Bolshevism. I then went down to Dr. Friedheim, who lent me *Poetry and Truth* for my imprisonment, and made me a present of a packet of expensive tobacco as consolation. The man is garrulous, vain, bank director, proud of his successes, over 60 years of age. "90 percent National Socialist"—anti-democratic, monarchist—otherwise very nice. Believes in Hitler's fall. Meanwhile the radio was on in the hospital next door. Eva summed up: Goebbels' speech will be repeated at half past twelve. We went into town, ate the "regular" at Pschorr, listened to the broadcast as well as we could with all the noise. The speech was already printed in the special edition, a bent, half-blind old woman handed it to us and said: "Our leader! He has had to bear it all alone, so as not to trouble his people!" Our very good, hard-working waiter said: "I was a prisoner in Siberia in the World War." — "What do you think now?" — Confidently: "The war will come to an end more quickly now." — What is the mood of the people? Always my same old question. How many think like the old woman and the waiter? For how many is it a debacle? How many will say, after a pause of two years, the Jewish-Bolshevist number has now been cranked up again? Now the treaty of friendship concluded with the Turks three or four days ago has become problematic? [. . .] When it got too noisy at Pschorr, we walked to the Ring and promenaded on the central reservation, while a loudspeaker preached from the streetlight suspended at the corner of Prager Strasse. Ribbentrop's note simultaneously appeared as a special edition. Back here toward three. Very tired and worn out. — Now into town again for supper and eight o'clock news.

Evening

General cheerfulness of the populace. Mood: "Triumphant we shall conquer France, Russia and the whole wide world." At our table in the Pschorr elderly, somewhat inebriated commercial traveler and dull, petit bourgeois married couple. The traveler: "Now we know where we stand, we'll get it over with more quickly—we're ready and armed, it's not like it was under the Empire. Only question is, what will Turkey do?" The petit bourgeois man: "We're ready for that too, we'll get it too." Then the traveler told awful anti-Nazi jokes, one after the other. "People have to tell jokes, as long as it stays within limits." The limits were drawn very wide, but it was told in high spirits and full of confidence in victory. — We got the packed E bus as far as the Toll House, walked home along Südhöhe. They were dancing in the Toll House, cheerful faces every-where. A new entertainment, a prospect of new sensations, the Russian war is a source of new pride for people, their grumbling of yesterday is forgotten [. . .].

July 6, Sunday

I am trying to work up in outline on the typewriter the terrible week, no eight days, in prison, June 23 till July 1. Since my return on Tuesday ex-hausted, dazed, overjoyed, incapable of doing anything. Perhaps this was the good thing about the time of tribulation, that we became conscious again of belonging together, of our happiness, of the absolute unimpor-tance of everything apart from being together. Short walks—an apple juice in the evening in the Toll House, chatting in the evening with Kätchen Sara, that's all. And housework of course, which after the nothingness now seems pleasant to me.

The Neumanns were here on Friday. [. . .] I read out part of the Front chapter. Debate on Zionism and Germany. Made friends with Dr. Fried-heim, who overwhelmed me with attentions (tobacco, wine). — Heavy pressure of the situation in Russia. [. . .] Not a line read out, not a line written. — I am interrupting the ongoing work on the Curriculum in favor of Cell 89, the typewritten copy of which now follows. It should be truth, not poetry and truth, does not have to be the final Curriculum text.

Cell 89, June 23–July 1, 1941

I began my long-pending police sentence in June: I had believed that once again it would only turn out to be something of a half measure like most of my experiences; but it proved to be horribly much the real thing.

On February 10 the window next to the desk was not blacked out. Until then, that is throughout 17 months of war we had always blacked out with the greatest care and always been annoyed at the countless instances of carelessness [. . .] which we encountered, first among our neighbors in Dölzschen, then on our return journeys to the Jews' House from supper in town. They've made a peace treaty of their own, Eva used to say, when we passed an illuminated window. There were repeated warnings and threats, the fines rose, there were to be prison sentences for repeated of-fences or particular malice—but the many half or fully illuminated win-dows remained, especially as before autumn and after November '40, there was not a single air raid warning here. It was our regular habit to black out both our rooms before darkness fell and before we went out for our afternoon walk. But on February 10, just as we were about to go out, we had a visitor who stayed a long time. It grew late, we had to be back at eight, at the station ancient waiters served at a snail's pace: so we hurried out. When we came back at eight, the night was like a black wall before the window, and we switched on the light as usual. Half an hour later a policeman rang the bell, one of the honest and friendly people from our station who carried out the supervision of the Jews very courteously. There was an illuminated window here. "Certainly not here," I said with a good conscience. Not until the man opened the window, did the omission occur to me. I asked him whether he could not leave it at a warning, otherwise with my J card I would have to pay an especially large fine. He could not fail to bring a charge, he replied, because the window had been drawn to his attention (there had been a denunciation in other words). I had to state the amount of my income and assets because that would determine the amount of the fine. "You will have to pay 200M," predicted Kätchen Sara, "a poor Jewish girl was recently sentenced to 180M for the same thing. You should have let your Aryan wife take the blame, then you would have gotten away more cheaply." But the next day she came home from her many visits with more favorable news: The average fine for both Yid and Christian was 20M. Weeks then passed, without notification of any penalty, and I was already beginning to think that the friendly policeman had not brought a charge after all. Then on March 13 it came: not a fine, but eight days in prison, for which I had to report within two weeks, unless I petitioned for a judicial decision. For a while I was shocked; I could not make up my mind to lodge an appeal, because what could I as a Jew expect from a judge? After much consideration I went to police headquarters, where I was given very friendly advice by junior officers. I would do well to accept the punishment, but at the same time to make a plea for leniency, after all this was a first and obvious oversight. Besides prison was not a cruel punishment, one was allowed to read, one was also allowed to write in pencil. Eva said that, at worst, it would amount to an enrichment of my Curriculum. I therefore submitted a petition, and when it had not been answered on the day my sentence was to begin, I again went to Schiessgasse, Room 197 on the 3rd floor, without any great fear. The same friendly policemen. My petition was "pending," it had been passed on with a recommendation, there was nothing more that could be done, a particular department head made the decision, I had to wait now. I went home relieved, and in the period that followed, the initial nightmarish pressure became ever lighter. Nowhere, nowhere even among the Jews, was there a known case of imprisonment for a first time blackout misdemeanor; the usual fine was now said to amount to 50M, possibly they would make it more for non-Aryans; money was needed, the prisons were overcrowded. Since additional funds had been transferred to me from Georg's blocked account and since police fines were tax free, I had hardly any need to fear the financial burden. I waited almost three months, and sometimes I forgot the small misfortune altogether. Even when the police decision came on June 12 [. . .] I opened the letter very calmly. My petition was rejected, I had to appear at Room 197, between eight and twelve A.M. on June 23, to begin my sentence and to pay 12M for meals, 3.50M duties. "If you do not appear at the proper time, you must expect to be presented by force." I felt very bitter, for I undoubtedly owed it solely to the J on my identity card, but I resolved to face the whole thing philosophically and regard it as an enrichment of my Curriculum. Police custody was not imprisonment, the police were not brutal like the Gestapo, and with the help of reading and writing the time would pass. Also I did not need to be especially worried about Eva, she was now firmly on her feet, and the irksome coal heaving of the winter was no longer necessary. From Dr. Friedheim I borrowed Goethe's volumes of autobiography, from my tiny reference library I took Moog's *History of German Philosophy in the 20th Century;* and since on my last free Sunday the outbreak of war with Russia mightily raised my spirits, I left the house on Monday after a late breakfast and a heartfelt leave-taking in a very reasonable state of mind. Eight days were no eternity, I would send greetings, a greeting, perhaps even be able to receive a visit. My courageous mood even held in the already familiar Room 197. The policeman was again very courteous, almost comically courteous. Please wait outside on the bench for a while, please be a little patient (I thought: eight days!). Then he read out a minute: "Commencement of sentence Monday, 11:30 A.M., release Tuesday, July 1, 11:30 A.M." and placed it in a blue-and-red-bordered envelope, on it in giant letters and with an exclamation mark the word "Custody." At the sight of this folder I was for the first time overcome by a slight feeling of nausea. "So, as far as I am concerned the case has now been dealt with, please come with me." — "Shall I be able to keep the books?" — "I certainly think so." We went down the three flights of stairs; to the left of the entrance was a large iron door with the inscription "Police Cells." The officer rang the bell, the door was opened, he led me in and immediately left again, the door was locked behind him, and now I was in a different world.

For a moment I thought: "Cinema." A huge rectangular hall; glass roof, six galleries with glass floors, railings of steel rods, wire nets between the individual floors, as if to break the fall of trapeze artists, but behind all the light transparency the uniform rows of dark spots, the handleless cell doors. I sat on a bench, a couple of men in prison clothes beside me; one of them whispered something to me in a foreign language. (Afterward I learned that many Poles were held here.) In the middle of the hall a policeman was writing in a booth, while all around there were shouts and words of abuse. From above came echoing calls, prisoners and turnkeys ran, moved along the galleries and up and down the stairs, there was an unpleasant noise everywhere. Opposite me was a door with the inscription "Police Doctor," beside it sat three decent-looking young women, behind me there appeared to be a cloakroom. I took all that in within the first few seconds, somewhat stupefied by the rattle as the mighty iron outer door was shut and by the unceasing din, but not yet really shocked: I still felt as if I were a spectator, and if the noise in the building was loud, it was hardly very different from the unforgettable hubbub of a barracks. Then I was standing in the cloakroom in front of a young policeman. — Should he have a bath? Probably unnecessary. "Undo your tie, unbutton your suspenders. Faster. In the time it takes you to remove your tie, I'd be completely undressed." It did not sound excessively brutal, but the order was roughly given. Only now did I know that I was not watching a film. "How shall I hold up my trousers?" — "With your hands. You can pull them tight somehow in your cell. Your briefcase. Nightshirt and toothbrush you can keep, hairbrush is superfluous, books and spectacles stay here." — "But I was told . . ." — "We make the rules here." — "But . . ." — "You would have to make an application. Ask at the counter." The man at the counter, half looking up, made a gesture with his elbow as if he wanted to push me away and shouted: "Clear off." Someone pressed a slip of paper into my hand, "Cell 89" was written on it, and said: "Three flights—Go!" Upstairs one of the dark doors was opened, behind me the double sound of the key turned in the lock and of a heavy latch bar falling into place. Then I was alone, and the loud voices outside merged and could not be separated anymore. Once again I had the feeling "cinema" and with it the memory of countless images, comic and tragic, of the prisoner in his cell. Then I was overwhelmed by the tragic novelty of the whole thing, the banal perception—all the most profound perceptions are banal, at most one man finds a somewhat more original expression for it than another man—that we know nothing at all except what we have experienced ourselves. Pity is such a shabby thing. I can torment myself with wanting to feel pity, and yet I don't succeed. How would I feel, Eva, if you were lying sick, if I knew you were on the operating table next to me? I wanted to feel pity, and my thoughts strayed, I would have liked to hit myself because of my lack of feeling, and my thoughts strayed here and there to trifles, became egotistical—I did not really feel pity. How could I know beforehand, what imprisonment, what a cell is? Only at the second that the door fell shut, that the latch fell into place, did I know it with a nameless fear. At that second the eight days turned into 192 hours, empty caged hours. And from then on the awareness of the heavy hours did not leave me again and became the real torment of these days. In translations of American novels, one usually finds the word Stop spelled out between each sentence of a telegram. Similarly, whether I liked it or not, slow-moving time again and again inserted itself between all my thoughts throughout this period: another 185 hours, another 184, another 183 . . . There was no getting away from it, and each one passed more slowly than the one before, and each had its particular restraint. But to be quite precise: This stop sign only began at hour 186, because only then did I discover a way of buttoning over my trousers so that they stayed on my hips; until then it was not Stop but: My trousers are slipping, my trousers are slipping. What good is all philosophizing about the inviolability of one's inner moral dignity? I experienced the misery of the slipping trousers, then of the tied-up trousers as the most extreme humiliation. And I did not remove my collar, even when it was very hot, because that gave me something at least to hold on to, because I did not want to be one of the "gentlemen without collars," who were not allowed to dance at Schramm's in Wilmersdorf. (Since there was no mirror I was hardly aware that my tie was missing.)

I came out of the shock of the door shutting because of a loud, regular, continuous hammering sound above my head, tap-tap-tap-tap. I realized immediately: The prisoner above me is pacing his cell. Familiar and yet completely new, only now reality, coming from the surface and penetrating deep inside. I matched the man's rhythm: four long strides from the door to below the high drop window. From side to side I could only manage three short strides, and there was no point at which I could do so in a straight line because of the pieces of furniture against the long sides. Anyhow the room was not so tiny. Also not oppressively low, it was certainly a good three yards to where the vaulted ceiling began, also bright and not—not unclean would probably be an exaggeration, but certainly not thick with dirt, no horrible medieval dungeon. But a cage after all, a dreary cage with bare gray-green walls and whitish ceiling, with opaque window panes and a barred peephole in the door, closed from the outside by a flap. It all emanated an oppressiveness, a rising increasing fear, which I dreaded. Was the romantic medieval dungeon really any more cruel? Perhaps one suffered less because the torment was greater. Straw and rustling rats and spiders, which one could observe, were, after all, a distraction from the self, the outside world, not the utter bareness, the abstract space of the cell, the naked idea of imprisonment. I had to break free of this idea of emptiness. The cell was my room, equipped with all that was necessary, I had only to study it in every detail. To the left on my walk to the window I had the bed. It hung folded up against the wall with two feet, held by staples like a bat, the bed cover, the woolen blanket, the sheet were spread over the edge of the bed, above it leaned the wedge-shaped headrest with the stenciled letters PPD, Polizeipräsident Dresden [Chief of Police Dresden]. I memorized the arrangement exactly, after all I would take it apart eight times and reconstruct it. Opposite on the right, also fastened to the wall, a tiny roughly made fold-up table with one leg, a tiny bench with one leg. In front of the table by the window a small shelf, on it a brown water jug, more precisely a coffee pot, a brown washbasin, a brown earthenware beaker, a half bar of ersatz soap, a tin spoon, a tin box with salt, beneath it a pegboard with three pegs, two empty, on the third a clean towel with the letters PPD. Behind the bench beside the door, two yards at most from the dining table, a lavatory. This was the only deviation from the superficial image of a cell familiar to me. Really it should be a pail standing here, instead it was a modern hygienic WC. Certainly the WC too soon made me feel my imprisonment: The flush could only be activated from outside, and this was done mornings and evenings. In between lay the warm summer day, the warm summer night, and only the top half of the drop window was opened. To the medieval dungeon there belongs stereotypically the pestilential stench. In this respect too the exalting and the stupefying were missing, one could breathe the air, it was merely stuffy and nasty. What else was there to see in Cell 89? I carefully had to fill the emptiness with every possible thing that presented itself. Opposite the lavatory, high up by the door the three pipes of the steam heating, just above the door, below the ceiling, a lightbulb; it was inside a barred cage—a scaled-down likeness, a symbol of my self and my lodging. Better not look in that direction! What else? A very crooked and clumsy swastika had been scratched on the wall behind the lavatory, engraved very regularly and skillfully in the table, a Soviet star. Par nobile. Anything else? Yes, all kinds of smudged scribbled names on the walls—I could not decipher them without spectacles. And above the table on a piece of card the house rules of the police prison—I could not decipher them without glasses. Or perhaps yes, I could take it off the wall, I could get the sheet in the right position, I could take my time over it; if it took a long time, if my eyes began to ache because of the blurred flickering—I would be resting my eyes for long enough. The deciphering must have got me through several hours, I moved back and forth with the sheet, constantly halting, constantly searching for the most favorable shaft of light, stretching each sentence so to speak by carefully thinking it over. The first went: "Prisoners are forbidden to use the German greeting." It was followed by the daily program. Wake-up time at six o'clock. The cell must be tidied by seven. Morning meal. At 11:30 midday meal, at 5:30 evening meal. The bed may only be used between nineteen hours and six hours. Then: All conversation is forbidden during exercise outside. Comforting: I would be exercised outside—an interruption, breathing in fresh air. Then: Applications to the House Inspector are to be made through the warders. Comforting: I would apply for my glasses and book to be released to me, I was only in custody after all, not in prison, there was a mistake on the part of subordinate officials. Both hopes were disappointed, but both did hold up for a little while and so helped me get over the beginning. I was not allowed exercise once in the 192 hours and it was impossible to make an application via the warder. "The warder" — these were police constables, who changed two or three times, old and young, bad-tempered, coarse, indifferent, almost courteous ones, and yet it was always essentially the warder. None was brutal or even inhuman, but each one endeavored to be unapproachable, tried to have as little as possible to do with the prisoner, not at any price to deviate from the minimum he had to do according to regulations. The door was opened a crack and immediately slammed shut again. Only a couple of times did I manage to call out in time: "Officer." The replies to my request went: The first time: "Must be done in writing, ask the officer tomorrow morning, it's too late now." The second time: "Monday is writing day." The third time: "I cannot give them back to you if they were taken away from you downstairs." The fourth time (a man with a very good-natured and intelligent face): "I'll consider it." After a while he came back and held out the *Freiheitskampf*: "Do you want to read?" — "But I can't without spectacles, officer." Then he pulled the newspaper back and closed the door. The fifth time (a particularly bad-tempered one): "Instead of sweeping out your cell, you make requests: you don't make requests in prison." — "But officer, I'm in custody." — "It's all the same. You are in prison, so you don't need spectacles." I made this attempt on Thursday and its failure had an unpleasant consequence.

The house rules ended with threatened punishments. Resistance, flight or attempted suicide would result in fetters or use of weapons. My trousers slipped again, the precautionary confiscation of suspenders and tie occurred to me again. I considered how one might commit suicide in such a cell; at first it seemed almost impossible to me (the window was barred, and they had carefully felt my pockets downstairs), after that child's play. A twisting thinner pipe led away from the uppermost of the three heating pipes, and a rope could easily be thrown around these pipes from the bottom end of the bed, and the rope itself—it did not have to be suspenders, probably handkerchief or briefs would do, but a twisted sheet would certainly work admirably well. If a warder did not happen to look through the peephole at the wrong moment. But the usual times of inspection would soon be familiar to one. And the resolve to go to the limit did not have to be summoned up here.

My cell was opened: "You, go over there!" Close by my cage a gangway crossed the middle of the hall, a large clock hung here, it was almost five, I had got through the first little bit of imprisonment. On the other side, between cells, was a warders' room. There I was measured, my teeth examined, impressions taken of all ten fingers and of both hands, everything evidently exactly as the necessary particulars of criminals are taken for the rogues' gallery. But in the circumstances the two ununiformed officials displayed an almost comical kindness. One loaned me his glasses so that I could sign the statement, which did not help me much, and consoled me, saying that I would certainly get my own back soon. The other, while taking the statement, asked: "Religion Mosaic?" The word Jew, stamped as a word of abuse, was avoided. It was as if here they did not want to accept the distinction between Aryan and non-Aryan, as if they wanted to have nothing in common with the Jewish persecution by the Gestapo and were a little ashamed of it. To the question as to religion I replied: "Protestant." Surprised look: "But your identity card?" — "By law, by descent." Silence, even greater politeness than before. I returned to my cell in better heart—but it was the cell. The lock rattled again, the latch bar fell. Immediately thereafter I heard loud steps, opening of doors, then my door was also opened again and someone called out: "Coffee pot!" Two men in prison clothes came past with a large hand-barrow, one put down several slices of bread and a little piece of margarine for me, a third followed with a huge can and poured something into the brown beaker. The door slammed shut again. The feeding, three times a day, which always took the same form, became my daily timekeeper. In the evening and at night I heard the strokes of the Kreuzkirche nearby, also more distant town clocks, during the day everything was drowned out in the roar of the city noise. The prison fare in itself did not bother me. We were well into the second year of the war, the phrase scarce commodity was just appearing, and if the Aryans got little of something, the non-Aryans got nothing at all. All in all I was fed no worse in prison than at home, in fact a couple of times better than at home. Besides during the first few days I felt no hunger at all, I felt so low that I did not even miss smoking. I ate entirely out of a sense of duty, so as not to become too exhausted. Later it happened that I would have liked to have a more ample meal in the evening. But then how often did I really eat my fill at home, as I would in peacetime? No, as far as diet went prison was no new experience for me. In the morning a thin porridge was poured into the coffee pot, and with it were a quarter pound of dry bread (I knew the weights exactly from the restaurants); in the evening some kind of herbal tea was poured into the coffee pot, a good half pound of bread was distributed, together with a half ounce of margarine or a little dish of jam or a little bowl of sugar. On such pleasant occasions a thin corn coffee replaced the herbal tea; I crumbled the bread into the sweet beverage, it was a very nice meal. Admittedly it had to last me all of thirteen hours. At midday too there was occasionally the call: "Coffee pot!" and the corn coffee was poured out for us; then there was a large bowl of jacket potatoes and tiny portion of cottage cheese with it. Mostly, however, a plate of gruel was handed out, and twice there were even small whole pieces of meat and fat floating in it. Yes and on Sunday evening there was even a thick slice of headcheese beside the half pound of bread. None of it meant any kind of vicious starvation for me, no especially unfamiliar Spartan condition. It was only the utensils, the form and receptacle of the food, that bothered me. The coffee cup was simultaneously the drinking glass and the mug for brushing my teeth, the gruel was handed over in a battered tin bowl, the only item of cutlery was an old tin spoon. If the margarine or the jam was to be put on the pieces of bread, then I had to spread it with the spoon handle or pass the bread over jam and margarine. And behind the naked dining table stood the lavatory. How many hands had already passed from the lavatory seat to the table on which I placed my bread! Washed hands? How often during the day was I able to wash my own hands? The jug of water was filled morning and evening (one had to put it quickly through the crack in the door at the right moment, quickly take it back the next time the door was opened), the jug was a coffee cup, and the water also had to suffice for drinking. Nevertheless even the primitiveness and repulsiveness attached to the feeding was not a lasting torment to me. It had all not been so very different in barracks and in the dugout very much worse. I quickly grew accustomed to it; by the second day I would no longer even have noticed at all, had it not been for the opening of the door a crack and the banging shut, closing, dropping of the latch bar, which repeatedly hammered imprisonment into me. But eventually I would have got over that too. A very old Third Reich joke, told to me by the long-escaped Gusti Wieghardt, gave me real consolation. Questionnaire of the fourth Reich: "When were you imprisoned under the previous government? If not, why?" It is honorable to be imprisoned now, it will be advantageous to any future character reference. I am not guilty of anything, I am not imprisoned because of my blackout misdemeanor, but I am in prison as a Jew. Nothing can truly humiliate me, every humiliation only raises me up and secures my future. I preach it to myself again and again, and it did help a little.

The only real torment, ever increasing and impossible to deaden, was the complete absence of activity, the awful emptiness and immobility of the 192 hours. There above me went the never ending tap-tap-tap-tap. Four steps at that pace, that was less than four seconds. How many steps were there in an hour?

After the meal on Monday, when the bowl had been put outside for the first time and the jug of water taken in, when the first night had begun for me in bright daylight, the despair, which had until then been repressed, rose up. Now I had already been here for an endless time, a truly endless time. That is something that cannot be described. What with? One can convey what happened, the least event, the least thought. But endlessness consists in what lies in between, in the simple feeling of being in a cage, of emptiness, in the nothingness of the four steps to the window and of the four steps to the door, in the conscious lack of feeling. Now it was six o'clock in the afternoon, now was the time when the most tolerable part of the day usually began for us. We went into town, a meal could normally be got in the Pschorr by the Reformed Church, customers chatted to one another, we picked up this or that and indulged in speculations about the popular mood; afterward we took the E bus up the Kohlenstrasse to the Little Toll House. There over an apple juice in the Wiesengarten we looked down on the city and the heights above the Elbe [. . .]. Then the long walk home along the Südhöhe, always the beautiful view, the many flowers in the front gardens, the croaking of the frogs from the demolished brickworks down below. Then at home the swapping of the day's experiences with Kätchen, talking politics over tea, then a little reading aloud, and then it is almost twelve, and so much shopping has to be done tomorrow, and I would very much like to keep a couple of hours for my Curriculum. The day is too short, I manage nothing. And now it was six, and an empty endlessness lay behind me, and it was not yet even one of the sixteen endlessnesses that had to be coped with, because the day was over, and there was still such a long time before night began. How could I save myself from this choking emptiness? What had other prisoners done? André Chénier and Paul Verlaine wrote the most beautiful verses in prison. I am no poet, it is thirty years since I believed myself to be one, I cannot think up even the most simple rhymes. Besides even Verlaine and Chenier will only have written poetry sometimes, and surely for them also the feeling of being in a cage and of emptiness will have lain between verse and verse. What did others do, more average men? One made friends with a spider. There are no spiders here. The prisoner has to keep his cell clean, it says in the house rules. In Ponten's *Students of Lyons* one prisoner spends his time watching the pigeons on the church roof outside his dungeon and baptizes each one with a name appropriate to its personality. This is no dungeon here, but the police prison in the Polizei Präsidium, Dresden. Through the one-eighth-open drop window I can, if I strain my neck, see a couple of the uppermost window frames and battlements of the main building; there are no pigeons. A couple of times and again just now I have heard aircraft rumbling very low over the building, but they remained invisible to me. (In the days that followed I turned it into an omen for myself: If I see an aircraft, I shall be given book and spectacles; I did not see a single one.) What else? Shortly before the outbreak of war a letter from Hans Meyerhof got through to us after a bizarre round trip; he spent 18 days in custody during Hitler's visit to Italy. "How many songs I sang in my lonely cell!" I am too unmusical for that; with the few tunes that I know, I go wrong after the first bars. I have also read about people who play chess with themselves, without a chess board. I lack the ability to imagine space. What else? Others have repeated mathematical theorems or solved arithmetical problems. That I cannot manage at all. Earlier I was hardly able to work out how many cell paces there are to the hour.

Again my description is wrong, the really bad thing is missing. How many cell paces also lay between each of these approaches, how many choking attacks of emptiness? Something flickered outside, I knew immediately that the peephole flap had been pushed aside. A voice, more fatherly than imperative in tone, called out: "Go to sleep!" It was bright daylight, it could be eight o'clock at most, eight o'clock summer time. If I lay down to sleep now, would I be able to sleep the whole night through? But it was an order after all, and making the bed ready was an activity at least, and perhaps the feeling of nothingness would lessen when I lay down. I fell asleep immediately. I woke up, and it was light. I thought: Early morning, the first night is behind me. It was very still, now the clock of the Kreuzkirche struck clearly, I counted on my fingers. First the four strokes of the full hour, then another nine, no more. When I was finished counting, I suddenly saw myself in Alvenslebenstrasse, where I had lived in 1910, when Eva was in the hospital. First the room was there and only then the stinging itch on shoulder and arm, which I had not felt since. Bedbugs! without a doubt bedbugs—not mosquito, not louse, not flea, I've got experience after all, I've been in Misdroy, in the dugout and in Spain. In fact I was not shocked at all. That was part of it, was a diversion at least. At worst I would spend some time out of bed and afterward sleep more soundly out of tiredness. I looked and found nothing, I scratched myself meekly and fell asleep again. Awoke again, at least it was dark now. Noise came through the window from below. The trampling of several horses, the engine sound of several wheels and of a vehicle, voices and footsteps.

Afterward voices, footsteps in the building and opening and shutting of cells. I then heard it every evening, new prisoners were being brought in. On a single occasion there were women screaming wildly, and a threatening bellowing, otherwise everything seemed to proceed in orderly and civilized manner. I also heard the horses and engines around five. The stables of the few mounted police seemed to be next to garages down in the courtyard. In the morning a third voice regularly joined in as well, the youthful bleating of a goat. It must have loving masters or friends, it was always enticed in an affectionate tone. Listening to the sounds outside entertained me for a while, but then I said to myself: You are clinging to the sounds of life, and I felt bitter.

When I woke up for the third time, it really was day, admittedly still very early, as yet nothing was stirring in the building. My first thought was the bedbugs, my second: I don't feel them anymore, I had already ceased to feel them when the prisoners were brought in during the night. I now examined my body, my underwear, the bed. I could find nothing. No inflamed, recurrently burning patches, no traces of blood, no living creatures. To relate the rest of this unsolved puzzle immediately: Every evening after falling asleep for the first time I was awakened by the mysterious vermin. I had to scratch myself for a long time, on my arm, my neck, my leg; I saw the large swellings and felt them, they were not, for example, a nervous delusion. But when the beasts had drunk their fill, they left me in peace for the remainder of the night and for the whole day and were gone, nowhere to be found. I made up a story about them. By analogy with the PPD I called them the PBD, the Police Bug Dresden. They were surely specially bred, in the coats of police dogs, trained by Rottweilers. They had special police characteristics: They remained hidden, their ill-treatment left no lasting marks. [. . .] [But] this whole story was no more than playing at gallows humor with myself. So I gave it up, and henceforth I only concerned myself with the PBD for one hour of the night, but did so regularly. But I should be grateful to it; after lying down to rest so very early, this strenuous interruption gave me a sleep of several hours.

On Tuesday morning I felt better than the evening before. By now I had served almost 18 hours, and perhaps the proverb according to which nothing is so hard as the beginning was right after all. (In general I tended rather to believe in its rougher opposite: The worst is still to come, and indeed so it proved this time.) I told myself it was a declaration of bankruptcy if I did not feel confident of coping with 192, no 174 hours, from which the night hours were also to be deducted, from my own resources. Above all I had to free myself from the obsession of counting the hours and start the day like a normal day. Had I not for many years worked out my timetable for the day every morning? Why not today as well? Yes, but without spectacles and book! It occurred to me how I had once dictated whole essays to my wife at the typewriter without notes—I would dictate this whole prison business to her, how it had come to pass, what I experienced here outside and inside myself, I would imagine her sitting there at the table, the typewriter in front of her, and the loathsome back and forward of the four steps between window and door were my usual free pacing while dictating: I would really put every sentence in its proper, final form. Whether I then also memorized it exactly as I had dictated it, did not matter very much—as long as I got rid of the feeling of being in a cage and stopped counting the hours. I made my bed, I washed myself—there was still no sound to be heard outside—who knows how long it still was until morning rations, how much of the first 18 hours was still to run? There was the counting again—it had to be completely banished, I would be able to summon up that much self-discipline. I began in a low voice: "My long-pending police sentence was enforced in June." As properly shaped dictation I never really got beyond this sentence, although I probably started twenty times at various points. This was no free walking around, these were the four cell paces, and I was addressing the empty table and the un-flushed closet. I had already been struggling in vain for a very long time and walked myself tired, the fear of emptiness was threatening to rise up again, before eventually outside there was the call "coffee pot." The hot porridge and the bread revived me a little, I dared not relax, I had to fill myself up and keep the emptiness out, otherwise . . . no, there was no otherwise. If the fictitious dictation did not work, then I would go over my intellectual assets.

What am I working on? From 1933 the minor activities of reviews and occasional literary journalism disappeared completely, from '35 the lectures also, I was used to concentrating on a single work de longue haleine (de longue haleine does not mean long-winded—is there a corresponding German expression? Hardly. Don't digress! Really, concentrate!) First of all, therefore, my Eighteenth Century. This was torn from my hands four years ago when I was on the last tenth of it. Because of the library ban. That I cannot draw out of myself. I must have the books of the century. And that is now so far away from me that later—in itself sufficient reason not to flirt with the heating pipe, I shall have to experience it at a later date—(don't digress, concentration!)—so far away therefore, that I shall have to study my completed manuscript like a completely unfamiliar work before I can go on with it. After that came the Curriculum. It was intended to be a short little volume and a refreshing sideline to my study of English. It grew and grew even further, the study of English was displaced long ago, the Curriculum has now accompanied me every day for two and a half years, two fat volumes have now almost been filled, I am only now carefully feeling my way toward the year 1919. The professorship and the Third Reich will get a third volume of their own. I have the broad outlines of it all clear in my mind, but to work up all the details I need my diaries, just as for the 18ième I need the authors of the time. And finally there is the third opus, still half a plan, half in a state of becoming, and perhaps it engages my mind even more intensively and incessantly than the Curriculum. I work on the Curriculum at certain hours of the day, at the desk, at the typewriter, reading and writing. But the Language of the Third Reich always surrounds me and does not let me go for a single moment; while reading the newspaper at mealtimes, on the tram, I live with it, I unintentionally collect and register material for it, when I wake up in the morning it occurs to me: Didn't the gentleman next to me yesterday say. . . . Establish their spirit from their language. That must yield the most general, the most infallible, the most comprehensive description. Thus I have become a philologist after all in my old age. The expressions I have collected so far, and admittedly also tried to interpret, are drawn only from the press and everyday language, are scattered through my diary [. . .] and I also do not know exactly when I began collecting and when the plan of one day making a book out of them came to me. I shall be able to begin the real work on it only when I study the books of the main authors of the movement and I shall be able to bring myself to do that without feeling sick, only when I have survived the whole thing, when I am no longer looking at torturers at work, but dissecting their brains. But in the meantime I do go on collecting continuously, since after all I associate every day that comes with this book of the future. What will it look like in the end? I frequently play with the idea of a Dictionnaire philosophique. Individual articles have already been sketched out at length, in the diary, in letters to Martin Sussmann in Stockholm, in the Rousseau section of my Dix-huitième. Foreign words, the definite article, fanatical . . . [. . .]. That is convenient and not so monotonous, one can fall dead over it at any moment, and what has been completed is still a whole, also no one demands that a dictionary be absolutely comprehensive. But it does of necessity lead to fragmentation and repetition, it cannot be a unified whole. . . . To what extent could I produce a systematic whole out of what I had so far collected and thought, what kind of structure would it have? The historical starting point is self-evident: the collapse, the convulsions, the beginning of reconstruction 1918–19. The most characteristic catchwords of the Weimar time have to be established. They want stability, calm, a safe haven. On the other side the final exaltation of Expressionism is raging, neo-Romanticism completely politicized and turned into madness by the war. [. . .]. Safe haven and turmoil, those are the two starting points of my language of the 3rd Reich, that is the double seed from which everything else develops, which seeks sustenance for itself, sucks up and assimilates matter. Out of the need for safe haven develops the language of discipline, the language of leadership, the encroachment of military terms on literally every area of life. The "literally every" must be demonstrated point by point: politics, literature (sub-sections!), economic life, everyday life, at its most everyday and intimate . . . LTI (fine scholarly abbreviation for Lingua tertii imperii, to be used in future), LTI knows indecencies like the health inspection in barracks—no, I must not be prudish here, like the cock parade therefore. Also and very seriously to be considered is the fact that military language is more that of the barracks and of the drill book than of war. Of course the actual language of war, which has become widespread in the passage of four years, is also utilized. From here it would be possible to link up with the "turmoil" section. No, not yet. The next section will be safe haven as assertion of tradition. Assertion of a circumscribed nationality, fundamental catchphrase Blood and soil [Blut und Boden], extremely close relationship to German Romanticism. Expand the distinction, suggested in the Curriculum, between German and Teutonic Romanticism. The LTI is tyrannically governed by the Teutonic, but not in such a way that the German is eliminated, but in a way that utilizes every detail, so that the latter is contaminated by the Teutonic. As long as I am dealing with safe haven, then I am also strictly dealing with the relationship to early Romanticism. In passing on to the turmoil section I presumably simultaneously incorporate neo-Romanticism and Expressionism. Hostility to Reason, emphasis and overemphasis on volition, action, hostility to scholarship. Work through branches of scholarship and the arts in detail. Again, contaminating exploitation everywhere. Scientia ancilla theologiae. The new theology, the German faith. Romanticism does not become national only through exclusion of the foreign. It also reaches out for the foreign, to enrich its own. The foreign models for the LTI. Avowedly only Italian Fascism. But behind it stands the enemy, Russian Bolshevism. My Rousseau chapter in the Dix-huitième. Russia takes over everything technical, commercial (in the widest sense), every propaganda method from America. Italy, Soviet Russia, United States leave their stamp everywhere on the LTI, are stronger than the original German. The political model (no matter whether the Führer has read it or not) is the *Contrat social*. In this respect I must make a fundamental change in my Rousseau chapter. I said: Just as Rousseau's leader of the people addresses the city-state in the agora, so Hitler addresses everyone through the radio. There is a tremendous difference. Rousseau's man and after him the men of the French Revolution speak to an assembly of the people, which is present, they can expect objections at every moment, they are parliamentary speakers, they cannot take too much for granted, they must discuss, justify, they are checked. The new leaders speak alone, no one can contradict them, they speak in front of a silent sham parliament just as they do on the radio, they need not fear any criticism in the press, they are completely unchecked. They seek to unscrupulously stupefy a silent mass, they seek to turn the multitude of animated individuals into the mechanized collective, which they call the people and which is the mass. Out of this unscrupulousness arises the coarseness and extravagance of the rhetoric and the dominant position of rhetoric in LTI. A special chapter on abuse, on the use of the superlative. The superlative has long been usual in Italian, presumably also in Russian, certainly in the American language of advertising; it corresponds to the character of the people, and so the effect is not excessively harmful, the language has been inoculated against it. In German it encounters a body that has never before been stricken by this illness. Curse of the superlative: It must constantly outbid itself. Proof in the speeches of Hitler and Goebbels. . . . Last part: particular characteristics, uniformity of the LTI.

Very few authors shape it in their writing and speaking, the mass is taught to imitate exactly . . .

"Coffee pot!" The thin corn coffee and the jacket potatoes were passed in, it was 11:30. I sat down triumphantly at table. One whole prison day, the first eighth was over, the last three hours had passed without my thinking about the time, without my even noticing the cell at all, it was as if I had been in my study. Why should I not get through the next seven days in the same manner? But this confidence did not survive the last mouthful from the coffee pot, which only washed down the potatoes and failed to stimulate me. I was tired now, the four paces in the cage, the cell in all its details, the counting of minutes were again there. Take my afternoon nap. Where? One was not allowed to fold down the bed, also it was not very tempting. But during the war in Leipzig had I not slept away the bad hour after my meal a hundred times in the Deutsche Bücherei with my head on the censor's table? Why would that not work here? Was the little bench so much more uncomfortable than the office chair there? No, but there the activity of the rest of the afternoon, the freedom of the evening lay before me, and here the constraint of the cell, another 168 cell hours. [. . .] Complete emptiness inside me and certainly far the greatest part of the afternoon around me. The fear I had felt yesterday rose up in me again. "You must let yourself fall, uncle." I heard the voice of my nephew Walter, as he had spoken to me twenty years ago. He wanted to become an actor, he meant falling down on stage, the skillful falling down, which appears natural and does not harm the person falling. "Your limbs must be completely relaxed, you must not offer any resistance." Why did I think of that now? What made me think of applying the word metaphorically? To let myself fall into the emptiness without resisting, without fear of the nothingness, without the will to fill up the minute, the hour, without the intention of thinking? I do not know what made me think of it, I only know that from now on right through the whole week I repeatedly spoke this "You must let yourself fall" out loud like a self-hypnotic formula, and that the formula was next to no help at all. It merged with the four paces, it only half stupefied me and did not accelerate the passing of the minutes. I did not succeed in letting myself fall, nor did I manage to go on thinking coherently and logically. No more than fragments of ideas emerged, sometimes I could identify what had produced them, sometimes they were there in as incomprehensible a way as Walter's voice earlier. If I was lucky, more exactly, perhaps, if I was feeling fresher, then I was able to take up such an involuntary thought, spin it into a string of ideas, which passed some time and displaced the counting of steps, the fear of the cage, the loathing of the cage. To let oneself fall—why is it so difficult? "My good man, what do you think about all day?" the professor asked the shepherd. "I'm not so stupid that I always have to be thinking something." . . . Dr. Friedheim told me about his imprisonment (in our circles everyone has something to say about doing time, it's part of our life): "I and my cell mate told each other jokes for hours and days on end." An inferior activity? (The Nazis maintain, a specifically Jewish one. One could just as well say, a specifically French one, a specifically American one. The Germans and the English go into too much detail, don't get to the point so quickly.) An inferior talent, one that is merely a product of reason? But there is a whole philosophy, a whole psychology behind every good joke. The professor and the shepherd, behind that stands the whole mendacious Rousseau business of the sickness of thinking, of the happiness of vegetating. Vegetating is not the desire to vegetate. The professor's back to nature is flirtation, an enjoyable playacting or torment. . . . But do I think all day long? Am I not for hours, often very pleasant hours, without thoughts? Yes, but not on command, not under duress. . . . And outside, can I think if I command myself to do so? Real ideas, creative inspiration—insofar as I am granted them at all—certainly not. They are simply a matter of inspiration, not of ideas, they are suddenly there, I cannot call them up. The rest, the conscious labor of thinking, is only working up, expansion, application, technique, there are secondary activities, which occupy a half, a quarter, an eighth of the intellect. . . . Why can I not busy myself here with such an eighth-part activity. . . . Because I am here, because I come up against the damned cage, because I can smell it. Equality before the law . . . today there is no law in Germany anymore, only arbitrary power, there is also no equality anymore before arbitrary power, the Aryan pays, the Jew does time. . . . [. . .] Now I have got through a little time and was really empty, was it perhaps ten minutes or twenty? Don't count the minutes! If only the famous spider were here. But there are three flies on the table, one has probably landed in this morning's porridge, it is cleaning itself, it laboriously pulls its legs forward . . . there are supposed to be six, then one should be able to see that through a magnifying glass . . . or in a film . . . we are also forbidden to go to the cinema . . . six legs, so here each minute pulls 60 sticky legs through the repulsive slime of this . . . what? If I say cell, then the image doesn't work, if I say sojourn then it is not an image. . . . At any rate an image that came to mind, something poetic. If I could still make verses, I would need to depict in a sonnet how the minute as a sixty-footed beast presses down with its heavy, unwieldy body, slowly crawls across my breast and squeezes the breath out of me . . . original idea? Haven't I seen something similar before? Where, when? Right: That's how Magnus Zeller in Kovno drew the plague of lice in the trenches. . . . What was it like in Kovno? I have only just looked at it again for my Curriculum, I want to bring it to mind again in detail . . . I want, then everything has disappeared, fallen into the barred hole. . . . [. . .] Eva is surely right, I must have the experience of this imprisonment for the Curriculum . . . but now I have had the experience, for something like 30 hours. There remain another 162, does habituation help? I think it is getting worse and worse. . . . Let oneself fall . . . now the evening food must be here soon . . .

That was the Tuesday afternoon, objectively and in retrospect the worst part of my imprisonment. During the night, after the anticipated scratch intermezzo, I made a new decision. One did not especially need to fear the

morning; I would be capable of getting through that with coherent thinking. Thinking—about what? It didn't matter. If the dictation did not work,
if nothing more on the LTI could be found, then I would start with whatever came to mind in the morning, something has always occurred to me
in the morning. The afternoon alone was to be feared. Now I would from
the first make no effort to go on thinking in the afternoon. Instead I would
recapitulate and carefully memorize what had gone through my head so
far. Learning by heart in such a way that I could later write it down exactly. Learning by heart is, to be sure, a secondary, uncreative activity, I
should therefore manage it in the weary afternoon. I have always found it
very difficult to learn things by heart. All the better, because then it will
take up more time.

The first thing before me in the morning was another old joke. The devout vagabond sings in his cell: "Thus far in his great mercy has God led
me." The joke gripped me, against my will and all the more firmly. For
decades I have refused to indulge in all speculation about the beyond,
considering it the most useless and unedifying, not to say improper waste
of time. But here wasting time doesn't matter, rather it's exactly what matters. On the other hand, if I now "go into myself," "seek God," as happens
in old-style accounts of imprisonment, then I am playing a comic role in
front of myself or feel that my brain is going soft; and if I rebel now, blas-
pheme against God or deny God, then I find that equally comic and senile.
But I can repeat what I had to know in philosophy for my doctoral examination and what I have since then added to this area through further
study. [. . .] It looks equally bad for yes and no, for God and no God, for
a gracious and a cruel God. And what is gained, if I replace *him* by the universe or animate matter and the creation by the state of always having
been there? And what is gained, if I appeal to feeling from the position of
failing reason? I hear *He is* just as often as *He cannot be.* No, there are only
two propositions, on which I fall back again and again as the only possibility; they are not modern, they are said to be superficial and made obso-
lete by philosophy, they are said to be un-German and nowadays even
Jewish and decadent—besides Montaigne had a Jewish mother, and in his
whole thinking at least Renan had Jewish kin—there are only these two
truths for me: Que sais-je and Tout est possible, même Dieu. For everything else I have to wait and see. And the fear of waiting in vain is my only
fear of death. I do not want to delude myself. Distinguo. I shall never be
rid of the fear of death, the constriction, the recoil of the living creature;
they need not have taken suspenders and tie away from me. No nervous
breakdown would drive me to suicide. Even if I did not want to go on living at any price in order to be together with Eva for every possible remaining hour, to see the end of these criminals, to write my couple of
books, even if I did not know that I shall get out of here in six days—the
convenient heating pipe up there would represent no danger to me. But
fear of death, thoughtful not instinctive fear of the beyond, of the judge?
That is completely incomprehensible to me. Only that I shall perhaps, or

never, receive an answer to the questions, which are at present insoluble, only the thought of being extinguished torments me. And I cannot console myself either with the popular notion of dissolution in the universe, with the popular notion of deliverance from the self. I only live as my own self, only as my own self can I ask and receive an answer. . . . If only I could grasp how millions of people with the same level of education, the same mental capacity as I, hold on to real faith, with God and the beyond. Am I different from them, worse or better, more stupid or more clever, do I lack grace or do they lack it? They cannot all be conscious or self-deceiving hypocrites. . . . Perhaps I am after all more free than they are, perhaps their thinking stops short at certain inherited illusions. Am I being presumptuous, if I say on my own account that I do not stop short at any traditional idea? I think not. . . . Tormenting skepticism—pleasurable skepticism, I have dealt with it a couple of times in my History of Literature and in my lectures; for my part I have probably always been on the side of pleasure. . . . Not always, neither with pleasurable doubt, nor with doubt altogether. At the front a number of certainties with regard to Fatherland and nation were unsettled in very painful fashion. They were reinforced afterward to such an extent that I was able to build my little bit of professional life's work on them, but in the last few years they have collapsed once more, with the result that now I sometimes think this whole life's work a mistake, that I often no longer care about the possibility of continuing with my work, that ultimately it is a matter of indifference whether I kill time at my desk or here in the cell.

With that I had arrived at awareness of my cell again, at the feeling of being in a cage. But I also already had the midday food bowl, I had two full days behind me. And now I would give memorizing a chance. It worked a little bit better than the dictation, but not much better. The torment of the four paces in a state of semi-stupefaction began again. They were accompanied by a single line of poetry, which I constantly repeated: "The feeling of his nullity pierces him." I became aware of it only after a while. I remembered how on first reading it as a twelve- or thirteen-year-old I had been unable to understand it at all, simply could not disentangle it linguistically; how soon afterward I had laughed at this childish inability to understand: in the tormenting, the fatally piercing feeling of his own superfluousness or nullity—it was so simple after all. Now it had a quite different meaning for me: a cage meaning: the nothingness around me because I am cut off from everything, the nothingness inside me because I think nothing, I feel nothing but emptiness.

But then something fell in from outside. Among the sounds reaching my cell in the course of these days there had a couple of times been radio talk, now heard faintly from the street, now louder from inside the building (presumably through the open door of an office or a guardroom, but always only unintelligible fragments). I had not been at all concerned. War reports no doubt, the usual victories, the usual ridicule and abuse of enemies—of what interest was it to me in my cage? The excitement with which

I normally waited for these reports was extinguished just as was the need to smoke. But now I clearly heard drum rolls and fanfares, then, after some words, which were again unintelligible, "Deutschland über alles" and the Horst Wessel Song. So a big routine, a special announcement, some very big success. Only now did I think of the Russian campaign, which I had used to raise my spirits on the last Sunday at home—how dreadfully long ago that was. And all at once I was afraid the final victory could be Hitler's and with it his permanent rule. I raised all the objections, which I had regularly raised to his previous victories, that he was winning-himself-to-death, that the blockade was unbreakable, the internal weakness, Napoleon's end, the end of the World War—nothing helped. Or rather it did help, that is, to kill time. Seasickness on a full stomach is not as bad as on an empty stomach? Nothingness stretches the minutes more than anxiety. I went back and forward for and against Hitler's victory until I was dead tired, for and against. Then incoherence. The caged lightbulb above the door . . . a similar image a couple of months ago . . . when, where. . . . It must have been longer ago . . . still in Dölzschen . . . Eva is sitting in her favorite place by the hall window . . . she hands me a periodical, Velhagen or Westermann: but that is written with something else at the back of my mind. You say "Encylcopaedic style." An illustrated article: Jan van Leyden in the cage, which is hanging outside the cathedral. When will our Jan van Leyden . . . for the present I am in the cage. . . . The Wilhelmplatz in Berlin, where does the Wilhelmplatz come from, I haven't seen it in decades, God knows if it still looks as it did in the last century. At the corners the four elegant and warlike generals of Frederick the Great with pigtails. One was called Winterfeldt, and the so gentle von Schulzendorf showed him to me and said he was related to him, and then I too felt a sense of belonging, for we were form-mates at the French Grammar School, and the Seven Years War was very much on my mind, and I was fighting it on the Prussian side—naturally, what other side was there . . . I cannot explain why he should have come to mind, but I fell asleep over General Winterfeldt.

On Thursday all politics, all program-making for the day had disappeared and I felt only a horrible exhaustion. I would most of all have liked to stay in bed. That was forbidden. Walking back and forth was too tiring. So, just as a prisoner should, I sat on the edge of the wretched little bench, my elbows on the wretched table, my face between my fists. My beard, unshaven since Monday, chafed and itched, I had been able to see my face a little in the water of the washbasin—truly a convict. Only the prison clothes were missing—but the tucked-up trousers with the pleats all wrong and the collar without a tie! I would not want any acquaintance to see me in this state of degradation. I, the professor, the senator, the state commissioner, with an entry in the Brockhaus Encyclopedia. One's self-esteem cannot be injured from outside? Talk! I can feel how injured it is, after all. Just as I feel my unshaven face. And I cannot smell too good either. Has the hygienic closet been flushed at all yet today? I cannot remember having thought anything else that whole morning. Perhaps because of the stifling heat. I must also mention as extenuating circumstance for what followed, that in the morning my daily request for my glasses had been finally and particularly rudely rejected. The cell door was opened at an unusual time, immediately after the midday meal. "Come out." Outside, fairly far away, on the nearside narrow gangway of the gallery, my wife was standing beside a white-bearded clerk. She looked very refined with the unaffectedly proud bearing, which she never loses. I should have been glad. Instead I was only dismayed. What was she doing here in these vile surroundings, why did she need to see me in this ignominy? The trousers, the collar without a tie, the smell. "Why have you come here?" I asked as I approached her, "I cannot help you in any way, I am quite helpless"—and more softly—"completely helpless, my glasses have been taken away." I immediately regretted this greeting, but that made me even more resentful. My wife was completely calm; she said, it's about the renewal of the food ration cards, the Jewish Community will not hand them out for the two of us, until mine are presented. I should have informed her of the whereabouts of my cards, I should have said how the Community was to be put off until my return, I should have . . . Only in my cell did all the things I should have said to my wife occur to me. And above all what I should not have said to her. But I only said again and again, I was helpless, and the Community had no right to hold back my wife's cards, and I was not pleased to see her here, and she would have to take care of everything herself until Tuesday, and I could not help at all. She listened to me with a calm face, but I could see that her arm was trembling. Then I felt sick at my lack of control, sick and afraid. "Until Tuesday then," I said, "take care," kissed her glove and ran back into the cell. On this Thursday I no longer suffered from nothingness, my time was full, amply and bitterly. At first only with reproaches at my momentary failure. Why had I not soberly provided the necessary information, why had I burdened her with my state of mind instead of assuring her, as was the truth, that I was not being treated brutally? The reproaches did not stop there. On the coming Sunday we would be together for 37 years, it would truly be the first wedding anniversary we had not spent together. Always, even in 1905! in the year of Roman exile, even during all the separations of the war years, it so turned out that we were able to spend June 29 together. We recently resolved to celebrate it all the more heartily after the event. Among all private and public red-letter days it has always been the real day of celebration for us, it has always filled me with the greatest gratitude to Eva. But also with a certain pride, a certain self-congratulation. I have always considered myself the most faithful, the most solicitous husband. I have always seemed glorious to myself on this one point of love and faithfulness. What remains of this splendid halo, when I reexamine my life? Where is the merit of love and faithfulness, if one finds everything, really everything that one has been looking for? A remark of poor Sonja Lerch occurred to me (no wonder that I thought of her in the cell): "He and I, we do not work together, with work only one person comes first and the other is always secondary." At the time I had thought, the poor people—Eva and I, we also have work in common. All these years I had taken it for granted that my writing came first, I had taken Eva's music making for granted as a pleasant sideline. How much was my love worth, when in Leipzig your musical need came more keenly to the fore with the urge to stand on an equal footing with my philology? I was only able to free myself of my egoism after hard inner struggle, and this struggle was not only an inner one, I allowed you to suffer from it for a long time. I was deplorably jealous of your music. Jealous love is a contradictio in adjecto—jealousy is the opposite of love, is envy, is selfishness. And then, in the twenties, how great was my sympathy when illness and accident expelled you from your true profession? It was considerable certainly, as considerable as sympathy can be, and that is not very great; but was I not often also jealous of your depression, did I not sometimes think back to our early days, when a single interest was enough for us? Each time I thought of what now stood in the way of our working together as completely as we had once done, each time I reproached myself forcefully for my egoism. And then, as you searched ever more desperately for a substitute for the music that was slipping away from you, for your reduced mobility, when it was a question of the garden, of a house of our own, how long did I resist, how belatedly—and almost too late—give way. Why? And suddenly my pride, which I had nourished the day before, collapsed. The villa! And I had believed myself free of the bonds of traditional ideas. A villa is something altogether unrespectable, is hubris, if it is not backed up by a very fat bank balance. How often did you calculate for me the possibility of building a simple house with limited financial means, how often list the practical advantages of a house of our own, how often point out to me all the houses being built by petit bourgeois clerks! The fantasy of a villa instilled in me the fear that it would be my downfall, the fear of financial entanglements and burdens held me back again and again. Can I grant myself extenuating circumstances, did this grappling with my own fear, did your depression perhaps cause me just as much suffering as it did yourself? Or are these only excuses? It's easy for Catholics, they fetch absolution for themselves. It's easy for anyone who can fetch forgiveness for himself somewhere. But if one settles accounts with oneself, forgiveness is self-deception. Can the intention, to do better in the future, help me? First of all, it is very questionable whether I still have a future (at 60 and in the clutches of the 3rd Reich), second, doing better never wipes out what one has done badly before, and third—I have always told myself that the opposite of every proverb is also true (the first step is always the easiest; you can teach an old dog new tricks . . .), but one, about the road to hell being paved with good intentions, is absolutely to the point. . . . Just don't miss the strokes of seven o'clock! Just get to bed and to sleep as soon as it is allowed, only scratch myself afterward when I have fallen asleep again! I awoke with a heavier burden on my soul than the day before. Today I would not defend myself against the nothingness,

I would be happy if I were able to doze away quite without thoughts. And then quite unexpectedly came the relief, the reversal of my whole situation and mood. Behind the coffee-pot bearer stood a turnkey, the very same policeman who had recently shouted "Clear off" at me at the counter, the only one who had treated me brutally during these days. "Do you want to be shaved?" he asked. "Please," I replied, and the mere prospect of getting rid of the beard was a small pleasure. But curiously the constable did not slam the door shut, but looked at me thoughtfully for a couple of seconds. "You are, you were professor at the TU—what are you actually inside for?" — "Blackout." — "So, as an absent-minded professor, you no doubt had to pay a fine half a dozen times before that?" — "No, it was the first oversight in one and a half years." — "Impossible." Pause. "Ah, then you are non-Aryan?" He looked almost sad. I spontaneously took advantage of the situation: "Officer, it is dreadfully hard for a professor to walk around here without any occupation whatsoever. I've been doing it for four days now. Book and glasses were taken away from me. But if I only had a pencil and a little paper." — "But you are supposed to be reflecting on your sins," he said laughing. Then he took a little pencil out of his pocket and looked at it. "I'll sharpen it and add a sheet of paper." He really did bring both immediately afterward. At that moment my life was just as much transformed as when the prison door slammed shut. Everything was lighter again, indeed had become almost light. Suddenly I realized that at midday of this Friday I would have the whole first half of my sentence behind me. Only another four days, and what was so terrible about them, now that I could occupy myself in almost accustomed manner? I could get a few notes down on paper even without spectacles, a great deal could be retained that way. And if nothing more occurred to me—then there were always the games of my days in Leipzig, making up words from one given word, geographical names. All morning long I did not need to use the pencil at all, simply making plans, the simple consciousness of possessing it filled me entirely. The remorse of the previous day had become much lighter, in fact it had disappeared entirely; in four days we would be together again—a great deal could be made better after all, extenuating circumstances and forgiveness were not worthless after all, and yesterday I had perhaps painted myself in colors that were too dark. Even after the midday meal, the pencil still remained unused for a while, being shaved was an event to be feasted on. It was not only that liberation from the tormenting stubble was a pleasure, the whole procedure was a boon. I had to go down to the entrance hall, have the 15 pfennigs for the barber given to me from my surrendered wallet, I then had to go up to the fourth floor, where the master and one assistant were working in the gallery. I had not seen so much for a long time, I had never before looked at the prison at such length. We, clients and convicts (few in prison clothing, all without suspenders and collar—only I had mine and had clung to it), stood six feet apart leaning against the wall between the cell doors; we were forbidden to talk to one another, we were forbidden to lean against the railings, but one could follow the constant activity in the building, the women's floor at the very top with its robust female warders drew the most glances, one could appraise one's neighbors (I could discover no criminal face, I did not have the impression that I was in bad company), it was simply change, it was life. I would gladly have had more men in line ahead. Again, as recently, I thought "cinema." But now I remembered Addison's theory that drama gave pleasure in that one experienced terrible things and at the same time knew that one was safe. Previously I had rejected that as a comically trite misunderstanding of catharsis, which consists precisely of really identifying with and living through [the events of the drama]; I now thought that the man was probably not so very far wrong. Not until later in the afternoon did I pick up the pencil—my first note, longer and more laden with pathos than all that followed, went: On my pencil I climb back to earth out of the hell of the last four days. Afterward I limited myself to single words. The white sheet of paper the constable had given me lasted only through Friday. Then I used the available toilet paper; it was thin and yellow and absorbed the pencil marks to the point of (at least provisional) illegibility. That meant a considerable restriction of my ability to pass the time. But even apart from that I was soon no longer quite so certain if the pencil really made the time go more quickly. And even now, when I think back, I cannot say with certainty if I got through the second part of my sentence more quickly than the first half. For sure, the feeling of deliverance still halfway held on the Friday and even for a couple of hours on Saturday. I made notes as precisely and as concisely as I could, always searching carefully for the most succinct and comprehensive catchword, before I put the precious stump to paper, for it was not certain whether a guard would sharpen the blunted stump for me, he could just as well take the forbidden writing material away from me—I noted down the content of the previous days; already I could no longer remember everything, an undifferentiated, excruciating eternity lay behind me. Then I turned to the games of my Leipzig days. How many words can be formed from tree frog, how many towns and rivers do I know beginning with the letter R. This did not hold my interest for long, after all the best thing about the childish game had been who could complete the longest list within a given time. I hit on a variant: How many famous names beginning with the same letter could I think of? I tried A: Alfieri, Alighieri, Andersen . . . Antonescu, the leader and army commander of the Romanians by Hitler's grace, who in ten years time will be remembered at most by the specialist scholar. Was that all? Had imprisonment so numbed my memory, was the knowledge contained in my head so modest? One should check how much of one's supposed knowledge is really present (put in business terms: is available from stock). Exercise: Which of Schiller's plays could I accurately and unhesitatingly summarize? *The Robbers?* Only very incompletely. What exactly is Amalie's role? *Fiesco?* Nothing whatsoever. Most easily perhaps *Wallenstein* and *Don Carlos.* But I do not remember the Eboli conspiracy clearly. Similar result with

Goethe, with Kleist . . . Am I uneducated? The old witticism: Being educated means knowing where to look things up. Entirely accurate; reduced
to a serious and succinct formula: Education is the ability to orientate oneself. . . . At the beginning of the semester I should like to present my seminar students with this exercise: "In the next ten minutes write down all
the famous names that occur to you, no matter from which area (sports or
literature or film or war, no matter from which country, which time)"—
then I would immediately know exactly what kind of students I was dealing with. . . . The tremendous break in the education of the generations,
contemporary youth are completely alien to me (certainly so completely
because I have no children). Certainly classical and scientific-technical education were already diverging in my day, but something of the classics
was required of everyone who considered himself educated, and the
scientific-technical was still usually considered professional knowledge.
And now, one has to know about the engine of a car and of an airplane,
one has to know something about the radio, otherwise one is truly uneducated, truly unable to orientate oneself. I feel it every day, it's no flirta-
tious Rousseau confession with a "Please, contradict me!" behind it, it is
the naked truth. And a classical education is regarded with a shrug of the
shoulders, at best with sentimental astonishment. [. . .] "Coffee pot!"
That was probably the best thing about my pencil, the knowledge that it
was there saved me from the obsessive search for thoughts. If nothing occurred to me, or if I was irritated because my mind was wandering, then I
could at any moment return to my word game again; I did not need to be
afraid of emptiness anymore, and so I no longer felt empty. Once the word
game had completely lost its modest charm, I fell to making up puzzles.
Words, whose letters are replaced by numbers, have to be guessed; if one
puts the decoded words in a certain order, then their first letters reveal a
particular quotation. That filled up the Sunday in particular, our June 29,
since I made an effort, though only half successfully, to make sure that the
self-torture of the Thursday was not repeated. I made up a puzzle as anniversary present, the first letters formed an early expression of affection
in our family language, 1,2,9,3—the philosopher at the beginning of the
series was of course Kant, because his statue stood in front of Königsberg
University and on the first picture postcard, which you sent to me from
Königsberg in July 1904. I followed it up with a longer and more complicated puzzle, which involved the war: 23 geographical names gave the
conclusion of a soldiers' song, which had been sung in 1914 and now had
a topical meaning again. The solution went: "Victorious we shall conquer
France, Russia and the whole wide world."

Now that I put down all these pastimes, I think there can be no doubt at
all that I found the lead-pencil half of my sentence much easier than what
had preceded it. And I also felt this relief again and again. And yet I certainly know that the minutes of the final days crept by on legs that were
even more slimy and bore down on me almost more oppressively than
those of the first days. I could accuse myself of presumption a hundred

times, I could console myself a hundred times, only another 80 hours, only another 79, it was no good. I was often so worn down that I felt more wretched than at the beginning.

The pencil really had made a profound difference to me. On Friday I had spooned up my midday meal for the first time without feeling completely full, afterward I had missed smoking for the first time, and in the evening I had lain down to sleep feeling real hunger and already tormented because I was unable to smoke. And the cell had smelled worse than before, and its walls had pressed in on me more than before. I had certainly clambered up out of hell on my pencil—but not as far as earth itself, only as far as limbo. I had only been liberated to the point where I felt the absence of complete freedom more strongly than when I was completely trammeled. If a few hours were more filled, the gaps between them yawned all the more emptily. I had hoped that the knowledge of having the second half, the mere remainder of the sentence before me, would help. It did not help at all. Only another three days, only another two? But that was still another three, two eternities. Also there was no getting used to it, on the contrary. In particular the afternoons seemed to stretch out more oppressively from day to day. My old subject: imagination and knowledge. Because I know about the length of this afternoon, know and fear it in advance, it gets more terrible each time. It is exactly the same as with the great highway between the Cape Verde Islands and Pernambuco. Because I knew that for nine whole days we would see only water and sky, the endlessness of the ocean made me happier than at other points at which it appeared just as boundless to my gaze. Because I now know how mercilessly slowly hour after hour drags itself toward evening, each one torments me more than at other times. [. . .] The French estheticians say that the French ear is unable to grasp more than 12 syllables as a unit of verse. Likewise I was unable to get beyond the unit of 48 hours. I told myself on Saturday: Now Sunday has almost begun, and on Sunday: Now it will soon be Monday, and then you will be on the brink of freedom. But even on Monday I did not feel the hoped-for anticipatory pleasure—after all, a great highway still lay before me, and I was so infinitely weary of it.

Tuesday arrived at last. I awoke with a feeling of fear, which I could not laugh away and only continued growing. What if they didn't release me. . . . If I had been forgotten in the great machinery, if some error had been made in the lists! How long would it take the subordinate officials to correct such an error in accordance with the rules—dear God! Or if I am placed in the hands of the Gestapo . . . With my J card I come under the jurisdiction of a special department. Or if meanwhile they have carried out another house search (how many now?) and this time someone has taken an interest in my manuscripts? This fear could not be laughed away and not argued away. It was so strong that the pencil did not help me at all. I only counted the passing of the seconds and minutes by the four paces, I was not capable of anything else, it was almost worse than the distant beginning. I had to be released at 11:30. I heard the steps outside and the opening and shutting of the cells for the midday meal. 11:30 therefore. Would I still receive my bowl, would I be able to get out immediately? The door was opened a crack as on the other days, the bowl passed in, the door locked again, double with key and latch. I shouted: "Constable, constable!" Calm voice from outside: "What's the matter?" — "Constable, I am being released at 11:30." — "It's a long time till 11:30." The man was not angry, not surprised, I need not be afraid, only wait a little while longer. I ate my porridge with a feeling of bliss. But now it must really be 11:30, no one came, and my fear returned and mounted to a furious palpitation. And then at last, I had not heard any steps, the latch was raised again, the lock turned back—I shall never again say the words "under lock and key" without emotion, as mere cliché: "Take your things with you, go downstairs." From this moment on everything was again and now too completely "cinema." How I was given my suspenders and tie again and put them on, how I sat on the same bench as eight days before and observed everything around me, while I waited for the certificate of discharge. Beside me sat two boys weeping bitterly. "What's the matter with you Polacks," asked a policeman with rough good humor, "no one's going to eat you." They did not understand him, an interpreter was fetched and comforted them. "They're only children," he said, "fifteen years old—they were with a farmer, with the horses, they couldn't manage the work." It did not become clear to me whether they were now being held prisoner here or were to be conveyed from here to other labor service. I felt sorry for them. — Really? Oh Addison, oh freedom. I was given my certificate, the outside door opened—the Polish boys were forgotten. I stepped onto the street, the sun was shining. My wife was waiting on the other side.

A couple of days of feeling absolutely happy. What was the war, what was the usual oppression to me? I was free, we were together. In the Jews' House I allowed myself to be fêted a little as a kind of martyr, I allowed myself to be looked after a little; I needed it, I had become a little haggard, and my nerves were not quite right. Then, spreading out my notes, I began this record. The further I got with them, the more my experience, my suffering dwindled away. No half measure, a fearfully whole thing I think I called it at the beginning. And what was it in the end, what torments did I report? How can it be compared with what is experienced by thousands upon thousands in German prisons today? Everyday life in prison, no more, a bit of boredom, no more. And yet I feel that for myself it was one of the most agonizing times of my life.

July 8

[. . .] The clichés about the Russians from before 1939 have been resumed again with a part comical, part sickening suddenness and comprehensiveness: people dead with hunger, atrocities, the fiendish Jew, sub-humans, even the "crime, to be allied with them." [. . .]

Since the day before yesterday I have been making a typewritten copy of my days in prison. They are fading as I do so, they are already remote.

Half apathetic puzzling over the Russian war and how much longer it will last. I consider it certain that Petersburg and Moscow will fall next week at the latest. [. . .]

July 9

[. . .]

Latest Jewish decree: They are not allowed to use the popular Elbe steamers.

Toward evening

News: USA occupies Iceland. That seems like direct entry into the war. We are experiencing world war for the second time. Knowing more and *with the other side.* Perhaps, probably, it is the greatest good fortune to experience so much world history. But shall we survive it? There is tremendous Jew-baiting. Litvinov–Wallach–Finkelstein is back again this evening too. Is there a pogrom in the offing? The government must be desperate, and desperadoes . . .

July 12, Saturday morning

Eva's birthday, the second in the Jews' House. Very oppressive heat, very depressed mood. I have been tormented since yesterday: What if Hitler does now finally win? Hochgemuth's version (cigars, lottery agent, freemason, anti-Nazi). Russia will be smashed militarily by the end of August, a line drawn east of Moscow, vast amount of land occupied. *That* is where they'll stop. (And so they'll have new triumphs, prospect of abundant food, free hand. Things can therefore go on for years.) — Brief congratulations from Annemarie. It is two years since she came to see us. My reserves with her will last until October. What then? [. . .]

Sodom and Gomorrah: Frau Paul; Kätchen Sara sat at our breakfast table, which *she* had decorated in petit bourgeois style for the birthday, flowers and little presents around Eva's plate, and talked. We have known her friend, Frau Paul, for a long time, a comical, good-natured, quite likable character. Very presentable woman in her fifties. Involved in a disagreeable divorce from her fourth husband, a drunken retired teacher (gambler). Her third husband was a respected businessman, Jew, he was the only one with whom she had been happy, he left her a villa and money, went to pieces in '34 because of the Jew-baiting. Suicide. She has a daughter by her first or second husband. The child's father was not completely Aryan, the Renate we know is not quite Aryan either. But she has been passed off as Aryan so as to be able to marry, her husband is a "one hundred and fifty percent" Nazi (one hundred and fifty percent—Lingua T.I.). Frau Paul has to let a room of her house, the case costs money, she would like a pensioner best. An old retired tax official is the best payer of those replying to the advert. The man informs himself about her, demands to know whether any non-Aryan daughter is present. She provides the information, she takes the tenant, precisely this one; not because she is forced to, but simply because he is the best payer. She says he is a very friendly tenant. Even if he hangs an oil painting of the Führer on the wall and puts a picture of Hitler on his desk. ("Himmler," says Frau Voss, "is not so bad—it's no more than a tear-off calendar picture!") How much more decent is the Widow of Ephesus. Whore is not the word for it. Whore of whores. And yet the woman is entirely anti-Nazi and very good-natured. But the tenant pays. And the tenant himself is supposed to be a good man, even a philo-Semite—but he fears for his pension.

July 13, Sunday morning

In part for my release from the PPD, in part for Eva's birthday, Lissy Meyerhof had sent a tiny amount of coffee and tea. (Her American relatives!) A remnant of it yielded two cups, one for Eva, one for Kätchen Sara, a glass of apple juice for me. That was the birthday party. In the evening the three of us sat in Hoppe's at the Neustadt railway station. Afterward on Frau Kreidl Sr.'s relatively cool garden veranda on the ground floor. Her son Paul there. He is now working on a highway on the border of Silesia and Saxony, comes for weekend leave every two weeks. I asked him what he sees, hears, thinks. He judges the situation in the East very differently from me. We were suffering tremendous losses, had underestimated the Russians' power of resistance, they appeared to be opening an attack on the oil wells in Romania, in terms of troops and also of armaments they were inexhaustible, they were not going to be overrun this summer. That seemed plausible to me for a while. Early this morning I awoke with the same conviction of a swift German victory as I had had before listening to Kreidl's speech. For days our military bulletins have been saying: "Operations are proceeding according to plan." Today, Sunday, there will certainly be—Goebbels' Sunday habit—to the accompaniment of fanfare, drum roll, Deutschland über alles and Horst Wessel Song the *special announcement* of a new triumph. The "curse of the superlative" has now also usurped the military bulletins. Last year phrases like "the greatest air battle," the greatest bombardment of all time, etc. were not included in the actual military bulletin. This time the report itself states: Bialystok-Minsk, *"the greatest battle of encirclement and attrition in world history."* — They are also searching (but in vain in pure linguistic terms) for means to intensify the newly revised Jewish-Bolshevist section. "Blow against the fortress of Judah" is the title of an article in the *Dresdner Anzeiger.* In it Stalin is on his fourth Jewish wife, Molotov (now Molotov as well, who was received in Berlin with Soviet flags and guard of honor!) has a wife with Jewish relatives.

[. . .]

In the newspapers for the first time in this war many announcements of deaths in the field. Noteworthy is the decreasing use of the formula "For Führer and Fatherland." (Also noteworthy, and that already for some time, the increasing frequency of "Good morning" and "Good-bye."

July 14, Monday morning

The dreaded Sunday special announcement came and exceeded all expectations. Stalin Line taken, in the south considerable forward advance from Romania (from Romania, away from the oil center, which was supposed to be under threat). Emphasis, and rightly so, evidently, that the war against Russia has been decided, that Hitler can carry on the war for years, that he is invincible master of the whole continent. Asia will be added to Europe. For us in a personal sense that means slavery until the end of our lives. Very depressed evening. On top of the catastrophic news there was the most extreme sultriness and, as usual on a Sunday, the food was especially gruesome and miserable. Nothing edible at Pschorr, other restaurants shut, finally the Neustadt railway station packed and suffocatingly hot.

[. . .]

July 16, morning

Shock effect of Sunday partly overcome—but only partly. Hitler will come to an end (there is talk of very heavy losses, of very poor internal morale, imminent USA), but it will take a *very long* time.

Yesterday evening at the stop for the D bus here, Fjodor Stepun (we both had to rack our brains for a long time for his name until Eva, not I, remembered it) greeted us cordially and quite naturally. I had seen him frequently in the meantime and avoided him, his role after all is ambiguous, although he retired a long time ago. He vacillates, he *must* vacillate between support for and opposition to the regime. He is Russian, was a Russian officer in the World War, worked in the Kerensky government, fled from the Bolsheviks (and was brought to Dresden by Kroner, the Teutonic Jew). More the born, involuntary actor than ever. In every movement of his big body, his broad face with its silvery fringe of hair under a floppy hat, in every note of his always loud and all too expressively declamatory voice. To the bus conductor no less than to us. The character actor, who behind a good mask plays the philosophizing Russian. — So yesterday his first and frequently repeated word was "complicated." How was he? "Complicated." What does he think of the situation? "Complicated." He said: The Germans will probably reach the Urals. They are meeting stronger resistance than expected, but the Russians lack generalship, Stalin had the best commanders shot. The Germans had already allocated every post of a Russian government along the lines of the Pétain regime. In the conquered territory, therefore, a government completely compliant with the German wishes would be set up, which would concede and deliver absolutely everything to Hitler. (He spoke contemptuously of Pétain, "he even handed over Thyssen" — on the other hand he is of course a friend of the émigrés now returning, enemy of the Bolshevists [. . .]. He is indeed in a "complicated" situation.) Germany will now obtain all the raw materials it needs in order to conduct the war against England. But the struggle will be prolonged for years, the outcome was impossible to predict, since the USA would undoubtedly intervene actively. The occupation of Iceland would now be followed by the landing of American troops in Ireland and Scotland . . . Then he talked about himself. He is working on an autobiography (of course!) "on broad foundations," it is intended to be a piece of Russian history. (I am sure that he will succeed.) He obtains books from Prague and several other places. So he has an advantage over me when it comes to library use; however, he is not allowed to publish either, because he has not been accepted by the Reich Chamber for Literature. — Was he still in touch with university people? Yes, with Janentzky and Kühn. Had I read Kühn's "little book on the meaning of the war"? I: "No—ever since he discovered the Nordic spirit of Frederick the Great, I no longer care to be instructed by him." Janentzky was working "on the tragic." He's been doing that for decades, it is the most imposing and deceptive impotence, mask: ponderousness and depth and laborious bringing to the light of all that is heavy, I also fell for him for years. Janentzky and Kühn are perhaps my deepest disappointments in matters German. At bottom they are both mendacious and fickle. Stepun is not so bad: Slav and an actor by nature, he does not fake, he plays himself. He is an amusing character. According to Stepun, Kühn, who always had a thing about Luther, is now lecturing on *Germanness and Christianity*. If he is allowed to give such a lecture course now, then it *must* be a betrayal of Germanness and Christianity . . . I: My situation is not complicated, but unambiguously bad, I do not know whether I shall be able to bear it much longer. He, not maliciously, undoubtedly from experience, but with the full pithy tone of his well-molded pronouncements: "The plebeian soul of man can bear so much." The word "simple" is missing from Stepun's dictionary.

[. . .]

July 18, Friday

LTI. Military bulletin of the seventeenth from the East: "Nine million are facing one another in a battle whose scale surpasses all historical imagination." Bialystok was recently "the greatest battle of attrition and annihilation in world history." Curse of the superlative, Barnum—cf. the style of the army reports in 1914.

Mood, situation? Food supply ever more difficult. No potatoes, now even we J-people have received a once only extra allowance of a pound of rice each. Our evening hunt for food ever more difficult. Neustadt railway station is so far away, takes up the whole evening. In the Pschorr yesterday at 6:15: our waiter, made sleek by many tips: the meat dumplings were finished, nothing else without meat coupons. In response to my entreaty: Did we want potatoes in horseradish sauce? We wanted. There then arrived *one* dumpling between the two of us, as well as very many new potatoes. Together with the kale soup (the "regular") and a little green salad ("scarce commodity") I then paid 3M. A gentleman beside us, "respectable gentleman": In two weeks all the difficulties will have been overcome and everything will be available in abundance. — ? — "It's just a matter of transportation—the battles in the East." — "And in two weeks?" — "We'll have finished them off, we'll have reached the Urals and the rolling stock will be free again." — How many people calculate, believe like him? Millions perhaps. The same millions who a year ago said: "Hitler will speak in London on August 1." The same people who said a month ago: "Our troops have been passing through our ally Russia for a long time. We have transit rights, Persia and India are the target." But how many millions are disappointed, embittered? Yesterday evening Kätchen Sara read out a letter from her brother-in-law Voss (the school man and Catholic) in Cologne. Constant clearing of monasteries. How was it possible that they could incense the believing population in such a fashion in this war, in which so many are suffering? The English planes were now coming night after night, there was much devastation in Cologne, "half of Münster flattened," Aachen destroyed in part.

July 19, Saturday morning

A pattern can now be established in the military bulletins. Throughout the week a slow winding up of tension: "Operations are going according to plan. . . ." "Favorable developments. . . ." "Great successes are in the offing. . . ." Each time accompanied by sentences (cf. July 18), which underline the tremendousness of the absolutely unprecedented world historical events. — Then, on Sunday afternoon, the "special announcement": Drum roll. . . . "There will now be a special announcement." . . . Another drum roll, fanfares, another pause. . . . At last. . . . Afterward the "Songs of the

Nation." All of that has been the fixed order for a long time now. For how much longer will it work? — Yesterday Hochgemuth, my cigar dealer, who is also lottery agent and freemason: Heavy losses, returning soldiers say prisoners are only taken at divisional strength, smaller units, even the wounded, are shot down—the Russians are fighting fiercely and are not giving any quarter either. "It's medieval. . . . But for God's sake be careful. My sales assistant is married to a Gestapo man. . . . I would not want to make trouble for anyone."

I now know why my piece, "Cell 89," on which I have been working since September 6, does not work. It is neither fish nor fowl, it is partly supposed to be a diary, partly already a finished part of the Curriculum, and the one gets in the way of the other.

July 20

Language. Latest words: *Scarce commodity.* For the month of July Jews also have received household cards. Scarce commodities are explicitly *not* supplied on these. They are valid only for potatoes. Vegetables, lettuce, lemons are "scarce commodities."

July 21, Monday

For years I was sanguine and Jewry around me was blackly pessimistic. Now it is quite the reverse. I am shocked by the victories in Russia, although I foresaw them and took them into account—they are too great and overwhelming. The Jews on the other hand. . . . For example Frau Kronheim yesterday, with whom we ate in a newly discovered little garden café in Königsbrücker Strasse—Hitler had lost the war. The most recent, very solid-sounding rumor: Japan had dropped out of the Triple Pact. (In the newspaper there was only: Change of cabinet in Japan, internal and foreign policy remain unchanged.)

[. . .]

"Cell 89" finished yesterday, almost 17 typewritten pages. I must read it out, in order to get an overall view. Work took exactly 14 days (but with what distractions!). Toward evening: Read "Cell 89" aloud all morning. Eva says it can be incorporated into the Curriculum as it stands, as a "novella," it was "a little work of art." The thing as a whole also makes a very good impression on me. That is a comfort. So now on with the long-interrupted copying of the Front chapter.

LTI. Characters. Today an article about the new "symbol" **V** = Victoria introduced a couple of weeks ago. On all locomotives and squares of the Protectorate of Bohemia and Moravia, in Holland, etc. Put next to Y and ⚡⚡ .

Frau Katz said recently: "Every Jew has his Aryan angel." This afternoon at Paschky's. Tins of sardines are being given out for the food coupons. "Your card, professor." — "That section has been cut off." — The man stiffens, mutters softly: "But that's . . . ," goes over to the fish counter and cuts me a piece of the extremely scarce and rare stock. At Vogel's I got a loaf without coupons. Uplifting, successful shopping day. But Fräulein Zwiener refused me tobacco. "Only to established customers, to those who have been 'registered.' " The usual joys and sorrows of shopping. When I come back, laden, squeezed into the bus, the rush begins for Eva. Everything has to be cooked immediately, so that the milk, the little bit of meat and fish don't go bad. In the meantime it's six o'clock. If we arrive in town now, most things have been crossed off the menu. But the fat reserve would not stretch to cooking at home, would result in *even* more dishes to wash and pots to scour.

July 23, Wednesday morning

LTI: "Jews unwelcome—Jews prohibited." In all restaurants with formula 1: [sign] de rigueur and milder [enforcement]. Formula 2: strict observance, disregard results in punishment. We no longer take offense at formula 1, it is unavoidable and well-worn. — Yesterday, in search of an evening apple juice: Toll House: "Shut on Tuesday." Café Weinberg: "Closed because of call-up" (sign on ever more shops, restaurants, etc.). Moreau Tavern: "Jews prohibited" (Seems to be a new sign, we were there a couple of times before.)

Situation with regard to Russia and USA puzzling. Abuse of Jews more immoderate, more repulsive than ever.

July 26, Saturday afternoon

LTI. Sunny. Our sunny, noble son . . . The sunny father of our little daughter . . . My sunny husband . . . In every third death notice, especially with the heroes' deaths (where, moreover, the "For Führer and Fatherland" is becoming less frequent. We count how often simply "For the Fatherland"). Perhaps a specifically Saxon (petit bourgeois) nonsense [. . .]. Every little Mötzsch and Zschiesche here is called Horst and is "sunny." Perhaps it goes back to the film *Sonny Boy* [German title of *The Singing Fool,* starring Al Jolson], but it's in a line with Baldur von Schirach. Emphatically Germanic affirmation of life—sun wheel—swastika. [. . .]

July 27, Sunday

Advance into Russia appears to have come to a standstill; everyone knows or spreads rumors about heavy German losses, the military bulletin [. . .] is economical and not triumphant.

New regulations about immigration into the USA. Our affidavit (which we have received twice!) is thereby invalid—the new procedure means effectively that it will be impossible to get out in any foreseeable future. That suits us entirely. All vacillation is now at an end. Fate will decide. As long as the war lasts we *can* no longer get out, *after* the war we shall no longer need to, one way or another, dead or alive.

Notification of the confiscation of typewriters. It *seems* for the time being only to concern businesses, not private persons. But Jewish private persons. . . . It will end as with the lamented car. Someone sees the typewriter here, and the next day I am rid of it. It would or will mean a heavy loss. Who can read my handwriting?

[. . .]

July 30, Wednesday

Eva's *Aryan clothing card.* This time as last year had 250 points, of which Eva used eleven for herself (a piece of material, forced on her by me, for her birthday). Everything else went to non-Aryans. Much of it in Denver: Frau Breit's woolen dress for the journey to the USA by way of Siberia and Japan. Much to Frau Voss. A coat for Lissy Meyerhof on her visit in April. The day before yesterday Lissy gave the last eleven points to her Aunt Sophie in Frankfurt, whose ninetieth birthday was celebrated in May. Aunt Sophie is said to be very hale and hearty, very concerned with her appearance. She lives in her dressing gown, collar and cuffs of the much loved garment have suffered from the passage of time. Since May, Frankfurt, Berlin, the whole of Germany has been searched for 32 inches of quilted silk. Thanks to Eva's clothing card, Lissy found what was necessary here.

[. . .]

August 3, Sunday

Yesterday afternoon the Reichenbachs were here—after a very long gap. What to offer them? The literally very last residue of real tea, eight apple cakes on 6 ounces of cake coupons. Frau Reichenbach has for several months been doing Labor Service at Zeiss-Ikon. She showed me her pass made out in the name of "Jewess Lotte Sara Reichenbach," permitting her to enter the plant. Half-time, 48 pfennigs an hour the rate for *everyone* (men and women, Aryans and Jews). Special room for Jews with Aryan foremen, yellow armbands, special stairs, divided off with wire netting, otherwise good treatment. Just *one* manual operation (several thousand times) on small components, presumably time fuses. — In the Aryan room there have been loudspeaker warnings against sabotage. Threat of imprisonment. Rumors that Hitler Youth attacks on Jews in Berlin called off.

Here too there are supposed to be isolated shouts against the Jews after inflammatory newsreels, but they don't find any response.

[...]

August 6, Wednesday morning

[...]

Yesterday evening on the Altmarkt Maria Kube, our beautiful Wend, wife of the harp maker. After many years. Still broken German, but altogether ladylike. Greatest friendliness, came toward us with arms outstretched. "Phoned in vain seven times." — Troubles and resentment of the Wend Catholics. Her husband in the field since December, now with the catering corps in Russia. In great danger of his life because the Russians single out the supply trains for attack. The Germans are wading terribly in Russian blood. — Priests imprisoned in this country. Little, talented Benno: out of the shut-down Catholic grammar school and into an elementary school, there degraded from an A grade student to an E grade one. . . . So many crimes, so much injustice against religion. . . . She rubbed her bare arms all the time: "It makes me shiver when I think about it. . . . But my mother said (Bible? Dream?): 'It will be all up with *him* in February '42.' " — She works for the army post office.

It is already getting darker and autumnal—we have hardly had a summer.

[...]

August 7, Thursday

Yesterday, in extreme Barnum style and with the familiar presentation of the special announcements, a survey of what has been achieved in the East so far: 895,000 prisoners, over 13,000 tanks, over 10,000 artillery pieces, approaching 10,000 airplanes—armies of millions annihilated, new operations under way, "our wildest expectations exceeded." But: "the toughest opponent so far," "fighting with tenacity and determination"—and *no* word about our losses and no longer, as still three weeks ago: After the Stalin Line there is nothing else for the Russians to fall back on until the Ural Mountains.

Among Jewry there is the greatest optimism everywhere; I cannot share it, whereas before, when everyone was in despair, I was confident. The double question is: How many such offensives can the Russians take? How many such victories can Germany take? The Jewish optimism trickles from a hundred springs. Kreidl Sr.: "My brother has written from Prague . . . (I got the envelope with the victory postmark: "Germany is victorious on every front for Europe.") Frau Voss: Herr Kussy was here from Holland and told Frau Aronade, the Germans had been stopped outside St. Petersburg, their losses . . . etc., etc.

August 10, Sunday

Just completed the copy of the Front chapter. That has taken since April 25—only interrupted by "Cell 89"—so little do I get down to work now. I will now be busy for at least another two weeks correcting 100 pages of typescript, before I start the next chapter, "Sup. Command East"; the preliminary work for it is finished, the first page is written too—but it all has to be brushed up first.

A new calamity: ban on smoking for Jews. There has been a great shortage in the city recently; in shops where one was not a regular customer one got nothing or a maximum of three cigarettes. Cigars, tobacco hardly at all. Often the reply: Merchandise doesn't arrive till one o'clock. Or: at five o'clock. Or: tomorrow. Yesterday at Walter's in Johannesstrasse, who has been a good supplier for me, the door handle was missing. Torn off by customers when he was shut. Apart from Walter, whom I acquired late and by chance, my principal suppliers were the ones I had used while still in Dölzschen, Zwiener and Hochgemuth, especially Hochgemuth, often mentioned here. Yesterday, with that solemnity familiar to me from Natscheff, the notification. As farewell he gave me four times the weekly ration of cigarillos (that is, 40) and a couple of packets of cigarettes. At first I thought it will be as it was with Natscheff: special precautionary measure on the part of someone considered "politically unreliable." But it seems that the sign "Jews prohibited" really is going to be hung on every shop door. Most of all I feel sorry for Eva. Perhaps she can buy something herself. But many shops don't give anything to women, and Hochgemuth will be afraid. I am deeply depressed.

Eva's health very poor. Swollen up for days because of jaw abscess and dental treatment.

Food ever more difficult. Nothing at home and ever less grub in the restaurants. Shortage of money on top of that.

Tremendous German victories in Russia. The war will last for years.

As Eva has to lie down so much, I have again been reading aloud a great deal. [. . .]

Since for Eva's sake I limit the amount of typing (and also because paper is becoming an ever more rare article), I shall go back to the "solid form" using an old diary. [. . .] I shall get the loose sheets to Annemarie as soon as possible.

August 15, Friday

The same situation for weeks now. According to the military bulletins tremendous successes in the East, one million prisoners, etc., battle at

Smolensk, now Ukraine, Odessa—nothing but annihilation of the Russians. According to what one hears otherwise, from the Jews, but also from Aryans (e.g., Eichler, the dentist), Germany's position most precarious, total victory over Russia before onset of winter impossible, lasting through the winter next to impossible, given shortage of raw materials. Who is right? For my part I am unable to work up any very great hopes. For which my very indifferent state of health is principally to blame. Also the ailments of old age and my bladder trouble. And the money worries. — Corrections going very slowly, otherwise nothing.

[...]

August 22, Friday

LTI. Lightning war [Blitzkrieg], final battle—superlative words. War and battle are no longer enough. At the same time the megalomania of numbers.
[...]

Frau Paul, whose 2nd or 3rd husband was Jewish, who is going through divorce proceedings with the 3rd or 4th, talks in despair about her mother, 89, who is showing signs of senile dementia. "I cannot put her in a hospital, she'll be killed there." There is widespread talk now of the killing of the mentally ill in the asylums. — How they are trying to relieve Frau Voss of her house, how it is always a matter of who has "better connections," like Estreicher, the Jewish connecting link between Gestapo and Jewish Community, who acts the tout and profits on commission—it could provide the material for a Russian *Government Inspector* comedy.

Yesterday the newspapers announced the new Winter Relief Fund: September 1, '41 till March 31, '42. No doubt related to that, the military bulletin today presented a summary of the first two months of the Russian campaign, which was stuffed full of superlatives, "The enemy's *unimaginably* bloody losses." Also 1,250,000 prisoners, etc. — "Unimaginable" in a German military bulletin! Not a word about our own losses. — But vox populi (apprentice at Vogel's): "Russia will be finished in two weeks." Perhaps the vox populi really is right.

September 2, Tuesday morning

The weather is immensely important. Fear of the winter. The *third.* It gets dark ever earlier, autumn has come exceedingly early, half of August was already autumnal. In fact rainy and cold throughout spring and summer, hot days a very rare exception. — The question everywhere: Will something decisive be achieved in Russia before the beginning of the autumn rain? It *hardly* looks like it despite all the certainly great and undoubtedly exaggerated victories. Our own losses are passed over in silence, but trickle through. True number from a senior medical authority is supposed to be:

by August first 300,000 dead, 700,000 wounded, 500,000 sick in the East. There has been continuous fighting since August 1. Ergo. . . . Morale in the Rhineland, which is constantly under air attack, and in Berlin, which is frequently attacked, is said to be catastrophic—one notices nothing of that in quiet Dresden. Recently from an "Aryan source": very great tension between SS and army, military clash in near future unavoidable. Every day rumors of untenable economic situation. — Against that: There is no starvation, foodstuffs are in short supply, in *very* short supply for us, but *no one is starving.* In Dresden and no doubt likewise in a hundred places there is calm and tranquility, and many hundreds of thousands undoubtedly believe in final victory and for all their antipathy to today's regime fear the chaos of tomorrow. So things can go on like this for *years.* — Our own position very gloomy: The absolutely necessary extra allowances up to the tax-free limit will last until November 1. What then? I live with this worry day after day. — The food in the restaurants ever scantier and more expensive; cooking at home hardly possible even once or twice a week. — I try to repress the feeling of dread. My mood and that in the Jews' House changes daily, almost hourly. England has occupied Iran: Up. Will Turkey go with Germany? Down. We count how many people in the shops say "Heil Hitler" and how many "Good afternoon." The "Good morning" or "Good afternoon" is said to be increasing. "At Zscheischler's bakery five women said 'Good afternoon,' two said 'Heil Hitler.' " Up. At Ölsner's they all said "Heil Hitler." Down. Kätchen Sara happy yesterday. At the tram stop an NSV welfare nurse said to her: "The Russians have blown up the Dnieper power station, southern Ukraine is flooded, thousands of Germans have drowned. It's not in the newspaper, it only writes about Russian prisoners . . . the war is lost . . . I know what the mood is, I get around. Good-bye, madam." — "Good-bye," not "Heil Hitler" — an NSV nurse! Up. But then comes the newspaper: Advance "toward Leningrad." Down. Etc., etc.

[. . .]

For weeks now we have had no luck with reading aloud. Admittedly we only get around to it for a few minutes in the evening when we are dead tired. For the greater part of the time Kätchen Sara sits here and relates in her confused way with a hundred repetitions what she has heard en route from strangers ("I play dumb"), from Aryan, from non-Aryan bridge partners. The Kreidls, the landlord and the young Kreidl, also come frequently "to discuss the situation." [. . .]

In the crowded trams now often conductresses with "Student Voluntary Service" on their cuffs.

[. . .]

September 7, Sunday

The newspaper vigorously denied Churchill's "lies about Russian victories," announced German successes everywhere. Frau Voss, always making acquaintances, meets a young girl, student, working in the Propaganda Ministry at the moment. She says: "Russia is terribly difficult, after all. In recent days it has been causing us a great deal of concern." Yet again Petersburg really seems about to fall. — We would be able to observe developments more calmly without the terrible pressure of our financial position. By all human calculations real starvation will begin for us in November. — Eva's nerves are now giving way very badly.

September 8, Monday morning

Yesterday evening ate in the Goldene Löwe in the Neustadt; long walk along the Priessnitz, toward the barracks. We now often make the Neustadt an object of study. On the way home we met Frau Paul in the tram: She told us—it is really supposed to be true, and if not or only half true, then the fact of the rumor is characteristic: A married couple in Ammonstrasse learn that all four of their sons have been killed in Russia. The father hangs himself, the mother hurls the picture of Hitler out of the window into the courtyard. Half an hour later she is arrested ("taken away").

At something like three o'clock at night we had the second air raid warning, the all clear soon came, nothing had happened.

This morning, distraught and pale, Frau Kreidl (the widow) brought the news, the Official Gazette of the Reich announced the introduction of the yellow Jewish armband. That means upheaval and catastrophe for us. Eva still hopes the measure will be stopped, and so I shall not write any more about it yet.

September 15, Monday

The Jewish armband, come true as Star of David, comes into force on the nineteenth. At the same time a prohibition on leaving the environs of the city. Frau Kreidl Sr. was in tears, Frau Voss had palpitations. Friedheim said this was the worst blow so far, worse than the property assessment. I myself feel shattered, cannot compose myself. Eva, now firmly on her feet, wants to take over all the errands from me, I only want to leave the house for a few minutes when it's dark. (And if there is snow and ice? Perhaps by then the public will have become indifferent, or che so io?) The newspaper justification: After the army had got to know, through Bolshevism, the cruelty, etc. of *the* Jew, all possibility of camouflage must be removed from the Jews here, to spare the comrades of the people all contact with them. — The true reason: fear of Jewish criticism because things look bad in the East or at least are at a standstill. And: rule of the terror people, of Himmler, because things look bad in the East. Wild rumors: Goering is a prisoner after an argument with Hitler. — Hitler has been shot in the stomach by a general. He had reviled the general, he had lain raving on the carpet and "chewed the tassels." [...]

There was yet another grave misfortune for us: Two weeks ago I was told at the Tax Office, I was free of income tax, would in the next few days even have an excess payment of 180M returned to me. [. . .] Now they are demanding "prepayment of 500M for the year '41" from me, immediately taking account from January 1 of the 1,200M Georg gave as a present, even though it only began to dribble through from May 16. That would eat up almost all of my reserves beyond the tax-free limit. — Then, seemingly a trifle, but in fact more painful than the tax business: Until now about once a week we got 5 pounds of flounder from Paschky; coupons were not needed for flounder, other fish could only be got with a "household card," which is not distributed to any Jewish household [. . .]. The flounder was a help in feeding the cat. On Saturday, a true thirteenth, I received the tax demand in the morning, in the afternoon at Paschky's the news that flounder no longer coupon free. Now the last bit of our meat ration will disappear into Muschel's little bowl, and the beast will still not be satisfied. — Finally the tobacco shortage has become so great that I have lived for two days without smoking at all—today is worse than ever. For the time being a couple of cigarettes (which do nothing for me) can still be picked up. Hochgemuth still supplies Eva, occasionally also gives her 5 extra cigarettes, occasionally I can still pick something up at Walter's in Moritzstrasse. (Mostly he is shut during the Jews' hour.) From Friday there will be nothing more from Walter, how long and how much will Hochgemuth still supply us? Eva too will soon be stymied in her smoking. — From Friday she will have to cook for us at home every day. What? The constraints are getting tighter, there are no potatoes, and it has been raining, raining, raining for weeks. — It is to be hoped, and to all appearances it is so, in Russia also.

In these days of extreme adversity, I have been suffering greatly from a kind of influenza. Today I am a little fresher, am shivering less. I am clinging to my work. Typewritten copy of the Kovno piece, making notes for the next part.

September 17, Wednesday

About two weeks ago, in the evening, at Postplatz, in the fourth restaurant in which we cannot find anything to eat, Delekat jumps up with very great cordiality: genuinely pleased to meet us, we should visit him in Radebeul. He himself long since retired as professor, as Confessing Pastor he is banned from speaking in public. I could not make up my mind on this visit. Now a somewhat pastoral letter arrived from him, dated September 13, tone: Consolation on the way to the gallows, "May God give you both the strength . . . may God be with you and your brave wife . . .," but very well meant and with the invitation "to discuss matters" with me "in the offices of the Confessing Church." I was reluctant to do so, I was also not quite certain of Delekat's complete altruism—was he afraid that I might visit him in his apartment wearing the star? — Eva persuaded me, it was at least interesting, so I went there yesterday sub specie curriculi.

Truly an interesting hour in the huge, labyrinthine and elegant apartment wing at Johann Georgen Allee 31, first floor, "offices of the Evangelical Confessing Church of Saxony," where I had frequently spoken with Richter because of the tax (he is now sergeant-major in the army medical service) and got to know Feder. (I have now almost completely fallen out with Feder over the Nazism of his narrow-minded wife, and because he did not want my taxes unless I paid them secretly, that is outside the tax-free limit.) Delekat, in tails and top hat, just come from a funeral, large, youthful, swarthy, perhaps a little more pastoral, a little less professorial than he used to be, sincere and cordial. He seems to be a leading figure in the "Fraternal Council of the Confessing Church."

Content of our conversation. General: One had to hold out. A complete victory by Germany "technically impossible." Either compromise peace now, only *without* Hitler. Or slowly bleeding to death. Impossible to say what will happen. Fear of Bolshevism ("the same thing under another name"), if it comes to bleeding to death. Concerning the Jewish star: Who knows how many "Rust" it will last? Rust (the Education Minister) a new unit of measurement, like "hertz" in physics. The teachers say: 'One Rust is the interval between a decree and its cancellation.' " — On the church tax: (Current position: This year I have to pay the "National Jewish Association" 279M. I *may* pay 112M of that to the Confessing Church, if I do not, it all goes to the Jews. Last year I *brought* the money to Richter, the treasurer, this time I would have to transfer it through the bank, because otherwise it would exceed my 320M "tax limit." Delekat: "If it's a constraint on your conscience, transfer it. If not, pay it to the Jewish Community." I: "You are afraid to be called a Jews' church? I am offended by that." He: "We are under surveillance, harassed, we fear a complete prohibition by the Gestapo, we have to think of the whole. We are thinking of setting up special Bible evenings for the Jewish Christians, e.g., in Düsseldorf." I: "So you too do not want someone with the Jew's star to come to your services?" He: "There are spies everywhere." Fear of ban of the whole organization. Also curfew for Jews during the hours of service could be the result. (As they have been prohibited from wearing medals.) I shall therefore pay the whole tax to the Jews. — Private: Delekat was surprised that I am still working, not "just burning myself up." LTI interested him too. Theologically it was interesting, how LTI excludes God everywhere, replaces divine workings with human beings. (I must ask him for material.) [. . .] When I mentioned the change in value of *fanatical,* he talked about *revolution.* Originates in the Renaissance, in astronomy, was for a long time pejorative in German (Luther only talks about "revolt"). Now revolution was a concept with a positive sign. (But surely already so in 1789?) — About Kühn and his war pamphlet—*I* called Kühn a traitor to scholarship—inwardly Kühn was a "skeptic," he had allowed himself to be carried along a little by the current of events, mixes a lot with officers, had repeated their opinions, had probably by now already changed his mind. Since childless, Kühn's wife doing labor service [. . .] as a librarian at Zeiss-Ikon (where there is a whole isolated section for Jews)—Delekat's own eldest boy, 19, at present doing labor service in Brest, can be called up at any moment, "a miracle" that he has not been already. Delekat himself wounded outside Verdun. A couple of months ago (after 25 years!) an abscess had developed on the old leg wound, which still contains splinters. Proudly, as if reporting some heroic deed: "I deliberately had myself examined by Dr. Kohlmann, whose wife is non-Aryan." (And today that really is a heroic deed.)

In the evening I was again momentarily depressed, since the Russian counteroffensive now appears to be broken and German thrust across the Dnieper and successes near Petersburg are announced. But then I said to myself: Bought with how many German blood sacrifices? And for what reason? Because there *must* be successes. Because yesterday tension with the USA increased even further. Roosevelt decree: Any U-boat that attacks or threatens American shipping between the USA and Iceland will be fired on. (But no declaration of war on either side!) On top of that the weather. The never ending downpours of rain. Fear for the potato harvest everywhere. — We talked to young Kreidl for a while. He said: Economically Germany cannot survive the winter. At Zeiss-Ikon sections are idle for hours because there is no material. Airplane instruments are made out of light metal because there is a steel shortage. Light metal is vulnerable to the weather. *Poor* wool substitute for soldiers' greatcoats—and now winter in Russia. There is a leather shortage. The postwoman complains about cracked shoes, does not get any new ones. No isolated case, anzi . . .

Daily event in the Jews' House: Frau Kreidl Sr. here in tears, she does not want to live anymore. Has to be comforted. Kätchen Sara's palpitations. Has to be comforted. Similar scenes between Eva and myself. With alternating roles. The comforter always says what he does not believe himself, and takes heart from his own words. For a couple of hours. Since the Star of David, which is due to rise on Friday, September 19, things are very bad. Everyone's attitude changing by turns, mine included: I shall go out proud and dignified—I shall shut myself in and not leave the house again. Eva plans as far as possible to be the "sabbath goy." How long will she be able to endure it? At best until the first black ice. She is now brave (plays music a lot), now deeply depressed. Muschel is starving. [. . .]

Yesterday a tobacco via dolorosa. On many shops: "No sale to Jews." At many the line hopeless. At a few: "No goods arrived yet." In one: "I can only serve my regular customers now." In a couple of places two or three loose cigarettes in the hand. Finally, at about four (Jewish closing time!), to Walter's once again, which had been shut earlier. Undreamed of luck: 60 cigarettes (sixty!) and a little packet of tobacco, 2 ounces, after I had already been without any smoking things for days. Also he gave advance notice of "Little Russians," Eva's favorite, and promised to hand them over to *her*. (Women are often not served.) He seemed to suspect my situation. But in the evening came the damper: Kreidl Jr. knew "for certain," tobacco cards would be issued on October 1. Naturally not for Jews.

Letter from Trude Scherk: Grete had not got out of her room all summer. She "dozes" at the window. Visitors are upsetting. She appears to be slowly dying away. Probably (hopefully) more agonizing for the onlooker than for her. I have had no more news from Änny Klemperer for months. Perhaps she took offense at a remark I made. I wrote, I was not very enthusiastic about emigration. I had suffered enough in my youth from financial dependence on family.

I do not read aloud much. We are very exhausted in the evenings, Frau Voss sits with us for a long time.

[. . .]

The tax business—on Monday I was at Sidonienstrasse Tax Office, where the officials' courteousness was exemplary—turned out passably for the time being. Admittedly the fact remains that Georg's 1,200M present is stuck on to my pension and as Jewish assessment costs 500M in tax, the worries about the winter also. But for the moment after everything was balanced only 67M were due, after that 125M, in December. What is the point in thinking any further ahead?

Kätchen Sara ostentatiously wears a cross at her neck (present from her Catholic husband, who was first a priest, then economist and became director of the Public Insurance Institute—she herself belongs to the Reformed Church), so as to paralyze the Jewish star.

The Jewish Cultural League in Berlin has been shut down, its property has been confiscated.

Today I interrupted work on the Curriculum for a whole diary morning—for the sake precisely of the Curriculum.

September 18, Thursday evening

The "Jewish star," black on yellow cloth, at the center in Hebrew-like lettering "Jew," to be worn on the left breast, large as the palm of a hand, issued to us yesterday for 10 pfennigs, to be worn from tomorrow. The omnibus may *no* longer be used, *only* the front platform of the tram. — For the time being at least Eva will take over all the shopping, I shall breathe in a little fresh air only under shelter of darkness.

Today we were outside together in daylight for the last time. First cigarette hunt, then on the tram (seat!) to Loschwitz over the suspension bridge, from there along the right bank down by the river toward town as far as the Waldschlösschen. In 21 years we have *never* taken this route. The Elbe, very high, broad, flowing strongly and quietly, a lot of mist, the park gardens behind the high walls autumnal with flowers and falling leaves. A first chestnut fell and burst at our feet. It was like a last day out, a last little bit of freedom before a long (how long?) imprisonment. The same feeling, as we ate in the Löwenbräu in Moritzstrasse.

When one occupant of this house visits another he rings three times. That has been agreed, so that no one catches fright. A simple ring could be the police.

[. . .]

September 19, Friday

[. . .]

Today the Jew's star. Frau Voss has already sewn it on, intends to turn her coat back over it. Allowed? I reproach myself with cowardice. Yesterday Eva wore out her feet on the pavements and must now go shopping in town and cook afterward. Why? Because I am ashamed. Of what? From Monday I intend to go shopping again. By then we shall certainly have heard what effect *it* has.

September 20, Saturday

Yesterday, as Eva was sewing on the Jew's star, I had a raving fit of despair. Eva's nerves finished too. She is pale, her cheeks are hollow. (The day before yesterday, for the first time in years, we had ourselves weighed. Eva was 123 pounds, six and a half pounds lighter than in the turnip winter of 1917—her normal weight was 154 pounds. I am still 148 pounds—it was 165 pounds before.) I told myself I must behave as after the car accident: straight back to the steering wheel! Yesterday after the evening meal a few steps outside with Eva only when it was completely dark. Today at midday I really did go to Ölsner's grocery shop on Wasaplatz and fetched soda water. It cost me a great effort to do so. Meanwhile Eva is constantly going on errands and cooking. Our whole life has been turned upside down, and everything weighs on Eva. How long will her feet hold out? — She visited Frau Kronheim. The latter took the tram yesterday—front platform. The driver: Why was she not sitting in the car? Frau Kronheim is small, slight, stooped, her hair completely white. As a Jewess she was forbidden to do so. The driver struck the panel with his fist: "What a mean thing!" Poor comfort.

Today the Germans captured Kiev. So the Russian counteroffensive has failed completely. What will happen when Hitler is finally victorious?

The weather has improved after weeks of rain (but autumnally cold).

That means: The Germans can keep going in Russia, the potatoes will *not* rot, that means, therefore, that Hitler has a good chance of winning.

Frau Kreidl downstairs going around weeping everywhere, does not want to go on living. Frau Kreidl upstairs, the Aryan one, shuts herself off brusquely from the community of Jews. Eva takes over smaller errands for the starred occupants of the house, on the street she gives them her arm, so that it is covered up. [. . .]

September 22, Monday

Yesterday shut in all day in glorious weather, in the evening sneaked out for a couple of minutes. [. . .] Even though I went to the grocer's on Wasaplatz on Saturday—as I went back to the wheel after the car accident—the dreadful aversion has not gone. Every step, the thought of every step is desperation. — Lissy Meyerhof writes from Berlin: Passersby sympathized with the star wearers. She also writes, we should be optimistic, Aryan friends told her, this was the final act. — I too believe it is the fifth act. But some plays in world literature, e.g., Hugo's *Cromwell*, have *six* acts.

[. . .]

On Kreidl's advice, I am now smoking the blackberry tea, which Eva drinks and which I loathe, in my pipe. For the Curriculum I am just working through the year 1917: increasing similarities with today.

[. . .]

September 23, Tuesday

Beginning of autumn with thick fog, could be the middle of October. — Old farmer Pfeifer, the big landowner up in Dölzschen, said to Vogel that never in his life had he seen such a pitiful potato harvest as this time. It has been announced in the papers that restaurants are banned from peeling potatoes. . . . I am reading the 1916–18 diaries for the Curriculum. Exactly the same notes as now, with similar (not quite so desperate) emotions— only today the fronts are reversed. Will the harvest be bad *enough,* will the weather in Russia be cold *enough,* etc., etc.?

Yesterday I really did go through the middle of town on the front platform and made purchases at Heckert's, Paschky's and Güntzel's. Nowhere a hurt—but the most wretched, bitter feeling.

September 25, Thursday evening

We had been told about a Jewish luncheon place in the Marschallstrasse, which also provided food around six o'clock. We arrived there hungry—it is not allowed to serve food in the evening. I sent Eva to a restaurant in the market hall, where she can get a plate of vegetables for a few pfennigs—I am not allowed in. At home I ate bread, of which there is never enough, and potato salad, for the third time today. On the way, on the front platform of the no. 5, as it got empty toward Zschernitz, the driver, man in his forties with war medals: "Leading us toward glorious times, isn't he? — it won't stay like this—another two years, at most another four—it'll turn out differently in the end. . . . Not so bad, your sign, at least you know who you're talking to, who you've got in front of you, you can speak your mind for once!" Then another passenger got on, and the driver was silent. — Yesterday Eva fetched our last reserves from Annemarie. Till November 1. What then?

I crisscross the city, on foot and by tram. It does not cease to be distressing.

September 27, Saturday

Herr von Loeben, the good-natured blatherer and busybody of the Confessing Church, came to visit and brought me, Frau Voss and young Kreidl as his little non-Aryan flock—he himself is half-Aryan—words of consolation from Herr Richter, who takes care of the administration of the Confessing Church and is now serving as a sergeant major in the medical corps. The letter is a confused sermon in purest pulpit style. Our Aryan fellow believers are tempted to deny us, we in turn are tempted to nurse unchristian thoughts of revenge, both must not be. Furthermore we should be proud of the Star of David, it demonstrates our kinship with David, that we are God's children. I told Loeben, I was not especially impressed by the Confessing Church, which denied us in public (no tax!) — Loeben said a few things about the general situation, which cheered me up a little. He said: The completely mendacious military bulletin is now talking about 600,000 prisoners at Kiev (this evening it's even 675,000!), but the first reports of the battle had said that four armies with approximately 200,000 men had been surrounded. He, Loeben, had inquired where the other hundreds of thousands came from. Answer: Kiev has 850,000 inhabitants, and the civilian prisoners have been included in the reckoning. — He went on: My cousin is laid up in a military hospital. Recently the high boots of all the wounded had to be handed over, they were given light shoes in return.

Such shortages! And despite them a winter campaign in Russia!

September 28, Sunday

[. . .]
    LTI. "From the Führer's headquarters, 9/27/41 . . . A victory in battle has thus been won, which is without parallel in history." Barnum ringing the

changes in hyperbole. This on the 665,000 prisoners at Kiev. In the same newspaper (*Dresdner Anzeiger,* September 27–28) a leading article on the anniversary of the pact with Japan. At the beginning: What a good position we are in, also *economically* "greater than ever," because based "on the strength of the whole of Europe." (!) At the end: Confidence, that Japan knows what it must do in its great hour, who its real enemy is. In the middle, however, the information that Japan has been negotiating with the USA for weeks. We "cannot blame" it for that, it is simply examining every approach. [. . .]

In the evening the Kreidls came up from downstairs. (Interruption by a police check, each in his lodging, glad that the officers were so courteous—y en a d'autres—then continuation of the conversation.) Paul Kreidl brought the news, which is already supposed to have been in the newspapers on Friday: "American assets in Germany have been blocked." With that there is virtually no prospect that I shall receive further payments from Georg's account. And that means that I shall be forced to sell the house, perhaps in January.

I also spoke to Kreidl about Loeben and learned this: The League of Non-Aryan Christians, which I was invited to join immediately after the Nürnberg Laws—I did not accept, to me it would have amounted to a recognition of Hitlerism—this League was soon banned; its place was taken, out of it grew the office of Pastor Grüber, with whom I repeatedly had dealings. The office was helpless, as Kreidl confirmed. *I* also had the worst experiences with Grüber's assistant, Miss Livingstone. This Pastor Grüber has been *locked up* since '39. — How far behind me already lie the years in which I endeavored to obtain a post abroad!

Extremely slow work on the section Book Control Office Leipzig.

[. . .]

October 1, Wednesday morning

There are warning notes here and there. The Czech prime minister (Elias) of a government compliant with Germany and closely supervised by it has been arrested for high treason, the Reich Protector, Neurath, "sick," replaced by SS Obergruppenführer Heydrich, Himmler's right hand, id aiunt: author of the Jew's star, bloodhound and Alba. — In Italy (*this* version and explanation is official) bread ration 7 ounces, for workers 10 ounces daily. It is not yet certain who counts as a worker, there had been reluctance to introduce the ration card because bread is *the* Italian staple food, what the potato is here. But the corn harvest is unfavorable, and Italy must also provide for Greece and Dalmatia, countries which have little grain and are dependent on imports.

From today considerable further limitation of bus services; so Lockwitz only gets a shuttle service to the no. 13 tram, which is in any case already overcrowded. Gasoline shortage! — The boom boom of the Wehrmacht must drown out all the warning notes. The greatest victory of world history at Kiev. Successes of *Italian*(!) troops in the East. (Is there more than one Italian division there? Is it kept anxiously in the background?) Great Italian air successes against the English fleet at Gibraltar. — Eva calls yesterday's report about bread rationing virtually a preparation for a separate Italian peace. I am not *that* optimistic, but I allow myself a little hope nevertheless. Hope is sorely needed, I am so wretchedly imprisoned after all. From today not allowed outside after eight again. Since I've been wearing this star . . . But I've already noted that down a dozen times.

October 4, Saturday

Yesterday to John Neumann's in Winckelmannstrasse. When we lived in Hohe Strasse, Frau Neumann, daughter of Alma Fink—acquaintance through Grete—used to take her two little children for walks. Now around 50, son New York machine fitter, 21; daughter 18, photographer, engaged to a Swede. I gave a recommendation to Sussmann (analogous fate to Hilde Sussmann-Jonson). The man mid-sixties. Neither Orthodox, but emphatically Jewish. Still they consented to their daughter's marriage. I borrowed Gronemann from them a couple of months ago. Now read out the Kovno section there. Good impression. The Neumanns still have their own apartment—but with three tenants. — Neumann very optimistic. The thing will collapse from the inside even before Easter—the tremendous losses in Russia—military dictatorship—democratic government waiting in London. — Favorable experiences with the star. Only a child of former acquaintances had run out full of fear: "Ugh, a Jew!" Horrified, the mother apologized, he had not heard it at home—presumably at kindergarten. — The child's fear could not be pacified.

I myself experienced this while shopping. Elderly woman, selling from a handcart. "Can I have some of the large radishes?" — "But of course!" — I glance longingly at the tomatoes, forbidden "goods in short supply." "They're not to be had without a card, are they?" — "I'll give you some, I know how things stand." Makes up a pound. Then reaches under her cart, pulls out a handful of onions, which are very rare: "Hold out your bag—so that's 60 pfennigs altogether." There is no doubt that the people feel the persecution of the Jews to be a sin.

Today communication from the Deutsche Bank, Berlin, that I have been allowed a further 1,200M in 200M installments from Georg's account. Incl. of Jewish tax more than 600M will be deducted from that, nevertheless it lifts a burden from me for the whole of the winter. What is the point in reckoning beyond that?

Frau Neumann had the simplest and most comprehensive comment on the star: Since that I have never been able to walk naturally on the street.

Woes of the time. The invitation to the Neumanns had read: "Bring your pipe, I have good tobacco." For two weeks now I have been smoking pure blackberry tea. Eva too is already mixing genuine cigarette tobacco with the tea and rolling her own. The number of ready-made cigarettes she gets from Walter and Hochgemuth is minimal, there is no tobacco to be found at all anymore—she has an emergency reserve of just 3½ ounces. So at the Neumanns I really did fill a pipe with genuine tobacco and even took away with me enough very good genuine tobacco for a dozen full pipes. I smoked some of it yesterday evening and early this morning— then it occurred to me that it could also be used for rolling cigarettes, and I went back to the blackberry tea.

October 7, Tuesday

Frau Voss heard as *vouched-for:* A chaplain is officiating in St. Hedwig's Cathedral in Berlin with the Jew's star on his vestment.

Frau Voss receives a bill from her health insurance, addressed to "Frau Käte *Lore* Voss." She signs the compulsory *Sara* in such a way that it looks like *Lore*. (Otherwise she would have had to give up the insurance a long time ago.) Similarly: turning back the coat over the Jew's star or walking with her umbrella up, even when it has stopped raining—because then her arm covers the star. Or a package or a bag pressed against it. (A circular from the Jewish Community has warned against it, it is severely punished.) The cross still dangling from her neck. At the same time the constant: "If my husband were still alive, I would not need to wear a star—I always have bad luck."

LTI. In his last speech to the Winter Aid Workers Hitler said: I shall return home from this war an even *more fanatical* National Socialist than I was before.

October 9, Thursday, toward evening

60 years. Vieillard. Ever since Berthold and Wally only managed to get to 59, I have never really believed that I would live to see the day. I am living through it in a very depressed mood. In normal times honors would have come to me, now I am wearing the Star of David.—And today of all days the newspaper is one long howl of triumph: Breaking through the middle of the Russian lines toward Moscow was the actual, true and complete annihilation of the Soviet Russians. Hitler's October 2 proclamation to the army *even* more Barnum-like than usual.

Stay calm, stay calm!

Annemarie visited us, the first time in about two years. She brought some new novel as a present; I asked her to exchange it for a summary of the World War. — Lissy Meyerhof sent a touching little packet of food, in it a couple of grams of coffee, Sussmann sent a long rambling letter. — I worked on a couple of lines of the Curriculum. Kätchen Sara baked me shortcake and gave me a bottle of wine, a little bottle of cognac, a pound of bread coupons. Commovente. Eva, terribly troubled by a cough, looking even more pinched than she did already, made potatoes lyonaise for the birthday dinner, managed to buy me an umbrella, a desk clock, a wallet replacement, two ties, is out from morning till evening hunting for food and tobacco goods.

Just stay calm!

In the evenings we are both regularly dead tired and exhausted. Mostly only small talk about same old things with Kätchen Sara or with Kreidl Sr. who tends to come downstairs (without his wife and without us having invited them or even only him) and who is somewhat intrusive. So the reading aloud often comes to a halt.

[. . .]

I am glad that this sixtieth is coming to an end, tomorrow is an ordinary day again. I intend to accept it as a fortunate dispensation of providence, as material for my Curriculum, as a gain, that I am experiencing all this ignominy on the spot.

What have I written between fifty and sixty? The *Corneille,* one and three-quarter volumes Dix-huitième, one and five-sixths volumes Curriculum, 1881–Easter 1917. C'est bien peu pour un sergeant.

[. . .]

October 13

The cobbler in Habsburger—no: Planettastrasse: "Please, let your wife come from now on. The guild has strictly forbidden us to do work for Jews—you are to go to the Jewish cobbler. But you are an old customer of mine."

The chilblains on my hands, which plagued me last winter, have already come back, and in an excruciating form.

October 25, Saturday

Ever more shocking reports about deportations of Jews to Poland. They have to leave almost literally naked and penniless. Thousands from Berlin to Lodz ("Litzmannstadt"). A letter from Lissy Meyerhof about it. And many stories from Kätchen Sara. Grotesque yesterday because of the way she jumped about from one thing to another. Tears, weak heart and pleasures all mixed up. A Jewish birthday coffee afternoon. Eighteen ladies. "Real coffee—but sooo strong, mocha, and cakes over and over, like in peacetime, home baked, saved up for. And letters read out from Berlin, Frankfurt, Essen. — This one's aunt has hanged herself—her sister wanted to throw herself in front of a train—I had palpitations—the cakes . . ."

Will Dresden be affected and when? It hangs over us all the time. — German advance continues in Russia, even though the winter has begun.

Latest version: After final victory over the Soviets, perhaps in the spring, there is a coup by the military and from the Right; the new government concludes a *good* compromise peace with England. I cannot believe it, not on the German side, nor on the English. [...] One who is of this opinion—it corresponds with his heart's desire—is here again, Ludwig Voss, Kätchen's brother-in-law, the Rhenish and Catholic headmaster retired. He abhors Hitler, but he abhors the English just as much. "In 1919 they forced us off the pavement with their riding whips. Servitude under Churchill would perhaps be even worse than under Hitler." Herr Ludwig Voss is not entirely sound after all. It gave him pleasure to put together his Proof of Ancestry: (*Proof of Ancestry: LTI.*) I always ask myself: Who among the "Aryan" Germans is really untouched by National Socialism? The contagion rages in all of them, perhaps it is not contagion, but basic German nature.

I am running around with an untidy head—hair much too long at the back of the neck and at the temples. I do not dare go into a barbershop, with the star they can refuse me. — Our food problem, in particular my shortage of bread, grows worse all the time.

October 27, Monday

The latest blows: *Smokers' cards,* only for men, not for Jews. With that we are quite defeated. It hits Eva even harder than it does me. I have already been accustomed to blackberry tea for weeks, cigarillos were a rare exception. So far she has still been rolling her cigarettes *half* with tobacco and only half with tea. I also gave her the last little packet of pipe tobacco. — Then yesterday, Sunday, after Eva had just cut my hair, letter from the Jewish Community, typewriters had to be handed over on Monday and Thursday. Agitated debates here, to what extent the machine is Eva's property, to what extent she has property of her own, whether our goods were divided or held in common. I ran to the Reichenbachs to get legal advice—he was working at the Community, she was deeply depressed. (The deportations!) Today, at the Community, the shady Estreicher told me I should make an application with respect to the typewriter, which, however, was unlikely to get anywhere.

On Saturday Paul and Ida Kreidl spent the evening with us. They have a daughter and sister in Prague, who is registered for Poland. On Saturday they were more composed than in the days beforehand. There was relatively positive news to hand from Lodz: clean barracks, good heating and food, decent treatment in the munitions factories. That is already reckoned a comfort.

Concepts of honor, of glory, of ambition—how dependent on social history: The Kreidls had a big sporting goods shop here, the father died a few years ago, the son already joint owner at 21. He explains with pride: "Father dealt in clothes, when he took over the shop he was still selling secondhand clothes, knew nothing about sports, about sports equipment. I enlarged it. We had 1,000 ski boots in stock. My successor doesn't have a single pair now—there's a ban on manufacturing them."

Letters from Trude Scherk and Änny Klemperer, as I had enquired about Grete. Consternation at the deportations. Änny Klemperer is racking her brains as to how she could possibly remit money for Grete to Poland, difficulties are already being raised for her here. Änny sees all the misery, and yet she writes: "It's a blessing that the Russians have not marched in—otherwise our life and all our culture would have been at an end." How can I go on complaining about the stupidity of the people, when my sister-in-law allows herself to be made just as stupid?

October 31, Friday

The typewriter was taken away on Tuesday. That hit me hard, it is virtually irreplaceable. I now want to finish a rough version of Volume II of the Curriculum by hand—perhaps I shall manage to do so by New Year, perhaps by February 12, '42 (I started on February 12, '39)—and then try to borrow a typewriter. — I was also offended that Eva again mistrusted my industriousness and herself went to the Community once again to claim back the typewriter as her personal and Aryan property.

LTI. Below an engagement notice in the *Dresdner Anzeiger* stood "Seaport Rostock." Every town has to have its own trade and symbol. Trade Fair City Leipzig, Spa Town X, etc. Borrowed from the Middle Ages. Peculiarity of tribes, towns, ranks, costumes.

November 1

Was for the first time subjected to some abuse the day before yesterday. At Chemnitzer Platz a section of Hitler Youth cubs. "A yid, a yid!" Yelling they run toward the dairy I am just entering, I can still hear them shouting and laughing outside. When I come out, they are lined up. I look calmly at their commander, not a word is spoken. Once I am past, behind me, but not called out loudly, one, two voices: "A yid!" — A couple of hours later at Lange's nursery, I am fetching sand for Muschel, an older worker: "You, mate, do you know Herrschmann? — No? — He's a Jew too, porter like me—I just wanted to say: It doesn't matter about the star, we're all human beings, and I know such good Jews." Such consolation is not very cheering either. But which is the true vox populi?

Today urgent warning card from Sussmann, he must have read something alarming about the deportations, I should immediately renew my USA application, he himself would see to it that I got an interim residence permit in Sweden, "if all conditions for the USA were fulfilled." I wrote back immediately, every route was now blocked. In fact we heard from several sources that a complete ban on all emigration has just been decreed on the German side. Besides a year and a day would pass before the new American conditions were fulfilled. No, we must wait here and see what our fate will be.

[...]

November 2, Sunday

[...]

[...] Headmaster Voss was with us yesterday. — Among other things he told us that the Bishop of Münster, Count Galen, had preached publicly against the Gestapo and the killing of the mentally infirm. The bishop had not been arrested on the grounds that "one does not want to make any martyrs," in truth, because they had "not dared to."

At home all day working on the Curriculum. Pitiful result: one written page [...]

LTI so uniform because the whole press has *one* director, because every word of the Führer and a few subordinate Führers is repeated mechanically and presented like a catechism. Everyone says: "stubborn," says "fanatical," says "sworn fraternity," says "matchless." (They're going to town on Hitler's allegory "General Winter" now.)

[...]

November 9, Sunday

[...] On Saturday evenings we are often downstairs with the Kreidls now or they come to us. Paul Kreidl, doing heavy laboring work constructing railway lines, the Jew's star on his sackcloth smock, can get a good sleep on Sunday. He talks a lot about life as a businessman (inherited sporting goods shop), something of a snob, but very interesting.

The deportations to Poland continue, the Jews everywhere deeply depressed. I met the Neumanns outside the teacher training college in Teplitzer Strasse, these usually plucky, optimistic people were utterly downcast, considering suicide. The possibility of getting to Cuba had just been offered to them when the complete ban on emigration came into force. Frau Neumann's uncle, Atchen Fink's older brother, a man late in his sixties committed suicide with his wife in Berlin, when they were to be deported. Neumann said to me he would rather be dead and know his wife dead, than see her "louse-ridden and rebuilding Minsk." Frau Neumann in tears: "We were just discussing where we could obtain veronal" ... I roused them with such fine words that I quite raised my own spirits. Five minutes to midnight ... our special courage ... rebuilding Minsk cannot be uninteresting, etc. They said it was a comfort to listen to me, God must have sent me to them. They will be our guests next Saturday. I recently wrote to Lissy Meyerhof that there are three kinds of preachers: those who do *not* believe and dissemble, those who really believe, and those who believe while they are speaking, and who speak in order to give themselves the pleasure of believing. I am one of the third kind.

Frau Voss is now suffering greatly from palpitations, she is subjected to attempts at extortion because of her house. The most recent threat, transmitted by Estreicher, was: "Within three days we can have you in a Polish ghetto and doing labor service."

Kreidl Sr. and Dr. Friedheim have not left the house since September 19, the day on which the Star of David rose. With Dr. Friedheim it's of his own free will, with Kreidl presumably the will of his Aryan wife, who does not want to be compromised. In good weather both are busy in the garden, but have now been shut in for quite a long while. They must go mad, and one can sense their tenseness.

November 11, Tuesday

LTI. Separate chapters: (1) The German schools reader and the history book in the 3rd Reich. (2) The anti-Semitic and racist press 1914–1933. (I come to this by way of the Curriculum note on Trotsky-Braunstein, cf. Litvinov-Finkelstein.)

The eternal: "He was very decent to me" (the policeman, some petty official or other, etc.) is appalling. People have no expectation anymore, hardly even hope of "decent" treatment.

A doctor from the Public Health Office was here for the second time to inspect the house, this time with a builder. We suspect expulsion. He was not allowed to say anything, replied the man to my question. Despair of the owner of the house, Kreidl Sr. *My* worry: the grand piano, the tomcat.

Yesterday Hitler's November 9 speech. Undisguised threat against the Bishop of Münster, undisguised fear.

November 18

The news of the Jewish deportations to Poland and Russia sounds catastrophic from several sources. Letter from Lissy Meyerhof to us, from Voss in Cologne to Kätchen Sara, word-of-mouth reports. We hear quite a lot. The Neumanns visited us. Frau Voss is doing labor service at Zeiss-Ikon— "voluntarily" because that is supposed to provide protection against deportation, also voluntarily without quotation marks, because it's like bridge, all her male and female friends work there. They punch holes or assemble some components or other, presumably measuring instruments for submarines and aircraft. (The Jewish section is supposed to have very good conditions.)

In the tram (rear cabin, the permitted front platform is not separated from the inside seats), I was addressed by Frau Kühn, whom I did not recognize at first. A courageous act, especially as a few days ago there is supposed to have been an explicit warning on the radio, supported by a Goebbels article, against any association whatsoever with Jews. He, Kühn, the historian, still has his post and is very well disposed to the regime. (His pamphlet on the meaning of the war.)

Preparation of new confiscations, which *this* time do not affect us. Apart from typewriters: opera glasses and cameras. (On the other hand the *complete* prohibition on using trams has *not* occurred.)

In exchange for the novel, Annemarie Köhler sent me an excellent unbiased and comprehensive survey: E. O. Volkmann, *The Great War 1914–1918*. My Curriculum has already benefited from his chapter on the last German offensive in the West, which confirms, extends the information in the diaries.

November 21, Friday

Kreidl Sr. summoned to the Gestapo the morning of the day before yesterday "for questioning," did not come back. His wife went there in the afternoon: arrest, PPD, in custody, political grounds. No one knows anything more. Supposition: the Czech unrest, Kreidl's name could have been found in some correspondence or other. He is completely harmless. He can be kept inside for weeks, even months. Everyone is threatened by the same fate at any moment.

November 23, Sunday

Kreidl Sr. still under arrest, no one knows the reason. Ironic circumstance: He absolutely did not want to go out on the street with the Jew's star, lived at home from September 19. His first walk: ordered to the Gestapo for "questioning." Detained there.
[. . .]

November 24, Monday evening

Frau Reichenbach—the Reichenbachs were our and Kätchen's guests yesterday—told us a gentleman had greeted her in a shop doorway. Had he not mistaken her for someone else? — "No, I do not know you, but you will now be greeted frequently. We are a group 'who greet the Jew's star.' "

November 28, Friday

Lissy Meyerhof unexpectedly included among those to be evacuated. Furniture confiscated for auction. Transport (to Poland or Russia) scheduled for November 27, postponed at the last moment, it is said until January. No one knows any details, not who will be affected, nor when, nor where to. Every day news from many cities, departure of large transports, postponements, then departures again, with sixty-year-olds, without sixty-year-olds—everything seems arbitrary. Munich, Berlin, Hanover, Rhineland ... The army needs the trains, the army has released trains ... Everyone wavers, waits from day to day. Today an urgent communication from the National Association: Who has war decorations? Will that be of any use against deportation?

I must go to the Clothes Store of the Israelite Community, following an application: "three pairs of *used* socks" have been allocated to me there.

Eva spends half the day scouring market hall and shops. Provisions, potato shortage. *Unavailable* apart from that: saucepans (not to be found *anywhere*), *heat resistant* wash-pots, *chromium-plated* knives, earthenware coffee mugs, deep plates. — Most extreme shortage of toilet paper.

Very great spectacle in Berlin for the Anti-Comintern Pact. Renewed after five years, 13 states. "The young nations," the "new Europe" against Jewish Bolshevism and Jewish England. Ribbentrop's speech: "We can wage war for thirty years."

Kreidl Sr. still under arrest. No one knows what he is accused of. His wife is not allowed to speak to him. An inspector at the PPD told her: "He talked." Kreidl's fate, Lissy's fate: at any hour it could be mine.

The alarm abroad about the deportations must be very great: Without having asked for them, Lissy Meyerhof and Caroli Stern received, by telegram, from relatives in the USA visa and passage to Cuba. But it doesn't help them; the German side is not issuing any passports. (Another assertion: only issued to the over-sixties. Everything uncertain, changing daily.) Cf. also Sussmann's card to me. We weighed matters up again. Result as always: stay. If we go, then we save our lives and are dependents and beggars for the rest of our lives. If we remain, then our lives are in danger, but we retain the possibility of afterward leading a life worth living. Consolation in spite of it all: Going hardly depends on us any more. Everything is fate, one could be rushing to one's doom. If, e.g., we had moved to Berlin in spring, then by now I would probably already be in Poland.

November 30, Sunday

My latest domestic activity: *brushing* jacket potatoes. (Unfortunately I cannot peel.) We have a hundredweight of potatoes, a blessing, shortage of potatoes everywhere, restaurants required three times a week to serve only potatoes in their jackets. — Questionnaire from the National Association: "Veteran? Decorations?" At the Community no one knows what it is about. Supposition in Berlin: Exemption from deportation, as well as from the Jew's star. Too nice to be true. Dropping the Jew's star would relieve Eva twice over: from the many shopping errands and from cooking. Cooking every evening, in particular, exhausts her very greatly (heating up of head, eyes, nerves).

When I fetched the socks—I got new ones moreover—the Community man there, an elderly educated man, front-line veteran, said: "From the Wars of Liberation onward, our papers don't go any further back, people from our family have taken part in all Germany's wars, '64, '66, '70"; evacuation of Dresden was not to be feared, because not worthwhile. "Only 1,000 Jews here, of whom 400 at Zeiss-Ikon, besides many children and people over seventy among the 600."

Today Lissy sent a touching little Christmas package (about ½ ounce of coffee, a piece of soap, a packet of black bread, green with mold, etc.), also lengthy letter: Chaotic conditions in the deportation business; transports leave, are canceled, leave after all. Those designated drag their suitcases to the station, drag them back, wait—in Hanover the women from an old people's home are sitting on their suitcases. — Uniformed police came to Lissy's room, searched it, took her vacuum cleaner and small carpets away with them.

Emigrants—Reich law since two days ago—declared stateless, their blocked accounts seized. The question now is, whether I shall still receive the 1,200M from Georg already assigned to me—so far the October installment has been paid to me. If nothing more follows, I have nevertheless hoarded a reserve of 1,000M over and above the tax-free limit, which would be sufficient for the enormous taxes, for mortgage and dentist until April. What is the point of making provision any further ahead than that?

I have the impression that terror and chaos are getting worse day by day. Ever new battles in the East, even though Russia is supposed to have been annihilated long ago, in Africa big English offensive in Cyrenaica, "Gondar, last Italian position" in Abyssinia has fallen. How much longer can Italy hold out?

December 4, Thursday morning

The diary must be out of the house. Yesterday Paul Kreidl brought news that a circular was on its way: *Inventory of household effects.* That means confiscations, perhaps also deportation. A house search can be expected immediately after the inventory statement. Eva is therefore to take my diaries and manuscripts to Annemarie. If necessary I shall have to stop the diary notes altogether. — Today I shall also leave my personal documents to be photocopied, since all documents are likely to be confiscated. (One turns into a Peter Schlemihl as it were.)

On Tuesday afternoon we were at the Neumanns for tea. An Aryan lady there, probably in her fifties, very anglophile, supplied with news from there. Situation of the English offensive in Africa is favorable.

Sussmann writes urgently again, I should pursue emigration. He had agreement by airmail from Georg, that he, Georg, was transferring the sum required by Sweden, maintenance for two persons for five years(!). Just now second card from Sussmann with 12 questions for the Foreign Ministry there. "If change of address likely, this could possibly be deferred by referring to imminent departure." Thus extreme disquiet abroad about our fate.

December 5, Friday

Nine tenths a false alarm: The circular merely contains the obligation to report every testamentary disposition of "movable goods," that is all Jewish property (every piece of furniture, etc.) is being *fixed*, nothing can be got to safety anymore. Bad enough—but not quite as bad and immediately threatening as an inventory. — But the "evacuations" continue, it can hit us any day. Also numerous house searches for foodstuffs, soap and skin cream are said to be taking place. — At all events diaries since 1933 will be out of the house today. And some manuscripts. And personal papers which, so it is said, the Gestapo like to take away with them.

Kätchen Sara in her nervousness: yesterday morning at about half past four flickering glow of fire outside the glass door of our bedroom. Eva up. Kätchen: "My God, did I get a fright!"; completely confused. Could not sleep, cigarette in bed, newspaper flared up—into the corridor with the burning sheet, attempt to extinguish—

December 7, Sunday

Eva was at Annemarie's the day before yesterday. Annemarie told her, Russian prisoners were searching garbage cans for food. Paul Kreidl had heard exactly the same story at work.

The new decree, which fixes our movable property—it states, inter alia, that what is permitted to be taken away on evacuation need *not* be notified!—furthermore the house searches for foodstuffs causing much anxiety. Kätchen is sticking "Pickling Vinegar" and "Vinegar" over wine-bottle labels. It was announced on the radio, Aryan persons who took Jewish property for safekeeping would receive prison sentences. Frau Pl . . . got into a hysterical panic, which she passed on to Kätchen Sara. What to do with the Persian lamb? — The church painting is a loan from her brother-in-law, to whom it was left by her late husband.

Today I saw a postcard with the postmark: "Litzmannstadt Ghetto." On it "the Elder of the Jews" made known that financial donations to evacuees were permitted. The card bore yet another stamp: "Litzmannstadt, biggest industrial city of the East."

[...]

Diary is kept in a folder of notes on the XVIIIme.

December 9, Tuesday morning

Big news yesterday evening. (1) Japan declared war on the USA on the eighth (or seventh?). Everything about it is inexplicable and incalculable. Why? (Triple Pact bound to respond: if war is declared on *it*?), why now? With what prospects? What effect on the relationship Germany-USA and what on Russia-Japan? Of course according to today's Japanese telegrams a whole US squadron has already been annihilated. Goebbels' and Asian style. — Paul Kreidl thinks: Now *all* opinion in the USA will be for war with Germany. (2) The military bulletin says, henceforth it is necessary to reckon on the winter and otherwise rest. Therefore the attack on Moscow and Petersburg appears to have been unsuccessful. And how often have they already said: Russia *completely* beaten. (Exactly like last year: England *is* already dead.) (3) From Africa only reports of continuing heavy fighting. In NS style that now means: The English offensive is gaining ground.

In addition Estreicher's arrest was announced yesterday. General rejoicing. The man is hated by everyone.

[...]

December 12, Friday morning

Yesterday, December 11, '41, Germany declared war on the USA. We properly heard of it only this morning (in the coal cellar from Frau Ludwig, Dr. Friedheim's Catholic-Aryan housekeeper). We already said it to each other yesterday, since Hitler had summoned the Reichstag to "receive a government declaration," and since the evening newspaper reported the reciprocal arrest of Germans in the USA and of US people in Germany.

Characteristic feature: At quarter to four I was at the grocer's on Wasaplatz. The shop empty, the owner fumbling around with something; the radio on in the back, I hear Hitler's voice without being able to understand it. I: "Has war been declared on the USA?" — The shopkeeper quite indifferent: "I don't know, I'm busy here." In 1918 in *just* the same way, at the Merkur in Leipzig, the racing results were hung over telegrams of the progress of the offensive. — In the newspaper nothing but announcements of great Japanese victories; ships sunk, cargos, etc.

[...]

Evening

"It was the Jew in all his Satanic vileness, which gathered around this man, but also to whom this man reached out." (Hitler on December 11, speech declaring war on Roosevelt.) LTI pushed to the point of absurdity. In this speech Hitler developed the concept of *Europe*. For him the beginning and *only* foundation is Greece, into which *Nordic* tribes entered. Jerusalem excluded, Hellas Germanized! Very interesting the stages Germany–Greater Germany–Europe, and how they have been climbed in the last few years. "Even Frenchmen" are fighting for Europe against Bolshevism, it is simply "a crusade" (in this last speech). The conclusion is yet again this time (as also the last time against the Bishop of Münster) a threat directed inward, in part in almost the same words: Whoever undermines or attacks the authority of the regime, no matter under what "camouflage," will die an ignominious death.

December 17, Wednesday

LTI. Lissy Meyerhof—still in Berlin, but constantly threatened by "evacuation," wrote that the '14–'18 war is lately being called the "*Little* World War." That is very LTIstic: What we are doing must be bigger than everything that went before. Consider at the same time this peculiarity: In the case of the war, it really is bigger—Japan, USA, Africa are much more strongly involved—and yet there is still an air of charlatanry about it. Even when they are telling the truth . . .

On Saturday young Kreidl, baptized, thoroughly European and German-minded, talked about the "Jewish nation." It shook me. Hitler is the most important promoter of Zionism, Hitler has literally created the "Jewish nation," "world Jewry," *the* Jew.

I walked down Caspar David Friedrich Strasse beside Frau Ida Kreidl; we were overtaken by an old mailman in uniform, a Christmas tree under his arm. He called out loudly to her, on the street, harmlessly: "When will we buy from you again? Me and my mates, old sportsmen, we bought so much from you. And such good quality. As mailman, I know, I delivered so many parcels to you. Such good quality!" The Kreidls had a shop in Galeriestrasse selling work clothes and sporting goods. It was Aryanized. — Vox populi?

Lissy's letter assumes war with the USA will make the war longer. The assumption appears widespread. But if I hang a heavier weight on a clock, then it runs down more quickly.

[. . .]

Today I wrote a very resigned letter to Sussmann. I quoted Kätchen Sara's favorite phrase: "I wonder what'll happen next." I wrote, that as last words they will turn out at least as beautiful as "More light" or "plaudite . . ."

December 22, Monday

Decrees yesterday—Paul Kreidl brings them up, circular from the Community, signature necessary: (1) *Prohibition on using public telephones.* (Private telephones were taken from us long ago.) (2) *Curfew* for all Jews from the morning of December 24 to January 1, "since provocative behavior of a Jew in public has caused outrage." Exempted is only the shopping hour three till four (Saturday twelve till one); so four of the eight days (the Christmas holidays, New Year's Day and Sunday) are days of complete imprisonment. — The one "outrageous" case is supposed to have been this (reports in agreement and incontestable): A Nazi cow shouts at an elderly gentleman: "Get down off the sidewalk, Jew!" He refuses, he has a right to be on the sidewalk. He is summoned to the Gestapo "for questioning" and imprisoned. This was told us by Paul Kreidl, whose workmate is a son of the man, who was present at the scene and was likewise summoned to the Gestapo. Kätchen, who worked with the man at Zeiss-Ikon, told exactly the same story.

This month the 200M installment from Georg's blocked account was no longer paid to me. The emigrants have now been expatriated, their assets confiscated. I have insisted that the sum given to me as a gift is my property—it will be no use. I have long been covering everything outside the tax exemption limit from my reserves. They were replenished by Georg's gift. Now there is still 1,000M left. Once that is used up, somewhere about April, I shall have to sell the house. — The Jews say, by April I shall be in the Polish ghetto.

New card from Sussmann: He has requested the $5,000 from Georg. He still believes we *could* and *want* to get out.

Paul Kreidl is now working on the railway main line; he says: many long ambulance trains. — The military reports subdued and obfuscatory: "Hard battles" in the East and heavy losses for the attacking Soviets; in North Africa "we are disengaging from the enemy, having repelled his attacks." Above that—East Asia plus Goebbels—endless Japanese victories, inaction and despair of England and America.

In our room for hours yesterday afternoon a minor shooting star from Kätchen's bridge party—a Herr Seliksohn. The man, mid-forties, interesting, but uncongenial mixture. Born Russian and Talmud Jew, until his lower school certificate at grammar school in Russia and "learned" at Talmud school. Then in Germany, volunteer at 17, wounded. Then Russian and Hebrew interpreter, knew Supreme Command East, Vilna, Arnold Zweig. Then Social Democratic journalist, bookseller, party official, employed at the "Vorwärts." Badly mistreated by the present government. Now gruesome mixture of Communism and Zionism. Naturally he considers me completely and doubly astray: bourgeois and German. I shall, he says, be a very poor and pitiable "Yid" when I ("in four months for sure") am sitting in a Polish or Russian ghetto.

Twelve midday

Kätchen Sara, returning from Zeiss-Ikon, has just rushed into the room: "Brauchitsch and Keitel resigned. Hitler assumes supreme command, proclamation to army and SS." Jubilation! Christmas present! New hope. Seliksohn told us the news yesterday evening as unconfirmed rumor, we must not pass it on to Kätchen, we did not believe it either. — Kätchen said Swiss stations had already been broadcasting the news yesterday.

December 23, Tuesday morning

In yesterday's newspaper, a call by the Führer and Goebbels to give all fur and woolen things, which could be spared, for the Eastern Front; to the Jews, however, insofar as they wear the star, order circulated through the Community, all fur and woolen things to be handed over "without compensation" by five o'clock this afternoon—"the authorities will carry out checks later." (Eva not affected, nevertheless as a precaution [took things] to Annemarie, because we shall certainly have a house search, because I literally have nothing to hand over.) — The bitterness at this new robbery disappears in the heart's joy at the *turnabout* (cf. the Kreidls' mood, and Kätchen's), because we regard Hitler taking over supreme command as a turnabout. It does not matter what lies behind it: discord between army and Party or refusal of responsibility for needless shedding of blood or whatever: It is a terrible sign of uncertainty, especially as the defeat in the East is hardly concealed anymore, that in Africa is plain to the whole world.

Hitler's proclamation to the army is a model example of LTI. Excessive piling up of the Barnum superlatives, underneath it uncertainty, fear. *Fanatical* twice. The form corresponds to the veiled, in part mysterious content. For consideration: A few weeks ago the Russians were officially "annihilated." Now they are to be annihilated in the spring. You merely need to hold on "fanatically" to what you have already conquered. Why "difficulties" just at this point, when the *world* power Japan (not *great* power) has annihilated(!) the USA's Pacific fleet? Why has the winter in Russia broken so unexpectedly early? — We, Eva and I, rack our brains: Have new Russian armies appeared, or has Germany sent troops to another front? To *which* one? I put my money on American threat to Scandinavia from Iceland. But everything remains obscure.

Certainty: *He* will fall. Uncertainty: (1) When? (2) Before we do?

Evening

Beresin, who delivered cigarettes to us in Dölzschen: Many weeks ago we were told, he was in the PPD. Later, that he was still inside, no one knew where or why. Today Kätchen brings the secret news from the Community: died in a concentration camp, his urn has been sent back. — Ernst Kreidl is still inside—one has already got used to it (*one*—but he?), no one asks much about him anymore.

This afternoon Eva was at Annemarie's. Her very welcome Christmas present: nearly eight pounds of bread coupons.

December 25, midday

Christmas and house arrest, and for the first time in 38 years no present for Eva. Nevertheless optimistic mood, because an end now seems in sight. The news from the East and from Africa daily more threatening. Yesterday the strongly vouched-for rumor that the garrison here was put on alert on the night of the twenty-third to the twenty-fourth—disturbances feared. Today Paul Kreidl reports, there is a reprint of an Italian article in the *Frankfurter Zeitung* which said the situation in the East was "serious," in Africa "very serious."

Eva had procured a little tree: second Christmas in the Jews' House, scantier and more optimistic than the first. We celebrated with Kätchen Sara, she donated a bottle of white wine. I got a pair of lined gloves from Eva and had *nothing* for her. Today and tomorrow she will eat carp in the restaurant, if there is still some to have. — Yesterday it was warm with driving rain all day long, thunderstorm in the evening. Today still stormy, but changing to snow and cold.

LTI. Paul Kreidl rightly says: If "heroes," "heroic," appear in the bulletin, then "it always sounds like an obituary" ("heroic resistance in Africa").

Barnumisms from Hitler's proclamation to the army on assuming supreme command (signed December 19, not made public until December 22, '41): "... The armies in the East, after their undying and in world history unparalleled victories against the most dangerous enemy of all times, must now, as a result of the sudden onset of winter, change from a campaign of movement into a war of position..." From now until spring, they must "*just as fanatically and tenaciously*" hold on to what they have gained so far. "... With my *fanatical* will as a simple German soldier I have succeeded in bringing the German nation together again after more than fifteen years work and of liberating it from the death sentence of Versailles ... My soldiers! You will thus understand that my heart belongs to you ... but that my reason and my determination know only the *annihilation* of the enemy, that is the victorious ending of this war ... But the Lord God will not refuse his *bravest* soldiers victory!" Why does Hitler console with the "annihilation of the Pacific Fleet" — he knows, doesn't he, that it is as little annihilated as the Russian army? [...]

How little fellow feeling there is, even for nearest and dearest. Ernst Kreidl, uncle, in-law, has remained in prison over Christmas. Very sad— but the Kreidls downstairs display a cheerful optimism, as do we. —

Richard Katz, the father-in-law, the cavalry man, ill for months, success-fully operated on a couple of weeks ago, is now tormented and con-demned: His wife hints, with barely an attempt at concealment, that he is suffering from cancer of the bladder and will be "in agony for years yet," but cannot be saved. Very sad—but the sense of optimism, the cheerful mood in the Kreidl household is no more subdued than ours. [. . .] I am hardly any younger than he is, I can be laid low tomorrow, as he is laid low today. Just produce another three works: Curriculum, Eighteenth Century and LTI! Vanitatum vanitas!

December 27, Saturday evening

On the twenty-fifth still storm and rain, since yesterday snow and frost. The Jews' House detention from December 24 till January 1 with excep-tion of the shopping hour means in fact complete seclusion on December 25, 26, 28 and January 1 as days of rest. On the twenty-fourth and twenty-fifth I did not leave the house, yesterday evening I walked three times round the snow-covered house inside the garden fence, at midday today was at Wasaplatz to buy potatoes.

Today I finished writing the chapter "War's End." My Curriculum achievement this year is very limited. [. . .] In total (including the prison study) I have managed about 160 manuscript pages (= 300 printed pages in the format of the literary history), all of it the war; but only the pieces up to and including Kovno have been typed and are the final version, about half therefore. It is my intention to get the last chapter, "Private Lecturer During the Revolution," down in outline in these last days of December and then to complete it by February 12. After that I shall attempt to borrow a type-writer and in about two months prepare a final version of the remainder of the volume. And beyond that I shall not make any further plans.

The general situation has not changed during the holidays. Heavy and disastrous battles everywhere; withdrawals and defeats in Russia and Africa concealed behind tarted-up Japanese victory reports.

December 28, Sunday

Continuing snowfall, frost.

Psychology of the Jews' House. We were imprisoned for two days and thus cut off from any news; after that yesterday's newspaper with telegrams very unfavorable to Hitler. Then in the evening Paul Kreidl came up "to discuss the situation" (an expression I introduced), in truth to let out his feeling of happiness. The thought of becoming free raised his spirits enor-mously. What was, what he planned before the 3rd Reich, what he plans now ("that is, if they don't" — gesture of throat cutting). The Sport House Kreidl on the Altmarkt; the father, died '34, was still essentially a clothing

Jew, he, Paul Kreidl, co-owner, then heir to the firm, dealt in sporting goods, was a fencer. Things flourished, twelve companies divided up the trade. Joint purchasing, this cartel kept three factories busy making swimsuits, bought 300,000, bought for 45 pfennigs what the retailer sold for 80 pfennigs. Finally, however, the factories themselves began to sell directly to the customers. (Witt, for example, the mail-order company, from which Eva bought so much.) Paul Kreidl's plans before the debacle: "A sports travel agency with professional advice from well-known sportsmen. (To be accounted for as advertising, the man given advice for free, buys 500M worth of goods from me.) A Sport House in which the various sports associations have their offices; develop our catalog into a monthly magazine. — Our own factories, first a ski factory, and our own shops. — Once the change comes, I'll first of all go to a ski factory for a year as a worker. There's a man in the Black Forest who's grown big because of us, with whom I've remained in touch—it's all agreed, he'll take me on. Later other goods as well—in 10 years I'll make a fortune for myself, just as my father rose after 1918. — Enforced disarmament and with it a boom in sports will come again as after 1918. — I have my plans, sometimes I feel so completely sure of success and everything is easy; sometimes I think I shall achieve nothing." — I told Paul Kreidl that I've felt like that for almost forty years with every book.

Other Jews' House themes: Dr. Friedheim, the embittered, arrogant banker, and his Catholic housekeeper, Fräulein Ludwig. Kätchen Sara's petit bourgeois jealousy of Fräulein Ludwig.

December 30, Tuesday

Frau Voss said yesterday: "At five o'clock in the morning on the tram to Zeiss-Ikon. Alone, driver sees star, soldier jumps on, recognizes the driver as a friend, does not notice me. The two greet each other boisterously, how is it going, I look the other way, try to be inconspicuous. 'You know, Emil, if we even just had a potato out there. Just eat our fill.' — 'We've got it up to here too.' — 'Man, out there in Russia, it's hell—wild horses won't get me away from here again—I know what I'm going to do . . .' He notices me, gets the shock of his life, can't say a word. — The driver, laughing: 'It's all right, you can talk . . .' I had to laugh too. I get off. Driver and soldier wave and call: "Good-bye, all the best!" — I don't think Kätchen Sara invents such stories or even embroiders them.

December 31, Wednesday

Résumé. Work: the war section of the Curriculi, Alphons School till the end of the war, half of it only in manuscript (cf. December 27), the prison piece. — The whole year long like a prisoner, not even longer summer walks possible, the situation ever more constrained and dangerous. The larger part of Georg's 3,000M gift lost. (200M installments, after 1,400 confiscation of emigrants' accounts; of these 1,400 at least 600 lost in taxes.)

Heaviest blow, heavier than the prison week in summer: the Jew's star since September 19, '41. Since then completely cut off. Eva does all the shopping, frequently eats alone in town at midday, cooks every evening for us. A lot of housework, washing up, scouring pots falls upon me. Restricted to a very few shopping errands on Chemnitzer Platz. Sitting at home for days on end. — Since about a month ago definite reversal in the war situation and increasing hope.

We celebrated New Year's Eve downstairs with the Kreidls, the wife of the imprisoned landlord was also there. (Friedheim, ill and bad-tempered, was not one of the party.) Very friendly reception, touching hospitality. Tea with cakes—then vermouth—toward twelve a real punch bowl. I made a serious little speech, so serious that when we toasted one another my hand was trembling. Hitler, the "Barnum of hell," as a proper circus director is always out for the "never before seen," thus instead of the usual seven lean years he had given us eight; this eighth could no longer be called lean, but a skeleton, since the mountains of corpses in the East were stinking to high heaven.

That it was our most dreadful year, dreadful because of our own real experience, more dreadful because of the constant state of threat, most dreadful of all because of what we saw others suffering (deportations, murder), but that at the end it brought optimism—I quoted widely: nil inultum remanebit. My adhortatio was: Head held high for the difficult last five minutes!

NOTES

1933

January 14—Rectoral election: The Technical University (TU) in Dresden had elected its rectors since 1890, when the original Royal Saxon Polytechnic at Dresden was awarded university status. Until the 1936–37 academic year the rector was elected annually.

Reuther: Dr. Oskar Reuther (1880–1954) was Professor of the History of Architecture at the TU from May 1920. He was rector in 1932–33 and 1933–34.

our section: Until 1941 the Dresden TU was divided into sections. The chairs, institutes and collections were grouped in these sections. Victor Klemperer was made Professor of Romance Languages in the General Section of the TU in 1920.

"Whispering Committee": The rectoral elections were often discussed confidentially in advance.

Beste: Professor Theodor Beste was Dean of the Cultural Sciences Section.

the house: At his wife's insistence Victor Klemperer had bought a plot of land in the village of Dölzschen, southwest of the city center, on which to build a house.

Eva's obsession: Eva Klemperer, née Schlemmer (1882–1951), from Königsberg, a pianist and musicologist, was Victor Klemperer's first wife. They were married in 1906.

The Hueber court case: The dispute with the Max Hueber publishing house in Munich evidently arose from the difficulties presented to the printers by Klemperer's handwriting (typescripts were still rare at the time).

the "Image of France": "Das neue deutsche Frankreichbild 1914–1933. Ein historischer Überblick" finally appeared in two parts in East Germany in 1961 and 1963.

Liesel Sebba: Julius Sebba had been a friend of the Klemperers since Victor Klemperer's days as a journalist before 1914 in Berlin. Julius Sebba was a lawyer born in Königsberg. Over the years the whole Sebba family had been drawn into the friendship—including Liesel Sebba.

the young Köhlers: Johannes Köhler, a young probationary teacher of German and Religion, and his wife, Ellen, were for a long time among the Klemperers' closest friends.

January 24—Annemarie: Dr. Annemarie Köhler, surgeon at the Johanniter (St. John's) Hospital in Heidenau. In 1937 moved to Pirna, near Dresden. Old friend of the Klemperers from their Leipzig days (1918).

Harms circle: A group of journalists in Leipzig whom Klemperer had gotten to know during his war service as military censor.

February 21—Hitler's appointment: President Hindenburg appointed Hitler Chancellor (i.e., prime minister) on January 30, 1933, as head of a coalition government.

Blumenfelds: Professor Walter Blumenfeld taught industrial psychology at the Pedagogical Institute (i.e., teacher training institute).

German Nationals: Deutschnationale Volkspartei, a "respectable" but antidemocratic conservative party. Coalition partners with the Nazis in Hitler's early administration. The party dissolved itself in June 1933.

Who will have the majority?: The Reichstag was dissolved on February 1, 1933, and elections were set for March 5.

the Thieles: Fritz Thiele was also one of the Harms circle.

the Köhlers, the "respectable" ones: The young Köhlers were married, unlike Annemarie Köhler, who lived with the doctor, Friedrich Dressel. The Klemperers jokingly distinguished between the "respectable" and the "unrespectable" Köhlers.

Wengler: Heinrich Wengler, teacher of Italian at the TU.

Young Frau Kühn: Wife of the historian Professor Johannes Kühn.

Breit: James Breit, a professor of law at the TU.

the beautiful Maria: Maria Kube, a former maid of the Klemperers, who kept in touch even through the most difficult times.

Baeumler: Professor Alfred Baeumler (1887–1968). In 1928, Chair of Philosophy and Pedagogics in Dresden; 1933, Professor of Political Pedagogy in Berlin. Director of the Scholarship Section in the office of Alfred Rosenberg ("Commissioner of the Führer for the Supervision of the Mental Training and Education of the National Socialist German Workers' Party, NSDAP").

Kriek: Professor Ernst Kriek, educationalist, founder of the Nazi theory of education.

March 10—Reichsbanner: A paramilitary organization set up to defend the constitution and the republic. It was supported by the "Weimar" parties—Social Democrats, Democrats, Zentrum—as well as by the Free Trade Unions. Essentially, however, it was a Social Democratic and trade union organization.

the clumsy business of the Reichstag fire: It is now known that the Reichstag fire was, in fact, the work of the lone Dutch anarchist, Marinus van der Lubbe, who set the building alight in protest against the Nazis. The latter were, however, immediately able to capitalize on the arson.

the Democrats: The German Democratic Party (DDP), a left-liberal party, whose size and influence had progressively shrunk in the course of the polarization of the Weimar years. In 1930 it had even gone so far as to amalgamate with the right wing Jungdeutscher Orden (Young German Order). By March 1933, it was no more than a shadow of the party that had won 18.6 percent of the vote in the first election of the Weimar Republic.

Zentrum: Catholic party. It had been of considerable significance in German politics since the "Kulturkampf" against the Catholic Church, initiated by Bismarck in the 1870s. Contained a wide spectrum of views from traditionalist conservatives to moderate-left trade unionists.

Dembers: Professor Harry Dember, physicist, and his wife, Agnes.

Horst Wessel: Wessel (1907–1930) was a Nazi Party/SA man and a petty criminal, active in the Berlin district of Friedrichshain. He was killed in a dispute with a pimp who was close to the Communist Party. Turned into a martyr by SA and NSDAP. A song he wrote—known as the Horst Wessel Song—became the Party anthem and after 1933, a second German anthem.

the dramaturge Karl Wolf: Wolf was senior dramaturge at the Schauspielhaus (theater) in Dresden.

the whole Saxon cabinet: Under the Weimar constitution, the various German states (Bavaria, Thuringia, Prussia, etc.) had their own governments within a federal system.

Que sais-je? (French): "What do I know?" Klemperer's favorite quotation from Montaigne.

Frau Schaps with the Gerstles: The Klemperers knew the Gerstles through Julius Sebba. Hans Gerstle, brother-in-law of Julius Sebba, was director of a flavored-coffee factory. Jenny Schaps was his mother-in-law.

March 17—the Weisseritz: A small tributary of the Elbe. Dresden, famously, is situated on the latter river.

the Thiemes: Johannes Thieme, whom the Klemperers had known since their Leipzig days, came to stay with them in 1920 and became their foster child soon after. For many years he called them father and mother.

SA men: SA, an abbreviation of Sturmabteilung, the Nazi paramilitary organization (the Brownshirts). Saw itself as the guardian of the radical aims of the Nazi revolution. Its power was broken in the purge known as the Night of the Long Knives. After that the SA was essentially an organization of Nazi activists.

Sachsenwerk: A large engineering plant in Dresden.

Okrilla: Small town north of Dresden.

Commissioner Killinger: Manfred von Killinger, Reich Commissioner for Security and Order in Saxony; he was personally involved in many crimes.

March 20—Father: Dr. Wilhelm Klemperer (1839–1912), rabbi in Landsberg an der Warthe and Bromberg; from 1890 second preacher of the Jewish Reform Community in Berlin.

"Act of State of March 21": Often called the Day of Potsdam. Hitler had chosen the Garnisonkirche (garrison church) in Potsdam, which had many associations with the Prussian monarchy, for the Reichstag opening ceremony. The formal handshake between Hitler and Hindenburg on the "Day of Potsdam" was supposed to demonstrate the convergence of "Prussianism" (Preussentum) and National Socialism.

Ebertstrasse: Ebert was the first president of the republic and a Social Democrat.

March 21—*Freiheitskampf:* "Struggle for freedom."

March 22—Wend Käthe: Member of a small Slav minority in the Lausitz area northeast of Dresden. Today usually referred to as Sorbs.

March 27—four "respectable" Köhlers: The young Köhlers, Ellen and Johannes, and their parents. Their father was a railway station inspector.

March 30—the National Socialist boycott: A general boycott of Jewish shops and stores—there had been haphazard and violent local boycotts—was announced in the *Völkische Beobachter* (the main Nazi paper), effective from 10 A.M. on Saturday, April 1.

Stahlhelm revolt: The Stahlhelm ("steel helmet") was a paramilitary organization of First World War and Freikorps veterans. (The Freikorps were quasi-legal military formations deployed in the years after the First World War to protect German interests in Eastern Europe and to suppress working class unrest within Germany.) It was associated with the German National People's Party and therefore distinct from the SA and SS of the Nazi Party. On March 27, 1933, armed SS and police units took action against an alleged putsch attempt by the Stahlhelm in Braunschweig (Brunswick). On March 28 the Stahlhelm was prohibited. The ban was lifted on April 1. The organization was incorporated into the SA on April 26.

Dr. Salzburg's: Friedrich Salzburg, lawyer and notary.

Herr Wollf: Professor Julius Ferdinand Wollf was for many years chief editor and publisher of the *Dresdener Neueste Nachrichten*.

March 31—the impressive letter: Klemperer is presumably referring to the appeal by the nationalist Reich Association of Jewish War Veterans.

Gusti Wieghardt's: Dr. Auguste Wieghardt-Lazar (1887–1970), author of books for children and young people, moved from Vienna to Dresden in 1920. From 1939, in exile in England, returned to Dresden in 1949.

April 3—since Lugano: Because of Eva Klemperer's deepening depression, the couple had taken a holiday in Lugano (March 9–28, 1931), which, however, only worsened her condition.

April 7—Albert Hirsch: Hirsch had been a student friend of Klemperer's in Munich.

April 10—the Meyerhofs: Victor Klemperer's friendship with the Meyerhofs dated from his time as an apprentice in Berlin. Hans Meyerhof was a fellow apprentice, and Klemperer remained in touch with the family.

April 12—Hugenberg: Alfred Hugenberg was a right-wing press and media baron in the Weimar Republic; he became leader of the German National People's Party.

Oberfohren: Ernst Oberfohren (1881–1933), leader of the parliamentary group of the German Nationals. A memorandum he wrote on February 27, 1933, published in the *Manchester Guardian* on April 29, alleged that the Reichstag fire had been deliberately started in accordance with a plan drawn up by Goebbels. On March 29 Oberfohren was forced to resign his seat, and he committed suicide some weeks later.

limpieza de la sangre (Spanish): "Purity of blood."

April 25—the Wieghardts: Auguste Wieghardt-Lazar and her stepson Karl Wieghardt.

April 30—that Georg had to go: Klemperer's eldest brother, Professor Georg Klemperer (1865–1946), eminent physician; at Moabit Hospital, Berlin, from 1906; forced to "retire" from all his posts on May 4, 1933.

Frau Lehmann: The Klemperers' cleaning woman.

May 15—Delekat: Professor Friedrich Delekat, pastor. Later a prominent member of the Bekennende (Confessional) Church, that part of the Lutheran Church that tried to maintain its autonomy within the Nazi state. It was openly critical of the Nazis' racial measures in particular. Some ministers became active resisters.

Kreuzkirche: Oldest church in Dresden; rebuilt in the baroque style and restored after the destruction of the Second World War.

Rüdiger: Klemperer had used his acquaintanceship with Gertrud von Rüdiger, a junior member of the TU's German department, to ask her brother, a major in the Reichswehr (the regular army), to use his influence on behalf of Hans Hirche.

May 22–May 16—The Klemperers were married in a civil ceremony on May 16, 1906.

Since Hitler's peace speech: On May 17, 1933, Hitler made his so-called "peace speech" to the Reichstag, in which he presented his foreign policy program.

June 17—Berthold: Victor Klemperer's brother, a lawyer in Berlin, who died in 1931.

coordination: The usual translation of Gleichschaltung, the Nazi term for the subordination of all aspects of public life, including professional associations, to the Nazi Party.

Scherner: Hans Scherner had also been part of the Leipzig circle.

D'altra parte (Italian): "On the other hand."

the Wenglers: Heinrich Wengler and his sister Ellen.

delightful Kiepura film: Jan Kiepura, Polish singer and comic actor, born 1902; international career from 1926; performed in opera throughout Europe and North and South America. First film appearance in Berlin, 1930. After 1940, worked largely in the United States.

I. Elbogen: Professor Ismar Elbogen (1874–1943), author of the highly regarded *Geschichte der Juden in Deutschland* (History of the Jews in Germany).

Otto Klemperer: The conductor Otto Klemperer (1885–1973) was a cousin of Victor Klemperer's.

June 29—First meeting 1904.

June 30—Reka: Rezidenzkaufhaus, a department store in Dresden.

July 20—the ceremony at the grave of the "Rathenau eliminators": On June 24, 1922, Walther Rathenau, the German foreign minister, was assassinated in Berlin by right-wing terrorists, partly because he was identified with a policy of fulfill-ment of the Versailles Treaty obligations but above all because he was a Jew. From 1930, after the Nazi Wilhelm Frick (later Hitler's Minister of the Interior) became Minister of the Interior in the state of Thuringia, ceremonies were held at Burg Saaleck, on the anniversary of the assassination, to commemorate the killers. Two of the assassins had been tracked down there and killed in a gun-fight with the police.

July 28—Gesslerhut: Reference to Schiller's play *Wilhelm Tell*. To humiliate the restless Swiss, Gessler, the Imperial governor in Schwyz, commands them to show as much respect to his hat mounted on a pole as to his own person.

That must have been before 1900: Adolf Wilbrandt's tragedy *Timandara* was not, in fact, performed until 1903.

Gumbinnen: Town in East Prussia; scene of a Russian victory at the beginning of the First World War. Soon to be followed by devastating defeats at the battles of Tannenberg and the Masurian Lakes. Prisoners of war from the armies of the Cen-tral Powers held in Siberia were unable to return to Europe immediately after 1917–18, when Russia dropped out of the World War because of the Russian Rev-olution and Civil War.

August 10—Stepun: Professor Fedor Stepun (1884–1965); expelled from the USSR 1922; Professor of Sociology in Dresden 1926–37. Taught Russian intellectual history in Munich from 1947.

August 19—Lössnitz: Now part of Radebeul to the northwest of Dresden.

serve . . . during the war: Victor Klemperer was a volunteer and first served with the Field Artillery on the Western Front; subsequently attached to the Censorship Section of Supreme Command East, first in Lithuania, then in Leipzig.

Michel: As John Bull was/is to England, so der deutsche Michel (the German Michael)—a plain, honest German—was/is to Germany. A representative carica-ture, essentially of the early- to mid-nineteenth century, Michel is usually pre-sented wearing a nightcap and as being a bit slow on the uptake, easily exploited by smarter nations.

the whole Jewish business of Löwenstein & Hecht: From 1887 to 1890, Klemperer was a commercial apprentice in this export company located in Alexandrinnen-strasse in Berlin.

September 6—Walter Jelski: Klemperer's nephew, son of his sister Marta.

Hettner: Hermann Hettner (1821–82), a liberal scholar of art and literature, was one of Klemperer's great models and stood in contrast to the nationalist views that dominated German scholarship of French literature.

Alliance israélite: Alliance israélite universelle (AIU), an international association founded in Paris in 1860, whose aims were to promote equal rights for Jews, to aid persecuted and oppressed Jews, and to finance and support educational establishments and scholarly research.

September 19—"blood flag" of 1923: Flag borne at the head of the column of insurgents during Hitler's failed putsch in Munich in 1923. The attempt to seize power was brought to an end when police opened fire, killing several of the marchers. The Nazi Party subsequently proclaimed the latter "martyrs," by whose blood the flag was supposedly stained.

October 9—the business with the pacifist Gumbel: During the Weimar Republic, Emil Julius Gumbel (1891–1966), professor of Statistics at Heidelberg, published several widely read books on right-wing extremist plots and assassinations. He was the subject of constant vilification.

Karen Michaelis: Danish writer (1872–1950); sheltered a number of German émigrés, including Bertolt Brecht, at her house on the island of Thurø.

Ulich: Professor Robert Ulich (1890–1977), assistant secretary in the Saxon Ministry of Education, chair at Dresden TU. He and his wife emigrated to the United States.

the three Sussmann daughters: Lotte, Hilde and Käte, daughters of Klemperer's youngest sister, Wally (1877–1936), who was married to Martin Sussmann, a doctor.

Erich Mühsam (1878–1934): Author, journalist, anarchist, bohemian. Arrested February 1933, murdered July 1934 in Sachsenhausen concentration camp, at Oranienburg near Berlin.

"Memories": Klemperer's memoirs, on which he began work in 1938, were published posthumously in 1989 under the title *Curriculum Vitae*.

October 23—"German Christians": Organization of Nazi Christians that was established before 1933. After the Nazi seizure of power it attempted to gain control of the Protestant churches in Germany and infuse them with the spirit of the National Socialist revolution. Partly through a mixture of force and fraud the Nazi Christians won control of important church offices in July 1933. This led to a large number of pastors setting up an informal organization, known as the Confessional Church, to oppose state intervention in church affairs. The German Christians were weakened by factionalism and internal disputes and faded into relative insignificance. The Nazi leadership was, in fact, not really interested in any kind of Christianity and given time would probably have embarked on determined repression of the Christian churches.

withdrawal . . . plebiscite . . . election: Germany withdrew from the League of Nations on October 19, 1933. A plebiscite to give assent to the one-party state and a Reichstag election were held on November 12. The turnout was 95.3 percent and the Nazis received 95 percent of the votes cast.

"Winter Aid": The Winter Aid was a social work program organized by the Nazis during the winter months on behalf of the needy. A large part of the funds was raised by public collection, involving members of various Nazi organizations rattling cans and demanding donations as a sign of commitment to national regeneration, etc. The Winter Aid campaigns were supervised by Goebbels' propaganda Ministry.

"National Work": Klemperer is probably referring to campaigns of job creation.

The November criminals: Popular derogatory term on the Right. It conflates the collapse of the Imperial government and the revolution of November 1918 with the democratic parties that accepted the conditions of the Versailles Peace Treaty.

November 2—Iduna: A large insurance company.

Janentzky: Professor Christian Janentsky (1886–1968), a colleague of Victor Klemperer's after the Second World War.

November 11—Frau Mark: Wife of a machine-tool manufacturer who was a friend of Harry Dember's.

Siemensstadt: District in Berlin where the principal factories of the Siemens electrical engineering company were—and to some extent still are—situated.

Rasser brothers: Should be Strasser brothers. Gregor Strasser (1892–1934), member of the Nazi Party from 1921; took part in the Munich putsch, 1923; involved in the attempt to establish a separate party in North Germany, 1925. Became head of propaganda for the whole of Germany in 1926. At the end of 1932 he advocated Nazi participation in a coalition government under the leadership of Kurt von Schleicher. He was subsequently sidelined and removed from all his offices. Murdered on the Night of the Long Knives, when the leadership of the SA was eliminated. Otto Strasser (1897–1974), under the influence of his brother, joined the Nazi Party in 1925; an advocate of an opening to the Left and of an anti-capitalist program, he broke with Hitler in 1930. Left Germany in 1933 and did not return until 1955.

November 14—"London says": The BBC.

December 31—"Tout est possible, même dieu" (French): "Everything is possible, even God."

Vossler: Professor Karl Vossler (1872–1949). Klemperer was Vossler's student in Munich before the First World War. Vossler was a decisive influence on Klemperer's decision to study the history of literature and language in the context of the history of culture as a whole.

1934

January 1—Sinclair Lewis: Klemperer was reading Lewis' novel *The Trail of the Hawk* (first published 1915, translated into German 1933).

January 27—the peace agreement with Poland: The German-Polish Non-Aggression Pact of January 26, 1934, committed both signatories to the peaceful settlement of differences, initially for ten years. The agreement was abrogated by Germany on April 28, 1939.

the Corridor: Usually referred to as the Polish Corridor. A strip of land allocated to Poland by the Treaty of Versailles, which gave the reconstituted state access to the Baltic Sea. However, as a result, the German province of East Prussia was separated from the rest of the country. In Germany, this was regarded as one of the most unreasonable impositions of the 1919 peace settlement.

Victor and Victoria: A 1933 musical comedy, written and directed by Reinhold Schünzel, a half-Jewish filmmaker who continued working in Nazi Germany before fleeing to Hollywood where he scraped out a living playing Nazi heavies. The film is now considered a classic. Blake Edwards made a new version in 1982 under the title *Victor/Victoria* with Julie Andrews in the title role.

February 2—the "Jew" Preuss: Hugo Preuss (1860–1925); constitutional lawyer and cofounder of the Democratic Party (DDP). Drew up the draft constitution of the new German republic (1919). Proposed abolition of Prussia, which occupied two thirds of the territory of the Reich, and the creation of fourteen "free states" of approximately equal size; however, on this issue his arguments did not prevail.

Lettres juives: Les lettres juives by Jean-Baptiste de Boyer, Marquis d'Argens (1703–1771), French writer and philosopher. D'Argens was a freethinker, whose work challenged authoritarian religion and scholasticism.

February 15—the heavy fighting in Austria: Brief civil war, most of the fighting taking place in Vienna between February 12 and 14, 1934. The Austrian chancellor

Dollfuss—usually referred to today as a "clerical Fascist"—provoked an uprising by part of the Social Democratic paramilitary force. Social Democratic strongholds in the capital were attacked and captured by right-wing paramilitaries and Austrian government troops. Subsequently, all political parties except Dollfuss' Fatherland Front were banned.

February 16—Reich Governor Mutschmann: Martin Mutschmann, lace manufacturer from Plauen; Gauleiter (Nazi title for head of a Gau or province) of Saxony from 1925 to 1945. (Before 1933, of course, he was in charge only of the Nazi Party.)

February 21—with a prominent scar by his right eye (did not go to a university): The wound is not a dueling scar, "won" as a member of a right-wing student fraternity.

Mecklenburg: Then, as now, a largely rural state in northern Germany.

March 2—Councillor of Commerce: Courtesy title given to prominent businessmen.

Leonie Meyerhof-Hildeck: Author; wrote as Leonie Hildeck (1858–1933).

Anselma Heine: Author (1855–1930); wrote under the pseudonyms Anselm, Selma or Feodor Heine.

March 19—qualified yourself: In German universities a special postdoctoral qualification, known as a habilitation, is required before an academic can be considered for a faculty appointment.

March 25—Cassirer: *Philosophie der Aufklärung* (The Philosophy of the Enlightenment). Ernst Cassirer (1874–1945) was an influential philosopher; he emigrated in 1933 via Britain and Sweden to the United States.

Grete: Grete Riesenfeld (1868–1942), Victor Klemperer's eldest, widowed sister.

Martin: Dr. Martin Sussmann, husband of Klemperer's sister Wally; physician.

April 24—Delille's *Gardens:* Jacques Delille (1738–1813), French poet, made famous by his didactic poem *The Gardens.* Klemperer's study appeared in 1955 under the title *Delilles Gärten, ein Mosaikbild des 18. Jahrhunderts* (Delille's Gardens, a mosaic of the eighteenth century).

June 13—Couéist: From Couéism, autosuggestion or self-hypnosis, after Émile Coué (1857–1926), a pharmacist and therapist, whose approach was characterized by use of autosuggestion, including frequent use of the formula "Every day, and in every way, I am becoming better and better."

Freudenheim-Bloch: Helene Bloch, née Freudenheim, dentist, grew up, like Eva Klemperer, in Königsberg. She was married to Joseph Bloch, editor of the Social Democratic *Sozialistische Monatshefte,* who died in Prague on December 14, 1936.

Par nobile fratrum (Latin): "What noble brothers," ironic phrase taken from the *Satires* of Horace (3, 243).

Rust, the Reich Education Minister: Bernhard Rust (1883–1945), teacher; 1933–34, Prussian Minister of Culture; 1934–35, Reich Minister for Science, Education and National Instruction. He committed suicide on May 8, 1945.

SA chief Röhm: Ernst Röhm (1887–1934) had risen to the rank of major during World War I; active in the Freikorps, he participated in the suppression of the Munich Councils Republic. Early supporter and advocate of Hitler, introduced him to bourgeois nationalist circles in the Bavarian capital. Built up the Nazis' paramilitary force (SA), very close to Hitler, but also a rival, since under his leadership the fighting organization retained a degree of autonomy from the Party. Absent from Germany 1925–30. After his return he was increasingly in conflict with Hitler because he was opposed to the latter's concept of a "gradual revolution" under cover of legality.

"do what is necessary": In June 1934, a "holiday" of one month was decreed for the SA in order to prevent "uncontrolled" actions.

y todo (Spanish): And everything.

DLZ: Deutsche Literatur Zeitung (German Literary Newspaper.)

June 15—bellum judaicum (Latin): "The Jewish War." An allusion to Josephus' *The History of the Jewish War,* which described the Jewish Revolt against the Romans A.D. 66–70 and was written shortly after the events. In his book on the language of the Nazi dictatorship, *LTI,* Klemperer entitled a chapter "The Jewish War." In it he wrote: "The Jewish War! The Führer did not invent it, and he certainly did not know anything about Flavius Josephus, he simply some time or other picked up from a newspaper or a shopwindow of a bookstore that the Jew Feuchtwanger had written a novel called *The Jewish War.*"

July 14—"Röhm Revolt": Usually known in English as the Night of the Long Knives. On June 30 and July 1, 1934, Ernst Röhm and other senior figures of the SA were shot on Hitler's orders for supposedly planning an uprising. Hitler used the occasion to eliminate a number of other political opponents including the former chancellor, Kurt von Schleicher, Gregor Strasser, Erich Klausener (Catholic Action) and Edgar Jung (a friend and colleague of von Papen). At a stroke, the SA lost its power and the way was open for Hitler to come to an agreement with the only remaining non-Nazi force in the country, the army. The SA ceased to be an unpredictable paramilitary organization with—sometimes—left-populist leanings. From then on Hitler would rely on the army and the SS. The latter was a tightly disciplined elite force and much more single-mindedly oriented toward racial issues.

Theodor Wolff: Wolff (1868–1943) was chief editor of the daily *Berliner Tageblatt* from 1906 to 1933. He emigrated to France but was arrested by the German occupation authorities in 1943. He was sent to Sachsenhausen concentration camp but died in the Jewish Hospital in Moabit, Berlin.

Jan van Leyden: Leyden (1509–1536) was one of the leaders of the Anabaptist revolt in Münster, 1534–35, during the Reformation. The Anabaptists believed they were founding the kingdom of a thousand years. Leyden was executed in 1536.

Rienzi: Cola di Rienzo (1313–1354); Tribune of the People in Rome; in 1347, expelled the leaders of the aristocratic party and proclaimed the revival of the Roman Republic. He was brought down by the opposition of the pope, regained power in 1354 but was killed in a popular uprising. Rienzi is the eponymous hero of Wagner's first successful opera.

scilicet tertii imperii (Latin): Naturally, of the Third Reich.

July 27—Dollfuss killed: Engelbert Dollfuss (1892–1934), Austrian politician; modeled his Christian Social Party on the Italian Fascists. Chancellor 1932, crushed the Social Democratic Party in a brief civil war in February 1934. He was murdered in an attempted putsch by the Vienna SS July 25, 1934.

July 29—Colonel Hindenburg: Colonel Oskar von Hindenburg (1883–1960), President Hindenburg's son, who used his influence on his increasingly senile father to have Hitler appointed Chancellor.

Papen: Franz von Papen (1879–1969); right wing Zentrum (Catholic Party) leader. Chancellor June–December 1932; vice-chancellor in Hitler's cabinet 1933–34. Papen was one of the conservatives who gave Hitler his chance of power in the belief that they could use the Nazi Party to destroy democracy and the threat from the Left while continuing to be in control themselves.

August 2—Franz Joseph: Austrian Emperor Franz Joseph II who died in 1916 after reigning 68 years.

August 4—plebiscite will take place: Hitler had announced a referendum for August 19, the purpose of which was to confirm him as head of state by popular assent.

August 7—the Hindenburg-Tannenberg ceremonies: President Field Marshal Paul von Hindenburg (1847–1934) was laid to rest at the memorial at Tannenberg in East Prussia to the German victory over the Russians at the end of August 1914.

Hindenburg, called out of retirement, had been the commander of the German forces. The engagement was immediately followed by another German victory, the Battle of the Masurian Lakes.

General Reichenau: Walther von Reichenau (1884–1942); Reichswehr general; key figure in the secret rearming before 1933 and of the subsequent integration of the army into the Nazi state.

September 4—black-white-red one: The flag of the pre-1918 German Empire, rather than the Nazi flag with the swastika or the black-red-gold flag of the constitutional republic.

Gustav Adolf: Usually called Gustavus Adolphus in English texts. Swedish king (1594–1632) who intervened against the imminent victory of the Imperial and Catholic forces in the Thirty Years' War. He defeated the Imperial forces under Wallenstein at Lützen in 1632. Although he himself was killed in the battle, it founded the period of Swedish dominance in Northern Europe. The immediate effect of his intervention, however, was to prolong the Thirty Years' War, bringing even greater destruction and misery to the population of Central Europe.

September 12—Du côté de Voltaire, Du côté de Rousseau (French): "From Voltaire's side, From Rousseau's side."

September 27—Forsechè sì, forsechè no (Italian): "Maybe yes, maybe no."

Trude Öhlmann: Loyal friend from the Klemperer's Leipzig days.

HJ: The Hitler Jugend, youth organization of the Nazi Party, frequently abbreviated to HJ.

September 29—as far as the Pucelle poem: "La Pucelle d'Orléans," mock-heroic poem (1755) by Voltaire about Joan of Arc.

Lettres persanes: "Persian Letters" by Montesquieu (1721).

October 6—*Don Carlos:* Play (1787) by Friedrich von Schiller, which intertwines the oppressiveness of the court of Philip II of Spain with the oppression of the Netherlands under Spanish rule and makes a plea both for freedom of the sentiments and for political freedom.

October 8—*Frankfurter Zeitung:* Leading liberal newspaper (founded 1856), particularly in the Weimar Republic. Survived until 1943, though by then a mere shadow of its former self.

Blubo: Abbreviation of Blut und Boden "blood and soil," itself a condensation of a central tenet of Nazi ideology, the rootedness of race in particular landscapes or territories.

October 10—Fedor Mamroth: Theater critic and novelist, died 1907. Klemperer wrote about him more than once in the years before the First World War.

October 14—Good Templar: Organization founded in 1852 in the United States to combat the evils of alcohol; it subsequently spread throughout the world.

October 30—*William Tell:* The play by Schiller.

November 20—*Lettres provinciales: Les provinciales ou lettres écrites par Louis de Montalte à un provincial de ses arnis . . .*, "Letters to a Friend in the Provinces" (1656–57) by Blaise Pascal.

December 4—Gaspary: Italian Dante scholar; author of a literary history of Italy.

December 16—Saar Plebiscite: After the First World War (Versailles Treaty) the coal and steel region of the Saar had been placed under League of Nations administration for fifteen years. The plebiscite of 1935, determining the territory's future, produced a 90 percent vote in favor of return to Germany.

December 30—June 30 da capo (Italian): Perhaps a repeat of June 30 (Night of the Long Knives).

cioè (Italian): "To wit."

1935

January 1, 1935—Lutze's New Year message to the SA: Viktor Lutze (1890–1943) was chief of staff of the SA after the execution of Ernst Röhm.

February 9—Max Liebermann: Liebermann (1847–1935) was perhaps the best known German painter of the early twentieth century. An artist often associated with Berlin, where he largely lived, he was enormously successful in his own lifetime. Today, his naturalistic scenes of labor and Impressionist landscapes and gardens can seem a bit tame, though his portraits and self-portraits still retain considerable force.

February 13—all of Wassermann: Jakob Wassermann (1873–1934), German novelist. Among his works is the autobiography *Mein Weg als Deutscher und Jude* ("My Path as German and Jew") published in 1921.

Roth, the Austrian officer novel: Joseph Roth's novel *Radetzky March.*

the Galsworthy trilogy: John Galsworthy's *The Forsyte Saga,* first published in German in 1933.

the second part of *Morath:* Klemperer probably means *Morath verwirklicht einen Traum* ("Morath realizes a dream"), the second of two *Morath* novels by Max René Hesse (1885–1952), adventurer, physician and author.

February 21—Bayle: Pierre Bayle (1647–1706), French philosopher famous for his *Dictionnaire historique et critique,* which expresses skepticism of orthodox Christianity and advocates religious tolerance. The "Dictionary" was much admired by Klemperer. It consists largely of quotations, anecdotes, commentaries and erudite annotation. This oblique method of subversive criticism was adopted by the eighteenth-century Encyclopedists, and Klemperer saw a revival of the "Encyclopedic style" in the way information was received and read under the conditions of dictatorship. The approach of the Dictionnaire also influenced Klemperer's own work on language and ideology in Nazi Germany, which culminated in the book *LTI* "Lingua tertii imperii," published in 1947.

"Confessional Front": The Confessional Church officially came into existence in May 1934 at the Synod of the Protestant Church in Barmen. (See notes for May 15 and October 23, 1933.)

The Commune: A term widely used in Germany for the Communist Left.

February 27—a little Hoche: Klemperer was reading the autobiography of Alfred Erich Hoche (1933), a psychiatrist in Freiburg.

March 4—the *Esprit des Lois:* "De l'Esprit des Lois," Montesquieu's treatise on the theory of the state, published in 1748.

cunctator (Latin): The irresolute or procrastinating person.

March 17—Weissberger: Arnold Weissberger (1898–1952) lived in the same pension in Munich as the Klemperers in 1919. Studied chemistry, went into research, was about to qualify as a university teacher in 1933 but emigrated to England and later to the United States.

April 17—*Der Stürmer:* Nazi paper, founded in 1923, devoted to anti-Jewish hate stories and illustrations. It was published by Julius Streicher (1885–1946) who was sentenced to death at the Nürnberg war crimes trials.

"The Jews are our misfortune": Phrase coined by the nineteenth-century historian Heinrich von Treitschke.

Kovno: Now usually given as Kaunas, a city in Lithuania.

Münchener NN: Münchener Neueste Nachrichten, a Munich daily newspaper.

April 22—the "election victory" in Danzig: In the Danzig election of April 7, 1935, the National Socialists won a majority. Danzig, now Gdansk, a port city at the mouth of the Vistula, within the band of territory known as the "Polish Corridor," allocated to Poland by the Versailles Treaty. Danzig, however, was declared a Free City and placed under the authority of the League of Nations, (a) because its population was overwhelmingly German, (b) so that Polish exports and imports would nevertheless flow through it without restriction. The Poles, however, built a new port a few miles along the coast—Gdynia.

Stresa: In April 1935, provoked by the reintroduction of universal conscription in Germany, which broke the conditions of the Versailles Treaty, Italy, France and Britain came to an agreement, known as the Stresa Front, to counter German expansionist aims. The Front came to nothing, first because of the Anglo-German Naval Agreement, by which Britain assented to German naval expansion and second, because Italy invaded Abyssinia, in direct opposition to British and French interests.

May 4—Tillich: Paul Tillich (1886–1965), theologian; 1929, Professor of Philosophy at Frankfurt am Main University; emigrated to the United States in 1933 and taught in New York and Chicago.

May 7—Anhalter Bahnhof: Until the destruction of the Second World War and the decisive division of the city in 1961, one of the main railway termini of Berlin.

May 15—"Je ne peux ni ne veux être autre chose . . .", etc. (French): "I cannot nor do I want to be anything other than German" into "I have never thought of being anything other than German."

Curtius: Ernst Robert Curtius (1886–1956), distinguished scholar, particularly of French literature and culture and comparative literature.

May 30—Privy Councillor Demuth: Secretary in Zürich of the "Notgemeinschaft deutscher Wissenschaftler im Ausland" ("Emergency Society of German Scholars Abroad").

June 11—Bastei: Beauty spot in the Saxon Switzerland southeast of Dresden, an area noted for its unusual sandstone rock formations.

"family record": A document including genealogical details, i.e., proof or otherwise of "racial purity."

July 21—m'ont devancé mes neveux (French): "My nephews have outstripped me."

Reymont's: Wladyslaw Stanislaw Reymont (1867–1925), author of *The Peasants* (first published in Poland 1902–09). Reymont won the Nobel prize for literature in 1924.

August 11—in Plauen: District of Dresden immediately below Dölzschen and not the town of the same name.

September 16—Blomberg: Werner von Blomberg (1878–1946), general. As Minister for the Reichswehr, he had the army swear allegiance to Hitler after President Hindenburg's death. From 1935, Minister of War and commander in chief of the Wehrmacht (i.e., the renamed armed forces). Made Field Marshal 1936. Discharged in 1938 for a marriage inappropriate to his position.

Reichenau: See note August 7, 1934, p. 470.

Fritsch: Werner, Freiherr von Fritsch (1880–1939), general. As commander in chief of the army 1935–38, bore a large part of the responsibility for German rearmament. In 1937, he and Blomberg expressed reservations about Hitler's expansionist policies. In 1938, excluded from the army for alleged homosexuality, subsequently cleared by a court of honor but not fully rehabilitated.

September 17—laws on German blood and honor: The annual congress of the Nazi Party in Nürnberg concluded on September 15 with a session of the Reichstag that passed three laws—the so-called "Nürnberg Laws"—including the "Law for the protection of German blood and German honor."

Schiwe sizn (Yiddish): The custom of sitting on a low stool at home for a week after the death of a close relative.

October 5—Lessing: Gotthold Ephraim Lessing (1729–81); playwright, critic and esthetician. *Nathan the Wise* is his most famous play.

Memel: Coastal strip of East Prussia, detached from Germany by the Versailles Treaty to allow Lithuania access to the sea, it was seized by the latter in 1923. Germany pressed for return of the territory, but Hitler was not able to compel its reincorporation into Germany until March 1939.

Beginning of the Abyssinian War: On October 3, 1935, Italian forces attacked Abyssinia, advancing from the colonies of Eritrea and Somalia.

on the Bückeberg: Hill near Hameln; from 1933 to 1937, on a slope forming a natural amphitheater, the main festival of harvest thanksgiving was held here with Hitler present. The ceremony symbolically linked peasantry and state.

October 19—BDM: Bund Deutscher Mädel: "League of German Girls," the girls' section of the Hitler Youth.

October 26—In Greek mythology, Laocoön, a priest, offended the gods. He and his two sons were punished by being crushed to death by two great sea serpents.

October 31—Have begun Rosenkranz: Karl Rosenkranz's *Diderots Leben und Werke* ("Diderot's Life and Work"), two volumes (Leipzig, 1866). In his *Literary History*, Klemperer describes this work as "fundamental and unsurpassed by any subsequent general monograph."

November 9—who fell at the Feldherrnhalle in 1923: Those killed in the course of the Nazis early attempt to seize power in Munich in 1923.

the capital city of the movement: Munich.

Hitler's thanks to the Stahlhelm, which has just been dissolved: From June 1933, members of the right-wing Stahlhelm under the age of 35 were incorporated into the SA; in April 1934, the remainder of the Stahlhelm was renamed the "Nationalsozialistischer Frontkämpferbund" ("National Socialist Veterans Association"), The Stahlhelm was finally dissolved in November 1935. Its leader Franz Seldte (1882–1947) had been appointed Reich Commissioner for the Labor Service in 1933.

November 11—the Naumann Jews: In 1921 Max Naumann founded the militant, right-wing Association of National German Jews, which called on Jews to surrender their Jewish identity. Naumann was hostile to eastern Jews whom he described as "dangerous immigrants from the East" and as harmful bacteria in the body of the German nation, racially and intellectually far inferior to German Jews. Naumann also attacked the Zionists. In 1935 the Gestapo dissolved the Association because of attitudes supposedly "hostile to the state."

Heinz Machol: The son of Klemperer's sister Hedwig who had died in 1901.

December 31—Oberammergau: Village in the Bavarian Alps in which a famous passion play is performed every ten years.

Agnes: Had for many years been the Klemperers' maid.

comme si de rien n'était pas (French): "As if nothing were wrong."

the Cacouac supplement: In his *Geschichte der französischen Literatur im 18 Jahrhundert* (History of French Literature in the C18, Vol. 1), in a chapter entitled "The opponents," Klemperer describes how Jean Nicolas Moreau's *Cacouac* became the epitome of mockery of the Enlightenment philosophers and Encyclopedists.

1936

February 11—a Jewish student: By assassinating the Nazi official Wilhelm Gustloff on February 4, 1936, the student, David Frankfurter, wanted to avenge the murder of Jews in Germany.

the Olympic Games: The Winter Olympics, which in 1936 were held in Garmisch-Partenkirchen in Bavaria.

March 6—Felix's eldest: Kurt, son of Felix Klemperer, no longer saw any possibility of becoming a lawyer in Germany and left for Brazil in 1934.

Betty Klemperer: Felix Klemperer's widow, went to Cleveland, Ohio.

March 8—the occupation of the Rhineland: Under the Versailles Treaty, the Rhineland was demilitarized and placed under Allied military occupation. The Locarno Treaty (October 1925) brought a guarantee by Britain and Italy, and signatures by France, Belgium, and Germany, of the post-1919 frontiers between the three signatories, and the demilitarization of the Rhineland. In 1936, Hitler used the excuse of the Franco-Soviet pact to declare the Locarno Treaty void and to order German troops into the demilitarized zone. There were only weak foreign protests.

March 23—the Kroll Opera is called the Reichstag: After the Reichstag fire, the new Nazi "parliament" used the Kroll Opera House, which was less prestigious than the other Berlin opera houses, for its sessions.

March 31—the plebiscite: The plebiscite on March 29, 1936, on the remilitarization of the Rhineland resulted in a 99 percent vote in favor.

April 24—*Zaïre:* Tragedy (1732) by Voltaire.

Heiss: Heiss was Klemperer's predecessor both at the Technical University and in owning a car.

dawke or proprio (Yiddish and Italian): Effectively an expression of defiance—"now or never."

May 3—*Contrat social:* Rousseau's "The Social Contract" (1762).

May 10—Schlageter: Albert Leo Schlageter (1894–1923). Active in right-wing military organizations (Freikorps) after 1918. During the 1923 French and Belgian occupation of the Ruhr, he was arrested for sabotage, sentenced to death by a French military court, and shot. Presented as a martyr in nationalist propaganda.

May 16—the Hindenburg offensive: The German offensive in the early weeks of the war that repelled the Russian incursion into East Prussia and culminated in the German victories of Tannenberg and the Masurian Lakes.

May 21—d'une passion dévorante (French): "With a consuming passion."

May 24—after his return from Lenin: Klemperer's brother Georg was repeatedly summoned to Moscow by the Soviet government during 1922–23 to treat Lenin. The distinguished doctor gave an exact diagnosis of Lenin's illness.

June 28—Blum: Léon Blum (1872–1950) founded the Socialist Party with Jean Jaurès in 1902 and reestablished it in 1918. As prime minister of France, 1936–37, he carried out fundamental social reforms and banned Fascist paramilitary organizations. Arrested by the Vichy government in 1940 and imprisoned in German concentration camps 1943–45. He was prime minister once more in 1946–47.

Litvinov-Finkelstein: Maksim Maksimovich Litvinov (1876–1951); People's Commissar for Foreign Affairs 1930–39. Advocate of a system of collective security to oppose the threat of Nazi Germany and Fascist Italy. His real name was Meier Walach and not Finkelstein.

Emile: Novel (1762) by Rousseau.

July 16—Auerbach: Erich Auerbach (1892–1957); his foremost work, *Mimesis: The Representation of Reality in Western Literature,* was first published in 1946 while Auerbach was still a professor in Istanbul and before he moved to the United States.

Dimillenario Orazione. Stet Capitolium fulgens. (Italian and Latin): Two-thousandth birthday of Horace. "May the Capitol still stand as a beacon."

Triple Alliance: Alliance between Germany, Austria-Hungary and Italy before 1914. In 1915, Italy broke with its partners and declared war on them, since the Allies promised it territories claimed from Austria-Hungary.

Ignazio Silone's: Silone (1900–1978); Italian writer, whose first novel, *Fontamara,* was published in German in 1930 and attracted a great deal of attention.

July 17—Münchner Platz: The police prison at Münchner Platz.

Croce: Benedetto Croce (1866–1952); Italian philosopher, historian and politician. Before Fascism, Croce was minister of education several times. From 1943 to 1952 leader of the Liberal Party. Klemperer had met him in 1914, when he was teaching in Italy.

League of Nations sanctions and then the victory in Abyssinia: When Italy invaded Abyssinia in October 1935, the League of Nations imposed rather ineffectual sanctions on the aggressor, which did not prevent Italy from suppressing resistance and occupying the country by May 1936 (capture of Addis Ababa).

July 18—KDF: Kraft durch Freude "Strength through joy." The name of the Nazi leisure organization which, among other activities, organized cheap mass travel.

July 30--Heidenau gave us . . . : The "unrespectable" Köhlers in Heidenau.

Economie politique: Rousseau's *De l'économie politique* (1755).

August 13—the Danzig business has only been postponed: The German claim for Danzig to be reincorporated in the Reich was expressed with increasing vociferousness after the Nazi Party won a majority in the city government in 1933.

Gamelin: Maurice Gustave Gamelin (1872–1958); commander-in-chief of the French armed forces, 1938–40; from September 1939, commander-in-chief of Allied forces in France.

The third Napoleon began his war of desperation over Spain: The Franco-Prussian War of 1870–71, which began when Napoleon III, losing popularity at home, was easily provoked by the German chancellor, Bismarck, into declaring war over the question of succession to the Spanish throne.

August 24—Darré: Walter Darré (1895–1953); Nazi Minister for Food and Agriculture 1933–42.

September 5—Deutsche Bücherei: Deutsche Bücherei ("German Library") in Leipzig, one of the deposit libraries for German-language publications.

September 9—The Jewish Cultural Leagues: The Cultural League of German Jews was founded in Berlin in June 1933 and subsequently in other cities. On April 27, 1935, all the local organizations were forcibly amalgamated into the Reich Association of Jewish Cultural Leagues. In 1936, the Association had 168 branches in Germany with 180,000 members.

September 27—Lilly Jelski de Gandolfo: Eldest daughter of Klemperer's sister Marta Jelski.

Erzgebirge: "Ore Mountains"; low mountain range on the border of Germany and Czechoslovakia to the southwest of Dresden.

Galicians: Jews from the former Austrian province of Galicia in present-day southern Poland and northeastern Ukraine.

è pagato (Italian): "It's been paid for."

October 10—Ilse Klemperer: Daughter of Klemperer's brother Felix.

cf. the happy times of 1906: 1906 was the year the Klemperers married; at that time they were living in Berlin.

con gli amici (Italian): "With his friends."

October 18—Milch: Erhard Milch (1892–1972), Field Marshal; 1933–44, State Secretary in the Reich Air Ministry; 1941–44, Inspector-General of the Luftwaffe. In 1947 Milch was tried and sentenced to life imprisonment by a U.S. Military Tribunal in a proceeding subsequent to the International Military Tribunal in Nürnberg. He was released in 1954.

Mary Wigman: Wigman (1886–1973) was a pioneering performer and teacher of modern dance.

November 24—Creizenach: A standard work on modern drama by Wilhelm Creizenach.

the Spanish affair: After Francisco Franco began his revolt against the legitimate center-left Spanish government, he was given military support by Germany, Italy and Portugal. The Franco regime was recognized as the Spanish government by Germany and Italy on November 18, 1936, while the Civil War was still being fought.

Fiamme dal ciel (Italian): "Flames from heaven" (i.e., May fire fall from heaven).

Renner's: A department store in Dresden.

December 13—*Der Bettelstudent:* The film has a theme that occurs in a number of German films at this time—the Polish struggle against Russia.

New Year's Eve 1936—Friz Mauthner: Mauthner (1849–1923) was a philosopher and writer, famous, above all, for his book *Der Atheismus und seine Geschichte im Abendland* (Atheism and Its History in the Occident).

Muncker: Franz Muncker (1855–1926), Professor of History of German Literature in Munich for over 40 years; supervised Klemperer's doctoral thesis.

Hermann Paul: Paul (1846–1921) was a Germanist; professor in Freiburg and Munich.

Professor Pringsheim: The musician Klaus Pringsheim (1883–1973) was a pupil of Gustav Mahler and was for many years musical director of the Max Reinhardt theaters in Berlin; from 1931 he was conductor and teacher at the Imperial Conservatory in Tokyo. Pringsheim was Thomas Mann's brother-in-law.

1937

January 10—speech on January 18: On the anniversary of the establishment of the German Empire, that is, of a unified Germany, on January 18, 1871.

April 25—In lingua veritas (Latin): "The truth lies in language"; Klemperer is varying the old saying "in vino veritas" (the truth lies in wine) originally derived from the Greek poet Alkaios.

May 12—Landsberg: Landsberg an der Warthe, today Gorzów Wielkopolski in Poland, a town to the east of Berlin. Landsberg is the setting of Christa Wolf's autobiographical novel *A Pattern of Childhood.*

When the zeppelin was destroyed: In 1937, the German airship LZ 129 (the *Hindenburg*) caught fire as it was docking at Lakehurst, N.J., near New York, and was completely destroyed. The disaster brought to an end trans-Atlantic passenger flights by airship.

May 22—to the dean of Bonn University: Thomas Mann's letter was addressed to the Dean of the Faculty of Philosophy at Bonn University. The Dean had informed Mann that since he had been stripped of German citizenship, his name would be struck from the list of honorary doctors.

the banned papal pastoral letter: Despite the Concordat concluded between the Vatican and Nazi Germany on July 20, 1933, the opposition of the Catholic Church to the Nazi regime's ecclesiastical policies grew. This phase reached a climax with Pope Pius XI's encyclical, co-authored with the German bishops, "With Burning Sorrow" (March 1937). The consequence was the arrest of many priests and the expropriation of church publishing houses and presses.

scandalous trials of churchmen: A campaign against monasteries began in May 1936. Two hundred seventy-six members of religious orders were put on trial accused of homosexual offenses.

June 2—Saint-Simon: Louis de Rouvroy, Duc de Saint-Simon (1675–1755); writer famous for his *Mémoires; not* the later utopian Socialist Henri de Saint-Simon.

the bombardment of Almería: Ships of the German navy bombarded Almería, Spain, in Republican-held territory, on May 31, 1937, in retaliation for an air attack on May 29 on the pocket battleship *Deutschland* anchored off Ibiza.

June 11—Cuxhaven: Port and resort at the mouth of the Elbe on the North Sea coast of Germany, more than 200 miles downstream from Dresden as the crow flies.

June 28—in Albrechtstrasse: In Berlin.

Hedwig's death: Klemperer's sister Hedwig died in March 1891, a few days after the birth of her first child, Heinz Machol.

Hannele: Play by Gerhart Hauptmann.

Notre commencement soit au nom du Père qui a fait le ciel et la terre (French): "Our beginning is in the name of the Lord, who has made heaven and earth. . . ."

July 19—*Nathan:* Lessing's play *Nathan the Wise,* published in 1779 and first performed in 1783, is an Enlightenment plea for tolerance.

August 6—the Vauvenargues by Lanson: Gustave Lanson, *Le Marquis de Vauvenargues* (Paris, 1930).

Monglond: André Monglond, *Le préromantisme français* (Paris, 1930).

August 8—Fü-Li: Fürstenhof Lichtspiele, "Fürstenhof Movie Theater."

Gordian the Tyrant: Bavarian comedy.

August 17—the agitation of Ahlwardt and Stoecker: Hermann Ahlwardt (1846–1914) was a populist anti-Semite. Author of numerous publications, he was sentenced several times for his slanders. Adolf Stoecker (1835–1909) was Court and Cathedral Chaplain in Berlin; on the extreme wing of the German Conservative Party "Deutschkonservative Partei," he advocated a militant anti-Semitism. The two men helped lay the foundations of an anti-Jewish campaign in Germany.

August 29–September 5—Riesengebirge: "Giant Mountains"; low mountain range, sometimes called the Sudeten Mountains, on the border between Silesia and Bohemia, i.e., present-day Poland and the Czech Republic.

Assekuranz-Bunzl: An insurance company.

September 5—Holtei: Karl Holtei (1798–1880) was a minor German poet and writer.

September 11—Signum temporis (Latin): "Sign of the times."

the Frankes: In his childhood, Victor Klemperer spent many happy hours with the family of his uncle Eduard Franke, a brother of Klemperer's mother. Klemperer was especially fond of his cousin Walter Franke.

September 12—The *Völkische Beobachter:* "The People's Observer," the official Nazi Party newspaper, a daily.

October 27—Fanny Lewald: Lewald (1811–1889) was a novelist and storyteller.

Börne: Ludwig Börne. Pseudonym of Löb Baruch; Börne (1786–1837) was a German critic and writer from a Jewish family and a leading radical of the period after the end of the Napoleonic Wars.

Auerbach: Berthold Auerbach (1812–1882), real name Moses Baruch Auerbacher, was a novelist and dramatist.

Liberalism: In this sense Liberalism is the constitutional movement for German unity opposed to the reactionary rulers of the various German states.

Young Germany: Radical literary and political movement of the period before the 1848 Revolutions.

November 28—*Zu neuen Ufern*: Detlef Sierck's penultimate film before leaving Germany, a delirium musical, largely set in Australia; Sierck was ultimately to reinvent himself as the Hollywood director Douglas Sirk.

December 28—Sholem Asch: Asch (1880–1957) was a Yiddish novelist and dramatist.

Manacorda: Guido Manacorda was an Italian Germanist; professor at the University of Naples when Klemperer was a lecturer there at the beginning of the First World War.

d'outre-tombe (French): "From beyond the grave"; probably a playful reference to Chateaubriand's posthumous *Mémoires d'outre-tombe.*

1938

January 8—the new Fascism in Romania: Klemperer was following the first signs of such a development in Romania, which culminated in the setting up of a pro-Fascist royal dictatorship by King Carol II in February 1938; the king established close relations with Germany.

the Warburg Institute: A research institute whose basis was the library of the history of art and culture collected by Aby Moritz Warburg (1866–1929). Founded in Hamburg in 1926, it moved to London in 1933.

January 11—Among the documents: Klemperer included letters and drafts of letters and documents with his diaries.

January 18—Teruel: Scene of very heavy fighting during the Spanish Civil War. A Republican offensive in the area was repelled and ground recovered by the Franco forces.

January 31—*Habañera*: Detlef Sierck's (Douglas Sirk) final German film.

February 19—has dismissed Blomberg and Fritsch: On February 4, 1938, Hitler shuffled the leadership of state and army. Hitler assumed supreme command of the armed forces; Blomberg, the Minister for War, was forced out and Walther von Brauchitsch replaced Fritsch as Commander in Chief of the Army; Wilhelm Keitel was appointed to the new post of Chief of the High Command of the Armed Forces; and Joachim von Ribbentrop became Foreign Minister.

Austria is now halfway incorporated: On February 16, Hitler forced Schuschnigg, the Austrian chancellor, to accept the Nazi Arthur Seyss-Inquart as Minister for the

Interior and for Security, thus paving the way for the "Anschluss" of Austria to Germany.

February 23—Eden is going, Chamberlain is negotiating: Klemperer is referring to Chamberlain's policy of appeasement, which Eden opposed, and which culminated in the Munich Agreement later in 1938.

March 1—Versailles cross: Cross erected after Versailles Treaty (after World War I) as a sign of mourning for German losses, especially territorial ones.

March 20—the annexation of Austria: Following an ultimatum from Hitler, Seyss-Inquart became Austrian chancellor on March 11, 1938, allowing the entry of German forces and completing the incorporation of Austria into the Third Reich. Seyss-Inquart thereupon became Reich governor of the Ostmark, as Austria was now officially to be called.

April 5—Braunau: Hitler's birthplace in the Austrian province of Upper Austria.

April 10—The "election" today, the "Day of the Greater German Reich": Hitler announced a plebiscite on the annexation, or Anschluss, of Austria, to be held on April 10, 1938. The annexation, which had, of course, already taken place, was supported by an overwhelming majority.

the proclamation of the Emperor in Versailles: In January 1871, after Prussian-German victory over France in the Franco-Prussian War of 1870, German unification was sealed by the acclamation of Wilhelm I of Prussia as Emperor Wilhelm I of Germany by the rulers of the German states.

The Conqueror of Berlin: Before the Nazi seizure of power, Goebbels had been in charge of the Nazi Party in Berlin, and organized both the election and propaganda campaigns there and the street fighting against the Left and the working class.

April 18—I read from Sayers: Klemperer is referring to Dorothy L. Sayers' *Gaudy Night*.

May 3—Poveretto d'un re d'Italia (Italian): "What a poor little king of Italy."

May 25—The Czech conflict: After the incorporation of Austria, Hitler concentrated on the dismemberment of Czechoslovakia.

June 1—panem et circenses . . . Pro pane circenses (Latin): "Bread and games (circuses)"—games (circuses) instead of bread.

June 29—Les enfants, c'est pour les femmes malheureuses . . . et pour les hommes malheureux (French): "Children are for unhappy women . . . and for unhappy men."

Inventory of Assets of Jews: Para 1 of the "Decree on the Registration of Assets of Jews of April 26, 1938" stipulated that all Jews had to register their total assets at home and abroad. The assets of non-Jewish spouses also had to be registered, and the assets of each person required to register had to be declared separately.

July 12—Harden's: Maximilian Harden (1861–1927), political journalist who founded and edited the political weekly *Die Zukunft* "The Future." He attacked Kaiser Wilhelm II for weakness and the Emperor's advisers Moltke and Eulenburg and defended Bismarck. He faced several prosecutions for libel, in which he was largely successful. After the First World War, he became a radical Socialist. He survived an assassination attempt in 1922.

Sudeten Deutsche Partei: "Sudeten German Party," the name of the Nazi Party in German-speaking areas of Czechoslovakia before the dismemberment of the country as a result of the Munich Conference.

July 27—Now England is intervening in Czechoslovakia on behalf of the Sudeten Germans: After increasing provocation by the supporters of Henlein, leader of the Sudeten German Party, the British government sent an observer, Lord Runciman, to the Sudetenland. Runciman was soon on better terms with Henlein than with Beneš, the Czech President. Runciman went on to recommend greater autonomy for the Sudeten Germans, then self-determination.

racial theory and anti-Semitism have been officially instituted in Italy as well: In July 1938, the Italian Fascist state adopted the racial ideology it had previously rejected.

August 10—all Jewish doctors have been struck from the Medical Register: In accordance with the "Fourth Decree supplementary to the Reich Citizen Law of July 25, 1938," with effect from September 30, 1938, with the exception of wives and children through marriage, Jews were allowed to treat only Jews.

An identity card for Jews: This became compulsory in accordance with a proclamation of July 23, 1938. It had to be obtained from the relevant police authority by December 31, 1938.

August 24—the just published law on Jewish forenames: In accordance with the Regulation of the Reich Minister of the Interior of August 18, 1938, Jews who were German citizens or stateless had to bear forenames taken from a list of Jewish names. If they bore names not on the list, then these had to be suffixed with Israel or Sara and henceforth used in all business and official correspondence.

September 20—Chamberlain flies to Hitler for the second time tomorrow: After two meetings between Hitler and Chamberlain (September 15, 1938, Berchtesgaden; September 22, Bad Godesberg), Chamberlain declared that England, France and the Soviet Union would stand by the Czech people, if Hitler used force.

October 2—a second threatening telegram from Roosevelt: On September 26 Roosevelt appealed to Hitler and Beneš to resolve their dispute peacefully. The English government then issued a statement saying that it and France strongly urged President Beneš to cede the territories demanded by Hitler without delay.

Four-power meeting today: On September 29, 1938, Hitler, Mussolini, Chamberlain and Daladier, the French Premier, met in Munich without any Czech representative being present. It was agreed that Czechoslovakia had to surrender the Sudetenland and the German-speaking territories on the former Austrian frontier. Czechoslovakia also had to surrender all military installations to Germany undamaged. The German army crossed the frontier on October 1.

October 5—Sudermann: Hermann Sudermann (1857–1928) was a leading Naturalist dramatist and storyteller, very popular in the early part of the century. His story *The Excursion to Tilsit* was also the basis of Murnau's famous Hollywood film *Sunrise.*

October 9—Jeremias Gotthelf: Gotthelf (1797–1854), a Swiss writer, is one of the leading German novelists of the nineteenth century.

November 22—the Grünspan shooting business: On November 7, 1938, Herschel Grynszpan, a young Polish Jew, assassinated a senior official of the German Embassy in Paris to draw attention to the suffering of Jews in Germany. On October 27, without warning, 18,000 Jews of Polish nationality, including relatives of Grynszpan, had been rounded up and taken to the Polish border and dumped in no-man's-land. The Nazis used the assassination as an excuse for the pogroms of November 9, 1938, the so-called *Kristallnacht* (Crystal Night).

November 25—Buchenwald, I think: Buchenwald concentration camp had been set up in June 1937.

the synagogue here had been "spontaneously" burned to the ground: During the night of November 9–10, 520 synagogues in Germany were wrecked or set on fire. The "crowds" that carried out the attacks and arson were usually groups of SA men, who were also usually able to prevent looting (by any unauthorized groups or individuals, that is). The police were prevented from intervening, and the fire brigade was allowed to protect only the homes of Aryans from being damaged by the synagogue fires.

December 2—the billion-mark fine: "Decree on the atonement payment of Jews of German citizenship of November 12, 1938. The hostile attitude of Jewry toward the German people, which does not shrink from cowardly deeds of murder, demands uncompromising measures of defense and hard atonement. In accordance with the Decree on the Execution of the Four-Year Plan of October 18, 1936 (. . .) I therefore decree the following: Para 1 The payment of a contribution of

1,000,000,000 Reichsmarks to the German Reich is imposed on Jews of German citizenship. Regulations regarding execution will be issued by the Reich Finance Minister in consultation with the relevant ministers of the Reich."

December 3—ghettoization and limitations on the free movement of Jews in Berlin: On November 28, 1938, the Berlin Chief of Police ordered that German and stateless Jews were not allowed to enter certain public places and certain areas of the city. (Jews resident in these areas were required to remove themselves by July 1, 1939.) The public places listed included all theaters, cinemas, cabarets, public concert and lecture halls, fairgrounds, all sports stadiums and fields, and private and public swimming pools. The areas of the city from which Jews were excluded were mainly those around government buildings in central Berlin.

December 6—*Die vier Gesellen:* The original title is *Les gens du voyage,* and it was made by the popular French filmmaker Jacques Feyder (1888–1948).

Police Minister Himmler: Heinrich Himmler (1900–1945) was both head of the SS and Chief of Police. Later in charge of the "Final Solution" of the Jewish question.

purtroppo (Italian): "Unfortunately."

December 15—Piccolo mondo moderno (Italian): "How small the modern world is."

New Year's Eve '38—Rétif: Rétif (or Restif) de la Bretonne (1734–1806), French novelist.

Berghof: Hitler's retreat above Berchtesgaden in the Bavarian Alps.

1939

January 8—the district of Hultschin: Part of the Sudetenland territories allocated to Germany by the Munich Agreement.

January 17—Spiero: Heinrich Spiero (1876–1947) was a literary historian and writer. In 1935 the Nazis appointed him head of the Cultural Association of Non-Aryans of Christian Confession.

March 14—the Slovakian business: On March 14, 1939, following German military pressure, an "independent" Slovakian state was established. On the fifteenth, German troops occupied the remaining Czech territories, and on the sixteenth, the latter were transformed into the "Reich Protectorate of Bohemia and Moravia."

the Wars of Liberation: The term generally used in Germany to describe the campaigns conducted by Prussian forces to overthrow French hegemony after Napoleon's disastrous invasion of Russia in 1812.

April 7—political touring exhibition: "The Eternal Jew": On March 24, 1939, Gauleiter Martin Mutschmann opened the propaganda exhibition "The Eternal Jew" in Dresden. The exhibition had already been seen in Munich, Vienna, Berlin and Bremen.

April 9—the bloody attack on Albania: On April 7, 1939, Italian troops occupied Albania and united it with the Italian crown.

April 20—Roosevelt's message: The American president made a final effort to avert war. On April 15, 1939, he approached both Hitler and Mussolini and requested that they refrain from attacking thirty listed states for a period of ten years. Further, he proposed the convening of an international conference to discuss international disarmament and regulating the world economy. Neither Hitler nor Mussolini gave an official reply to this message.

Hinc impedimentum (Latin): "Hence the difficulty."

May 3—The Polish business: On March 21, 1939, Hitler made certain demands of Poland: The city of Danzig, whose supreme authority was the League of Nations, was to be reincorporated into Germany and an extraterritorial link to East Prussia established. (The Versailles Treaty had separated East Prussia from the rest of Germany, so as to allow Poland access to the sea.) These demands were rejected by Poland. On March 23, Hitler forced Lithuania to return the territory of Memel, which had been under Lithuanian control since 1924. On March 31, 1939, England and France gave Poland a guarantee of support. On April 28, Hitler terminated the German-Polish Non-Aggression Agreement and the Anglo-German Naval Agreement.

June 7—celebrating the Condor Legion: The Condor Legion referred to the totality of German armed forces (air, tank, information, and transport units as well as training groups) deployed to support General Franco during the Spanish Civil War. After Franco's victory on April 1, 1939, the Condor Legion was welcomed home by Hitler with a victory parade.

June 20—sourdement s'aggravant (French): "Getting dully worse."

June 27—*Thibaults:* Cycle of novels by Roger Martin du Gard (1881–1958), who won the Nobel prize for literature in 1937; translated into English as *The World of the Thibaults.*

July 4—the West Wall: Better known in English as the Siegfried Line.

August 14—Pastor Grüber's Office: Heinrich Grüber (1891–1975), Protestant theologian. In 1937, he set up an "Aid Office for Christian Jews" in his parsonage in Berlin. This was permitted by the state, and the Office helped Jews to emigrate to the Netherlands. In 1940, Grüber was interned in Sachsenhausen concentration camp; 1941–43, in Dachau concentration camp. From 1945, Provost of the Marienkirche, Berlin (East), from 1949 to 1958, he was the official representative of the Protestant Church in Germany to the government of the German Democratic Republic (GDR—East Germany).

National Association of Jews: Klemperer writes "Reichsbund der Juden," probably in error for Reichsvereinigung der Juden in Deutschland, an umbrella organization for all Jewish communities, previously called Reichsvertretung der deutschen Juden.

August 29—the pact with the Russians: A German-Soviet Non-Aggression Pact was signed on August 23, 1939, with a secret protocol defining each power's spheres of interest in Eastern Europe.

Ribbentrop: Joachim von Ribbentrop (1893–1946) was German foreign minister from 1938 to 1945. He was sentenced to death at the Nürnberg War Crimes Trial in 1946.

September 10—y en a x (French): "There are any number of them."

September 14—Richter: Martin Richter, Secretary of the Confessing Church. After the war he was mayor of Dresden.

Pourtalès: Guy de Pourtalès (1881–1941); Swiss-French author.

September 18—Russians march into eastern Poland: On September 17 the Soviet Union, which had just concluded an armistice with Japan in an undeclared conflict on the Manchurian-Soviet border, attacked Poland from the east. On September 28, foreign ministers Ribbentrop and Molotov signed a friendship treaty that also regulated frontiers between the two powers.

September 29—Vox populi communis opinio (Latin): "The voice of the people is the general opinion."

October 6—Emil Ludwig: Ludwig (1881–1948) was the author of novel-like biographies, an essayist, and a playwright. In the 1920s one of the most widely read authors in the world. His books were among those publicly burned in 1933.

The *Cruises of the Goeben:* At the outbreak of World War I, the German battle cruiser *Goeben*, and its accompanying cruiser, were in the western Mediterranean. The warships escaped into Turkish waters, were incorporated into the Turkish Navy, and henceforth saw action in the Black Sea.

November 12—the attempt to assassinate Hitler in the Munich Bürgerbräu: On November 8, 1939, Georg Elser, a carpenter, detonated a homemade bomb in the ,Bürgerbräu beer cellar in Munich. Hitler was speaking there at the annual ceremony to commemorate the failed right-wing putsch of November 8–9, 1923. The bomb exploded after Hitler had left the room. Seven people were killed and 63 injured. Elser was arrested as he tried to cross the border into Switzerland. On Himmler's orders, he was executed on April 9, 1945.

confessional bigamy: At his civil marriage to Eva, Klemperer had provided only his birth certificate and not his baptismal certificate, and so was married as belonging to the "Mosaic Confession."

December 9—guaio: "Misfortune."

The coupons for gingerbread and chocolate: The sale of chocolate and gingerbread products to Jews was banned by order of the Minister of Food and Agriculture on December 2, 1939.

fetch all provisions from one specified place in the city: A circular of September 13, 1939, provided for the "allocation of special food shops for Jews." According to the circular the mere presence of Jews in food lines was provocative. "No German could be expected to stand in line with a Jew outside a shop."

December 24—the Wilbrandt: Klemperer's monograph on Wilbrandt was published in 1907 on the occasion of the latter's seventieth birthday.

my *Corneille*: Klemperer's monograph *Pierre Corneille*, which was published in 1933.

New Year's Eve '39—Di doman (Italian): Abbreviation of Di doman non è certezza "there is no certainty about tomorrow."

1940

January 13—from among those being repatriated: As part of the Nazi-Soviet pact, ethnic Germans from areas under Soviet control were voluntarily or forcibly resettled in Germany or German-held territory. There was a similar agreement with Italy with respect to the South Tirol.

February 11—Dios dirà (Spanish): "God will speak" (i.e., It's in God's hands).

March 17—Russo-Finnish peace treaty: After Finland had refused to give way to demands to allow Soviet troops to be stationed in the country, the Soviet Union attacked on November 30, 1939 (and was expelled from the League of Nations). After a bitterly fought "Winter War," the Finns were forced to cede territory, including Karelia, in a peace treaty signed on March 12, 1940.

March 31—The Lublin business: The persecution of the Jewish population of Poland began immediately on the conclusion of the Polish campaign. In winter 1939–40 Jews from those areas incorporated in the Greater German Reich were deported to the district of Lublin in the so-called "Generalgouvernement," the Nazi administrative designation for that area of central Poland that had not been incorporated directly into Greater Germany. Conditions were chaotic. There was starvation and poor hygiene, which gave rise to epidemics. The death rate rose rapidly. It was at this time too that the first deportations of German Jews (as from Stettin) to the Generalgouvernement began, though at this point the death camps had not yet been set up.

May 8—Paléologue: Klemperer was reading Maurice Paléologue's *Czar Alexander I.*

May 11—the offensive through Holland and Belgium: Violating the neutrality of the Netherlands, Belgium and Luxembourg, Hitler launched a surprise attack, using highly mobile tank formations, with the strategic aim of striking the French lines of defense at their weakest point.

May 26—Lanson and Scherer and Meyer: Literary histories and reference books.

May 31—"Blessing at Cohns": (Gottes Segen bei Cohns) Card game popular in middle-class families.

the Protectorate: The Nazi designation for occupied Bohemia and Moravia, that is, the rump of Czechoslovakia, minus the Sudeten German territories and Slovakia, which formally had the status of an independent state but was a German satellite.

June 11—Italy in the war: Italy declared war on Britain and France on June 10, 1940.

June 23—the Forest of Compiègne: On November 11, 1918, the armistice between Germany and the Allied powers was signed here. To humiliate France, Germany required the armistice between France and Germany to be signed in the same place on June 22, 1940.

Foch's Pullman car: In 1918, Foch was Supreme Allied Commander, and the unconditional armistice imposed on Germany was signed in his railway car. Following the 1940 armistice, it was brought to Berlin as a trophy. (During the Napoleonic Wars Napoleon's traveling coach was displayed by the victors after his defeat at Waterloo, while Napoleon himself ordered that the quadriga atop the Brandenburg Gate in Berlin be transported to Paris after the defeat of Prussia at Jena and Auerstedt in 1806.)

July 6—Churchill: Churchill had become British prime minister and defense minister on May 10, 1940.

Felsenkeller: "Rock cellar."

July 7—Count Ciano: Galeazzo Ciano (1903–1944); Mussolini's son-in-law; Italian foreign minister from 1936. Argued for Italian neutrality on outbreak of World War II, helped force Mussolini's resignation in 1943 but fled to Germany and was interned; subsequently handed over to the Italian Fascist authorities, and shot.

July 14—Train upon train with troops . . . was rolling eastward: It has only recently been established that this was not mere rumor. Elements in the German High Command wanted to launch a surprise attack on the Soviet Union immediately after the conclusion of the western campaign and began to move forces eastward at a time when Hitler apparently saw the decisive blow against Russia being struck some years in the future.

July 26—annoscolare (Italian): "School years," i.e., years as a teacher.

August 30—Pionkowski: Siegfried Pionkowski, former commercial traveler, then employee of the Jewish Community.

November 7—brutal evacuation of Jews from Württemberg: Supposedly as a preliminary stage to a forced settlement in Madagascar, Jews were deported from southwestern Germany to the south of France on October 22 and 23, 1940. They were placed in former internment camps at the foot of the Pyrenees. The continuation of the war in any case made the plan impossible to execute.

Roosevelt's election: In 1940, Franklin Roosevelt was elected to a third term as United States president, thus defying the convention that United States presidents served only two terms.

November 11—Molotov's Berlin visit: Molotov had been invited with the aim of persuading the Soviet Union to join a four-power pact with Germany, Italy and Japan. Molotov, who was in Berlin on November 12 and 13, 1940, had instructions not to enter into any new commitments.

November 21—senza niente (Italian): "Without anything."

December 10—Lugano trip: The holiday actually took place in March 1931.

Jew Süss and the *Eternal Jew*: Anti-Semitic films, the former a feature film, the second in the form of a documentary. Both date from 1940 and were produced to prepare the population for more radical measures against Jews.

Herzl's racial theory: Theodor Herzl (1860–1904); Austrian writer and journalist who was the founder of political Zionism, the aims of which are presented in *The Jewish State*. Called the First Zionist World Congress in Basel in 1897 and was elected first president of the Zionist World Congress. Its goal was the establishment of an independent Jewish national state.

December 20—(The day will come.): From the Fourth Book of Homer's *Iliad:* "The day will come, when holy Troy sinks into the dust."

December 26—*Stechlin:* Novel by Theodor Fontane (1819–98).

1941

January 31—Krasnow, *Endless Hate:* Pjotr Nikolajewich Krasnow, Russian writer.

February 13—αὐτὸς ἔφη (Greek): "Autos efe" (he says it himself).

February 20—Gobineau: Joseph-Arthur, comte de Gobineau (1816–82) developed a theory of racial determinism and racial purity that was enormously influential. He believed that "Aryan" societies flourish to the degree that their racial character remains undiluted.

February 25—anzi (Italian): "On the contrary."

March 1—Bulgaria had joined the Tripartite Pact; It had joined the Axis powers. This occurred on March 1, 1941, after Hungary, Romania, and Slovakia had also joined the Pact.

March 4—*100 Percent: 100%: The Story of a Patriot,* title of a novel by Upton Sinclair.

March 27—Conclusion of the Tripartite Pact with Yugoslavia: The adherence of Yugoslavia to the pact on March 25, 1941, led to a coup d'état two days later. On April 5, the new government signed a friendship treaty with the USSR. The Balkan campaign that began on the sixth was now directed against both Greece and Yugoslavia. By April 17, the whole of Yugoslavia was in German and Italian hands. By May 11, Greece had also been overrun despite British assistance.

The Young Germany—the Young Italy of Gutzkow and Mazzini: Young Germany and Young Italy were radical literary and political movements opposed to reactionary princely rule in the larger and smaller states into which both countries were divided. Karl Gutzkow (1811–78) was a leading figure in Young Germany; Mazzini founded Young Italy in 1831 and in 1848, became one of the intellectual leaders of the 1848 Revolution.

April 10—Bergson's psychology: Henri Bergson (1859–1941) was a French philosopher who had a great influence on the intellectual life of his time. Klemperer entitled the introductory chapter of the second volume of his history of French literature in the nineteenth and twentieth centuries, "Bergson as Representative Figure."

the Wandervögel: Youth movement in German-speaking countries, which began in Berlin in 1896 and largely involved grammar school youth in an activist ideology that promoted a return to nature, camping, folk music, etc. The various Wandervögel associations displayed both right- and left-wing elements and tendencies.

April 20–April 21—"system period": Derogatory Nazi term for the democratic system of the Weimar period.

May 15—Sammy Gronemann: Gronemann (1875–1952) was a Berlin lawyer and writer and one of the leading figures of the Zionist movement in Germany. In 1924, he published *Hawdoloh und Zapfenstreich* (Havdalah and Last Post), humorous memories of Supreme Command East, and especially of Kovno, during the First World War. Klemperer also served at Supreme Command East, as did Arnold Zweig, Herbert Eulenburg and Magnus Zeller, whom Klemperer frequently met.

May 21—They have built a special crematorium: First experiments in gassing were carried out on Germans classified as mentally ill. The lessons learned were subsequently applied in the "Final Solution."

May 24—Wilhelm: Wilhelm II, the last German Emperor. When a republic was declared in November 1918, he went into exile at Doorn, in the Netherlands.

Prien's U-boat: Günther Prien was a submarine commander. In October 1939, his boat sank the British battleship *Royal Oak,* apparently in safe harbor at Scapa Flow. His submarine was sunk on March 7, 1941, during an attack on a convoy.

June 9—the De Gaulle troops have marched into Syria: Free French and British forces occupied Syria (and Lebanon), then under Vichy French control, and declared it independent. However, Allied forces did not leave until 1946.

June 14—in vinculis (Latin): "In chains."

June 18—the Biesterfeld man: Bernhard, Prince of Lippe-Biesterfeld (born in 1911) married Princess Juliana of Orange-Nassau, heir to the Dutch throne, in 1937. He went into exile in 1940 when German forces invaded the Netherlands.

June 22—It's starting with Russia: Hitler attacked the Soviet Union on June 22, 1941.

Poetry and Truth: "Dichtung und Wahrheit," an autobiographical work by Goethe.

July 6—at Schramm's in Wilmersdorf: Klemperer is referring to his years in Berlin before the First World War.

Par nobile: Par nobile fratrum "What noble brothers."

Ponten's *Students of Lyons:* Studenten von Lyon, a novel by Josef Ponten (1883–1940).

Polizei Präsidium Dresden: "Police headquarters Dresden."

Alvenslebenstrasse: In Schöneberg in Berlin.

Misdroy: Resort on the Baltic Coast; today Miedzyzdroje.

de longue haleine (French): "At length and exactingly."

Scientia ancilla theologiae (Latin): "Science is the maid of theology."

Distinguo (Latin–Italian): "I distinguish."

Jan van Leyden in the cage: See note p. 469.

poor Sonja Lerch: In *Curriculum Vitae,* Klemperer describes the tragic fate of the Social Revolutionary Sonja Rabinowitsch-Lerch, wife of his colleague Eugen Lerch, who was arrested for agitation against the First World War. She hanged herself while in custody.

my Leipzig days: Toward the end of World War I, Klemperer was a censor for the Book Examination Office of Supreme Command East and based in the Deutsche Bücherei in Leipzig.

Addison: Joseph Addison (1672–1719), best known for his *Tatler* and *Spectator* essays.

July 9—Litvinov–Wallach–Finkelstein: The emphasis on obviously Jewish names was part of the anti-Jewish campaign.

July 12—The widow of Ephesus: Character from Petronius' novel *Satyricon.*

July 16—he even handed over Thyssen: The industrialist Fritz Thyssen had been a supporter and financier of Hitler but turned away from Nazism because of its anti-Catholicism and persecution of the Jews and fled to Switzerland in 1939. In 1941 Thyssen and his wife were arrested in Vichy France, handed over to Germany and imprisoned in a concentration camp until the end of the war.

July 21—Japan had dropped out of the Triple Pact: This was no more than a rumor. In the face of the threat of a larger conflict with the Soviet Union, Japan had simply chosen to concentrate its forces in the southern theater of war with its rich raw material resources. Japan held to this position after Nazi Germany attacked the Soviet Union.

July 26—Baldur von Schirach: Schirach (1907–1974) was Reich Youth Leader from 1931 to 1940, subsequently Gauleiter in Vienna; he bore responsibility for deportations of Jews. Sentenced to twenty years imprisonment at the Nürnberg war crimes trials in 1946.

July 27—New regulations about immigration into the USA: The tightening limitations on the emigration possibilities of Jews came to a climax with a decree from the Reichssicherheitshauptamt of August 23, 1941. The emigration of Jews was to be prevented with immediate effect except when permission for individual Jews to emigrate might be of positive benefit to the Reich.

September 2—NSV nurse: NSV—Nationalsozialistische Volkswohlfahrt (National Socialist People's Welfare), a Nazi health and welfare organization.

September 8—the introduction of the yellow Jewish armband: The police ordinance on the "Identification of Jews" of September 1, 1941, stipulates:
Para. 1
1. Jews above the age of six are forbidden to show themselves in public without the Jews' star.
2. The Jews' star consists of a black-edged, six-pointed star of yellow cloth, as large as the palm of the hand, with the word 'JUDE' in black. It must be clearly visible, firmly sewn to the left breast of the piece of clothing.
Para. 2
Jews are forbidden, a) to leave the boundaries of the community in which they are resident, without carrying written permission from the local police authority, b) to wear decorations, medals or other insignia.
[...]
Para. 4
1. Whoever contravenes the ban in para. 1 and 2, whether deliberately or through negligence, will be fined up to 150 RM or be given a prison sentence of up to 6 weeks.
2. Further police security measures such as penal provisions, by which a higher sentence is incurred, remain unaffected."

September 15—che so io (Italian): "What do I know?"

September 17—sub specie curriculi (Latin): "From the point of view of the Curriculum."

"sabbath goy": A gentile who takes care of household matters that in a strict religious household are prohibited to a Jew.

The Jewish Cultural League . . . shut down: The Jewish Cultural League was banned on September 11, 1941, its property confiscated, and the remaining officials and employees arrested.

September 28—y en a d'autres (French): "There are others."

I also had the worst experiences with . . . Miss Livingstone: There are quite different assessments of the work of Miss Livingstone. Elisabeth Gumpert, member of a banking family in Brandenburg, was able to get her brother Wolfgang out of Dachau concentration camp and make it possible for him to leave Germany, with the help of Miss Livingstone. Elisabeth Gumpert: "This brave woman dared go to Gestapo headquarters in Prinz Albrecht Strasse [in Berlin]. There she kept on negotiating until Wolfgang Gumpert was first transferred to Buchenwald and then released." (*Märkische Allgemeine Zeitung* 12/7/90)

October 1—*the Reich Protector Neurath:* Konstantin, Baron von Neurath (1873–1956), German foreign minister 1932–38, subsequently Reich Protector for Bohemia and Moravia. Neurath was summoned to Berlin on September 27, 1941, and forced to resign. He was sentenced to fifteen years imprisonment at the Nürnberg War Crimes Trial but was released in 1954.

SS Obergruppenführer Heydrich: Reinhard Heydrich (1904–42) was head of the Reichssicherheitshauptamt (effectively chief of the Security Police). He was assassinated by resistance fighters parachuted into Czechoslovakia. In retaliation, in June 1942 the German authorities razed the village of Lidice and massacred the male inhabitants.

id aiunt (Latin): "It is said."

Alba: Fernando, Duke of Alba (1507–82), ruthless Spanish general who carried out successful campaigns of conquest in Europe. Notorious above all for his attempts to crush the Dutch in their war of independence against Spain.

October 7—*A chaplain . . . with the Jews' star on his vestment:* A rumor that distorts the courageous actions of the Catholic bishop of Berlin, Bernhard Lichtenberg, who repeatedly preached against the persecution and deportation of the Jews during 1941. He was imprisoned for some time and died as he was being taken to Dachau concentration camp.

October 9—Vieillard (French): "Old man."

Commovente (Italian): "Touching."

C'est bien peu pour un sergeant (French): "It's not much for a sergeant," i.e., I haven't really achieved much.

October 25—*deportations of Jews to Poland:* On July 31, 1941, Goering appointed Heydrich to take charge of the "Total solution of the Jewish question in the German area of influence in Europe." Goering's letter states, among other things: "In addition to the task already entrusted to you by decree of January 24, 1939, of achieving the most favorable possible solution to the Jewish question in the form of emigration or evacuation, depending on circumstances, I now hereby charge you with effecting all necessary preparations, whether organizational, practical or material, for a total solution of the Jewish question in the German area of influence in Europe."

"Litzmannstadt": A Nazi invention as Germanization of the name of the Polish town.

Proof of Ancestry: A Proof of Ancestry (Ahnenpass) was required of all Germans to demonstrate their Aryan "blood."

November 2—Count Galen: Clemens August, Count von Galen (1878–1946), was Bishop of Münster in Westphalia from 1933. He spoke out publicly against the church and racial policies of the Nazi regime, in particular, euthanasia.

November 11—Trotsky-Braunstein: In *Curriculum Vitae,* Klemperer noted that during the First World War the *Leipziger Neueste Nachrichten* newspaper regularly referred to "Herr Trotsky-Braunstein" or even "Herr Trotsky-Braunstein, the Talmudic scholar" among other anti-Semitic designations.

November 18—supported by a Goebbels article: In an article of November 16, 1941, entitled "The Jews are to blame," Goebbels had once again justified the deportation of the Jews: "The Jews wanted their war and now they've got it. But now the prophecy, which the Führer made in the German Reichstag on January 30, 1939, is also coming to pass, that if international finance Jewry should once more succeed in plunging the nations into a world war, the result will not be the Bolshevization of the earth and the victory of Jewry, but the extermination of the Jewish race in Europe. We are even now living through the consummation of this prophecy and the fate of Jewry is thereby fulfilled, one that is indeed hard, but more than deserved. Pity or even sorrow is quite misplaced. . . ."

November 28—Anti-Comintern Pact: On November 25, 1941, the Anti-Comintern Pact was renewed in Berlin for a further five years. Germany, Japan, Italy, Manchukuo (the Japanese puppet state in Manchuria), Hungary and Spain were joined by seven new members.

November 30—Germany's wars '64, '66, '70: The German-Danish War of 1864, the Austro-Prussian War (or German Civil War or Seven Weeks War) of 1866, and the Franco-Prussian War of 1870–71.

December 4—Peter Schlemihl: Character in the story of the same name by the German Romantic writer Adelbert von Chamisso (1781–1838). The hero forfeits his shadow to the devil.

December 7—Frau Pl . . . : Frau Paul. Klemperer presumably altered the name—somewhat transparently—for safety's sake.

December 9—Japan declared war . . . on the eighth (or seventh?): On December 7, 1941, the Japanese launched a surprise attack on the American naval base at Pearl Harbor in Hawaii, destroying a significant part of the American Pacific Fleet, though not its aircraft carriers. The United States and Great Britain thereupon declared war on Japan on December 8, 1941.

December 17—"More light" or "plaudite": "More light" were supposedly Goethe's last words on his deathbed. "Plaudite" (Latin) is a reference to the supposed words of the Roman Emperor Augustus on *his* deathbed, "Clap your approval, if the performance pleased you."

December 22—Arnold Zweig: Zweig (1887–1968) was a notable German-Jewish writer and novelist. Among his many works is a cycle of novels utilizing his experiences at Supreme Command East.

"Brauchitsch and Keitel resigned": After the opening of the Soviet winter offensive on December 5, 1941, the falling back of the German forces and Hitler's call for "fanatical resistance," it was only a matter of time before the German army command was deprived of power. Brauchitsch resigned and Hitler himself took over as Commander in Chief of the Army. However, Keitel never resigned his position until the surrender of May 1945.

December 31—nil inultum remanebit (Latin): Meaning that nothing will go unpunished.

adhortatio (Latin): Words of encouragement.

CHRONOLOGY

1881—Victor Klemperer born in Landsberg an der Warthe (today Gorzow Wielkopolski in Poland) on October 9. Father: Rabbi Dr. Wilhelm Klemperer; mother: Henriette Klemperer (née Franke).

1884—The family moves to Bromberg (today Bydgoszcz in Poland).

1890—The family moves to Berlin to 20 Albrechtstrasse, in the old center of the city. His father becomes second preacher of the Berlin Reform Congregation.

1893—Attends the French Grammar School in Berlin.

1896—Attends the Friedrich-Werdersche Grammar School. The family moves to 26 Winterfeldstrasse in the Schöneberg district of Berlin.

1897—Begins a commercial apprenticeship in the haberdashery and fancy-goods export company of Löwenstein & Hecht at 2 Alexandrinnenstrasse.

1900–1902—Attends the Royal Grammar School in Landsberg an der Warthe, and takes the final examination.

1902–1905—Studies philosophy, and Romance and German philology in Munich, Geneva, Paris, and Berlin.

1905–1912—Works as a journalist and writer in Berlin.

1906—Marries Eva Schlemmer, a pianist and musicologist.

1912—Takes up his studies again in Munich.

1913—Takes his doctorate with Franz Muncker. Embarks on his second stay in Paris. Studies Montesquieu for an habilitation thesis (qualification as university teacher).

1914—Completes his habilitation under Karl Vossler.

1914–1915—Becomes an assistant at the University of Naples as a private, un-salaried lecturer of the University of Munich.

Publishes two-volume work, *Montesquieu*.

1915—Serves at the front as a volunteer from November 1915 until March 1916.

1916–1918—Works as a censor in the Book Examination Office of the Press Section of the Military Government of Lithuania, first in Kovno then in Leipzig.

1919—Named an associate professor at the University of Munich.

1920–1935—Appointed a professor at the Technical University, Dresden.

1923—Publishes *Moderne Französische Prosa* (Modern French Prose).

1925–1931—Authors *Die französische Literatur von Napoleon bis zur Gegenwart* (French Literature from Napoleon to the Present) in four volumes (new edition issued in 1956 under the title *Geschichte der französischen Literatur im 19. und 20. Jahrhundert* [History of French Literature in the 19th and 20th Centuries]).

1926—Publishes *Romanische Sonderart. Geistesgeschichtliche Studien* (Romance Particularity. Studies in Intellectual History).

1929—Publishes *Idealistische Literaturgeschichte. Grundsätzliche und anwendende Studien* (Idealist Literary History. Basic and Applied Studies) and *Moderne Französische Lyrik* (The Modern French Lyric).

1933—*Pierre Corneille* is published.

1935—"Retired from his duties" in accordance with the Law to Re-establish a Professional Civil Service.

1945–1947—Reappointed a professor at the Technical University Dresden.

1947—Publishes *LTI—Notizbuch eines Philologen* (LTI—Notebook of a Philologist).

1947–1948—Professor at the University of Greifswald.

1948–1960—Takes on a professorship at the University of Halle.

1951—Eva Klemperer dies on July 8.

1951–1954—Professor at the University of Berlin.

1951—Receives honorary doctorate from the Technical University Dresden.

1952—Marries Hadwig Kirchner.

1953—Becomes a member of the German Academy of Sciences in Berlin.

1954—*Geschichte der französischen Literatur im 18. Jahrhundert, Bd. I: Das Jahrhundert Voltaires* (History of French Literature in the 18th Century, vol I: The Century of Voltaire) is published.

1956—Publishes *Vor 33/Nach45. Gesammelte Aufsätze* (Before 33/After 45. Collected Essays).

1960—Victor Klemperer dies in Dresden on February 11.

1966—*Geschichte der französischen Literatur im 18. Jahrhundert, Bd. II: Das Jahrhundert Rousseaus* (History of French Literature in the 18th Century, vol II: The Century of Rousseau).

1989—*Curriculum vitae. Erinnerungen eines Philologen 1881–1918* (Curriculum Vitae. Memoirs of a Philologist) is published.

1995—*Ich will Zeugnis ablegen bis zum letzten. Tagebücher 1933–1945* (I Will Bear Witness unto the Last. Diaries 1933–1945) is published.

1996—*Und so ist alles schwankend. Tagebücher Juni bis Dezember 1945* (And so Everything Is in the Balance. Diaries June–December 1945) and *Leben sammeln, nicht fragen wozu und warum. Tagebücher 1918–1932* (Collecting Life, Not Asking What For and Why. Diaries 1918–1932) are published.

INDEX

ABOUT THE TYPE

The text of this book was set in Palatino, designed by the German typographer Hermann Zapf. It was named after the Renaissance calligrapher Giovanbattista Palatino. Zapf designed it between 1948 and 1952, and it was his first typeface to be introduced in America. It is a face of unusual elegance.